Lecture Notes in Computer Science   **11581**

Commenced Publication in 1973
Founding and Former Series Editors:
Gerhard Goos, Juris Hartmanis, and Jan van Leeuwen

T0075636

More information about this series at http://www.springer.com/series/7409

Vincent G. Duffy (Ed.)

Digital Human Modeling and Applications in Health, Safety, Ergonomics and Risk Management

Human Body and Motion

10th International Conference, DHM 2019
Held as Part of the 21st HCI International Conference, HCII 2019
Orlando, FL, USA, July 26–31, 2019
Proceedings, Part I

 Springer

Editor
Vincent G. Duffy
Purdue University
West Lafayette, IN, USA

ISSN 0302-9743   ISSN 1611-3349   (electronic)
Lecture Notes in Computer Science
ISBN 978-3-030-22215-4   ISBN 978-3-030-22216-1   (eBook)
https://doi.org/10.1007/978-3-030-22216-1

LNCS Sublibrary: SL3 – Information Systems and Applications, incl. Internet/Web, and HCI

This Springer imprint is published by the registered company Springer Nature Switzerland AG
The registered company address is: Gewerbestrasse 11, 6330 Cham, Switzerland

Foreword

The 21st International Conference on Human-Computer Interaction, HCI International 2019, was held in Orlando, FL, USA, during July 26–31, 2019. The event incorporated the 18 thematic areas and affiliated conferences listed on the following page.

A total of 5,029 individuals from academia, research institutes, industry, and governmental agencies from 73 countries submitted contributions, and 1,274 papers and 209 posters were included in the pre-conference proceedings. These contributions address the latest research and development efforts and highlight the human aspects of design and use of computing systems. The contributions thoroughly cover the entire field of human-computer interaction, addressing major advances in knowledge and effective use of computers in a variety of application areas. The volumes constituting the full set of the pre-conference proceedings are listed in the following pages.

This year the HCI International (HCII) conference introduced the new option of "late-breaking work." This applies both for papers and posters and the corresponding volume(s) of the proceedings will be published just after the conference. Full papers will be included in the *HCII 2019 Late-Breaking Work Papers Proceedings* volume of the proceedings to be published in the Springer LNCS series, while poster extended abstracts will be included as short papers in the HCII 2019 *Late-Breaking Work Poster Extended Abstracts* volume to be published in the Springer CCIS series.

I would like to thank the program board chairs and the members of the program boards of all thematic areas and affiliated conferences for their contribution to the highest scientific quality and the overall success of the HCI International 2019 conference.

This conference would not have been possible without the continuous and unwavering support and advice of the founder, Conference General Chair Emeritus and Conference Scientific Advisor Prof. Gavriel Salvendy. For his outstanding efforts, I would like to express my appreciation to the communications chair and editor of *HCI International News,* Dr. Abbas Moallem.

July 2019   Constantine Stephanidis

HCI International 2019 Thematic Areas and Affiliated Conferences

Thematic areas:

- HCI 2019: Human-Computer Interaction
- HIMI 2019: Human Interface and the Management of Information

Affiliated conferences:

- EPCE 2019: 16th International Conference on Engineering Psychology and Cognitive Ergonomics
- UAHCI 2019: 13th International Conference on Universal Access in Human-Computer Interaction
- VAMR 2019: 11th International Conference on Virtual, Augmented and Mixed Reality
- CCD 2019: 11th International Conference on Cross-Cultural Design
- SCSM 2019: 11th International Conference on Social Computing and Social Media
- AC 2019: 13th International Conference on Augmented Cognition
- DHM 2019: 10th International Conference on Digital Human Modeling and Applications in Health, Safety, Ergonomics and Risk Management
- DUXU 2019: 8th International Conference on Design, User Experience, and Usability
- DAPI 2019: 7th International Conference on Distributed, Ambient and Pervasive Interactions
- HCIBGO 2019: 6th International Conference on HCI in Business, Government and Organizations
- LCT 2019: 6th International Conference on Learning and Collaboration Technologies
- ITAP 2019: 5th International Conference on Human Aspects of IT for the Aged Population
- HCI-CPT 2019: First International Conference on HCI for Cybersecurity, Privacy and Trust
- HCI-Games 2019: First International Conference on HCI in Games
- MobiTAS 2019: First International Conference on HCI in Mobility, Transport, and Automotive Systems
- AIS 2019: First International Conference on Adaptive Instructional Systems

Pre-conference Proceedings Volumes Full List

1. LNCS 11566, Human-Computer Interaction: Perspectives on Design (Part I), edited by Masaaki Kurosu
2. LNCS 11567, Human-Computer Interaction: Recognition and Interaction Technologies (Part II), edited by Masaaki Kurosu
3. LNCS 11568, Human-Computer Interaction: Design Practice in Contemporary Societies (Part III), edited by Masaaki Kurosu
4. LNCS 11569, Human Interface and the Management of Information: Visual Information and Knowledge Management (Part I), edited by Sakae Yamamoto and Hirohiko Mori
5. LNCS 11570, Human Interface and the Management of Information: Information in Intelligent Systems (Part II), edited by Sakae Yamamoto and Hirohiko Mori
6. LNAI 11571, Engineering Psychology and Cognitive Ergonomics, edited by Don Harris
7. LNCS 11572, Universal Access in Human-Computer Interaction: Theory, Methods and Tools (Part I), edited by Margherita Antona and Constantine Stephanidis
8. LNCS 11573, Universal Access in Human-Computer Interaction: Multimodality and Assistive Environments (Part II), edited by Margherita Antona and Constantine Stephanidis
9. LNCS 11574, Virtual, Augmented and Mixed Reality: Multimodal Interaction (Part I), edited by Jessie Y. C. Chen and Gino Fragomeni
10. LNCS 11575, Virtual, Augmented and Mixed Reality: Applications and Case Studies (Part II), edited by Jessie Y. C. Chen and Gino Fragomeni
11. LNCS 11576, Cross-Cultural Design: Methods, Tools and User Experience (Part I), edited by P. L. Patrick Rau
12. LNCS 11577, Cross-Cultural Design: Culture and Society (Part II), edited by P. L. Patrick Rau
13. LNCS 11578, Social Computing and Social Media: Design, Human Behavior and Analytics (Part I), edited by Gabriele Meiselwitz
14. LNCS 11579, Social Computing and Social Media: Communication and Social Communities (Part II), edited by Gabriele Meiselwitz
15. LNAI 11580, Augmented Cognition, edited by Dylan D. Schmorrow and Cali M. Fidopiastis
16. LNCS 11581, Digital Human Modeling and Applications in Health, Safety, Ergonomics and Risk Management: Human Body and Motion (Part I), edited by Vincent G. Duffy

34. CCIS 1033, HCI International 2019 - Posters (Part II), edited by Constantine Stephanidis
35. CCIS 1034, HCI International 2019 - Posters (Part III), edited by Constantine Stephanidis

http://2019.hci.international/proceedings

10th International Conference on Digital Human Modeling and Applications in Health, Safety, Ergonomics and Risk Management (DHM 2019)

Program Board Chair(s): **Vincent G. Duffy,** *USA*

- Stephen Baek, USA
- André Calero Valdez, Germany
- H. Onan Demirel, USA
- Stephen J. Elliott, USA
- Afzal A. Godil, USA
- Ravi Goonetilleke, Hong Kong, SAR China
- Akihiko Goto, Japan
- Hossam Haick, Israel
- Hiroyuki Hamada, Japan
- Dan Högberg, Sweden
- Thorsten Kuebler, USA
- Noriaki Kuwahara, Japan
- Byung Cheol Lee, USA
- Kang Li, USA
- Claudio Loconsole, Italy
- Masahide Nakamura, Japan
- Sergio Nesteriuk, Brazil
- T. Patel, India
- Caterina Rizzi, Italy
- Beatriz Santos, Portugal
- Juan A. Sánchez-Margallo, Spain
- Meng-Dar Shieh, Taiwan
- Leonor Teixeira, Portugal
- Renran Tian, USA
- Anita Woll, Norway
- Kuan Yew Wong, Malaysia
- S. Xiong, Korea
- James Yang, USA
- Rachel Zuanon, Brazil

The full list with the Program Board Chairs and the members of the Program Boards of all thematic areas and affiliated conferences is available online at:

http://www.hci.international/board-members-2019.php

HCI International 2020

The 22nd International Conference on Human-Computer Interaction, HCI International 2020, will be held jointly with the affiliated conferences in Copenhagen, Denmark, at the Bella Center Copenhagen, July 19–24, 2020. It will cover a broad spectrum of themes related to HCI, including theoretical issues, methods, tools, processes, and case studies in HCI design, as well as novel interaction techniques, interfaces, and applications. The proceedings will be published by Springer. More information will be available on the conference website: http://2020.hci.international/.

General Chair
Prof. Constantine Stephanidis
University of Crete and ICS-FORTH
Heraklion, Crete, Greece
E-mail: general_chair@hcii2020.org

http://2020.hci.international/

Contents – Part I

Work Modelling and Industrial Applications

Risk Assessment and Safety

Contents – Part II

Quality of Life Technologies

Health Dialogues

Health Games and Social Communities

Anthropometry and Computer Aided Ergonomics

A Comparison Between Virtual Reality and Digital Human Modeling for Proactive Ergonomic Design

Salman Ahmed$^{(\boxtimes)}$, Lukman Irshad, H. Onan Demirel, and Irem Y. Tumer

Oregon State University, Corvallis, OR, USA
ahmedsal@oregonstate.edu

Abstract. Proactive ergonomics can improve the overall performance and well-being of the user and has the potential to improve the product quality and reduce the cost of resources. Application of Digital Human Modeling (DHM) is a pathway for proactive ergonomics. However, DHM has the issue of fidelity and it is yet not in the level of simulating human perceptions and emotions accurately. In this study, we have proposed an ergonomics approach that is used to infuse human factor engineering (HFE) guidelines during the early design process. The approach utilizes Virtual Reality (VR), Computer Aided Design (CAD) objects, and human-subjects to proactively filter design ideas, during the conceptualization phase, before functional prototypes are built. A comparative study between full computational prototyping and mixed prototype using VR is performed by (a) designing cockpit packaging and (b) assessing human performance during a fire in cockpit emergency situation. It is found that the cockpit design based on the two prototyping strategies provide similar outcomes. However, the computational prototyping approach is more suitable in design space exploration and the mixed prototyping is more relevant for communicating design ideas. Further, it is found that the computational prototyping approach cannot simulate the change in human performance due to emergency whereas the mixed prototype is able to simulate the change in human performance due to the emergency situations.

Keywords: Proactive ergonomics · Human factor ·
Digital Human Modeling · Virtual Reality · Design · Prototyping ·
Cockpit · Emergency

1 Introduction

Incorporating ergonomics approach early in the product development not only reduces the risk of injury and discomfort but also has the potential to improve the user performance and overall production cost [1]. Despite the benefits of ergonomics, it is sometimes not clear for many companies how to apply ergonomics or Human Factor Engineering (HFE) principles early in the design process [2]. A great deal of research in the design literature shows that designers often perceive adding ergonomics into the design process with an increase in the

ⓒ Springer Nature Switzerland AG 2019
V. G. Duffy (Ed.): HCII 2019, LNCS 11581, pp. 3–21, 2019.
https://doi.org/10.1007/978-3-030-22216-1_1

workload and additional engineering constraints. Also, many believe ergonomics is not part of a designer's core job [3]. There are also few studies show that many engineers think that there is not enough time to consider ergonomics within the product design process [4].

In addition to the above limitations, there is also a significant disconnect between ergonomics theory and how it is incorporated within the design process. Specifically, there is a discrepancy between reactive and pro-active ergonomics approaches within product development. For example, the traditional reactive ergonomics design approach uses checklists which often requires the presence of a functional physical prototype and human-subject studies to assess the ergonomics performance [5]. This approach misses the opportunity to correctly utilizing the HFE within the product design. It is because physical prototypes are time-consuming and expensive to build which delays the evaluation and feedback loop. Any modification or retrofitting that are applied at late stages of the design process is time-consuming, costly to carry on, and sometimes infeasible to implement since most of the major design decisions are made early in the design process [6, 7]. Hence, the traditional reactive ergonomics approach causes designers to end-up with a sub-optimal product or workplace design [8].

The problems of traditional reactive approach can be partially mitigated by proactively applying ergonomics assessments early in the design, before the products built, via computational or virtual prototyping strategies. One of the promising proactive computational approach, Digital Human Modeling (DHM), can bring the advantage of using ergonomics and biomechanics simulation tools early in the design to explore human factors issues. This approach has the potential to reduce product lead time, improve quality and increase user-performance [9–11]. DHM technology offers designers the promise of running various what-if scenarios to simulate a large variety of human-product interactions, then correct any ergonomics issues early in the design phase [12].

Although DHM approach has the advantage of providing quicker evaluations and earlier feedback to the designer, it has limitations in predicting actual human performance measures with high-fidelity [13]. Another limitation is in its inability to assess human cognitive performance accurately [14]. One way to circumvent the limitations of computational prototyping due to DHM is to use mixed-prototyping via a human-in-the-loop strategy where users are immersed in a virtual workplace or environment (e.g., via using virtual reality) and execute tasks. Immersing a real human subject into a virtual workplace can mitigate some of the fidelity limitations found in DHM such as complex task generation, posture setup, and perception.

Hence, in this paper, an early design ergonomics methodology is proposed with the goal of injecting HFE into the design process and executing ergonomics evaluations, proactively, before committing into a final design. The approach utilizes Virtual Reality (VR), Computer Aided Design (CAD) objects, and human-subjects to proactively filter design ideas, during the conceptualization phase, before functional prototypes are built. In this paper, a comparison between the two prototyping strategies (i.e., a computational prototype using DHM and a mixed-prototype using VR, CAD, and human subject) are performed by going through a cockpit packaging case study, which is focusing on ergonomics performance assessments during an emergency situation - fire in a cockpit. Performance assessments are performed using two types of prototyping strategies, and the merits and demerits of both strategies regarding fidelity, time, and cost are presented.

The rest of the paper is organized as follows. Section 2 contains a literature review on prototyping and computational prototyping strategies. Section 3 illustrates the early design ergonomics methodology presented in this paper and Sect. 4 includes the design case study. Sections 5 and 6 present the result and discussion of the case study. Finally, Sect. 7 provides the limitations and future work.

2 Literature Review

2.1 Prototyping

Prototyping is defined as an artifact that is used to replicate features of a product, service or system for evaluation and development [15, 16]. In the context of human-centered design, prototyping is performed to assess the usability and ergonomics of concept ideas prior to committing a significant amount of resources such as time and money into the final design. There are various taxonomies and classifications of prototyping that exist in engineering, industrial design, and architecture literature. One of the common identifiers for many prototyping strategies is whether the prototypes are built for assessing the form or functionalities of a product [15, 17]. Alternatively, Stowe et al. proposed a three-level hierarchy system to classify prototyping strategies, which is based on (a) the variety of prototypes (i.e., physical prototype, computational prototype or a mixed prototype); (b) the complexity of prototypes (i.e., whether the complete product or a partial product is built); and, (c) the fidelity of prototypes which determines how accurately the prototype replicates or mimics the final product [18]. Beyond such mainstream taxonomies, Camburn et al. stated that some of the four most frequently cited objectives behind prototyping are: refinement, communication, exploration, and active learning [19].

The brief literature reveals that prototypes can be built in various ways. From the human-centered design perspective, it is crucial to determine how the prototypes should be built and what objectives should it be able to accomplish. A physical prototype can be of high fidelity, but it is time-consuming and expensive to build which causes delays in ergonomic evaluations. In contrast, a computational prototype can be built in a shorter period of time; however, it lacks fidelity. The contradictory findings give rise to the dilemma of what prototyping strategy to follow; however, currently, there are no widely accepted guidelines to assist designers for generating ergonomics assessments [20]. Therefore, many designers rely on previous experiences and trial-and-error on various prototyping strategies to execute ergonomics analysis before products are built. The next section presents computational and mixed prototyping practices in human-centered design.

2.2   Computational Prototyping: Digital Human Modeling

There are several ways to perform ergonomic analysis computationally. This study focuses on a prototyping approach where the workplace or product representation is created using Computer Aided Design (CAD) software and ergonomic assessment is performed using Digital Human Modeling (DHM) packages. DHM is defined as a methodology to perform computational ergonomic assessment by inserting a digital manikin inside a computer or virtual environment to simulate the performance and safety of a worker. It also includes graphical visualization of humans with math and science in the background [14,21]. From the perspective of research, DHM is defined as a mathematical model to represent human behavior through a real-time computer graphic visualization in response to a minimal command input by a user [22]. DHM consists of anthropometric libraries that represent various demographic populations. These libraries enable designers to perform design decisions based on ergonomic evaluations applied to the specific populations. Some of the common ergonomic assessments include lower-back (L4/L5 - the lower 4th and 5th lumbar section) analysis, posture analysis, energy expenditure, vision, reaching zone, etc.

DHM has been used as a computational ergonomics method in various design studies including aviation, automobile, space, and health-care. Some of the recent examples that used DHM to perform ergonomic evaluations early in design are as follows. For example, Khayer et al. performed an ergonomic evaluation of manual weeding using wheel hoe to reduce work-related musculoskeletal disorders. Posture and biomechanical behavior of the workers were studied. The study revealed that a larger group of male population (50th–95th) are assuming more uncomfortable postures. Also, L4/L5 forces are found to be higher on both male and female workers [23]. Another recent study from Ford Research and Advanced Engineering presents how DHM is used to assess and design new vehicles. This study reports that using real human appraisal during new vehicle design is subjective, qualitative, and might not be accurate. Their proposed methodology includes capturing human motions and compare how human motion changes due to new designs. These motions are then used to drive the digital manikins and generate a swept volume of the corresponding body segments. The swept volumes are used to find out the minimum clearance between the human body segments vehicle components [24]. Another human motion data study uses DHM along with Kinect to automate the human engineering simulations. The study claims that simulating a human posture solely using DHM has two drawbacks. The first drawback is setting up and simulating a complex human posture is time-consuming and also the fidelity or accuracy of the posture simulation depends on the designer's expertise and knowledge in the DHM software. To minimize time and bias of the designer during posture construction and simulation, Jun et al. have automated the simulation by capturing human postures through multiple Kinects and feeding the motion data to a DHM motion compiler [25]. In a slightly different study, Irshad et al. proposed a methodology that couples DHM with function failure and human error analysis to enable ergonomic assessments early in the design process [26]. The method uses the results from the Human Error and Functional Failure Reasoning (HEFFR) [27,28] to guide designers towards choosing the appropriate DHM analysis through an iterative process. The authors conclude that while DHM enables ergonomic assessments, it also provides a means to visualize human product interactions and predict unforeseen errors early in the design process.

Although DHM has the advantage of saving time and financial commitments, it has some limitations. Chaffin pointed out that a major issue of DHM is the lack of fidelity of the ergonomic evaluation [13]. Similarly, a study by Lamkull et al. states that DHM has acceptable fidelity when simulating simple postures, but during complex task simulations DHM lacks the fidelity [29]. Another limitation of DHM is predicting the cognitive or perceptual aspects of uses. When compared to physical DHM models, cognitive methodologies and tools within the DHM domain are still in an early developing stage [14].

2.3   Mixed Prototyping: Virtual Reality

Mixed prototyping is defined as a technology that mixes both the real and virtual components of a design to assess product interactions [30]. In mixed prototyping, a workplace or a product created using CAD and projected through a virtual reality system (e.g., head-mounted display), and actual users are asked to conduct product evaluations. Virtual Reality is defined as a technology that gives objects a spatial form and provides immersive experiences to the users. Interaction with the virtual objects provides the user with an impression of immersion rather than being only an observer [31,32]. Bordegoni et al. proposed a framework for mixed prototyping which consists of two independent domains, namely, prototype and user. Both of these domains have two states of being real and virtual which give rise to four settings: (1) real user - real prototype; (2) real user - virtual prototype; (3) virtual user - virtual prototype; and, (4) virtual user - real prototype. Additionally, *real user - mixed prototype* was proposed as a hybrid setting which takes into a real person immersed in a prototype that contains virtual and physical components. These prototyping strategies were used for evaluating different types of products. Ergonomics and usability assessment were generated. It was concluded from the study that traditional physical prototypes do not allow generating both operational and emotional agents of ergonomics in a short period of time [30].

In conclusion, mixed prototypes have the advantages of assisting designers in performing ergonomics and usability assessments in a short period and has the potential to reduce the cost of prototyping. Since the workplace or product is represented virtually; thus, it also reduces the risk of injuries and stress of the user-workplace interactions [33]. However, mixed prototypes using virtual reality lacks the depth perception, haptic feedback and other multi-sensory feedback [34,35].

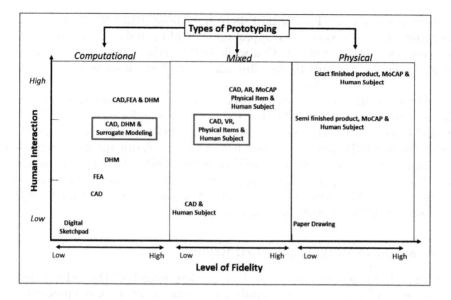

Fig. 1. Types of prototypes for designing workplace or product and assessing human performance adapted from [36]

3   Methodology

In this paper, two types of prototypes are studied namely, computational prototyping and mixed prototyping with the goal of performing (a) workplace design and (b) human performance assessments during an emergency case study. One can see that Fig. 1 illustrates various prototyping methodologies which are categorized based on their type and fidelity as shown in the horizontal axis. The vertical axis represents the level of interaction found on the product that is going to be prototyped. Figure 1 provides a partial guideline to a designer regarding how to build a prototype depending on the level of interaction of the product or workplace and the amount of fidelity desired. In this study, we evaluated two types of prototyping strategies, shown by the rectangular boxes, specifically: (1) full computational prototype created using CAD, DHM, and surrogate modeling technique; and, (2) a mixed prototype created using CAD, VR, physical objects and human subjects. The following sections describe how each of the prototypes is built to do workplace design and performance assessment during an emergency situation.

3.1   Computational Prototype

Workplace or Product Design: The computational prototype utilizes a surrogate model to express human performance as a function of some design variables of the workplace or product. This surrogate model is then explored and optimized to find configuration or design of the workplace that gives optimal human performance. The computational prototyping method starts with creating the CAD model that represents the workplace or product, then importing it to a DHM (Siemens JACK [37]) for ergonomics analysis. Next, the designer needs to know what design variables of the workplace or product affect the designer's performance. So, several probable design variables are selected and varied to find the change in human performance. Once the design variables are identified, several workplaces or product concepts are created by varying design variables. Later, the corresponding human performance for each concept is measured quantitatively. This procedure allows the creation of a surrogate model which models the human performance to design variables of the concepts using mathematical equations. The surrogate model can be explored and solved to identify the configuration, i.e., design variables of the workplace or product that gives the optimal human performance. This computational prototype is explained in detail in Ahmed et al. [38].

Performance Assessment: The computational prototype is also used to simulate the performance of a user/designer during an emergency situation. Similar to the workplace design using computational prototype, a CAD model of the workplace or product is created and imported into DHM. Additionally, a sense of the emergency situation is created by inserting elements of emergency such as fire, smoke, alarm, light etc into the workplace. A digital manikin is inserted into the workplace and his performances are measured both during an emergency situation and non-emergency situation. In this paper, performance is assessed by identifying the changes in posture for a sequence of reaching task due to emergency situation compared to a non-emergency situation. Only upper body posture analysis is performed through Jack's comfort assessment tool.

3.2 Mixed Prototype

Workplace or Product Design: As shown in Fig. 1, the mixed prototype consists of a CAD model of the workplace or product, virtual reality (HTC Vibe [39]), physical objects and human subject. In order to have consistency, the same CAD model of the workplace or product is used in both the prototypes. The CAD model is imported to SimLab virtual reality [40] which is a platform that converts the workplace or product into an immersive virtual world through VR. The attribute of interacting virtual objects in VR is exploited in this study so that the designer can design the workplace or product by changing the configuration of the virtual objects in such a way that ensures optimal performance. This approach would include direct manipulations (such as moving, rotating or changing spatial configuration of the virtual product) in a VR environment according to designer's or customer's own ergonomic requirements. Though the designer can interact and design the workplace according to the designer's ergonomic requirement, there is a limitation on quantifying the ergonomic assessment. Since the performance cannot be quantitatively measured in SimLab so the newly designed workplace or product is imported to DHM (JACK) and the performance is measured quantitatively. Similar to having the same CAD model in both types of prototypes, the same anthropometric manikin and human subject is used in both prototypes respectively to have consistency. An Asian-Indian human subject and manikin of 168 cm height and 73 kg weight are used respectively.

Performance Assessment: The mixed prototype is also used to simulate and compare human performances during an emergency situation and a non-emergency situation. Similar to the computational prototype, a sense of emergency is instilled in the workplace by putting elements of emergency such as fire, smoke, alarms, lights etc. The human subject performs the same sequence of the task as the digital manikin performed in the computational prototype. The performance is assessed by identifying the difference in reaching task posture arises due to emergency and non-emergency situations. The postures of the human subject can not be measured through the mixed prototype setup. So Microsoft Kinect is used as a marker-less motion capture device that is connected to Jack for quantitative posture analysis. An upper body posture analysis is performed in both types of prototypes using Jack's comfort assessment tool.

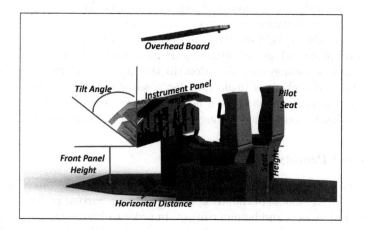

Fig. 2. CAD of Boeing 767 Cockpit

Table 1. Design variables and design objectives

Design variables	Ranges
Instrument Panel Height	47–80 [cm]
Instrument Panel Tilt Angle	0–30 [degree]
Horizontal Seat Distance	30–55 [cm]
Vertical Seat Height	34–53 [cm]
Design objectives	**Minimize reach gap & Minimize vision obscuration**

4   Case Study

Cockpit packaging and fire in the cockpit of a Boeing 767 is taken as a case study to demonstrate the methodology of designing for ergonomics and simulating human performance in an emergency situation using both the computational and mixed prototyping. The aviation sector is widely known for utilizing human factors engineering guidelines in order to improve pilot performance and reduce errors. Also, the advent of smart technologies such as touch displays and digitized controls causes the cockpit control area to undergo changes in future models and variants. The new layouts and designs should be evaluated from an ergonomics perspective to assess human performance. In this design case study, the height and tilt angle of the instrument panel and the horizontal and vertical distance of the pilot seat are considered as design variables as shown in Fig. 2. The explanation for selecting these design variables are given in [38].

The objective in cockpit packaging design is to improve the reachability to the instrument panel and improve the pilot's vision through the windshield. The ranges of each design variable and the objectives of the design are shown in Table 1. The maximum and minimum ranges of the design variables are extracted from aviation databases corresponding to civilian aircraft [41].

The objective in simulating human performance during an emergency situation is to identify which types of prototypes can accurately capture the pilot's posture during an emergency situation. During a fire in the cockpit, the pilot goes through a series of tasks such as reaching oxygen mask box on the left console, reaching for the instrument panel, and reaching auxiliary power on the overhead board. Details about the fire in Boeing 767 cockpit is given in [36]. Simulating these reaching task using both the prototypes and identifying postural differences will let designers understand which type of prototypes is better suited to prototype emergency situations. Sections 4.1 and 4.2 discusses how these two prototypes are used for cockpit packaging design and human performance assessment during the fire in cockpit emergency situations.

4.1   Computational Prototype

The CAD model of a Boeing 767 cockpit as shown in Fig. 2 is imported into DHM, i.e. Siemens JACK, as shown in Fig. 3(a). A digital manikin which represents the designer's anthropometry is inserted in the cockpit, and ergonomic assessment of instrument panel reachability and vision obscuration analyses are performed by changing the design variables. Details about the ergonomic assessment performed in DHM are provided in the Result Section. Additionally, performance (e.g., posture analysis of the designer/pilot during an emergency situation and non-emergency situation) is evaluated using JACK's comfort assessment tool. Figure 3(b) shows a spherical bubble in the cockpit which represents the smoke and fire produced during the emergency situation. Human performance assessment is assessed by comparing the postures for reaching (a) oxygen mask, (b) instrument panel, and (c) overhead board during an emergency and non-emergency situation.

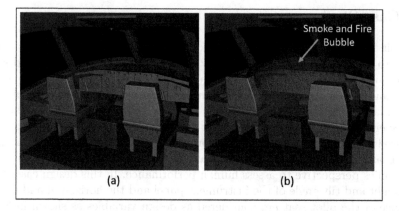

Fig. 3. Boeing 767 CAD imported to Jack for ergonomic design and performance assessment during emergency situation

4.2   Mixed Prototype

Similar to the computational prototype, the CAD model of a Boeing 767 shown in Fig. 2 is imported into SimLab as shown in Fig. 4(a). The designer then puts the HTC Vive VR headset on to get immersed inside the CAD cockpit. In the immersive virtual cockpit, the designer interacts with the instrument panel and pilot seat using the wand (hand control) by translating and rotating the objects according to his ergonomic requirement. Once the designer finalizes the cockpit arrangements in VR, the final cockpit configuration is exported to JACK to measure the performance of reachability and vision quantitatively. Figure 4(b) shows the fire in the cockpit scenario by placing a dynamic fire and smoke inside the CAD model using SimLab software. This approach replicated the fire in the cockpit emergency and the designer/pilot's performance is assessed by measuring the upper-body postures as discussed in the computational prototype. The postures of the designer are captured using Kinect and posture angles are measured using JACK.

Fig. 4. Boeing 767 CAD imported to SimLab for ergonomic design and performance assessment during emergency situation

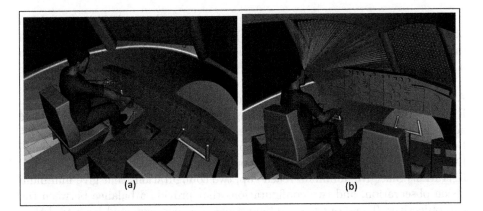

Fig. 5. Cockpit design using computational prototype (Color figure online)

5   Result

5.1   Cockpit Design Using Computational and Mixed Prototype

In the computational prototype, multiple cockpit configurations are created by changing the design variables. In each cockpit configuration, the same manikin is inserted and ergonomic assessment of reachability and vision is performed as shown in Fig. 5. Figure 5(a) shows the manikin is reaching towards the instrument panel and the reach gap between the index finger and instrument panel is measured. Similarly, vision obscuration is measured as shown in Fig. 5(b). The green rays show visibility and red rays show obscuration. The reach gap and vision obscuration for each cockpit configuration are used to create a surrogate model. The surrogate model is explored and optimized to identify the minimum reach gap and minimum vision obscuration. The surrogate modeling technique is described in Ahmed et al. [38].

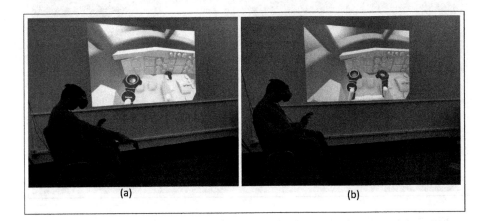

Fig. 6. Ergonomic evaluation using mixed prototype

Furthermore, the mixed prototype is used to assess the reachability and vision obscuration as shown in Fig. 6(a) and (b) respectively. The designer is immersed in the virtual cockpit where he can position himself in the pilot's seat and sits on a physical chair. From the seated position, the designer can use the wand to do a reach assessment and move his head around for vision obscuration assessment. Also, the designer can interact with objects to create new cockpit configurations. Figure 7 shows the designer is translating and/or rotating the instrument panel according to his ergonomic need. The designer can create an optimal configuration of the cockpit by spatial manipulation of the pilot seat and instrument panel. In this study, the designer created six optimal cockpit configurations: two configurations that give minimum reach gap, two configurations that give minimum vision obscuration, and two configurations that provide a balance between the two objectives. These optimal configurations are then exported back to JACK to get a quantitative measurement of reach gap and vision obscuration.

Figure 8 shows a plot of percentage vision obscuration versus reach gap for both types of prototypes. The surrogate model of the computational prototype is explored and used to create the plot. Some of the reach gap values are negative which implies that the manikin is positioned in such a way that the index finger goes beyond the instrument panel when the hand is stretched. The reach gap and vision obscurations obtained from the six cockpit configurations designed via mixed prototype is superimposed on Fig. 8 for comparison purpose. One can see that the ergonomic assessment from mixed prototype closely overlaps with the ergonomic assessment obtained from the computational prototype. An independent sample Student's t-test is used to compare the ergonomic assessment obtained from the two prototypes. The results are given in Table 2. The p-values are greater than 0.05 which suggest that mean ergonomic values or reach gap and vision obscuration obtained from the two prototypes are not significantly different, or in other words, ergonomic assessments from the two prototypes are close to each other.

Fig. 7. Interacting with objects to design the cockpit using mixed prototype

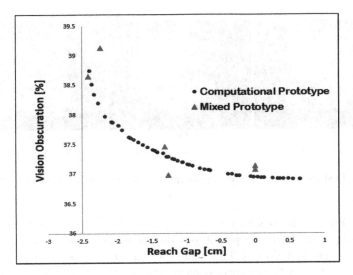

Fig. 8. Cockpit design comparison between computational and mixed prototype

5.2 Posture Assessment in Emergency Situation Using Computational and Mixed Prototype

As mentioned in Sects. 4.1 and 4.2, posture assessment for reaching (a) oxygen mask, (b) instrument panel and (c) overhead panel during non-emergency and emergency situation are performed using both types of prototypes. The emergency situation of fire in the cockpit is created by placing a smoke bubble in JACK and a dynamic fire in SimLab as shown in Figs. 3(b) and 4(b) respectively. It is observed in the JACK, i.e., the computational prototype that there is no posture change of head and upper arm angle, due to the emergency situation. However, in the mixed prototype, the designer showed different postures for the reaching task during an emergency situation as compared to non-emergency situations. The postures during emergency situation using mixed prototype are

Table 2. Statistical analysis between computational and mixed prototyping

	Reach gap		Vision obscuration	
	Computational	Mixed	Computational	Mixed
N	50	6	50	6
Mean	−0.941	−1.203	37.332	37.740
SD	0.918	1.042	0.450	0.917
F-value	0.014		11.119	
t -value	0.588		−1.072	
p-value	0.578		0.330	
CI	−0.828 to 1.352		−1.368 to 0.553	

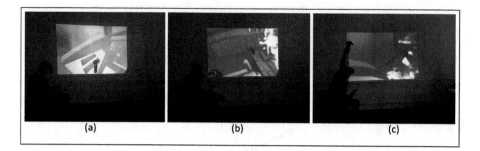

Fig. 9. Posture assessment during emergency situation using mixed prototype

shown in Fig. 9. The reaching task is repeated three times, and the average posture angles for both the prototypes during non-emergency and emergency situation is shown in Table 3. This table shows that the posture angle in JACK is exactly the same whether there is an emergency or not but the postures identified through mixed prototype is different. The Intra-Class Correlation (ICC) test is performed to statistically analyze the body segment joint angles for emergency and non-emergency situations. The ICC test measures how strongly two groups correlate to each other. The ICC value ranges from 0 to 1. A value of 0 means no correlation and value of 1 shows perfect correlation [42–44]. In this study, the ICC value is 0.656, which is a fair correlation. This value suggests that the posture of the human subject during an emergency situation is not exactly equal to that of during non-emergency situation.

Table 3. Posture analysis and intra-class correlation test between non-emergency and emergency situations

Reach	Body segments	Computational		Mixed	
		Non-emergency posture angle	Emergency posture angle	Non-emergency posture angle	Emergency posture angle
Oxygen mask	Head	30.2	30.2	0.9	5
	Upper arm	3.8	3.8	5.6	2.3
Instrument panel	Head	17.6	17.6	12.7	6.5
	Upper arm	55.2	55.2	33.5	18.5
Overhead board	Head	−4.9	−4.9	−0.15	2
	Upper Arm	125.4	125.4	36	16
ICC		N/A		0.656	
CI		N/A		−0.04 to 0.941	
Sig.		N/A		0.037	

6 Discussion

This study compared the ergonomic design and human performance assessment capabilities during an emergency of a cockpit fire by using two types of prototypes namely, a full computational prototype and a mixed prototype. The methodology presented in this study is illustrated by cockpit packaging design and posture assessment during a fire in the cockpit situation. The cockpit packaging design based on the ergonomic assessment outcomes of the reach gap and vision obscuration when using the computational prototype and mixed prototype are found to be close to each other as shown in Fig. 5 and Table 2.

Although the ergonomic assessment resulted in relatively similar outcomes, the time spent and resources allocated during a design case study for each prototype is significantly different. For example, the computational prototype requires the creation of multiple cockpit configurations according to Latin Hyper Cube Sampling (LHS) method and then performing ergonomic simulation in each of the configurations. It is estimated that it takes around 5 min for an expert DHM user to perform each simulation. Thirty cockpit configurations are created using LHS; thus, it adds up to around 150 min. Furthermore, surrogate modeling and optimization techniques are used to identify the cockpit configurations which takes an additional 200 min for a programmer/coder. So in total, the computational prototype takes a total of 320 min. Also, the cost of the software license for JACK and MATLAB or other programming software adds to the overall cost of resources used on the computational prototype.

On the other hand, the mixed prototype is created using SimLab and HTC Vive and Microsoft Kinect which are less resource intensive as compared to the computational prototype. There are only six cockpit configurations created using mixed prototype which is sufficient to replicate the result from the full-computational prototype. Each cockpit configuration takes approximately 7 min in SimLab, and an additional 5 min is required in Jack to generate each quantitative assessment, which adds up to a total of approximately 72 min. Furthermore, the SimLab educational license is free for two years and HTC Vibe costs around 500 USD. Therefore, the mixed prototype produces similar results to the computational prototype with much fewer resources. It should be noted that the cost of the CAD model and stipend for the designer is not included in this analysis as these two are present in both types of prototypes.

In addition to cockpit packaging design, posture assessment during an emergency situation is also simulated using these two prototypes. Table 3 shows that the comparison between the two prototypes in terms of posture assessments during emergency situations. The computational prototype using JACK is unable to simulate the changes in the posture angles due to fire and smoke in the cockpit. It is because, given that the starting and initial points are the same, JACK always uses the same inverse kinematic algorithm to simulate the posture. Hence, it shows no change of posture due to the fire and smoke in the cockpit. However, the mixed prototype is able to capture the differences in the posture angles due to fire in the cockpit emergency. It is because the fire and smoke presented in the cockpit hinders the vision of the designer and the sense of emergency creates an urgency. These two effects cause the designer to attempt reaching postures that are different than that of during non-emergency situation.

Although the mixed prototype is less resource intensive and generates reach gap and vision obscuration results similar to the computational prototypes, it has several shortcomings. First, the result obtained from mixed prototype carries subjective input or biased opinion of the designer. Human subjects/designers of the same anthropometric properties may create different outcomes due to their subjective ergonomic requirements or perceptions. Second, the SimLab used in mixed prototyping strategy does not generate quantitative assessment. The six cockpit designs generated in the mixed prototyping is exported to JACK for quantitative assessment of the reach gap and vision obscuration. Third, the number of cockpit concept design generation using mixed prototype is limited and depends on the designers. This makes the mixed prototyping approach inefficient in design space explorations. Whereas, the computational prototype is efficient in terms of the design space exploration and generating concepts that give an optimal human performance when coupled with the optimization technique. In contrast, because of the subjectivity associated with mixed prototyping, it can not be coupled with optimization techniques for measuring quantitative human performances.

As found in the literature, Camburn et al. stated about the different objectives of building prototypes [19], the computational prototype can be used for the objective of design exploration and the mixed prototype can be used for communication purposes. The mixed prototyping strategy is less resource intensive and the designer feels immersed in the design so it can be used for effectively and efficiently communicating design ideas with other design teams and users or customers. On the other hand, the computational prototyping strategy is resource intensive and can create numerous design concepts so it can be used for design exploration purposes. Therefore, the two types of prototypes have their own merits and demerits that can complement each other, so both of them should be used according to the desired objectives.

7   Limitations and Future Work

One of the major limitations of this methodology is the lack of validation. Neither the computational prototype nor the mixed prototype has been validated. Validation can be done by comparing the result obtained from this study with the designs created using physical prototype and human subjects. Some other limitations include using the designer as the only human subject to design the cockpit using virtual reality. This study mainly serves as a proof of concept where the designer is used as one human subject to conduct a pilot study. Incorporating multiple human subjects to design the cockpit and comparing with the computational prototype is another avenue for a future study. Another limitation is the low fidelity of the CAD model of the cockpit and the low fidelity of Microsoft Kinect used as a motion capturing device. Improving the fidelity of the CAD model and using a marker-based motion capture device can give a deeper insight into the cockpit design and human posture assessment during a fire in the cockpit emergency situation.

References

1. Zare, M., Croq, M., Hossein-Arabi, F., Brunet, R., Roquelaure, Y.: Does ergonomics improve product quality and reduce costs? A review article. Hum. Factors Ergon. Manuf. Serv. Ind. **26**(2), 205–223 (2016)
2. Bernard, F., Zare, M., Sagot, J.C., Paquin, R.: Integration of human factors into the design process of helicopter maintainability. Hum. Factors Ergon. Manufact. Serv. Ind. (2019)
3. Kim, S., Seol, H., Ikuma, L.H., Nussbaum, M.A.: Knowledge and opinions of designers of industrialized wall panels regarding incorporating ergonomics in design. Int. J. Ind. Ergon. **38**(2), 150–157 (2008)
4. Wulff, I.A., Rasmussen, B., Westgaard, R.H.: Documentation in large-scale engineering design: information processing and defensive mechanisms to generate information overload. Int. J. Ind. Ergon. **25**(3), 295–310 (2000)
5. Regazzoni, D., Rizzi, C.: Digital human models and virtual ergonomics to improve maintainability. Comput. Aided Des. Appl. **11**(1), 10–19 (2014)
6. Dul, J., Neumann, W.P.: Ergonomics contributions to company strategies. Appl. Ergon. **40**(4), 745–752 (2009)
7. Alexander, D.: The Cost Justification Process. Auburn Engineers, Inc., Alabama (1999)
8. Andrews, D.: Simulation and the design building block approach in the design of ships and other complex systems. Proc. R. Soc. London A Math. Phys. Eng. Sci. **462**, 3407–3433 (2006)
9. Naumann, A., Rötting, M.: Digital human modeling for design and evaluation of human-machine systems. MMI-Interaktiv **12**, 27–35 (2007)
10. Chaffin, D.B.: Improving digital human modelling for proactive ergonomics in design. Ergonomics **48**(5), 478–491 (2005)
11. Duffy, V.G.: Handbook of Digital Human Modeling: Research for Applied Ergonomics and Human Factors Engineering. CRC Press, Boca Raton (2016)
12. Chaffin, D.B.: Digital human modeling for workspace design. Rev. Hum. Factors Ergon. **4**(1), 41–74 (2008)
13. Chaffin, D.B.: Some requirements and fundamental issues in digital human modeling. In: Handbook of Digital Human Modeling, vol. 2, p. 1 (2009)
14. Sundin, A., Örtengren, R.: Digital human modeling for CAE applications. In: Handbook of Human Factors and Ergonomics, pp. 1053–1078 (2006)
15. Otto, K.N., et al.: Product Design: Techniques in Reverse Engineering and New Product Development (2003)
16. Drezner, J.A., Huang, M.: On prototyping (2009)
17. Michaelraj, A.: Taxonomy of physical prototypes: structure and validation (2009)
18. Stowe, D.: Investigating the role of prototyping in mechanical design using case study validation (2008)
19. Camburn, B., et al.: Design prototyping methods: state of the art in strategies, techniques, and guidelines. Des. Sci. **3** (2019)
20. Camburn, B., et al.: A systematic method for design prototyping. J. Mech. Des. **137**(8), 081102 (2015)

21. Demirel, H.O., Duffy, V.G.: Applications of digital human modeling in industry. In: Duffy, V.G. (ed.) ICDHM 2007. LNCS, vol. 4561, pp. 824–832. Springer, Heidelberg (2007). https://doi.org/10.1007/978-3-540-73321-8_93
22. Zhang, X., Chaffin, D.B.: Digital human modeling for computer-aided ergonomics. In: Handbook of Occupational Ergonomics, pp. 1–20. Taylor & Francis, London; CRC Press, Boca Raton (2005)
23. Khayer, S.M., Patel, T., Ningthoujam, B.: Ergonomic postural and biomechanical analysis of manual weeding operation in agriculture using digital human models. In: Chakrabarti, A. (ed.) Research into Design for a Connected World. SIST, vol. 135, pp. 451–462. Springer, Singapore (2019). https://doi.org/10.1007/978-981-13-5977-4_38
24. Wan, J., Wang, N., Kozak, K., Gomez-levi, G., Mikulionis, L.: A method of utilizing digital manikins to assist passenger vehicle design. In: ASME 2017 International Design Engineering Technical Conferences and Computers and Information in Engineering Conference, pp. V001T02A043–V001T02A043. American Society of Mechanical Engineers (2017)
25. Jun, C., Lee, J.Y., Kim, B.H., Do Noh, S.: Automatized modeling of a human engineering simulation using kinect. Robot. Comput. Integr. Manuf. **55**, 259–264 (2019)
26. Irshad, L., Ahmed, S., Demirel, O., Tumer, I.Y.: Coupling digital human modeling with early design stage human error analysis to assess ergonomic vulnerabilities. In: AIAA Scitech 2019 Forum, p. 2349 (2019)
27. Irshad, L., Ahmed, S., Demirel, O., Tumer, I.Y.: Identification of human errors during early design stage functional failure analysis. In: ASME 2018 International Design Engineering Technical Conferences and Computers and Information in Engineering Conference, pp. V01BT02A007–V01BT02A007. American Society of Mechanical Engineers (2018)
28. Irshad, L., Ahmed, S., Demirel, H.O., Tumer, I.: Computational functional failure analysis to identify human errors during early design stages. J. Comput. Inf. Sci. Eng. **19**, 031005 (2019)
29. Lämkull, D., Hanson, L., Örtengren, R.: A comparative study of digital human modelling simulation results and their outcomes in reality: a case study within manual assembly of automobiles. Int. J. Ind. Ergon. **39**(2), 428–441 (2009)
30. Bordegoni, M., Cugini, U., Caruso, G., Polistina, S.: Mixed prototyping for product assessment: a reference framework. Int. J. Interact. Des. Manuf. (IJIDeM) **3**(3), 177–187 (2009)
31. Riel, A., Draghici, A., Draghici, G., Grajewski, D., Messnarz, R.: Process and product innovation needs integrated engineering collaboration skills. J. Softw. Evol. Process **24**(5), 551–560 (2012)
32. Robles-De-La-Torre, G.: Principles of haptic perception in virtual environments. In: Grunwald, M. (ed.) Human Haptic Perception: Basics and Applications, pp. 363–379. Springer, Heidelberg (2008). https://doi.org/10.1007/978-3-7643-7612-3_30
33. Grajewski, D., Górski, F., Zawadzki, P., Hamrol, A.: Application of virtual reality techniques in design of ergonomic manufacturing workplaces. Procedia Comput. Sci. **25**, 289–301 (2013)
34. Lawson, G., Salanitri, D., Waterfield, B.: Future directions for the development of virtual reality within an automotive manufacturer. Appl. Ergon. **53**, 323–330 (2016)

35. Renner, R.S., Velichkovsky, B.M., Helmert, J.R.: The perception of egocentric distances in virtual environments - a review. ACM Comput. Surv. (CSUR) **46**(2), 23 (2013)
36. Ahmed, S., Zhang, J., Demirel, O.: Assessment of types of prototyping in human-centered product design. In: Duffy, V.G. (ed.) DHM 2018. LNCS, vol. 10917, pp. 3–18. Springer, Cham (2018). https://doi.org/10.1007/978-3-319-91397-1_1
37. Paul, G., Quintero-Duran, M.: Ergonomic assessment of hospital bed moving using DHM Siemens Jack. In: Proceedings of the 19th Triennial Congress of the International Ergonomics Association. International Ergonomics Association (2015)
38. Ahmed, S., Gawand, M.S., Irshad, L., Demirel, H.O.: Exploring the design space using a surrogate model approach with digital human modeling simulations. In: ASME 2018 International Design Engineering Technical Conferences and Computers and Information in Engineering Conference, pp. V01BT02A011–V01BT02A011. American Society of Mechanical Engineers (2018)
39. Niehorster, D.C., Li, L., Lappe, M.: The accuracy and precision of position and orientation tracking in the HTC Vive virtual reality system for scientific research. i-Perception **8**(3), 2041669517708205 (2017)
40. Sell, R., Seiler, S.: SimLab: towards ten years of successful Estonian-German cooperation. In: 2015 16th International Conference on Research and Education in Mechatronics (REM), pp. 221–226. IEEE (2015)
41. Goossens, R., Snijders, C., Fransen, T.: Biomechanical analysis of the dimensions of pilot seats in civil aircraft. Appl. Ergon. **31**(1), 9–14 (2000)
42. Flisher, A.J., Evans, J., Muller, M., Lombard, C.: Brief report: test-retest reliability of self-reported adolescent risk behaviour. J. Adolesc. **27**(2), 207–212 (2004)
43. Tzannes, A., Paxinos, A., Callanan, M., Murrell, G.A.: An assessment of the interexaminer reliability of tests for shoulder instability. J. Shoulder Elbow Surg. **13**(1), 18–23 (2004)
44. Demirel, H.O., Duffy, V.G.: Incorporating tactile cues into human-centered virtual product design. Hum. Factors Ergon. Manuf. Serv. Ind. **27**(1), 5–16 (2017)

Comparison of Digital Human Model-Based Ergonomic Software Using Eye-Tracking Methodology – Presenting Pilot Usability Tests

Mária Babicsné Horváth[1(✉)], Károly Hercegfi[1], and Tamás Fergencs[2]

[1] Department of Ergonomics and Psychology, Budapest University
of Technology and Economics, Magyar Tudosok krt. 2, Budapest 1117, Hungary
{bhorvathmaria, hercegfi}@erg.bme.hu
[2] Information Studies Master's Program, Aalborg University,
A. C. Meyers Vænge 15, 2450 Copenhagen, Denmark
tferge18@student.aau.dk

Abstract. Nowadays, analysis software for ergonomics are more and more wide spread among researchers and ergonomists. There are several different ergonomic software available on the market, and it would be important to know which one to choose in various applications. Although data on the capabilities of the software can be found easily, a comparison regarding their ease of use and the quality of their user interface cannot be found in the literature. In this article, a methodology for comparison is presented along with the results of a pilot tests. For the pilot tests, a cloud based software, ViveLab was chosen. We could draw conclusions for the software and the methodology, as well. Regarding the usability of the software, many suggestions can be made, however, not all function was tested. We could interpret the eye movements in the model space only with strong limitations. Based on the experiences of the pilot tests, we will insert a short subtask into the protocol of the real usability tests, when we will ask the participants not to move in the model space. In conclusion, except a few changes, the method can be considered as applicable for the further usability tests.

Keywords: Usability testing · Eye-tracking ·
Human Factors and Ergonomics (HFE) · Digital human model ·
Computer Aided Anthropometric Design (CAAD) ·
Software for ergonomic risk assessment · ViveLab

1 Introduction

Nowadays, analysis software for ergonomics are more and more wide spread among researchers and ergonomists. These can be used for anthropometric design (fit tests, reachability analysis, etc.), and ergonomic risk assessment [1]. These are most often used for evaluating manufacturing processes [2], or in the field of human-machine interaction, e.g., in vehicle design [3]. There exist several different ergonomic software available on the market, and it would be important to know which one to choose in various applications.

© Springer Nature Switzerland AG 2019
V. G. Duffy (Ed.): HCII 2019, LNCS 11581, pp. 22–32, 2019.
https://doi.org/10.1007/978-3-030-22216-1_2

Although data on the capabilities of these software can be found easily, a comparison regarding their ease of use and the quality of their user interface cannot be found in the literature. Therefore, a comprehensive study about the usability of these software tools could mean scientific novelty. NB, in a research done in Sweden [4], digital human models were compared, and in another examination in the Czech Republic [5], production workplace models were tested, focused on comparing the carrying, lifting-lowering, and biomechanical conditions. There also exist a research for comparison of different lifting tools to estimate spine loads during static activities [6], however, in this case, they did not always use digital human model. Our research focuses on the different features of the different ergonomic software and the usability of the interfaces.

We developed a methodology for comparison. In this article, the methodology is presented along with the results of a pilot research. For the pilot, a cloud based software, ViveLab [7] was chosen, because it is a new, Hungarian software with notable features, and it was easily accessible for us. It is primarily used for risk assessment of industrial workplaces, ergonomic evaluation of products, reachability tests, and path review (with spaghetti diagram).

For the future tests we plan to use the current version of Jack [8], as probably the most known ergonomic software, and as many other software as we can reach e.g. RAMSIS, SAMMIE, DELMIA, Anybody, SANTOS, IMMA [9].

2 Methods and Tools

During the pilot phase of the research several methods were used. Before the usability test, three experts were interviewed. During the test, we apply eye-tracking method with think aloud technique, and, after that, each participant was interviewed.

2.1 Eye-Tracking

The eye-tracking methodology in human-computer interaction is a well-known tool for measuring usability or user experience [10]. Several researches was made in the field of web design [11] and other human-computer interaction fields [12, 13]. This method can give us additional information about the users' behavior [14]. Combining the conventional usability test with the eye-tracking method, more data can be acquired; furthermore, its visualization techniques, can support us to interpret these data in a relatively efficient way.

In our research, we used a monitor based Tobii T120 eye-tracking device. There are two cameras in the monitor, one is to record the participants' movements, gestures, and facial expressions, and another one to determine the gaze. The device also record the computer screen, and as a result we can get a video with the eye movement, heatmaps [15], AOI (Area of Interest) statistics [16, 17], and gaze plot diagrams [18].

2.2   ViveLab

ViveLab is a digital human model-based software for ergonomic analysis. The software was released in 2015. This is a cloud-based software, which is one of its main advantages. It means the shared model spaces (so called "virtual labs" or simply "labs") can be available from all countries, only a utility software, Citrix Receiver must be installed. Everyone can register on the webpage [7] and get a one-hour trial license.

After login, we can create labs, and work with coworkers in the same lab at the same time. The built-in human model has a database of accurate body dimensions. We can adjust the percentile, age, somatotype, and acceleration of our human mannequin. The parameter of acceleration means we can adjust the birth year of the human, since, over the decades, the later they are born the higher they will be. There is an opportunity for import xsens motion capture file, and we can create our own animation manually as well. The software includes three implemented risk assessment methods (RULA, OWAS, NASA-OBI), two implemented standards (ISO 11226, EN 1005-4), and two other analysis techniques (reachability zone, spaghetti diagram). After analyzing the human motion and/or postures, we can generate risk assessment documents and ask for statistics.

3   Protocol of the Pilot Tests

The pilot research was made exactly like the planned real tests. We defined a divided user profile, and the participants were recruited in accordance of it: University students and university teachers both were among the participants. Six person was participated, three students and three teachers.

In the case of the actual six participants, the students had much more active experiences with CAD programs than the teachers had, which could give us better task completion time or error-free rate. On the other hand, the teacher participants usually had much more knowledge about risk assessment and anthropometric fit.

The protocol of the pilot tests was the following. After the calibration of the eye-tracker, the participants have to complete the given tasks. The tasks for the participants were the following:

1. Ergonomic verification of a product in the design stage. The aim is to analyze the reachability and the differences in the measurements of the components.
2. Ergonomic risk assessment for a body posture in the use of a product or for a particular posture during work.

The particular tasks targeted ergonomic analysis of an adjustable height table. The required steps were the following:

- Opening the given ViveLab project.
- Importing the given object to the lab as a model of a machine.
- Placing a human model.
- Setting the body posture of the human model to "stand – typing on computer".
- Placing the human model near the table. The forearm should be over the table top.

- Adjusting the properties of the human model to the specific parameters: work clothes; female; Swedish; database: Bodyspace; age: 27; percentiles: 5%. Participants did not have to change other attributions.
- Setting the height of the table top to touch it with the forearm of the human. Determining whether the end stops of the adjustable table allow this proper height or not.
- Modifying the properties of the human to another specific parameters: male; percentiles: 95%; without any changes in other attributions.
- Repeating the task in accordance to the new human: Setting the height of the table top to touch with the forearm of the human; determining whether the bumpers allow this to be carried out.
- Ascertaining the anthropometric compliance of the table.
- Opening the RULA risk assessment tool.
- Determining the load caused by the angle of the neck based on the RULA tool.

The simplicity of the task (assessing just a simple adjustable table, not a complex machine), and the level of detailing the steps in the protocol were necessary to carry the sessions in a comfortable period and with a reasonable effort by novice users as well. However, we consider these steps as representative for practical, industrial usage of the main feature of the tested software and the other pieces of software to be tested later.

4 Results of the Pilot Tests

As the results of the tests, we have identified many usability problems regarding the software. We gained two types of data: qualitative and quantitative. The qualitative data came from the eye-tracking visualization techniques (heatmaps, gaze plots) and interpretation of the statistics of AOI. The quantitative data came from the task completion time and the success rate.

4.1 Qualitative Results from the AOIs, Heatmaps, and Gaze Plots

The first subtask was opening the software, which was almost the easiest subtask, though there was one problem regarding the completion time. According to the fast and wide saccades, we could identify a searching behavior of the participants. This means they assumed that the program will indicate how much time left or the status of the loading.

Importing the CAD model was the next subtask. This subtask was one of the hardest. Based on their previous experiences with other similar programs (CAD programs), all participants searched for a file menu. Therefore, they tried to find this tool mainly the top left corner and under the "Main" menu as we can see on the heatmaps. (See Fig. 1.)

According to two participants' individual gaze plots showed in Fig. 2, we can see the eye movements on the horizontal menu bar. The particular participants returned and searched again on the same part of the user interface. That means they were sure that

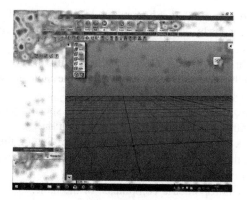

Fig. 1. Importing the CAD model – aggregated heatmap for all participants.

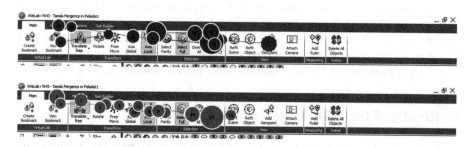

Fig. 2. Importing the CAD model – gaze plots: saccade regressions for two participants.

the menu should be there, but they could not find it, or the pictograms were not evident enough. Some of them tried the "drag and drop" method unsuccessfully.

Two of the participants found the "Add machine" menu, however, they did not click on it. After the moderator informed the participants that the software considers the CAD model as a machine, all of them found the correct user interface element in 8 s.

Inserting a human model was the next problematic subtask. The label of the correct button was "Diving suit" and not "Add human" or "Create human". This was confusing especially for the students. The Heatmap showed by the left image of Fig. 3 also confirms, with the red parts, the long fixation time and the inactivity, which indicates the difficulty of interpretation of the object.

The AOI analysis of the fixation counts also confirms the difficulty of this task. Right image of Fig. 3 displays the selected AOIs, where the red one is the menu for creating a human model. Let's see a particular participant's data as an example: the time to first fixation was 2.84 s, the number of fixations was 36, and 17 visits were counted. So, the participant looked at the right part relatively early, however, they clicked on it later, after many visits and fixations.

The next problem was to change the posture of the human model. In average, the students were faster than the teachers. As we can see from the two aggregated gaze

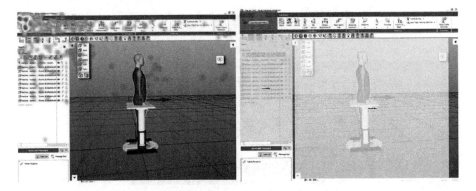

Fig. 3. Creating a human model – aggregated heatmap for all participants (left); selected AOIs (right). Red AOI: create human menu; green AOI: model tree; yellow AOI: model space. (Color figure online)

plots for teachers and for students in Fig. 4, it can be stated, that all participants searched in the human model context menu, however, the teachers first scanned the "Human Properties" tool. The real user interface elements to use are located in the main menu.

During posturing the human model, a software error was occurred. In isometric view, after opening the side toolbar, the ratio of the model space had change, and the coordinate system of the selected models didn't function until the next zoom in or zoom out operation.

Adjusting the table surface to the correct height subtask was the most time consuming. The longest time was more than 5 min. The default setting is the "Select full" interaction mode, which means that the users can shift and rotate the whole model, but they have to click on the "Select partly" button to move only one part, or they can select the part from the model tree. In this subtask, the students examined the model tree and the horizontal menu bar as well, and the teachers focused only on the menu bar.

Table 1 shows the AOI data of this subtask. According to the data, it can be stated, most of the participants did not think that the solution is in the main menu. We selected three areas to analyze: menu bar, model tree, model space. The fixation count of the model space AOI was always at least two or three times higher than the fixation count of the menu bar AOI or the model tree AOI. This result refers to the fact that the participants intended to complete the task using the mouse, for example double click or right click on the parts. Those who chosen the "Select partly" command needed help from the moderator.

The RULA risk assessment tool was easy to find, mostly because during the previous subtasks they had seen it. The determination of the angle of the neck was relatively easy subtask, but one problem has occurred. The participants firstly searched for the angle directly on the human model, but later they found the solution in the RULA tool. For two participants, the View More Options tab was not opened, making it difficult to find information about the body parts (see Fig. 5).

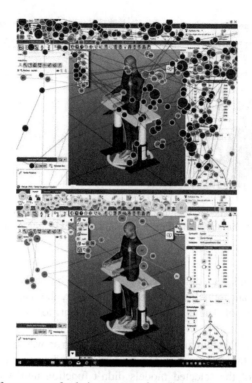

Fig. 4. Gaze plots of two types of solution strategy for adjusting the posture of the human body: searching for a variety of areas, primarily the Human Properties window (left, showing gaze plots of two teacher participants), and focusing on the menu bar (right, showing gaze plots of two student participants).

Table 1. Adjusting the table surface to the correct height– AOI data.

		Time to first fixation (s)			Fixation count (piece)			Visit count (piece)		
		Menu bar	Model tree	Model space	Menu bar	Model tree	Model space	Menu bar	Model tree	Model space
Student	1	33.38	35.25	0.03	41	92	221	17	21	22
	2	26.66	19.91	0	67	64	190	13	24	17
	3	49.67	30.53	0	1	24	322	1	8	15
Teacher	1	4.43	75.49	0	40	64	261	10	9	21
	2	3.69	47.94	0	60	5	206	21	3	17
	3	23.13	35.14	2.23	77	94	582	22	21	28

Deleting the models and closing the program was the final subtask. All of the participants completed this task successfully, but two of them missed the function of the "DEL" button and none of them used the more time-effective "Delete all objects" command.

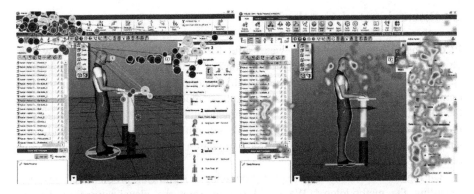

Fig. 5. Finding RULA risk assessment tool – aggregated gaze plots (left); determination of the angle of the neck – aggregated heatmap (right).

4.2 Quantitative Results from the Task Completion Time and the Success Scale

In order to quantify the efficiency completing the tasks, we applied two metrics: the task completion time and the level of the subtask's success. The level of success scale was a Likert scale from 0 to 3.

In our research, we defined the levels of the success scale as the followings:

3 – The participant could complete the task without help.

2 – The participant could complete the task with little help from the moderator or the use of the help system.

1 – The participant could complete the task with significant help from the moderator.

0 – The participant could not complete the task, intervention of the moderator was necessary.

Regarding the task completion time, the data of the first student participant during posturing the human model was inaccurate because of the previously mentioned software error. All the other data are correct. According to the task completion time and the success scale, it can be stated, the hardest subtask was to import a CAD model. The second hardest subtask was to move the table top.

The participants acquired routine already in these short sessions: it can be concluded from the task completion time and the successes of the two repeating subtasks. They completed the second similar subtask much earlier and they were more successful. The experience in other similar program was also important. Those who wasn't experienced or have not used these kind of software recently finished the tasks in average later than those who had fresh experience.

5   Discussion and Conclusion

In conclusion, the pilot research was useful for both purpose. We could draw conclusions for the software and the methodology as well. Regarding the software, many suggestions can be made, however, not all function was tested. Based on the task completion time, which was around 15 min, the complexity of the task was correct, and the continuation of this list of steps is recommended, however, it can be expanded with more tasks while the complexity of the task will not significantly change. Additional subtasks would probably take more task completion time, but would also give more results.

During the evaluation and the post processing, a significant problem had observed regarding the methodology. We could not interpret the visualizations of the eye movements in the model space in spite of the simple objects and subtasks. (See Fig. 6.) The reason for this problem is the nature of the model space. The participants can rotate the whole model and the virtual space too. In a usability test every user could rotate, shift and zoom as they like, therefore will not be one same view, which means we have to evaluate for each participant separately. Furthermore, evaluation has to be based on dynamic videos of screen- and eye-tracking recordings instead of static screenshots.

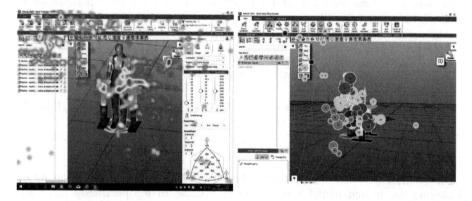

Fig. 6. A problem during the evaluation. Heatmaps and gaze plots are not interpretable in the model space because of the potential movements. Aggregated heatmap (left); aggregate gaze plots (right).

After this experience of the pilot, we will insert a new, short phase into the protocol of the planned usability tests, when the participants will be asked neither to move in model space nor to move the model.

For the further usability tests, it can be stated, the number of the involved participants (six) is correct, however, at least one unexperienced student participant is recommended, thus the correlation between the age, the experience and the task completion time can be observed. For instance, this is confirmed by the fact that the students had found the function of change the body posture of the human model faster than the teachers.

References

1. De Magistris, G., et al.: Dynamic control of DHM for ergonomic assessments. Int. J. Ind. Ergon. **43**, 170–180 (2013). https://doi.org/10.1016/j.ergon.2013.01.003
2. Santos, J., Sarriegi, J.M., Serrano, N., Torres, J.M.: Using ergonomic software in non-repetitive manufacturing processes: a case study. Int. J. Ind. Ergon. **37**, 267–275 (2007). https://doi.org/10.1016/j.ergon.2006.10.022
3. Bergman, C., Castro, P.R., Högberg, D., Hanson, L.: Implementation of suitable comfort model for posture and motion prediction in DHM supported vehicle design. Procedia Manuf. **3**, 3753–3758 (2015). https://doi.org/10.1016/j.promfg.2015.07.816
4. Sundin, A., Örtengren, R.: Digital human modeling for CAE applications. In: Handbook of Human Factors and Ergonomics, pp. 1053–1078. Wiley, Hoboken (2006). https://doi.org/10.1002/0470048204.ch39
5. Polášek, P., Bureš, M., Šimon, M.: Comparison of digital tools for ergonomics in practice. Procedia Eng. **100**, 1277–1285 (2015). https://doi.org/10.1016/j.proeng.2015.01.494
6. Rajaee, M.A., Arjmand, N., Shirazi-Adl, A., Plamondon, A., Schmidt, H.: Comparative evaluation of six quantitative lifting tools to estimate spine loads during static activities. Appl. Ergon. **48**, 22–32 (2015). https://doi.org/10.1016/j.apergo.2014.11.002
7. ViveLab Ergo. http://vivelab.cloud/
8. Blanchonette, P.: Jack Human Modelling Tool: A Review. Air Operations Division Defence Science and Technology Organisation DSTO-TR-2364, Air Operations Division DSTO Defence Science and Technology Organisation, Fishermans Bend (2010)
9. Berlin, C., Adams, C.: Production Ergonomics: Digital Human Modeling (2017). https://doi.org/10.1007/978-3-642-21799-9
10. Poole, A., Ball, L.: Eye tracking in human-computer interaction and usability research: current status and future prospects. In: Encyclopedia of Human-Computer Interaction (2006). https://doi.org/10.4018/978-1-59140-562-7
11. Romano Bergstrom, J.C., Olmsted-Hawala, E.L., Jans, M.E.: Age-related differences in eye tracking and usability performance: website usability for older adults. Int. J. Hum. Comput. Interact. **29**, 541–548 (2013). https://doi.org/10.1080/10447318.2012.728493
12. Józsa, E., Hámornik, B.P.: Find the difference! Eye tracking study on information seeking behavior using an online game. J. Eye Track. Vis. Cogn. Emot. **2**, 27–35 (2012)
13. Michalski, R.: Information presentation compatibility in a simple digital control panel design: eye-tracking study. Int. J. Occup. Saf. Ergon. **24**, 395–405 (2018). https://doi.org/10.1080/10803548.2017.1317469
14. Wang, J., Antonenko, P., Celepkolu, M., Jimenez, Y., Fieldman, E., Fieldman, A.: Exploring relationships between eye tracking and traditional usability testing data. Int. J. Hum. Comput. Interact. 1–12 (2018). https://doi.org/10.1080/10447318.2018.1464776
15. Tula, A.D., Kurauchi, A., Coutinho, F., Morimoto, C.: Heatmap explorer: an interactive gaze data visualization tool for the evaluation of computer interfaces. In: Proceedings of the 15th Brazilian Symposium on Human Factors in Computing Systems, pp. 24:1–24:9 (2016). https://doi.org/10.1145/3033701.3033725
16. Conradi, J., Busch, O., Alexander, T.: Optimal touch button size for the use of mobile devices while walking. Procedia Manuf. **3**, 387–394 (2015). https://doi.org/10.1016/j.promfg.2015.07.182

17. Orquin, J.L., Ashby, N.J.S., Clarke, A.D.F.: Areas of Interest as a signal detection problem in behavioral eye-tracking research. J. Behav. Decis. Making (2016). https://doi.org/10.1002/bdm.1867
18. Räihä, K.-J., Aula, A., Majaranta, P., Rantala, H., Koivunen, K.: Static visualization of temporal eye-tracking data. In: Costabile, M.F., Paternò, F. (eds.) INTERACT 2005. LNCS, vol. 3585, pp. 946–949. Springer, Heidelberg (2005). https://doi.org/10.1007/11555261_76

A Full-Chain OpenSim Model and Its Application on Posture Analysis of an Overhead Drilling Task

Jing Chang[1], Damien Chablat[2(✉)], Fouad Bennis[1], and Liang Ma[3]

[1] Ecole Centrale de Nantes, Laboratoire des Sciences du Numérique de Nantes (LS2N), UMR CNRS 6004, 44321 Nantes, France
[2] CNRS, Laboratoire des Sciences du Numérique de Nantes (LS2N), UMR CNRS 6004, 44321 Nantes, France
`damien.chablat@cnrs.fr`
[3] Department of Industrial Engineering, Tsinghua University, Beijing 100084, People's Republic of China

Abstract. Biomechanical motion simulation and kinetic analysis of human joints and muscles provide insights into Musculoskeletal disorders. OpenSim is an open-source platform that give easy access to biomechanical analysis, especially of muscles. The biomechanical analysis in OpenSim is based on pre-defined human models. Among the dozens of models available right now, none covers the muscles and joints of all the body parts. In view of the fact that most human motions are systemic, the lack of a comprehensive model prohibits synthesized and systematical biomechanical analysis. The aim of this research is to develop an OpenSim model which enables the full-chain dynamic analysis of tasks involving multi-bodies. The model is developed based on two existing models. It consists of 45 body segments, 424 muscles and 39 degrees of freedom. The model was then used to simulate an overhead drilling task. Six drilling postures are analyzed, and the estimated joint moments and muscle activations are compared .

Keywords: Biomechanical analysis · OpenSim model · Joint moment · Muscle activation · Overhead work · Drilling posture · Posture analysis

1 Introduction

Biomechanical analysis of human positions and motions enables investigations on the neuromusculoskeletal system even beyond experiments. It provides insights into many concerned issues, such as musculoskeletal Disorders (MSDs), which makes up the vast proposition of the occupational diseases [1]. When conducting biomechanical analyses, we have to bear in mind that human body is systematic: bodies and muscles are inter-connected as a whole kinematic chain. The state of one part may influent another without physical contact. For example, in a task of self-balance, the arm motions would influence the transversal pelvis-thorax moment up to 30% [2]. The full kinematic chain should be considered in biomechanical analysis.

© Springer Nature Switzerland AG 2019
V. G. Duffy (Ed.): HCII 2019, LNCS 11581, pp. 33–44, 2019.
https://doi.org/10.1007/978-3-030-22216-1_3

Over the past decades, many tools have been developed for biomechanical simulation and analysis. OpenSim [3] is one of the virtual human modeling software that have been widely used [4,5]. There are immense amount of data and dozens of musculoskeletal models available, such as the running model [6] which includes muscles of the lower extremities and the torso, the lumbar spinal model [7] which contains the eight main muscle groups of the lumbar spine, the arm model [8] that covers 50 muscles on the right upper extremity. However, no musculoskeletal model has included the full kinematic chain of human body. There is a need of a full-chain model that enables synthesized and systematical biomechanical analysis. For example, using a muscle fatigue model [9] and a recovery model [10], it is possible to determine the maximum working time by knowing, the maximum voluntary contraction, the fatigue and recovery parameters as well as the activation rate of each muscle. With this model, we can also do posture optimization using worker fatigue and comfort indexes [11] as well the maximum endurance time for static posture [12] or dynamic posture [13]. This method was partially applied in an OpenSim model to study fatigue while walking in [14].

The aim of this research is to develop a full-chain OpenSim musculoskeletal model that includes segments and muscles of torso and all limbs. The model is then used to simulate an overhead drilling task. Six different postures are analyzed, and comparisons are made in view of joint moments and muscle efforts. Specially attention is paid to the full chain effect.

Next section presents the full-chain OpenSim musculoskeletal model. The simulation of an overhead task is reported in Sect. 3. Section 4 is devoted to the analysis of the simulation results. Finally, Sect. 5 presents a discussion of results and their application for ergonomic analysis.

2   Model Development

The full-chain model is developed based on two existing models: Raabe's Full-body Lumbar-spinal model [15] and Saul's 7 degree-of-freedom arm model [16]. The former includes muscles of the lumbar and the lower extremities, with 21 segments, 30 degrees-of-freedom, and 324 muscle actuators. It is characterized by a detailed description of the trunk musculature. Its geometry is obtained from a male of 180 cm and 75.3 kg. The latter, Saul's Arm model represents the right shoulder, arm and hand of a male of 177 cm and 75.0 kg, with 7 segments and 50 muscles.

To build up the full-chain model, we conjoint the two models above, and reconstruct the left upper extremity to endue it with the same segment structure and musculature as the right one. The entire model consists of 424 muscles, 46 body segments, with 39 degrees of freedom, shown in Fig. 1. Its segment mass parameters are derived from the 3-D scanned geometries of a 31-year-old male of 177 cm and 77.0 kg [17]. Validation tests were performed to validate this model with an ART motion capture system. Only the muscles of the neck are not present in this model which does not allow to include the movements of the head to see the task to be carried out in our study. The OpenSim model is

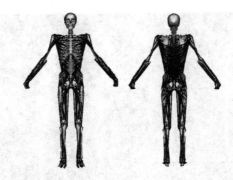

Fig. 1. The whole-body model visualized in OpenSim

defined in an XML file with links to the bone geometry for graphics rendering. The position of the motion capture markers can also be changed.

3 Simulation of an Overhead Task

3.1 Overhead Work

Overhead work is constantly accused by epidemiologists for its close relationship with shoulder disorders [18,19]. It is always accompanied by abnormal postures (for example, upper arm flexion or adduction 60 [18]) and forceful exertions. For some occupations like welder [20] and driller [21], these tasks are sometimes impractical to be avoided. An alternative plan would be to optimize the working posture.

An optimized posture is characterized by lower physical load. When estimating posture loads, attention should be payed to the integrity of human body. There is a possibility that some postures would reduce load from one part of body while bring in extra load to another.

In this study, we use the full-chain OpenSim model to simulate a typical overhead drilling task. Six task postures are analyzed. In each case, joint moments and muscle activations are checked. The sum of activations of all muscles is viewed as the index of posture load. Hypothesis is made that the index varies with different postures.

3.2 Simulation Setup

Overhead drilling is a common task in industry. Workers hold a driller in hand while applying an force upwards. For a specific task, workers' drilling postures vary with the spatial position of the target point. Postures that vary in the sagittal plane are the main concerns [22]. In this study, we simulate an overhead drilling task about 30 cm higher over head. Six postures are applied,

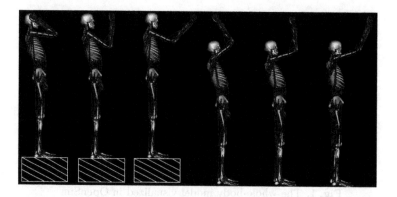

Fig. 2. Simulations of six drilling postures where L means a low hand posture and H a high hand posture with respect to the human body. From left to right: low close reach (L-C); low middle reach (L-M); low far reach (L-F); high close reach (H-C); high middle reach (H-M); high far reach (H-F).

which represents 6 possible combinations of two factors: reach height (with/without stepladder) and reach distance (close reach/middle reach/far reach), shown in Fig. 2.

The "stepladder" is 30 cm high. It enables the "low-reach" postures with the wrist height at eye-level in comparison with the "high-reach" ones. In aspects of the reach distance, "close-reach", "middle-reach", "far-reach" are used to denote positions with wrist aligned with the pelvis mass center, aligned with tiptoes, and 15 cm further away from tiptoes, respectively. Settings of the model's joint space is presented in Table 1. The unmentioned joint coordinates are set to zero. An external force of 44 N is applied downwards on the proximal row of the right hand, which simulates the load of a 2.27 kg portable drill together with a compression force of 22 N [22]. Ground reaction force is applied evenly on the two feet.

Table 1. Model joint space settings. [Unit: degree]

Coordinates	Permitted joint motions	Postures					
		L-C	L-M	L-F	H-C	H-M	H-F
Flex_extension	Lumbar extension	5	5	0	5	5	0
Elv_angle	Shoulder adduction	80	80	80	80	80	80
Shoulder_elv	Shoulder elevation	75	50	70	120	100	110
Elbow_flexion	Elbow flexion	145	120	60	80	70	40
Flexion	Wrist flexion	−45	−45	−45	−45	−45	−45
Deviation	Wrist deviation	0	−5	−10	0	−5	−10

Inverse dynamics are conducted, which computes joint moments; muscle forces and activations are estimated on optimizing the sum of total muscle activations.

4   Results of Simulation

Shoulder moment is the main concern of the overhead work. The simulation with the Whole-body OpenSim model permits not only the estimation of the shoulder elevation moment but a comprehensive overview of joint moments in all coordinates, as shown in Table 2.

Table 2. Estimated joint moments of six simulations. [Unit: $N.m$]

Coordinates	Postures					
	L-C	L-M	L-F	H-C	H-M	H-F
Shoulder elevation	12.27	13.87	13.90	11.58	14.39	13.17
Shoulder rotation	−7.78	−6.60	−6.96	−5.95	−7.26	−6.66
Shoulder adduction	−0.48	−0.43	0.65	−0.39	−0.27	0.62
Elbow flexion	−2.40	−4.04	−6.18	−5.57	−6.22	−7.26
Hand flexion	−3.10	−3.92	−2.03	−4.00	−4.25	−3.24
Hand deviation	2.07	9.97	−4.41	−13.40	9.69	−4.64
Hand pronation	6.38	−1.69	−6.27	4.34	0.06	−3.47

Results shows that as far as the shoulder, the rotation moment is considerable beside of the elevation moment. The high close reach posture is estimated to lead to the least shoulder moment (17.92 N.m in total), while the high middle reach posture is related to the most (21.92 N.m in total). The elbow flexion moment varies substantially (from 2.40 N.m to 7.26 N.m). So is the wrist moment, which varies from 11.35 N.m to 21.74 N.m. It is notable that it is the high close reach posture which brings about the least shoulder moment that leads to the largest wrist moment.

Muscle activations are computed on optimizing the sum of total muscle activation while counteracting the joint moments. Table 3 presents the sum of activations of some muscle groups and of whole-body muscles in the six simulations. As a whole, the sum of all muscles' activations varies from 11.88 to 29.35, which indicates a variation of average muscle activation from 2.8% to 6.9%. This suggests that the muscles exert efforts of different levels in different postures. Posture optimization would be a efficient way to interfere with muscle-related disorders.

The upper arm and shoulder muscle group (shown in Fig. 3(a)) is the primary concern of overhead works. The simulation results show that the average activation of muscles in this group varies from 2.2% (low close reach) to 8.6% (high far reach). It can also be figured out that the muscles of lower arm could be activated in varying degrees as well (averages vary from 1.2% to 8.6%).

The simulation results also highlight the roles played by muscles of latissimus dorsi (shown in Fig. 3(b)) and hip abductor (shown in Fig. 3(c)). Significantly asymmetrical activation levels are shown between left and right side of the two muscle groups. For the latissimus dorsi, muscles of the right side are more activated than that of the left. And for the hip abductor, muscles of the left side are intensively activated (about 16.8% in average in every posture) while that of the right side are almost relaxed (about 0.3% to 0.4% in average). It is also notable that the activations of the right latissimus dorsi muscles vary with postures. For the low middle reach and the high middle reach, right latissimus dorsi shows far less activation than in other postures.

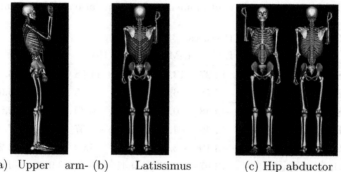

(a) Upper arm-shoulder   (b) Latissimus dorsi   (c) Hip abductor

Fig. 3. Locations of three muscle groups

As far as overhead works, the activation of some specific muscles such as the biceps, the triceps, the deltoids have concerned researchers. In the current study, the activations of these muscles are estimated, as shown in Table 4. The biceps and posterior deltoids are not significantly activated while the anterior deltoids exerts considerable efforts in all the six simulations. The lateral deltoids is activated enormously with high close reach and high far reach posture, whereas

Table 3. Estimated muscle activations of muscle groups

Muscle group	No. of muscles	Mean muscle activation					
		L-C	L-M	L-F	H-C	H-M	H-F
Right lower arm	18	6.88%	3.96%	1.20%	8.60%	3.18%	1.42%
Right upper arm-shoulder	22	2.18%	4.92%	8.18%	8.31%	6.38%	8.59%
Right Latissimus dorsi	14	82.29%	0.39%	81.64%	40.95%	0.43%	78.97%
Left Latissimus dorsi	14	0.09%	0.06%	0.84%	0.10%	0.06%	0.65%
Right hip abductor	10	0.34%	0.32%	0.41%	0.38%	0.32%	0.37%
Left hip abductor	10	16.77%	16.77%	16.77%	16.77%	16.77%	16.77%
Whole-body	424	5.81%	2.80%	6.43%	5.29%	3.62%	6.92%

Table 4. Estimated activations of individual muscles

Muscle	Muscle activation rate					
	L-C	L-M	L-F	H-C	H-M	H-F
Biceps long head	0.00%	0.36%	0.00%	0.00%	0.36%	0.00%
Biceps short head	0.39%	0.36%	0.00%	0.00%	0.36%	0.00%
Anterior deltoids	22.06%	18.93%	24.37%	13.37%	36.98%	19.95%
Lateral deltoids	19.69%	0.00%	19.02%	100.00%	7.70%	66.49%
Posterior deltoids	0.39%	0.36%	0.46%	0.43%	0.36%	0.42%
Triceps long head	0.39%	8.98%	0.00%	0.00%	0.00%	0.00%
Triceps medial head	0.39%	5.83%	16.15%	30.54%	13.28%	18.39%
Triceps short head	0.39%	5.72%	15.69%	30.00%	13.01%	17.06%

makes trivial exertions with low middle reach posture. The long head of triceps does not exert markable effort except with the low middle reach posture; the medial and short head of triceps are most activated with high close posture (about 30%), and least activated with low close reach posture (about 0.4%).

5   Discussions

5.1   The Full Chain Effect

When evaluating work loads of the shoulder joint, ergonomists pay much attention to the moment of shoulder elevation and abduction, rather than the rotation [18,19]. For example, Anton et al. [22] studied an overhead drilling task with similar posture configurations with the current simulation, in which the shoulder elevation moments that are calculated from measurements taken on still video frames are used as the only indicators of posture loads, whereas results of the current simulation imply that shoulder rotation moment is also considerable. To evaluate the moments of multi-degrees-of-freedom joints, the use of refined musculoskeletal models are strongly suggested.

The full-chain effect is underlined by the simulation results. Significant activations of the right hip adductors go with all the six postures, hypothetically because of the asymmetric loads between the left and right arm. Intensive activations of the right latissimus dorsi are found in postures with forward or backward arm reach, other than the neutral. This result implies the possible relationship between back loads and arm positions.

Low back pain is an important and costly health problem in industry [23,24]. Among all occupations, the highest recurrence rate is reported in nurses and drivers [25,26]. Both of the two occupations require lots of forward or backward arm reaches. Among the enormous efforts to study the ergonomic risk factors of low back pain [27,28], very little has been made on the arms. We suggest more attention to arms with regards to low back pain, and also a synthesized point of view in future ergonomic researches.

5.2   The Full-Chain Model as a Way of Ergonomic Posture Analysis

One of the main findings of the overhead work simulation is that sum of all muscles' activation level varies significantly with different working postures. Here the muscle activations are estimated while solving the muscle-moment redundancy problem. Currently, the commonly used methods for this problem include static optimization (SO), computed muscle control (CMC) and neuromusculoskeletal tracking (NMT) [29]. These methods are based on optimizations to minimize a given performance criterion. For SO and CMC, the criterion is the sum of squares of muscle activations [30], and for NMT, the criterion is the cumulative muscle efforts expressed in a cost function (see Eq. 11 in Seth and Pandy [31]). The current study takes the SO method, which incorporates time-instant instead of time-dependency cases. It is very computationally efficient, and as concluded by Anderson and Pandy [30], it provides reasonable predictions of muscle forces and is hereby effective. The generated muscle activation could fairly be used as a representation of muscle effort.

The posture analysis benefits also from the whole-body muscle model. As illustrated above, the full-chain effect should be considered in physical assessments. The engagement of the whole-body muscle model would avoid the case that the position reduces efforts on one part while bring in extra efforts on another. The sum of all muscles' activation can be an good indicator of posture load when conducting posture analysis.

5.3   Overhead Working

Simulations of the six working postures indicate that the forward/backward reach (the L-C, L-F, H-C and H-F) postures are much more effort-demanding than the neutral reach (the L-M and H-M) postures (Table 3) in the overhead drilling task. This result suggests that the efforts spent on horizontal body balance takes a great portion in total efforts. The study of Maciukiewicz et al. [32] indicates that for upward overhead drilling, further forward reach distance results in greater muscle demands (measured by EMG of upper extremity muscles). Similar results were reported by Shin and Yoo [33]: overhead work with a forward reach distance of 30 cm leads to stronger EMG activities of upper trapezius, lower trapezius, anterior deltoid and serratus anterior than that with the distance of 15 cm.

The EMG activity of anterior deltoid was found to be less intensive with backward reach overhead drilling posture than that with neutral reach ones by Anton [22]. The finding is different from the result of current simulation (Table 4). Anton's work was based on an experimental task simulation with 20 volunteers. One explanation is that in experiments, the subjects would turn their head right and look up towards the drilling point. Whereas in our simulation, no head movement is considered due to model limitation (Fig. 4). The small difference would probably influent the anterior deltoid, which works to connect the neck and shoulder. Future work should be done to refine the movement of head and neck of the full-chain model.

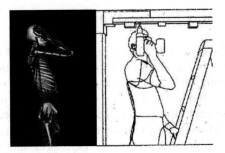

Fig. 4. Backward drilling posture in current simulation (left) and in Anton's work (right) [22].

Most previous researches on overhead drilling postures reported a significant difference in efforts demanded by low reach and by high reach [22,33]. There are also exceptions. In the study of Maciukiewicz et al. [32], with the same working height, the standing posture with lower arm reach is found to go with more intensive muscle activities in compare with the sitting posture with higher arm height. In current simulation, the lower reach height is estimated to go with a bit more muscular efforts than the higher reach height in the case of far forward reach. The diverse results indicate the complexity of posture analysis. No universe principle could apply to all practical cases. Biomechanical analysis based on detailed posture configuration should be conducted for job design.

Besides, the simulation result also reveals significantly different activation states for various heads of a muscle branch (Table 4), which indicates different roles played by different heads of a muscle. Therefore, it is suggested that future researches avoid vague terms such as biceps, deltoids, but rather precisely down to the head of muscles.

Concerning the study of the muscle fatigue, an activation rate equal to 100% means the worker cannot keep this posture because his muscle capacities will decrease quickly. Conversely, a low activation rate means the worker can keep longer this posture. During usual tasks, it is often request to be under 20% of activation rate. So, for this task, only the L-M posture is feasible for drilling operations.

Indeed, if we compare the for the whole body, the estimated muscle activation, the L-C and H-C postures are mostly the same. However, for the L-C posture, maximal activation rate permits to the worker a short activity but not for the H-C posture.

This last remark permits us to write a future optimization problem: minimize the whole body muscle activation under constraint to the maximal value of local muscle activation. This problem need to find new realistic human postures and the computation of the inverse dynamic model at any steeps of the computation to determine new muscle activation rates.

6   Conclusions and Future Works

This research introduces a full-chain OpenSim model. It consists of 45 body segments, 424 muscles and 39 degrees of freedom. This model was used to simulate an overhead drilling task. Results suggest that beside of shoulder elevation moment, shoulder rotation moment is also considerable during overhead drilling; and back muscles play an important role. In addition, the total muscle activations vary markedly with different postures for this task. Conclusions are drawn that the full-chain OpenSim model facilities biomechanical analysis in three aspects: (i) a comprehensive estimation of multi-degree-of-freedom joints' moments; (ii) understanding how the muscles across body cooperate in motions; (iii) optimizing working posture in view of total muscle efforts.

Future works will be done to optimize working postures under constraint of maximal muscle activity to minimize the worker fatigue or to adjust the behavior of exosqueleton mechanism attached to the worker. Indeed, a local assistant can remove local muscle constraint but increase the muscle activity, for another part body, and yields to new musculosqueleton disorder. Thus, the full-body muscle model with a motion capture system can also predict the dynamic muscle endurance times for complex task where many muscles are activated to produce the motion.

Acknowledgments. This work was supported by INTERWEAVE Project (Erasmus Mundus Partnership Asia-Europe) under Grants number IW14AC0456 and IW14AC0148, by the National Natural Science Foundation of China under Grant numbers 71471095 and by Chinese State Scholarship Fund.

References

1. Eurogip: Declaration des maladies professionnelles: problematique et bonnes pratiques dans cinq pays europeens, p. 44 (2015). https://www.eurogip.fr/images/documents/3906/Rapport_DeclarationMP_EUROGIP_102F.pdf
2. Robert, T., Chèze, L., Dumas, R., Verriest, J.P.: Validation of net joint loads calculated by inverse dynamics in case of complex movements: application to balance recovery movements. J. Biomech. **40**(11), 2450–2456 (2007)
3. Delp, S.L., et al.: OpenSim: open-source software to create and analyze dynamic simulations of movement. IEEE Trans. Biomed. Eng. **54**(11), 1940–1950 (2007)
4. Thelen, D.G., Anderson, F.C.: Using computed muscle control to generate forward dynamic simulations of human walking from experimental data. J. Biomech. **39**(6), 1107–1115 (2006)
5. Kim, H.K., Zhang, Y.: Estimation of lumbar spinal loading and trunk muscle forces during asymmetric lifting tasks: application of whole-body musculoskeletal modelling in opensim. Ergonomics **60**(4), 563–576 (2017)
6. Hamner, S.R., Seth, A., Delp, S.L.: Muscle contributions to propulsion and support during running. J. Biomech. **43**(14), 2709–2716 (2010)
7. Christophy, M., Senan, N.A.F., Lotz, J.C., O'Reilly, O.M.: A musculoskeletal model for the lumbar spine. Biomech. Model. Mechanobiol. **11**(1–2), 19–34 (2012)

8. Holzbaur, K.R., Murray, W.M., Delp, S.L.: A model of the upper extremity for simulating musculoskeletal surgery and analyzing neuromuscular control. Ann. Biomed. Eng. **33**(6), 829–840 (2005)

9. Ma, L., Chablat, D., Bennis, F., Zhang, W.: A new simple dynamic muscle fatigue model and its validation. Int. J. Ind. Ergon. **39**(1), 211–220 (2009)

10. Ma, L., Chablat, D., Bennis, F., Zhang, W., Guillaume, F.: A new muscle fatigue and recovery model and its ergonomics application in human simulation. Virtual Phys. Prototyping **5**(3), 123–137 (2010)

11. Ma, L., Zhang, W., Chablat, D., Bennis, F., Guillaume, F.: Multi-objective optimisation method for posture prediction and analysis with consideration of fatigue effect and its application case. Comput. Ind. Eng. **57**(4), 1235–1246 (2009)

12. Ma, L., Chablat, D., Bennis, F., Zhang, W., Hu, B., Guillaume, F.: A novel approach for determining fatigue resistances of different muscle groups in static cases. Int. J. Ind. Ergon. **41**(1), 10–18 (2011)

13. Sakka, S., Chablat, D., Ma, R., Bennis, F.: Predictive model of the human muscle fatigue: application to repetitive push-pull tasks with light external load. Int. J. Hum. Factors Model. Simul. **5**(1), 81–97 (2015)

14. Chang, J., Chablat, D., Bennis, F., Ma, L.: Muscle fatigue analysis using opensim. In: Duffy, V.G. (ed.) DHM 2017. LNCS, vol. 10286, pp. 95–106. Springer, Cham (2017). https://doi.org/10.1007/978-3-319-58463-8_9

15. Raabe, M.E., Chaudhari, A.M.: An investigation of jogging biomechanics using the full-body lumbar spine model: model development and validation. J. Biomech. **49**(7), 1238–1243 (2016)

16. Saul, K.R., et al.: Benchmarking of dynamic simulation predictions in two software platforms using an upper limb musculoskeletal model. Comput. Methods Biomech. Biomed. Eng. **18**(13), 1445–1458 (2015)

17. Chang, J., Chablat, D., Fouad, B., Ma, L., Bennis, F.: Using 3D scan to determine human body segment mass in opensim model. In: 20th International Conference on Human-computer Interaction. arXiv preprint arXiv:1805.05330 (2018)

18. Van Rijn, R.M., Huisstede, B.M., Koes, B.W., Burdorf, A.: Associations between work-related factors and specific disorders of the shoulder–a systematic review of the literature. Scand. J. Work Environ. Health **36**(3), 189–201 (2010)

19. Bernard, B.P., Putz-Anderson, V.: Musculoskeletal disorders and workplace factors; a critical review of epidemiologic evidence for work-related musculoskeletal disorders of the neck, upper extremity, and low back (1997)

20. Herberts, P., Kadefors, R., Andersson, G., Petersén, I.: Shoulder pain in industry: an epidemiological study on welders. Acta Orthop. Scand. **52**(3), 299–306 (1981)

21. Rempel, D., Star, D., Barr, A., Blanco, M.M., Janowitz, I.: Field evaluation of a modified intervention for overhead drilling. J. Occup. Environ. Hyg. **7**(4), 194–202 (2010)

22. Anton, D., Shibley, L.D., Fethke, N.B., Hess, J., Cook, T.M., Rosecrance, J.: The effect of overhead drilling position on shoulder moment and electromyography. Ergonomics **44**(5), 489–501 (2001)

23. Walker, B.F.: The prevalence of low back pain: a systematic review of the literature from 1966 to 1998. Clin. Spine Surg. **13**(3), 205–217 (2000)

24. Dagenais, S., Caro, J., Haldeman, S.: A systematic review of low back pain cost of illness studies in the united states and internationally. Spine J. **8**(1), 8–20 (2008)

25. Andersson, G.B.: Epidemiological features of chronic low-back pain. Lancet **354**(9178), 581–585 (1999)

26. June, K.J., Cho, S.H.: Low back pain and work-related factors among nurses in intensive care units. J. Clin. Nurs. **20**(3–4), 479–487 (2011)

27. Tissot, F., Messing, K., Stock, S.: Studying the relationship between low back pain and working postures among those who stand and those who sit most of the working day. Ergonomics **52**(11), 1402–1418 (2009)
28. Hoogendoorn, W.E., et al.: Flexion and rotation of the trunk and lifting at work are risk factors for low back pain: results of a prospective cohort study. Spine **25**(23), 3087–3092 (2000)
29. Lin, Y.C., Dorn, T.W., Schache, A.G., Pandy, M.G.: Comparison of different methods for estimating muscle forces in human movement. Proc. Inst. Mech. Eng. Part H J. Eng. Med. **226**(2), 103–112 (2012)
30. Anderson, F.C., Pandy, M.G.: Static and dynamic optimization solutions for gait are practically equivalent. J. Biomech. **34**(2), 153–161 (2001)
31. Seth, A., Pandy, M.G.: A neuromusculoskeletal tracking method for estimating individual muscle forces in human movement. J. Biomech. **40**(2), 356–366 (2007)
32. Maciukiewicz, J.M., Cudlip, A.C., Chopp-Hurley, J.N., Dickerson, C.R.: Effects of overhead work configuration on muscle activity during a simulated drilling task. Appl. Ergon. **53**, 10–16 (2016)
33. Shin, S.J., Yoo, W.G.: Effects of overhead work involving different heights and distances on neck and shoulder muscle activity. Work **51**(2), 321–326 (2015)

Design and Evaluation of the System Device for Mitigation of the Low Back Pain Among Veterinarians

Tzu-Lien Chou[(✉)], Hsi-Jen Chen, and Fong-Gong Wu

Department of Industrial Design, National Cheng Kung University,
No. 1, University Road, Tainan 701, Taiwan
jaskl234tw@gmail.com

Abstract. This Study proposes an innovative auxiliary device to solve the low back pain (LBP) caused by veterinarian's poor work posture. In recent years, with the heightened status of pets in people's lives, the demand in animal hospitals has increased significantly, and the occupational hazards of veterinarians have also emerged gradually. Veterinary work environment is complex and diverse, and working hours are overly long, which can easily cause the issue of the LBP. Among the patients with the LBP, many people are classified as non-specific low back pain (NSLBP). This means that there is no known pathological anatomy for the LBP itself, and its principle is strongly related to the compressive load of the spine. NSLBP should be considered as a change in the structure of the whole body's spine. Poor posture can lead to imbalance of curvature of the spine and damage to soft tissues. This Study begins with the posture state of the veterinary surgery, where biomechanics and physiological anatomy are used to target the interaction of the lower back and shoulder flexion angles during the operation of the veterinarian, and to consider the results of the blood flow when the muscles are tight. This Study will design an auxiliary device for the veterinary surgery to effectively reduce the mechanical load on the spine, overstretch the muscles and promote blood circulation, thereby improving the fluency of the veterinary surgery and slowing the veterinarian's NSLBP.

Keywords: Veterinary · Non-specific low back pain · Assistive device

1 Introduction

The high suicide risk among doctors and veterinarians has been widely documented due to the overly long man-hours and dramatic changes in work patterns [1]. Fritschi [39] and Platt et al. [40] point out that veterinarians have a three-fold higher risk of suicide than normal people, and the proportion of veterinarians committing suicide is higher than that of pharmacists, dentists, and other medical practitioners [2], mainly because of the complicated working environment and long working hours, coupled with social pressure, sense of incompetence/helplessness and mistakes, etc., which leads to the relatively complex occupational risk factors faced by veterinarians [3].

This Study hopes to find the best way and design elements to systematically integrate the veterinary surgical posture, so as to create an improved design of device to

© Springer Nature Switzerland AG 2019
V. G. Duffy (Ed.): HCII 2019, LNCS 11581, pp. 45–58, 2019.
https://doi.org/10.1007/978-3-030-22216-1_4

tackle with the non-specific low back pain (NSLBP) suffered by the veterinarian and to promote the efficiency and quality of the veterinarian. The background and purpose of this study will be detailed below.

1.1 Background

Studies indicate that 50% of veterinarians in New Zealand suffer from chronic musculoskeletal problems, mainly because of the long hours of work. In recent years, musculoskeletal discomfort (MSD) has become a disease in the veterinary industry [4]. However, Fritschi et al. do not define the MSD among the veterinarians and the details of the MSD in relation to their body parts, so follow-up studies conduct a more indepth investigation of veterinarians in different parts of New Zealand and find that 96% of veterinarians have encountered the MSD-related issues, where 67% says their life is affected and 18% can no longer work, and the most affected part of the body is the lower back, accounting for 73% of the entire population in this study [5].

According to the occupational injury system records managed by the Ministry of Labor in Taiwan from 2008 to 2013, 3477 occupational diseases were reported, of which 873 were related to lumbar vertebrae, and the number of cases related to the low back pain (LBP) was also increasing year by year [6]. However, although the work-related musculoskeletal disorder will not cause harm immediately, long-term accumulation will make it a major cause of disability in a veterinarian, which can then lead to more diseases, the most common of which is the LBP. In the United States, the lifetime prevalence of the LBP is 60–85% [7], costing about $100 billion [8].

LBP is just a symptom, not a disease. It can be caused by multiple causes [9]. Common causes include soft tissue damage or inflammation of the back fascia, including the back muscles, ligaments, tendons, acute and chronic strains, sprains, contusions, and the risk of the head's lifting posture and waist and back injuries are also focused on in many studies [10]. Thus, it is known that the LBP is not just a single disease, but a symptom caused by multiple causes [11]. The most common form of the LBP is the NSLBP, which means that the LBP itself does not have a known cause from the perspective of pathological anatomy. Thus, approximately 85% of cases are classified as the NSLBP [12]. As a result, the doctor's diagnosis process or the patient's testing process will cause a large medical cost. NSLBP should be regarded as a change in the structure of the whole body's spine. Poor posture can lead to pathological changes between the bones of the spine and soft tissues, so the analysis cannot be restricted to the lumbar region [13].

1.2 Purpose

Poor posture among veterinarians during prolonged surgery can easily cause the NSLBP. This Study will learn how to maintain the correct posture and improve the joint mobility during the veterinary surgery from Literature Review to improve the issue of the NSLBP among veterinarians. An innovative assessment method will be produced to consider the spine angle and blood flow during the veterinary surgery, and summarize those factors during the procedure of surgery into a posture classification system. The posture classification system can be used as a tool to assess posture stress and prevent the NSLBP among veterinarians, including the hands, arms, neck and lower back, as well as the time period of remaining in the posture. Based on biomechanics and physiological anatomy, the posture state can be used to explain the interaction between the lower back and shoulder flexion angle and the mechanics during the operation, and the result of blood flow when the muscle is tight will be considered as well. Minimizing discomfort can help to reduce the risk of the LBP [14] among veterinarians.

The purpose of this study will be summarized into the following four points:

1. Maintain or control joint movements and reduce the problem of slouching due to overly reliance on the vision.
2. Provide an upward moment that supports the torso, and reduce the angle of the spine and the mechanical load, thus reducing the force on the lower back and neck.
3. Promote blood circulation in the hands of the veterinarian during the surgery to help reduce excessive muscle tension and improve mobility of the shoulder joints compared to that in the general state.
4. Improve the quality and efficiency of veterinary work, increase work comfort and slow down the occurrence of the NSLBP.

2   Literature Review

Nowadays, most of the research and design for mitigation of the LBP are based on drug therapy and physical stimulation. There is no discussion about the physiological mechanisms and correlations of factors that may induce the LBP. Therefore, this study will re-examine the influence of trunk changes on the severity of NSLBP, which is briefly described as follows:

2.1   Spinal Changes

The NSLBP is not just a symptom. There are many possible reasons, like the psychological factors [15], biomechanical factors [16] and many others. Studies in the human body have found that the magnitude of compression loads on spine is strongly correlated with the injury caused by the LBP among the patients [17].

The spine will absorb or transfer the force between the upper and lower limbs when the body is in a certain posture, and the proper dynamic balance will be maintained in combination with appropriate visual motion control [18, 19]. The functional unit of the spine contains two adjacent vertebrae and soft tissues in between, and the vertebral body is the structure mainly subjected to the compressive load (Fig. 1). Some studies have also linked the flexion posture to the underlying mechanisms of the LBP. As the flexion posture can change the passive mechanical properties of the trunk and weakens the trunk's proprioception [20, 21], it can damage the active neuromuscular control of the spine. These changes may cause the spine to become overloaded and unstable, thus increasing the risk of lumbar injury [22].

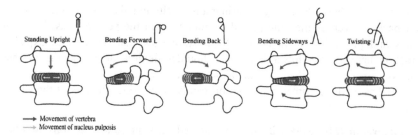

Fig. 1. Different positions may damage your spine. (Sequence Olgakabel [42]-Reorganized by this Study)

There are quite a lot of research literatures on the biomechanical model of the lower back. The biomechanical law uses the mechanical model to estimate the stress on the lower back and joints. This way, the force on each part can be clearly known, and the patterns related to the lower back mainly include the biomechanical model proposed by Chaffin in 1969, which divided the main body into seven links. Without considering the influence of inertia, the angle of each joint is taken by photography to calculate the force on the spine. The principle of force and moment balance, where torque equals force times distance ($T = F * L$) and $M_{muscle} = F_{muscle} * d$, is adopted to compare the calculated value at L5/S1 and verify the result of joint reaction and torque [23]. The study conducted by the National Institute for Occupational Safety and Health (NIOSH) also points out that if the force on the L5/S1 intervertebral disc exceeds the action limit by 3400 Newtons, it will increase the risk of injury caused by the LBP [24]. It can be seen that the factors inducing the NSLBP are no longer limited to the lesions in the lumbar spine, but are more related to the curvature of the spine and the changes in the trunk [25], The more curved position requires more muscle strength to offset the moment about the lower back, so how to reduce the moment about the lower back through analysis of the posture structure of different parts of the trunk, thus reducing the total compressive stress acting on the spine (Fig. 2) will be the focus of this study.

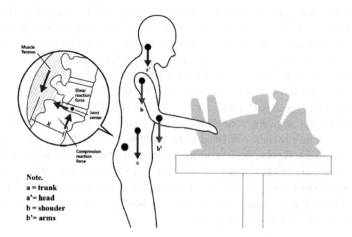

Fig. 2. The biomechanics of the human spine

2.2   Soft Tissue Changes

Experts point out that prolonged spinal flexion can lead to back muscle fatigue, and studies have shown that in this position, the torso extensor muscles will creep. The back muscles also reflexively contract to limit the angle of the spine, thus protecting the spine from injury [26]. Under the high static load for a long period, ischemia and hypoxia will cause energy loss and pain in muscles or tendons [27]. And if the work involves fine hand movements, the pain should be related to the vasodilation of the trapezius muscle [28].

In recent years, studies have delved into the relationship between the angle of the back, the degree of shoulder flexion and different levels of discomfort for different muscle groups. It has been found that the angle of shoulder flexion and the angle of elbow flexion has a significant influence on the level of discomfort for different muscle groups [29]. Therefore, the design must consider how to reduce the interaction between the MSDs, so as to reduce the risk effect.

Through the concept of back extensions, we can understand the relationship between muscles (Fig. 3) and locations. It is found that when there is a change in the muscles of the hand, it actually affects the muscle groups in charge of the shoulders and lower back. If the relationship between the trapezius muscle and the shoulder angle is discussed, as the shoulder angle and the height of the arm increase, the trapezius muscle will be overactive, resulting in a decrease in the blood flow [30]. If the trunk is in a tight, stressed state for a long time, the state of poor blood circulation will be extended to the whole body. If the nerves between the cervical vertebrae are pressed again, the muscles will be tense, the shoulders and necks will be sore, and the headache and arm numbness will be indirectly caused. Studies have shown that skin temperature contributes to thermal comfort and autoregulatory response throughout the body [31]. In a low temperature environment, maintaining a stable hand and body temperature above a certain level is an important key to maintain operational ability [32]. Studies have also pointed out that the standing posture can affect the muscles and blood flow, so the interaction of the shoulder flexion angle, elbow flexion angle and back angle should be considered. It has an important impact on the stability of the spine [30].

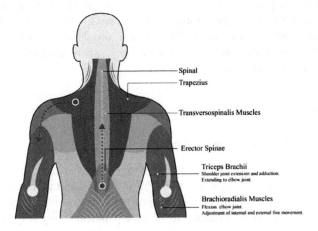

Fig. 3. Back muscle anatomy

Bru, Svebak, Mykletun & Gitlesen also suggested that in order to reduce the back pain of the medical staff, attention should be paid not only to the source of external physical load, but also how to relieve neck and shoulder pain. Studies on the LBP should not only start with the waist, but combine the biomechanics principles of the back with the physiological concepts to maintain normal body temperature regulation and thermal comfort in order to control the blood flow between muscles and achieve homeostasis.

2.3 Postural Control

Existing research shows that the NSLBP can affect the capabilities in postural control, emphasizing that motion control can affect a person's ability to proces postural control, and the LBP patients are prone to damage to their central nervous system [33]. The stability in the posture of the NSLBP patients will be worse than that of healthy subjects. Postural Control reduces the coordination of the back muscles and over-stretches the muscles [34]. Therefore, maintaining a balance between static and dynamic postures in any work activity can prevent the LBP problem from occurring. In addition, the veterinarian will inevitably maintain the surgical posture to some extent. As the shoulders are shrunk for a long time, and the trunk is not used to support the body, the core mucles can be debilitated to cause muscle paralysis and reduced shoulder mobility. Core mucles activey has been recognized as a way to reduce damage and increase tissue health [35].

Many designs that address the LBP will lead to compensatory patterns [36]. As the movement of any segment of the spine is limited, other segments may suffer damages. Meanwhile, most of the existing products do not consider the correlation between lumbar motion and the whole body. As the job task involves exercise of the whole body, it is necessary to analyze the influence of spinal exercise on the lower back during work. The Swiss neuroscientist, Brügger [41], uses the gear mechanism to illustrate the chain reaction caused by the spine posture, which is also known as the Brugger Sitting Posture. In the past, we used to see only the relevant areas or nearby tissues upon occurrence of the pain and disease. However, the body is actually working as a whole and each part will affect another. Therefore, Brugger divides the spine into several parts, using a simple gear rotation mechanism to illustrate the chain reaction caused by the spine posture, where the cervical vertebrae, thoracic vertebrae and lumbar vertebrae are considered a coherent system, where changes to one part can affect the overall alignment of the spine.

3   Methods

3.1 Veterinary Hospital Observation

Through interviews and observations with veterinarians, it is easy to understand that veterinarians are prone to changes in lumbar curvature and soft tissues due to the poor surgical posture. The influencing factors include the actual operations of the veterinarian, environmental design and conditions of the equipment in use (Fig. 4). Regarding the follow-up observations and step analysis of the veterinary procedure for ovario-hysterectomy (OHE) of animals, the following shows the results of observation and analysis: (a) un-balanced standing posture, indentation and lifting of the shoulders; (b) Step 1: Use tweezers and the scalpel to cut the abdominal wall layer by layer. (c) Step 2: Use the hook to find the uterus and ovary and take them out. (d) Step 3: Use the needle to suture the wound.

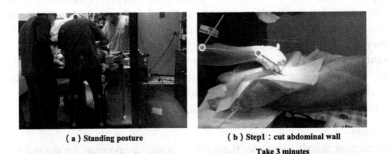

(a) Standing posture

(b) Step1 : cut abdominal wall

Take 3 minutes

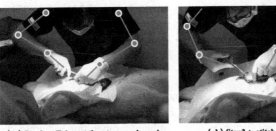

(c) Step2 : Take out the uterus and ovaries

Take 15 minutes

(d) Step3 : stitch up the wound

Take 10 minutes

Fig. 4. Analysis of the OHE posture and process

3.2   Expert Interview

The influence of the spine curvature, soft tissue status, and visual angle on the basic operating mechanism of the NSLBP and the impact and limitations of spine research are established based on the advice obtained from interviewing a physiotherapist in National Cheng Kung University. Also, through Literature Review, the direction of this study is clearly defined. Expert Interview also helps clarify whether NSLBP among veterinarians is caused by the poor posture that skews the curvature of the spine and damages the soft tissues. Veterinarians will also increase the load on the lower back due to the long period of suspending the hands in the air. Design which is commonly seen only addresses the compensatory patterns or the inability to cure over the part of the lumbar spine. The above interviews will provide details and be used as the focus in the follow-up design and experiment of this Study.

3.3   A New Assistive Design for the Thermal Comfort

Through Literature Review, it is found that maintaining a stable hand and body temperature above a certain level is an important key to maintaining operational ability Through evaluation of the skin temperature, we can understand the thermal comfort relationship between the human body and the environment [37]. In the initial stage of veterinary hospital observation, it was found that the ambient temperature in the operating room was low, which may cause the veterinarian's hand fluency to decrease during the surgery and make the posture more flexed during operation. However, in the initial observation, we can only understand the problem of posture buckling during the veterinary surgery, but we cannot explore in depth the association between the skin temperature and thermal comfort, so this Study will design a assistive device to evaluate the veterinary surgery and the relationship between the skin temperature and the Blood Flow and discuss whether the balance in the skin temperature can promote blood circulation and mitigate muscle tensions.

Participants

This experiment mainly simulates the posture of the veterinarian during the veterinary surgery. Therefore, the subjects will mainly be students aged between 22 and 25, and there will be 5 participants in the Evaluation Experiment. The subjects suffer no other obstacles to their actions and they take no muscle relaxation drugs (such as NSAID) that can affect their central nervous systems.

Site Planning

The experimental site is set in the Ergonomics and Interaction Design Lab under department of industrial design National Cheng Kung University, where the environment is deemed as a control factor (with the ambient temperature maintained at $20-24°$, the ambient humidity maintained at 50–60%, and lighting) to achieve a unified status for simulation of the surgery for the subjects.

Evaluation Model

This Study is aimed at veterinarians in Taiwan who show changes in the curvature of the trunk posture and the state of soft tissues during the surgery. After the observation and interview in the veterinary hospital, the OHE in the surgical content will be the Evaluation Model. As the OHE is relatively standardized and highly frequent in Taiwan, the veterinary hospital with a large number of visitors may arrange a series of operations in a day, which may take a longer time than other diagnostic and surgical operations.

Evaluation Equipment

This study utilizes the Human Computer Interaction Method, where the temperature sensors are combined with the carbon fiber heating sheets through Arduino (Fig. 5), to make a wearable device that can evaluate whether the skin temperature of the hand is maintained at the normal temperature or $32°$ [38]. If the skin temperature of the hand is lower than the normal temperature, the heat generating sheet will be utilized to make the temperature reach equilibrium based on the concept of thermal comfort, so that the skin temperature can be maintained within the normal range (Fig. 6). Making the temperature sensor based on Arduino can also allow us to have a better understanding of the human body at low temperatures, as well as the changes in the values of the skin temperature and the relevant status. Afterwards, the Bi-Directional Pocket Doppler with the LCD Display (Model: ES-100 V3, HADECO, JAPAN) is used for measurement and evaluation of the blood flow status.

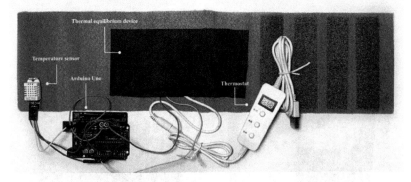

Fig. 5. Wearable thermal comfort assistive device

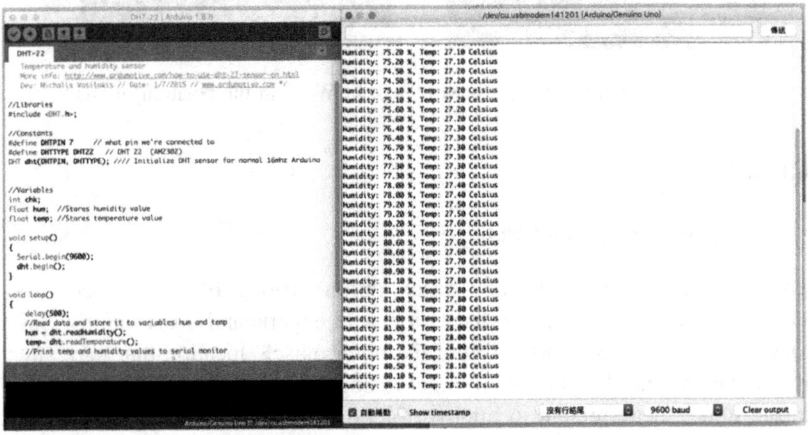

Fig. 6. Temperature control data

Evaluation Process

With the previous understanding of the concept of back muscle extension, in this Study, the subjects will simulate the OHE on the animal models, and each process will take 30 min, with the interval of 10 min for resting. This Study will test (1) New Type 1: no device intervention; (2) New Type 2: the thermal comfort device worn in the position of triceps brachii (TB, inside the upper arm) (Fig. 7a); and (3) New Type 3: the thermal comfort device worn in the position of brachioradialis (BH, inside the forearm) (Fig. 7b) to assess the effect of intervention or no intervention with the device on blood circulation in the hands. The subjects wear the designated clothes, which is convenient to wear and photograph, and starts the simulation of the OHE within the specified time limit. Afterwards, an evaluation of the blood flow status is conducted on the brachial artery to compare whether the intervention of the wearable thermal comfort device can adjust the skin temperature, maintain body temperatures within the normal range and control the blood flow between muscles to achieve homeostasis.

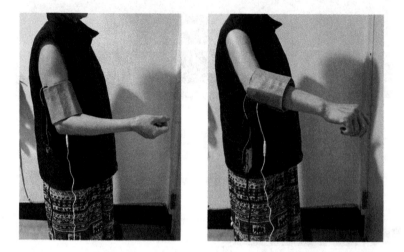

Fig. 7. a: Worn in the position of TB, b: Worn in the position of BH

4   Results

4.1   Variations in the Blood Flow

Design and analysis are performed based on the Blood Flow obtained from the Evaluation Experiment, as well as discussion with experts and observations. Based on the concept of thermal comfort, we find the main muscle location that may affect the blood circulation, and the parts with larger changes in values as the main stimulation site in the future measurement to improve blood circulation. This Study aims to conduct statistical analysis on (1) New Type 1: no device intervention; (2) New Type 2: the thermal comfort device worn in the position of TB; and (3) New Type 3: the thermal comfort device worn in the position of BH. One-way ANOVA is conducted on the above 3 categories (Table 1) to analyze the significant difference between the mean blood flow rate and mean blood flow volume. The results show that there are significant differences with $P < 0.05$, thus rejecting the null hypothesis. The evaluation device proves that compared with the situation where there is no intervention of any device, wearing the device designed by this Study can help maintain the skin temperature and thermal comfort and bring about significant benefits to the blood flow status.

Table 1. Evaluation - Pre-test result

		Sum of squares	df	Mean square	F	Sig.
MN	Between groups	39.232	2	19.616	9.819	.003
	Within groups	23.972	12	1.998		
	Total	63.204	14			
MN'	Between groups	135.525	2	67.763	9.366	.003
	Within groups	84.412	12	7.034		
	Total	219.937	14			

Note. MN: Mean of velocity (cm/s); MN': Mean of volume flow (ml/s); Pre-MN: Previous mean of velocity (cm/s); Post-MN': Post mean of volume flow (ml/s).
[*]The mean difference is significant at the 0.05 level.

Therefore, this Study goes further for post-hoc verification and uses Multiple Comparison Analysis Testing to understand significant differences exist between which groups when there is a significant difference in the mean numbers of multiple sets of samples. Table 2 shows the blood flow data in different states. It can be found from the data in the table that there is a positive relationship between the mean blood flow rate and the mean blood volume, and the data obtained from the thermal comfort device worn in the position of TB exhibit more significant differences than that obtained from the thermal comfort device worn in the position of BH. This study proves that the wearable device worn in the position of TB can more significantly promote blood circulation than that worn in the position of BH. This is also consistent with the findings proposed by Hellig [30] and Frank et al. [31] previously, where excessive muscle stretching will cause the blood flow status to decrease, but if thermal comfort is maintained for the hands, it will promote blood circulation and improve the operational competence of the hands.

Table 2. Multiple comparisons

Dependent variable	(I) Phase	(J) Phase	Mean difference (I-J)	Std. error	Sig.	95% confidence interval	
						Lower bound	Upper bound
MN (cm/s)	1.00	2.00	−3.76	0.8939	0.004	−6.252	−1.268
		3.00	−2.96	0.8939	0.02	−5.452	−0.468
MN' (ml/min)	1.00	2.00	−6.96	1.6774	0.005	−11.636	−2.284
		3.00	−5.56	1.6774	0.02	−10.236	−0.884

Note. MN: Mean of velocity (cm/s); MN': Mean of volume flow (ml/s); Pre-MN: Previous mean of velocity (cm/s); Post-MN': Post mean of volume flow (ml/s).
[*]1.00 = Non-thermal comfort; 2.00 = Thermal comfort TB; 3.00 = Thermal comfort BH.
[*]The mean difference is significant at the 0.05 level.

5 Discussion

This Study creates a new assessment method that considers the spine angle and blood flow during the veterinary surgery, and summarizes those factors during the procedure of surgery into a posture classification system. Through analysis in the Evaluation Experiment, it is proved that maintaining the skin temperature and thermal comfort of the hands can effectively improve blood circulation, and that the wearable device worn in the position of TB can more significantly promote blood circulation than that worn in the position of B. This could be caused by the fact that TB is a bridge between the shoulder muscles and the elbows, so the effect on blood flow status is more obvious. This is also consistent with the findings proposed by Hellig and Frank et al. (2018; 2009) previously, where excessive muscle stretching will cause the blood flow status to decrease, but if thermal comfort is maintained for the hands, it will promote blood circulation and improve the operational competence of the hands.

This study needs further data collection and observation to understand the effects of the NSLBP among veterinarians on the biomechanics changes of the trunk and the state of blood circulation. This Study analyzes the existing LBP assistive devices and factors that may influence the NSLBP. Design guidelines are thus established, and the Focus Group is implemented to allow participation of experts in biomechanics and anatomy, so that the follow-up design proposals can be made to select appropriate device designs and soothing means.

6 Conclusion

This Study achieves blood flow status boost to the lower back muscles by maintaining thermal comfort of TB. This study will subsequently evaluate the biomechanical rule for the veterinary surgical posture, and use the motion capture system to assess the stress and angle of posture. In this study, we explore the principles, combine the concepts of biomechanics and physiological anatomy, and use innovative aids to solve the issue of NSLBP among veterinarians.

References

1. Fink-Miller, E.L., Nestler, L.M.: Suicide in physicians and veterinarians: risk factors and theories. Curr. Opin. Psychol. **22**, 23–26 (2018)
2. Hong, P.C., Lin C.-C.: Investigations on occupational health of veterinarians for small animals. Institute of Labor, Occupational Safety and Health, Ministry of Labor, Research plan number ILOSH102-H504 (2005)
3. Bartram, D.J., Baldwin, D.S.: Veterinary surgeons and suicide: a structured review of possible influences on increased risk. Vet. Rec. **166**(13), 388–397 (2010)
4. Fritschi, L., et al.: Inj. Austr. Vet. **56**(3), 199–203 (2006)
5. Scuffham, A.M., et al.: Prevalence and risk factors associated with musculoskeletal discomfort in New Zealand veterinarians. Appl. Ergon. **41**(3), 444–453 (2010)

6. Tsung, P.Y., Liang, K.Y.: Investigations on occupational health of veterinarians for small animals. Institute of Labor, Occupational Safety and Health, Ministry of Labor, Research plan number ILOSH103-H504 (2005)
7. Krismer, M., van Tulder, M.: Low back pain (non-specific). Best Pract. Res. Clin. Rheumatol. 21(1), 77–91 (2007)
8. Katz, J.: Lumbar disc disorders and low-back pain: socioeconomic factors and consequences. JBJS 88(Suppl. 2), 21–24 (2006)
9. Maher, C., Underwood, M., Buchbinder, R.: Non-specific low back pain. Lancet 389(10070), 736–747 (2017)
10. Hlavenka, T.M., Christner, V.F.K., Gregory, D.E.: Neck posture during lifting and its effect on trunk muscle activation and lumbar spine posture. Appl. Ergon. 62, 28–33 (2017)
11. Borczuk, P.: An evidence-based approach to the evaluation and treatment of low back pain in the emergency department. Emerg. Med. Pract. 15(7), 1–23 (2013)
12. O'Sullivan, P.: Diagnosis and classification of chronic low back pain disorders: maladaptive movement and motor control impairments as underlying mechanism. Man. Ther. 10(4), 242–255 (2005)
13. Papi, E., Bull, A.M.J., McGregor, A.H.: Is there evidence to use kinematic/kinetic measures clinically in low back pain patients? A systematic review. Clin. Biomech. 55, 53–64 (2018)
14. Dul, J., Douwes, M., Smitt, P.: Ergonomic guidelines for the prevention of discomfort of static postures based on endurance data. Ergonomics 37(5), 807–815 (1994)
15. Gatchel, R.J., Polatin, P.B., Mayer, T.G.: The dominant role of psychosocial risk factors in the development of chronic low back pain disability. Spine 20(24), 2702–2709 (1995)
16. Kerr, M.S., et al.: Biomechanical and psychosocial risk factors for low back pain at work. Am. J. Publ. Health 91(7), 1069–1075 (2001)
17. Marras, W.S., et al.: Spine loading characteristics of patients with low back pain compared with asymptomatic individuals. Spine 26(23), 2566–2574 (2001)
18. Grasso, R., Zago, M., Lacquaniti, F.: Interactions between posture and locomotion: motor patterns in humans walking with bent posture versus erect posture. J. Neurophysiol. 83(1), 288–300 (2000)
19. Lee, L.-J., Coppieters, M.W., Hodges, P.W.: Anticipatory postural adjustments to arm movement reveal complex control of paraspinal muscles in the thorax. J. Electromyogr. Kinesiol. 19(1), 46–54 (2009)
20. Gade, V.K., Wilson, S.E.: Position sense in the lumbar spine with torso flexion and loading. J. Appl. Biomech. 23(2), 93–102 (2007)
21. Wilson, S.E., Granata, K.P.J.S.: Reposition sense of lumbar curvature with flexed and asymmetric lifting postures. Spine 28(5), 513 (2003)
22. Panjabi, M.M.: The stabilizing system of the spine. Part I. Function, dysfunction, adaptation, and enhancement. J. Spinal Disord. 5, 383 (1992)
23. Mehrizi, R., et al.: Using a marker-less method for estimating L5/S1 moments during symmetrical lifting. Appl. Ergon. 65, 541–550 (2017)
24. Konz, S.: NIOSH lifting guidelines. Am. Ind. Hyg. Assoc. J. 43(12), 931–933 (1982)
25. Ning, X., et al.: Influence of asymmetry on the flexion relaxation response of the low back musculature. Clin. Biomech. 26(1), 35–39 (2011)
26. Sánchez-Zuriaga, D., Adams, M.A., Dolan, P.: Is activation of the back muscles impaired by creep or muscle fatigue? Spine 35(5), 517–525 (2010)
27. Palmerud, G., et al.: Intramuscular pressure of the infra- and supraspinatus muscles in relation to hand load and arm posture. Eur. J. Appl. Physiol. 83(2), 223–230 (2000)
28. Strøm, V., Røe, C., Knardahl, S.: Work-induced pain, trapezius blood flux, and muscle activity in workers with chronic shoulder and neck pain. PAIN® 144(1), 147–155 (2009)

29. Lim, C.-M., Jung, M.-C., Kong, Y.-K.: Evaluation of upper-limb body postures based on the effects of back and shoulder flexion angles on subjective discomfort ratings, heart rates and muscle activities. Ergon. **54**(9), 849–857 (2011)

30. Hellig, T., Mertens, A., Brandl, C.: The interaction effect of working postures on muscle activity and subjective discomfort during static working postures and its correlation with OWAS. Int. J. Ind. Ergon. **68**, 25–33 (2018). https://doi.org/10.1016/j.ergon.2018.06.006

31. Frank, S.M., Raja, S.N., Bulcao, C.F., Goldstein, D.S.: Relative contribution of core and cutaneous temperatures to thermal comfort and autonomic responses in humans. J. Appl. Physiol. **86**(5), 1588–1593 (1999). https://doi.org/10.1152/jappl.1999.86.5.1588

32. Tian, Y., et al.: Effects of EVA glove on hand dexterity at low temperature and low pressure. Appl. Ergon. **70**, 98–103 (2018)

33. Salavati, M., et al.: Effect of dual-tasking on postural control in subjects with nonspecific low back pain. Spine **34**(13), 1415–1421 (2009)

34. Ershad, N., Kahrizi, S.: Balance and posture in chronic low back pain patients. Bimon. J. Res. Rehabil. Sci. **3**(1), 8–16 (2008)

35. Kisner, C., Colby, L.A., Borstad, J.: Therapeutic Exercise: Foundations and Techniques. F. A. Davis Co. (2017)

36. Hernandez, A., Gross, K., Gombatto, S.: Differences in lumbar spine and lower extremity kinematics during a step down functional task in people with and people without low back pain. Clin. Biomech. **47**, 46–52 (2017)

37. Priego Quesada, J.I., et al.: Effects of the cycling workload on core and local skin temperatures. Exp. Ther. Fluid Sci. **77**, 91–99 (2016)

38. White, M., et al.: Human body temperature and new approaches to constructing temperature-sensitive bacterial vaccines. Cell. Mol. Life Sci. **68**(18), 3019–3031 (2011)

39. Fritschi, L., Morrison, D., Shirangi, A., Day, L.: Psychological well-being of Australian veterinarians. Aust. Vet. J. **87**(3), 76–81 (2009). https://doi.org/10.1111/j.1751-0813.2009.00391.x

40. Platt, B., Hawton, K., Simkin, S., Mellanby, R.: Systematic review of the prevalence of suicide in veterinary surgeons. Occup. Med. **60**(6), 436–446 (2010)

41. Brügger, A.: Gesunde Haltung und Bewegung im Alltag: mit Regeln zur Wiederherstellung und Bewahrung der gesunden Körperhaltung; moderne Rückenschule und Rückenturnen aus der Sicht von Dr. Alois Brügger: A. Brügger (1996)

42. Olgakabel: Rolling up from a standing forward bend can damage your spin. sequencing basics, teaching tips, yoga for your body (2013). https://sequencewiz.org/2013/08/14/rolling-up-from-a-standing-forward-bend-can-damage-your-spine

Research on Body Pressure Distribution of Office Chair with Different BMI

Pu Hong[1], Yinxia Li[1(⊠)], Huimin Hu[2,3], and Mengjing Cai[1]

[1] School of Mechanical Engineering, Zhengzhou University,
Zhengzhou, Henan, China
Hongup1001@163.com, liyxmail@126.com,
1223274297@qq.com
[2] Ergonomics Laboratory, China National Institute of Standardization,
Beijing, China
huhm@cnis.gov.cn
[3] AQSIQ Key Laboratory of Human Factors and Ergonomics, Beijing, China

Abstract. The office chair is one of the most important sittings in the office, life and learning process. When people use uncomfortable office chairs, it can have a negative impact on people's work efficiency and health. The body pressure distribution of the office chair is one of the most common objective measures index of office chair comfort. Therefore, in order to improve the comfort of the office chair, it is necessary to study the differences in the pressure distribution and the differences in comfort evaluation of people with different BMI. The Pliance pressure test system was used to collect the seat pressure and contact area of 18 subjects with different BMI, and a subjective score for office chair of each subject was recorded. Through difference analysis, we found that the mean pressure and mean contact area of subjects with different BMI were significantly different ($P < 0.05$) and positive correlation were found for mean pressure and BMI, for mean contact area and BMI. But no correlation were found for BMI and subjective comfort scores ($p > 0.05$). According to the experimental data, the pressure distribution diagram was drawn, the pressure distribution characteristics of subjects with different BMI were summarized.

Keywords: Pressure distribution · Office chair · BMI

1 Introduction

Nowadays, working in an office chair is ubiquitous. Approximately three-quarters of all employees in industrialized countries now have jobs that require working in a sitting position. A good seat can not only properly support for hip and distribute the weight of the human body, but also improve work efficiency. An increasing amount of time is spent seated, especially in office environments, where sitting comfort are increasingly important due to the prevalence of musculoskeletal disorders [1].

At present, the methods for measuring the comfort of the office chair seat surface mainly include objective measurement and subjective evaluation. In the literature, various objective methods (e.g. pressure measurements, measurements of posture, EMG etc.) can be used to quantify the subjective comfort/discomfort of an office chair [2].

© Springer Nature Switzerland AG 2019
V. G. Duffy (Ed.): HCII 2019, LNCS 11581, pp. 59–70, 2019.
https://doi.org/10.1007/978-3-030-22216-1_5

Objective methods have the advantage of being less time consuming, less dependent on a large number of subjects and less prone to measurement error [3]. The seat surface is the main interface between the user and the seat, and is an important part that affects the comfort of the user. The body pressure distribution of the office chair is one of the most common objective measures of office chair comfort [4].

However, technical methods to objectively determine sitting comfort/discomfort are always indirect and, at best, can provide only an indication of a chair user's feeling of comfort/discomfort. The comfort/discomfort of the seat is based on subjective feelings and is difficult to quantify. Subjective assessment is possible to gain an indication of the level of sitting comfort and discomfort. Vergara and Page reported that subjective evaluation is the effective way to determine changes in comfort and pain [5].

Chen Yuxia, Zhou Min, Hou Jianjun and others used the method which combined pressure distribution measurement and subjective comfort evaluation to study the relationship between objective data and subjective comfort evaluation of sofa and seat respectively. The factors affecting the comfort of sofa and chair are analyzed. Tianyi [8] also used the method which combined body pressure distribution and subjective evaluation to study the influence of sitting posture on seat comfort. This proves the effectiveness of the combination of subjective and objective evaluation.

At present, the distribution ratio of Chinese adult BMI is 1 (thin): 5 (normal): 4 (fat). The distribution of the seat surface pressure of people with different BMI is different. The pressure distribution of fat people is relatively uniform, and the highest pressure values of thin people are seen at the hip ischial tuberosity [9]. It can be seen that the individual BMI difference has an effect on the seat pressure distribution [10]. Therefore, in order to improve the comfort of the office chair, it is necessary to further study the difference in the pressure distribution of people with different BMI.

Based on the above analysis, the combined method of subjective and objective was used in this study. The pressure test system was used to measure the seat surface pressure, and the seat surface was subjectively evaluated for comfort. The experimental data was analyzed for differences. This study will provide reference and basis for the office chair seat surface design to improve the comfort of the office chair.

2 Method

2.1 Experimental Design

In this study, according to the Chinese BMI index classification criteria, 18 subjects of three types were recruited. They were divided into thin group (BMI < 18.5), normal group (18.5 ≤ BMI < 23.9) and fat group (BMI ≥ 24) respectively. The most common office chair with moderate seating hardness was selected as the experimental sample. The subjects provided their evaluation on comfort of the seat surface after sitting for 20 min. The subjective comfort experience evaluation was scored by using a 5-level comfort meter (1 point - very uncomfortable, 2 points - uncomfortable, 3 points - general, 4 points - comfortable and 5 points - very comfortable). Then, the subjects sit in the office chair in accordance with the requirements of the "reference sitting posture [11]". The reference seating posture is as follows:

- The sole of the foot placed on the floor;
- The foot forms an angle of approximately 90° with the lower leg;
- The lower leg is approximately vertical;
- The lower leg forms an angle of approximately 90° with the thigh;
- The thigh is almost horizontal;
- The thigh forms an angle of approximately 90° with the trunk;
- The trunk is erect.

Subjects were required to be in contact with the office chair only by buttocks and thighs, try to ensure that the rest of the body and the office chair is not in contact to reduce the influence of extraneous factors on the pressure distribution test of the seat surface. Finally, the Pliance pressure test system of German Novel Company was used to collect pressure distribution data of each subject for 30 s, and 15 s stable pressure distribution data was selected to extract mean pressure values, peak pressure values and mean contact area. One-way analysis of variance was used to compare mean pressure, peak pressure and mean contact area of people with different BMI, and the correlation between BMI and seat comfort was determined based on Spearman correlation analysis (Fig 1).

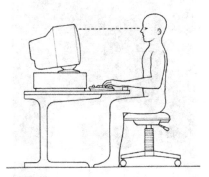

Fig. 1. The reference seating posture

2.2 Subject

In this study, according to the Chinese BMI index classification criteria, 18 subjects of three types were recruited. They were divided into thin group (BMI < 18.5), normal group (18.5 $\leq$ BMI < 23.9) and fat group (BMI $\geq$ 24) respectively. All subjects were required healthy, with no spine and hip related medical history and experimented with good physical and mental condition. All subjects provided written informed consent prior to participation in this study. Subjects' information see Table 1.

Table 1. Subjects' information

	Thin group			Normal group			Fat group		
	Range	Mean	SD	Range	Mean	SD	Range	Mean	SD
Age (years)	20–32	23	4.1	21–32	24	3.7	23–46	32	9.2
Height (cm)	156–176.5	167.8	7.4	160–185	168.9	8.4	153.6–185	165.2	11.8
Weight (kg)	45–54.7	50.3	4.1	54–74.2	61.3	7.5	62–104	79.2	15.2
BMI	17.5–18.4	17.9	0.4	20.7–23	21.4	0.8	26.3–30.4	28.7	1.6

2.3   Main Apparatus

Pressure Test System. The body pressure distribution test was carried out by the Pliance body pressure test system (see Fig. 2) of Germany Novel. The computer software used with the system can visually display 2D and 3D color pictures of pressure distribution. And the pressure values of each sensor is contained in the picture (see Fig. 3).

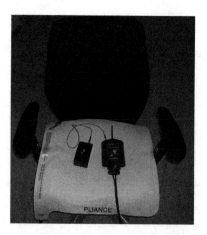

Fig. 2. The main hardware of Pliance body pressure measure system

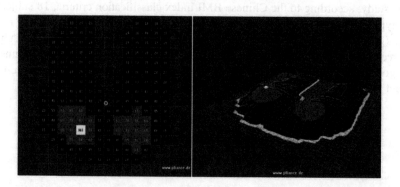
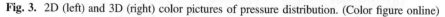

Fig. 3. 2D (left) and 3D (right) color pictures of pressure distribution. (Color figure online)

Office Chair. The seat surface hardness of 15 office chair were measured for selecting office chair by the Shore F Durometer (a device for measuring the surface hardness of soft materials such as sponges, see Fig. 4). We found that the seat surface hardness of 11 office chair is mainly concentrated between 35HD and 42HD, and the mean hardness is 40.18HD. So the office chair with 40HD and adjustable height was selected for experiment (see Fig. 5).

Fig. 4. Shore F durometer

Fig. 5. Office chair

2.4 Task and Procedure

1. Each subject was informed about the study and gave a written informed consent,
2. Before the test, the subjects were informed of experiment purpose, experiment contents and way of testing, and assistance was given to them to get familiar with the subjective comfort rating scale.

3. The gender, age, and height and weight of the subjects were record.
4. The subjects provided their evaluation on comfort of seat surface after sitting for 20 min.
5. Adjust the seat surface of the office chair to the appropriate height. The subjects sat in the office chair in accordance with the requirements of the "reference sitting posture" (see Fig. 6) while back does not contact with the backrest without using the armrest (hands on their lap).
6. Contact pressure and contact area between chair seat and buttock was measured within 30 s.

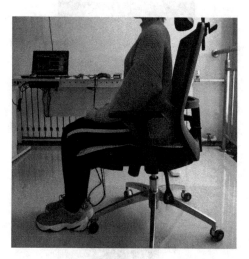

Fig. 6. The experimental scene. The subject kept the "reference sitting posture" while back does not contact with the backrest without using the armrest (hands on their lap) for 30 s. Measure the pressure distribution during this period.

2.5   Data Analysis

Subjective scores of different BMI subjects were counted. Peak pressure values, mean pressure values and mean contact area of the sensors during the measurements were extracted from the Novel software. One-way analysis of variance was used to determine whether there was a difference between pressure distribution and BMI. Spearman correlation analysis was used to determine correlation between subjective comfort scores and BMI, mean pressure and BMI, peak pressure and BMI, mean contact area and BMI. The significance was determined at a 0.05 level.

3   Results

Significant differences were found for mean pressure and mean contact area of people with different BMI ($p < 0.05$). See Table 2 for significant results. Positive correlations were found for mean pressure and BMI, for Mean contact area and BMI (see Table 3).

Table 2. Pressure and contact area of different group and difference results.

	Group	N	Mean	SD	Sig.
Mean pressure (kPa)	Thin group	6	4.02	0.34	0.004
	Normal group	6	4.71	0.48	
	Fat group	6	5.20	0.45	
Peak pressure (kPa)	Thin group	6	12.96	3.80	0.568
	Normal group	6	11.58	2.89	
	Fat group	6	11.17	2.03	
Mean contact area (cm^2)	Thin group	6	922.38	37.52	0.000
	Normal group	6	1011.42	36.16	
	Fat group	6	1164.48	112.74	

Table 3. Correlation between subjective comfort scores and BMI, mean pressure and BMI, peak pressure and BMI, mean contact area and BMI.

		Mean pressure	Peak pressure	Mean contact area	Subjective scores
Spearman's rho	Correlation coefficient (R)	0.893*	−0.133	0.828*	0.026
	Sig.	0.000	0.598	0.000	0.919
	N	18	18	18	18

*Correlation is significant at the 0.01 level. $R > 0.8$ means strongly correlated.

3.1   Mean Pressure

Mean pressure of thin group was the lowest (4.02 kPa). Mean pressure of fat group was the highest (5.20 kPa). Mean pressure of normal group was somewhere between the two (4.71 kPa). And positive correlations were found for mean pressure and BMI ($R > 0.8$, $p < 0.05$). In Fig. 7, the distribution of mean pressure is shown. And the trend of mean pressure with BMI can be seen from the dotted line in the figure. So, mean pressure increases with increasing BMI.

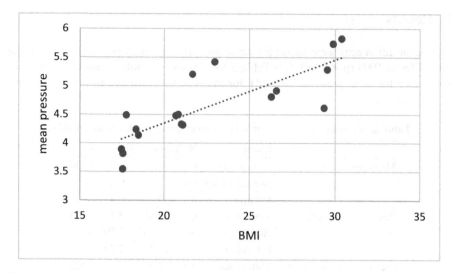

Fig. 7. Mean pressure scatter diagram of 18 subjects. And the dotted line represents the trend line of mean pressure with BMI

3.2   Peak Pressure

No significant differences were found for peak pressure of people with different BMI ($p > 0.05$). And no correlations were found for peak pressure and BMI ($p > 0.05$). It can be seen from Fig. 8 that with the increase of BMI, there is no obvious change trend of peak pressure.

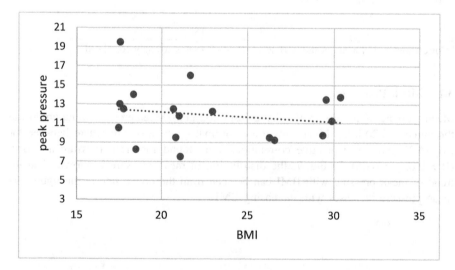

Fig. 8. Peak pressure scatter diagram of 18 subjects. And the dotted line represents the trend line of peak pressure with BMI

3.3 Mean Contact Area

The mean contact area of the fat group was the largest (1164.48 cm^2). The mean contact area of the thin group was the smallest (922.38 cm^2), and the mean contact area of the normal group was between the two (1011.42 cm^2). Positive correlations were found for mean contact area and BMI (R > 0.8, p < 0.05). It can be seen from Fig. 9 that as the BMI increases, the mean contact area has a significant increase trend. The higher the BMI is, the larger the volume of the subject is. So the contact area between the hip and the office chair is larger.

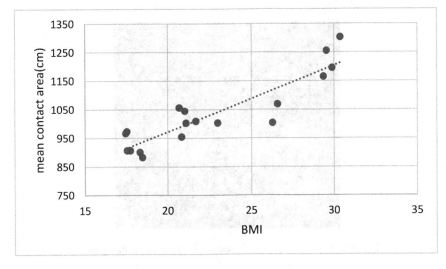

Fig. 9. Mean contact area scatter diagram of 18 subjects. And the dotted line represents the trend line of mean contact area with BMI

3.4 Subjective Score

No significant correlations were found for subjective scores and BMI (p > 0.05). At present, only one office chair with moderate hardness is selected in the experiment. It is possible that this office chair has met the comfort requirements of all the subjects. And López-Torres [12] reported comfort is an extremely complex concept that involves the absence of discomfort and the presence of a series of positive perceptions. Some participants in the experience said that this office chair did not cause discomfort, so they thought that this office chair is comfortable, which may lead to no difference in subjective scores, or there was indeed no significant correlation between subjective score and BMI. Studies have shown that subjective comfort evaluation may take at least 1 h to distinguish the change of comfort [13], and the experience of this experiment is only 20 min, which may not be enough to get an effective subjective score in a short time. Therefore, it is necessary to carry out experiments with longer experience in the future, so as to obtain accurate subjective scores.

3.5   Pressure Distribution

The difference in pressure distribution between subjects with different BMI can be clearly seen from Figs. 10, 11 and 12. The seat contact area of thin subject is the smallest, and the highest pressure values are seen at the hip ischial tuberosity. The seat contact area of normal subject is slightly larger than that of thin subject, and larger pressure values are distributed near the hip ischial tuberosity. The seat contact area of fat subject is the largest, and larger pressure values are also distributed near the ischial tuberosity, but the area is larger than normal, and the pressure distribution of fat subject is more evenly distributed.

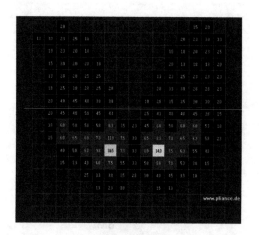

Fig. 10. Typical example of pressure distribution in thin group.

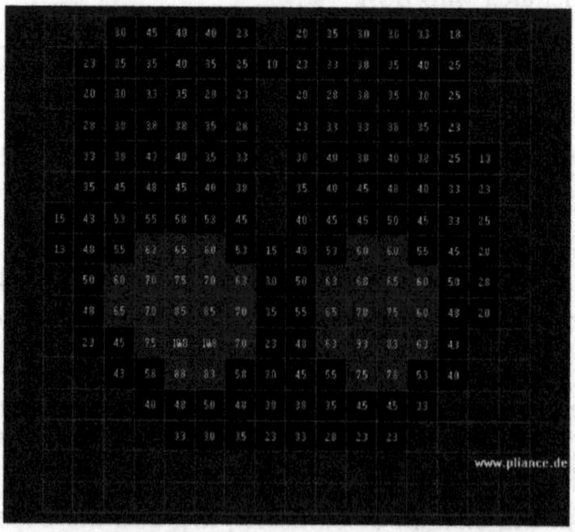

Fig. 11. Typical example of pressure distribution in normal group.

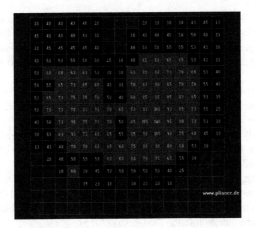

Fig. 12. Typical example of pressure distribution in fat group.

4   Conclusion

Research shows [3] that the pressure distribution of car seats is correlated with subjective score, so it can be hypothesized that the same conclusion may hold for other seats (like office chair) as well, although the association between pressure distribution and (dis)comfort in other seats is yet to be determined. And the seating pressure distribution of groups with different BMI was different. Therefore, people with different BMI have different feelings on the comfort level of the same office chair. Li Juan reported there were different pressure distribution in different hardness of the seat surface. This study found that the mean pressure of different BMI groups is different. Therefore, in order to improve the comfort of office chairs, it is necessary to design office chairs with different seating hardness for people with different BMI.

Acknowledgments. This research is supported by 2016 revised national standard project plan project (20162676-T-469) and China National Institute of Standardization through the "special funds for the basic R&D undertakings by welfare research institutions" (522017Y-5278 and 522016Y-4488).

References

1. Zemp, R., Taylor, W.R., Lorenzetti, S.: Seat pan and backrest pressure distribution while sitting in office chairs. Appl. Ergon. **53**, 1–9 (2016). https://doi.org/10.1016/j.apergo.2015.08.004
2. Zemp, R., Taylor, W.R., Lorenzetti, S.: Are pressure measurements effective in the assessment of office chair comfort/discomfort? Rev. Appl. Ergon. **48**, 273–282 (2015). https://doi.org/10.1016/j.apergo.2014.12.010
3. De Looze, M.P., Kuijt-Evers, L.F.M., Van DieN, J.: Sitting comfort and discomfort and the relationships with objective measures. Ergonomics **46**(10), 985–997 (2003). https://doi.org/10.1080/0014013031000121977

4. Zhang, Z., Yuan, Q., Xu, Z., Huang, S., He, Y.: A study on the ride comfort of vehicle seats based on body pressure distribution. Automot. Eng. **36**(11), 1399–1404 (2014)
5. Vergara, M., Page, A.: Relationship between comfort and back posture and mobility in sitting-posture. Appl. Ergon. **33**(1), 1–8 (2002). https://doi.org/10.1016/s0003-6870(01)00056-4
6. Chen, Y., Shen, L.: Discuss about the evaluation method on sofa comfort degree. J. Northwest Forest. Univ. **22**(02), 179–183 (2007). https://doi.org/10.3969/j.issn.1001-7461.2007.02.046
7. Min, Z.: The study on the interface pressure distributions and the temperature between the testee and the seat. Doctoral dissertation, Nanjing Forestry University (2007). https://doi.org/10.7666/d.y1196137
8. Tianyi, H., Liming, S.: Comfort and supporting ability of waist and haunch by using office chair in forward sitting position. J. Anhui Agric. Univ. **41**(1), 173–178 (2014)
9. Lingling, H., Zuoxin, L., Jilei, Z.: The study of sitting pressure distribution for subjects with different BMI. Furniture & Interior Design (6) (2015)
10. Xinzhu, H.: Research on individual differences of the seat surface comfort effect. Doctoral dissertation, Beijing Institute of Technology (2015)
11. BS ISO 24496:2017 Office furniture-Office chair-Methods for the determination of dimensions
12. López-Torres, M., Porcar, R., Solaz, J., Romero, T.: Objective firmness, average pressure and subjective perception in mattresses for the elderly. Appl. Ergon. **39**(1), 123–130 (2008). https://doi.org/10.1016/j.apergo.2006.11.002
13. Carcone, S.M., Keir, P.J.: Effects of backrest design on biomechanics and comfort during seated work. Appl. Ergon. **38**(6), 755–764 (2007). https://doi.org/10.1016/j.apergo.2006.11.001
14. Li, J., Xu, B., Lian, J., Wang, C.: Seat comfort characterization by body—seat interface pressure distribution. Mech. Sci. Technol. Aerosp. Eng. **33**(9), 1298–1303 (2014). https://doi.org/10.13433/j.cnki.1003-8728.2014.0904

Design Method of 3D-Printable Ergonomically Personalized Stabilizer

Ryota Kawamura[✉], Kazuki Takazawa[✉], Kenta Yamamoto[✉], and Yoichi Ochiai[✉]

University of Tsukuba, Digital Nature Group, Tsukuba, Japan
ryota.kawamura@digitalnature.slis.tsukuba.ac.jp

Abstract. In photography and videography, it is a challenge to align a sight toward the target continuously and steadily, as considerable practice and experience are required. Blurry photographs are often captured by camera users who lack the necessary skills. To address the problem, stabilizers have been developed. However, conventional stabilizers involve a steep learning curve because they are designed to be mass produced, and thus not tailored according to an individual. We herein present the design method of a three-dimensional printable personalized stabilizer. It is optimized ergonomically through topology optimization, which is a typical method to optimize the shape of materials.

Keywords: Digital fabrication · Personalization · Design · Personal fabrication

1 Introduction

In photography and videography, it is a challenge to align a sight toward the target continuously and steadily, as considerable practice and experience are required. Blurry photographs are often captured by camera users who lack the necessary skills. To address the problem, stabilizers have been developed. Conventional stabilizers involve a steep learning curve because they are designed to be mass produced, and thus not tailored according to an individual. For example, in filming a location, large equipment or considerable manpower have been used to move a photographer smoothly, primarily because conventional stabilizers have less customizability for various uses. It is noteworthy that stabilizers for professional users are heavy, in general, that a photographer cannot perform any actions other than photographing. The spread of image sharing applications has resulted in increased camera users. Non-personalized stabilizers bring out the result to lack of user experiences. For example, some users suffer from holding a camera with their hands for a prolonged time. To achieve the goal where all users can operate stabilizers comfortably and enjoy photographing without any stress, we must build a design framework of personalized stabilizers without any costs such as transport or human power produced by a simplified manufacturing

© Springer Nature Switzerland AG 2019
V. G. Duffy (Ed.): HCII 2019, LNCS 11581, pp. 71–87, 2019.
https://doi.org/10.1007/978-3-030-22216-1_6

line that can be customized without any stress. Hence, it is necessary to conduct shape-optimization based on a user's physical features for personalized stabilizers, and form it through digital fabrication technologies. The system formulates the problem internally as topology optimization, and subsequently forms it using three-dimensional (3D) printing technologies using different materials.

2 Related Work

2.1 Commercial Strategies for Supporting Photography

Currently, camera photography and videography can be observed in some situations such as when people capture a photograph of everyday life or when a professional photographer shoots a film. To support photography and videography, camera shake correction techniques are now available on many cameras, which benefits users. Camera shake corrections are divided into two methods: a *software-based* approach that realizes correction with electronic calculations such as electronic image stabilizing, and a *hardware-based* approach that realizes the correction with optical image stabilization. Thus, each image stabilizing method installed on camera presents its own advantages. However, disadvantages also occur for these methods, in that users cannot receive any photography support unless they own the camera because different cameras involve different image stabilizing techniques. Old and cheap cameras most likely do not possess any of these techniques; hence, the quality of photography and videography would depend on a user's skills.

Electronic image stabilization techniques installed on camera can be defined as a *software-based* approach, and numerous investigations based on software have been conducted [6,13,14].

Meanwhile, optical image stabilization techniques installed on camera can be defined as a *hardware-based* approach, and numerous investigations based on hardware have been conducted [4,8].

Commercial stabilizers have been developed to avoid such a hardware dependency, as shown in Fig. 1. A stabilizer is a photographic instrument directly installed on the body of a photographer. It enables a smooth operation even with a large camera. Many commercial stabilizers can reduce camera shake from handheld devices to devices attached to users. Although a handheld stabilizer is light, it lacks stability. Therefore, professional photographers tend to use a heavy stabilizer. Because they must operate it for a long time, it leads to user fatigue. Thus, the weight of a stabilizer has been related to user fatigue. Currently, brushless gimbals have been used to reduce camera shake and user burden. A steadicam is a conventional device to support camera users and is slightly heavier, whereas brushless gimbals are lighter than a steadicam because their gimbals are controlled computationally. Thus, this device depends on the proficiency of the user, and subsequently the scope of use is limited to professional photographers. To our knowledge, no method exists that specializes in designing stabilizers for amateur individuals, and they are only shared as 3D models created by volunteers in the design repository.

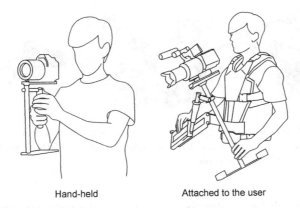

Hand-held   Attached to the user

Fig. 1. Examples of 2-type camera stabilizers. Left: a hand-held device. Right: a device attached to the user to fix a camera for a long time in situations like a film shooting.

2.2 Optimization with Digital Fabrication

The spread and development of computers have diversified computational design methods. Further, the affinity between digital fabrication and optimization is high, thereby resulting in the development of some products. Koyama et al. presented a computational design method to automatically optimize and create a 3D-printable connector between two different objects [7]. In their study, they provided a simple user interface to users so that they would not be confused. They were only required to adjust the fix-position of two objects and the length between them, and they could choose the suitable design from presented candidate designs. We also adopted the concept to allow end-users to design a personalized stabilizer easily.

Fabrication researchers are also interested in the internal mechanism of 3D objects. Several studies have been conducted widely on balancing 3D objects under certain circumstances such as underwater [10,16], in air [15], etc. Changing the internal mechanisms of 3D objects also enabled them to stand on a plane [11,16].

2.3 Topology Optimization

Shape optimization is important in computational design. In particular, topology optimization is a typical shape-optimization method. Several professional software are available to support the generative design in the market such as ANSYS[1] and the components in the framework of Grasshopper plugin[2,3]. Topology optimization, in which inefficient materials are removed iteratively from a

---

[1] https://www.ansys.com/products/structures/topology-optimization (Last accessed: 2019-02-15).

[2] http://www.grasshopper3d.com/forum/topics/stress-topology-optimization-with-millipede (Last accessed: 2019-02-15).

[3] https://www.food4rhino.com/app/ameba-rhino (Last accessed: 2019-02-15).

Fig. 2. Left: All of parts we prepared. They consists of a monopod, harness, bungee code, and 3D-printed components. Center: assembly phase of these parts. Right: the user is equipped with our instrument.

structure while efficient materials are added to the structure simultaneously, obtains the best layout of materials within a limited design space, and maximizes the system performance. Optimized structures sometimes exhibit limitations regarding shape, thereby rendering them difficult to reproduce on an industrial scale. However, a breakthrough in reproduction was achieved from digital fabrication [1]. The design method to optimize shape by topology optimization has often been investigated in human-computer interaction. For instance, Chen et al. [2] presented a user-driven generative design method using topology optimization. Kazi et al. [5] also used topology optimization and function for a sketch-based generative design. We also used topology optimization in the method describe herein this paper, which is on the Grasshopper as an add-on. When using the add-on and realizing topology optimization on Grasshopper, some components functions are used as the inputs of topology optimization. Thus, our method of conducting topology optimization is conventional from the viewpoint of direct inputs.

3   Exo-Balancer

In this section, we introduce the Exo-Balancer, our previous design method for a personalized stabilizer, and the results. Next, we enumerate some issues that are to be addressed. Subsequently, we describe the implementation in detail.

3.1   Implementation

In this section, we introduce our implementation, which is divided into two parts: calculation that considers the moments of forces between the user and some instruments, and personalized fabrication using the simulated result. Our system consists of a calculation to investigate the suitable fixed position and some instruments to mount a camera. These instruments include a harness, monopod, and camera, two bungee cords, and an assembly of connectors printed with a 3D printer (see Fig. 2 center). Figure 2 (left) shows the model of components between a harness and monopod.

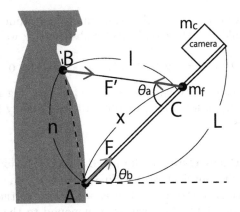

Fig. 3. Simple configuration image of our instrument. This image includes the applied forces, the masses of a few instruments, and the angles when the user is equipped with our instrument.

Calculation Using Body Data. Our goal is to personalize a stabilizer such that users can capture photographs without any stress. Hence, we focus on the moments of forces. We present a design method to obtain a suitable position for each user from a balance relation between forces and moments according to their body data and the fixed angles of an object. First, users input the length from their shoulder to lumbus (its value is n, see Fig. 3) as their basic body data, the angle θ_b that sets the upward-facing horizontal as positive, and fixes a camera. According to the horizontal and vertical equilibrium of forces, the following equations are obtained:

$$F = m_f g \cos \theta_b + F' \cos \theta_a + m_c g \cos \theta_b \tag{1}$$

$$F' \sin \theta_a = m_c g \sin \theta_b + m_c g \sin \theta_b \tag{2}$$

where F is the force on the point-on-contact between a harness and monopod, while F' is that on the point-of-contact around the shoulder of the user. L is the length from a harness to a camera, while x is the length from a harness to the point that supports a monopod; l is the length from point to A. We ask the user to hold a camera in advance, and measure the distance from the camera position to where the harness is to be attached (its value is L, see Fig. 3). We apply L to the measured value. As shown in Fig. 3, θ_a is the angle between the line segment from B to C and the line segment from A to a camera. The moment of forces around C is as follows:

$$\frac{x - L}{2} m_f g \sin \theta_b = (L - x) m_c g \sin \theta_b \tag{3}$$

From Eqs. (1) to (3), we gain equations about x as follows:

$$x = \frac{(2m_c + m_f)L}{2(m_c + m_f)} \tag{4}$$

We define the equation $F = F'$ as the requirement that minimizes the forces on the user body and calculate them on Unity[4]. Subsequently, we solve the following equation:

$$2l^3 + nl^2 - 2l(n^2 + x^2) - n(x^2 - n^2) = 0 \tag{5}$$

Our system optimizes the two equations above by inputting x and l, which are based on specific user values. Thus, we obtain the optimally fixed position of a camera for the users.

Assemble Some Parts Using Calculated Results. Next, the users externalize the data to the physical world. First, we attach the harness, which is typically used to set an instrument such as a camera, to the body. A harness comprises a mounting plate; thus, we set a monopod to the mount (see Fig. 2 right). We printed out the models on a 3D printer (5th generation printer) using regular polylactic acid filaments. We set its infill rate to 100% because it must withstand some forces and support some parts.

3.2 Evaluation

In this section, we describe the experimental evaluation of our approach. Our evaluation involved a qualitative evaluation to interview the participants in our experiment about the practicability of our instrument and a quantitative evaluation based on a three-axis acceleration sensor to measure the shakiness of a camera. First, we asked the participants to capture videos for 30 s to verify the effect of our personalization. The participants conducted this phase four times: hold a camera by their hands, hold a camera with our method, hold a camera with our method while changing x slightly from the calculated results. Thus, we investigated whether our design method had resulted in personalization. Next, we conducted an interview and some questionnaires. In addition to the quantitative evaluation, we compared the impact on a camera with that on our instrument as a qualitative evaluation. We measured the values on a three-axis acceleration sensor attached to a camera and compared them.

Participants. To verify the practicability of our method, we recruited college students (1 female, 7 males) as participants. They had different physique. They were aged between 18 and 25 years (M = 20.4, SD = 2.0) and were not familiar with the stabilizer of a camera.

Experimental Procedure. To calculate the parameters for personalization, we first equipped the participant with a harness and adjusted the length to fit to their bodies. We measured two lengths: one is between the shoulder and the mount of a harness (n, as mentioned in the section, "Simulation using body data"), and the other is between the mount of a camera and the mount of a

---

[4] https://unity3d.com (Last accessed: 2019-02-15).

Fig. 4. Left: the camera used in our experiment. Center: iPhone 6 attached to the camera in order to measure the gravitational acceleration from its acceleration sensor inside it. Right: a scene of our experiment. (Color figure online)

harness (L, as mentioned in the section, "Simulation using body data"). To define L, we asked the participants to hold a smartphone when they capture a photograph. We input these values for the participants' own data and calculated x and l. Finally, we assembled the parts and equipped them on the body of the participants based on these values. We projected a video in which a red ball was bouncing onto the wall for 30 s. In our experiment, the participants continued with shooting such that he/she could observe the ball in the middle of the angle of view (see Fig. 4 center). It is noteworthy that the ball speed changes randomly when it bounces off the wall (see Fig. 4 right).

Usability in Personalizing Shootings. As a quantitative evaluation, we interviewed the participants. The purpose of this interview was to reveal how the users felt when using our instrument. To investigate the usability and enjoyability, we asked them to rate each question in a five-point Likert scale, from "strongly disagree" to "strongly agree." In addition, we asked for details with free-description questions. We used the two-tailed Wilcoxon signed-rank test, which is non-parametric method and evaluated at an alpha level of 0.05. Scores of each question were analyzed on a five-point Likert scale. We also analyzed two cases derived from our method similarly when we changed the value of x deliberately to verify the propriety of our method (see Fig. 5, Q1–Q4). In addition to these questions, to investigate the usability, we prepared two questions regarding the enjoyability (see Fig. 5, Q5, Q6). Finally, we asked the participants for details with free-description questions.

3.3   Results

Figure 5 shows the results from all six questions. These questions aim to reveal the usability (Q1–Q4) and enjoyability (Q5, Q6). The first question pertained to the operability when the participants captured a photograph. In the conventional style, they are required to hold a camera at all times with both hands while bending a little and look into the finder. However, our method is different, in that we only need them to hold a camera with one hand and operate the other

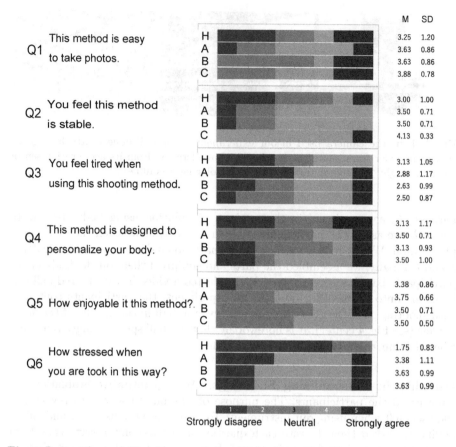

Fig. 5. Rating the usability of personalizing shootings compared to another 3 methods. Our instrument is used in method A. In method B, x is set to plus 5 cm. On the other hand, it is set to minus 5 cm in method C. Each question is scored on a 5-point Likert scales.

instruments with another hand while grasping a monopod. The Wilcoxon signed-rank test demonstrated no statistical significance between methods A and H ($Z = -0.79$, $p > 0.05$), A and B ($Z = 0.00$, $p > 0.05$), and A and C ($Z = -0.63$, $p > 0.05$).

The second question pertained to the stability when the participants captured a photograph. We focused on whether the participants felt stable to explore the usability. The Wilcoxon signed-rank test demonstrated no statistical significance between methods A and H ($Z = -1.89$, $p = 0.06$), A and B ($Z = -1.19$, $p > 0.05$), and A and C ($Z = 0.00$, $p > 0.05$).

The third question pertained to the fatigue when the participants captured a photograph. Fatigue is an important element while investigating the usability. Operability and stability are considered to reduce significantly when fatigue increases. The Wilcoxon signed-rank test indicated no statistical significance between methods A and H ($Z = -0.42$, p > 0.05), A and B ($Z = -0.54$, p > 0.05), and A and C ($Z = -0.83$, p > 0.05).

The fourth question pertained to the personalization of participants. The definition of personalization is obscure; thus, we asked them to determine whether these methods were designed for personalizing their bodies. The Wilcoxon signed-rank test demonstrated no statistical significance between methods A and H ($Z = -1.00$, p > 0.05), A and B ($Z = -1.13$, p > 0.05), and A and C ($Z = 0.00$, p > 0.05). Unlike Q1, Q2, Q3, and Q4, we set two questions to understand the participants' enjoyability. We verified the enjoyability from different viewpoints.

The fifth question pertained to the viewpoint of the photographer. For instance, some people are motivated to capture a photograph to satisfy their desire in using an exclusive camera, while others are motivated by the opportunity to communicate with friends through an image-sharing application. Thus, we must investigate the positive effect of our method in sustaining people motivation in photography. The Wilcoxon signed-rank test demonstrated no statistical significance between methods A and H ($Z = -1.34$, p > 0.05), A and B ($Z = -1.41$, p > 0.05), and A and C ($Z = -1.00$, p > 0.05).

Meanwhile, the sixth question was based on the viewpoint of the participant. People tend to be daunted when surrounded by large photographic equipment. Meanwhile, they are often relaxed when captured with a smartphone. Thus, we must confirm that our method does not cause mental stress. The Wilcoxon signed-rank test demonstrated no statistical significance between methods A and B ($Z = -1.00$, p > 0.05), and A and C ($Z = -1.00$, p > 0.05). Meanwhile, a statistical significance exists between methods A and H ($Z = -2.41$, p > 0.05). Overall, all the results are attributed to insufficient power.

In addition, according to the participants' personal opinions from the free descriptions, a few participants felt stressed when they captured a photograph using our method. The majority opinions are provided below. P (participant) 7: "*I felt slightly nervous to be targeted by devices that I have not seen*". In method B, a participant struggled at capturing an upper photograph. P8: "*When I tried to capture an upper photograph, I felt inconvenienced because I had to bend my body backwards.*" In method C, a few participants felt a slight tightness when equipped with the instrument. P2: "*It was difficult to capture pictures on the bottom because my body was pulled up.*" P4: "*I felt a monopod sticking in my chest and it was slightly painful when I was equipped with the instrument.*" P6: "*The mounted position of the camera is slightly far from me when using methods A to C; therefore, I felt the weight. However, it was relatively easy to operate the instrument because its distance was the shortest in these methods.*" P7: "*I felt tightness and discomfort around my chest.*"

Analysis of Each Shaky Phenomenon. In addition to a quantitative evaluation using the Likert scale, we conducted a qualitative evaluation that analyzes the values of acceleration sensors that were built into an iPhone. The application

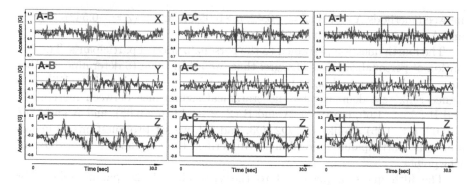

Fig. 6. Results from captured 3-axis position of a camera. Note that graphs of x-axis, y-axis, and z-axis are shown separately in order to compare each method. Besides, red line represents method A and blue line do the others, and black frames do the areas that surround the characteristic range of difference between 2 methods. (Color figure online)

we used for this user study was AccelerationLogger[5]. We attached iPhone6 to the top of a camera (see Fig. 4 left). The data of the participant are shown in Fig. 6, in which the difference in values among the methods was remarkable. In comparison with methods A and H or A and B, a slightly difference was observed. However, we found an interesting difference in comparison with methods A and C. The shake from method C was reduced on all axes rather than that from method A. As described in the next section, method C contributed to the improvement in operability while imposing a burden on the user by reducing x.

3.4 Limitations and Discussions

Through the user study, we asked the participants and verified the usability and enjoyability. Consequently, we found the areas for improvement: reselection of equipment and expansion of experimental situation. Our quantitative evaluation revealed that method C was the most appreciated. Method C is less 5 cm from the value of x, which was calculated, and the reason that the participants appreciated can be attributed to the harness usage. In our experiment, we used a rubber harness because we wanted to detract from the participants' wearability and maintain their lightness as much as possible. However, rubber expands and contracts easily; therefore, a monopod was set slightly looser than the simulated result in method A. Consequently, the score of the five-point Likert scale revealed that method C was the most appreciated by the participants. Another limitation of this study is that our instrument cannot include all participants. Further, x was a few centimeters larger or smaller than the range of our instrument when we experimented one strapping man and one smallish woman. Henceforth,

---

[5] https://itunes.apple.com/jp/app/id340777156 (Last accessed: 2019-02-15).

the fundamental reselection of the ready-made instruments or selecting them ourselves using digital fabrication tools such as a 3D printer and laser cutter result in enhanced practicability.

Meanwhile, through our qualitative evaluation, a camera held in a participant's hand reduced the shake the most. Our study is at the prototype stage of achieving the personalized design method; therefore, we focus on exploring the design method for personalization to adapt to the user body and enrich user experience further. Thus, we do not focus on stabilizing more than the existing stabilizers. However, the prototype presented herein may be useful at times, for instance, when a user captures a photograph when they are not standing steadily. We conclude that this approach offers great promise to be useful under such a situation and can improve the performance as a stabilizer.

3.5 Summary

Exo-Balancer is the rudimentary design method for a personalized stabilizer. Based on their physical data, it calculates and presents one of the best fix-positions for users to operate comfortably without any stress. In exploring the position, we considered the moments of forces between the users and equipment such as a harness, monopod, and camera, two bungee cords, and some connectors generated by 3D printers. Subsequently, we recruited participants of different physiques and obtained some results from the quantitative evaluation based on three-axis acceleration sensors on the camera, as well as a qualitative evaluation based on the statistical analysis of the questionnaire.

1. **Low durability because of the property of ready-made goods.** A harness is a typical photography-assisting tool; however, the part that is attached to the body stretches when loads are added because it is made of rubber. Therefore, a camera mounted on a stabilizer generates a large torque, resulting in low usability.
2. **Low adaptability for physically characterized people.** Ready-made goods are not necessarily customable especially when their specifications are limited. In our method, for example, it is impossible to adjust an equipment (e.g., monopod length) slightly when our participants are extremely fat or small.
3. **Low stabilizing ability.** To our knowledge, Exo-Balancer was the first to explore the design space to combine digital fabrication with personalization in producing a stabilizer. Therefore, we first focused on building the whole structure without applying loads compared to conventional commercial stabilizers. Thus, we provided the users an opportunity to experience it as a simple prototype, and expected a specific stabilization mechanism to be the next step.

4 New Approach

We adopted topology optimization, the typical shape-optimization method, as our new approach to address *issue1* and *issue2* described above. We aim to realize

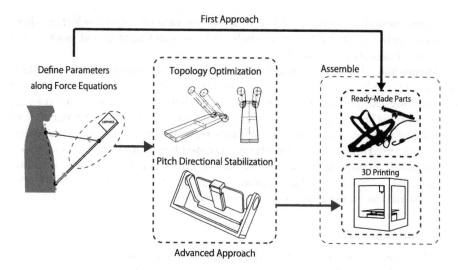

Fig. 7. System overview.

a high optimization and end-to-end output by shifting the size optimization of ready-made goods into computational shape-optimization while maintaining the mechanical constraints proposed previously (see Fig. 7). Regarding *issue3*, we described the structure that enabled pitch directional stabilization when using a compact camera.

4.1   Topology Optimization

First of all, *structural domains* mean the smooth area occupied by structures. In topology optimization, we introduce fixed structural domains D and expand the shape-optimization problem from to D. Therefore, topology optimization can be generally formulated as follows:

$$\inf_{\Omega} F = \int_D f(x, u) \chi(x) \, d\Omega \tag{6}$$

where χ represents a characteristic function which value is 1 if the area is in D, and 0 if not as follows:

$$\chi(x) = \begin{cases} 1 & if \ \forall x \in \Omega \\ 0 & if \ \forall x \in D \backslash \Omega \end{cases} \tag{7}$$

We designed a personalized stabilizer on Grasshopper using add-on *ameba*, developed for 3D topology optimization. *Ameba* is based on the bi-directional evolutionary structural optimization (BESO) technology. Bi-directional evolutionary structural optimization [12,18] is a finite-element method based on topology optimization, and is significantly more efficient than evolutionary structural

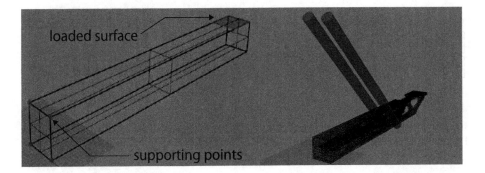

Fig. 8. System on grasshopper. Left: The supporting points is a red dot, and the green surface is loaded to the Z-axis negative direction. Right: The result model and two supporting poles. (Color figure online)

optimization [17] in terms of material removal. First, we defined the basic shape of a stabilizer prior to optimization, and both the points to support and the surface on which the load was placed as shown in Fig. 8 left. It is noteworthy that we allowed the users to hold the steering with both hands in this case to improve operability although Exo-Balancer used both shoulders as a fulcrum (see Fig. 8 right). Figure 9 right shows the Python component of the Exo-Balancer algorithm. The input values to the component consist of camera mass (c_mass), weight of the overall instrument (m_mass), length of user fuselage (bLength_n), and length between their abdomen and the position (mLength_L). According to the algorithm, calculation was conducted for the component. Subsequently, outputs from the component was used for the size optimization of a fundamental stabilizer. Finally, we conducted topology optimization for the shape optimization of a stabilizer. It is noteworthy that loads corresponding to a camera was applied to the Z-axis negative direction as shown in Fig. 8 right, the green surface. All parameters including the load for optimization are shown in Fig. 9 left.

The result is shown in Fig. 8 right. It can be exported as STL or OBJ file for 3D-printing. The shape transition for each iteration is shown in Fig. 10.

Pitch Directional Stabilization for Compact Camera. In this paragraph, we describe the structure that enables pitch directional stabilization as the first approach to address *issue3*. When a photographer moves in a certain direction, maintaining the equilibrium according to the direction by his/her own weight stabilizes the pitch direction. Some patents to explore and develop the method have been pended and granted. In particular, we focus on the patent pended by Da-Jiang Innovations Science and Technology Co., Ltd. (DJI)[6]. They filed many patents and invented a connecting device and a gimbal apparatus [9]. Following their idea, we attempted to generate a 3D-printable camera mount on which the structure for stabilization was installed. We designed it on Fusion360,

---

[6] https://www.dji.com (Last accessed: 2019-02-15).

Camera mass	Stabilizer mass	n	L
400g	480g	48cm	43cm

Fig. 9. Left: Fundamental parameters. Right: we input these parameters into the Python component. Exo-Balancer algorithm is implemented in that component.

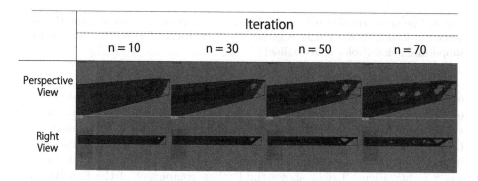

Fig. 10. Results through each iteration.

a notable 3D computer-aided design software. Figure 11 shows the output through MakerBot Replicator. Our proposed model was divided into two, and we used a commercial bearing to connect with these parts.

5   Discussion and Limitations

In this section, we firstly summarize our implementation, and then discuss some limitations and future work.

We chose topology optimization for shape-optimization to realize the personalized stabilizer without altering the shape of fundamental stabilizer. Topology optimization for the structure we define in Fig. 9(a) can be limited when applied loads to supporting or load-bearing positions within the structure. In other words, it is desirable that these structures corresponding to user's physical characteristics. Therefore, we need to have several basic structures, and then we use the different one depending on each user. We will also attempt to develop the system with automatic parameter tweaking functions for designing personalized stabilizer. It is generally known that not only the topology optimization but also almost all shape-optimized models are often coarse and not practical. Therefore, it is necessary to smoothen such coarse parts on a model. Laplacian smoothing algorithm [3] is one of the algorithms to smoothen a polygonal mesh.

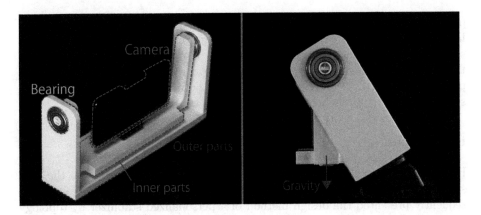

Fig. 11. Concept image of the structure which realize the pitch directional stabilization for compact camera. These parts unite into one by using a commercial bearing.

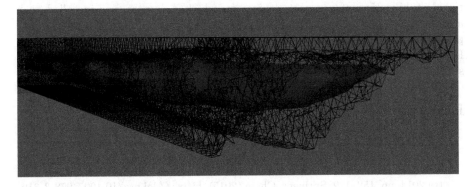

Fig. 12. Wireframes show the meshes of 3D model on which we conducted topology optimization, and its inside 3D model shows the one after laplacian smoothing.

According to the common recognition, we also smoothed our model. However, we tend to have more non-manifold edges in our models, therefore we could not conduct the process smoothly as shown in Fig. 12. More practical design will require more strict smoothing process based on Laplacian algorithm.

We developed a camera mount for pitch directional stabilization, and it is used for compact camera. However, it does not function when you use a camera with heavy lens because the center of gravity shifts remarkably.

Our future work requires practical experiments for various shooting situations. We conducted the shooting experiment in advance, in which a photographer stood still while a target object was moving. On the contrary, we can consider a shooting situation in which only the photographer moves while the target object is stationary, such as capturing a picture in the same pose or scanning a static object with a 3D scanner. Both the photographer and target object are stationary in the shooting situation, such as when photographing a landscape, and vice versa, such as when photographing a running athlete. Thus, several shooting situations exist, and must recruit specific participants such that their photographic skills can be divided into three ranks: professional, semi-professional, and novices. We will be able to gain more useful results through such a type of comprehensive user study.

6 Conclusion

Herein, we first reported the experimental results of Exo-Balancer, the first study pertaining to the design method of a personalized stabilizer, and subsequently presented the design method of a personalized stabilizer by topology optimization. Our primary contribution was to design personalized stabilizers through topology optimization method to establish ant end-to-end design framework that removed materials efficiently and render stabilizers 3D-printable. As a sub-contribution, we designed a fundamental structure for the pitch directional stabilization of compact devices on which a camera was installed such as smartphones. A comprehensive user study of camera users having different photographic skills in several shooting situations will be performed in the future. In addition, we will compare our method to conventional photographic methods such as commercial stabilizers or hand-held camera photography.

References

1. Aage, N., Amir, O., Clausen, A., Hadar, L., Maier, D., Søndergaard, A.: Advanced topology optimization methods for conceptual architectural design. In: Block, P., Knippers, J., Mitra, N.J., Wang, W. (eds.) Advances in Architectural Geometry 2014, pp. 159–179. Springer, Cham (2015). https://doi.org/10.1007/978-3-319-11418-7_11
2. Chen, X.A., et al.: Forte: user-driven generative design. In: Proceedings of the 2018 CHI Conference on Human Factors in Computing Systems, CHI 2018, pp. 496:1–496:12. ACM, New York, USA (2018). https://doi.org/10.1145/3173574.3174070
3. Field, D.A.: Laplacian smoothing and delaunay triangulations. Commun. Appl. Numer. methods. **4**(6), 709–712 (1988)
4. Furukawa, H., Tajima, A.: Image stabilizing optical system having a variable prism. US Patent 3,942,862, 9 March 1976
5. Kazi, R.H., Grossman, T., Cheong, H., Hashemi, A., Fitzmaurice, G.: DreamSketch: early stage 3D design explorations with sketching and generative design. In: Proceedings of the 30th Annual ACM Symposium on User Interface Software and Technology, UIST 2017, pp. 401–414. ACM, New York (2017). https://doi.org/10.1145/3126594.3126662
6. Ko, S.J., Lee, S.H., Jeon, S.W., Kang, E.S.: Fast digital image stabilizer based on gray-coded bit-plane matching. IEEE Trans. Consum. Electron. **45**(3), 598–603 (1999)
7. Koyama, Y., Sueda, S., Steinhardt, E., Igarashi, T., Shamir, A., Matusik, W.: AutoConnect: computational design of 3D-printable connectors. ACM Trans. Graph. **34**(6), 231:1–231:11 (2015). https://doi.org/10.1145/2816795.2818060

8. Oshima, M., et al.: VHS camcorder with electronic image stabilizer. IEEE Trans. Consum. Electron. **35**(4), 749–758 (1989)
9. Pan, P., Yanchong, Z.: Connecting Device and a Gimbal Apparatus, US Patent 9,657,897, 23 May 2017
10. Prévost, R., Bächer, M., Jarosz, W., Sorkine-Hornung, O.: Balancing 3D models with movable masses. In: Proceedings of the Conference on Vision, Modeling and Visualization, VMV 2016, pp. 9–16. Eurographics Association, Goslar (2016). https://doi-org.ezproxy.tulips.tsukuba.ac.jp/10.2312/vmv.20161337
11. Prévost, R., Whiting, E., Lefebvre, S., Sorkine-Hornung, O.: Make it stand: balancing shapes for 3D fabrication. ACM Trans. Graph. **32**(4), 81:1–81:10 (2013). https://doi.org/10.1145/2461912.2461957
12. Querin, O., Steven, G., Xie, Y.: Evolutionary structural optimisation (ESO) using a bidirectional algorithm. Eng. Comput. **15**(8), 1031–1048 (1998)
13. Rousso, M.I.B., Peleg, S.: Recovery of ego-motion using image stabilization (1993)
14. Shi, J., et al.: Good features to track. In: Proceedings of 1994 IEEE Computer Society Conference on Computer Vision and Pattern Recognition, CVPR 1994, pp. 593–600. IEEE (1994)
15. Umetani, N., Koyama, Y., Schmidt, R., Igarashi, T.: Pteromys: interactive design and optimization of free-formed free-flight model airplanes. ACM Trans. Graph. **33**(4), 65:1–65:10 (2014). https://doi.org/10.1145/2601097.2601129
16. Wang, L., Whiting, E.: Buoyancy optimization for computational fabrication. Comput. Graph. Forum **35**(2), 49–58 (2016). https://doi-org.ezproxy.tulips.tsukuba.ac.jp/10.1111/cgf.12810
17. Xie, Y.M., Steven, G.P.: Basic evolutionary structural optimization. Evolutionary Structural Optimization, pp. 12–29. Springer, London (1997). https://doi.org/10.1007/978-1-4471-0985-3_2
18. Young, V., Querin, O.M., Steven, G., Xie, Y.: 3D and multiple load case bidirectional evolutionary structural optimization (BESO). Struct. Optim. **18**(2–3), 183–192 (1999)

Size North America – The New North American Anthropometric Survey

Thorsten Kuebler[✉], Andre Luebke, Jamie Campbell,
and Tim Guenzel

Human Solutions of North America, Inc., Morrisville, NC 27560, USA
contact.usa@human-solutions.com

Abstract. Size NorthAmerica is the new North American anthropometric survey, the latest and most representative survey of 18,000 men, women, children and elderly people of the United States and Canada. It is the largest civilian size study to date that provides over 100 body measurements, compliant with ISO 8559 and ISO 7250, and extensive socio-demographic information of all participants. For the first time ever, a representative number of children 6–18 and elderly people >65 years is collected. It is also the only size survey that includes a representative amount of people with different ethnic backgrounds from different regions of both countries.

The size survey has been conducted over the last two years by Human Solutions of North America, Inc. partnering directly with industry and universities. The United States portion is finished, and data is available. 14,460 persons have been scanned and surveyed across the USA. A data pool of 57,840 whole body scans, far more than double the number of scans compared to any other survey. These representative results form the basis for an up-to-date anthropometry database including a secular growth prognosis model which will last until 2040. All data is delivered by means of the online-portal iSize, easily accessible through www.portal.i-size.net. The portal provides partnering companies access to all results, with comprehensive functionality for data analysis. The purpose of this paper is to give an overview on the still on-going project and to describe the data that has been collected and processed so far for the USA population.

Keywords: Size NorthAmerica · Anthropometry

1 Introduction

Anthropometry plays an important role within the area of Human Factors and Ergonomics. It is important for consumer product design and workplace design alike. Especially in the application of Digital Human Modeling (DHM) anthropometry is one major input to build accurate virtual human representation. In the early stages of human modeling back in the 80s, available anthropometric data was insufficient for the complete definition of a comprehensive 3-D human figure model. To create the RAMSIS model Seidel 2004 reports that in the beginning they had to overlay 2 and 3-D data images and adjust length, thickness, and circumferences of each human body element until the scanned data was completely congruent with the corresponding digital human

© Springer Nature Switzerland AG 2019
V. G. Duffy (Ed.): HCII 2019, LNCS 11581, pp. 88–98, 2019.
https://doi.org/10.1007/978-3-030-22216-1_7

model [1]. Today DHM tools are widely used in the industry. Various tools are available. The human figure models are based on available anthropometric data. In many cases, due to the lack of specific measurements, values to build the models have to be extrapolated.

To provide good ergonomics, safety and comfort for the end-user, the correct anthropometry layout for products and workplaces is essential. Product and workplace designers need accurate and up-to-date anthropometric data of their actual target population to provide the best solutions that are appropriate for their customer's needs.

To date, available anthropometric data sets are not satisfying. Not only in terms of accuracy for the creation of 3-D DHM. For various studies it is questionable if they are actually representative. Prior studies lack critical groups like children and elderly people. Furthermore, the population has changed significantly within the last decades. The increase in overweight and obese individuals has affected 70.7% (2013/2014) and 71.6% (2015/2016) of 20-year-old adults, as reported by the National Center for Health Statistics [18]. It can be questioned if other surveys reflect these changes especially for surveys that involve military personnel.

In order to provide the industry with representative and up-to-date anthropometric data, it is the goal of Size NorthAmerica to:

- Collect appropriate data for technical ergonomics and apparel design
- Collect data of age groups between 6–75 years
- Represent regional and ethnic diversity
- Include extensive socio-demographic information
- Surveying consumer satisfaction and trends
- New acceleration prediction for future trends
- Make data accessible from anywhere via iSize web portal

The purpose of this study is to assess the anthropometric evolution of the USA and Canadian population. A longitudinal study of nearly 18.000 men, women and children from 6 to 75 years is performed to get a comprehensive look at today's population to provide vital information of body shapes and sizes to the industry. The study will meet and exceed any requirements for products in Automotive, Apparel, Consumer, Digital, Medical and Military industries.

2 Methods

The objective of Size NorthAmerica is the acquisition of true, representative data for the North American population for use in technical ergonomics primarily in the apparel and transportation industries. Three key methods have been defined for the concept of the serial measurement collection [15]:

1. Measurement must take place solely with the help of body scanners in accordance with the ISO 20685. Standard body shapes must also be analyzed as a supplement to body dimensions.

2. The analysis of the body dimensions must take place in compliance with the market standards for technical ergonomics in accordance with ISO 7250 and for the apparel industry in accordance with ISO 8559.
3. The results are made available in the form of a web-based, interactive data portal, enabling companies to carry out product-specific analyses online. The guidelines of the ISO 15535 were also incorporated.

2.1 Assure True and Representative Data Collection

The United States of America, with a population estimate of around 330M (United States Census Bureau, population estimate, July 1st, 2018, (V2018)) [17], is the 3rd largest population in the world. Only 6.1% of the population is in the age 5 years and under, 22.6% is 6–17 years that is an interesting market of 50 Million young people. The main portion of the population is 18–65 years, 205M. Elderly people 66–80 years represent 16.7%, 37M. Consequently, these subpopulations 6–18 and >65 years represent around 30% of the consumer market. The US market is constantly growing, with a 6% growth from 2010 to 2018 and a population projection of over 400M in 2060. Natural increase in average is around 545 thousand per year (US fertility rate 1.9) and net international migration is over 1 Million per year. The United States is a country with large ethnic diversity. With further immigration the market becomes more diversified. The ethnic diversity of the US population shows regional differences from the West to the Northeast, the Midwest and the South [17].

In order to collect a representative sample size for all these different aspects of the population, the concept incorporates recommendation of the ISO 15537 (Principles for Selecting and Using Test Persons for Testing Anthropometric Aspects of Industrial Products and Designs). The population was divided into subpopulation by gender, age and region. The overall number of sampling groups is 108 (2 (gender) * 9 (age groups) * 6 (regions) = 108). With age strata of 6–10, 11–13, 14–17, 18–25, 26–35, 36–45, 46–55, 56–65, 66+. The regions are 4 regions in the United States (Northeast, Midwest, South and West) and two regions in Canada (Quebec and Non-Quebec).

Ethnicity diversity was not a separate stratum but covered by collecting scans in different regions (see Fig. 1).

Based on the accuracy requirements of $\alpha \pm 10$ mm for body height and 95% confidence ($c_\%$ is 1.96) the minimum sample size for each subpopulation was calculated using formula 1. The total number of persons is $n_{Size\ NA} = 17{,}820$ subjects (2).

$$n = \left(c_\% * \frac{\sigma_{stature}}{a} \right)^2, \sigma_{stature} = 65.5 \text{ mm} \tag{1}$$

$$n_{Size\ NA} = gender * age\ groups * regions * n \tag{2}$$

Each combination of gender, age and region will be kept as one category. The quality assurance reviewed the participant demographics on a regular basis to ensure that sufficient data is collected to accurately represent each group. Recruiting of the participants was done parallel through local advertisement at the scanning locations, flyers and handouts, social media, media coverage and in cooperation with partner

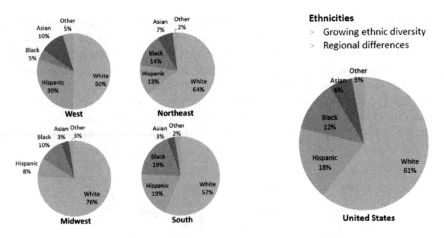

Fig. 1. United States – population facts

companies and market research institutions. To ensure the intended active sampling strategy, it was necessary to invite participants with specific characteristics to fill up all groups equally. The partnering market research institutions have a vast database of people who want to participate in research studies. This partnership allowed an efficient and accurate connection between Human Solutions of North America and specific test persons. Different incentives were given to each participant depending on the scanning location and specific needs.

2.2   Measurement Technology and Procedure

The ISO Standard 20685 (3-D scanning methodologies for internationally compatible anthropometric databases) was introduced in 2006. The standard specifies the technical requirements for the measurement equipment in the acquisition of human body shape data and measurements that can be extracted from 3-D scans [6]. The intended audience is everybody who uses 3-D scanners to create 1-D anthropometric databases as well as the users of 1-D anthropometric data from 3-D scanners.

Data acquisition is based on highly accurate 3D body scanners. All body dimensions are extracted from 3D body surface data. The scanning equipment used in the Size NA study are VITUS Smart XXL body scanners together with ANTHROSCAN software from Human Solutions. The equipment is compliant with ISO 20658 and has been used in previous size studies. The VITUS Smart XXL is a four-column, 3D body scanner which uses the optical triangulation measurement principle (laser technology and 100% safe for the eyes). The 8 sensor heads have a measuring range of 2100 mm height, 1000 mm depth and 1200 mm width (see ISO 20685). The level of accuracy of the system is very high - it has an average error (circumference) of less than 1 mm. Within just 12 s of scanning time, the sensors capture a density of 27 points/cm^2; approx. 550,000 3D points for each person are thus measured. Yet another advantage the system has mobility. The weight of the measuring columns is less than 100 kg and the floor space required is only around 4.8 m^2.

ISO 20685 suggests scanning poses for an accurate extraction of all necessary body measures specified in ISO and ASTM standards. Figure 2 shows the four scanning poses that were used in the study. The test persons had a visual instruction inside the scanner and the scan operators described verbally each pose. After each scan the scan PC showed the scanning result and the operator checked the result for correct posture of the test person and eventual artefacts. If a problem was found the pose was rescanned. In addition all scans were checked for correct posture and artefacts by a separate person on a daily basis. Using a standardized quality assurance document each scanning operator got a daily feedback on the results of the previous day.

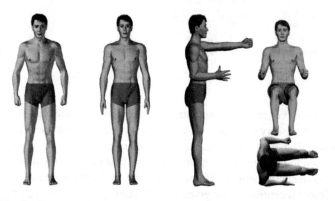

Fig. 2. Four scanning poses: standard, relaxed, reach and sitting pose

Together with the scanning procedures all participants had to submit a questionnaire with extensive socio-demographic information. This additional data and information of the test subjects provides a realistic profile of how physical and characteristic data correlate amongst the participants.

Participants had to fill out the questionnaire prior to their scheduled scanning date. The survey questionnaire was completely anonymous, no personal data is registered during the process.

The final quality control of the scanning data and the extraction of the body measurements and data processing was done at the Human Solutions headquarters in Germany by body scanning specialists and statisticians. The ANTHROSCAN software has been used in various size surveys all over the world and has proven its capabilities to process scans and extract 1-D and 2-D measurements accurately, quickly and cost efficient. The advantage of this method compared to traditional measuring is that there is no physical contact that can lead to compression of tissue and reading errors such as parallax and estimation. The extracted measurements were compiled in a Size NorthAmerica database that is now available through the iSize web portal.

3 Results

3.1 Survey Status

The results presented in this paper are a status report as of November 15th, 2018. Remaining data sets are currently processed, and measurements are extracted. The complete USA dataset will be available in early 2019. The vast demographic information of all test subjects and the remaining measurements will be implemented into the iSize web portal. The data for the Canadian population will be available by the end of 2019. Another 6,000 persons are to be surveyed and scanned until September of 2019.

The survey for the US population has been completed on November 3rd, 2018. 14,460 persons participated in various locations at different events across the United States.

Over two years the project raised attention of the media. Local Broadcasting stations interviewed participants and scanning operators who presented the scope of the project and the 3-D body scanning technology.

3.2 Data Analysis

The following results have been analyzed based on a subset of 10,866 subjects that already have been quality assured, processed and implemented into the web portal iSize. This data is now available, partner companies of the apparel and transportation industry are already working on updating their size tables and gradings as well as their digital human models. In total the data pool contains a number of 57,840 3-D body scans. The analysis of the demographic composition of the survey data shows a higher number of female participants. 6,427 in this first data set are females, 4,439 males. This corresponds to 59% female participants and 41% male participants. Data sets with other information than male or female where not included into the results. The following diagram shows the demographic composition for the 6 adult and 3 children age groups (Fig. 3).

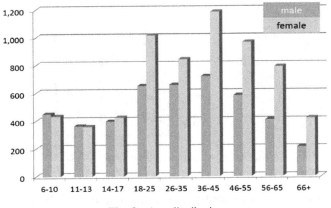

Fig. 3. Age distribution

To represent the geographic differences and the differences in the ethnical composition, body scans were gathered in 4 regions of the United States in the Northeast, Midwest, the South and the West. The following diagram shows the number of scans that were collected in these four regions (Fig. 4).

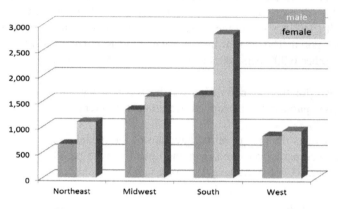

Fig. 4. Regional composition of the size survey

The largest group was the Non-Hispanic White ethnic group with 2961 females and 2220 males. The second largest ethnic group were African-Americans with 1509 females and 888 male participants. Data from 1955 Hispanic persons includes 1180 females and 775 males, 789 Americans with Asian background (454 females, 335 males) and 221 other ethnicities have participated (Fig. 5).

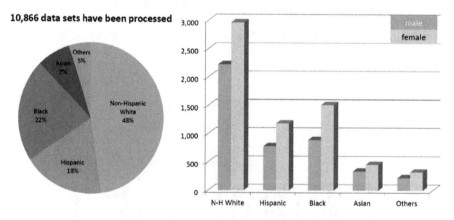

Fig. 5. Representation of ethnicity groups

Body measurements that have been extracted from the 3-D body scans are compliant with the technical standard ISO 8559 for apparel and ISO 7250 for ergonomics. In total, 38 body measurements for the application in apparel design and 42 body measurements for ergonomics have been extracted. Furthermore, several body measurements have been extracted especially for the RAMSIS DHM software to generate 3-D digital human figure models. The following tables show the different body measurements that are available in iSize (Table 1).

Table 1. 38 body measurements have been extracted for application in apparel design in compliance with ISO 8559, 42 body measurements for ergonomics in compliance with ISO 7250 and to generate digital human models in the ergonomic design software RAMSIS.

Body measurements Apparel

BMI	Knee Girth	Shoulder Slope
Back Width	Knee Height	Thigh Girth
Bust/Chest Girth	Lower Knee Girth	Total Crotch Length
Bust/Chest Height	Maximum Waist Girth	Trunk Length
Calf Girth	Middle Forearm Girth	Upper Arm Girth
Cervical Height	Middle Hip	Upper Arm Length
Cervical to Knee Hollow	Minimum Leg Girth	Upper Knee Girth
Crotch Length Front	Neck Base Diameter (front view)	Waist Girth
Elbow Girth	Neck Base Girth	Waist Height
Head Girth	Neck Girth	Waist to Hip
Height	Outside Leg Length	Weight
Hip Girth	PROP Waist Girth / Hip Girth	Wrist Girth
Inside Leg Length	Shoulder Length	

Body measurements Ergonomics

BMI	Crotch height	Thigh clearance, sitting
Head breadth	Chest depth, standing	Knee height, sitting
Head height	Body depth, standing	Abdominal depth, sitting
Head length	Chest breadth, standing	Thorax depth at the nipple
Foot breadth	Hip breadth, standing	Buttock-abdomen depth, sitting
Upper arm length	Sitting height (erect)	Forearm-fingertip length
Foot length	Eye height, sitting	Buttock-popliteal length (seat depth)
Chest breadth	Cervical height, sitting	Buttock-knee length
Forearm circumference	Shoulder height, sitting	Neck circumference
Upper arm circumference	Elbow height, sitting	Chest circumference
Chest depth	Shoulder-elbow length	Waist circumference
Foot height	Elbow-wrist length	Wrist circumference
Stature (body height)	Shoulder (biacromical) breadth	Thigh circumference
Eye height, standing	Shoulder (bideltoid) breadth	Calf circumference
Shoulder height, standing	Hip breadth, sitting	
Elbow height, standing	Lower leg length (popliteal height), sitting	

The body measure stature (body height), which is defined as the vertical distance from the floor to the highest point of the head (vertex) according to ISO 7250, was extracted from the subject standing fully erect with feet together and the head oriented in the Frankfurt plane. The results show a range for all genders from 1039 mm to 2039 mm (3′5″–6′8″). The adult women range from 1358 to 1881 mm (4′6″–6′2″) and the adult men range from 1444 to 2039 mm (4′9″–6′8″).

The body weight ranges from 16.5 kg up to 199.3 kg that corresponds to 36.4 lbs and 439.4 lbs for the entire test sample presented herein. The adult women range from 37.2 kg to 199.3 kg (82 lbs–439.4 lbs) and the adult men range from 39.8 kg to 194.3 kg (87.7 lbs–428.4 lbs).

3.3 iSize Web Portal

One of the important innovations by Human Solutions was to provide anthropometric data for the first time in an easily accessible online portal. iSize was initiated with the Size Germany survey in 2008. iSize not only allows the user to access results but also to filter and analyze data and use the results for their product design. For industrial applications it is not suitable and not valuable to provide a pool of data and statistical numbers. iSize gives anthropologists, designers, engineers and specialists the possibility to break down the data specifically to represent the intended target market. Since its development, the iSize web portal has been established as an application for apparel design. Fashion companies use the online tool to generate up-to-date size tables and to create avatars. The results can be imported into the human simulation software Vidya and the ergonomic design software RAMSIS. For specific application various filters for demographic data and body measurements can be applied to all available databases. For each selection a representative number of persons for the target market is calculated and the user gets a qualitative feedback whether the data is representative for the market or not.

4 Conclusion

Size NorthAmerica is the biggest size survey of the USA and Canadian civilian population. For the first time ever a true, representative dataset of anthropometric measurements together with extensive socio-demographic information for each subject is available for the industry. In comparison with other size surveys of the US population, Size NA is the only survey that complies with important industry standards such as ISO 20685 for internationally compatible anthropometric databases and ISO 15537 for selecting and using test persons for testing anthropometric aspects of industrial products and designs. With 14,460 persons scanned in 4 postures Size NA has collected more than double the number of 3-D body scans than every other size survey of the US civilian population ever before. Body measurements extracted from the 57,848 scans are compliant with ISO 7250 for ergonomics and ISO 8559/ASTM D5219 for apparel design. Therefore, the data is better applicable for the design and development of consumer products. CAESAR reports an actual number of scanning subjects for North America of 2375 vs. a planned sample size of 3384 including 188 per strata. Ethnic groups "Black" and "Other" are low represented [14, 15]. Previous surveys collected data for adults and neglected the important market of people under 18 and over 65 which is more than 30% of the US population. Size NorthAmerica for the first time covers those age groups and provides rich data about this untouched consumer market.

Size NorthAmerica is the new American anthropometric survey that replaces all former studies. For the first time, representative anthropometric important data from children 6 years and up as well as elderly people (up to 75) is available.

Human Solutions provides efficient and accurate products, as well as the expertise for sizing surveys worldwide. The anthropometric data of the Size NorthAmerica study is available through the iSize web portal together with anthropometric databases from other countries around the world. The iSize web portal gives users an easy and effective overview and the ability to compare and analyze anthropometric and socio-demographic data of their target market. Major companies have already begun to use the data to optimize ergo guidelines, human figure models, size charts and target market specifications. The data will also become available within the digital human modeling software RAMSIS to create 3D virtual avatars to represent a product's end user within a human-centric product development and design validation.

For the first time, companies which offer their products worldwide will be able to use the latest anthropometric data to develop these products ergonomically - addressing the specific needs of their customers in multiple regions concurrently.

References

1. Seidl, A.: The RAMSIS and ANTHROPOS human simulation tools. In: Delleman, N.J., Haslegrave, C.M., Chaffin, D.B. (eds.) Working Postures and Movements – Tools for Evaluation and Engineering, pp. 445–453. CRC Press, Boco Raton (2004)
2. DIN 33402: Koerpermaße des Menschen. Part 1–3 (1978)
3. Godil, A., Ressler, S.: Shape and size analysis and standards. In: Duffy, G.V. (ed.) Handbook of Digital Human Modeling. Research for Applied Ergonomics and Human Factors Engineering. CRC Press, Boco Raton (2009)
4. ISO 15535:2003. General requirements for establishing anthropometric databases
5. ISO 15537:2004. Principles for selecting and using test persons for testing anthropometric aspects of industrial products and designs
6. ISO 20685:2006. 3D scanning methodologies for internationally compatible anthropometric databases
7. ISO 7250:1996. Basic human body measurements for technological design
8. ISO 8559:1989. Garment construction and anthropometric surveys – body dimensions
9. Juergens, H.W., Aune, I.A., Pieper, U.: Internationaler Anthropometrischer Datenatlas. Schriftenreihe der Bundesanstalt fuer Abreitsschutz. Fb 587 (1989)
10. Juergens, H.W.: Anwendung anthropometrischer Daten. Direkte und indirekte Anwendung. In: Schmidtke, H. (ed.) Handbuch der Ergonomie (A - 3.3.1). Hanser Verlag (1992)
11. Lewin, T., Juergens, H.W.: Ueber die Vergleichbarkeit von anthropometrischen Maßen. Zeitschrift Morph. Anthrop., 61 (1969)
12. Robinette, K.M., Daanen, H.A.M., Zehner, G.F.: Three dimensional anthropometry. In: Delleman, N.J., Haslegrave, C.M., Chaffin, D.B. (eds.) Working Postures and Movements, pp. 29–49. CRC Press LLC, Boco Raton (2004)
13. Seidl, A., Bubb, H.: Standards in anthropometry. In: Karwowski, W. (ed.) Handbook on Standards and Guidelines in Ergonomics and Human Factors, pp. 169–196. Lawrence Erlbaum Associates Publishers, New York (2005)

14. Blackwell, S., et al.: Civilian American and European Surface Anthropometry Resource (CAESAR), Final report, vol. 2 (2002)
15. Robinette, K., et al.: Civilian American and European Surface Anthropometry Resource (CAESAR), Final report, vol. 1: Summary (2002)
16. Seidl, A., Trieb, R., Wirsching, H.J., Smythe, A., Guenzel, T.: SizeNorthAmerica—The New North American anthropometric survey: conceptual design, implementation and results. In: Goonetilleke, R., Karwowski, W. (eds.) Advances in Physical Ergonomics and Human Factors. AISC, vol. 489, pp. 457–468. Springer, Cham (2016). https://doi.org/10.1007/978-3-319-41694-6_46
17. United States Census Bureau. https://www.census.gov/quickfacts/fact/table/US/PST045218. Accessed 20 Jan 2019
18. CDC

Research on the Characteristic and Gender Differences in Adult Foot Shape in China

Jing Zhao[1], Jingjing Wang[2], Haitao Wang[1], Fan Zhang[1],
Chao Zhao[1], and Gang Wu[1(✉)]

[1] China National Institute of Standardization, Beijing, China
{zhaoj, wugang}@cnis.gov.cn
[2] School of Mathematical Sciences, Capital Normal University, Beijing, China

Abstract. The purpose of this study was to obtain some new knowledge for manufacturing a sizing system for adult men's and women's shoes. In this paper, five quantitative indicators are used to describe the difference between male and female foot shapes. They are foot length, foot breadth, medial malleolus height and foot oblique width and ankle circumference. Firstly, descriptive statistical analysis are conducted to describe adult's foot shape characteristics and how they differ among different age groups. The result showed that four indicators for adult men and women vary gently with age growing, other than the ankle circumference. At the same time, Empirical CDF (Cumulative Distribution Function) are plotted to compare the percentage difference for male and female among the five variables. The results showed that other than ankle circumference, percentile (5th to 95th percentile) of the other four variables are significantly different among men and women. Additionally, we conduct univariate t-tests to analyze the difference among the five variables. The results showed that when the level of significance is 0.05, the five variables for men and women are all significantly different and foot length has a higher difference among them. Overall the foot shape of male and female is different. At last, multivariate discriminant analyses are conducted to classify a large sample of individuals by gender. When the absolute values of the data were used to predict gender, the correct rate of the classifier is 91.5% (90.7% of the time for men and 92.3% of the time for women). Based on our study, we recommend that shoe manufacturers should mainly consider the effects of gender compared to age bracket when making adult shoes.

Keywords: Descriptive analysis · Univariate t-test · Discriminant analysis

1 Introduction

It is commonly recognized that a suitable shoe can be obtained by matching the shape of the shoe to the shape of the foot [2]. Therefore, studies of the gender differences in foot shape are essential to the proper design of men's and women's shoes. Traditionally, women's sport shoes have been made using a small version of a men's shoe last with all dimensions proportionally scaled according to foot length [2]. However, if women's feet differ in shape from men's feet, it is an inappropriate model for a women's shoe last and could lead to improper shoes in women [3]. In 1993, the

© Springer Nature Switzerland AG 2019
V. G. Duffy (Ed.): HCII 2019, LNCS 11581, pp. 99–110, 2019.
https://doi.org/10.1007/978-3-030-22216-1_8

American Orthopaedic Foot and Ankle Society's Women's Shoe Survey [4] reported that 88% of the healthy women surveyed were wearing shoes smaller than their feet (1.2 cm average in length), 80% of the women surveyed said they had foot pain while wearing shoes, and 76% had some sort of foot deformity [5]. These statistics advocate a greater focus on the shape and fit of women's shoes. So far, most attention has focused on the design and fit of dress shoes and the negative impact of high heels. However, although women are increasingly involved in recreational activities and are increasingly aware that sports have the potential to cause special harm to women, little attention has been paid to matching women's shoes to feet. Other research referred to foot anthropometric study, please see literatures [1, 4, 6]. Here, we give some suggestions on the correct design of women's sports shoes [7] based on the study of gender differences in foot shape.

The samples used in this study are from the Chinese adult body size database, which contains 4000 human body samples, of which 50% are male and 50% are female. The subjects' ages range from 18 to 60 years old. There are five variables related to the foot shape in this paper: foot length, foot breadth, ankle circumference, medial malleolus height and foot oblique width.

2   Basic Statistical Analysis

2.1   Numerical Analysis

Table 1 is the total mean of each variable for all women and the mean of all age groups of each variable for women.

Table 1. Mean value table for women' foot shape

Item	Means of women by age category					
	≤ 20	>20 ≤ 30	>30 ≤ 40	>40 ≤ 50	>50	Total mean
Foot length	228.62	228.50	228.56	226.57	227.61	228.25
Foot breadth	87.64	87.43	88.31	88.65	87.50	87.95
Ankle circumference	210.86	205.72	207.80	207.98	208.06	207.36
Medial malleolus height	66.53	65.88	66.20	65.06	66.44	65.95
Foot oblique width	91.89	91.93	92.65	92.28	91.28	92.23

Table 2 is the total mean of each variable for all men and the mean of all age groups of each variable for men.

From Tables 1 and 2 we can conclude that: (1) For each variable, no matter men or women, the mean for each age group fluctuated around the mean. (2) Overall, the mean value of the five variables for men are bigger than women.

Table 2. Mean value table for men' foot shape

Item	Means of men by age category					
	≤ 20	>20 ≤ 30	>30 ≤ 40	>40 ≤ 50	>50	Total mean
Foot length	245.35	248.53	246.33	245.32	243.78	246.73
Foot breadth	94.43	95.82	95.79	96.17	95.70	95.74
Ankle circumference	210.57	210.14	209.90	211.16	208.57	210.18
Medial malleolus height	73.91	74.76	74.37	73.73	74.44	74.37
Foot oblique width	98.93	100.80	100.67	101.17	100.34	100.63

2.2   Graphical Analysis

Line Graph. Figure 1 shows the change of the mean in each variable for males and females of all age groups. A line graph can visually show the trend of the average of each variable in each age group.

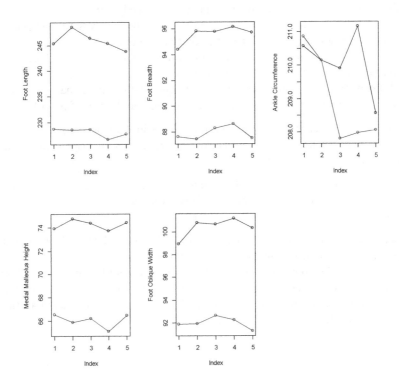

Fig. 1. Line chart of the mean of each variable for men and women of all age. Note: (1) Women are represented by red lines, and men are represented by blue lines. (2) On the x-axis, 1 represents a population of 18 to 20 years old, 2 represents a population of 21 to 30 years old, 3 represents a population of 31 to 40 years old, 4 represents a population aged 41 to 50 years, and 5 represents an age group of 51 and 60 (Color figure online).

From Fig. 1, we can obtain:

(1) **Men.** With the increase of age, the foot length of men increases first and then decreases. In the 20–30 years old period, the foot length of men reaches its maximum value.

    Women. Female foot length remains stable until the age of 40, then decreases between the age of 40 and 50, and then increases. At the age of 40 or 50, the length of a woman's foot reaches the minimum.

(2) **Men.** The male foot breadth increases before the age of 30 and does not change much after the age of 30.

    Women. Female foot breadth rises before the age of 50, peaks around 50 years old, and falls after 50 years old.

(3) **Men.** With the increase of age, the ankle circumference of male decreases at first, then increases and then decreases, and the fluctuation is very large.

    Women. As the age increases, the female's ankle circumference decreases at first and then increases, and finally tends to be stable. The drop point is 20 to 30 years old.

(4) **Men.** As the age increases, the medial malleolus height of male rises at first, then falls and finally rises. The overall change is relatively flat.

    Women. The medial malleolus height of the female falls between the ages of 40 and 50, while it remained constant in other age groups.

(5) **Men.** With the increase of age, the foot oblique width of the male foot rises first and then remains flat after the age of 30.

    Women. With the increase of age, the oblique width of the female foot rose first and then decreased, and reached its highest point at the age of 30–40.

Conclusion: (1) There are significant differences in the characteristics of the foot between men and women. (2) There is also a difference in foot shape data of different age groups in the same gender.

Histogram. Figures 2 and 3 show histograms of each variable for men and women. The histogram can show the distribution of each variable.

From Figs. 2 and 3 we can conclude that:

1. Regardless of male or female's foot shape data, the five variables of the foot data are approximately following the normal distribution.
2. Mean and standard deviation. In the five variables, except for ankle circumference' standard deviation, the mean value and standard deviation of the male were higher than those of the female. It shows that the degree of change in female foot shape is relatively smaller than that of males.

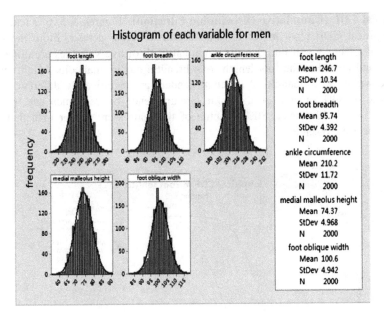

Fig. 2. Histogram of each variable for men

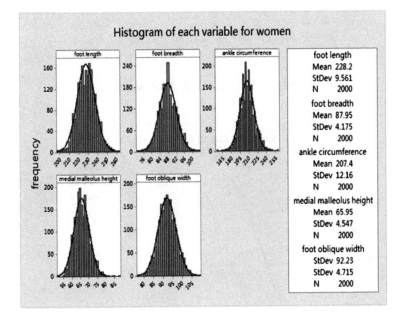

Fig. 3. Histogram of each variable for women

Empirical CDF (Cumulative Distribution Function). Figures 4, 5, 6, 7 and 8 show the empirical CDF plots for each variable with different gender. From the plot of Empirical CDF, we can find that the empirical CDF of five variables are different for women and men. For the foot length, foot breadth, medial malleolus height and foot oblique width, 80% quantile of different genders are significantly different, and the difference of 80% quantile in the ankle circumference between men and women is relatively small. Moreover, 80% quantile of the male were higher than that of the female for each variable.

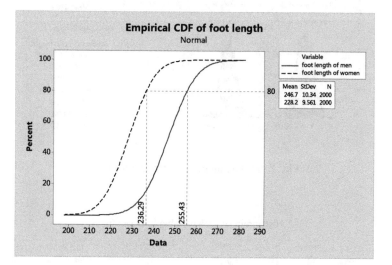

Fig. 4. Empirical CDF of foot length

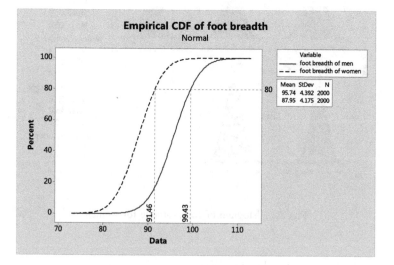

Fig. 5. Empirical CDF of foot breadth

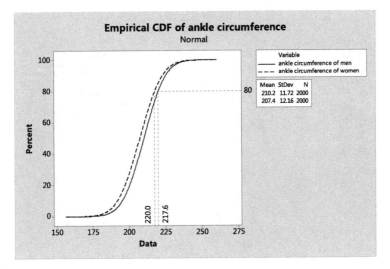

Fig. 6. Empirical CDF of ankle circumference

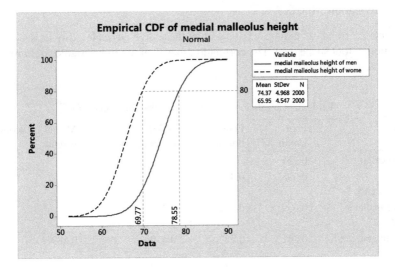

Fig. 7. Empirical CDF of medial malleolus height

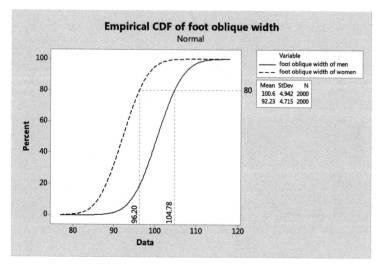

Fig. 8. Empirical CDF of foot oblique width

2.3 Correlation Matrix

Of course, correlation maybe exists within these five variables. So let's study the correlation of foot shape data. The correlation matrix of the five variables of human foot shape data is as follows:

Table 3. Correlation matrix of variables for human' foot

Items	Foot length	Foot breadth	Ankle circumference	Medial malleolus height
Foot breadth	0.741			
Ankle circumference	0.398	0.466		
Medial malleolus height	0.639	0.601	0.347	
Foot oblique width	0.741	0.932	0.479	0.589

From Table 3, we can find that positive correlations exist between the five variables of the foot data. There is a strong positive correlation between foot breadth and foot oblique width. There are also positive correlations between foot length and foot breadth, foot length and foot oblique width, but they are not too strong.

3   Univariate Analysis

We performed a univariate t-test on five variables for men and women. The test results are shown in Table 4. Table 4 shows the difference estimates of male and female for the five variables, the 95% confidence interval for the difference, and the P-value of testing, etc.

Not surprisingly, each of the 5 variables is both significantly different between men and women. The difference of foot length between male and female is the biggest, followed by medial malleolus height, foot oblique width and Foot breadth; the difference of ankle circumference between male and female is the least.

Table 4. Two-sample T-test and CI between men and women

Items	Estimate for difference	95% CI for difference	T-value	P-value
Foot length	18.481	(17.863, 19.099)	58.68	0.000
Foot breadth	7.787	(7.521, 8.053)	57.47	0.000
Ankle circumference	2.824	(2.084, 3.564)	7.48	0.000
Medial malleolus height	8.422	(8.127, 8.717)	55.93	0.000
Foot oblique width	8.393	(8.094, 8.692)	54.96	0.000

Furthermore, we compared the density distribution of foot length between men and women. The histogram of foot length is shown in Fig. 9.

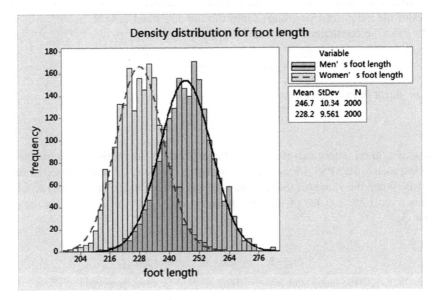

Fig. 9. Density distribution of foot length for men and women

Figure 9 shows that on average, the foot length of men is about 18.5 mm longer than that of women. It also shows that the data of foot length are more concentrated in men.

4 Linear Discriminant Analysis (LDA)

Here, we use Linear Discriminant Analysis (LDA) method [8], which is a generalization of Fisher's linear discriminant, a method used in statistics, pattern recognition and machine learning to find a linear combination of features that characterizes or separates two or more classes of objects or events. The basic idea is projection. The resulting combination may be used as a linear classifier, or, more commonly, for dimensionality reduction before later classification. Let us introduce LDA for two groups briefly. Assume that random samples of N_1 and N_2 observation vectors are drawn independently from respective multi-normal populations with mean vectors μ_1 and μ_2 and a common covariance matrix $\sum$. We wish to construct a linear compound or index for summarizing observations from groups on one-dimension scale that discriminates between the populations by some measure of maximum separation. If $\bar{x}_1$ and $\bar{x}_2$ are the sample mean vectors and S is the pooled estimate of $\sum$, we shall determine the coefficient vector a of the index $a'x$ as that which gives the greatest squared critical ration

$$t^2(a) = \frac{[a'(\bar{x}_1 - \bar{x}_2)]^2 N_1 N_2/(N_1 + N_2)}{a'Sa} \tag{1}$$

or, equivalently, which maximizes the absolute difference $|a'(\bar{x}_1 - \bar{x}_2)|$ in the average values of the index for two groups subject to the constraint $a'Sa = 1$.

Resolve the constrained optimization problem, we have

$$a = S^{-1}(\bar{x}_1 - \bar{x}_2) \tag{2}$$

and the linear discriminant function is

$$Y = (\bar{x}_1 - \bar{x}_2)S^{-1}x. \tag{3}$$

Nowadays, many statistical analysis packages contain programs for discrimination analysis, such as R, SPSS, Minitab, etc. Here we use Minitab to conduct discrimination analysis. When the values of the data are used to predict gender, the correct rate of the classifier is 91.5% (90.7% of the time for men and 92.3% of the time for women) (Table 5).

Table 5. Summary of classification

True group	Put into group		Total N	N	Correct proportion
	1	2			
1	1815	154	1969	1815	0.922
2	185	1846	2031	1846	0.909

We also establish a discriminant function and the results are shown in Table 6. It has been observed that the foot breadth, the foot length and medial malleolus height have a greater influence on the gender discrimination, and the influence of the ankle circumference and the foot oblique width is less.

Table 6. Linear discriminant function for groups

Item	1	2
Constant	389.51	332.86
Foot length	1.59	1.47
Foot breadth	2.81	2.54
Ankle circumference	0.24	0.39
Medial malleolus height	1.3	0.98
Foot oblique width	−0.29	−0.42
Linear method for response: lass		

5 Discussion and Conclusion

The results of this study suggest that we can use foot size to distinguish men and women reliably. This discovery has certain guiding significance to the design of male and female sports shoes. Our analysis of foot data shows that there are significant differences in the shape of feet between men and women. These findings suggest that women's shoes should not be just a smaller version of men's shoes. At the same time, the foot shape of different age groups are slightly different. This paper also has some limitations. One limitation of the present paper is that the variables used may not fully represent the entire set of three dimensional shape differences that exist between men and women. In some cases, in order to make sports shoes more compatible with the foot, other measurements such as foot thickness can be considered. Future studies should expand the set of measurements, focusing on areas identified as functionally important in this and other studies.

Acknowledgements. This research was supported by National Key Technology R&D Program (2017YFF0206503, 2017YFF0209004, 2016YFF0204205) and China National Institute of Standardization through the "special funds for the basic R&D undertakings by welfare research institutions" (522018Y-5941, 522018Y-5948, 522016Y-4681, 712016Y-4941-2016).

References

1. O'Connor, K., Bragdon, G., Baumhauer, J.F.: Sexual dimorphism of the foot and ankle. Orthop. Clin. **37**(4), 569–574 (2006)
2. Miller, R.G., Redwood, S.R. (eds.): Manual of Shoemaking, 4th edn., pp. 44–70. C. & J. Clark Ltd., Bristol (1976)
3. Stewart, S.F.: Footgear: its history, uses and abuses. Clin. Orthop. **88**, 119–130 (1972)

4. Frey, C., Smith, J., Sanders, M., Horstman, H.: American orthopaedic foot and ankle society women's shoe survey. Foot Ankle **14**, 78–81 (1993)
5. Frey, C.: Foot health and shoewear for women. Clin. Orthop. Relat. Res. **372**, 32–44 (2000)
6. Frey, C., Coughlin, M.J.: Women's shoe wear: an orthopaedist's advice. J. Women's Health **8** (1), 45–49 (1999)
7. Wunderlich, R.E., Cavanagh, P.R.: Gender differences in adult foot shape implications for shoe design. Med. Sci. Sports Exerc. **33**, 605–611 (2001)
8. Klecka, W.R.: Discriminant Analysis, vol. 07–019, pp. 52–53. Sage Publications, Newbury Park (1980)

Motion Prediction and Motion Capture

Exploring the Feasibility of Classifying Fundamental Locomotor Skills Using an Instrumented Insole and Machine Learning Techniques

Toyin Ajisafe[(✉)] and Dugan Um

Texas A&M University – Corpus Christi, Corpus Christi, TX, USA
toyin.ajisafe@tamucc.edu

Abstract. Movement interventions commonly feature Fundamental locomotor skills (FLSs) like hopping. These skills are thought to positively shape physical activity (PA) trajectory in children. However, the extent to which children who are at risk for overweight and obesity deploy these skills during leisure time PA is often unknown. Direct observation methods are cost-prohibitive. Step count from commercial activity trackers fail to capture these movements. This paper explored the feasibility of using an instrumented insole and machine learning algorithms to classify hopping, running, sprinting, and walking. A subject (age: 40 years; mass: 81 kg; height: 1.7 m) walked, hopped, and sprinted while wearing an instrumented insole. The insole features two pressure sensors and a mechanical housing. The mechanical housing held an Arduino/Genuino 101 programmed using Arduino Software Integrated Development Environment (IDE). An artificial neural network (ANN) training and real-time classification software was written in Arduino IDE and downloaded onto the Arduino 101's non-volatile memory. The ANN used pressure and time derivative data from a dual sensor array and was tested with various statistical parameters. The moving average, standard deviation, min, max, time derivative and acceleration proved most significant for effective training and precision realtime classification. The on-line validation produced mixed accuracy: walking, running, and sprinting were classified with higher than 70% accuracy, but hopping was classified with only 25% accuracy. It is concluded that insole instrumentation with supervised machine learning seem promising to help track FLS deployment. The lower classification accuracy associated with hopping may be due to higher signal variability.

Keywords: Machine learning · Locomotor skills · Movement classification · Foot pressure · Neural network

1 Introduction

Physical activity (PA) interventions pervade many multi-setting programs, including school-based programs, aimed at preventing or controlling obesity [1]. Given recommendations that children and youth engage in 60 min or more of predominantly moderate to vigorous PA every day [2], PA patterns should expectedly feature

© Springer Nature Switzerland AG 2019
V. G. Duffy (Ed.): HCII 2019, LNCS 11581, pp. 113–127, 2019.
https://doi.org/10.1007/978-3-030-22216-1_9

recurrent deployment of fundamental locomotor skills (FLSs) like hopping, jumping, and running (including variations like sprinting). These movements cost more than six times the energy expended from sitting quietly for one minute and can facilitate neuromuscular and cardiorespiratory fitness [3, 4]. When implemented in children, trainings that involve agility (e.g., sprinting) and plyometric movements (e.g., hopping) are designed to facilitate mastery of FLSs and projected to positively shape physical activity trajectory [5, 6]. Fundamental movement skills include FLSs and are thought to be positively related to PA behavior [7]. The presence of FLSs and children's PA behavior content has typically been investigated through direct observation [8]. This method is cost and temporally prohibitive. More commonly, accelerometer-based devices are used to output number of steps taken. This method lacks details on activity structure and the specific types of movements that are deployed. Therefore, there is a need for a research device that will allow researchers to directly investigate, understand, and model the relationship between ad hoc interventions and subsequent locomotor behaviors.

PA is any bodily movement generated by skeletal muscle and results in energy expenditure [9]. It has been suggested that motor skill competence mediates engagement in PA [10] and is associated with health-related physical fitness across childhood (i.e., in children aged 4−13 years) [11]. Chen et al. [12] concluded that health-related physical fitness components like trunk lift, push-up, and curl-up tests were linked with students' engagement in PA during physical education, recess, and sports outside school. Castetbon and Andreyeva [13] found that gross motor skills, which involved vertically translating the body's center of mass (e.g., skipping a minimum of eight consecutive steps, jumping from a standing start, and hopping unilaterally over five consecutive repetition) were inversely associated with obesity and standardized BMI scores. FLSs like jumping, hopping, leaping, and running form the foundation necessary to acquire sport-specific skills and engage in PA across the lifespan [10]. For example, jumping is integral to performing complex activities in a number of sports, including volleyball, basketball, and soccer [14–16]. Unlike walking, which emerges automatically across the developmental trajectory, FLSs are acquired through instruction, structured training, context-specific exposure and practice [11]. When adequately developed, these skills can facilitate joint stiffness regulation and powers, which are optimal for many metabolically demanding bipedal movements [17]. Deficits in these skills can engender low self-confidence and can constitute a barrier to PA [18].

While some longitudinal studies have assessed self-reported PA behavior among children who participated in such interventions, others have measured PA behavior using more objective means like accelerometers [19]. The challenge is that while there is some evidence that FMS proficiency may mediate PA behaviors, the specific mechanisms are not lucid. This relationship is further complicated by factors such as health-related physical fitness and ecological factors, including park density and park amenities, which have also been linked with PA behavior. Therefore, it is important to pose more specific questions regarding the relationship between FMS interventions and the deployment frequency and duration of targeted skills. Because FLSs tend to be metabolically expensive, thereby engendering high energy expenditure, it is important to understand whether interventions that promote FLSs among children result in increased deployment frequency and duration.

Wundersitz et al. [20] previously classified activity types using time and frequency domain features of gyroscope and accelerometer signals and multiple approaches, namely Logistic Model Tree, Random Forest, and Support Vector Machine. Their Logistic Model Tree algorithms showed the highest classification accuracy (79−92%) a walk, tackle, standing stationary, sprinting, jogging, change of direction, and a countermovement jump. However, their movement capture durations varied between 0.5 to 1.5 s [20]. Shorter duration capture was considered optimal for accelerometer-based classification training, because they exclude non-pertinent movement data (i.e., noise) [20]. It is unclear whether this method would remain accurate during longer duration movements. While instrumented insoles have been used to extract spatiotemporal gait features [21] and detect fall events [22], they have yet to be implemented to classify FLSs and associated temporal features.

To that end, the current work explored the feasibility of implementing artificial intelligent technologies to classify different modes of human locomotion using input from an instrumented insole. Although various wearable PA tracking devices are pervasive, many use accelerometers and gyroscopes and are typically worn around the wrist. As such, they are subject to artifacts and require many more features (upwards of 37), in order to accurately classify lower extremity-driven movements [20]. This requires greater processing power and time [20]. Additionally, activities like riding outdoor bicycles or stationary indoor exercise bikes become difficult to detect or quantify, because the upper limbs are generally stationary in these contexts (the hands usually grasp the handle bars for support stability). In contrast, this work focuses on using pressure-related data from an instrumented insole to classify locomotor modes, especially considering that these movements are primarily undertaken using the lower extremities. This method is expected to require fewer features for classification.

This study has two primary aims: (1) present the design of an instrumented insole that uses foot pressure data from a dual sensor array to classify three FLSs (i.e., hopping, running, and sprinting) and a non-fundamental locomotor skill (i.e., walking), and (2) present an initial feasibility assessment by means of accuracy estimates of the ad hoc ANN's classification of the foregoing locomotor modes. The device and proposed method could allow researchers track and answer elusive questions regarding the relationship between FLS training and movement competency interventions and locomotor activity behavior and structure, especially during unsupervised play in children. The device could also allow researchers model the relationship between FLS deployment frequency and weight trajectories, especially among children.

2   System Development

2.1   Mechanical Design

To fulfill the requirements for an ergonomic design of a wearable system for FLS classification and motion triggering, the physical interaction between the human users and the elements of the system needed be carefully taken into account. Most wearable devices are parallel and physically coupled with a human limb. Therefore, the ergonomic design of wearable sensor/actuator devices, in particular, should be compliant with the human model in terms of anatomical, anthropometric and biomechanical characteristics. In order to make the wearable device comfortable, we designed the device to wrap around the tarsus. Pressure sensors were placed to coincide with the first metatarsal head and medial rear foot, in order to optimally sense foot pressure. While the average adult tarsus radius helped informed the dimensions of the current insole, its dimensions can be easily modulated to suit a variety of foot sizes. The design of the mechanical housing of the wearable device is shown in Fig. 1. Notably, the ankle-mounted mechanical housing is fairly bulky in size; however, it contains all of the mechanical and electrical devices in multi-layered housing for ease of maintenance and operation.

Fig. 1. Mechanical housing of the wearable device

2.2   Electrical Design

The brain of the real time ANN is an Arduino 101 (Intel Corporation, Santa Clara, CA). The Arduino/Genuino 101 is a development board, which contains the Intel® Curie™ Module, designed to integrate the core's low power-consumption and high performance with the Arduino's ease-of-use.

In order to make the wearable device wireless, we used the 101 Bluetooth Low Energy technology. The Arduino/Genuino 101 is programmable using the Arduino Software (IDE), our Integrated Development Environment common to all our boards. These ran both online and offline. The overall electrical diagram is shown in Fig. 2.

The ANN training and real-time classification software was written in IDE and downloaded onto the non-volatile memory. Two thin (0.2 mm) circular (diameter 9.53 mm) force sensitive resistors (i.e., FlexiForce A301 sensors) (Teksan, South Boston, MA) capable of measuring up to 25 lbs. were connected through the analog inputs. Two vibrator actuators were connected through the Arduino relay shield. Although shown in pertinent figures, further information on the vibration actuators is not presented, as it is outside the scope of this paper. The force range of the Flexiforce sensors were adjustable by varying the voltage drive applied and the resistance of the feedback resistor. A 6 V battery with a power on/off switch on the housing was integrated, in order to drive the force sensor amplifier.

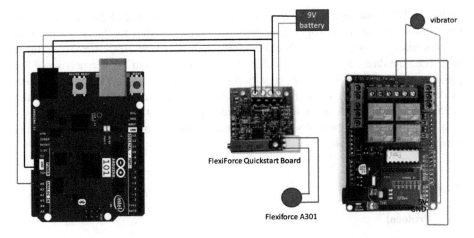

Fig. 2. Electrical diagram

2.3 Artificial Neural Network (ANN) Design

ANNs are a very rough model of how the human brain is structured. ANNs are composed of units of calculation called neurons. These artificial neurons are connected by synapses with weighted values.

ANN emerged as a more meaningful approach to solving problems, given increased computer processing power and the availability of big data. Among the core enablers is the backpropagation mechanism that helps train an ANN to solve specific non-linear

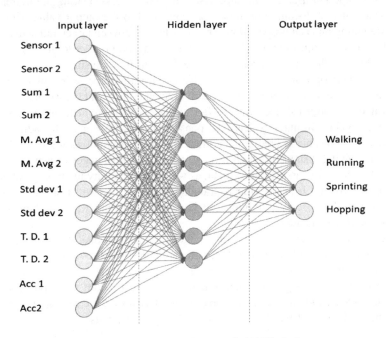

Fig. 3. Artificial Neural Network (ANN) design

problems. When the result is unexpected, an error is calculated, and the values at each neuron and synapse are propagated backwards through the ANN for the next time. This process takes big data for an ANN to be trained correctly. In an ANN, there is an input layer (i.e., the data), a hidden layer, and an output layer. From the perspective of the problem scope of the locomotion classification, we start with an assumption that one hidden layer suffices to solve the problem. After several iterations, we finalized the ANN structure with 12 inputs nodes, 8 hidden nodes and 4 output nodes as follows (Fig. 3). The details of the ANN design are finalized during the ANN training, which is detailed in the next section.

3   Experiment

3.1   Protocol

A college age young adult male (age: 20 years; height: 1.7 m; mass: 74 kg) wore their regular running shoes fitted with the instrumented insole on their dominant side. They then walked for 33 s, ran for 28 s, sprinted for 19 s, and hopped unilaterally for 42 s on a single belt Merax JK1603E treadmill (Merax Fitness, City of Industry, CA). The Texas A&M University – Corpus Christi Institutional Review Board approved this study.

3.2   ANN Training

The supervised training was used. In the training phase, the correct class for each record was kept and used for the supervised training process. During the training, the target value of each locomotion mode was compared to the output value with 0.5 of initial weighting on each propagation. The error terms between target and actual output were then used to adjust the weights in the hidden layers, in order to drive subsequent outputs closer to the target values (i.e., a feedforward mechanism).

A key feature of neural networks is an iterative learning process in which data cases (rows) are presented to the network one at a time, and the weights associated with the input values are adjusted each time. After all cases are presented, the process often starts over again. During this learning phase, the network learns by adjusting the weights so as to be able to predict the correct class label of input samples. As shown in Fig. 5, the training data have a high level of noise. The advantages of neural networks include their high tolerance to noisy data, as well as their ability to classify patterns on which they have not been previously trained. Therefore, we will test the ANN classification with data used for training (off-line validation) and with data not used for training (on-line validation).

The network processes the records in the training data one at a time, using the weights and functions in the hidden layers, then compares the resulting outputs against the desired outputs. Errors are then propagated back through the system, causing the system to adjust the weights and apply them to the next record to be processed. We trained the ANN 1000 times and compared the total least square error with the desirable goal. The goal value of the ANN was set to 15 with 12 inputs.

Input Layer. The input layer of the ANN was composed of 12 data sets as listed in Table 1. Note that some networks did not learn. This could be because the input data did not contain the specific information from which the desired output was derived. Therefore, we tested different sets of input data starting with the raw sensor data. As a result, a total of 12 sets of data were identified for the adequate classification accuracy of up to 70% (Table 1). Networks also do not converge, if there is not enough data to enable complete learning. Ideally, there should be enough data so that part of the data can be held back as a validation set. We trained the ANN with the average number of data set of 100 for each locomotion mode. Therefore, a total of 400 data were used to refine the ANN weights. The front and rear sensors were positioned to approximately coincide with the first metatarsal head and medial tubercle of the calcaneus, respectively (Fig. 4).

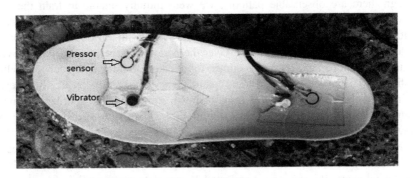

Fig. 4. Sensor implementation at insole

Table 1. Input data structure

Set 1	Rear sensor data	Sum of last 20 data	Moving average	Standard deviation	Time derivative	Acceleration
Set 2	Front sensor data	Sum of last 20 data	Moving average	Standard deviation	Time derivative	Acceleration

Output Layer. We tested two possible configurations of the output layer. One was the single node of decimal value from 0 to 4. The other was the digital 0, 1 value of each node with 4 nodes to cover 5 different locomotion layers. The latter turned out to be more accurate in classification. Therefore, we structured the output layer of the ANN with 4 neurons as listed in Table 2.

Table 2. Output data structure

Output	Locomotion mode
0000	Staying
0001	Walking
0010	Running
0100	Sprinting
1000	Hopping

4 Preliminary Data Analysis

In order to train the ANN, we collected data across four locomotor modes (Fig. 5). Although there are observable patterns, we were initially unable to train the ANN successfully; the classification accuracy was only up to 30%. In order to enhance the classification accuracy, we trained and tested the ANN with various statistical parameters to find the most significant ones. Over the period of experiments, we discovered several significant parameters (i.e., features) for effective training and precision realtime classification. Therefore, we explored parameters that were statistically relevant/ meaningful to the training objective from the raw locomotion data, in order to bring the classification accuracy up to 70%. As listed in Table 1, we identified six features from the raw data from each sensor. A total of 12 features served as input to the ANN. Each input is shown in Figs. 6, 7, 8 and 9. In order to generate all six features, we processed the raw data by following the data processing sequence as shown (Fig. 10). Each data was sampled every 100 ms, so we collected 10 raw data per second.

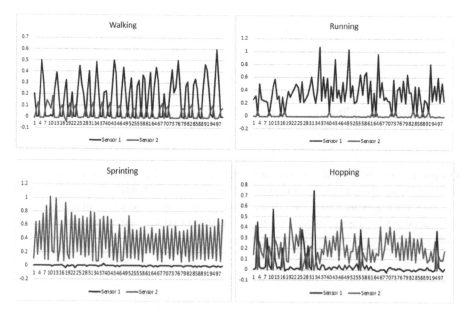

Fig. 5. Raw data for 4 locomotion modes

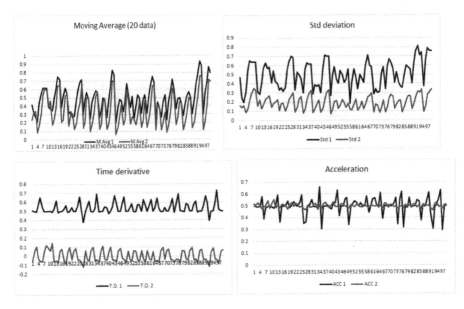

Fig. 6. Walking data

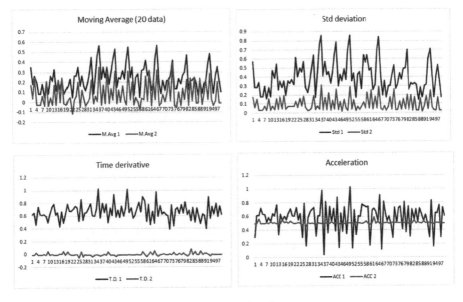

Fig. 7. Running data

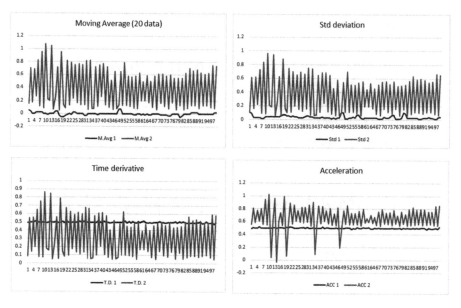

Fig. 8. Sprinting data

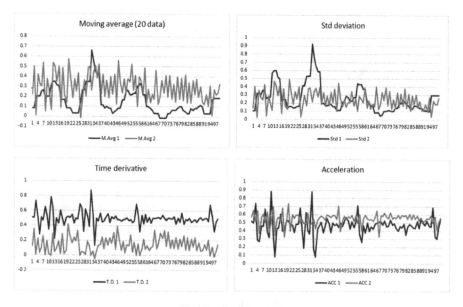

Fig. 9. Hopping data

Fig. 10. Data processing sequence

5 Results and Discussion

5.1 ANN Classification

In this section, we share the results and discuss the ANN classification. Notably, the off-line validation, which used the same data as the training, demonstrated 100% for all four locomotion modes. In on-line validation, most of the locomotion modes were classified with greater than 70% accuracy, except hopping. As shown in Fig. 5, the noise level in hopping tended to be very high compared to other locomotion modes. This may be primarily due to the fact that the wearer likely did not depress the two sensors in a consistent pattern during the stance phase of each hop. Specifically, the participant appeared to depress the sensor at the medial tubercle of the calcaneus with relatively more variable pressure during each hop. Tables 3 and 4 show the off- and on-line validation outputs for each of the four locomotor modes.

This work attempted to classify FLSs by solely using force-sensitive resistors (FSR) sensors. A system designed to track FLS deployment duration and frequency during leisure time PA among children has to be wearable and practical. Therefore, excluding additional sensors like accelerometers was an important initial hardware consideration to minimize the systems' cumbersomeness and energy requirements. However, the lack of other opportunistic sensor integration may have detracted from the current classification outcomes. Cates et al. [22] recently designed a multi-sensor insole by integrating four force-sensitive resistors and an inertial measurement unit accelerometer to detect high acceleration fall events from low acceleration activities of daily living. Their algorithm involved 45 features, and 15 of these were from FSR data. Although they concluded that a multi-sensor system produced increased classification accuracy, they conceded that such design is associated with increased user discomfort. Their work also underscored the challenge of classifying comparably high acceleration movements using accelerometer data features. Running, jumping, and hopping are consistent with high acceleration movements; therefore, it is unclear whether integrating accelerometry and related vector magnitude features may boost relative classification accuracy in the current design [22].

Table 3. Off-line validation

a. Walking (100%)

Output 1	Output 2	Output 3	Output 4
0	0	0	1
0	0	0	1
0	0	0	1
0	0	0	1
0	0	0	1
0	0	0	1
0	0	0	1
0	0	0	1
0	0	0	1
0	0	0	1

b. Running (100%)

Output 1	Output 2	Output 3	Output 4
0	0	1	0
0	0	1	0
0	0	1	0
0	0	1	0
0	0	1	0
0	0	1	0
0	0	1	0
0	0	1	0
0	0	1	0
0	0	1	0

c. Sprinting (100%)

Output 1	Output 2	Output 3	Output 4
0	1	0	0
0	1	0	0
0	1	0	0
0	1	0	0
0	1	0	0
0	1	0	0
0	1	0	0
0	1	0	0
0	1	0	0
0	1	0	0

d. Hopping (100%)

Output 1	Output 2	Output 3	Output 4
1	0	0	0
1	0	0	0
1	0	0	0
1	0	0	0
1	0	0	0
1	0	0	0
1	0	0	0
1	0	0	0
1	0	0	0
1	0	0	0

Table 4. On-line validation

a. Walking (80%)

Output 1	Output 2	Output 3	Output 4
0	0	0	1
0	0	0	1
0	0	0	0.997
0	0	0	0.998
0	0	0	1
0	0	0	1
0	1	0	0
0	0	0	1
0	0	0	1
0	1	0.007	0

b. Running (75%)

Output 1	Output 2	Output 3	Output 4
0.002	0	0.999	0
0	0	1	0
0.004	0.001	0.975	0.001
0	0	0.973	0.022
0	0	1	0
0.004	0	0.998	0
0	0	1	0
0	0.001	1	0
0	0	1	0
0	0	1	0

c. Sprinting (100%)

Output 1	Output 2	Output 3	Output 4
0	1	0	0
0	1	0	0
0	1	0	0
0	1	0	0
0	1	0	0
0	1	0	0
0	1	0	0
0	1	0	0
0	1	0	0
0	1	0	0

d. Hopping (25%)

Output 1	Output 2	Output 3	Output 4
0.011	0	0	0.999
0.001	0.999	0.001	0
0	0	1	0
0.056	0.011	0.854	0.003
0	0	1	0
0.996	0.01	0.001	0.001
0.018	0.96	0.002	0
0.012	0.945	0.006	0
0	0	1	0
0.085	0.012	0.775	0.002

6   Limitations

The current work is has several limitations. The insole only has two integrated FSR sensors. Considering the placement of these sensors, pressure data from the midfoot region was likely not captured. Capturing and integrating pressure data across more foot regions may enhance the accuracy of classifying more variable movements like hopping. The training data was relatively diminutive and originated from one participant.

There is need to collect more data, in order to optimize the algorithm training. Further, additional instrumented insole data features, including ones in the frequency domain should be explored, in order to potentially improve hopping classification accuracy up to 70% or higher. Future research will aim to classify additional FLSs like jumping and non FLS lower extremity-based movements like bike riding.

7 Conclusion

This paper explored the feasibility of using data from an instrumented insole to classify running, hopping, sprinting, and walking. During the off-line validation, we achieved 100% classification accuracy; however, the on-line validation produced mixed accuracy. Walking, running, and sprinting were all classified with higher than 70% accuracy in the on-line validation, but hopping was classified with a 25% accuracy. The level of variability in hopping tended to be high compared to other locomotor modes. This may have been due to the fact that the wearer did not depress the sensors using similar pressure patterns during each hop. It is concluded that an ANN technology using features generated from foot pressure data appears promising to classify the locomotor modes that are often the subject of many movement competency interventions. This may provide important insight into children's FLS deployment and their overall movement content, particularly during leisure time PA. This knowledge may help inform movement competency interventions and how these may shape moderate to vigorous PA behaviors, especially in the context of preventing or controlling overweight and obesity. The device overcomes some limitations associated with wrist worn activity trackers, including artifacts and decreased predictability of upper extremity movement patterns during primarily lower extremity-driven movements. It also minimizes the need for excessive features, which was previously reported to increase processing time.

Although the wearer did not report any discomfort associated with the device, future work will aim to miniaturize the mechanical housing and assess its usability.

Acknowledgement. This work was funded by Texas Comprehensive Research Fund from Texas A&M University-Corpus Christi Division of Research and Innovation.

References

1. Bleich, S.N., Vercammen, K.A., Zatz, L.Y., Frelier, J.M., Ebbeling, C.B., Peeters, A.: Interventions to prevent global childhood overweight and obesity: a systematic review. Lancet Diabetes Endocrinol. **6**, 332–346 (2018)
2. Armstrong, B., Lim, C.S., Janicke, D.M.: Park density impacts weight change in a behavioral intervention for overweight rural youth. Behav. Med. **41**, 123–130 (2015)
3. Myer, G.D., Faigenbaum, A.D., Ford, K.R., Best, T.M., Bergeron, M.F., Hewett, T.E.: When to initiate integrative neuromuscular training to reduce sports-related injuries and enhance health in youth? Curr. Sports Med. Rep. **10**, 155–166 (2011)
4. Cattuzzo, M.T., et al.: Motor competence and health related physical fitness in youth: a systematic review. J. Sci. Med. Sport **19**, 123–129 (2016)

5. Pereira, S.A., Seabra, A.T., Silva, R.G., Zhu, W., Beunen, G.P., Maia, J.A.: Correlates of health-related physical fitness levels of Portuguese children. Pediatr. Obes. **6**, 53–59 (2011)
6. Stodden, D.F., True, L.K., Langendorfer, S.J., Gao, Z.: Associations among selected motor skills and health-related fitness: indirect evidence for Seefeldt's proficiency barrier in young adults? Res. Q. Exerc. Sport **84**, 397–403 (2013)
7. Bremer, E., Cairney, J.: Fundamental movement skills and health-related outcomes: a narrative of longitudinal and intervention studies targeting typically developing children. Am. J. Lifestyle Med. **20**, 1–12 (2016)
8. Han, B., Cohen, D., McKenzie, T.L.: Quantifying the contribution of neighborhood parks to physical activity. Prev. Med. **57**, 483–487 (2013)
9. Caspersen, C.J., Powell, K.E., Christenson, G.M.: Physical activity, exercise, and physical fitness: definitions and distinctions for health-related research. Public Health Rep. **100**, 126–131 (1985)
10. Stodden, D.F., et al.: A developmental perspective on the role of motor skill competence in physical activity: an emergent relationship. Quest **60**, 290–306 (2008)
11. Stodden, D.F., Gao, Z., Goodway, J.D., Langendorfer, S.J.: Dynamic relationships between motor skill competence and health-related fitness in youth. Pediatr. Exerc. Sci. **26**, 231–241 (2014)
12. Chen, W., Hammond-Bennett, A., Hypnar, A., Mason, S.: Health-related physical fitness and physical activity in elementary school students. BMC Public Health **18**, 195 (2018)
13. Castetbon, K., Andreyeva, T.: Obesity and motor skills among 4 to 6-year-old children in the united states: nationally-representative surveys. BMC Pediatr. **12**, 1–9 (2012)
14. Mcerlain-Naylor, S., King, M., Pain, M.T.G.: Determinants of countermovement jump performance: a kinetic and kinematic analysis. J. Sports Sci. **32**, 1805–1812 (2014)
15. Ryan, W., Harrison, A., Hayes, K.: Functional data analysis of knee joint kinematics in the vertical jump. Sports Biomech. **5**, 121–138 (2006)
16. Domire, Z.J., Challis, J.H.: Maximum height and minimum time vertical jumping. J. Biomech. **48**, 2865–2870 (2015)
17. Lazaridis, S., Bassa, E., Patikas, D., Giakas, G., Gollhofer, A., Kotzamanidis, C.: Neuromuscular differences between prepubescents boys and adult men during drop jump. Eur. J. Appl. Physiol. **110**, 67–74 (2010)
18. van Schijndel-Speet, M., Evenhuis, H.M., van Wijck, R., van Empelen, P., Echteld, M.A.: Facilitators and barriers to physical activity as perceived by older adults with intellectual disability. Intellect. Dev. Disabil. **52**, 175–186 (2014)
19. Pate, R.R., et al.: An intervention to increase physical activity in children: a randomized controlled trial with 4-year-olds in preschools. Am. J. Prev. Med. **51**, 12–22 (2016)
20. Wundersitz, D.W., Josman, C., Gupta, R., Netto, K.J., Gastin, P.B., Robertson, S.: Classification of team sport activities using a single wearable tracking device. J. Biomech. **48**, 3975–3981 (2015)
21. Crea, S., Donati, M., De Rossi, S.M., Oddo, C.M., Vitiello, N.: A wireless flexible sensorized insole for gait analysis. Sensors (Basel) **14**, 1073–1093 (2014)
22. Cates, B., Sim, T., Heo, H.M., Kim, B., Kim, H., Mun, J.H.: A novel detection model and its optimal features to classify falls from low- and high-acceleration activities of daily life using an insole sensor system. Sensors (Basel) **18**(4), 1227 (2018)

Classifying Non-elementary Movements in Vietnamese Mõ Dances

Mustapha Bourahla[1], Abdelmoutia Telli[2], Salem Benferhat[3(✉)],
and Ma Thi Chau[4]

[1] LMPA Laboratory, University of M'Sila, M'Sila, Algeria
[2] Biskra University, Biskra, Algeria
[3] CRIL-CNRS, Artois University, Arras, France
benferhat@cril.fr
[4] HMI Lab, University of Engineering and Technology, Hanoi, Vietnam

Abstract. This paper proposes a method to classify non-elementary movements in Vietnamese dances. This classification method uses an OWL ontology called VDM (Vietnamese Dance Movements) recently developed by the authors. The VDM defines a taxonomy of dance movement classes and their relationships for the traditional Vietnamese dances taking into account the semantics of its art and its cultural anthropologists. The VDM terminology describes elementary movements (poses) as a dataset ontology importing the ontology VDM. These poses are results of dance sequences segmentation (using segmentation techniques). In this paper, we support the initial ontology VDM by complex classification rules written with SWRL (Semantic Web Rule Language, which is the OWL complementary language) to classify non-elementary movements. The objective is to entail classes of movement phrases, which are non-elementary basic movements with complete meaning and illustrated using Mõ dances. The classification result is the initial dataset VDM ontology augmented with class descriptions of non-elementary movements, which can be queried using the query language SQWRL (Semantic Query Web-enhanced Rule Language).

Keywords: Ontology · Description logics ·
Traditional Vietnamese dances

1 Introduction

Recently, there is a great interest in using ontologies for video processing. Ontologies have been developed in the domain of multi-media with different goals as information retrieval and annotation. Based on the ontology, one may might develop multimedia information query applications for classifying vietnam traditional dances for instance. The use of ontologies is important to understanding, managing and querying videos by using high level semantic concepts and their relations in the context of the video analysis.

© Springer Nature Switzerland AG 2019
V. G. Duffy (Ed.): HCII 2019, LNCS 11581, pp. 128–139, 2019.
https://doi.org/10.1007/978-3-030-22216-1_10

There is a large number of works that uses ontologies in videos/images processing. For instance, ontologies have been using for analysis of soccer videos [4], image retrieval system and video events detection [25], video-surveillance [17]. In [20] the authors provide an algorithm that allows unsupervised segmentation of image sequences, video indexing and retrieval using ontologies.

Besides, different works have been developed the use of ontologies for modeling the human movements (specifically dance movements) from video sequences. For instance, the authors in [9] propose an outline of collective dance consciousness into a dance ontology. The authors in [11] presented a knowledge-based system for describing and storing dances that takes advantage of the expressivity of description logics. In [12] the authors discussed key elements of a semantic dance move representation model based on rule and extractions of logical descriptions from existing Labanotation system [6]. Furthermore, in [10] the authors presented an approach for semantic annotation of movement in the videos based on ontology model and semantic concept classifiers. They used the BMN (Benesh Movement Notation) system for building Video Movement Ontology (VMO). On other hand, an ontology-based approach for browsing the heritage collection of Indian dance videos using Multimedia Web Ontology Language (MOWL) is presented in [19]. In [18] the authors proposed an ontology for learning scheme, which is a combination of standard techniques for multimedia analysis with knowledge drawn from conceptual meta data to learn a domain specific multimedia ontology for exploration of multimedia content. Similarly, in [13] the authors created an ontology transferring the semantics of Labanotation into OWL entities. In addition, authors in [6] evaluated the impact of the choreographic language agent and the digital dance archives on dance ontology.

In this paper, we extend our previous work in [23], which proposed an OWL ontology called "VDM" (Vietnamese Dance Movements), to define a taxonomy for the traditional Vietnamese dances taking into account the semantics of its art and its cultural anthropologists. The objective of this extension is to develop a searchable knowledge base that enables us to search for non-elementary movements in dances.

Our starting inputs are sequences segmentation of videos (produce of movements). These movements are represented as a dataset (assertions) using the terminology ontology "VDM" for the purpose to develop a knowledge base that describes traditional Vietnamese dances and enables us to search for specific movements in dance. However, this "VDM" ontology only contains a description of elementary movements (or poses).

This paper goes one step further and proposes a tool that supports the "VDM" ontology with classification rules. These rules are developed with the OWL complementary language SWRL (Semantic Web Rule Language) to entail movement phrases, which are basic movements with complete meaning. The SWRL [16] is a language for the Semantic Web that can be used to express rules as well as logic, combining OWL DL or OWL Lite with a subset of the Rule Markup Language.

The dataset ontology containing pose descriptions can be queried using the query language SQWRL (Semantic Query Web-enhanced Rule Language), which is an extension of SWRL to retrieve implicit dance knowledge. The description of these dances will allow us to express complex relations for inferring on the domain of human movements to extract implicit knowledge from explicit one. These complex relations will be described as SWRL [16] rules. These SWRL rules represent additional description for the dance OWL ontology, to entail implicit knowledge as movement classification.

We specify queries on dance ontologies using the language SQWRL [21], which is based on the SWRL rule language and uses SWRL's strong semantic, where set of operators can be used to perform closure operations as failure, counting, and aggregation. Then, a SQWRL query can be specified to retrieve particular dance information using inference on the dataset ontology, which imports the "VDM" ontology and its classification SWRL rules.

The rest of paper is organized as follows. Sections 2 and 3 cares about the classification of elementary and non-elementary dance movements with illustrative examples, and Sect. 4 concludes the paper.

2 Classification of Elementary Dance Movements

2.1 Motivation

Traditional Vietnamese intangible cultural heritage values are always present in life. Each cultural heritage has its own nuance in each region, clearly showing its own needs and identity. Traditional festivals, performances, folk games, customs, habits, beautiful lifestyle of people have been actively researched, collected, restored and protected. However, due to the impact of the market mechanism and the integration process, many cultural and social organizations are being doped and gradually eroded. Even many folk songs, traditional dances, traditional musical instruments, folk festivals, some traditional handicrafts and daily means of transport are lost, the rest are also being under great competition pressure. The documents and materials mentioned in each field of storage are not much, the rest are scattered, no conditions for collecting and gathering. Artists and artisans who are professional are older.

Therefore, it is important to preserve and promote the intangible cultural heritages and make that heritage "live" in the midst of life, as its nature, contributing to preserving ethnicity's cultural identity, bringing culture to become the spiritual foundation of society. Vietnam has a huge folk dance source of massive ethnic groups exploited to build a professional dance industry. Like other forms of intangible culture, folk dance is also being eroded and needs to be preserved and promoted.

In the context of classifying videos dances, ontologies could be used to annotate dance videos automatically. The constructing elements of the ontology and their relationships to construct the dance model may be based on the semantics of the Labanotation system [5], a widely-applied language that uses symbols, which are identified by concepts and relationships created with the language OWL to denote and reason on dance choreographies.

2.2 Mõ Dance

Mõ is a very popular folk musical instrument, used usually by a very special messenger in old villages, when go through the village for announcing an important notice to villagers. Mõ is also hang on buffalos so the buffalos do not get lost. Mõ is used as an instrument in dance because of its joyful sound. Mõ dance is often a playful dance with many dancers. Mõ dance, a combination of Mõ dance basic units (Inviting, Toe touching, Foot dragging, Rotation jumping, and Exchanging), are actually existing only in the Red river delta, performed in old village's festivals. "Mõ dance under the moon" is a Mõ dance danced in moon cake festival by children. The dance having 20 steps is performed by 4 groups of dancers [24].

2.3 Brief Refresher: VDM Ontology

This section provides a brief refresher on the ontology concepts defined in [23]. First, We chose the representation and analysis of aspects of the folk Vietnam dance movement type Mõ[1], which expresses cultural knowledge, spiritual and daily life.

The terminological box (TBox) in our dance ontology is the concepts and roles which are defined beforehand. While, the assertional box (ABox) is each pose of body parts described by its positions. We use this dataset ontology to entail implicit knowledge from the explicit knowledge to answer queries on dance movements. The reasoning procedure is based on classification rules, which are developed using training datasets.

In order to express complex relationships and rules of inference for the realm of human movements we used OWL to represent Mõ dance ontology (we called by VDM ontology). This ontology development process follows the steps proposed in [14] and [15]. We apply body parts based on Labanotation [8] division in the dance analysis. Then, we represented formally in description logic the dance where the reasoner supports answering different queries on Vietnamese folk-dance.

Description Logics (DLs) [2,3,22] are a family of knowledge representation languages that can be used for representing and reasoning with ontologies. They have two components to build a DL knowledge base: a terminological base TBox, which represents conceptual knowledge by providing a vocabulary for a domain of interest together with axioms that describe semantic relationships between the vocabulary items [7]. An assertional base ABox containing facts (assertions) storing data about the concept and role names introduced in the TBox [26]. We chose DL-Lite family [1] as logic for lightweight ontologies to represent knowledge of vietnamese traditional dances. The choice of this important tractable family of DLs is based on its query answering, which is done in an efficient way.

We defined each basic unit as the smallest movement with a complete meaning *MovementPhrase*:

$$Dance \equiv \forall hasPhrase.MovementPhrase$$

---

[1] https://www.youtube.com/watch?v=3sO-WkNxjZc.

This is means that the (*Dance*) concept is related to movement phrase by the abstract role *hasPhrase*.

There are two main types of movements, corresponding to basic actions:

- *BodyMovement*: makes the position of the whole body of dancer changed in space where the dancers move and change their positions on a stage. They are composed of movement phrases *MovementPhrase*, which include displacement (a point), translation (a line) and rotation (an arc).
- *BodyPartMovement*: makes the position of different parts of dancer's body changed. the movements primitives represented by the concept *MovementPrimitive* are quick movements, which change the position of body parts (hand movements, arm movements, feet movements, leg movements, head movements, and combined arm-leg movements). it is a movement between main dance poses and it considers the part of body as a local coordinate.

We consider that each part of human body has its right side and its left side. Mõ dance includes concepts, concepts properties and relationships between concepts to provide a formal description of a domain. For instance:

- *Movement*: considered as the root of the movement aspect (related to body and body part) of the dance.
- *Region*, *Message* and *Clothing*: represent regional information, dance content, and transmitted messages.
- *TimeOf*, *Orientation* and *Pose*: represent the position and orientation of body or body part in every moment.

On other hand, there are certain types of relationships between dance concepts such as:

- $HasSegment(a, b)$: means that $Mouvement(a)$ belongs to $Segment(b)$
- $PosDancer(a, b)$ means that $Dancer(a)$ is at the $Position(b)$
- $HasMessage(a, b)$ means that $Dancer(a)$ transmit the $Message(b)$

Since a dance pose is a particular position of the dancer's body. We defined the following setting of each movement, where $Pose_I$ is one of predefined poses:

$$PoseDance \equiv \left\{ \begin{array}{l} A : DancerBody, P : MovementPhrase, \\ B : MovementBodyPart, \\ (A, P) : HasPose, (P, time) : timeOf, (P, B) : Pose_I \end{array} \right\}$$

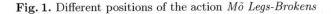

(a) Both legs in orientation 1 and left leg before right leg by 50cm.   (b) Leg left is straight, right leg is in broken position on the rise 20cm   (c) Leg left is straight, right leg is in broken position on the rise 50cm

Fig. 1. Different positions of the action *Mõ Legs-Brokens*

We suggest in this example the motion description of legs for the left part of dancer body, which are represented in the following Figs. 1a, b and c as follows:

$$1a \equiv \left\{ \begin{array}{l} A : DancerBody, P : MovementPhrase, (A, P_1) : HasPose, \\ (P_1, 1) : timeOf, (P_1, Legs) : Orientation1Pose, \\ (P_1, RightLeg, LeftLeg) : BeforePose \end{array} \right\}$$

$$1b \equiv \left\{ \begin{array}{l} A : DancerBody, P : MovementPhrase, (A, P_2) : HasPose, \\ (P_2, 2) : timeOf, (P_2, LeftLeg) : StraightPose, \\ (P_2, RightLeg) : HalfBrokenPose \end{array} \right\}$$

$$1c \equiv \left\{ \begin{array}{l} A : DancerBody, P : MovementPhrase, (A, P_3) : HasPose, \\ (P_3, 3) : timeOf, (P_3, LeftLeg) : StraightPose, \\ (P_3, RightLeg) : BrokenPose \end{array} \right\}$$

3   Classification of Complex Dance Movements

Till now, we described the elementary dance movements in the Vietnamese dance Mõ. The aim of this section is to describe complex (non-elementary) movements which can be viewed as parallel combinations of different poses of basic movements (elementary movements) from body parts. A complex movement can be also a result of a movement achieved by a set of dancers. The concepts *Group*, *Groupshape*, and *memberOf* encode the informations of groups of dancers in a dance.

3.1   Example of Non-elementary Movement

In Vietnamese dance Mõ, a group of dancers can have a shape created by two relations:

(a) Move forward and left side to the centre. (b) Move forward and Back to the centre (c) Stopping forward and facing the centre

Fig. 2. Positions formed the Line Relation

- *LineRelation* represents the sequences of the positions of the dancers that form a line or an arc. The descriptions given in Figs. 2a, b and c for the movement directions of the dancers form a straight line. These movements poses are represented by the individuals LP_1, LP_2 and LP_3 from the concept *MovementBodyPart*, wich correspond to the image of Fig. 2. To give complete formal description, we assume that each dancer ($A : DancerBody$) makes the same basic movements. Thus, their DL descriptions are as follows.

$$2a \equiv \left\{ \begin{array}{l} (A, LP_1) : hasPose, (LP_1, 0) : timeOf, (LP_1, A) : LeftSideCentre, \\ (LP_1, arms) : UpPose, (LP_1, Legs) : StraightPose \end{array} \right\}$$

$$2b \equiv \left\{ \begin{array}{l} (A, LP_2) : hasPose, (LP_2, 2) : timeOf, (LP_2, A) : BackCentre, \\ (LP_2, arms) : DownPose, (LP_2, Legs) : StraightPose \end{array} \right\}$$

$$2c \equiv \left\{ \begin{array}{l} (A, LP_3) : hasPose, (LP_3, 3) : timeOf, (LP_3, A) : FacingCentre, \\ (LP_3, arms) : HexaPose, (LP_3, Legs) : StraightPose \end{array} \right\}$$

- *CircleRelation* can represent the sequences of the positions of the dancers that form a circle. All these relations are declared individuals as shown in Figs. 3a, b, c and d. Logically, this relation is formulated by:

$$3a \equiv \left\{ \begin{array}{l} (A, CP_1) : hasPose, (CP_1, 0) : timeOf, (CP_1, A) : Orientation1Pose, \\ (CP_1, arms) : StraightPose, (CP_1, Legs) : StraightPose \end{array} \right\}$$

$$3b \equiv \left\{ \begin{array}{l} (A, CP_2) : hasPose, (CP_2, 2) : timeOf, (CP_2, A) : Orientation1Pose, \\ (CP_2, arms) : HexaUpPose, (CP_2, Legs) : StraightPose \end{array} \right\}$$

$$3c \equiv \left\{ \begin{array}{l} (A, CP_3) : hasPose, (CP_3, 3) : timeOf, (CP_3, A) : Orientation1Pose, \\ (CP_3, arms) : HexaPose, (CP_3, Legs) : StraightPose, \\ (CP_3, Hands) : OrthUpPose \end{array} \right\}$$

(a) Assembly

(b) The arms are raised in hexagonal form

(c) The arms are down and straight;

(d) The arms are down in hexagonal form

Fig. 3. Positions formed of the Circle Relation

$$3d \equiv \left\{ \begin{array}{l} (A, CP_4) : hasPose, (CP_4, 4) : timeOf, (CP_4, A) : Orientation1Pose, \\ (CP_4, arms) : HexaDowenPose, (CP_4, Legs) : StraightPose \end{array} \right\}$$

Now, according to the example Sect. 2.2 we present the parallel combination between the actions of the feet with the actions of the hands or arms in a complete corporal movement. These non-elementary movements execute in a repetitive way that is what we apply in the annotation of the movements.

$$a \equiv \left\{ \begin{array}{l} (A, P_1) : hasPose, (P_1, 1) : timeOf, (P_1, Legs) : Orientation1Pose, \\ (P_1, RightLeg, LeftLeg) : BreakPose, (P_1, Arms) : UpPose, (P_1, Hands) : OpenPose \end{array} \right\}$$

$$b \equiv \left\{ \begin{array}{l} (A, P_2) : hasPose, (P_2, 2) : timeOf, (P_2, LeftLeg) : StraightPose, \\ (P_2, RightLeg) : HalfBrokenPose, (P_2, Arms) : DowenPose, (P_2, Hands) : OpenPose \end{array} \right\}$$

$$c \equiv \left\{ \begin{array}{l} (A, P_3) : hasPose, (P_3, 3) : timeOf, (P_3, LeftLeg) : StraightPose, \\ (P_3, RightLeg) : BrokenPose, (P_3, Arms) : DowenPose, \\ (P_3, Hands, Lengs) : UnderPose, (P_3, Hands) : ClosePose \end{array} \right\}$$

3.2 Rule-Based Classification of Non-elementary Movements

We use the ontology concepts defined in [23] to classify the movement poses ($MovementPose$), the movement primitives ($MovementPrimitive$), the movement phrases ($MovementPhrase$) and dance movements. For the classification, we propose a set of rules written using declared abstract roles (*poseClass, primitiveClass,* and *phraseClass*). This allows to associate a class with each movement pose, primitive or phrase, respectively. Using abstract roles is important for a compact representation of rules.

Rules are of the form of an implication between an antecedent (body) and consequent (head). The intended meaning can be read as: whenever the conditions specified in the antecedent hold, then the conditions specified in the consequent must also hold. Both the antecedent (body) and consequent (head) consist of zero or more atoms. Atoms in these rules can be of the form $C(x)$, $P(x,y)$, $sameAs(x,y)$ or $differentFrom(x,y)$, where C is an OWL concept (class), P is an OWL property, and x,y are either variables, OWL individuals or OWL data values. There are many built-in atoms.

An example of a SWRL rule used to classify the poses is described below (the rules below are presented with the premise-conclusion form).

$$\frac{DancerBody(?d) \ \wedge \ hasPose(?d,?p) \ \wedge orientation8Pose(?p, LeftFoot) \ \wedge}{poseClass(?p, LegsPose1)}$$
$$orientation2Pose(?p, RightFoot) \ \wedge straightPose(?p, Legs)$$

If a dancer body specified by the variable d has a movement pose p and this movement pose satisfies the description specified by the atoms in the rest of rule body then it is classified by the class specified by the second argument of the atom *poseClass*. The same thing applies for classification of arms poses.

A sequence of movement poses can create a predefined movement primitive. The consecutive legs poses will create for example, a primitive of legs movements, which is of class *LegsPrimitive*. The SWRL rule to create this primitive is below.

$$DancerBody(?d) \ \wedge \ hasPose(?d,?p1) \ \wedge \ poseClass(?p1, LegsPose1) \ \wedge$$
$$hasPose(?d,?p2) \ \wedge \ poseClass(?p2, LegsPose2) \ \wedge \ hasPose(?d,?p3) \ \wedge$$
$$poseClass(?p3, LegsPose3) \ \wedge \ hasPose(?d,?p4) \ \wedge$$
$$poseClass(?p4, LegsPose4) \ \wedge \ hasPose(?d,?p5) \ \wedge$$
$$poseClass(?p5, LegsPose5) \ \wedge \ timeOf(?p1,?t1) \ \wedge \ timeOf(?p2,?t2) \ \wedge$$
$$timeOf(?p3,?t3) \ \wedge \ timeOf(?p4,?t4) \ \wedge \ timeOf(?p5,?t5) \ \wedge$$
$$add(?t2,?t1,1) \ \wedge \ add(?t3,?t2,1) \ \wedge \ add(?t4,?t3,1) \ \wedge$$
$$add(?t5,?t4,1) \ \wedge \ makeOWLThing(?pr,?d)$$

$$MovementPrimitive(?pr) \ \wedge \ primitiveClass(?pr, LegsPrimitive) \ \wedge$$
$$hasPrimitive(?d,?pr) \ \wedge \ hasPose(?pr,?p1) \ \wedge \ hasPose(?pr,?p2) \ \wedge$$
$$hasPose(?pr,?p3) \ \wedge \ hasPose(?pr,?p4) \ \wedge \ hasPose(?pr,?p5) \ \wedge$$
$$beginTime(?pr,?t1) \ \wedge \ endTime(?pr,?t5)$$

Queries on dance dataset ontologies are specified with the language SQWRL [21], which is based on the SWRL rule language and uses SWRL's strong semantic. SQWRL takes a standard SWRL rule antecedent and treats it as a pattern specification for a query. It replaces the rule consequent with a retrieval specification. For example, the query:

$$Query(pose, time, image) \leftarrow phraseClass(phrase, MoFootDragging) \wedge$$
$$hasPrimitive(phrase, primitive) \wedge hasPose(primitive, pose) \wedge$$
$$timeOf(pose, time) \wedge video(pose, image)$$

retrieves the poses, their times and their video sequences (images) of the basic movement Mõ foot-dragging of the Vietnamese dance Mõ and it can be specified using the query language SQWRL as

$$Query : phraseClass(?phrase, MoFootDragging) \wedge$$
$$hasPrimitive(?phrase, ?primitive) \wedge hasPose(?primitive, ?pose) \wedge$$
$$timeOf(?pose, ?time) \wedge video(?pose, ?image) \rightarrow$$
$$sqwrl : select(?pose, ?time, ?image) \wedge sqwrl : orderBy(?time)$$

where *video* is OWL datatype relating a movement pose to a string representing a file. The left hand side of a SQWRL query operates like a standard SWRL rule antecedent with its associated semantics. The atoms in the SQWRL will not match only all direct OWL individuals in the ontology, but will match also individuals that are entailed by the ontology to be OWL individuals. The core SQWRL operator $sqwrl : select(?pose, ?time, ?image)$ builds a table using its arguments as columns of the table. This query returns tuples of poses, times and video sequences with one row for each tuple. The results are ordered by time $(sqwrl : orderBy(?time))$.

4   Conclusions

This paper has presented a work for the classification of non-elementary movements in Vietnamese Mõ Dances. The elementary dance movements (called dance poses, which are extracted from video sequences) are described by an initial dataset ontology based on a defined terminology in [23] using the OWL description language. These pose descriptions are inputs for a set of classification rules to construct non-elementary movements classes.

Then, the extended dataset ontology by non-elementary movements classes can be used to answer specific queries for replaying complex dance movements. The perspective of this work is its integration within an application for reproducing dance movements as for dance training.

Acknowledgments. This work has received support from the European project H2020 Marie Sklodowska-Curie Actions (MSCA) research and Innovation Sta Exchange (RISE): AniAge (High Dimensional Heterogeneous Data based Animation Techniques for Southeast Asian Intangible Cultural Heritage Digital Content), project number 691215.

References

1. Artale, A., Calvanese, D., Kontchakov, R., Zakharyaschev, M.: The DL-Lite family and relations. J. Artif. Intell. Res. **36**, 1–69 (2009)
2. Baader, F., Calvanese, D., McGuinness, D., Patel-Schneider, P., Nardi, D.: The Description Logic Handbook: Theory, Implementation and Applications. Cambridge University Press, Cambridge (2003)
3. Baader, F., Sattler, U.: An overview of tableau algorithms for description logics. Stud. Logica **69**(1), 5–40 (2001)
4. Bai, L., Lao, S., Jones, G.J., Smeaton, A.F.: Video semantic content analysis based on ontology. Institute of Electrical and Electronics Engineers (2007)
5. Barbacci, S.: Labanotation: a universal movement notation language. J. Sci. Commun. **1**, 1–11 (2002)
6. Blades, H.: Creative computing and the re-configuration of dance ontology. In EVA (2012)
7. Botoeva, E., Kontchakov, R., Ryzhikov, V., Wolter, F., Zakharyaschev, M.: When are Description Logic knowledge Bases Indistinguishable? AAAI Press (2015)
8. Brown, A.K., Parker, M.: Dance Notation for Beginners. Princeton Book Co. Pub., Hightstown (1984)
9. Clarance, A.: A proposal for the creation of a dance ontology. In: Brooks, A.L., Ayiter, E., Yazicigil, O. (eds.) ArtsIT 2014. LNICST, vol. 145, pp. 86–99. Springer, Cham (2015). https://doi.org/10.1007/978-3-319-18836-2_11
10. De Beul, D., Mahmoudi, S., Manneback, P., et al.: An ontology for video human movement representation based on benesh notation. In: 2012 International Conference on Multimedia Computing and Systems (ICMCS), pp. 77–82. IEEE (2012)
11. El Raheb, K., Ioannidis, Y.: A labanotation based ontology for representing dance movement. In: Efthimiou, E., Kouroupetroglou, G., Fotinea, S.-E. (eds.) GW 2011. LNCS (LNAI), vol. 7206, pp. 106–117. Springer, Heidelberg (2012). https://doi.org/10.1007/978-3-642-34182-3_10
12. El Raheb, K., Ioannidis, Y.: From dance notation to conceptual models: a multilayer approach. In: Proceedings of the 2014 International Workshop on Movement and Computing, MOCO 2014, pp. 25:25–25:30. ACM, New York (2014)
13. El Raheb, K., Papapetrou, N., Katifori, V., Ioannidis, Y.: Balonse: ballet ontology for annotating and searching video performances. In: Proceedings of the 3rd International Symposium on Movement and Computing, MOCO 2016, pp. 5:1–5:8. ACM, New York (2016)
14. Fernandez-Lopez, M., Gomez-Perez, A., Juristo, N.: Methontology: from ontological art towards ontological engineering (1997)
15. Gangemi, A., Steve, G., Giacomelli, F.: Onions: an ontological methodology for taxonomic knowledge integration. In: ECAI 1996 Workshop on Ontological Engineering, Budapest, vol. 95 (1996)
16. Horrocks, I., Patel-Schneider, P.F., Boley, H., Tabet, S., Grosofand, B., Dean, M.: SWRL: a semantic web rule language combining OWL and RuleML. W3C Member Submission, May 2004. http://www.w3.org/Submission/SWRL/. Accessed Dec 2008
17. Kazi Tani, M.Y., Lablack, A., Ghomari, A., Bilasco, I.M.: Events detection using a video-surveillance ontology and a rule-based approach. In: Agapito, L., Bronstein, M.M., Rother, C. (eds.) ECCV 2014, Part II. LNCS, vol. 8926, pp. 299–308. Springer, Cham (2015). https://doi.org/10.1007/978-3-319-16181-5_21

18. Mallik, A., Chaudhury, S.: Acquisition of multimedia ontology: an application in preservation of cultural heritage. Int. J. Multimed. Inf. Retr. 1(4), 249–262 (2012)
19. Mallik, A., Chaudhury, S., Ghosh, H.: Nrityakosha: preserving the intangible heritage of indian classical dance. J. Comput. Cult. Herit. (JOCCH) 4(3), 11 (2011)
20. Mezaris, V., Kompatsiaris, I., Boulgouris, N.V., Strintzis, M.G.: Real-time compressed-domain spatiotemporal segmentation and ontologies for video indexing and retrieval. IEEE Trans. Circ. Syst. Video Technol. 14(5), 606–621 (2004)
21. O'Connor, M., Das, A.: SQWRL: a query language for OWL. In: Proceedings of the 6th International Conference on OWL: Experiences and Directions, OWLED 2009, Aachen, Germany, vol. 529, pp. 208–215 (2009). http://www.CEUR-WS.org
22. Robinson, A.J., Voronkov, A.: Handbook of Automated Reasoning, vol. 1. Elsevier, Amsterdam (2001)
23. Telli, A., Chau, M.T., Bourahla, M., Tabia, K., Benferhat, S.: An ontology for classifying vietnamese dance movements. In: Proceedings of the International Conference on Pattern Recognition and Artificial Intelligence, pp. 23–29. ACM (2018)
24. Thinh, N.D.: Regional Culture and Culture Zoning in Vietnam. Science and Society Publisher/Ho Chi Minh Youth Publisher, Hanoi (1993)
25. Town, C.: Ontological inference for image and video analysis. Mach. Vis. Appl. 17(2), 94 (2006)
26. Van Harmelen, F., Lifschitz, V., Porter, B.: Handbook of Knowledge Representation, vol. 1. Elsevier, Amsterdam (2008)

Periodicity Detection of Quasi-Periodic Slow-Speed Gait Signal Using IMU Sensor

Jayeeta Chakraborty[(✉)] and Anup Nandy

Department of Computer Science and Engineering,
Machine Intelligence and Bio-Motion Research Lab, NIT Rourkela,
Rourkela, India
jayeeta.iem2012@gmail.com, nandy.anup@gmail.com

Abstract. Wearable sensors have emerged as low-cost portable gait assessment tools in the past decade. However, it is necessary to process the signal collected from the sensors to analyze the human gait. Different spatio-temporal features for example, stride length, step length etc. can be obtained by detecting specific events in a gait cycle. Extraction of a single cycle is an important step for detection of events such as heel strike, foot flat, toe off, and mid-swing. Existing methods assume gait signals are fully periodic, whereas they are actually quasi-periodic. This quasi-periodicity increases with decrease in walking speed. Individuals with abnormal gaits are unable to walk in high speed. We propose a novel approach to extract cycles from gait signals with varying periodicity which are appropriate for low gait speed. To discriminate normal and abnormal gait pattern, we consider normal and equinus gait data in experimental analysis. Three participants walked normally, two participants simulated walking with equinus on the right leg, and two participants simulated walking with equinus on both legs. We have used two Sparkfun 9DoF Razor Inertial Measurement Unit (IMU) sensors having sampling frequency of 200 Hz. The performance of proposed approach is demonstrated through statistical error analysis. It outperforms the existing techniques, specially in case of low speed gait data. The complexity analysis is also presented to evaluate the efficiency of the proposed algorithm. Finally, Fisher's Discriminant Ratio is applied on the entire feature set to identify most prominent features to discriminate between normal and abnormal gait pattern.

Keywords: Human gait · Quasi-periodicity ·
Slow-speed gait analysis · Gait event detection · IMU sensor ·
Gait abnormality

1 Introduction

Gait analysis has recently gained significant attention for several applications such as medical diagnostics, bio-metric identification, robotics, animation etc.

© Springer Nature Switzerland AG 2019
V. G. Duffy (Ed.): HCII 2019, LNCS 11581, pp. 140–152, 2019.
https://doi.org/10.1007/978-3-030-22216-1_11

Among different gait assessment tools, 3D-motion capture systems are considered the best tool because of their high accuracy and reliability. Unfortunately, it is not affordable for clinics, specially in developing and poor countries. Wearable sensors such as, Inertial Measurement Unit (IMU) may be considered as a low-cost gait analysis tool in the clinical domain [1–4].

Inertial Measurement Unit. An Inertial Measurement Unit (IMU) consists of a tri-axial accelerometer, a tri-axial gyroscope and a tri-axial magnetometer. The accelerometer data provides the information about acceleration of the sensor, gyroscope measures the angular velocity of the sensor, and magnetometer measures the magnetic field vector with respect to the gravity vector. Additionally, the information about orientation of the sensors can be obtained by integrating the angular velocity. Presence of magnetic disturbances can limit the accuracy of the estimated orientations. In our experimental setup, we have used wearable IMUs as a cost-effective approach.

Periodic vs. Quasi-periodic. Periodic signals are the signals that recur the same behavior after regular intervals. In signal processing, quasi-periodic signals are defined as signals that show periodicity microscopically, but may not be periodic macroscopically i.e. one period is more similar to its adjacent periods than the periods at farther away in time. Non-stationary processes that changes in time generates quasi-periodic signals. Gait signal is also quasi-periodic in nature, specially when captured for a long duration and slower speed [5,6]. This is mainly due to the fact that walking in lower speed permits the candidate to change the time intervals to complete a gait cycle. This changing periodicity poses as a challenge while detecting a full gait cycle during gait analysis (here by periodicity, we refer to the time interval to complete a gait cycle).

Gait Cycle Events. A gait cycle consists of two phases: (1) stance phase (60% approximately) and (2) swing phase (40% approximately). Each of these phases consists of sub-phases i.e. initial contact, loading response, mid-stance, terminal stance, pre-swing, initial swing, mid-swing, terminal-swing. These phases can be distinguished with events like heel strike, foot flat, heel off, toe off, mid-swing. To obtain spatio-temporal features like stride length, step length etc., detection of the previously mentioned events are important. Gait cycle extraction can be used to detect these events.

In this paper, we proposed a new approach which is used for extracting gait cycles taking the varying periodicity of a long gait signals of slow walking pattern. We collected normal and equinus gait data as samples using wearable IMU sensors. Equinus gait has been simulated by the participants due to lack of availability of medical gait data. A comparison between the existing methods and proposed method for slow speed gait data with different speeds is presented. We compared the feature values extracted, and presented a comparison of standard errors caused due to each methods. We also analyzed complexity of the proposed method. We performed a statistical analysis among the features extracted. In Sect. 2, we discuss the data acquisition procedure and pre-processing of the

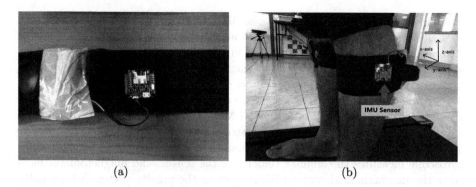

Fig. 1. (a) A closer look at Sparkfun 9DoF Razor IMU sensor. (b) Placement of the two IMU sensors around the shank of both legs of the candidate walking on the treadmill.

acquired data. In Sect. 3, we briefly explain the existing methods for gait cycle extraction. Next in Sect. 4, we propose a new approach that considers varying periodicity. In Sect. 5, we analyze and discuss the results. Finally, we conclude our study and state our future plans in Sect. 6.

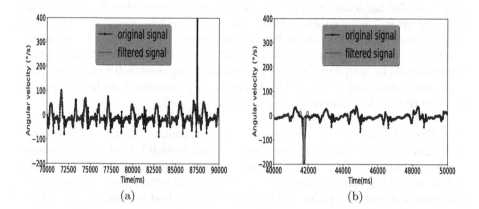

Fig. 2. Sample clips of a signal: filtered vs. original (a) for 3 km/h (b) for 1.5 km/h.

2   Data Collection and Pre-processing

For our experimental setup, we have used wearable IMUs as a cost-effective approach. Two Sparkfun 9DoF Razor IMU sensors having sampling frequency of 200 Hz were attached with a band along with batteries and on-board memory chip. These bands were tied around the shanks of both legs of each participant. Figure 1a is an image of the used IMU sensor. The gyroscope in IMU measures the angular velocity of the sensor. Signal values in gyroscope "X"-axis is ignored because movement in x-axis is negligible. Figure 1b shows placement of the IMU sensors and gyroscopic axes for both shanks. We performed our analysis on three categories of gait: normal gait, equinus gait on both legs and equinus gait on right leg only. Due to lack of medical gait data, we simulated equinus gaits. Three participants walked normally, two participants simulated walking with equinus on the right leg, and two participants simulated walking with equinus on both legs. The candidates were asked to walk on a treadmill with two different pre-specified speeds: normal (1.5 km/h) and high (3 km/h). We did not opt for higher speed considering it will be difficult for a differently-abled person to walk with higher speed.

The preprocessing of the data was done in three steps: (i) Clipping: During the process of capturing signal data, the person is in standing position before starting walking and after stopping. The signals occurred during this phase is discarded in the clipping process. (ii) Interpolation: The collected data does not have equal time intervals. We interpolated the signal data using linear interpolation method. (iii) Filtering: The signal data collected from the IMU contains high frequency noise. To remove high frequency noise, we filtered the signal using high-pass filtering with help of convolution process. Figure 2 shows the original signals and filtered signals for left shank gyroscope z-axis data of both leg equinus gait at 3 km/h and 1.5 km/h respectively.

3   Gait Cycle Extraction

For a fully periodic signal, periodicity can be utilized to extract complete cycles. Periodogram is used to identify the highest occurring periodicity in a signal. There are two general methods to generate periodogram: a. circular auto-correlation method [7–9], b. spectrum analysis using Fast Fourier Transform (FFT) [10,11].

3.1   Circular Auto-correlation

In this method, correlation value of a time series to itself with increasing lag is computed. For a discrete signal y, it is defined as,

$$ACF_l(y) = \sum_{n \in L} y(n) * \bar{y}(n - l), \tag{1}$$

where L is the signal length and l is the lag. Figure 3 represents normalized cACF plots with 400 lag in sample signals shown in Fig. 2. As it can be observed that the peaks are not at regular intervals, specially in Fig. 3(b) i.e. normalized cACF plot of slower speed gait data, signifying that gait signals are not fully periodic. In the periodogram, the highest peak is at lag 0 because the correlation between same signals is 1 and the next highest peak is considered as the most dominant period.

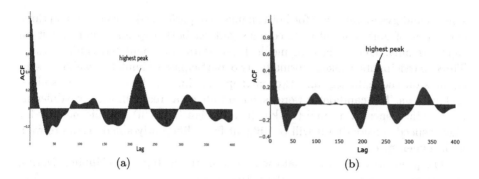

Fig. 3. Circular auto-correlation values of sample clips of (a) 3 km/h (b) 1.5 km/h respectively.

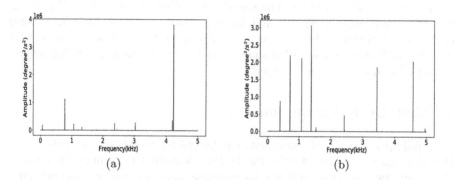

Fig. 4. Spectrum analysis after Fourier transformation of sample clips of (a) 3 km/h (b) 1.5 km/h respectively.

3.2   Spectrum Analysis

In spectrum analysis method, first the signal is converted to frequency domain using FFT. The periodogram is generated by plotting the spectrum or power distribution against different frequencies. Figure 4 are spectrum distributions against frequency for sample signals shown in Fig. 2. The dominant frequencies are easily observable from the plot. We observe that number of peaks in Fig. 4(b) is larger than number of peaks in Fig. 4(a). It shows that quasi-periodicity of gait signals increase as the speed decreases which leads to multiple periodicity values.

4   Proposed Method

The traditional methods considers a fixed periodicity and segments the signal of equal size. Due to wrong segmentation, cycles extracted are not always complete. For example, a cycle may be missing one or more phases e.g. heel strike and again, some cycles may contain two heel strikes. Only complete cycles are selected for further processing. During this process, if the data is highly quasi-periodic, there is higher chance of information loss as many cycles will remain undetected. Our objective is to track the varying time intervals taken to complete each gait cycle of the signal. Pseudo-code for the proposed process is shown as *GetVarPeriodicity* procedure in Algorithm 1. A graphical representation of the whole process is shown in Fig. 5.

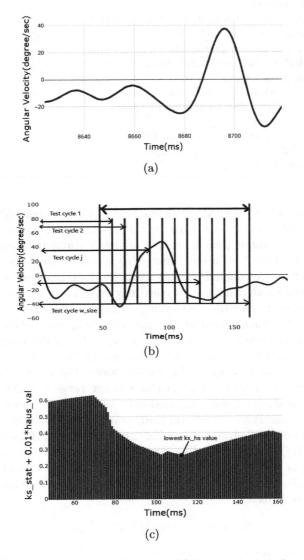

Fig. 5. (a) A base cycle under consideration, (b) Test cycles' window range (w_size) in a single iteration (c) Generated combined value of Kolmorogrov-Smirnov (KS) tests and Hausdorff's distance

Algorithm 1. Proposed algorithm

```
 1: procedure GETVARPERIODICITY(signal, init_period)
 2:     sig_len ← length of signal
 3:     last_index ← init_period
 4:     est_per ← init_period
 5:     base_cycle ← signal[1 : init_period]
 6:     while ((last_index + est_per) < sig_len) do
 7:         min_cmbdist ← Inf
 8:         for (j in range(0.5 * est_per, 1.8 * est_per)) do
 9:             test_cycle ← signal[last_index : j]
10:             k_stat, p_val = kstest(base_cycle, test_cycle)
11:             h_dist = hausdorff_dist(base_cycle, test_cycle)
12:             if p_val > thres_prob then
13:                 cmb_dist = k_stat + 0.01 * h_dist
14:                 if cmb_dist < min_cmbdist then
15:                     saved_j ← j.
16:                     min_cmbdist ← cmb_dist.
17:         last_index ← last_index + saved_j.
18:         periodlist ⊃ saved_j.
```

In our approach, we use the pre-defined knowledge of a complete gait cycle. Initially, a complete cycle, called base cycle (*base_cycle*), is taken as reference. Along with it, an initial period i.e. *init_period* is required as input which is the time length of the base cycle. Figure 5(a) is base cycle of the example signal from Fig. 2(b). Considering the microscopic property of quasi-periodic signals, it is expected that adjacent cycles may have more or less similar time period. Therefore, to find the next cycle, a window is taken into account that depends upon the time-period of the previous complete, within which it is assumed the next cycle lies. In our case, we have taken the window range to be $(0.5 * est\_per, 1.8 * est\_per)$, where *est_per* is the estimated time period of the previously detected cycle. Figure 5(b) shows the window range for the text cycles. Signals corresponding to this window range is taken sequentially as test cycles (*test_cycle*) and compared with base cycle as shown in Fig. 5(b). To measure the similarity of pattern, some statistical tests are performed. Discretized Kolmorogrov-Smirnov test or KS test (*kstest*), and Hausdorff distances (*hausdorff_dist*) have been used for dissimilarity measurement. The purpose of KS test which is based on empirical distribution function is to find out whether two samples follows the same distribution or not [12]. KS value for two discrete sets X and Y is defined by

$$d_{ks}(n, m) = sup_x \| F_{1,m}x - F_{2,n}x \| \tag{2}$$

where sup is the supremum function, and $F_{1,m}$ and $F_{2,n}$ are empirical distributions of the two samples respectively, with m and n to be the sizes of two samples respectively. KS test generates a statistical value that is the measure of similarity and a p-value (*p_val*) that is the measurement of confidence associated with each hypothesis. Hausdorff distance measures how much two subsets of a metric space are distant from each other [13]. Hausdorff value for two subsets X and Y is defined by

$$d_{ks}(X, Y) = max\{sup_{x \in X}\{inf_{y \in Y}d(x, y)\}, \\ sup_{y \in Y}\{inf_{x \in X}d(x, y)\}\} \tag{3}$$

where sup is the supremum function and inf is the infimum function and d is the distance metric used. For our approach, KS statistical values only with p-value more than a threshold probability is taken into consideration. Both Hausdorff and KS statistical values are combined after normalization process, denoted as *cmb_dist*. Plot in Fig. 5(c) shows how the combined value of KS test and Hausdorff distance is changing for the test signals in the window range. The test cycle generating minimum combined distance (*min_cmbdist*) is selected as the final complete cycle.

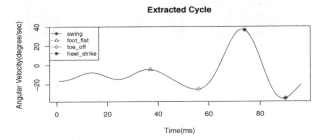

Fig. 6. A complete single cycle extracted from a signal with highlighted features i.e. maximum foot flat, toe off, maximum swing, and heel strike.

Gait Features Selection. After gait cycles are extracted, values of the signal at events such as toe off, heel strike, foot flat were computed from each gait cycle. Then average values of these features for all extracted gait cycles are taken as feature representation of a particular signal and has been used for statistical comparison. We discarded outliers from the feature values before averaging process. Figure 6 shows an example of the features selected from an individual cycle.

5   Result Analysis and Discussion

A gait cycle is considered complete if it consists of the following gait events: heel strike, foot flat, toe off, and mid-swing. Table 1 shows a comparison based on the percentage of 'complete gait cycles' extracted by each of the methods for different gait types with respect to speed. We define 'complete gait cycles' by the cycles which contains all four events i.e. swing, toe-off, heel strike, and foot flat. Any cycle missing even one of the feature values is considered as incomplete gait cycle. From Table 1, it can be observed in most of the cases, performance of FFT is average. Although it produces large number of cycles, but large portion of these cycles are incomplete cycles. ACF on the other hand, shows a remarkable performance for z-axis gyroscopic data, but fails to perform for y-axis gyroscopic data, specially for low speed gait. However, we can observe a consistent good performance of our method for all types of gait data even for slow speed gaits. A clearer representation of the performance of all three methods are presented in Fig. 7 for both high and slow speed.

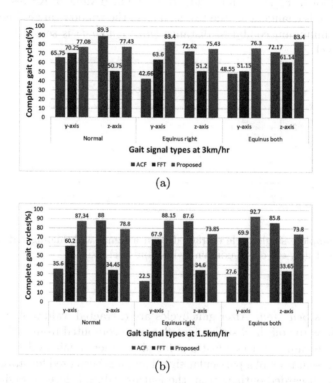

(a)

(b)

Fig. 7. Percentage of complete gait cycles extracted by ACF, FFT and proposed method for different types of gait data with (a) 3 km/h and (b) 1.5 km/h

We analyzed the feature values produced by each methods and a comparative study of the standard error values of each feature for different gait signal categories are shown in Table 2. Standard error (se) is defined by

$$\frac{sd(x)}{\sqrt{\sum_{i=1}^{n}(x)}}, \tag{4}$$

where sd is the standard deviation and x is a vector of numerical observations. From Table 2 it can be observed, while the performance of cACF and FFT is

Table 1. Percentage of complete gait cycles extracted by ACF, FFT and proposed method for different types of gait data with 3 km/h and 1.5 km/h speeds.

Speed	Gait type	Gyroscope	Number of complete gait cycles		
			ACF (%)	FFT (%)	Proposed (%)
3 km/h	Normal	y-axis	65.75	70.25	**77.08**
		z-axis	89.3	50.75	77.43
	Equinus right	y-axis	42.66	63.6	**83.40**
		z-axis	72.62	51.2	**75.43**
	Equinus both	y-axis	48.55	51.15	**76.30**
		z-axis	72.17	61.14	**83.40**
1.5 km/h	Normal	y-axis	35.60	60.20	**87.34**
		z-axis	88.0	34.45	78.80
	Equinus right	y-axis	22.5	67.9	**88.15**
		z-axis	87.6	34.6	73.85
	Equinus both	y-axis	27.6	69.9	**92.70**
		z-axis	85.8	33.65	73.80

inconsistent for different conditions, performance of our proposed method is on average good throughout all the test case situations. For low speed gait signals, when the signal is expected to be highly quasi-periodic, both cACF and FFT succeeds occasionally, for example, normal swing phase y-axis data, or equinus both heel strike z-axis data, but fails to perform on most of the other cases. For better understanding, mean and standard deviations of the error values of each methods are also presented as summary in Table 3. From Table 3, lower standard deviation of standard error in low speed gait supports the fact that our proposed method worked well on the overall data compared to cACF and FFT.

To analyze the features extracted by the proposed method, Fisher Discriminant Ratio (FDR) of each of the features are examined. FDR is used to find the contribution of features to distinguish between classes. It is defined by

$$\frac{\sum_{k=1}^{C} p_k (\mu_k - \mu)^2}{\sum_{k=1}^{C} \sigma_k^2}, \tag{5}$$

where C is the number of classes, p_k is the probability of class k and μ_k and σ_k is the standard deviation of each class, whereas μ is the overall mean. FDR values of each feature extracted by our proposed method is presented in Table 4. Heel_strike has the highest FDR value, swing amplitude being the second highest FDR value. We can conform from this analysis, these two features are more significant than the rest of the features.

Complexity Analysis

The computational complexity of cACF method is $O(L^2)$, where L is length of the signal. While using the spectrum analysis method, the signal goes through

Table 2. Standard errors of features generated by ACF, FFT (Spectrum Analysis) and proposed method for different gait types (normal, equinus right, equinus both) of different gait speeds

Speed	Gait type	Method	Swing		Foot flat		Toe off		Heel strike	
			y-axis	z-axis	y-axis	z-axis	y-axis	z-axis	y-axis	z-axis
3 km/h	Normal	ACF	2.12	3.23	1.24	1.12	1.69	1.64	1.46	1.57
		FFT	2.01	3.69	1.47	2.12	1.98	6.18	1.62	2.32
		Proposed	**2.35**	**2.85**	**1.46**	**1.49**	**1.74**	**2.91**	**1.34**	**3.69**
	Equinus right	ACF	2.18	3.07	0.99	1.92	1.40	1.37	1.52	2.41
		FFT	1.79	3.69	1.08	1.96	1.16	4.20	1.26	2.20
		Proposed	**2.04**	**3.52**	**1.46**	**1.28**	**1.30**	**2.03**	**1.39**	**2.50**
	Equinus both	ACF	2.45	2.80	1.13	1.75	2.13	3.35	1.52	4.11
		FFT	1.63	3.28	0.81	2.14	1.10	4.23	1.04	5.42
		Proposed	**1.75**	**2.66**	**1.04**	**1.61**	**1.36**	**3.39**	**1.23**	**3.16**
1.5 km/h	Normal	ACF	1.92	3.17	1.51	1.14	2.24	2.97	1.73	1.55
		FFT	1.68	5.34	1.39	3.06	2.11	7.20	1.43	3.62
		Proposed	**2.37**	**3.94**	**1.49**	**1.60**	**2.12**	**3.26**	**2.05**	**3.28**
	Equinus right	ACF	5.82	4.63	2.04	1.26	3.33	2.76	1.76	2.64
		FFT	1.72	6.83	1.34	3.75	1.26	6.30	1.25	4.07
		Proposed	**2.28**	**4.81**	**1.70**	**1.95**	**1.70**	**4.11**	**1.43**	**3.32**
	Equinus both	ACF	4.35	5.10	2.24	1.47	2.59	3.78	2.34	2.27
		FFT	4.58	4.30	2.26	1.54	2.93	5.31	2.55	2.08
		Proposed	**2.15**	**4.31**	**1.84**	**1.08**	**2.38**	**4.46**	**1.89**	**2.83**

Table 3. Mean and standard deviations of the standard errors of ACF, FFT and proposed method

Speed	ACF		FFT		Proposed	
	Mean	sd	Mean	sd	Mean	sd
3 km/h	2.008	0.811	2.433	1.442	**2.064**	**0.824**
1.5 km/h	2.692	1.252	3.247	1.873	**2.598**	**1.079**

Table 4. Fisher Discriminant Ratios (FDRs) of the gait features extracted by the proposed method

Speed	Gyroscope	Swing	Foot flat	Toe off	Heel strike
1.5 km/h	y-axis	0.01934	0.00524	0.01802	0.06522
	z-axis	0.03246	0.0243	0.02201	0.03217
3 km/h	y-axis	0.02348	0.01933	0.01629	0.03113
	z-axis	0.03345	0.01187	0.02879	0.03636

Fast Fourier Transform which has time complexity of $O(L*logL)$, where L is length of the signal [14]. In our algorithm, apart from signal length, the complexity depends upon the length of testing range, w_{size}, and the complexity of similarity measurements. Distance calculation methods depends on the length of the vectors, i.e. in our case is length of the base cycle(b_l) and the test cycles(t_l) which is again dependent on w_{size}. Therefore, we can say the similarity measurement is of complexity $O(b_l*w_{size})$. Finally, the total complexity of the proposed method becomes $O(L*b_l*w_{size}{}^2)$. When the signal is too long, b_l can be ignored compared to L and the complexity reduces to $O(L*w_{size}{}^2)$. For small length gait signals, complexity of the proposed method is less than ACF. When w_{size} is very small compared to length of the signal, L, the proposed method shows lower time complexity than spectrum analysis.

6   Conclusion

For modeling different types of abnormal gait, it is required to capture slow speed gait data from the participants having gait abnormality. In our experimental research we observed that slow speed gait is of highly quasi-periodic nature. Existing methods considering singular periodicity are able to detect relatively less number of complete cycles for quasi-periodic signals which may lead to major loss of information. A varying periodicity detection algorithm has been proposed to address this issue. It has been understood from the comparative result analysis that the proposed approach is able to extract more number of complete gait cycles with significant feature information. For feature analysis, a statistical technique, FDR, has been applied to evaluate the reliability of extracted features for discriminating normal and abnormal gait pattern. From the complexity analysis, the following observations can be stated: (i) Circular ACF is more computationally intensive than the proposed method. (ii) Spectrum analysis method has lower computational complexity for small length signals. For long-duration gait data, our method demonstrates lower computational complexity than spectrum analysis. The proposed algorithm shows promises to be used to extract cycles from other quasi-periodic signals such as electro-myography (EMG) signals of muscles activity or electroencephalography (EEG) signals from brain, with the prior knowledge of the repetitive pattern.

Acknowledgments. We are extremely grateful to Science and Engineering Research Board (SERB), DST, Govt. of India to support this research work. The IMU sensors used in our research experiment are purchased from the project funded by SERB with FILE NO: ECR/2017/000408.

References

1. Cooper, G., et al.: Inertial sensor-based knee flexion/extension angle estimation. J. Biomech. **42**(16), 2678–2685 (2009)
2. Favre, J., Jolles, B.M., Aissaoui, R., Aminian, K.: Ambulatory measurement of 3D knee joint angle. J. Biomech. **41**(5), 1029–1035 (2008)

3. Ong, Z.C., Seet, Y.C., Khoo, S.Y., Noroozi, S.: Development of an economic wireless human motion analysis device for quantitative assessment of human body joint. Measurement **115**, 306–315 (2018)
4. Seel, T., Raisch, J., Schauer, T.: IMU-based joint angle measurement for gait analysis. Sensors **14**(4), 6891–6909 (2014)
5. Lauer, R.T., Smith, B.T., Betz, R.R.: Application of a neuro-fuzzy network for gait event detection using electromyography in the child with cerebral palsy. IEEE Trans. Biomed. Eng. **52**(9), 1532–1540 (2005)
6. Sundaresan, A., RoyChowdhury, A., Chellappa, R.: A hidden Markov model based framework for recognition of humans from gait sequences. In: Proceedings of 2003 International Conference on Image Processing, ICIP 2003, vol. 2, p. II-93. IEEE (2003)
7. Bowers III, S.V., Skeirik, R.D.: Analysis of periodic information in a signal, 17 October 2017. US Patent 9,791,422 (2017)
8. Ergun, F., Muthukrishnan, S., Sahinalp, S.C.: Sublinear methods for detecting periodic trends in data streams. In: Farach-Colton, M. (ed.) LATIN 2004. LNCS, vol. 2976, pp. 16–28. Springer, Heidelberg (2004). https://doi.org/10.1007/978-3-540-24698-5_6
9. Moe-Nilssen, R., Helbostad, J.L.: Estimation of gait cycle characteristics by trunk accelerometry. J. Biomech. **37**(1), 121–126 (2004)
10. Beck, Y., Herman, T., Brozgol, M., Giladi, N., Mirelman, A., Hausdorff, J.M.: SPARC: a new approach to quantifying gait smoothness in patients with Parkinson's disease. J. Neuroeng. Rehabil. **15**(1), 49 (2018)
11. Hatkar, S.P., Kadam, S.H., et al.: Analysis of various periodicity detection algorithms in time series data with design of new algorithm. Int. J. Comput. Appl. Technol. Res. **3**(4), 229–239 (2014)
12. Arnold, T.B., Emerson, J.W.: Nonparametric goodness-of-fit tests for discrete null distributions. R J. **3**(2), 34–39 (2011)
13. Barnsley, M.F.: Fractals Everywhere. Academic Press, Cambridge (2014)
14. Lohne, M.: The computational complexity of the fast Fourier transform (2017)

Using Foot and Knee Movement and Posture Information to Mitigate the Probability of Injuries in Functional Training

Rafael de Pinho André[✉], Alberto Raposo, and Hugo Fuks

Pontifícia Universidade Católica do Rio de Janeiro, Rio de Janeiro, Brazil
randre@puc-rio.br
http://www.inf.puc-rio.br

Abstract. Foot and Knee pain have been associated with numerous orthopedic pathologies and injuries of the lower limbs. From street running to CrossFit functional training, these common injuries correlate highly with unevenly distributed plantar pressure and knee positioning during long-term physical practice and can lead to severe orthopedic injuries if the movement pattern is not amended. Therefore, the monitoring of foot plantar pressure distribution and the spatial and temporal characteristics of foot and knee positioning abnormalities is of utmost importance for injury prevention. This work proposes a wearable platform to provide real-time feedback of functional exercises, aiming to help users and physical educators to mitigate the probability of injuries during training. We conducted an experiment with 12 diverse volunteers to build a Human Activity Recognition (HAR) classifier that achieved about 87% overall classification accuracy, and a second experiment to validate our physical evaluation model. Finally, we performed a semi-structured interview to evaluate usability and user experience issues regarding the proposed platform.

Keywords: Human Activity Recognition · Health and ergonomics · Wearable computing and sensing

1 Introduction

Over the last 10 years, functional training exercises became a popular method to improve muscular and cardiovascular fitness, and many studies, such as [5] and [9], point out the benefits of this type of training regimen - while also suggesting that functional training practitioners have increased risk of foot, knee and lower back pain and related injuries. Nevertheless, works such as [17] and [14] point out a twofold increase of the prevalence of knee pain injuries, whereas works such as [8] show a threefold increase of the prevalence of lower back pain and injuries. Foot and Knee pain have been associated with numerous orthopedic

© Springer Nature Switzerland AG 2019
V. G. Duffy (Ed.): HCII 2019, LNCS 11581, pp. 153–169, 2019.
https://doi.org/10.1007/978-3-030-22216-1_12

pathologies and injuries of the lower limbs. From high intensity functional training (HIFT), such as CrossFit, to Extreme Conditioning Programs, lower limb injuries correlate highly with unevenly distributed plantar pressure and knee positioning during long-term physical practice and can lead to severe orthopedic injuries if the movement pattern is not amended. Therefore, the monitoring of foot plantar pressure distribution and the spatial and temporal characteristics of foot and knee positioning abnormalities is of utmost importance for injury prevention. Common methods employed by physical educators for the diagnosis of plantar pressure and knee positioning abnormalities are based on human observational approach, predominantly subjective, which is neither reliable nor scalable to a large group of individuals.

Human Activity Recognition (HAR) research on posture and movement information has seen an intense growth during the last ten years, drawing attention of fields such as mobile healthcare and ergonomics. Researchers investigate the recognition of human movement patterns and behaviors to better understand our actions and their context, to detect misguided action and to help people perform better in their daily life or professional activities. Traditionally, the equipment used to track and process these movements patterns were invasive, expensive and unsuited for outdoor experiments, but the development of Internet of Things (IoT) wearable technologies allowed researchers to investigate HAR related questions without the constrains of a laboratory environment.

This work presents a study for foot and knee movement and posture analysis of individuals to help them assess and correct their movements during training, aiming to mitigate the probability of repetitive strain injuries (RSI). Our solution employs an IoT wearable device with a novel sensor array and a machine learning HAR activity classifier for movement pattern recognition. The wearable device comprises three components: an US men's size 8 insole that houses the plantar pressure sensors, an external protective case that houses the microcontroller and the foot sensors and a knee band that houses the knee sensors. It is equipped with a set of 16 sensors and can collect detailed foot and knee movement and posture information every 20 ms, providing a feature-rich stream of data for local processing at the microcontroller or remote processing at an application server. The machine learning HAR activity classifier employs an individually tailored decision tree algorithm, when processing data locally, or a Random Forest, when processing data at the server, to recognize, within a set of 13 activities, whether the movement pattern is correct or inaccurate. The experimental results show that the HAR classifier achieves an overall accuracy of 87.08% for local processing. After classification, the IoT wearable device uses a component that provides haptic feedback to the user to warn whenever an inaccurate movement pattern is performed.

We conducted an experiment to build our machine learning HAR activity classifier, employing twelve volunteers carefully selected for their diverse characteristics, since a common limitation of the surveyed works that is the prevalence of homogeneous participants. We employed participants from both genders and diverse age categories, some of which with disabilities, such as class II obesity, severe knee injury and blindness. Each participant performed 3 sessions of 30 min of functional training supervised by a certified physical educator, following a routine consisting of the 13 activities of our activity model. We conducted a second experiment with the same participants to validate our HAR classifier, consisting of a 30-min session followed by a semi-structured interview to evaluate usability and user experience questions. Our experiment demonstrates the feasibility of our real-time feedback system and the supporting role it can perform for early intervention and prevention of orthopedic injuries, by providing a mobile, easy to use and affordable long-term monitoring of individuals.

2   Literature Review

This section presents a literature review about wearable-based research projects using feet and knee information for the detection of exercise execution errors. We conducted the literature review in four steps: (i) definition of a research question and its sub questions, (ii) formulation of a search query string, (iii) definition of exclusion criteria and (iv) completion of a quantitative and qualitative data analysis. The research question posed in this work is: What are the wearable-based research projects conducted in recognition of exercise execution to help prevent or treat sport-related injuries? This research question was broken down into four sub-questions:

- How the incorrect execution of exercises was addressed?
- How the activity model was structured?
- What activity classifier was built?
- What hardware and software setting types, quantities and locations of the sensors were assembled?

The surveyed works may be grouped into three distinct research categories: (i) user feedback and performance assessment, (ii) activity recognition and (iii) prevention or treatment of injuries and diseases.

2.1   User Feedback and Performance Assessment

The study presented in [13] uses off-the-shelf devices, such as the Microsoft Kinect, to evaluate posture and analyze users movement in order to help them assess and correct their movements during a CrossFit training session. Although the experiment focused on only one exercise within a restricted context, the study suggests that the proposed application provides a coach-like feedback useful in the absence of such an expert. The works proposed by [6] and [2] use upper and lower body accelerometer data to provide, respectively, feedback to swimmers and rowers. In [6], a sensor system is used to extract lap times and stroke counts for each lap of the pool, achieving good overall results. However, in [2], even though the experiment was successfully conducted by providing users with immediate feedback, no improvements were found for performance-related parameters. One other work focused on rowers collects femur and lower back kinematic data through an accelerometer-based body sensor network (BSN) [10]. The proposed system was used, alongside optical tracking, to distinguish between good and poor rowing techniques. Also, in [4], an experiment was conducted with professional swimmers to help improve their performance. The researchers used acceleration sensors to monitor relevant swimming parameters for a continuous performance evaluation, while also offering visual, audio and haptic feedback to swimmers. After testing four feedback modes, visual signs were chosen for their fastest reaction time. In the ongoing work presented by [43], an experiment was conducted with professional skiers aiming at improving the trainer-athlete relationship. Through the usage of wearable sensors and visualization software, participants were able to share their observations and impressions. Another work aiming at benefiting athletes with immediate feedback during training is presented by [19]. The researchers propose feedback systems for rowing, table tennis and biathlon professional athletes, providing detailed hardware information.

2.2 Activity Recognition

Many works, such as [21, 23, 25, 35] and [22], rely on plantar FSR pressure sensors to classify user activity according to a previously elaborated activity model. Other works, such as [28, 42] and [23], rely on inertial motion units (IMUs) located on user's feet for that purpose. Sensor fusion - FSRs and IMUs - is employed by works such as [32, 49, 53] and [39], achieving good overall results. Only a few of the surveyed works used sensors other than ground contact force (GCF) sensors and IMUs, such as infrared sensors [36] or capacitive sensing technology [29] and [41]. Henceforth, the main difference being these works is the machine learning algorithms applied and the context of the experiments. Differently, [54] proposes a novel approach using ultrasonic sensors in a wearable platform to monitor lower limb movements and patterns. Although it is an ongoing work, the results show that ultrasonic systems may be successfully used for gait analysis in running and jogging. The researchers in [16] use in-shoe Ground Contact Force (GCF) sensors to evaluate patients with postural instability making use of a posturography. The wearable-based sensor technology used in their experiment allowed for static and dynamic posturography in clinical and home environments an important assessment for orthopedic diagnosis. There is evidence showing a strong correlation between dynamic in-shoe sensor data acquisition and static pressure plate data acquisition.

The work in [15] presents an extensive research using wearable sensors to understand the best signal processing, sensors and classification methods for classifying health-enhancing physical activities such as walking, running and cycling. It discusses how each activity is best characterized and what sensors should be used to recognize them. Likewise, in the work proposed by [7], activity recognition using wearable sensors provides lifestyle feedback regarding health-enhancing physical activities. However, contrary to the previous study, this one focuses on non-lab activities and sports in unsupervised settings. Considering the proposed activity model, results showed that using both unsupervised and supervised data for machine learning yields similar results to using only supervised data. The work in [37] proposes an optimal sensor set for gait identification of patients with dropped foot for clinical evaluation. This sensor set consists of three IMUs capable of six degrees of freedom, placed onto users thigh, shank and foot of the impaired leg. The study identifies the best sensor orientations and attachment positions, whilst accurately identifying gait events. Finally, it suggests that the system could be used to analyze other walking conditions during daily activities.

Some other shoe-based wireless sensor platforms, such as the SmartStep [34], were used by many different healthcare-related works. In [33], the former platform was used to develop an Android application to capture data from the wearable device and provide real time recognition of a small set of activities. In [48] and [50], the SmartShoe platform is used for energy expenditure estimation after the classification of the activities performed by the user, and in [51] it is further used to predict body weight. The same platform is then used by [27] and [26] to identify activity levels and steps in people with stroke.

Many of the surveyed studies that were conducted in the recognition of activities were related to healthcare and well-being, such as (i) the research presented in [38], that aims at recognizing caregiver's patient handling activities (PHA) and movement activities to help prevent overexertion injuries, (ii) the work presented in [55], that measures activity in people with stroke, (iii) the work presented in [24], that recognizes activities and postures to provide behavioral feedback to patients recovering from a stroke, and (iv) the research proposed by [44], in which researchers present a pair of shoes that offer low-cost balance monitoring outside of laboratory environments and uses features identified by geriatric motion study experts. This lightweight smart shoes platform is based on the MicroLEAP wireless sensor platform [18], and uses an IMU and FSR pressure sensors embedded inside each insole for data acquisition.

2.3 Prevention and Treatment of Injuries and Diseases

The prevention and treatment of injuries and diseases is the most prevalent theme of research found in this literature review. The research presented in [11] and [12] recognizes that the first step to reduce caregivers risk of overexertion injuries is to identify patient handling activities [PHA]. It proposes an eTextile fabric with 48 plantar pressure sensors and an IMU capable of nine degrees of freedom motion sensing to detect user activity and identify awkward postures that might lead to injuries. Despite the complexities of the interaction between users and loads (e.g., patients and instruments), both studies show promising results.

In works such as [1] and [3], researchers propose an accelerometer-based wearable framework for recognizing athletes activities in outdoor training environments. They aim at identifying (i) potential injury or performance determining factors, (ii) users in the early stages of a developing injury and (iii) a predisposition to injury based on movement patterns. In this work, the researchers performed an experiment to monitor thigh and shank movement and posture during jogging, achieving good overall results. In [44], the researchers present a pair of shoes that offer low-cost balance monitoring non-lab environments. The shoes use features identified by geriatric motion study experts to monitor balance and predict fall risk, demonstrating the feasibility of a model of instability assessment. They are based on a wireless sensor platform using IMU and FSR pressure sensors embedded inside each insole for data acquisition.

3   Building the HAR Classifier

On this Section, we describe the stages followed to develop the HAR classifier: (i) prototyping the wearable IoT Device, (ii) conducting the experiment to acquire use data, (iii) processing the acquired data, (iv) extracting and selecting features, (v) building models and (vi) validating the selected model.

3.1   Wearable IoT Device Prototype

On this section, we present the wearable device prototype used to collect functional training data. To allow for the reproduction of this research, we provide detailed hardware information - types, quantities and models for each component.

Aiming at a user base as diverse as possible, we followed the prototyping principles discussed in [46] and [47]. To reach this goal, we (i) developed a low power consumption easy-to-use wearable IoT device with only a power button and (i) that required only one functional foot to collect and analyse user data. This allowed for extended operation and ease operation during the experiments. The use of only one foot to collect user data was discussed in [46] and does no incur any significant loss of accuracy, reduces prototyping costs and broadens our user base. The wearable device comprises three components: (i) an US men's size 8.5 insole that houses the plantar pressure sensors, (ii) an external protective case that houses the microcontroller and the foot sensor array and (iii) an external protective case that houses the knee sensor array.

The insole employs six GCF sensors following the literature's recommendations for placing discussed in [45,52] and [40], in addition to the lessons learned from the prototypes presented in [46] and [47]. We used the FSR 402, by Interlink Electronics - a PTF (Polymer Thick Film) device that exhibits a decrease in resistance as the force applied to its active surface increases - and Amphenol FCI Clincher Connectors to avoid melting or distorting the silver traces of each sensor. As in [47], to create a variable voltage for the microcontroller's Analog to Digital Converter (ADC) inputs of each sensor, we embedded six $10\,k\Omega\,\frac{1}{4}\,W$ static resistors inside the insole next to them.

The main component of the foot external protective case is the Electron, a 3G-enabled microcontroller from Particle.io that collects data from the foot sensor array and transmits the data to the remote database. For the accelerometer, gyroscope and magnetometer sensors responsible for monitoring the feet posture, we used the SparkFun 9DoF IMU LSM9DS1 Breakout, a system-in-package component that houses a 3-axis accelerometer, 3-axis gyroscope, and 3-axis magnetometer sensor array that is capable of digital communication with the Electron microcontroller. The barometer selected for the experiment is the MPL3115A2, by Freescale Semiconductor, a low power, high-precision altitude and pressure. For the range finder sensor we used two of the RFD77402 3D ToF (Time of Flight) by Simblee, a low-cost accurate sensor that allows millimeter readings up to two meters. The RFD77402 uses an infrared VCSEL (Vertical Cavity Surface Emitting Laser) module to measure the amount of time the emitted light takes to bounce off a target.

The Electron microcontroller and its board, along with the MPL3115A2 and RFD77402 sensors mentioned above, were positioned in the ABS 3D printed external protective case. The prototype is powered by a 2,200 mAh lithium ion battery pack by Sparkfun Electronics, allowing for an easier, faster replacement and improved usability. We did not take any measures to address the sensor drift over time of this prototype, as discussed in [47].

The knee external protective case houses a second SparkFun 9DoF IMU LSM9DS1 Breakout and is connected to the foot external protective case by a flexible cable.

The software model used in this work is based on the model proposed in [46] and [47], comprising two components: (i) the embedded software running on the microcontroller, responsible for acquiring, structuring and transmitting raw sensor data over 3G to the application server, and (ii) the application server itself, responsible for processing and logging the streamed data to Firebase NOSQL database - tasks not suitable for the embedded microcontroller due to its hardware limitations. The authors made available the complete and commented source code of the application server in [46].

3.2   The First Experiment

The first experiment, aimed at building the HAR classifier, was conducted with twelve volunteers carefully selected for their diverse characteristics. One prevailing limitation of the surveyed the works is the employment of homogeneous participants in their experiments. This study tries to circumvent this problem with the participation of people with disabilities and mature adults. Table 1 below summarizes participants information.

Since the insole and shoes are US men's size 8.5, we selected participants in the 7.5 to 9.0 shoe size range. We collected 18 h of activity data - 90 min of feet and knee posture and movement data from each volunteer. The number of subjects in our study is not that different from the surveyed works others, considering the median of 6 found in the literature. However, the number of samples in our study - over 1.2 million - is significantly higher than the median number of samples - around 50,000 - found on the surveyed works.

The activity model we developed for the experiment comprises 13 activities: walking straight (2 km/h), slow jogging (6 km/h), hopping, ascending stairs, descending stairs, standing, Basic Squat, Sumo Squat, Squat Hold, Basic Step

Table 1. Experiment 1 participant profiles.

Participant	Age	Gender	Height	Weight	Observations
Participant 1	35	Male	1.85 m	136 kg	Class II Obesity; Lesion: Right Knee
Participant 2	28	Male	1.74 m	73 kg	Attention Deficit Hyperactivity Disorder
Participant 3	29	Male	1.76 m	72 kg	-
Participant 4	32	Male	1.81 m	81 kg	-
Participant 5	27	Female	1.77 m	61 kg	Lesion: Left Knee/Left Ankle
Participant 6	45	Female	1.64 m	87 kg	Class II Obesity
Participant 7	62	Male	1.93 m	110 kg	Overweight
Participant 8	28	Male	1.74 m	70 kg	-
Participant 9	37	Female	1.67 m	59 kg	Professional Runner
Participant 10	35	Male	1.54 m	65 kg	Overweight
Participant 11	34	Male	1.89 m	90 kg	Professional Skater
Participant 12	33	Female	1.61 m	52 kg	-

Up, Front Lunge, Side Lunge and sitting. The experiment was conducted in 3 distinct 30-min sessions, where participants performed a set of the planned activities supervised by a certified physical education professional. Following the advice of the physical educator, no participant performed more than 1 session per day and sessions were spaced by at least 48 h. All sessions were performed in a personal training studio.

At each session, participants performed 6 cycles of 5-min routines. In the first session, participants were required to interweave walking, jogging, hopping, ascending stairs, descending stairs, standing and the execution of the Basic Step Up functional exercise. In the second session, participants were required to interweave walking, standing, sitting and the execution of the Basic Squat, Sumo Squat and Squat Hold functional exercises. In the third session, participants were required to interweave walking, standing, sitting and the execution of the Front Lunge and Side Lunge functional exercises. Subjects were free to perform the activities - the wearable prototype did not restrict in any sense their movement. All routines were developed jointly with the certified physical education professional, who provided clear instructions of how the activities were to be performed during the experiment. We focused on the time that each participant should spend performing the proposed activities, rather than the number of repetitions, as the physical conditioning of each participant varied significantly. Table 2 below details the performed activities:

Since the classifier proposed in [46] performed well, achieving 93.34% overall accuracy, we were confident to extend the original activity model of 6 activities to the current activity model of 13 activities for this experiment. The results showed a drop of 6.26% in the overall accuracy, when compared to the first

Table 2. Experiment session routines.

Session	Cycle	Routine
1	1	1 min walking, 2 min ascending stairs, 1 min walking, 1 min standing
1	2	1 min walking, 2 min descending stairs, 1 min walking, 1 min standing
1	3	1 min walking, 2 min Basic Step Up, 1 min walking, 1 min standing
1	4	1 min walking, 2 min Jogging, 1 min walking, 1 min standing
1	5	1 min walking, 2 min Hopping, 1 min walking, 1 min standing
1	6	1 min walking, 2 min Basic Step Up, 1 min walking, 1 min standing
2	1	1 min walking, 2 min Basic Squat, 1 min standing, 1 min sitting
2	2	1 min walking, 2 min Sumo Squat, 1 min standing, 1 min sitting
2	3	1 min walking, 2 min Squat Hold, 1 min standing, 1 min sitting
2	4	1 min walking, 2 min Basic Squat, 1 min standing, 1 min sitting
2	5	1 min walking, 2 min Sumo Squat, 1 min standing, 1 min sitting
2	6	1 min walking, 2 min Squat Hold, 1 min standing, 1 min sitting
3	1	1 min walking, 2 min Front Lunge, 1 min standing, 1 min sitting
3	2	1 min walking, 2 min Side Lunge, 1 min standing, 1 min sitting
3	3	1 min walking, 2 min Front Lunge, 1 min standing, 1 min sitting
3	4	1 min walking, 2 min Side Lunge, 1 min standing, 1 min sitting
3	5	1 min walking, 2 min Front Lunge, 1 min standing, 1 min sitting
3	6	1 min walking, 2 min Side Lunge, 1 min standing, 1 min sitting

activity model. We accompanied all participants during the sessions to monitor the wearable IoT device data collection and for logging any unusual occurrence. Hypoallergenic socks were used to avoid skin allergies.

3.3   Data Acquisition

During the data acquisition stage, a stream of unprocessed sensor signals is built from the combination of the insole's sensors and the knee's sensors, and it is stored in the microcontroller in JSON format. This raw data combines two accelerometers, two gyroscopes, two magnetometers, six FSR sensors, altitude, pressure and two range finder sensor signals, resulting in 28-feature set entries to the dataset. We used a 20 Hz sampling rate to recognize between similar activities and subtle variations in execution style [31]. The JSON formatted data was periodically sent to the application server in small packages of 200 KB to reduce energy and data usage.

3.4   Data Processing, Feature Extraction and Selection

A data processing pipeline of two steps, similar to the one proposed in [46] and [47], was employed. No experiment data is discarded, given that the prototype starts collecting feet movement and posture information immediately after it is powered. First, the dataset is labelled for supervised learning, and activity class information is appended to each entry according to the activity performed in the experiment. Finally, all sensor data is normalized to make their scales equivalent for the model building.

In the feature extraction stage, we used descriptive statistics - standard deviation, variance, minimum, maximum and average values - to generate derived features from each of the 28 original features:

- Six FSR sensor readings;
- Six gyroscope axis data;
- Six magnetometer axis data;
- Six accelerometer axis data;
- Six accelerometer axis data;
- Altitude reading;
- Pressure reading; and,
- Two range finder sensors reading.

Moreover, (i) the cumulative difference between samples for each feature and (ii) the Euler angles of pitch, roll and yaw are also used to generate additional derived features, for a total of over 200 features for selection.

As in [46] and [47], we employed Hall's algorithm [30] based on correlation for feature selection, using its default "Best Fit" backtracking greedy strategy configuration. In total, 22 features were utilized to build the classifier: 2 axis of the foot gyroscope, 2 axis of the foot magnetometer, 1 axis of the foot accelerometer, 4 FSRs, 2 Euler angles of the foot, 3 axis of the knee gyroscope, 2 axis of the knee magnetometer, 2 axis of the knee accelerometer and the maximum and minimum of the two range finder sensors. Based on the surveyed related works, we already expected to see accelerometer, gyroscope, magnetometer, Euler angles and FSR features showing high correlation and being used in the building of the classifier. However, as in [36,46] and [47], the range finder sensors were successfully employed and improved the average accuracy of our results. Unlike the classifier proposed in [46] the altimeter was not employed by the classifier.

3.5   Classification and Validation

We experimented different strategies to build the HAR classifier model, as in [46] and [47], and once more the Random Forest Algorithm achieved better results - with an overall classification accuracy of about 87%. To validate the model, we applied the Leave-one-out Cross Validation in attempt to increase the robustness of the model - since this method guarantees that both training and test splits does not share any example data. The individual validation results for each of the 12 examples were: 81.11%, 79.26%, 94.33%, 92.21%, 84.18%, 82.72%, 87.51%, 90.12%, 96.44%, 74.71%, 89.49% and 92.90%.

We experimented several time window sizes to build the classifier and decided to use a 3-s window based on our model validation results. Although [20] recommends window sizes within the 0.25 s–0.50 s range for single activity recognition, our activity model consists of complex single activities, and smaller window sizes did not achieve good overall classification accuracy.

4   Validating the HAR Classifier

On this Section, we describe the stages followed to validate the HAR classifier: performing a second experiment and a semi-structured interview to evaluate usability and user experience.

4.1   The Second Experiment

During the second experiment we employed 9 of the 12 original first experiment volunteers - three of them were not available at the time it was conducted. Table 3 below summarizes participants information.

Table 3. Experiment 1 participant profiles.

Participant	Age	Gender	Height	Weight	Observations
Participant 1	35	Male	1.85 m	136 kg	Class II Obesity; Lesion: Right Knee
Participant 2	28	Male	1.74 m	73 kg	Attention Deficit Hyperactivity Disorder
Participant 3	29	Male	1.76 m	72 kg	-
Participant 6	45	Female	1.64 m	87 kg	Class II Obesity
Participant 7	62	Male	1.93 m	110 kg	Overweight
Participant 8	28	Male	1.74 m	70 kg	-
Participant 9	37	Female	1.67 m	59 kg	Professional Runner
Participant 10	35	Male	1.54 m	65 kg	Overweight
Participant 12	33	Female	1.61 m	52 kg	-

The goal of the second experiment was to validate the HAR classifier and its capability to assess if the movement pattern of a particular functional training exercise was performed correctly by the user. To achieve that goal, we used the same wearable IoT device employed to build the model with two modifications: (i) we added a SparkFun Haptic Motor Driver with the DRV2605L by Texas Instruments, together with a vibration motor, and (ii) we altered the embedded code to send packages of the collected data to the application server for data processing and waiting for a return code that indicated if the activity was performed correctly. The second experiment was conducted in a 30-min session, where participants performed a set of the planned activities supervised by the physical educator responsible for the first experiment. This session was performed at the same personal training studio used for the first experiment. No data was collected during the second experiment.

At the session, each participant performed 6 cycles of 5-min routines. The routines consisted of all 13 activities of our activity model, and were also developed jointly with the certified physical education professional, who did not provide instructions of how the activities were to be performed during the experiment. A few participants that were performing correctly every activity of the proposed routines were asked to alter the movement pattern to replicate the most common execution errors found during a functional exercise practice. This was done for no more than 3 repetitions for each activity - since the repetitions were performed without extra weights on foam mat floor tiles, the physical educator ensured that no harm would befall those participants. Once more, we focused on the time that each participant should spend performing the proposed activities, rather than the number of repetitions, as the physical conditioning of each participant still varied significantly. Table 4 below details the performed activities:

Table 4. Experiment session routines.

Session	Cycle	Routine
1	1	1 min walking, 2 min Basic Step Up, 1 min standing, 1 min sitting
1	2	1 min walking, 2 min Basic Squat, 1 min standing, 1 min sitting
1	3	1 min walking, 2 min Sumo Squat, 1 min standing, 1 min sitting
1	4	1 min walking, 2 min Squat Hold, 1 min standing, 1 min sitting
1	5	1 min walking, 2 min Front Lunge, 1 min standing, 1 min sitting
1	6	1 min walking, 2 min Side Lunge, 1 min standing, 1 min sitting

During each cycle, participants performed only one of the 6 specific functional exercises of our activity model. We configured the server application to assess only the matching functional exercise each cycle, sending a return code of 0 if the movement pattern was performed correctly and 1 otherwise. A return code of 1 activated the vibration motor, warning the user of the movement pattern performed. After each session, we analyzed the application server log and the physical educator notes - the classifier detected between 6 and 7 incorrect executions out of every 10, per participant.

4.2   The Interview

After the second experiment, we performed a semi-structured interview to evaluate usability and user experience. We interviewed all 9 participants and the physical educator. Below, the questions that were asked:

- Did the device or the haptic feedback hinder in any way the execution of the activities?
- Do you perceive the haptic feedback as a help to perform the proposed activities?

– Do you think that the physical assessment platform proposed is necessary or adequate for your regular physical training program?

The participants did not consider that the device hindered the execution of the activities, since it is lightweight and the flexible cable connecting the knee band and the foot external protective case was well positioned and of adequate length. However, 3 of the 9 respondents reported that they were over overzealous with their movements to prevent any damage to the wearable IoT device, so in their perception the device hindered their focus. Of those 3 respondents, 2 reported that the impaired focus may have been the cause of some execution mistakes. The participants knew that there was only one prototype available and that the research group did not receive any grant to fund the research. The haptic feedback was perceived as a help factor to perform exercises more correctly by 8 of the 9 respondents, although 6 of those respondents pointed out that a human feedback is more helpful since it enables them to understand the reason why an execution was performed incorrectly. All seven physically active participants train without the individual supervision of a physical educator and agreed that (i) a physical assessment platform is necessary and that (ii) the proposed platform, after adjustments necessary for production, is adequate for their training needs. The physical educator did not perceive the device or the haptic feedback to hinder in any way the execution of the proposed activities or the other common functional exercise activities he is used to supervise. The haptic feedback was perceived as a very helpful feature, even considering the real-life accuracy below 70%, since the key factor regarding RSI prevention is the detection of repeated mistakes, not the detection of a single poor execution. In addition to that, (i) a typical functional exercise class equipped with a physical assessment platform could be supervised by only one physical educator, able to make better use of his time helping the users instead of monitoring every aspect of the execution and (ii) some aspects of the execution, such as plantar pressure distribution, are not easily assessed by an observational approach.

5   Conclusion

This work proposes a platform for physical evaluation of functional exercise activities with real-time feedback to help reduce injury risk. We conducted two experiments: (i) the first with 12 volunteers, to build a HAR classifier of a 13-classes activity model based on foot and knee movement and posture information and (ii) the second with 9 volunteers, to validate the physical evaluation model and investigate usability issues of the proposed wearable IoT device. The platform was considered helpful by the experiment participants and the supervising physical educator.

The main contributions are:

– A comprehensive literature review about wearable-based HAR research using feet and knee movement and posture information for the detection of exercise execution errors;

– A platform and a model that can be used to assess the quality of execution of different lower limb functional exercises; and,
– A wearable IoT device blueprint with a comprehensive and novel sensor fusion selection that can be used for lower limb HAR.

Currently, we are evolving the proposed wearable IoT device prototype and broadening the activity model of the HAR classifier to use it in two studies. The first study aims at assessing collective engagement in Physical Education and Sports programs at the high school education level. The second study is an extension to this work and aims at reducing back and shoulder injury risk during functional exercise sessions. Our goal is to progressively provide real time feedback of the whole athlete's body during the practice of functional exercises.

References

1. Ahmadi, A., et al.: Automatic activity classification and movement assessment during a sports training session using wearable inertial sensors. In: 2014 11th International Conference on Wearable and Implantable Body Sensor Networks (2014)
2. Anderson, R., et al.: Rowing: accelerometry-based feedback - can it improve movement consistency and performance in rowing? Sports Biomech. 4(2), 179–195 (2005)
3. Auvinet, B., et al.: Runners stride analysis: comparison of kinematic and kinetic analyses under field conditions. Sci. Sports 17, 92–94 (2002)
4. Bächlin, M., et al.: SwimMaster: a wearable assistant for swimmer. In: UbiComp 2009 (2009)
5. Bergeron, M.F., et al.: Consensus paper on extreme conditioning programs in military personnel. In: Consortium for Health and Military Performance and American College of Sports Medicine (2011)
6. Davey, N.P., et al.: An accelerometer based system for elite athlete swimming performance analysis. In: Smart Structures, Devices, and Systems II, Proceedings of SPIE, vol. 5649. SPIE, Bellingham (2005)
7. Ermes, M., et al.: Detection of daily activities and sports with wearable sensors in controlled and uncontrolled conditions. IEEE Trans. Inf. Technol. Biomed. 12(1), 20–26 (2008)
8. Freburger, J.K., et al.: The rising prevalence of chronic low back pain. Arch. Intern. Med. 169(3), 251–258 (2009)
9. Haddock, C.K., et al.: The benefits of high intensity functional training (HIFT) fitness programs for military personnel. Mil Med. 181(11), e1508–e1514 (2016)
10. King, R.C., et al.: Body sensor networks for monitoring rowing technique. In: 2009 Body Sensor Networks (2009)
11. Lin, F., et al.: Automated patient handling activity recognition for at-risk caregivers using an unobtrusive wearable sensor. In: 2016 IEEE-EMBS International Conference on Biomedical and Health Informatics (BHI) (2016)
12. Lin, F., et al.: Towards unobtrusive patient handling activity recognition for injury reduction among at-risk caregivers. IEEE J. Biomed. Health Inform. 21(3), 682–695 (2016)
13. Lisboa, C.L., et al.: A study for postural evaluation and movement analysis of individuals. In: 2016 XVIII Symposium on Virtual and Augmented Reality (2016)

14. Nguyen, U.S.D.T., et al.: Increasing prevalence of knee pain and symptomatic knee osteoarthritis. Ann. Intern. Med. **155**(11), 725–732 (2011)
15. P., et al.: Wearable static posturography solution using a novel pressure sensor sole. IEEE Trans. Inf. Tech. Biomed. **10**(1) (2006)
16. R., et al.: Activity classification using realistic data from wearable sensors. In: 2014 IEEE (2014)
17. Wallace, I.J., et al.: Knee osteoarthritis has doubled in prevalence since the mid-20th century. Proc. Natl. Acad. Sci. U.S.A. **114**(35), 9332–9336 (2017)
18. Au, L.K., Wu, W.H., Batalin, M.A., McIntire, D.H., Kaiser, W.J.: MicroLEAP: energy-aware wireless sensor platform for biomedical sensing applications. In: Biomedical Circuits and Systems Conference, BIOCAS, pp. 158–162. IEEE (2007)
19. Baca, A., Kornfeind, P.: Rapid feedback systems for elite sports training. In: Published by the IEEE CS and IEEE ComSoc 2006 (2006)
20. Banos, O., Galvez, J.M., Damas, M., Pomares, H., Rojas, I.: Window size impact in human activity recognition. Sensors **14**(4), 6474–6499 (2014)
21. De Santis, A., Gambi, E., Montanini, L., Raffaeli, L., Spinsante, S., Rascioni, G.: A simple object for elderly vitality monitoring: the smart insole. In: Mechatronic and Embedded Systems and Applications (MESA), ASME, pp. 1–6. IEEE (2014)
22. Doppler, J., et al.: Variability in foot-worn sensor placement for activity recognition. In: International Symposium on Wearable Computers, ISWC 2009, pp. 143–144. IEEE (2009)
23. Drobny, D., Weiss, M., Borchers, J.: Saltate!: a sensor-based system to support dance beginners. In: CHI 2009 Extended Abstracts on Human Factors in Computing Systems, pp. 3943–3948. ACM (2009)
24. Edgar, S.R., Swyka, T., Fulk, G., Sazonov, E.S.: Wearable shoe-based device for rehabilitation of stroke patients. In: 2010 Annual International Conference of the IEEE Engineering in Medicine and Biology Society (EMBC), pp. 3772–3775. IEEE (2010)
25. El Achkar, C.M., Massé, F., Arami, A., Aminian, K.: Physical activity recognition via minimal in-shoes force sensor configuration. In: Pervasive Computing Technologies for Healthcare, pp. 256–259. ICST (2013)
26. Fulk, G.D., Edgar, S.R., Bierwirth, R., Hart, P., Lopez-Meyer, P., Sazonov, E.: Identifying activity levels and steps in people with stroke using a novel shoe-based sensor. J. Neurol. Phys. Ther. **36**(2), 100 (2012)
27. Fulk, G.D., Sazonov, E.: Using sensors to measure activity in people with stroke. Top. Stroke Rehabil. **18**(6), 746–757 (2011)
28. Ghobadi, M., Esfahani, E.T.: Foot-mounted inertial measurement unit for activity classification. In: Engineering in Medicine and Biology Society, EMBC, pp. 6294–6297. IEEE (2014)
29. Haescher, M., Matthies, D.J., Bieber, G., Urban, B.: CapWalk: a capacitive recognition of walking-based activities as a wearable assistive technology. In: International Conference on PErvasive Technologies Related to Assistive Environments, p. 35. ACM (2015)
30. Hall, M.: Correlation-based feature subset selection for machine learning. Thesis submitted in partial fulfillment of the requirements of the degree of Doctor of Philosophy at the University of Waikato (1998)
31. Harasimowicz, A., Dziubich, T., Brzeski, A.: Accelerometer-based human activity recognition and the impact of the sample size. In: Advances in Neural Networks, Fuzzy Systems and Artificial Intelligence, pp. 130–135 (2014)

32. Hegde, N., Bries, M., Swibas, T., Melanson, E., Sazonov, E.: Automatic recognition of activities of daily living utilizing insole based and wrist worn wearable sensors. IEEE J. Biomed. Health Inform. **22**(4), 979–988 (2017)

33. Hegde, N., Melanson, E., Sazonov, E.: Development of a real time activity monitoring android application utilizing SmartStep. In: 2016 IEEE 38th Annual International Conference of the Engineering in Medicine and Biology Society (EMBC), pp. 1886–1889. IEEE (2016)

34. Hegde, N., Sazonov, E.: SmartStep: a fully integrated, low-power insole monitor. Electronics **3**(2), 381–397 (2014)

35. Holleczek, T., Ruegg, A., Harms, H., Troster, G.: Textile pressure sensors for sports applications. In: 9th IEEE Sensors Conference, Kona, HI (2010)

36. Jiang, X., Chen, Y., Liu, J., Hayes, G.R., Hu, L., Shen, J.: Air: recognizing activity through IR-based distance sensing on feet. In: International Joint Conference on Pervasive and Ubiquitous Computing: Adjunct, pp. 97–100. ACM (2016)

37. Lau, A., Tong, R.: The reliability of using accelerometer and gyroscope for gait event identification on persons with dropped foot. Gait Posture **27**(2), 248–257 (2008)

38. Lin, F., Song, C., Xu, X., Cavuoto, L., Xu, W.: Sensing from the bottom: smart insole enabled patient handling activity recognition through manifold learning. In: Connected Health: Applications, Systems and Engineering Technologies (CHASE), pp. 254–263. IEEE (2016)

39. Lin, F., Wang, A., Zhuang, Y., Tomita, M.R., Xu, W.: Smart insole: a wearable sensor device for unobtrusive gait monitoring in daily life. IEEE Trans. Industr. Inf. **12**(6), 2281–2291 (2016)

40. Martinez-Nova, A., Cuevas-Garcia, J.C., Pascual-Huerta, J., Sanchez-Rodriguez, R.: BioFoot in-shoe system: normal values and assessment of the reliability and repeatability. Foot **17**(4), 190–196 (2007). https://doi.org/10.1016/j.foot.2007.04.002. http://www.sciencedirect.com/science/article/pii/S0958259207000338

41. Matthies, D.J., Roumen, T., Kuijper, A., Urban, B.: CapSoles: who is walking on what kind of floor? In: Proceedings of 19th International Conference on Human-Computer Interaction with Mobile Devices and Services (2017)

42. McCarthy, M., James, D., Lee, J., Rowlands, D.: Decision-tree-based human activity classification algorithm using single-channel foot-mounted gyroscope. Electron. Lett. **51**(9), 675–676 (2015)

43. Michahelles, F.: Sensing and monitoring professional skiers. In: Published by the IEEE CS and IEEE ComSoc 2005 (2005)

44. Noshadi, H., Dabiri, F., Ahmadian, S., Amini, N., Sarrafzadeh, M.: HERMES: mobile system for instability analysis and balance assessment. ACM Trans. Embed. Comput. Syst. (TECS) **12**(1s), 57 (2013)

45. Perry, J., Burnfield, J.M.: Gait analysis: normal and pathological function. Dev. Med. Child Neurol. **35**, 1122 (1993)

46. de Pinho Andr, R., Diniz, P.H., Fuks, H.: Bottom-up investigation: human activity recognition based on feet movement and posture information. In: iWOAR (2017)

47. de Pinho Andr, R., Diniz, P.H., Fuks, H.: Investigating the relevance of sensor selection: recognition of ADLs based on feet movement and posture information. In: Sensor Devices (2018)

48. Sazonov, E., Hegde, N., Browning, R.C., Melanson, E.L., Sazonova, N.A.: Posture and activity recognition and energy expenditure estimation in a wearable platform. IEEE J. Biomed. Health Inform. **19**(4), 1339–1346 (2015)

49. Sazonov, E.S., Fulk, G., Hill, J., Schutz, Y., Browning, R.: Monitoring of posture allocations and activities by a shoe-based wearable sensor. IEEE Trans. Biomed. Eng. **58**(4), 983–990 (2011)
50. Sazonova, N., Browning, R.C., Sazonov, E.: Accurate prediction of energy expenditure using a shoe-based activity monitor. Med. Sci. Sports Exerc. **43**(7), 1312–1321 (2011)
51. Sazonova, N.A., Browning, R., Sazonov, E.S.: Prediction of bodyweight and energy expenditure using point pressure and foot acceleration measurements. Open Biomed. Eng. J. **5**, 110 (2011)
52. Shu, L., Hua, T., Wang, Y., Li, Q., Feng, D.D., Tao, X.: In-shoe plantar pressure measurement and analysis system based on fabric pressure sensing array. IEEE Trans. Inf. Technol. Biomed. **14**(3), 767–775 (2010). https://doi.org/10.1109/TITB.2009.2038904
53. Tang, W., Sazonov, E.S.: Highly accurate recognition of human postures and activities through classification with rejection. IEEE J. Biomed. Health Inform. **18**(1), 309–315 (2014)
54. Wahab, Y., Bakar, N.: Gait analysis measurement for sport application based on ultrasonic system. In: 2011 IEEE 15th International Symposium on Consumer Electronics (2011)
55. Zhang, T., Fulk, G.D., Tang, W., Sazonov, E.S.: Using decision trees to measure activities in people with stroke. In: 2013 35th Annual International Conference of the IEEE Engineering in Medicine and Biology Society (EMBC), pp. 6337–6340. IEEE (2013)

Extraction of the Graceful Feature from Classical Dance Motion Focused on Dancer's Perspective

Yuki Inazu[1], Yuya Tsukigata[1], Etsuko Ueda[1(✉)], Kenichi Iida[2],
Kentaro Takemura[3], Takayuki Nakamura[4], and Masanao Koeda[5]

[1] Osaka Institute of Technology, Osaka, Japan
`etsuko.ueda@oit.ac.jp`
[2] National Institute of Technology, Nara College, Nara, Japan
[3] Tokai University, Hiratsuka-shi, Kanagawa, Japan
[4] Wakayama University, Wakayama, Japan
[5] Osaka Electro-Communication University, Osaka, Japan

Abstract. This research focuses on "gracefulness" and aim for the extraction and modeling of the graceful motion feature using classical dance. We consider that dancers decide their position and orientation based on their foot movement and decide their posture based on the movement of their limbs. Hence, in this paper, we describe extracting the gracefulness feature, not just from the motion data acquired by the motion capture system analyzed so far, but from the data separated into "position/orientation" and "movement of limbs". Firstly, we analyzed the curved surface made by a dancer's arm movement and showed that its area is strongly related to gracefulness. Next, we visualized its curvature using the Gauss map and quantified. Using the mapping distance, we indicated that the separation emphasizes the movement feature of both forearms. Finally, we showed that change in orientation is also an important factor of gracefulness using position/orientation data.

Keywords: Graceful motion · Motion capture · Motion analysis · Human-robot interaction

1 Introduction

In the near future, the main market of robots will be in the services field, such as nursing care, communication, etc. Robots that co-exist with humans are currently becoming more widespread in the fields of production in factories and nursing care services. For people and robots to co-exist, the robots must not be a source of uneasiness, but due to their mechanical movements, many people tend to feel a sense of fear and anxiety towards them. Hence, for robots that co-exist with humans to be able to work in the same space as people, aside from their functionality, safety, and operability, it is also essential for them to have movements that do not give a sense of fear or uneasiness to people.

© Springer Nature Switzerland AG 2019
V. G. Duffy (Ed.): HCII 2019, LNCS 11581, pp. 170–181, 2019.
https://doi.org/10.1007/978-3-030-22216-1_13

With this background, research regarding people looking at motion and the impression they receive from such motions has been increasing. For example, Matsumaru [1] and Nakata [2] implemented features representing emotions obtained based on Laban Movement Analysis on a small robot and are studying the impressions of people upon seeing these features. Hugillz [3] and Fink [4] investigated if women could judge what emotions were being expressed upon seeing a male dancer dancing a dance that expresses particular emotions. These studies are conducted with motions created by the researchers and motions created by the dancers' own sense. McCarty [5] analyzed what kind of dance gives a good impression to people, focusing on the joint angles. In addition, Yokoi [6] implemented the motion wherein the robot hands a small box to a person, and is studying the influence of the difference in motion orbit on human psychology.

We focus on "gracefulness", one of the adjectives that describes human motion, and aim for the modeling and extraction of the graceful motion feature using classical dance motion. Research on motion analysis of classical dance has been carried out by various approaches. Sakata [7] researched on the correspondence relationship between the subjective information obtained by the sensitivity evaluation experiment on Japanese dance and the physical information obtained by the motion capture system; Kai [8] researched on the extraction of the "choreography" part in Japanese dance and the quantitative understanding of personality based on it. These studies are aimed at extracting the features related to feelings from the "choreography" of Japanese dance motions. In addition, Ikeura [9] studied a method of implementing Japanese dance motions on a robot. Although studies targeting classical dance such as these have so far been conducted, in order to implement human-like movements to the robot, an approach where graceful motion is extracted from classical dance motion and implemented on the robot has yet to be done.

We inspired by wheeled humanoid robots such as Pepper, who decide their form based on a change in position, orientation, and movement of limbs at a given moment, we considered that dancers decide their position and orientation based on their foot movement and decide their posture based on the movement of their limbs. In this study, the aim is to try to extract the gracefulness feature, not just from the motion data acquired by the motion capture system analyzed so far, but from the data separated into "position/orientation" and "movement of limbs".

2   Motion Analysis Target

2.1   Acquiring Motion Data

The classical dance motion to be analyzed are the following 5 types: Japanese dance, Hula Dance, Indian Dance, Balinese Dance, and Myanmar dance, with one piece of motion data by one professional dancer for each type of dance. The motion data was obtained using an optical motion capture system. The data loss due to occlusion was interpolated using linear interpolation. The sampling rate was 120 Hz.

Table 1. Motion number and their feature

No.	Motion sequence	No.	Motion sequence
1	Raise arms, change orientation **score 0.133**	11	Move arms in figure 8 shape **score -0.032**
2	Wave arms **score 0.110**	12	Move both arms left and right **score 0.034**
3	Raise arms and move them sideways **score 0.153**	13	Move right arm diagonally forward **score -0.154**
4	Raise arms to the left and right **score -0.244**	14	Raise one arm repeatedly **score -0.098**
5	Pull arms obliquely downroad **score -0.021**	15	Clap hands **score 0.136**
6	Lower arms in a circle **score 0.210**	16	Maintain arms in the center of the body **score 0.130**
7	Raise arms directly above **score -0.170**	17	Change orientation of both arms **score 0.252**
8	Maintain arms in the center of the body **score -0.098**	18	Move both arms diagonally upwards **score -0.370**
9	Move the right arm **score 0.235**	19	Slide the right arm in a semicircular shape **score 0.309**
10	Quickly change the orientation of the right arm **score -0.415**		

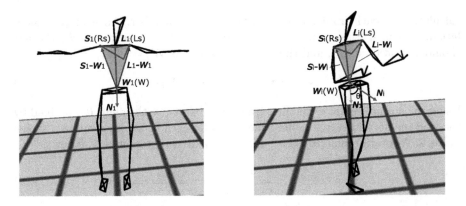

Fig. 1. Definition of the normal vector   Fig. 2. Definition of the rotation angle

2.2 Factor Score on Classical Dance and Gracefulness of Arm Motion Used in Analysis

Distinctive movements from 5 types of dance motion were selected; 1000 frames before and after these were cut out, and 19 kinds of animations showing stick figures of the arms only were prepared. Table 1 shows the 19 types of classical dance motion numbers and the features of the motions. These animations were presented to 60 test subjects (male and females from their teens up to sixties), and their impression was evaluated by the SD method using 10 pairs of adjectives. Factor analysis of the impression evaluation results was conducted, and the factor score for "gracefulness" was calculated. The correspondence of the motion-number and factor score on "gracefulness" are also shown in Table 1. Motion analysis is carried out using these 19 types of motion, and the quantification method was verified by the correlation between factor scores and quantified features.

3   Motion Data Separation

3.1   Definition of Data Separation

The normal vector of the plane formed by the position coordinates of both shoulders and the sacrum is taken as the reference vector of that frame. Position/orientation: Data extracted from the position of the sacrum on the xz-plane of the dancer, and from the rotation around the y-axis of the reference vector only. Motion of limbs: Data extracted from the movements of the dancer's limbs, and the rotation around the xz-axis of the reference vector only. In this paper, we call the original motion capture data as "pre-separation motion".

3.2   Extraction of Position/Orientation

The basis surface is defined using both shoulders position and a sacrum position of the pre-separation motion. Its normal vector $N_i = (x_{Ni}, y_{Ni}, z_{Ni})$ is calculated for each frame. Here, i shows a frame number. An example calculation, shown in Figs. 1 and 2, has the right shoulder position as $\boldsymbol{S}_i$, the left shoulder position as $\boldsymbol{L}_i$, and the sacrum position as $\boldsymbol{W}_i = (x_{Wi}, y_{Wi}, z_{Wi})$.

$$\boldsymbol{N}_i = (\boldsymbol{S}_i - \boldsymbol{V}_i) \times (\boldsymbol{L}_i - \boldsymbol{V}_i) \tag{1}$$

Using the normal vector of the first frame as a reference, the angle θ_i obtained by rotating the normal vector around the y-axis for each frame is calculated, shown in Eq. 2. A rotation matrix $\boldsymbol{R}_i$ around the y-axis is represented as follows,

$$\theta_i = \cos^{-1}\left(\frac{x_{N1}x_{Ni} + z_{N1}z_{Ni}}{\sqrt{x_{N1}^2 + z_{N1}^2}\sqrt{x_{Ni}^2 + z_{Ni}^2}}\right) \tag{2}$$

$$\boldsymbol{R}_i = \begin{bmatrix} \cos\theta_i & 0 & -\sin\theta_i \\ 0 & 1 & 0 \\ \sin\theta_i & 0 & \cos\theta_i \end{bmatrix} \tag{3}$$

Furthermore, translational vector $\boldsymbol{T}_i$ is obtained from the moving distance of the sacrum position $\boldsymbol{W}_i$ on the xz-plane from the first frame.

$$\boldsymbol{T}_i = \begin{bmatrix} x_{wi} \\ y_{w1} \\ z_{wi} \end{bmatrix} \tag{4}$$

When the sacrum position set to the origin, each joint's position vector of T-pose is defined as $\boldsymbol{p}_{Tj}$. Here, j shows the joint ID. The converted position vector $\boldsymbol{p}_{ij}$ can be obtained by multiplying $\boldsymbol{p}_{Tj}$ by the homogeneous transformation matrix $\boldsymbol{H}_i$. $\boldsymbol{H}_i$ consists of the rotation matrix $\boldsymbol{R}_i$ and the translational vector $\boldsymbol{T}_i$.

$$\boldsymbol{H}_i = \begin{bmatrix} \cos\theta_i & 0 & -\sin\theta_i & x_{wi} \\ 0 & 1 & 0 & y_{w1} \\ \sin\theta_i & 0 & \cos\theta_i & z_{wi} \\ 0 & 0 & 0 & 1 \end{bmatrix} \tag{5}$$

$$\boldsymbol{p}_{ij} = \boldsymbol{H}_i \boldsymbol{p}_{Tj} \tag{6}$$

3.3   Extraction of the Movement of the 4 Limbs

Using the first frame as a reference, the coordinates of each joint are converted so that the position coordinates of the sacrum do not move in the y-axis direction. Concretely, the position vector $\boldsymbol{p}_{ij}$ (the frame no. i, the joint ID j) is converted to the position vector $\boldsymbol{O}_{ij}$ as the following equation.

$$\boldsymbol{O}_{ij} = \boldsymbol{p}_{ij} - (\boldsymbol{W}_{ij} - \boldsymbol{W}_{1j}) \tag{7}$$

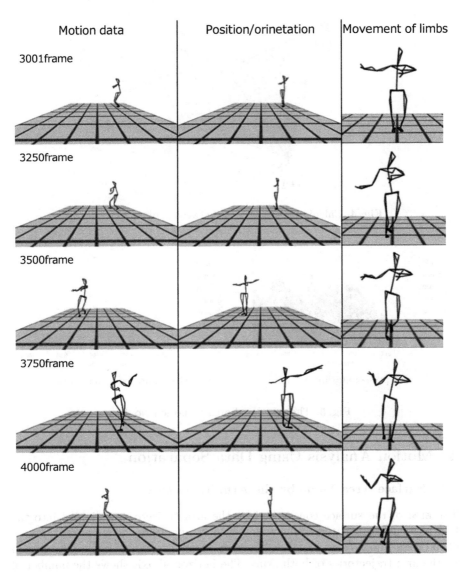

Fig. 3. An example of the motion data separation

The movement of the limb is obtained by multiplying the position coordinate by the inverse matrix of rotation matrix $\boldsymbol{R}_i^{-1}$ obtained in Sect. 3.2.

$$\boldsymbol{L}_i = \boldsymbol{R}_i^{-1}\boldsymbol{O}_i \tag{8}$$

A separation example is shown in Fig. 3.

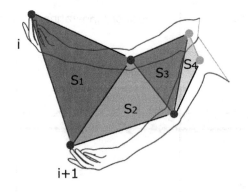

Fig. 4. Calculated surface area between frame i to $i + 1$

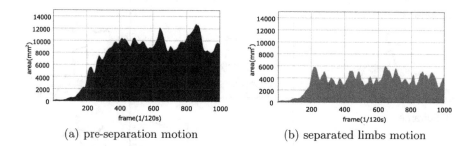

(a) pre-separation motion   (b) separated limbs motion

Fig. 5. The calculated area of motion No. 9

4   Motion Analysis Using Data Separation

4.1   Surface Area Made by the Arm Trajectory

The area of the surface constituted by the arm trajectory is divided into the four parts and calculated as shown in Fig. 4. It quantifies the amount of motion of the arm. Figures 5 and 6 shows an example of the change in the area formed by the arm trajectories of both arms. The horizontal axis shows the number of frames; the vertical axis shows the area between frames (Figs. 5 and 6).

For the 19 classical dance motions shown in Table 1, the scatter diagrams between these surface area and the factor score of gracefulness are shown in Figs. 7 and 8. For the surface area, the sum of the areas of the two arm trajectories for 1000 frames was used. The correlation coefficient between the area created by the trajectory and the factor score of gracefulness was 0.67 before separation and 0.51 for the movement of the limbs only, both of which had a positive correlation. It was found that the magnitude of arm movement is strongly related to gracefulness.

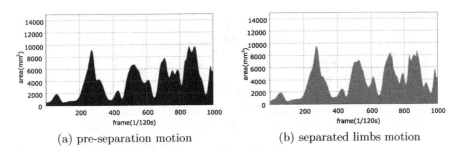

(a) pre-separation motion   (b) separated limbs motion

Fig. 6. The calculated area of the motion No. 14

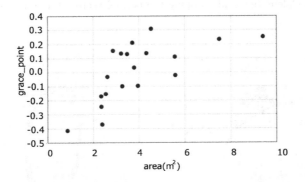

Fig. 7. Correlation between the calculated area and the gracefulness score (pre-separation motion)

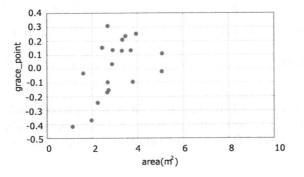

Fig. 8. Correlation between the calculated area and the gracefulness score (separated limbs motion)

4.2 Gauss Map

Gauss map is mapping that associates a point on a curved surface with a particular point on the surface of a unit sphere. When the starting point of the unit normal vector at an arbitrary point on the curved surface is moved to the

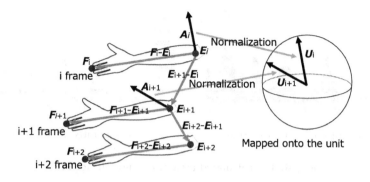

Fig. 9. Calculation and mapping the normal vector onto a unit sphere

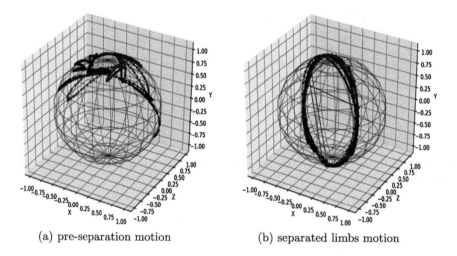

(a) pre-separation motion   (b) separated limbs motion

Fig. 10. The Gauss map of the left forearm of the motion No. 9

origin point of a unit sphere, the endpoint is as the corresponding point. The unit normal vector U_i is calculated by the following equations using the positions of the elbow E_i, E_{i+1} and the position of the hand tips F_i, as shown in Fig. 9.

$$A_i = (F_i - E_i) \times (E_{i+1} - E_i) \tag{9}$$

$$U_i = \frac{A_i}{|A_i|} \tag{10}$$

Then, we map it on the unit sphere and create the Gauss map which visualizes the curvature of the surface constructed by arm motion. The Gauss map results of the pre-separation motion and the limb motion data are shown in Figs. 10 and 11.

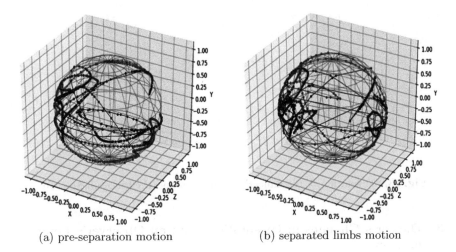

(a) pre-separation motion   (b) separated limbs motion

Fig. 11. The Gauss map of the left forearm of the motion No. 14

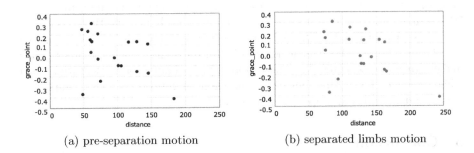

(a) pre-separation motion   (b) separated limbs motion

Fig. 12. Correlation between the calculated area and the gracefulness score

The mapping distance is defined as the sum of the distance between the points plotted on the unit sphere and quantifies the curvature of the curved surface constituted by the arm movement. The mapping distance is long where the curvature increases and is short where the curvature decreases. For the 19 types of classical dance motion shown in Table 1, the scatter diagrams of the mapping distance and the factor score of gracefulness are shown in Fig. 12. The horizontal axis is the mapping distance, and the vertical axis is the factor score of gracefulness. The correlation coefficient was -0.43 before separation, and -0.41 for the limb motion only; both had a weak negative correlation. From the scatter plot, it was found that the mapping distance becomes larger on the limb movement data than on the pre-separation motion data. It can be said that the separation can emphasize and extract the movement of changing the orientation of both forearms.

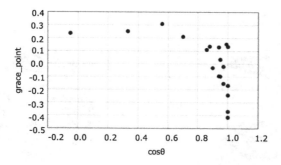

Fig. 13. Correlation of the dancer's orientation and the gracefulness score

4.3 Dancer's Changes in Orientation from an Observer's Point of View

For the 19 kinds of classical dance motions shown in Table 1, we quantified the change of body orientation from the first frame using the inner product. The body orientation change was taken as the average value of the inner product in 1000 frames. The scatter plot of the body orientation change and the gracefulness score is shown in Fig. 13. The correlation coefficient was -0.59 with a negative correlation. Those who change their orientation while dancing tends to have higher gracefulness scores than those who did not change their orientation much while dancing. Hence, this shows that change in orientation is also an important factor that provides an impression of gracefulness.

5 Conclusion

In this study, to extract the gracefulness feature from classical dance motion, we analyzed the curved surface consists of a dancer's arm trajectory and the dancer's body orientation change. The motion data obtained using an optical motion capture system analyzed was separated into position/orientation data and limb movement data, and then some features were extracted. It was found that the gracefulness feature appears in both the before/after separation. However, there was no significant difference brought about by the separation. In the future, a further study on the feature quantity extraction method and modeling will develop.

Acknowledgment. This work was supported by JSPS KAKENHI Grant Number JP17K00393.

References

1. Matsumaru, T.: Discrimination and implementation of emotions on zoomorphic robot movements. SICE J. Control Meas. Syst. Integr. (JCMSI) **2**(6), 365–372 (2009)
2. Nakata, T., Mori, T., Sato, T.: Analysis of impression of robot bodily expression. J. Robot. Mechatron. **14**(1), 27–36 (2002)
3. Hugill, N., Fink, B., Neave, N., Besson, A., Bunse, L.: Women's perception of men's sensation seeking propensity from their dance movements. Personality Individ. Differ. **51**(4), 483–487 (2011)
4. Fink, B., Weege, B., Flugge, J., Roder, S., Neave, N., McCarty, K.: Men's personality and women's perception of their dance quality. Personality Individ. Differ. **52**(2), 232–235 (2012)
5. McCarty, K., et al.: Optimal asymmetry and other motion parameters that characterise high-quality female dance. Sci. Rep. **7**, 42435 (2017). EP
6. Yokoi, K., Arisumi, H., Komoriya, K.: Gentle motion of robot manipulator - how does human feel hand-over motion of a robot? J. Mech. Eng. Lab. **52**(4), 149–155 (1998). (in Japanese)
7. Sakata, M., Marumo, Y., Hachimura, K., Kojima, K., Yoshimura, M.: An attempt to process KANSEI information found in physical movements in Japanese traditional dance -measurements and analysis using motion capture-. IPSJ SIG Computers and the Humanities Technical report, No. 7, pp. 49–56 (2004). (in Japanese)
8. Yoshimura, M., Sakai, Y., Kai, T., Yoshimura, I.: A trial for identifying and characterizing typical parts of Japanese dancing. Trans. Inst. Electron. Inf. Commun. Eng. D-II **84**(12), 2644–2653 (2001). (in Japanese)
9. Ikeura, R., Nakazato, H., Inooka, H.: Motion planning for dancing robots based on human's dancing motion. J. Robot. Soc. Jpn. **15**(6), 927–933 (1997). (in Japanese)

Homologous Mesh Extraction
via Monocular Systems

Mohamed Fateh Karoui[1,2(✉)] and Thorsten Kuebler[1]

[1] Human Solutions of North America, Morrisville, NC 27560, USA
Thorsten.Kuebler@human-solutions.com
[2] North Carolina State University, Raleigh, NC 27606, USA
mfkaroui@ncsu.edu

Abstract. Pose estimation of humanoid objects in monocular systems is a non-trivial problem that has been at the forefront of the human-computer interaction field. The ability for a computer to not only to detect the presence of a humanoid shape within an image but also to infer relative location and configuration has particular use for many applications. We explore a novel approach to solving this task by introducing a multi-stage preprocessing algorithm and a constrained pose estimator.

Keywords: Homologous · Mesh · Monocular ·
Convolutional neural network · Generative adversarial network · Regression

1 Introduction

Here at Human Solutions of North America, we have developed a novel multi-tiered approach to detecting and estimating poses in monocular system of humanoid objects using state of the art deep learning architectures and extensive domain knowledge through our commercial body scanners and Size North America proprietary data. Using a U-Net architecture we are able to segment an image to classify which pixels belong to a humanoid and which pixels belong to the background. The U-net architecture is ideal for this task and is considered the state of the art when it comes to image segmentation tasks. It is an encoder-decoder architecture that introduced a technique called a skip step that allows the propagation of feature locality throughout the network in order to classify what kind of subject a particular pixel belongs to. We then clip each detected subject and pass the image into a Convolutional Neural Network (CNN) to infer demographic information. This particular portion of the approach allows us to pick a good "initial guess" as to the structure of the subject. We extract information such as race, age, weight, and body morphology. Thusly, we choose a homologous mesh that has been statistically generated from our Size North America database for that particular demographic. The Size North America database consists of submillimeter precision three dimensional body scans of approximately 18,000 subjects distributed evenly across various demographics. This database allows us to produce a statistically representative three dimensional meshes of each demographic across multiple morphologies. Finally, we pass the homologous mesh into a deep neural network and

V. G. Duffy (Ed.): HCII 2019, LNCS 11581, pp. 182–197, 2019.
https://doi.org/10.1007/978-3-030-22216-1_14

produce a final mesh that represents the pose of the subject. This last step acts as a regressor and deforms the homologous mesh to fit the initial body pose of the subject.

This novel approach allows us to estimate the pose of multiple subjects that are within view of a monocular system as well as letting us infer a globally plausible body shape for occluded portions of the subject. This approach also opens the door for soft body simulation on subjects within an image. Applications of this methodology are wide and far impacting from three dimensional scene reconstruction and point of view visualization, to high fidelity motion capture from low cost systems.

2 Materials and Methods

2.1 Image Segmentation

Training a deep encoder-decoder neural network is rather tricky. This is caused by the conflicting nature of the requirements of the neural network versus the drawbacks of backpropagation. The U-Net architecture requires a maximization of information for semantic segmentation to be successful. This means that the standard methods of model regularization can no longer be utilized.

One major issue of deep neural networks is a tendency for overfitting. This is due to their large parameter space. The standard way to combat this issue is through dropout. During training we employ a process that stochastically stops gradients from propagating backwards through the layers in the neural network. This effectively kills neurons and forces the neural network to perform at a deficit. Many have theorized that this method causes the neural network to generate strong sub-classifiers in earlier layers. The late stage layers then ensemble these subnetworks to produce a final prediction. Unfortunately, structural information will be lost that act as input for later layer in the decoder network. Therefore, this method cannot be used.

To reduce computational cost, many neural networks, employ a Max Pooling layer whereby neurons of a previous layer are pooled together into a single neuron by taking the highest output signal from the group. This has the effect of reducing computational complexity while preserving the gross structure of the information. Unfortunately, local adjacency information is not preserved with this technique and fine image details that are important for classifying humans are lost.

We initially take a 512×256 three channel image, referred to as the source image, and pass it through a specialized "encoder-decoder" convolutional neural network referred to as a U-Net architecture [1]. The U-Net architecture introduces a tensor concatenation operator that allows structural information about identified classes to propagate throughout the neural network that is used to reconstruct a pixel-wise classification tensor. This concatenation operation is referred to as a "skip-step". Because we are dealing entirely with rank three tensors the concatenation operations occur along the third axis or the channels axis and are computationally cheap (Fig. 1).

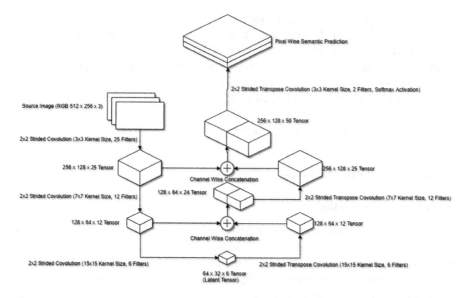

Fig. 1. Shows the general architecture for the U-Net Convolutional Neural Network. On the left hand side show the encoder network. On the bottom center is the latent tensor representation of the source image. On the right hand side is the decoder side of the neural network. In the center we have the concatenation operations that allow the structural information of the source image to propagate.

To reduce computational complexity, we employ a strided convolution that acts similarly to max pooling. The difference is our kernel size is always larger than the stride. This allows us to include adjacent information that is outside the "pooling" region while reducing the number of computations by power of two.

Since we are unable to use dropout to regularize our neural network we employed a method of streaming subsets of our original dataset, this is also referred to as incremental learning [1]. The Common Objects in Context (COCO) dataset [2], includes 330 thousand images that are semantically labeled by object class. The dataset is excellently curated and provides a large variety of examples to train on (Fig. 2).

Our activation function, which provide the non-linear capacity for our neural network, was chosen specifically to remove the need for batch normalization [3]. SELU, or scaled exponential linear units belong to a class of self-normalizing activation functions. This activation function allowed us to remove the need for additional normalization layers without losing the benefit that normalization has to solving the vanishing gradient property.

SELU is defined as

$$f(x, \alpha) = \lambda \begin{cases} \alpha(e^x - 1), & x < 0 \\ x, & x \geq 0 \end{cases}$$

Where λ is a learned parameter that acts as a scaling factor to boost gradient propagation.

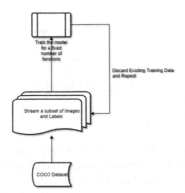

Fig. 2. The iterative training process allows us to define a dynamic set of images to train on. This removes the issue of training over fit without having to perform dropout and other model regularization techniques.

2.2 Clipping

Once a class is identified within the source image we must clip the class object into a separate image to extract demographic information. This clipped form of the image isolates the subject from external sources of information that may add undue noise during the subsequent processes.

Clipping is performed using a masking methodology on a low-pass canny filter. Initially we take a source image and pass a Gaussian Kernel Convolution across the source image to remove high frequency information from the image. This will have the effect of reducing the number of possible edges, as shown in Fig. 3.

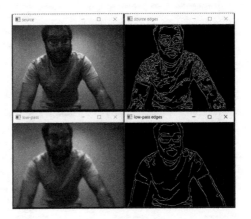

Fig. 3. Shows the canny edge filter as applied directly on the source image (top right) versus being applied after a low pass filter operation on the source image (bottom right).

Once we extract edges we apply a pixel-wise multiplication of our region proposal. The result of the operation yields a very clean image that contains only the subject to be passed on later processes (Fig. 4).

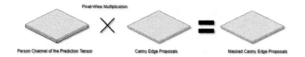

Fig. 4. Edge masking allows us to focus on edges that we think belong to a human.

2.3 Demographics Estimation

The demographics of a detected subject plays an important role in selecting the right initial conditions for the mesh regression procedure. Extracting the demographics of a subject is done using three convolutional neural networks. Each one is responsible for extracting a prediction for age, race, and gender. The CNN's use two principles to achieve better than human performance when classifying demographics. A decaying special drop rate, and an expanding kernel size.

To regularize the neural networks and prevent over fit, we employ a high drop rate in the earlier stages of the neural network and a low dropout rate in the later stages of the neural network. This improves the ability of strong subnetworks to be generated for extracting low level features. In the later stages we want the layers to act as an ensembling mechanism. Secondly, expand the kernel sizes to capture local features within the image at earlier stages and global features in later stages.

The result of the convolutional neural networks is then concatenated to produce a final prediction vector to be used in subsequent steps (Fig. 5).

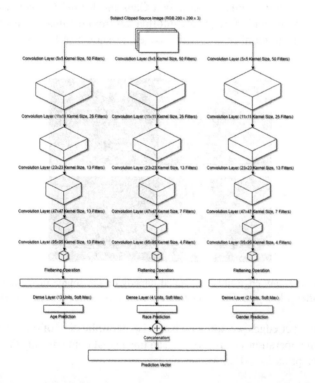

Fig. 5. Highlights the key architecture of the set of Convolutional Neural Networks that are responsible for extracting demographic information from the subject after clipping.

2.4   Homologous Mesh Generation

During our product developments we conducted a size survey called Size North America which consisted of scanning eighteen thousand diverse subjects using millimeter precision body scanners. The subject takes a quick demographic survey and then change into skin-tight under garments. They then enter our body scanner whereby multi-laser optical measurements occur across the entire length of the body producing High Density Point Cloud (HDPC) data. Using propriety software, we aggregated our HDPC data into statistically representative and vertex uniform meshes called homologous meshes (Fig. 6).

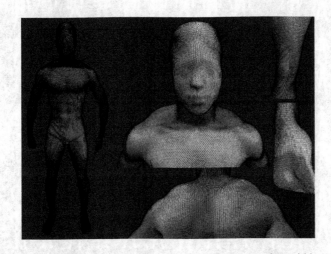

Fig. 6. Showcases the vertex uniformity of the homologous meshes within our dataset.

2.5   Homologous Mesh Estimation

Given a demographic prediction vector P_i about a particular subject then a reasonable estimate about a subject's mesh M_i can be given by an inner product of the prediction vector with the basis B of the space representing all possible human meshes. We approximate the basis of this space using out homologous mesh's extracted from our Size North America survey.

$$M_i = \frac{P_i \cdot B}{P_i \cdot P_i}$$

Where B is the basis set of meshes defined as

$$\{B_{g,r,a} | B_{g,r,a} \in M^{n \times 3 \times 160,785}, g \in Z\ r \in Z, a \in Z\}$$

and P_i is the prediction vector defined as

$$\{P_i | P_i \in \mathbf{R}^n\},$$

for a subject i (Fig. 7).

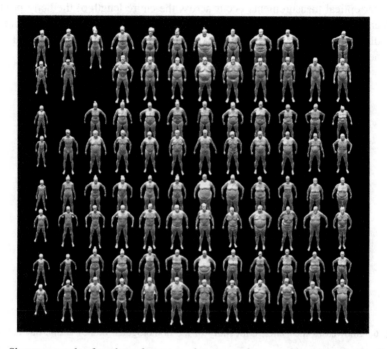

Fig. 7. Shows a sample of our homologous meshes across demographic range. Starting from the top we show meshes for Female African Americans, Male African Americans, Female Asians, Male Asians, Female Others, Male Others, Female White, Male White. Each mesh across a row is a statistically representative model of our age group classes. Starting from the left we show meshes for ages 0–11, 12–17, 18–23, 24–29, 30–35, 36–41, 42–47, 48–53, 54–59, 60–65, 66–71, 72+ respectively.

In essence this process is a weighted average operation of all the homologous meshes across our demographic classes. The weights are determined by the probabilities produced by the neural network.

2.6   Pose Estimation

Pose estimation was accomplished using a Convolutional Neural Network on clipped source images. Preprocessing the image to remove background information allowed us to reduce the complexity of our neural network. Since pre-clipping removes background information, our neural network did not need to learn what a person looks like.

We posit that the pose estimator works by simply regressing a central skeleton into the contour provided. Our neural network's final layer simply had 22 degrees of freedom. We constructed a constrained skeleton layer based on pre-existing anatomical models which greatly reduced the regression times and improved overall accuracy when compared to a standard dense layer output. Our constraints are defined by medically accepted normal ranges of motion (Tables 1, 2, 3, 4, 5, 6 and 7).

Table 1. Describes the normal range of motion for the hip.

Type	Minimum angle (Deg.)	Maximum angle (Deg.)
Flexion	0	125
Extension	115	0
Hyperextension	0	15
Abduction	0	45
Adduction	45	0
Lateral rotation	0	45
Medial rotation	0	45

Table 2. Describes the normal range of motion for the knee.

Type	Minimum angle (Deg.)	Maximum angle (Deg.)
Flexion	0	130
Extension	120	0

Table 3. Describes the normal range of motion for the ankle.

Type	Minimum angle (Deg.)	Maximum angle (Deg.)
Plantar flexion	0	50
Dorsiflexion	0	20

Table 4. Describes the normal range of motion for the foot.

Type	Minimum angle (Deg.)	Maximum angle (Deg.)
Inversion	0	35
Eversion	0	25

Table 5. Describes the normal range of motion for the shoulder.

Type	Minimum angle (Deg.)	Maximum angle (Deg.)
Flexion	0	180
Extension	0	50
Abduction	0	90
Adduction	90	0
Lateral rotation	0	90
Medial rotation	0	90

Table 6. Describes the normal range of motion for the elbow.

Type	Minimum angle (Deg.)	Maximum angle (Deg.)
Flexion	0	160
Extension	145	0
Pronation	0	90
Supination	0	90

Table 7. Describes the normal range of motion for the wrist.

Type	Minimum angle (Deg.)	Maximum angle (Deg.)
Flexion	0	90
Extension	0	70
Abduction	0	25
Adduction	0	65

2.7   Rigging Homologous Meshes

Once pose estimation is complete applying the pose to the mesh involves regressing the mesh skeleton which applies a system of linear transformations to the mesh allowing the mesh to be regressed into the desired pose.

To simplify the rigging process of the homologous mesh we used the software Unity. By defining the key points of a skeleton we are able to apply transformations to the entire mesh through the 3D rendering software (Fig. 8).

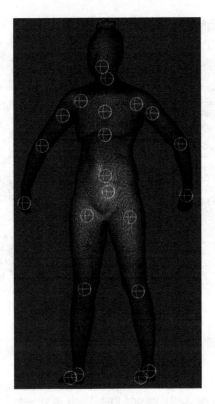

Fig. 8. Showcases the control points of the skeleton defined in Unity. These will act to define a system of linear transformations that will be applied to each vertex on the mesh.

3 Results

The image segmentation network was particularly difficult to train as great care had to be taken when dealing with class weights. Code was developed to dynamically calculate class weight upon each batch. The class weights were calculated by counting pixels belonging to people versus pixels belonging to the background. This added procedure cause training times to be much higher, but yielded very good results (Fig. 9).

The clipping operation yielded expected results whereby 83% of human subjects in validation data were clipped from the source image. This is largely sufficient for images in the wild. We expect the use case for this algorithm to be mostly situated in controlled well lit environments (Fig. 10).

Fig. 9. Showcases very hard validation examples of the image segmentation process. Input images are shown in column 1, the ground truth labels in column 2, and the neural network results in column 3. Background pixels are represented in green, while pixels belonging to people are represented in blue. (Color figure online)

Fig. 10. Shows a sample of the clipping process in a non-trivial test case where the subject has intersecting edges with a background. The subject also has a wide variety of occluding features such as facial hair with no discernable variation from his shirt.

Training the demographic convolutional neural networks yielded a significantly greater than random accuracy for each network. We trained these networks using the UTKFace dataset [16] which provides a well curated set of faces with race age and gender annotations (Figs. 11, 12 and 13).

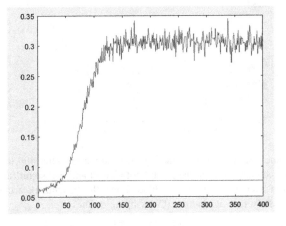

Fig. 11. Outlines the train curve for extracting age estimations after 400 training epochs. The top one prediction accuracy for 13 classes plateaued after the 150th epoch. The jitter in accuracy is caused by the dropout rate in earlier layers as compared to the training step size (1e-3). The line in blue shows the benchmark accuracy if the neural network were to classify age at random. (Color figure online)

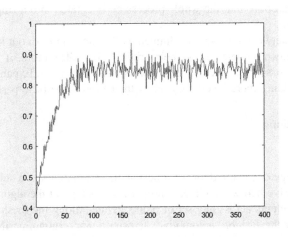

Fig. 12. Outlines the train curve for extracting gender estimations after 400 training epochs. The top one prediction accuracy for two classes plateaued after the 60th epoch. The line in blue shows the benchmark accuracy if the neural network were to classify gender at random. (Color figure online)

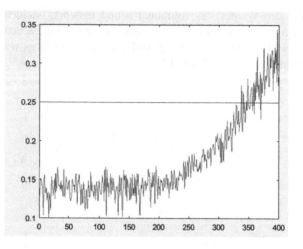

Fig. 13. Outlines the train curve for extracting race estimations after 400 training epochs. The top one prediction accuracy for four classes did not plateau and had significant trouble attaining greater than random accuracy. The line in blue shows the benchmark accuracy if the neural network were to classify race at random. (Color figure online)

4   Discussion

4.1   Improvements

One major drawback that this methodology has is the multistage approach. Computationally speaking this is not efficient and may suffer when implemented on lower end hardware. We propose that the whole process be integrated into a single feed forward neural network.

Our neural network size was also limited by the capabilities of our hardware. Source images were down sampled from their original sizes. Therefore, it is reasonable to expect a major loss of fine details that are crucial to the process. Expanding the number of filters and adding more layers may allow the neural network to perform better.

4.2   Applications

Mobile Sizing
Our methodology opens the door for robust sizing estimations of a subject without the need for expensive hardware. Given a proper reference point the algorithm can extract length measurements across any set of points defined along the mesh. This has direct applications for the fashion, automotive, aerospace, and ergonomic industries.

An example scenario for the fashion industry would be at the retail level. A boutique fashion store can setup or use existing camera systems to build mesh estimates for all their customers. When a customer selects a garment they can instantly view a simulation of how the garment looks and moves on their body. This removes the risk of exposing expensive apparel to the customer and allows the store to reduce inventory while catering to a higher range demographics.

In ergonomic research, a key area of the field that is lacking is the ability to rapidly prototype designs on computer systems. The ability to develop ergonomic products that can be easily be tested on specific demographics plays an important role. Our technology has particular use when the designer(s) does not have access to an expensive demographics sizing database. They will be able to easily produce simulation ready meshes from any images.

Social Networking and Information Pivoting

The ability search information broker databases allow one to leverage limited knowledge about a subject to expand their information. Unfortunately, traversing these databases becomes an intractable computational nightmare. Searching social media databases is nearly impossible when looking for a particular subject. The ability to narrow down the search space for a human subject greatly reduces search times.

When this methodology is paired with other information gathering techniques, such as natural language processing, one may be able to extract knowledge about a human subject just by having a simple conversation with the subject. This has direct applications in law enforcement. During an interrogation the interviewer's task is to extract information that might otherwise be hidden or obscured. Real time information validation plays a very crucial role. Our system can be used to search and validate a person's identity in real time. Information such as age, gender, race, height, body morphology can be used as filtering terms to search offender databases without the need to rely on the human subject to provide accurate information.

Motion Capture

The motion capture industry has barrier of entry in terms of cost of equipment and education. High fidelity motion capture systems requires dedicated studios with dedicated hardware and a very knowledgeable team to maintain [18]. With our pose estimation and mesh regression we are able to produce reasonably accurate motion capture that can later be fed game development projects and movie studios. Our system's ability to produce homologous mesh's allows for easy integration with pre-existing animation and rendering pipelines. The vertex uniformity of the mesh lets studios perform soft-body and hard body simulations to produce highly realistic scene renderings at a fraction of the cost.

4.3   Privacy Implications

The sensitive nature of extracting demographic data from images has grave privacy implications. The applications for this technology should be selected to align with the public good. Such a technology could be used to leverage into personal and private details. The methods discussed by this paper are not the edge cases for the potential application of this technology. Such methods can be used to estimate data protected by legislation such as medical history. With the right combination of inputs bad actors may use this technology to perform identity theft and other more malicious acts.

Age has particularly strong privacy implications if this technology is used in public facing systems. The ability to extract identifying features from the minority subset of the population without parental approval can breach many local and federal regulations. Such a system must have filters in place to ignore subjects that have reasonable evidence that they are below the age of majority.

Race plays an important role in the system's ability to extract fine details with a high degree of accuracy. Initial structural features that reduce regression times are highly dependent on race. There are many downsides to a system that relies on accurately classifying race. If the convolutional neural network is trained on data that has a class imbalance between races the network may miss-identify a race or the race in particular may become under or over represented within the prediction vector. This will negatively impact the quality of the results. In terms of morality, threat analysis systems and the like that rely on race for identification and classification may compound race inequalities. Therefor the author proposes that systems that are used to predict human behavior should abstain from using race qualifiers.

Gender, like race, is a predictive qualifier for estimating body structure. The very trivial example is bust size. If an initial guess for a female subject was not statistically representative for a female, the regressor would likely need more iterations for a fixed step size to optimize the initial mesh to fit a female bust. Choosing the correct gender is crucial to an accurate representation of a subject. Unfortunately, it is very difficult to represent the subset of the population that is gender ambiguous. By the very definition a transgender subject crosses the boundaries between classes and can cause even the most perceptive humans to think twice. This poses a very difficult technological problem and may also exacerbate the political issues around transgender rights.

Many of the examples presented show the need for a good demographic classifier, but we must take particular care when these systems are applied to public applications. We must not give public institutions and regulatory bodies technological justifications to widen the gap of inequality. Nor must we employ these technologies prematurely when they have a direct impact on a person's life and liberty.

Acknowledgements. A large effort was made to collect the data presented here in the paper. The authors would like to thank Human Solutions of North America for the continuous effort to provide high quality scan data. In particular Dylan Hendricks, a key account manager at Human Solutions of North America, for his critical role in the generation of the homologous meshes. The authors would also like to extend great appreciation for the open source community that has developed around the field of machine learning. Their continued effort in providing key systems made our research possible.

References

1. Pasquale, G., Ciliberto, C., Odone, F., Rosasco, L., Natale, L.: Are we done with object recognition? The iCub robot's perspective. Robot. Auton. Syst. **112**, 260–281 (2019)
2. Lin, T.Y., et al.: Microsoft COCO: common objects in context. In: Fleet, D., Pajdla, T., Schiele, B., Tuytelaars, T. (eds.) ECCV 2014. LNCS, vol. 8693, pp. 740–755. Springer, Cham (2014). https://doi.org/10.1007/978-3-319-10602-1_48
3. Ruiz-Garcia, A., Elshaw, M., Altahhan, A., Palade, V.: A hybrid deep learning neural approach for emotion recognition from facial expressions for socially assistive robots. Neural Comput. Appl. **29**(7), 359–373 (2018)

4. Lee, D., Nakamura, Y.: Motion recognition and recovery from occluded monocular observations. Robot. Auton. Syst. **62**(6), 818–832 (2014)
5. Sarafianos, N., Boteanu, B., Ionescu, B., Kakadiaris, I.A.: 3D Human pose estimation: a review of the literature and analysis of covariates. Comput. Vis. Image Underst. **152**, 1–20 (2016)
6. Kang, M.-J., Lee, J.-K., Kang, J.-W.: Combining random forest with multi-block local binary pattern feature selection for multiclass head pose estimation. PLoS ONE, 1–24 (2017). https://doi.org/10.1371/journal.pone.0166749
7. Ariz, M., Villanueva, A., Cabeza, R.: Robust and accurate 2D-tracking-based 3D positioning method: application to head pose estimation. Comput. Vis. Image (2019, in press)
8. Zhu, S., Mok, P.Y., Kwok, Y.L.: An efficient human model customization method based on orthogonal-view monocular photos. Comput. Aided Des. **45**(11), 1314–1332 (2013)
9. Yu, J., Guo, Y., Tao, D., Wan, J.: Human pose recovery by supervised spectral embedding. Neurocomputing **166**, 301–308 (2015)
10. Kim, H., Lee, S.-H., Sohn, M.-K., Kim, D.-J.: Illumination invariant head pose estimation using random forests classifier and binary pattern run length matrix. Hum.-Centric Comput. Inf. Sci. **4**(1), 9 (2014)
11. Zhang, Z., Zhao, R., Liu, E., Yan, K., Ma, Y.: Scale estimation and correction of the monocular simultaneous localization and mapping (SLAM) based on fusion of 1D laser range finder and vision data. Sensors **18**(6), 1948 (2018)
12. Piccirilli, M., Doretto, G., Adjeroh, D.: Framework for analyzing the whole body surface area from a single view. PLoS ONE, 1–31 (2017). https://doi.org/10.1371/journal.pone.0166749
13. Droniou, A., Ivaldi, S., Sigaud, O.: Deep unsupervised network for multimodal perception, representation and classification. Robot. Auton. Syst. **71**, 83–98 (2015)
14. Hu, R., Savva, M., van Kaick, O.: Functionality representations and applications for shape analysis. Comput. Graph. Forum **37**(2), 603–624 (2018)
15. Hussein, A., Elyan, E., Gaber, M.M., Jayne, C.: Deep imitation learning for 3D navigation tasks. Neural Comput. Appl. **29**, 389–404 (2018)
16. Zhang, Z.S.: Age progression/regression by conditional adversarial autoencoder. In: IEEE Conference on Computer Vision and Pattern Recognition (CVPR) (2017)
17. Jáuregui, D.A.G., Horain, P.: Real-time 3D motion capture by monocular vision and virtual rendering. Mach. Vis. Appl. **28**(8), 839–858 (2017)
18. Kim, Y., Kim, D.: Real-time dance evaluation by markerless human pose estimation. Multimedia Tools Appl. **77**(23), 31199–31220 (2018)
19. Basu, S., Poulin, J., Acton, S.T.: Manifolds for pose tracking from monocular video. J. Electron. Imaging **24**(2), 023014-1–023014-21 (2015)
20. Biasotti, S., Cerri, A., Bronstein, A., Bronstein, M.: Recent trends, applications, and perspectives in 3D shape similarity assessment. Comput. Graph. Forum **35**(6), 87–119 (2016)
21. Calderita, V.L., Bandera, J.P., Bustos, P., Skiadopoulos, A.: Model-based reinforcement of kinect depth data for human motion capture applications. Sensors **13**, 8835–8855 (2013)
22. Chen, C., Zhuang, Y., Xiao, J.: Silhouette representation and matching for 3D pose discrimination – a comparative study. Image Vis. Comput. **28**(4), 654–667 (2010)
23. Xia, S., Gao, L., Lai, Y.K., Yuan, M.-Z., Chai, J.: A survey on human performance capture and animation. J. Comput. Sci. Technol. **32**(3), 536–554 (2017)
24. Xu, C., Nanjappa, A., Zhang, X., Cheng, L.: Estimate hand poses efficiently from single depth images. Int. J. Comput. Vis. **116**, 21–45 (2016)

Machine Learning to Estimate the Amount of Training to Learn a Motor Skill

Moisés R. Santos[1], Eduardo D. F. Souza[1], Mateus B. F. Carvalho[1],
Alexandre C. M. Oliveira[1], Areolino de Almeida Neto[1], Marco R. Curado[2],
and Paulo R. A. Ribeiro[1(✉)]

[1] Universidade Federal do Maranhão, São Luís, Maranhão, Brazil
`moisesrs@lacmor.ufma.br`, `eduardo.dorneles.fs@gmail.com`,
`mateusbfrota@gmail.com`, {`alexandre.cesar,areolino`}`@ufma.br`,
`paulo.ribeiro@ecp.ufma.br`
[2] AbbVie Deutschland GmbH & Co. KG, Knollstrasse, Ludwigshafen, Germany
`marco.curado@abbvie.com`

Abstract. Machine Learning (ML) has been widely and successfully employed in different fields to estimate information from datasets. However, the necessary time to learn a motor task or to rehabilitate is mainly determined by the professional experience of medical doctor, physiotherapist and so on. Thus, this work introduces a software to measure the performance of subjects on a experiment performing a tracing task, which requires motor learning, and uses ML algorithms on the dataset acquired during this experiment. The task is divided into 1 session that has 3 blocks and each block is composed of 10 trials whereas each trial is one word. Furthermore, ML algorithms - namely k-nearest neighbours, decision tree, support vector machines and multilayer-perceptron neural network - are applied on the collected data from the experiment to estimate which block the subject currently is. The results demonstrated that there was motor learning, as well as that is possible to apply classification models to predict the block of the subject with decision tree achieving statistically significant (p-value < 0.01) best predictions. The proposed approach may be useful for health professionals when estimating the amount of training a patient requires to learn a motor task or rehabilitate.

Keywords: Motor learning · Rehabilitation · Machine Learning

1 Introduction

An enormous part of the Brazilian population has some kind of motor disease. According to the Brazilian Institute of Geography Statistics, its 2010 national census [18], 7% of the Brazilian population has some kind of motor disease,

V. G. Duffy (Ed.): HCII 2019, LNCS 11581, pp. 198–209, 2019.
https://doi.org/10.1007/978-3-030-22216-1_15

e.g. stroke, cerebral palsy and congenital disorders. Then, neuroscience studies emphasizing motor learning and rehabilitation may pave the way to reveal solutions for these patients.

Some aspects of how motor learning may occur have been studied, e.g. [24] has a review of some relevant works, presenting the main components of motor learning: information extraction, classes of control, decisions and strategies. Furthermore, [24] also presents some processes of motor learning: error-based learning, reinforcement learning and use-dependent learning.

During motor rehabilitation sessions, the professional experience - from medical doctor, physiotherapist and so on - is the predominant information about the necessary time that a patient may require to rehabilitate or improve his/her performance. The absence of more details and information may demotivate the patient and create false expectations about his/her own progress.

Machine Learning (ML) can estimate patient's data from a historical dataset [8,17,20]. These ML algorithms have been widely employed in different fields such as health, education, economy, science, technology and logistic [5]. Furthermore, these algorithms might be used to predict the necessary time that a patient may require to learn a motor task or rehabilitate.

Thus, in addition to the professional experience, other information may be used to infer patient improvement, for example historical data from rehabilitation sessions of others patients. Then, Machine Learning algorithms may be convenient for this problem once they can be used to make predictions and estimate patients improvements from a historical dataset.

This paper presents a software tool to measure and compute the performance of subjects in a tracing task [12], as well as it compares different classifiers to estimate the amount of training to learn a motor skill.

This work is divided into five sections. Section 2, Motor Learning and Models of Prediction, details some aspects of Motor Learning as well as presents some works on Models of Prediction Applied to Motor Learning and Rehabilitation. Section 3, Material and Methods, explains how the experiment was conducted. Section 4, Results, presents and discusses the experiment assessment. Finally, Sect. 5, Conclusion, summarizes the work and presents some future works.

2 Motor Learning and Models of Prediction

2.1 Motor Learning

The main studies on motor learning present three components: information extraction, classes of control, decisions and strategies [24]. These components define how motor learning may occur. Information extraction is responsible for the capabilities that the motor learning system has to influence sensory organs [15]. Another interesting aspect of information extraction is how the brain filters information. People are only able to realize changes in the environment, while performing some motor task, when the change is related to the task in execution [22]. As a result, the need to extract information or process it only happens when it is relevant to execute actions of interest to the motor task.

Any kind of motor task demands decision making from extracted information, strategies are formulated to finish the task successfully considering how or when the movement must be performed [24]. In decision making experiments a decision variable is used to represent: the experience accumulation, an evidence and a value that must be interpreted by the decision rule to finally generate a choice for the participant [4]. A decision maker is interest in obtain positive feedback while avoids negatives. Positive feedback can be understood as correct decisions while negative feedback are errors, waste of time or efforts.

Classes of control are related to the means of how optimize the motor performance, they are subdivided in predictive control, reactive control, and biomechanical control [24]. Predictive control is associated to the sensorimotor outcome delays, the prediction is kept based on the individual's experience. Meanwhile, the reactive control is related to the updates in motor commands during the execution course after new sensory perception. Finally, the biomechanical control is related to the limbs movements that have a considerable factor in motor improvement. All the three classes are adaptable and contribute to the motor learning, depending on the task that has been performed is possible that some classes contribute in a more significant manner than others.

The processes of motor learning may indicate how motor learning is acquired in neurons while focus in the used information, they are: error-based learning, reinforcement learning and use-dependent learning [24]. The sensorimotor is capable to realize if the movement outcome has been performed as expected in the error-based learning. Sensory prediction errors are interesting because they show the causes for the failure. Reinforcement learning, differently from the error-based learning, takes positives and negatives values for each performed action, without any information regarding how the motor commands should be changed for a better performance. Reinforcement learning offers the advantage of contributing more to skill learning acquisition because of its rewards signals [1]. However, reinforcement learning mechanisms are not well understood yet and a better comprehension of what might be considered a reward to the motor system still exists [24]. Use-dependent learning refers to the capability of learning based on pure movements repetition even when there is no outcome information available [24].

2.2 Models of Prediction Applied to Motor Learning and Rehabilitation

A prediction model to evaluate stroke progression using Functional Independence Measure (FIM) score has been used and collected data from a motor rehabilitation center in Japan. A prediction model was built with Stepwise Multiple Regression and obtained a 0.68 correlation coefficient [23].

Another work that intended to predict FIM has used some characteristics from 87 patients in rehabilitation after stroke. In this case, a multiple linear regression has been adopted and obtained a 0.88 correlation coefficient [20].

A prediction model to estimate the level of independence in routine activities after stroke was created. A dataset with characteristics of 65 patients - with parameters such as age, time since stroke, functional independence measure motor subscale score, functional independence measure cognitive subscale score, stroke impairment assessment set score, Berg balance scale score, and vitality index - was used to predict the future functional independence measure motor subscale score. They used Multiple Stepwise Regression to obtain the model and had a coefficient of determination computed of 0.60 [17].

Rather than using 3 level resolution per item on the Fugl-Meyer Assessment (FMA), [6] proposed another approach using 14 levels, i.e. obtaining more resolution, aiming to detect patient's smaller improvements. The proposed was to use 14 fractional digits resolution instead of 3, in 6 upper-extremity FMA items, so the patient's minor improvements could be more accurately detected. Some predict models were used - such as Linear Regression, Bayesian Linear Regression, Neural Network Regression, Boosted Decision Tree Regression and Decision Forest Regression - to convert these 3 levels to the 14 levels that were proposed. The best result was with a Neural Network Regression that obtained a 0.58 Pearson Correlation Coefficient.

Support Vector Machine has been used to predict the patients functional damage with stroke and achieved a 0.85 of accuracy [3]. This work shows how Machine Learning approaches may be used in rehabilitation scenarios.

Another interesting approach evaluates the applications of collected data from inertial wearable sensors to support decision making in rehabilitation clinics [21]. The collected data were used to predict the FIM from patients in rehabilitation. Machine learning algorithms were trained with 20 patients data in order to predict their FIM. The methods used were: Support Vector Regression (SVR), Linear Regression and Random Regression Forest. The algorithm with the best result was SVR with a 0.97 Pearson Correlation Coefficient.

Machine Learning was also employed to predict improvements of 55 patients in first stage treatment after stroke. The attribute to compute patient improvement was Motor (FIM) and the machine learning algorithm applied was the Support Vector Regression - which had three different kernels i.e. Polynomial, Gaussian and Linear - with a Pearson Correlation Coefficient between 0.71 and 0.81 [16].

3   Materials and Methods

3.1   Participants

The participants of this experiment were students at Federal University of Maranhão (UFMA). Initially a group of 3 healthy people, i.e. people without motor constraint, were volunteers in this experiment. All participants provided written authorization in order for their data to be used in a publication whereas at the same time this work maintains the confidentiality of the participants.

For the selection of participants, a neurological history was also carried out. They were asked about any constraint to perform a motor task. Subjects with any motor problem would be excluded from this study. This questionnaire is used to know which hand is used in daily living activities. The subject must use his/her non-dominant hand, which in this case was the left hand and was measured with the "Edinburgh Handedness Inventory" [2], once only right-handed participants were considered in this study. The use of the non-dominant hand created the environment to learn a motor skill necessary to accomplish the task.

3.2   Study Design

A software for the Tracing Task, which was a task proposed by [12], was developed. The experiment replicated the Tracing Task once it is an interesting task to study motor learn. The software was developed using the Pygame Framework [19] of the Python programming language [14].

The task consists of subjects drawing a series of words with the aid of a Wacom tablet with their left hand, i.e. their non-dominant hand. The Tracing Task is depicted on Fig. 1.

Fig. 1. Tracing Task. The participant traces a word that is shown on the screen whereas the cursor on it is controlled with a pen on a tablet. Image Source: Own Authors

Each subject experiences one session, which has 3 blocks and each block is composed of 10 trials whereas each trial is one word. All the subjects performed the same words. The words used were chosen from a free database (Invoke IT Limited[1]). They are the most common words of 5 letters of the Brazilian Portuguese language. The words were written with a free font (League Script[2]).

The template and the traced word undergo a process of blurring so that participants who do not perfectly match the shape of the drawing are not harmed.

---

[1] https://invokeit.wordpress.com/frequency-word-lists/.
[2] https://www.theleagueofmoveabletype.com/.

The blurring process consists of a convolution of each image with a Gaussian kernel of size 50 × 50 pixels. These filtered images are thresholded, i.e. they are converted to binary images, and later a metric (percentage error), which is a difference between these binary images, is generated. This whole process is illustrated on Fig. 2.

Fig. 2. Method to calculate the error in the Tracing Task. (A) is an example of a trial, the image above is the template image whereas the image below is the traced image. **(B)** presents the filtered images. **(C)** is the thresholding of the images. **(D)** shows the subtraction of the images. Percentage error is obtained from **D**. Image Source: Own Authors

After the data was acquired, they were formatted in Comma Separated Value (CSV) so that processing and analysis can be done. The CSV format was chosen for simplicity and for being widely used in statistical analysis.

3.3   Complementary Samples

Complementary samples were created from those obtained by the experiment in order to verify how the result would may be with more subjects. These samples were related to the average performance of the 3 blocks, for the two measures of performance: necessary time to trace the word and the percentage error.

A Gaussian noise with zero mean and standard deviation 0.01 (value defined based on the magnitude of the data) was added to the real data. A new dataset was generated, which contained 18 participants generated based on the 3 real subjects, i.e. for each one of these 3 participants 6 subjects were generated.

3.4   Classification Models

A subject performs a training, which is composed of session, blocks, and trials. ML algorithms are used - based on error and the time to perform the task - to predict the amount of blocks that the subject has performed. Classification models were built using the following algorithms: k-nearest neighbours (KNN), decision tree (AD), support vector machines (SVM) and multilayer-perceptron neural network (MLP) [9,10].

The scikit-learn [11] was used: (i) the K value in KNN was set to 3 and with Euclidian distance; (ii) the default configurations of decision tree were used; (iii) for SVM, the radial basis kernel was used; and (iv) MLP neural network used the logistic sigmoid function activation, the hidden layer size was set to 10, the max number of epochs was 10000 and the solver function chosen was Quasi-Newton method.

3.5   Validation

The validation method for the constructed models was 5-fold cross-validation whereas accuracy, recall, and specificity were used as evaluation metrics.

For statistical analysis the models were executed 10 times by randomly blending the dataset. An Analysis of Variance (ANOVA) was carried out to determine whether there was a statistically significant difference between the classifiers. The statistical analyzes were carried out using the R programming language. All statistical tests were two-sided and a p-value < 0.01 was used as statistically significant.

4   Results

4.1   Motor Learning

The results shown on this subsection are from the 3 real subjects. The motor learning characteristic can be observed on Fig. 3. According to [7] and [13], the motor learning occurs when there is a balance between speed and accuracy in performing a task, as depicted on Fig. 3.

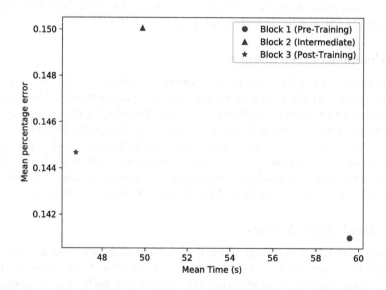

Fig. 3. Motor Learning. The red dot represents the average performance of participants in Block 1 (Pre-Training). The green triangle represents the average performance of participants in Block 2 (Intermediate). The blue star represents the average performance of participants in Block 3 (Post-Training). The mean performance is a function of the mean time of movement (abscissa) and the mean percentage error per block (ordinate). Image Source: Own Authors (Color figure online)

On Fig. 3, it can be seen that there is a motor learning comparing Pre-Training with Post-Training. In Pre-Training, the participants had on average a small percentage error but the average execution time was greater in comparison to the other blocks. In the Intermediate training, the participants decreased the average time but increased the average percentage error. In post-training it is possible to observe a balance between time and average percentage error. Thus, there was motor learning between Block 1 and Block 3.

4.2 Comparative Analysis of Models

The results shown on this subsection are from the 18 simulated subjects. Figures 4, 5 and 6 show the performance for three different metrics - Accuracy, Specificity and Recall, respectively - for different classification models: Neural Network Multi Layer Perceptron (MLP); Support Vector Machine (SVM) with kernel RBF; K-Nearest Neighbors (KNN); and Decision Tree (AD).

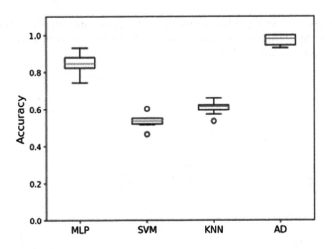

Fig. 4. Box plot of the performance for different classification models and the metric is Accuracy. The models are Neural Network Multi Layer Perceptron (MLP); Support Vector Machine (SVM) with kernel RBF; K-Nearest Neighbors (KNN); and Decision Tree (AD). Image Source: Own Authors

The Decision tree algorithm presented a superior performance compared to the others with: an average accuracy of 0.97; specificity (0.98); and recall (0.95). The mean performance of the neural network MLP was: accuracy = 0.84, specificity = 0.88 and recall 0.78. The performance of the SVM method was: accuracy = 0.53, specificity = 0.55 and recall 0.55. The performance of the KNN method was: accuracy = 0.60, specificity = 0.66 and recall 0.51.

It can be seen, Table 1, that there was a statistically significant difference between, i.e. p value was less than 0.01, the classifier for all the metrics (accuracy, specificity and recall).

A post hoc test, Tukey multiple comparisons of means, was performed to verify the statistical difference between the results and it is shown on Table 2.

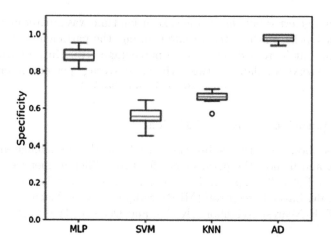

Fig. 5. Box plot of the performance for different classification models and the metric is Specificity. The models are MLP; SVM with kernel RBF; KNN; and AD. Image Source: Own Authors

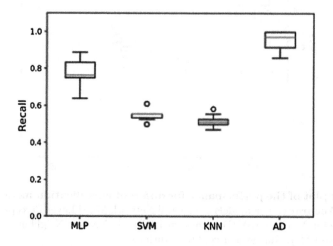

Fig. 6. Box plot of the performance for different classification models and the metric is Recall. The models are MLP; SVM with kernel RBF; KNN; and AD. Image Source: Own Authors

It can be seen that for almost all combinations the difference was statistically relevant (p-value < 0.01), i.e. the decision tree was the best estimate model whereas MLP was the second better. KNN was the third better algorithm when using the accuracy and specificity metrics. However, there was no statistically significant difference between KNN and SVM for the recall metric.

Table 1. ANOVA for Classification Models. Df stands for Degrees of Freedom, Df.res is the residue of the Degrees of Freedom, Sum Sq is the sum of squares, Sum Sq.res is the residue of the sum of squares, Mean Sq are the Mean Squares and Pr(>F) is the p-value.

Metric	Df	Df.res	Sum Sq	Sum Sq.res	Mean Sq	Pr(>F)
Accuracy	3	36	1,247	0,054	0,415	$2 * 10^{-16}$
Recall	3	36	1,275	0,093	0,425	$2 * 10^{-16}$
Specificity	3	36	1,147	0,057	0,382	$2 * 10^{-16}$

Table 2. Post hoc test - Tukey multiple comparisons of means

Algorithms	P (Accuracy)	P (Specificity)	P (Recall)
KNN-AD	0,0000000	0,0000000	0,0000000
MLP-AD	0,0000001	0,0000366	0,0000000
SVM-AD	0,0000000	0,0000000	0,0000000
MLP-KNN	0,0000000	0,0000000	0,0000000
SVM-KNN	0,0018110	0,0000126	0,4004624
SVM-MLP	0,0000000	0,0000000	0,0000000

5   Conclusion

This work introduced a software to measure the performance of subjects on a tracing task. This task and setup replicated an interesting previous work from motor skill learning. However, the present work went beyond the replicated study. The collected data with the software was also used on classification algorithms rather than only to indicate motor learning during the task, which was also demonstrated. This data was employed to predict the block a subject is using his/her dataset.

The results suggest that is possible to apply classification models to correlate the movement time and the percentage error with the number of blocks. This approach, which is proposed on this work, might be useful to estimate the number of trials, blocks, and sessions a patient requires to rehabilitate. Future works will be devoted to have more subjects as well as to use the proposed approach with patient.

Acknowledgment. The authors acknowledge FAPEMA for the financial support for this research specially for scholarship and Proc. UNIVERSAL-01294/16.

References

1. Abe, M., Schambra, H., Wassermann, E.M., Luckenbaugh, D., Schweighofer, N., Cohen, L.G.: Reward improves long-term retention of a motor memory through induction of offline memory gains. Curr. Biol. **21**(7), 557–562 (2011)

2. Espírito-Santo, H., Pires, C.F., Garcia, I.Q., Daniel, F., Silva, A.G.d., Fazio, R.L.: Preliminary validation of the Portuguese Edinburgh Handedness Inventory in an adult sample. Appl. Neuropsychol. Adult **24**(3), 275–287 (2017)
3. Forkert, N.D., Verleger, T., Cheng, B., Thomalla, G., Hilgetag, C.C., Fiehler, J.: Multiclass support vector machine-based lesion mapping predicts functional outcome in ischemic stroke patients. PloS ONE **10**(6), e0129569 (2015)
4. Gold, J.I., Shadlen, M.N.: The neural basis of decision making. Annu. Rev. Neurosci. **30**, 235–274 (2007)
5. Jordan, M.I., Mitchell, T.M.: Machine learning: trends, perspectives and prospects. Science **349**(6245), 255–260 (2015)
6. Julianjatsono, R., Ferdiana, R., Hartanto, R.: High-resolution automated Fugl-Meyer Assessment using sensor data and regression model. In: 3rd International Conference on Science and Technology-Computer (ICST), pp. 28–32. IEEE (2017)
7. Kitago, T., Krakauer, J.W.: Motor learning principles for neurorehabilitation. Handb. Clin. Neurol. **110**, 93–103 (2013)
8. Lin, W.Y., et al.: Predicting post-stroke activities of daily living through a machine learning-based approach on initiating rehabilitation. Int. J. Med. Inf. **111**, 159–164 (2018)
9. Marsland, S.: Machine Learning: An Algorithmic Perspective. CRC Press, Boca Raton (2015)
10. Norvig, P., Russell, S.: Inteligência Artificial, vol. 1, 3rd edn. Elsevier, Rio de Janeiro (2014)
11. Pedregosa, F., et al.: Scikit-learn: machine learning in Python. J. Mach. Learn. Res. **12**, 2825–2830 (2011)
12. Prichard, G., Weiller, C., Fritsch, B., Reis, J.: Effects of different electrical brain stimulation protocols on subcomponents of motor skill learning. Brain Stimul. **7**(4), 532–540 (2014)
13. Reis, J., et al.: Noninvasive cortical stimulation enhances motor skill acquisition over multiple days through an effect on consolidation. Proc. Nat. Acad. Sci. **106**(5), 1590–1595 (2009)
14. Rossum, G.: Python reference manual. Technical report, Amsterdam, The Netherlands (1995)
15. Sailer, U., Flanagan, J.R., Johansson, R.S.: Eye-hand coordination during learning of a novel visuomotor task. J. Neurosci. **25**(39), 8833–8842 (2005)
16. Sale, P., et al.: Predicting motor and cognitive improvement through machine learning algorithm in human subject that underwent a rehabilitation treatment in the early stage of stroke. J. Stroke Cerebrovasc. Dis. **27**(11), 2962–2972 (2018)
17. Sato, A., Fujita, T., Ohashi, Y., Yamamoto, Y., Suzuki, K., Otsuki, K.: A prediction model for activities of daily living for stroke patients in a convalescent rehabilitation ward. J. Allied Health Sci. **7**(1), 1–6 (2016)
18. SDH/PR: Cartilha do censo 2010 pessoas com deficiência. Secretaria de Direitos Humanos da Presidência da República (2012). http://www.pessoacomdeficiencia.gov.br/app/sites/default/files/publicacoes/cartilha-censo-2010-pessoas-com-deficienciareduzido.pdf
19. Shinners, P.: Pygame (2011). http://pygame.org/
20. Sonoda, S., Saitoh, E., Nagai, S., Okuyama, Y., Suzuki, T., Suzuki, M.: Stroke outcome prediction using reciprocal number of initial activities of daily living status. J. Stroke Cerebrovasc. Dis. **14**(1), 8–11 (2005)
21. Sprint, G., Cook, D.J., Weeks, D.L., Borisov, V.: Predicting functional independence measure scores during rehabilitation with wearable inertial sensors. IEEE Access **3**, 1350–1366 (2015)

22. Triesch, J., Ballard, D.H., Hayhoe, M.M., Sullivan, B.T.: What you see is what you need. J. Vis. **3**(1), 9 (2003)
23. Tsuji, T., Liu, M., Sonoda, S., Domen, K., Chino, N.: The stroke impairment assessment set: its internal consistency and predictive validity. Arch. Phys. Med. Rehabil. **81**(7), 863–868 (2000)
24. Wolpert, D.M., Diedrichsen, J., Flanagan, J.R.: Principles of sensorimotor learning. Nat. Rev. Neurosci. **12**(12), 739 (2011)

Capture of Stability and Coordination Indicators in Virtual Training Scenarios for the Prevention of Slip, Trip, and Fall (STF) Accidents

Anika Weber[1,2,3(✉)], Peter Nickel[3], Ulrich Hartmann[1], Daniel Friemert[1], and Kiros Karamanidis[2]

[1] Department of Mathematics and Technology, University of Applied Sciences Koblenz, Remagen, Germany
weber4@hs-koblenz.de
[2] School of Applied Sciences, London Southbank University, 90 London Road, London SE1 6LN, UK
[3] Institute for Occupational Safety and Health of the German Social Accident Insurance (IFA), St. Augustin, Germany

Abstract. The aim of the project is to develop and evaluate a training environment for the prevention of falls with the help of an application in virtual reality (VR). The participants of our study walk on a treadmill with fall protection while immersing into a virtual scenario where they should cross virtual obstacles. Potential parameters reflecting the plasticity of the neuromotor system are investigated in order to search for possible learning effects and their stabilization. In addition, it will be determined how many perturbations (i.e. obstacles) are necessary to establish a learning process. The results will be used to check the experimental setup and to prepare a main study for the development of a training program that helps preventing slip, trip, and fall (STF) accidents using a VR environment. So far two pilot measurements have been completed and parameters that may indicate learning effects were calculated. Initial results do not reveal clear learning effects, however, they inform about relevant adjustments for setting up systematic investigations and provide important details about strategies for data acquisition and analysis.

Keywords: Accident prevention · STF hazards · Virtual reality · Transfer effects · Gait perturbation · Behavioral training

1 Introduction

In Germany, about 20% of all accidents at work are associated with slipping, tripping and falling (STF). A significant percentage of the 176,000 STF accidents in 2015, i.e. almost 3,500 led to such serious injuries that those affected received an accident pension [1]. In addition to painful injuries and even permanent damage to those affected, the accident insured companies incur additional expenses because of lost working days of their employees. Therefore, the prevention of STF accidents has high

© Springer Nature Switzerland AG 2019
V. G. Duffy (Ed.): HCII 2019, LNCS 11581, pp. 210–219, 2019.
https://doi.org/10.1007/978-3-030-22216-1_16

relevance not only for occupational health and safety (OSH) but also for economic and social reasons.

Statistics show that a majority (about 60%) of falls take place on ground level resulting from slips and trips [1]. Causes of accidents in this group are manifold and diverse. They may refer to damages of the ground floor, slippery walking ways or left over working and operating equipment on the ground floor. Sometimes, accidents seemingly occur for no reason on stairs or paths. Preventive measures should be based to the hierarchy of controls (STOP model) and take into account a structural redesign that prevents STF hazards as far as possible (e.g. work areas without steps, anti-slip floors). Furthermore, organizational and personal measures (e.g. tidying up work areas and work shoes as personal protective equipment) must not be neglected [2, 3].

In addition to the above-mentioned prevention measures, behavioral prevention measures are particularly suitable for actively involving a large number of potentially affected employees in prevention activities. There are fall prevention programs aiming at training of balance, orientation and reactivity. Investigations carried out in these trainings point to slight improvements in dynamic balance and responsiveness [4]. Recent findings in the development of training concepts to reduce STF hazards indicate that some of the disadvantages of training (e.g. decreasing motivation and endurance of participation, high and long-lasting expenditure of time, availability of training equipment) must be overcome to improve the outcome.

Mechanical training with older people (65 ± 7 yr) has already shown that the neuromotor system has a high plasticity for repeated unexpected perturbations and has the ability to maintain adaptations over longer periods of time (about 1.5 years) [5]. Effects of the use of mechanical perturbation were found to be long-term effects with low training effort and they were rated to reduce the risk of fall injuries [5]. Training studies with perturbations show that the neuromotor system adapts and learns to deal with situations by continuous repetition [6]. Acquired behavioral strategies in trainings are probable to provide long-term fall prevention.

Simulation techniques such as virtual reality (VR) have increasingly being used in training research and for the development of training programs. This is due to easy access to physical training devices in VR, more flexibility for training programs in terms of location and time, and, in addition to modeling options for realistic contexts of training scenarios that may also result in options for the implementation of training content [7].

With the help of VR, several training programs have already been developed that appear relevant and effective in the context of STF accident prevention. Simple training with visual stimuli and postural standing training in a virtual environment resulted in improved static equilibrium parameters (e.g. in terms of limits of stability and confidence ellipse) [8]. Over time, however, these effects are gradually diminishing. In VR-supported training for people with Parkinson's disease, gait parameters improve. In addition, characteristics of cognitive performance improve in terms of better planning capabilities when dodging objects [9]. Treadmill training, in which perturbation is triggered by a sudden inclination of the virtual image, lead to a better interception strategy during transfer into real slipping situations. This can reduce the occurrence of falls. However, long-term effects were not investigated [10]. In another study, visual perturbations were used and compared to visual combined with physical perturbations.

The adjustment and variability in gait induced by purely visual perturbations caused compensatory changes in gait parameters like those obtained in response to physical perturbations [11].

Stimulated by these positive findings, the present study is investigating whether and to what extent criteria from real training settings can depict and reflect aspects of learning success from virtual settings.

2 Methods

2.1 Participant Preparation and Training Procedure

Two healthy young adults participated in the pilot study (Table 1). Participants provided informed consent to take part in the pilot study. They reported adequate or corrected visual acuity, color and stereo vision. Participants did not report orthopedic or neurological impairments.

Table 1. Participant characteristics

	Participant 1	Participant 2
Age (years)	22	26
Sex	Female	Male
Height (m)	1.72	1.79
Body mass (kg)	70	91

Investigations were conducted in the biomechanical laboratory of the University of Applied Sciences Koblenz, RAC, Department of Technology and Mathematics. The participants walked through a virtual course of obstacles on a real treadmill (pluto med, h/p/cosmos, Germany) as an endless walking distance and they stepped over virtual obstacles in recurring sections while walking. For the participant's safety they wore a safety belt on the upper body and the virtual environment included hand rails mapped to the physical handrails of the treadmill. The virtual scene is shown in Fig. 1. A motion capturing system (Qualisys, Sweden) in combination with the VR software system Unity (Version 2018.2.18f1, Unity Technologies, USA) supported acquisition and logging of measurement data. Unity also served for modeling and simulating the virtual environment, which also presented perturbations to the participant on a virtual tour wearing the head mounted display (HMD) HTC Vive Pro (HTC Corporation, Taiwan) with a wireless adapter. In addition, data from the motion capturing system was used to visualize the schematic human body in VR. The virtual environment was constructed using assets in Unity. The handrail was built with Solidworks (Education Edition, Dassault Systems, France) and imported in Unity. Potentially relevant movement parameters for the plasticity of neuromotor systems were recorded, especially during crossing of virtual obstacles (e.g. toe clearance, toe distance and crossing versus precrossing stride length) [12].

The treadmill speed was set to 1.3 m/s according to the speed of the virtual environment. In intervals of about 15 s to 25 s chosen at random, after initially hitting the ground with the foot, a perturbation obstacle was generated 1.5 m in front of the participant. The dimensions of the obstacle were 100 mm by 100 mm by 4000 mm. Stepping over the obstacle triggered an event in the motion capturing software Qualisys Track Manager (QTM). Participants were required to always step over the obstacle with the right foot. Before the measurement was started, the participants were asked to move randomly for about 15 s. This information was used to create an AIM (automatic identification of markers) model that is needed for the visualization of the participants' body in VR. At the beginning, participants walked for about 3 min on the treadmill using VR without perturbations to get used to walking on the treadmill with HMD and VR. Afterwards, the perturbation session started. The participant walked on the treadmill for 50 perturbations.

Fig. 1. Reproduction of participant stepping over an obstacle in VR.

As participants walked on the treadmill, gait kinematics were measured using an 8-camera Qualisys motion capture system. Kinematic data was recorded at 120 Hz using a 42-marker modified dynamicus alaska model. Four infrared markers were placed on the HMD and six markers were placed on the trunk (right and left acromioclavicular, C7, T10, clavicle and sternum). Four markers were placed on the pelvis (right and left anterior and posterior superior iliac spine). 10 markers were placed at the left and right arms (elbow lateral, elbow medial, wrist lateral, wrist medial, third meta head).

22 markers were placed at the left and right legs (medial knee, lateral knee, tibia, medial ankle, lateral ankle, heel, back foot medial, back foot lateral, second meta head, fifth meta head and toe). A fully equipped participant is shown in Fig. 2.

Fig. 2. Measurement setup on the treadmill with a participant wearing markers. The participant is safeguarded against fall by a safety belt on the upper body attached to the beam of the treadmill.

2.2   Data Analysis

Human gait is characterized by a cyclic pattern of toe offs (TO), and touch downs (TD) on alternating sides of the body. The time at which the toe leaves the ground is called TO. TD is the time frame at which the foot initially hits ground. TO and TD can be identified by analyzing the changes in position of kinematic markers placed on the participant. From these events, temporal parameters such as step length (SL: distance from TD to TO of the opposing feet) and step width (SW: distance from medial to lateral distance between the feet) can be determined. The quantification of gait characteristics can be used to investigate the participant's ability to control balance during exercise and to study balance compensation in response to external disturbances.

Anatomical markers from the motion capture system were labeled and processed in QTM. All calculations were performed using a customized routine written in MATLAB (Version 9.3.0, The Mathworks Inc., Natick, USA).

The calculated parameters are shown in Fig. 3. Toe clearance is calculated as the height of the toe marker when the marker is above the leading edge of the perturbation obstacle minus the height of the obstacle. Critical toe clearance is calculated as the minimum distance between toe and heel marker and front and rear edge of the perturbation obstacle. Lead and trail foot distance are calculated as the horizontal distance between the toe markers and the leading edge of the obstacle at toe off. TD and TO where determined using the foot contact algorithm (FCA) [13]. Therefore, data is filtered with a low-pass filter set at 50 Hz. To identify different types of foot strikers, time frames of the vertical position of the heel and the fifth meta head markers are compared. A time interval around this minimal position is defined. To estimate touch down, FCA uses a characteristic maximum in the vertical acceleration curve of the target marker in the given approximation interval. For toe off, a local maximum in the vertical acceleration of the toe marker is detected and compared to the minimal vertical position of the toe marker. A logical operation selects the event that occurs earlier in time, which is then used to estimate the time of toe off.

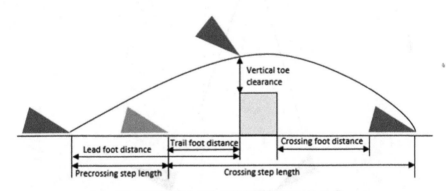

Fig. 3. Recorded gait parameters for both feet when crossing obstacles.

2.3   Margin of Stability (MoS)

In the static case, a body is stable when the center of mass (CoM) is located within the boundaries of support (BoS).

The dynamic balance control is characterized by the fact that the CoM is kept within the bounds of the feet during the gait cycle. A CoM outside the bounds of the feet represents a more unstable system and carries the risk of falling. To maintain balance under unstable conditions, healthy participants typically increase step width and MoS, and decrease step length [14].

To determine MoS, the movement of the CoM is represented as an inverted pendulum [15]. The CoM position can be determined as the average of the four pelvis markers at the time frame of TD. Extrapolated center of mass (XCoM) is calculated according to Eq. 1 [16]:

$$XCoM = CoM_{Position} + \frac{CoM_{Velocity}}{\omega_o} \tag{1}$$

$$\omega_o = \sqrt{\frac{g}{l}} \tag{2}$$

Equation 2 consists of the gravitational constant 'g' and the equivalent pendulum length 'l', which is taken as the distance from the lateral heel marker to the COM at heel strike. MoS is defined as the vertical distance between XCoM and the anterior boundary of support, which is visualized in Fig. 4.

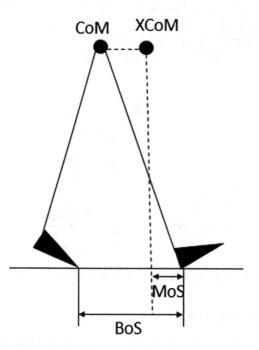

Fig. 4. Margin of stability

3   Results, Challenges and Limitations

The above-mentioned setup and data analysis could be performed without any problems. The evaluation routines are now available for further measurements in order to determine the mentioned parameters.

Future studies will also contain measuring muscular activity via EMG of the leg muscles to quantify proactive and reactive changes due to training. EMG can show co-contractions of muscles which indicate a more stiff and unstable gait.

Since the obstacles are not visible in Qualisys, they have to be calculated from given data. For this, the time at which the event was created in Qualisys is used. At this time, the toe marker is located exactly above the front edge of the obstacle. The position, speed and dimensions of the perturbation obstacle can be used to calculate the position at any time. However, the accuracy of these calculations still needs to be validated. This allows calculation of parameters such as the critical clearance for the toe and heel marker, as well as the distance to the obstacle.

The human gait has the disadvantage that the CoM lies high above a small BoS. Small deviations from a perfect body orientation lead to significant gravitational moments that accelerate the body away from this orientation and can easily move the CoM away from the BoS, which then leads to falls. In the sagittal plane, the body moves the CoM outside the BoS during each of the single support phases of the gait cycle. Therefore, it can be assumed that when this pattern is interrupted, e.g. by a suddenly appearing object or the slipping of a foot, a fall often occurs. In addition to a good reactivity, it is necessary to have a good interception strategy should a trip occur. This also requires a good general ability to balance and control appropriate muscles. Therefore, many of the STF prevention trainings use balance and strength training but they do not prevent the actual trip. Toe and heel clearance as well as critical clearance, are important parameters because they show if a trip would have occurred. In a normal learning process, participants would first step high over the obstacles but then reduce the distance to the obstacle because the body always wants to move in an efficient way.

Initial results with two participants do not reveal specific learning effects after 50 perturbations. This could be due to different reasons. One reason that parameters chosen do not indicate a learning effect could be due to VR. The field of view is restricted by the VR googles. When looking through the HMD the field of view is restricted to 100° horizontal and vertical. Therefore, in contrast to human behavior in reality, in VR participants were required to bend the head in order to look at their feet. With the restricted field of view in VR, participants cannot see the perturbation obstacles when looking straight forward/ahead. In reality, perturbations or obstacles would be visible because the field of view is about 150° vertical and 210° horizontal [17]. There are already VR glasses with a field of view of 130° vertical and 210° horizontal, which also have a better resolution than the HTC Vive. With the aim to develop training procedures for use at the shop floor or at home, the preferred choice for the HMD would rather be a cost effective consumer product. Another VR issue is related to the realism of the virtual environment and a potential impact on human behavior. The scenario could be improved by changing the lighting and using a humanoid avatar instead of a stick figure to create body presence. In this scenario, it would also be possible to use photorealistic models of the environment and the obstacle. In order to find out more about this issue, a usability study should inform about the quality of the virtual environment and its use as a training scenario in the present context.

Maybe the training period was too short to determine training effects. Therefore, it is possible to do three training periods of 15 min length with a break of 5 min between them.

The task may have been too difficult at given treadmill speed, so that the participants were predominantly concentrating at holding their balance while walking on the treadmill with VR. While VR only influences postures while working stationary by small margins [18], several studies have already shown gait changes while walking in virtual reality [11], e.g. a reduced SL and increased MoS indicating an unstable gait, a reduced treadmill speed may result in improvements in training parameters.

In future measurements, it will be investigated whether participants no longer need to hold on to the handrails with reduced speed of the treadmill so that participants no longer need to hold on to the handrails. In addition, the familiarization period with VR and the treadmill should be extended. This should lead to the participants walking at the right speed themselves and therefore no longer having to hold onto the handrails. Then it is also possible to determine MoS, which is a very reliable parameter for dynamic balance.

Another effect could possibly be diminished by reducing the speed of the treadmill. Longer Treadmills have to be considered so that participants do not have to walk in the rear of the treadmill, as otherwise they would come up against the cover of the treadmill motor when crossing obstacles.

4 Conclusion

The prevention of STF accidents is not only of utmost importance from an occupational safety and health point of view, but also very relevant for economic and social reasons. The project is in the process of developing a VR training program that should enable fall prevention possibly after only a single training session. Several studies have shown VR to be a promising tool to support behavioral learning in virtually hazardous situations in a safe environment [10, 11]. When a training effect can be demonstrated, our approach should be able to serve a solid basis for conducting training courses for example as part of events to promote health and safety at the workplace. A desirable aim is to develop recommendations for further actions.

Initial results do not reveal clear learning effects, however, they inform about relevant adjustments for setting up systematic investigations and provide important details about strategies for data acquisition and analysis in the calculated parameters.

References

1. DGUV: Statistik. Arbeitsunfallgeschehen 2015. Deutsche Gesetzliche Unfallversicherung (DGUV), Berlin (2016). https://publikationen.dguv.de/dguv/pdf/10002/au_statistik_2015.pdf
2. Lehto, M.R., Cook, B.T.: Occupational health and safety management. In: Salvendy, G. (ed.) Handbook of Human Factors and Ergonomics, pp. 701–733. Wiley, Hoboken (2012). ISBN 978-0-470-52838-9
3. EU OSH Framework Directive 89/391/EEC of 12 June 1989 on the introduction of measures to encourage improvements in the safety and health of workers at work. Official Journal of the European Union L 183, 29/06/1989, pp. 1–8 (2008)
4. Mohr, J.-O.: Fit gegen das Stolpern – Projektstudie der HFUK Nord. In: Ellegast, R. (ed.) 6. DGUV Fachgespräch Ergonomie. Zusammenfassung der Vorträge vom 2/3, November 2016, pp. 125–127. Deutsche Gesetzliche Unfallversicherung e. V. (DGUV), Berlin (2017). ISBN 978-3-86423-201-5

5. Epro, G., Mierau, A., Mccrum, C., Leyendecker, M., Bruggemann, G.-P., Karamanidis, K.: Retention of gait stability improvements over 1.5 years in older adults: effects of perturbation exposure and triceps surae neuromuscular exercise. J. Neurophysiol. **119**(6), 2229–2240 (2018). https://doi.org/10.1152/jn.00513.2017

6. Pai, Y.-C., Yang, F., Bhatt, T., Wang, E.: Learning from laboratory-induced falling: long-term motor retention among older adults. Age **36**(3), 1367–1376 (2014). https://doi.org/10.1007/s11357-014-9640-5

7. Hale, K.S., Stanney, K.M. (eds.): Handbook of Virtual Environments: Design, Implementation, and Applications. CRC Press, Boca Raton (2015). ISBN 9781138074637

8. Duque, G., et al.: Effects of balance training using a virtual-reality system in older fallers. Clin. Interv. Aging **8**, 257–263 (2013). https://doi.org/10.2147/cia.s41453

9. Mirelman, A., Maidan, I., Herman, T., Deutsch, J.E., Giladi, N., Hausdorff, J.M.: Virtual reality for gait training: can it induce motor learning to enhance complex walking and reduce fall risk in patients with parkinson's disease? J. Gerontol. Ser. Biol. Sci. Med. Sci. **66A**(2), 234–240 (2010). https://doi.org/10.1093/gerona/glq201

10. Parijat, P., Lockhart, T.E., Liu, J.: Effects of perturbation-based slip training using a virtual reality environment on slip-induced falls. Ann. Biomed. Eng. **43**(4), 958–967 (2014). https://doi.org/10.1007/s10439-014-1128-z

11. Riem, L., Van Dehy, J., Onushko, T., Beardsley, S.: Inducing compensatory changes in gait similar to external perturbations using an immersive head mounted display. In: Proceedings of the 2018 IEEE Conference on Virtual Reality and 3D User Interfaces (VR), pp. 128–135. IEEE, New York (2018). https://doi.org/10.1109/vr.2018.8446432

12. Rietdyk, S., Rhea, C.K.: The effect of the visual characteristics of obstacles on risk of tripping and gait parameters during locomotion. Ophthalmic Physiol. Opt. **31**(3), 302–310 (2011). https://doi.org/10.1111/j.1475-1313.2011.00837.x

13. Maiwald, C., Sterzing, T., Mayer, T.A., Milani, T.L.: Detecting foot-to-ground contact from kinematic data in running. Footwear Sci. **1**(2), 111–118 (2009). https://doi.org/10.1080/19424280903133938

14. Hak, L., et al.: Speeding up or slowing down? Gait adaptations to preserve gait stability in response to balance perturbations. Gait Posture **36**(2), 260–264 (2012). https://doi.org/10.1016/j.gaitpost.2012.03.005

15. Winter, D.: Human balance and posture control during standing and walking. Gait Posture **3**(4), 193–214 (1995). https://doi.org/10.1016/0966-6362(96)82849-9

16. Hof, A.L., Gazendam, M.G.J., Sinke, W.E.: The condition for dynamic stability. J. Biomech. **38**(1), 1–8 (2005). https://doi.org/10.1016/j.jbiomech.2004.03.025

17. Traquair, H.M.: An Introduction to Clinical Perimetry. Henry Kimpton, London (1938)

18. Friemert, D., Saala, F., Hartmann, U., Ellegast, R.: Similarities and differences in posture during simulated order picking in real life and virtual reality. In: Duffy, Vincent G. (ed.) DHM 2018. LNCS, vol. 10917, pp. 41–53. Springer, Cham (2018). https://doi.org/10.1007/978-3-319-91397-1_4

Effect of Selective Training Device in the Mono-Articular Muscle of Lower Limbs

Takashi Yoshikawa[1]([✉]), Ryuga Sadaoka[1], Tadashi Akehi[1],
Tomonori Inoue[1], Yuichi Suzuki[2], and Takamasa Omori[2]

[1] National Institute of Technology, Niihama College, Yagumocho 7-1, Niihama,
Ehime, Japan
yosikawa@mec.niihama-nct.ac.jp
[2] Matsuyama Rehabilitation Hospital, Matsuyama, Japan

Abstract. In rehabilitation, muscle weakness in long-term bed resting is remarkable in the mono-articular muscle, but in the conventional muscular strength training, a strong load is also applied to the bi-articular muscle, and selective strengthening of the mono-articular muscle is often difficult in many cases. Therefore, utilizing the output direction control characteristics of the human body lower limbs, we developed a selective training device in the mono-articular muscle of lower limbs that even one patient can use. After being evaluated at the actual clinical site, it was used as training for hospitalized patients and confirmed the effectiveness as a device.

Keywords: Mono-articular muscle · Output force distribution ·
Rehabilitation device

1 Introduction

As a role of rehabilitation for joint diseases, walking necessary for early social reintegration and reacquisition of lower limb muscle activity are indispensable. Postoperative patients such as lower limb bone fracture, total knee arthroplasty (TKA), total hip arthroplasty (THA), etc. are accompanied by surgical invasion and long-term bedding, and single joints that are considered to be anti-gravity muscles compared with bipartite muscles Muscle contraction of the muscle is remarkable, and selective training of a mono-articular muscle is also an important matter of a physical therapist. However, knee joint extension movement with weight load applied to the distal end of the lower limb at the sitting posture, which is performed as a voluntary training other than training time, causes excessive contraction in the rectus femoris muscle (RF), a bipartite muscle It is difficult to say that it is effective as a selective training of the medial vastus muscle (VM), which is a mono-articular muscle, as voluntary training to be performed by the patient himself.

To solve this problem, we modeled the musculoskeletal system of the human being with a single articulated muscle and a bi-articular muscle [1], and utilize the output direction control characteristic [2] clarifying the relationship between the output distribution of the lower limb tip and each muscle activity It has been suggested that it can be applied to selective strength training [3, 4]. Using this output direction control characteristic, we developed a selective training device for the lower extremity mono-articular

V. G. Duffy (Ed.): HCII 2019, LNCS 11581, pp. 220–229, 2019.
https://doi.org/10.1007/978-3-030-22216-1_17

muscle which patients can use as self-training in rehabilitation [5], aimed at actual use after clinical evaluation In this case, since we used the device for patients who are actually hospitalized for social rehabilitation and carried out the confirmation of the effect, we report on it.

2 Development of Selective Training Device for Lower Extremity Mono-articular Muscle

2.1 Output Direction Control Characteristics of Lower Limb

According to the output direction control characteristic by Kumamoto et al. [4], when extending the lower limb from the posture shown in Fig. 1, if exercising at the maximum effort of 30 to 40% or more is done, the hip joint single muscle group In the activity, the direction of the lower thigh axis (C), the direction connecting the ankle joint and the hip joint (B) in the activity of the knee joint mono-articular muscle group, the direction parallel to the thigh axis in the activity of the femoral bi-articular muscle group (A).

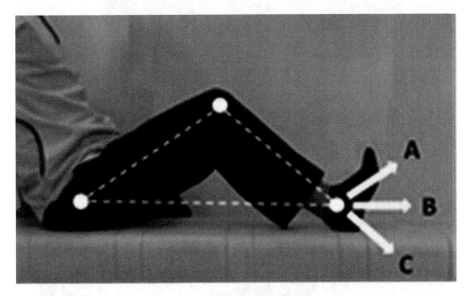

Fig. 1. Output direction control characteristics

By utilizing this characteristic, if the output direction and the load amount can be set by the device, each muscle group of the lower limb can be selectively trained.

2.2 The Developed Lower Limb Mono-Articular Muscle Training Machine

As shown in the previous section, we think that it is possible to selectively train active muscle groups by arbitrarily adjusting the extension direction (angle) of the lower limbs. Therefore, we prepared a device that can be used by the patient at the bed end sitting position or the wheelchair sitting position, and furthermore, the output direction can be adjusted.

Figure 2 shows the configuration of the training device developed this time. The guide shown in this figure is for determining the direction of extension of the lower limbs, and it is possible to adjust the height and angle of the guide.

A guide
plate

An angle
Adjustment bar

A   height
adjustment
bar

Fig. 2. Selective training device

The loading amount was made to be able to be worn through a dedicated belt with a rubber band that is frequently used clinically. As a result, consideration has been given so that the rehabilitation staff can adjusted sensuously. Figures 3(a), (b) and (c) show a rubber band, the fixing belt, and the state where the rubber band and the belt are attached to the waist respectively.

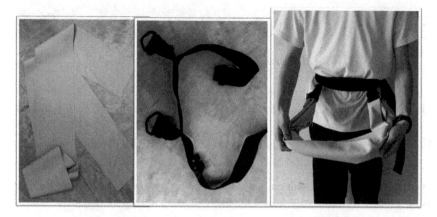

Fig. 3. (a) A rubber band, (b) The fixed belt, (c) A state of wearing the belt on the waist.

Figure 4 shows the state of the developed device and the load applied to the lower limbs, that is, the state before starting the training at the wheelchair sitting position.

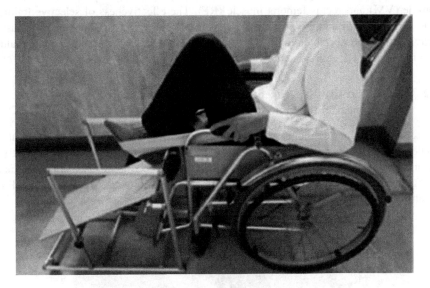

Fig. 4. Examples of using the developed device.

In order to maximize the effect of this device, it is important to adjust the angle of the guide by the rehabilitation staff. In order to minimize the vector component in the direction A caused by the activity of bipartite muscle shown in Fig. 1, it is necessary to determine the output in the direction C. However, this matter shows the activity of a mono-articular muscle in the knee joint Since the vector component in the B direction decreases, it is reasonable to decide the output between the B direction and the C direction. Therefore, when determining the output angle, the rehabilitation staff palpates the rectus femoris muscle (RF), which is the bipartite muscles of the thigh, and the medial vastus muscle (VM), which is the mono-articular muscle of the knee joint, and the muscle activity It is desirable to adjust the angle of the guide from the state.

3   Verification of Effect of Developed Device

3.1   Measurement Method of Muscle Activity

In this study, with the approval of Matsuyama City Rehabilitation Hospital Ethics Committee, subjects fully explained the research and obtained consent to the subjects. Subjects were 1 patient with THA postoperative without any neurological disease who was hospitalized at Matsuyama Rehabilitation Hospital recovery hospital. The EMG master used was EMG Master (manufactured by Ozawa Medical Instrument Co., Ltd.), sampling frequency was set to 1 kHz, and the electrode pasting site was treated with sufficient skin, then recommended by Shimono [6].

Assuming 40 [%] of the maximum effort for both loads, we perform integral EMG (IEMG) analysis in the middle 3 s when holding at the final limb position for 5 s to obtain the muscle activity amount. The desired active muscle group is the medial broad muscle (VM) and rectus femoris muscle (RF). The effectiveness of selective training was verified by dividing VM muscle activity amount during training by RF muscle activity amount and calculating VM/RF value. If the VM/RF value shows a high value, this means that RF muscle activity is suppressed.

3.2   A Comparative Experiment of the Muscle Activity Amount with Respect to the Output Angle

As a preliminary experiment, we perform an experiment to find the optimum output angle (θ [rad] in the figure). As a selective training, use the device developed at the sitting position as shown in Fig. 5, and carry out the knee joint extension movement along the guide. At that time, 10° of flexion of the knee joint was taken as the final limb position.

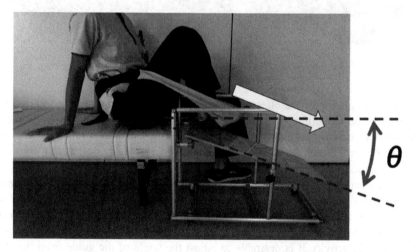

Fig. 5. Selective training with developed apparatus.

The output angle (θ) of selective training is determined by using IEMG analysis. The output angle is measured in four stages of 0 [rad] in the horizontal direction and $\pi/12$ [rad], $\pi/6$ [rad], $\pi/4$ [rad] in the downward direction. The VM and RF muscle activity ratios of each angle with respect to the muscle activity amount of output angle 0 [rad] are obtained by dividing the muscle activity amount of each output angle in VM and RF by the muscle activity amount of output angle 0 [rad]. Moreover, by comparing with the VM/RF value, we confirm the change of the muscle activity amount at the output angle and investigate the optimum output angle.

3.3   Comparative Experiment with Conventional Training Method

Figure 6 shows the weight load training method that has been practiced in clinical practice. This method is an extension movement from $\pi/2$ [rad] flexion position of the knee joint in which the weight load is added to the distal end of the lower leg at the side sitting position.

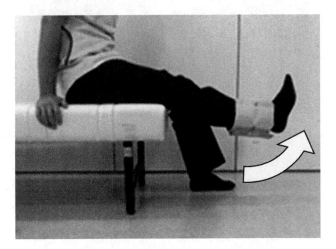

Fig. 6. Traditional weight type training.

4   Results

4.1   Selection of Optimum Output Angle

By the selective training method shown in Fig. 5, the activity amount of the mono-articular muscle (VM) and the bipartite muscle (RF) with respect to the output angle was measured. Figures 7 and 8 show the integrated EMG of VM and RF when the output angle (θ) is $\pi/4$ [rad]. The horizontal axis of the figure is 3 s measured at 1 [kHz], and the vertical axis is the myoelectric potential [mV]. The RMS value of the VM was 0.012 [mV], and the RF was found to be 0.010.

Similarly, Table 1 shows the result of integrating electromyogram analysis in each output direction. The muscle activity ratio and the VM/RF value in the case where the muscle activity amount in the 0 [rad] direction which is the maximum value is 100 are shown.

It was found that VM, RF muscle activity rate and VM/RF value tended to decrease with increase of output angle in selective training. The higher the VM/RF value, the more selective training effect is shown. Therefore, an output angle of 0 [rad] with a higher VM/RF value and the highest muscle activity rate of VM is determined as an optimum angle.

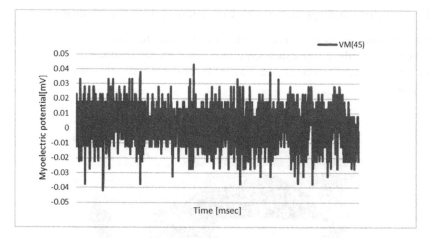

Fig. 7. Output of π /4 [rad] direction of mono-articular muscle group.

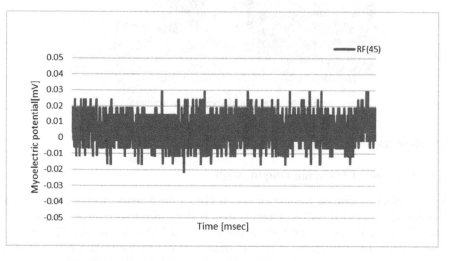

Fig. 8. Output of π /4 [rad] direction of bipartite muscle group.

Table 1. Muscle activity amount per output direction

Angle [rad]	$\Sigma|VM|$[mV]	$\Sigma|RF|$[mV]	VM/VM_0	RF/RF_0	VM/RF
0	103.5	63.8	100	100	1.62
$\pi/12$	84.9	62.3	82.1	97.7	1.36
$\pi/6$	31.7	24.3	30.7	38.1	1.31
$\pi/4$	27.5	23	26.6	36.0	1.20

4.2   Effectiveness Verification of Selective Training

Table 2 shows the selective training at the output angle 0 [rad] determined in the previous section (Fig. 5) and the muscle activity amount and VM/RF value of the conventional type of weight load training (Fig. 6). It can be seen that the amount of activity of the VM in the conventional training method is larger than that of the selective training method and the RF activity is also very large. However, the VM/RF value is 0.44 for the weight load training and 1.62 for the selective training. In other words, by training with the optimum output angle using the selection training device produced this time, it was about 4 times higher than the conventional method.

Table 2. Effect of selective training.

Training type	$\Sigma|VM|$[mV]	$\Sigma|RF|$[mV]	VM/RF
Selective	103.5	63.8	1.62
Traditional	177	404.1	0.44

5   Discussion

Figure 9 shows VM/RF values at four output angles of the selective training method and the VM/RF value in conventional weight load training. The change in VM/RF value for each output angle shown in the same figure is similar to the tendency of the execution muscle force in the output direction of the lower limb tip for the healthy persons of Oshima et al. [1, 2] and the lower limb output direction. We believe that regulation of lower limb output direction is effective as selective training of muscle fr this postoperative patient. On the other hand, in order to suppress the vector in direction A shown in Fig. 1 which occurs during RF activity, we considered that it is effective to adjust the output angle in the C direction. However, in the case of 0 [deg] indicating B direction, the output angle became optimum. This is considered to be due to the fact that the decrease in the muscle activity rate of VM was marked more than the RF in this case with the increase of the output angle.

In addition, the VM/RF value shows a high value at all output angles of selective training compared with the value of the conventional weight load training. The weight load training compared in this study seems to have promoted the muscle activity of RF, because the initial motion output includes many vector components in direction A shown in Fig. 1. Especially postoperative patients who are forced to stay in bed for a long period of time, VM's muscle contraction tends to be more pronounced, I believe that it is partly due to the fact that who are difficult to activate VMs.

On the other hand, many users intuitively understand the convenience of weight load training considering preparation time and storage place. Therefore, although the developed selective training device has an advantage as an effect, it is thought that it is necessary to improve against the convenience of the user. Devices that are not used in the clinical setting have no existential value and can not be neglected to listen to the user's voice in developing the device.

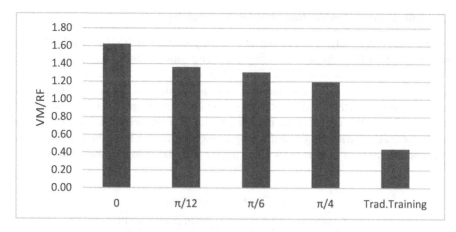

Fig. 9. VM/RF activity rate against difference in output angle.

6 Conclusions

In this study, compared with the weight load training, we confirmed the effect of selective training of the lower limb mono-articular muscle in hospitalized patients using the developed device. As a result, I got the following conclusion.

(1) By using the device developed this time, the patient can be used in the bed end sitting position or the wheelchair sitting position, and the output direction can be adjusted to make the unipolar muscle group dominate over the bipartite muscle group.

(2) In postoperative patients who are forced to lie longer for a long time, the VM/RF tends to decrease as the output angle (θ [rad] in Fig. 5) increases.

(3) From the conventional weight load training, the VM/RF value becomes higher when the selective training method using the developed device is used. That is, the activity of the mono-articular muscle group can be made larger than the activity of the bipartite muscle group.

References

1. Oshima, T.: Muscular strength evaluation by function by muscle coordinate system including one joint muscle and bipartite muscle - output of muscular strength and limb tip. J. Precis. Eng. **65**(12), 1772–1777 (1999)
2. Oshima, T., et al.: Muscle strength evaluation by leg function by muscle coordinate system including one joint muscle and bipartite muscle - estimation of effective muscle strength by function from output distribution. Precis. Eng. J. **67**(11), 1824–1828 (2001)
3. Oshima, T.: Possibility of application to rehabilitation and modeling of human musculoskeletal system. J. Precis. Eng. **73**(3), 309–312 (2007)
4. Kumamoto, W., et al.: Bi-Articular muscle - motor control and rehabilitation, pp. 146–175. Igaku-Shoin Ltd. (2008)

5. Yoshikawa, T., et al.: Development of selective training device in lower extremity mono-articular muscle. 2nd Dissertation Paper of the Kyushu Branch of the Japanese Welfare Engineering Society, pp. 20–21 (2017)
6. Shimono, T.: Surface EMG Manual Basics, 1st edn, pp. 81–114. Sakai Medical Co., Ltd. (2004)

Work Modelling and Industrial Applications

The Neuroeducational Principles of the SEE BEYOND Method Applied on the Materialization of a Fashion Collection Designed by Visually Impaired Fashion Designers

Geraldo Coelho Lima Júnior[1]([⊠]) [iD] and Rachel Zuanon[2]([⊠]) [iD]

[1] Graduate Program in Design, Anhembi Morumbi University, São Paulo, Brazil
glimadesign58@gmail.com
[2] Art Institute, State University of Campinas (UNICAMP), Campinas, Brazil
rzuanon@unicamp.br

Abstract. The SEE BEYOND teaching-learning method is hinged on studies of Neuroscience and Neuroeducation, so as to expand the structures of project-based methodologies conventionally applied in higher education Design courses in Brazil. This method centres on the needs of the user's body, with a view to ensure their well-being, their quality of life and their health.

This article focuses on the main contributions of the SEE BEYOND method to the Materialization aspect of the product. This occurs through the articulation between all project design stages and the ten principles underlying the method, namely: [A] Connection with the brain's nature; [B] Homeostatic Regulation; [C] Transversalities of the method; [D] Sensory-motor perception; [E] Multidimensional Abstraction; [F] Perceptive-emotional dynamics; [G] Motivational flows; [H] Connection with the individual brain; [I] Connection with the social brain; [J] Critical reflexive positioning.

This articulation is demonstrated here through the Materialization of the fashion collection "Parque Contemporâneo" (Contemporary Park), conceived by visually impaired designers. The main results of the aforementioned articulation include: [a] positive impacts relating to the exercise of the designer's role and actions in the project-oriented process; [b] greater correspondence between the product and the user's needs; [c] enhancement of the product's functional and aesthetic potential; [d] enhancement of the use experience provided by the product.

Keywords: Design · Neuroscience · Neuroeducation · SEE BEYOND · Visual impairment

1 Introduction

In our contemporary times, the Neurosciences, as a particularly beneficial field of knowledge for cooperation with other fields of applied science, has been making significant contributions to the expansion of these limits. The lens of Behavioural and

© Springer Nature Switzerland AG 2019
V. G. Duffy (Ed.): HCII 2019, LNCS 11581, pp. 233–250, 2019.
https://doi.org/10.1007/978-3-030-22216-1_18

Cognitive Neuroscience broaden the comprehension of the mechanisms that engender human behaviour and cognition, as they delve, respectively, into the study of neural structures that produce behaviours and other psychological phenomena like emotion; and into more complex mental capacities, such as language, self-consciousness, memory, etc. [1] Within the ambit of the Neuroscience-Education relationship, the contributions made by Tokuhama-Espinoza [2] can be highlighted. The author records 14 basic principles, all of which are proposed as being conducive to the activities inscribed within the scope of Neuroeducation. These principles articulate studies derived from Neuroscience, Psychology and Education as their fundamental basis, and acknowledge that: "[a] students learn a lot more when they are highly motivated than when they have no motivation; [b] stress exerts considerable impact on learning; [c] anxiety disrupts learning opportunities; [d] depressive states can interfere with learning; [e] other people's tones of voices are quickly judged in the brain as threatening or non-threatening; [f] people's faces are judged almost instantly (i.e., good or bad intentions); [g] feedback is important for learning; [h] emotions play a key role in learning; [i] movement can potentiate learning; [j] humour can potentiate learning opportunities; [k] nutrition exerts impact on learning; [l] sleep has impact on the consolidation of memory; [m] learning styles (cognitive preferences) derive from each individual's unique brain structure; [n] different classroom practices are justified by the varied intelligence of students".

In addition to these principles, which refer both to the learner's individuality and to the teacher's didactic approach in the classroom, Tokuhama-Espinosa [2] adds twenty-two new principles to this scope. These new principles were formulated to widen the spectrum of performance of the previous ones by providing non-linear connections between both, as follows: "[I] each brain is unique and uniquely organized; [II] brains are specialized and not equally good at everything; [III] the brain is a complex and dynamic system, which undergoes changes on a daily basis according to each individual's experiences; [IV] brains are considered 'plastic' and continue to develop and reshape themselves throughout their lives; [V] learning is partly based on the brain's ability to self-correct and learn from experience, through the analysis of data and self-reflection; [VI] the search for meaning is innate to human nature; [VII] the search for meaning occurs through 'patterning'; [VIII] learning is based in part on the brain's ability to detect patterns and make approximations to learn; [IX] emotions are critical for detecting patterns; [X] learning is based in part on the brain's ability to create; [XI] learning is potentiated by challenge and inhibited by threat; [XII] the brain processes parts and wholes simultaneously (it is a parallel processor); [XIII] brains are designed for fluctuations rather than constant attention; [XIV] learning involves both focused attention and peripheral perception; [XV] the brain is social and grows in interaction (as well as in personal reflection); [XVI] learning always involves conscious and unconscious processes; [XVII] learning is developmental; [XVIII] learning engages the whole physiology (the body affects the brain and the brain controls the body); [XIX] different memory systems (short-term, long-term, work-related, habit-related, emotional, spatial) learn in different ways; [XX] new information is archived in various areas of the brain and can be evoked through different access routes; [XXI] the brain remembers best when facts and skills are embedded in natural contexts; and [XXII] Memory + Attention = Learning".

In its turn, the SEE BEYOND teaching-learning method [3–5] resides within the context of Design-Neuroeducation cooperation. This method is composed of three modules: Foundation [3]; Enhancement [4] and Materialization, all of which have a view to incorporating sensory-motor stimuli into the stages of creation and development of projects. Stemming from these stages, SEE BEYOND expands the structure of project-oriented methodologies conventionally applied in higher education Design courses in Brazil. For this purpose, this method proposes ten guiding principles, as follows: [A] Connection with the brain's nature; [B] Homeostatic regulation; [C] Transversalities of the method; [D] Sensory-motor perception; [E] Multidimensional abstraction; [F] Perceptive-emotional dynamics; [G] motivational flows; [H] Connection with the individual brain; [I] Connection with the social brain; [J] Critical reflexive positioning.

This article focuses on the major contributions of the SEE BEYOND method to the Materialization stage of the "Parque Contemporâneo" fashion collection, conceived by designers with visual impairments. In this sense, the article intends to present relevant elements to project-oriented conception and practice, with the aim of ensuring well-being, quality of life and health to the collection's potential users.

2 Methodology

The methodology of this research study articulates the main principles of the SEE BEYOND method to the stages of the Materialization process of the "Parque Contemporâneo" fashion collection. The articulations that have been carried out are specified below:

- **Data collection | [A]; [B]; [C]; [E]; [I]** – Means: online questionnaire. Sample collected: 154 (one hundred and fifty-four) participants;
- **Definition of target audience | [A]; [B]; [C]; [E]; [I]** – Gender: female. Lifestyle/Values/Behaviour: higher education level (72% complete and 28% incomplete), the majority of which are workers (79%), who lead an active way of life as they live in major Brazilian cities (83% in São Paulo and 17% in other cities). Context of use: casual, practical clothing destined for work-related activities, followed by leisure. Need: to include women with physical impairments, wheelchair users. Market segment: casualwear;
- **Concept definition (Briefing) | [A]; [B]; [C]; [E]; [F]; [G]; [H]; [I]; [J]** – "Parque Contemporâneo". Concept: the paradoxical place of leisure and work in the metropolises [nature × shopping centres]. Keywords: pleasant, pleasure and freedom;
- **Creation of the garments | [A]; [B]; [C]; [D]; [E]; [F]; [G]; [H]; [I]; [J]** – Definition of source materials/fabrics and trimmings: denim, cotton stretch fabric, satin crepe and georgette crepe. Colour palette: indigo and royal blue [both of which are the dominating colours], black and off-white. Definition of the mix of products: number of looks: 7. Quantity of garments: 15, which consist of 7 items of clothing for covering the upper body and arms (top = 1 blouse, 2 shirts, 1 tanktop shirt, 1 cropped top, 1 blazer, 1 jacket), 7 items of clothing for the lower body and legs

(bottom = 1 jeans shorts, 1 mini skirt accompanied by 1 cotton knit shorts, 1 mini skirt, 3 pairs of slacks or trousers), and 1 single-piece garment (dress). Creative development: given that the visually-impaired designers are not able to draw the items, the pieces of clothing are conceived by way of mental formulation and textual description.

- **Technical specifications sheets | [A]; [B]; [C]; [D]; [G]; [H]** – technical design on tactile boards [relief-textured surface], with the respective detailing of the items of clothing;
- **Patternmaking and grading | [A]; [B]; [C]; [D]; [E]; [G]; [H]; [I]** – carried out by an outsourced professional;
- **Prototyping | [A]; [B]; [C]; [D]; [G]; [H]** – fabrication of prototypes, manufactured by an outsourced professional;
- **Product evaluation | [A]; [B]; [C]; [D]; [E]; [F]; [G]; [H]; [I]; [J]** – carried out with a professional model. Corrections of the fit. Modifications of details in the items of clothing. Approval of the first "proto" sample garment.
- **Finishing/trimmings/haberdashery | [A]; [B]; [C]; [D]; [G]; [H]; [I]** – Textile printing techniques: stencil dyeing and hand painting;
- **Final adjustments | [A]; [B]; [C]; [D]; [G]; [H]; [I]; [J]** – Final composition of the looks: combination between the items of clothing;
- **Launch | [A]; [B]; [C]; [D]; [E]; [F]; [G]; [H]; [I]; [J]** – collection presented in two exhibitions: [a] 7th Inclusive Fashion Competition – International Edition, in October 2015; [b] Virada Inclusiva (Accessibility All-Night Event), held on December 2015. Both events are sponsored by the State Secretariat for the Rights of People with Disabilities, São Paulo, Brazil.

3   Results and Discussions

This section expands on the main results obtained and the discussions generated in the process of Materialization of the "Parque Contemporâneo" fashion collection, in articulation with the principles of the SEE BEYOND method.

[A] Connection with the Brain's Nature

Traditionally, to work on the project of a fashion collection involves dealing with challenges that tangentially touch on aesthetic, ergonomic and sociocultural issues. Within the ambit of the "Parque Contemporâneo" collection, these issues gain another dimension when they connect to the needs of the user's body, needs that are intrinsic to the **nature of the human brain**. In this sense, to conceive, design and deliver products that respect the nature of the brain demands that the designer turn his attention to the field of Neuroscience. In other words, it entails seeking theoretical-practical tools in this field of scientific knowledge for anchoring their creative process and the project-oriented development. This attitude involves qualifying the design of an item of clothing as something beyond its primary function of clothing a body, treating it as an object that fosters body-brain-environment interaction. That is, an instrument that potencializes the cerebral mechanisms of neuroplasticity, perception, emotion and feeling, cognition and memory. Within the context of the "Parque Contemporâneo" collection, this principle drives and permeates all project stages described in the Methodology section.

[B] Homeostatic Regulation

Homeostasis encompasses a set of simultaneous processes that result in the biological regulation of life and in the states resulting from well-regulated life. The homeostatic machine, as an innate and automated equipment of life governance, has become increasingly sophisticated over the course of the biological evolution of human beings. Its mechanism incorporates a range of functions, from an organism's simple actions of approaching/retracting or excitability/rest in relation to a certain object, to complex actions with the involvement of responses that are competitive or competitiveness-related. Both these types of actions perform a crucial role in the management of life.

In synthesis, the homeostatic reactions act on the detection of difficulties or opportunities, and, in turn, solve the 'problem' through simple or complex actions, either by the elimination of difficulties or by the opportunities [6, 7]. The designer works in alignment with **homeostatic regulation**.

In conceiving, designing and delivering products that corroborate to the well-being, quality of life and health of their users, the designer works in synchrony with the body's homeostatic machine, and corresponds to the physiological engagement necessary for survival. In other words, the user's need and the designer's motivation articulate themselves for the regulation of life. In this process, the body in the mind (cerebral maps) brings extraordinary contributions to the management of the various different behaviours assumed in the most distinct situations, which are capable of threatening the integrity of the human organism and compromise its life [7].

Within the ambit of the Materialization of the "Parque Contemporâneo" collection, the pieces of clothing conceived mentally by the designers with visual impairments aim to achieve the homeostatic balance of their users, once they are commited to providing them with feelings of satisfaction, pleasure and freedom (in alignment with the key words of the theme: pleasant, pleasure and freedom). In this case, this commitment translates itself into the choices of source materials; in the ergonomic aspects of patternmaking and grading; and in the quality of the finishing of the manufactured garments.

Homeostatic regulation, like the connection with the brain's nature composes the group of principles of the SEE BEYOND method that guide and shape all stages of the project.

[C] Transversalities of the Method

Over the course of their project-oriented working process, the designer's body-brain 'displaces' itself in multiple directions and in multiple planes to meet the progression, retreat, repetition, combination and recombination movements of their proposals, driven by their own curiosity [8]. Unlike what common sense supposes, these movements do not operate in the linearity of a 'production line'. On the contrary, the actions of the creative body-brain cut across linear thought and construct conceptual and applied transversalities. In the words of Damásio [7], the human organism (the body and the brain) interacts with the objects, and the brain reacts to this interaction. This reaction translates itself into a record, which is not restricted to the structure of the entity, but to the various consequences of the organism's interactions with the entity's organism. In other words, the brain extrapolates the record of the object's visual structure to map out the sensory-motor patterns associated to vision, touch and manipulation, the evoking of previously acquired memories, and to emotions and feelings triggered by this particular object.

Within the context of the "Parque Contemporâneo" collection, the application of the SEE BEYOND method ensures the construction of the abovementioned conceptual and applied transversalities, seeing that the method recovers the stages that compose the three dimensions (Foundation, Enhancement and Materialization) in a non-linear manner. Just as the preceding principles, the **transversalities of the method** permeate and extend throughout all project stages (Fig. 1).

Fig. 1. Principles of the SEE BEYOND method that are present in all project stages: [A] Connection to the brain's nature; [B] Homeostatic Regulation; [C] Transversalities of the method. Source: the authors.

[D] Sensory Motor Perception

The impossibility of seeing is not an obstacle to the designers with visual impairments in the process of identifying and selecting the source materials that compose the project of the "Parque Contemporâneo" fashion collection (such as, for example, fabrics and trimmings). Within this domain, the sensory motor perception acts as a protagonist in the **sensitisation and enhancement of tactile perception**. Beyond the circumscribed context of source materials, the stimulus to the sensory motor system permeates the majority of stages that comprehend the creation and execution processes of the aforementioned collection [definition of the colour palette; definition of the mix of products; creative development; finishing and trimmings; elaboration and identification of the information on the technical specifications sheets; patternmaking and grading; prototyping; final fitting; final looks]. Within this domain, it is also worth emphasizing its role in the sensory perception of colours and in fostering both the formation of mental images and the reduction of the temporal space for abstraction. With regards to the sensory perception of colours, sensory panels composed of objects of various different natures trigger tactile, olfactory, auditory and gustatory stimuli in the designers, incapable of perceiving colour as light (visual stimulus). These stimuli enhance perception and the command of the chromatic scales by the designers [4]. As regards to the formation of mental images and the reduction of the temporal space for abstraction, the sensory motor perception reveals itself to be crucial for overcoming the considerable difficulty of performing temporal abstraction faced by visually-impaired individuals. That is, of creating new elaborations (creative process) based on consolidated memories [9–11]. For this purpose, the sensory contact with the project-based elements and the association of these elements with the references that are present in the memory enable the designers to construct mental registers throughout this whole process [5] (Fig. 2).

Fig. 2. Sensory motor perception: tactile stimuli. Source: the authors.

[E] Multidimensional Abstraction

With regard to the patternmaking and grading, the relationship between the two-dimensional and three-dimensional planes reveals itself as a fundamental strategy to stimulate spatial perception and the capacity for relational abstraction of the visually impaired designers [5]. By identifying the item of clothing on the dress form (dummy), and then separating its parts and displacing them to the two-dimensional model, the designers acquire full understanding of the connection between the two dimensions. This connection, in turn, expands itself to encompass a comprehension of the relationship between inside and outside applied to the human body. In this case, three-dimensionality offers the opportunity that the two-dimensional design does not afford. In other words, "(…) the interior-exterior connection that is intrinsic to the relation between the garment, the body and the context, as support-structure of the design object, (…) the status of the garment, as the continent space of a body, and the passage from the garment in a plane situation to the third dimension" [12].

Moreover, the perception of the human body in natural scale (1:1) brings greater knowledge and command over it. It also promotes familiarity with its morphology and proportions, and develops the perception of scale [13], which reveals itself as extremely useful for the dimensioning of wearable products by the visually impaired. For example, by analysing certain models of blazers in this scale (1:1), the designers are capable of perceiving the common structure, besides being able to differentiate details in the patternmaking and grading, fabric, fit, texture, volume, length and forms that

Fig. 3. Multidimensional abstraction: relationship between the two-dimensional and three-dimensional planes. Source: the authors.

compose the garment. This command is essential in the fitting process, as spatial perception and relational abstraction are applied to the correlation between that which is idealized and the result of the manufactured garment (Fig. 3).

[F] Perceptive-Emotional Dynamics

The fitting process represents a moment of **challenge-threat [potencialization-inhibition of the creative process]** for the visually impaired designers. While this stage elicits the recognition of the creative results related to the fit, texture and the patternmaking and grading of the items of clothing, it also presents itself as a test to the very skill of recognizing all this information almost entirely through the sense of touch, without the aid of vision. In the words of Sacks [14] "(…) the world of objects needs to be learnt by means of experience and activity: (…) touching, handling, correlating the impressions conveyed by objects with their appearance". Within this sphere, the **action of emotions and feelings** generated during the formulation of mental images [6, 7] of these creative results, act and interfere in the sensorial perception of the prototypes. This interference denotes positive and/or negative impacts, which can either be incorporated as qualities or as hurdles to the continuity of this process (Fig. 4).

Fig. 4. (a) Perceptive-emotional dynamics: clothes fitting. Source: the authors. (b) Perceptive-emotional dynamics: the fitting process. Source: the authors.

[G] Motivational Flows

In the words of Fornasier et al. [15], to think like a designer means to "perceive, analyse and understand the reality of situations to create products and processes", with a view to the real needs. In this sense, motivating the individuals to think like designers can be a key factor to stimulate and expand their creative potential, and consequently enhance their **self-confidence and self-esteem.**

Faced with the development of something new and full of uncertainties, such as the initial creation and development stages of a fashion collection, the sense of motivation, gradually built and underpinned over the course of the creative process, can be regarded as crucial for overcoming the feelings of fear, shyness, fragility and insecurity, frequently responsible for mental/creative blockage and for the abandoning of the project.

This gradual construction assimilates a gain in complexity, essentially mediated by a process of continuous repetition, of elaborating and re-elaborating, of doing and redoing the various activities that encompass the scope of a project. This process engenders a sense of motivation by **experience** and culminates in a gain of **familiarity**, which leads the designers to appropriate the information, consolidating it in their memory and evoking it whenever necessary [4, 5].

In other words, the motivational flows act as powerful stimuli for boosting positive emotions and feelings [6, 7] and, consequently, for the permanence of behaviours that bring about relaxation, humour, disinhibition, satisfaction, tranquillity and that promote the well-being and the health of the designers, of the members of the project team and other professionals involved.

This reverberation of motivational flows extrapolates the activities of everyday life. In other words, it gives rise to a movement that begins with the project of a fashion collection and which expands itself in responding to the everyday challenges of human survival (Fig. 5).

Fig. 5. Motivational flows: initial stage (left) and final stage (right) of the creative process of the fashion collection "Parque Contemporâneo". Source: the authors.

[H] Connection with the Individual Brain

To avail oneself of life stories, drawing on personal experiences as sources of reference for the creative process can turn out to be a fundamental strategy for the evocation and the consolidation of the memories [9–11] of the visually impaired designers. For example, the stage involving the mix of products, which encompasses the qualitative definition and the quantitative distribution of the items of clothing that compose the fashion collection, marks a point in the process of intense immersion into the **personal repertoires** of the designers. Within this ambit, the definition of the types of items and the respective quantities of each, both in alignment with the theme, act as a trigger for the process of rekindling and delving into the designers' individual memories.

In the case of the "Parque Contemporâneo" collection, two moments mark the definition of the mix of products: (A) the evoking and re-evoking of the designers' individual memories; and (B) the articulation of individual memories for the composition of the collection's mix of products. That is to say, the collectivity is structured using a **focus on individuality** as its starting point. And the **needs**, **skills** and **competencies** of the **individual brain** of these designers emerge from their repertoire of memories, going beyond the references. Together, all these singularities shape the referred collection (Table 1).

Table 1. Connection with the individual brain: final result of the collective composition (derived from their individual mental elaborations) of the mix of products of the "Parque Contemporâneo" collection. Source: the authors.

TOPS	
I. Cropped top	Corset fit, satin-lined bodice; heart neckline; belly button length; front opening with exposed zipper; straps crossed on the back; inverted "U" hemline with side; fabric: denim
II. Tanktop shirt	Close fit; crew neckline; zigzag stitch (aplique) with wire-cut fabrics (satin on denim) in "X", diagonally from the straps to the hemline; reverse-cut fabric; fabric: satiny crepe (blue) and denim
III. Sleeveless blouse	Close-fit; built-up mandarin collar, sleeveless, combination of fabrics (printed and plain); front buttoning, pocket lapels, back yoke in print denim; other parts of the blouse in plain denim
IV. Long-sleeved shirt	Snug fit; traditional neckline; front buttoning; combination of fabrics: mousseline and satiny crepe (colour: black); body and sleeves in mousseline; shawl colar neck, front pockets, cuffs and hemline (front and back) in satiny crepe
V. Long-sleeved blouse	Loose-fitting waste; round neckline; hip-length hem; front and back plackets, with alternation of fabrics; fabrics: mousseline and satiny crepe (colour: black)
VI. Jacket	Perfecto fit jacket draped cross-over front with diagonal zíper, waist-length; exposed zíper on front pockets near the hemline; fabric: printed denim
VII. Blazer	Semi-fitted, marked waist; hip length hemline; long sleeves with reverse cuffs; fabric: denim, alternating use of front and reverse sides of fabric; wire-cutting on the collar, body and sleeves; internal seam in reverse gathers and sides
BOTTOMS	
VIII. Minissaia	Tight fit; pockets and yoke (5 pockets) details; waistline with "x-shaped" beltloops; front opening: buttoning on the waistline and zip fly; finishing of pockets and zíper in blue satiny crepe; fabric: denim; miniskirt accompanied by stretch cotton shorts
IX. Knee-length skirt	Dirndl knee-length; combination of fabrics: denim and punto di Roma knit (front and back in denim, sides in punto di Roma knit); waistline in punto di Roma knit
X. Shorts	Close-fitting; hemline at waist with buttoning; front zip opening; frontside with curved-shaped pockets; back with yoke and plane pockets; side bands in satiny crepe (3 cm); fabric: denim
XI. Skinny pants	Skinny fit; five-pocket model; "x-shaped" beltloops on the waistband; zipper on the sides in bottom hemline; fabric: denim

(*continued*)

Table 1. (*continued*)

XII. Tailored pants	Straight, tapered cut, slim fit; side pockets, knife pleat; pockets lined with black satin; black satiny crepe belt loops on the waist; front-button closure, zip fly; fabric: denim (dark blue tone for the denim)
XIII. Pants (jeans and cotton mix)	Skinny fit; denim front; cotton knit back and waistband in punto di Roma stitch; fake pockets with exposed zipper
ONE PIECE	
XIV. Dress	Close fit and flared skirt; "V" neckline and draped collar; denim bodice with padding below bust, front zip opening; black mousseline slitted skirt; finishing with denim in slits

[I] Connection with the Social Brain

The access to all of the items of clothing that compose a collection by women with different physical biotypes, including those with some form of physical impairment is a concern that was widely debated throughout the creation and development processes of the "Parque Contemporâneo" collection. As a general rule, this is not a focus of attention among the different features of products offered by the fashion market. The absence of **empathy** in defining the target audience is still highly common in the design industry, that is, it has low priority in an industry that is still driven by programmed obsolescence.

Working in the opposite direction, the designers of this collection center the **individual-group-society relations** around difference and diversity, in such a way as to guarantee the functionality and useability of the items of clothing for everyone and by everyone (Universal Design) [16]. In this sense, the condition of this group of designers marked by the sensory difference of blindness, by their differences in age and by the diversity of their individual repertoires is conducive to the engendering of feelings of empathy, in other words, to the limitations and needs of the other.

Fig. 6. Connection with the social brain: definition of the target audience. Source: the authors.

The dialogue that emerges from the heterogenous shapes the **social brain of the group**. This reveals the **interactions** between the **skills** and competences of the group and the specific demands of the defined target audience (Fig. 6).

[J] Critical Reflexive Positioning

The designer's thought and creative activities are permeated by the challenge of **self-criticism**. A healthy dose of self-criticism enables them to ponder their initial ideas, evaluate their project-oriented choices and reflect about them. It also conduces the designer to identify problems and flaws, and consequently, make correction or come up with adjustments over the course of all project stages.

In speaking of visually impaired designers, such a challenge gains another dimension, since this **critical reflexive positioning** derives from somatosensory recognition of possible absences in the correspondence between the outlined idea, the planned project actions, the prototype developed and the finalized product [3–5] (Figs. 7 and 8).

Within the scope of the "Parque Contemporâneo" collection, we draw attention to the situation faced by the designers in the combination of items of clothing for the creation of final looks for two exhibitions, the first of which took place at the International Edition of the 7th Inclusive Fashion Competition, in October 2015; and the second at the all-night event Virada Inclusiva in December 2015. Both events are sponsored by the State Secretariat for the Rights of People with Disabilities, Sao Paulo, Brazil. In other words, the challenges to which we refer here demand multiple resolution plans: (A) the same items of clothing require different combinations for distinct looks, in view of the events' different exhibition proposals. Here it is important to highlight the challenge posed by the somatosensory perception of the items of clothing, which had to be integrated to the looks; (B) the different exhibition proposals of the events, which present the visually impaired designers with the challenge of assimilating the ideal location of the mannequins in the exhibition spaces of each event, both in relation to the association between the mental visualization of this space and the somatosensory perception of the products, in addition to the correlation of, and dialogue between, each look (Fig. 9).

Fig. 7. Critical reflexive positioning: setting up of the exhibition of the "Parque Contemporâneo" collection at the International Edition of the 7th Inclusive Fashion Competition. Source: the authors.

Fig. 8. Critical reflexive positioning: the exhibition of the "Parque Contemporâneo" collection at the International Edition of the 7th Inclusive Fashion Competition. Source: the authors.

Fig. 9. Critical reflexive positioning: setting up of the exhibition of the "Parque Contemporâneo" collection at the all night event Virada Inclusiva, in December 2015. Source: the authors.

4   Conclusion

The materialization of a product involves a process made up of various stages, specific to the different types of possible products. From the perspective of Design, traditionally this process is sustained by methodologies that structure it and drive definitions relating to its form, function and use experience in certain sociocultural context. These definitions are formulated from frames of reference guided towards responding to consumption and market desires, not necessarily in that order. This vision gives structure to the world as we know it, where 'more is better', and the needs of the target audience are not truly met, nor their desires truly understood. Contemporaneity calls for change. The messages are explicit: systemic air, water and land degradation; environmental catastrophes and the destruction of ecosystems; forced migratory flows [17], among many other impacts that threaten the homeostatic balance, and, consequently, our survival on this planet. At this point we must emphasize the responsibilities of Design and of the Designer, where that of Design lies in being a field of knowledge within the realm of applied science, and therefore capable of instrumentalizing human development in the socioeconomic and cultural spheres. The Designer, in turn, has a responsibility as a professional of this sector, who can act as a spokesperson for the application of this knowledge, and thus its role in structuring the bases that drive transformations in this sphere. The Design-Neurosciences relationship is built upon this set of responsibilities. The cooperation between these domains has revealed itself to be increasingly promising, strategic and adequate for spurring positive transformations aimed at development and social-economic sustainability. By unveiling the brain and neurophysiological mechanisms that engender human existence, the Neurosciences equip both Design and the Designers with the fundamental substrate for the comprehension of the real needs and desires of the end users relating to the products. And that is where the SEE BEYOND method enters into the picture. Through its process-based, procedural transversalities, this teaching-learning method applied to Design sees the 'mind-brain-body of the individuals who compose the Target Group as a strategic pillar for subsidizing the creative process guided towards the development of products. It is also worth emphasizing the extension of the referred method for capacitating designers with visual impairments.

Within this context, the Parque Contemporâneo (Contemporary Park) fashion collection, created by visually impaired designers, comes into being, based on the ten principles that constitute the SEE BEYOND method, all of which were articulated with each project stage (Table 2):

Table 2. Articulation between the principles of the SEE BEYOND method and the project stages of the "Parque Contemporâneo" collection. Source: the authors.

SEE BEYOND principles	Scope of action	Project stage of the collection
[A] Connection with the brain's nature	Aligns itself to the characteristics and to the cerebral processes of: neuroplasticity; singularity; selectivity; search for patterns, associations and meanings; consciousness and unconsciousness; emotions and feelings; memories; cognition; fluctuating attention; focused attention; peripheral perception; creativity; among others	Data collection Definition of target audience Choice of theme Designing of the garments Technical specifications Patternmaking and grading Prototyping Product evaluation Finishing/trimmings Final adjustments Launch

(continued)

Table 2. (*continued*)

SEE BEYOND principles	Scope of action	Project stage of the collection
[B] Homeostatic regulation	Encompasses physiological recruitment for the dynamic balance of body functions; the processes of regulation of life; the states resulting from a well-regulated life; detection and resolution of difficulties and opportunities	Data collection Definition of target audience Choice of theme Designing of the garments Technical specifications Patternmaking and grading Prototyping Product evaluation Finishing/trimmings Final adjustments Launch
[C] Transversalities of the method	Encompasses an expanded communications network: the transversal communications/feedbacks between people (designers/target audience); between the contents of subjects (transdisciplinarity); between concepts and applications; between physical and digital/online resources; flexibility between all stages and domains of the method	Data collection Definition of target audience Choice of theme Designing of the garments Technical specifications Patternmaking and grading Prototyping Product evaluation Finishing/trimmings Final adjustments Launch
[D] Sensory motor perception	Involves sensibilization for specialization and enhancement of tactile perception; sensory perception of colours; encourages the formation of mental images and the reduction of temporal space for abstraction	Designing of the garments Technical specifications Patternmaking and grading Prototyping Product evaluation Finishing/trimmings Final adjustments Launch

(*continued*)

Table 2. (*continued*)

SEE BEYOND principles	Scope of action	Project stage of the collection
[E] Multidimensional abstraction	Focuses on the relationship between the two-dimensional and three-dimensional planes as a stimulus for spatial perception and for the capacity for relational abstraction; encourages the formation of mental images and the reduction of temporal space for abstraction	Data collection Definition of target audience Choice of theme Designing of the garments Patternmaking and grading Product evaluation Launch
[F] Perceptive-emotional dynamics	Examines the action of emotions and feelings on perception; the threat-challenge mechanisms [inhibition-potentiation]	Choice of theme Designing of the garments Product evaluation Launch
[G] Motivational flows	Deals with self-confidence; self-esteem by experience; self-esteem by familiarity, etc.	Choice of theme Designing of the garments Technical specifications Patternmaking and grading Prototyping Product evaluation Finishing/trimmings Final adjustments Launch
[H] Connection with the individual brain	Connects itself to personal repertoires; reviews experiences as a strategy of appropriation and of memory consolidation; translates memory appropriation as a competence; addresses individuality within diversity; focuses on individual needs, skills and competencies	Choice of theme Designing of the garments Technical specifications Patternmaking and grading Prototyping Product evaluation Finishing/trimmings Final adjustments Launch

(*continued*)

Table 2. (*continued*)

SEE BEYOND principles	Scope of action	Project stage of the collection
[I] Connection with the social brain	Addresses the individual-group relation (deals with diversity within individuality; the social interaction); focuses on the needs, skills and competencies of the social group	Data collection Definition of target audience Choice of theme Designing of the garments Patternmaking and grading Product evaluation Finishing/trimmings Final adjustments Launch
[J] Critical reflexive positioning	Foments evaluation, self-reflection, self-criticism and fosters the consolidation of knowledge	Choice of theme Designing of the garments Product evaluation Final adjustments Launch

This articulation results from a process that is transversal, continuous, dynamic and interactive between the universes of the designers, the target audience and the product concept (briefing). Compared to other project-oriented methodologies applied to the development of products, the referred articulation makes it possible to observe qualitative gains, particularly in what concerns: [a] the designer's awareness of their own repertoire and their own competences; [b] the designer's commitment to and involvement in the stages of the project-based process; [c] the product's adherence to the organic needs of the user; [d] the aesthetic and functional refinement of the product; [e] the enhancement of the product's use experience.

It is also worth emphasizing that the visually impaired condition, as well as their commitment to the inclusion of people with physical disabilities in the collection's target audience group, reinforces the contributions that arise from the cooperation between the field of Design, Behavioural and Cognitive Neurosciences and the referred method.

Based on the implementation of this methodology centered on the needs of the user's 'mind-brain-body' and the results obtained, the present research suggests the application of this articulation (between the principles of the SEE BEYOND method and the project stages of a product) with sighted designers as a future development. Going beyond the expansion of the creative potential of these designers, we aim to lay emphasis on the role of the designer as a transformative agent in society, commited to the health, well-being and quality of life of its citizens.

References

1. Lent, R.: Neurociência da mente e do comportamento [Neuroscience of mind and behavior]. Guanabara Koogan, Porto Alegre (2008)
2. Tokuhama-Espinosa, T.N.: The scientifically substantiated art of teaching: a study in the development of standards in the new academic field of neuroeducation (mind, brain and education science). Doctoral Research. Capella University (2008). http://pqdtopen.proquest.com/doc/250881375.html?FMT=ABS. Accessed Jan 2019
3. Lima Júnior, G.C., Zuanon, R.: The foundation of the SEE BEYOND method: fashion design and neuroeducation applied to the teaching of the project methodology to students with congenital and acquired blindness. In: Streitz, N., Markopoulos, P. (eds.) DAPI 2017. LNCS, vol. 10291, pp. 528–546. Springer, Cham (2017). https://doi.org/10.1007/978-3-319-58697-7_40
4. Lima Júnior, G.C., Zuanon, R.: SEE BEYOND: enhancement – strategies in teaching learning as a stimulus to creativity in fashion design. In: Duffy, V.G. (ed.) DHM 2018. LNCS, vol. 10917, pp. 280–294. Springer, Cham (2018). https://doi.org/10.1007/978-3-319-91397-1_24
5. Lima Júnior, G.C., Zuanon, R.: SEE BEYOND contributions to the project-based practice of sighted and visually impaired students in the context of higher education in Design (2018). https://ppgdesign.anhembi.br/datjournal/index.php/dat/article/view/91. Accessed Jan 2019
6. Damásio, A.R.: In Search of Spinoza: Pleasure and Pain in the Science of the Senses. Companhia das Letras, São Paulo (2004)
7. Damásio, A.R.: E o cérebro criou o homem. [And the brain created man]. Companhia das Letras, São Paulo (2011)
8. Zeisel, J.: Inquiry by Design: Environment/Behavior/Neuroscience in Architecture, Interiors, Landscape, and Planning. W.W. Norton, New York (2006)
9. Estrela, J.B.C., Ribeiro, J.S.F.: Analysis of relationship between memory and learning construction of knowledge (2012). https://goo.gl/SqPSFP. Accessed Jan 2019
10. Izquierdo, I.: Memory. Artmed, Porto Alegre (2011)
11. Tabacow, L.S.: Contributions of cognitive neuroscience to the training of teachers and educationalists. http://www.bibliotecadigital.puc-campinas.edu.br/tde_arquivos/3/TDE-2006-06-30T115909Z-1178/Publico/Luiz%20Tabacow.pdf. Accessed Jan 2019
12. Saltzman, A.: El cuerpo diseñado: sobre la forma em el proyecto de la vestimenta. Paidós, Buenos Aires (2004)
13. Souza, W.G.: Modelagem no design do vestuário. [Modeling in clothing design] (2007). http://fido.palermo.edu/servicios_dyc/encuentro2007/02_auspicios_publicaciones/actas_diseno/articulos_pdf/A6045.pdf. Accessed Jan 2019
14. Sacks, O.: The Mind's Eye. Companhia das Letras, São Paulo (2010)
15. Fornasier, C.B.R, Martins, R.F.F., Demarchi, A.P.P.: O ensino da disciplina de desenvolvimento de projetos como sistema de gestão de conhecimento. [Teaching the discipline of project development as a knowledge management system] In: Pires, D.B. (org.) Design de Moda: olhares diversos. Estação das Letras e Cores Editora, Barueri (2008)
16. Martins, S.B., Martins, L.B.: Ergonomics, design universal and fashion (2012). https://www.ncbi.nlm.nih.gov/pubmed/22317450. Accessed Jan 2019
17. Loschiavo dos Santos, M.C.: Conectando ética e estética: reflexões sobre o design [Connecting ethics and aesthetics: reflections on design] (2016). http://pdf.blucher.com.br.s3-sa-east-1.amazonaws.com/designproceedings/ped2016/000-003.pdf. Accessed Jan 2019

First Impressions and Acceptance of Order Pickers Towards Using Data Glasses at a Simulated Workstation

Daniel Friemert[1]([✉]), Mirko Kaufmann[1,2], Ulrich Hartmann[1], and Rolf Ellegast[1,2]

[1] Department of Mathematics and Technology,
University of Applied Sciences Koblenz, Remagen, Germany
friemert@hs-koblenz.de
[2] Institute for Occupational Safety and Health of the German
Social Accident Insurance, St. Augustin, Germany

Abstract. In the field of logistics, data glasses might help to increase work efficiency and optimize workflows. However, their impact on physical and psychological stress has not been adequately investigated yet. 29 healthy participants worked for 40 min at a mock-up version of an industrial order picking workplace, distributing simulated tools represented as balls from one box to four surrounding boxes. Information's concerning amount and destination of the order pick were provided either from a monitor above the machine or from the display of data glasses. Before the measurements, the participants received questionnaires to rate their technical affinity and to obtain information's about their prior experiences concerning data glasses. After each measurement, additional questionnaires were issued to evaluate the perceived physical and mental workload and visual fatigue during the work as well as to evaluate the data glasses. For the comparison between the setups different repeated measures ANOVA-models (or alternatively a t-test) were applied. A significant higher strain was reported for the eyes while working with the data glasses. However, no significant differences were found when asking for specific eye parameters (e.g. blurred vision and dry eyes). Additionally, a lower significant strain was reported for the neck. When asked for general physical workloads due to the workplace setup no significant differences were reported which contradicts these results. Cognitive workloads were perceived significantly higher when using data glasses. No influence of the technical affinity could be found. Overall, it can be stated that the acceptance of data glasses in this study was quite positive, while differences in perceived physical or cognitive workload were reported in certain parameters. However, the subjective reports of increase in eye strain can be an indicator that the use of data glasses may lead to problems in this area. Especially since no significant differences were reported for a particular parameter further research has to be done.

Keywords: Ergonomics · Occupational safety and health · Analysis · Augmented reality · Acceptance · Logistics · Order picking · Smart glasses · Data glasses · Google glass

© Springer Nature Switzerland AG 2019
V. G. Duffy (Ed.): HCII 2019, LNCS 11581, pp. 251–265, 2019.
https://doi.org/10.1007/978-3-030-22216-1_19

1 Introduction

As the field of logistics is constantly seeking for an optimization of its workflow, the demand for modern technologies and the interest in further digitalization is accordingly high. One of the frequently discussed approaches is the use of data glasses: small head-mounted microcomputers that display context-sensitive information to the worker. This is realized by a small monitor placed in front of the worker's eyes enabling them to work hands-free. There has been news of companies claiming that data glasses can be a powerful tool for optimizing warehouse management processes, although studies, analyzing this in a controlled environment, do not exist to our knowledge. However, many of these studies focused on the effects of data glasses on work efficiency, while our approach sheds light on the effects of data glasses on physical workload, cognitive workload and user acceptance. Therefore, we have developed a simplified picking workstation in order to perform motion analysis and simultaneous evaluation of physiological and cognitive parameters under laboratory conditions. In this study we present the results of the assessment of self-reported workloads.

2 Related Work

Data glasses have been tested during the last five years in the areas of assembly and warehouse logistics, especially in large companies, as part of pilot studies. Meanwhile they are also used under real conditions [1–3]. In the field of logistics, the personnel of a German automobile manufacturer use data glasses for order picking in order to improve process reliability in production [4]. The main advantage of using data glasses according to this study is that the users have both hands free and as a consequence can reach a better performance. Another pilot project to investigate the use of data glasses was carried out under the leadership of a German logistics company [5]. Here the technology was used to implement "Pick-by-Vision" in warehousing. The company's employees were guided through the warehouse rack hall by means of graphics on the data glasses in order to accelerate the picking process and reduce errors. These two studies have shown that logistics can benefit from assisted reality tools by leading to a significant increase in efficiency during the picking process. The cited pilot studies, however, dealt exclusively with the influence of data glasses on work efficiency and process safety. On the other hand, few analyses were carried out on the effects of data glasses on physical and psychological stress in the workplace. Literature on this topic is therefore only available to a limited extent and strongly concentrated on assembly workplaces. Theis et al. 2015, investigated the aspect of physical stress caused by the use of data glasses for work support [6]. The study simulated assembly work on an automotive engine with the aid of data glasses. The work instructions were communicated either via data glasses or a tablet PC. Among other things, the authors of the study come to the conclusion that in order to avoid head and neck pain, the mechanical center of gravity of the spectacles should be balanced. Another relevant publication of the Federal Institute for Occupational Safety and Health (BAuA) describes two laboratory studies, whose focus was on mental stress during several hours of work with data glasses [7]. A construction task and a monitoring task were set in parallel and the work instructions were presented both by data glasses and a tablet PC. The authors stated that the decision as to whether data glasses should be used or not must always be made according to context and task. Another important aspect for the acceptance of data glasses by employees is the software ergonomics of the user interface. In the context of an interview-based study from the USA [8], which was conducted in various branches of industry, almost all respondents were of the opinion that poorly designed interfaces for data glasses distract employees. However, they saw great potential in the use of data glasses to improve safety and health at work. In another study analyzing information and interaction design, its impact on cognitive workload and visual comfort in the work environment was investigated [9]. The results of this study indicate that the established usability criteria for conventional screen work need to be adapted to the rapid development of data glass technology. But it is not only the software ergonomics that must react to the new challenges; the great advances in data glass technology require up-to-date examination methods. The next generation of data glasses, which are now about to enter the market, use laser-based methods that project directly onto the human retina or other innovative display technologies whose effects on humans have not been sufficiently investigated yet. In close cooperation with the Institute for Occupational Safety and Health of the German Social Accident Insurance (IFA), the University of Applied Sciences Remagen has been carrying out its own research on data glasses for several years now. Within the scope of comparative studies, the physical physical and cognitive workloads at order picking workplaces with and without the use of data glasses is measured and evaluated. The results, which are still preliminary, indicate that the use of data glasses can lead to a relief of the strain of neck muscles [10].

3   Methods and Materials

For the study presented a model of a picking environment was created. The structure is based on a real workstation at our partner company "wolfcraft", a hardware and tool manufacturer with its own logistics. In this article we focus on the fictitious use case for data glasses being used on this machine and the impressions people had in this scenario with data glasses.

3.1   Subjects

29 physically healthy subjects (11 male, 18 female) participated in this study containing a subgroup of 8 participants (0 male, 8 female) of professional (p) order pickers employed at the hardware tool manufacturer. The occupation of the non-professional (np) order pickers was diverse ranging from students through office workers to welders. Age (M = 35.1, SD = 12.5), height (M = 173.6, SD = 8.1), weight (M = 74.2, SD = 12.5) and BMI (M = 24.6, SD = 3.4) as well as occupations are reported in detail in Table 1.

Table 1. Subject information and list of non-order-picking occupations

Characteristics	M (SD)	Median	Min	Max
Total (n = 29)				
Age [y]	35.1 (12.5)	32	16	58
Height [cm]	173.6 (8.1)	173.8	155.8	189.9
Weight [kg]	74.2 (12.5)	73.9	55.3	101.6
BMI [kg/m^2]	24.6 (3.4)	23.3	19.2	31.9
Professional order pickers (n = 8)				
Age [y]	32.6 (11.8)	30.0	16	58
Height [cm]	175.9 (7.2)	177.2	164.5	189.9
Weight [kg]	74.3 (11.8)	73.0	57.8	101.6
BMI [kg/m^2]	25.6 (4.2)	28.0	19.2	31.9
Non-professionals (n = 21)				
Age [y]	41.6 (12.5)	47.0	20	57
Height [cm]	167.5 (7.5)	167.3	155.8	177.1
Weight [kg]	73.9 (15.3)	78	55.3	91.2
BMI [kg/m^2]	23.9 (2.9)	22.7	20.5	29.8
List of Participants Occupations for Non-professional order pickers				

• High School Teacher	• Graduate student
• Student (5)	• Pharmacist
• Metallworker – Welder	• Nurse
• Employee in public service (4)	• Manager at labour office
• Technical staff (electrician)	• Project manager (IT)
• Professor	• Office worker
• Agricultural trade koordinator	• Factory worker

3.2 Data Glasses

Prior to our study we evaluated different data glasses. The Vuzix M300 was found most suitable for our purposes. Especially the balanced design and the long-lasting battery lifetime were the main reasons for this decision. Subjects had the possibility of using the Vuzix M300 with a headband or with a frame (Fig. 1).

3.3 The Real-Life Workplace

Our laboratory workstation is a simplified copy of a real picking station at our partner company. Their workers, exclusively women,

Fig. 1. Subject using the Vuzix M300 with a headband

use this machine for fast, error-free and efficient order picking. The complete order picking system consists of three parts:

1. The storage facility

   The warehouse is a fully automatic high-bay warehouse with an area of several hundred square meters. The system software knows how to process all customer orders and places the desired products (contained in yellow boxes) on conveyor belts in an optimized sequence using storage robots. The products are then transported to the picking machine's exchange port. The warehouse was not rebuilt in our laboratory as it is not relevant for our investigation.

2. The interior

   The inside of the machine is the entry point for new cartons and the starting point for unused cartons and completed customer orders. The latter is automatically transported to the appropriate loading ramp. The machine interior can accommodate up to 48 customer containers and up to 12 product containers simultaneously.

3. The frontend

   The frontend (see Fig. 2) consists of five boxes. The middle row always contains the product box (Box M) coming from the warehouse, while all other boxes (Box LL, Box L, Box R, Box R, Box RR) are customer boxes. The monitor installed above Box M gives instructions to the employees. It informs them how many of the current products have been ordered by which customer and how many products remain in the product packaging. Then the employee selects the right number of products and places them in the appropriate customer box. After this step is completed by pressing the green button next to the customer box, the software checks if another customer has ordered the current product and displays the next command or changes the products and the cycle repeats itself. Since all work is done from the frontend, this part of the machine has been most realistically rebuilt in the laboratory.

Fig. 2. (left) Schematic portrait of the interior of the picking maching (right) worker during order picking at wolfcraft company (Color figure online)

3.4   Our Physical Mock-Up of the Picking Workplace

Our physical model (see Fig. 3) is built to scale, but is simplified in terms of product provision and the objects to be picked. Our most important requirement is to design the workstation interface for the test persons in such a way that it is as close as possible to the working environment of the real machine frontend. In order to automate and standardize the picking tasks, we have chosen wooden balls with different weights (60 g, 150 g, 250 g and 700 g) and diameters (40 mm, 60 mm, 80 mm and 100 mm) as picking objects instead of real products. The parameter range of our

Fig. 3. Subject doing order picking on our physical mock-up while wearing the CUELA system

counterfeit products (i.e. wooden balls) accounts for about 70% of all the products selected by the workers. A single picking task is defined as follows: Our machine delivers a defined number of products in Box M. According to the information on the monitor (see Figs. 2 and 3) mounted on the frame of the model, the products must be correctly sorted into four boxes (LL, L, R, RR). After completing the picking task for an output box, the subject must press a button to indicate that the box is ready for shipping. In our mock-up, this step is performed by pneumatic pistons, which mechanically empties all boxes. The complete setup is controlled and monitored by a customized software. All product sizes and boxes used were evenly distributed over the entire order. Work efficiency was monitored through the custom software in use.

3.5   Questionnaires

Several questionnaires were used to assess different subjective parameters that reflect the workers' attitude and acceptance when working with data glasses. Tailor-made questionnaires were created using the Delphi method [11]. Sensitivity, reliability and objectivity could not be evaluated in this study, but were discussed with a group of four experts in the field of ergonomics.

A specialized questionnaire was used to assess overall information about the subjects and their prior experience with digitalization and data glasses in order to retrieve information on their expectations. The questionnaire assessing workload was given to the participants twice: the first time after having worked with data glasses, the second time after having worked with a normal monitor setup. The questionnaire about data glasses was complemented by some questions about the usage of the glasses themselves and their impact on workload. Professional workers also answered several questions about how realistic their workplace was presented in the laboratory. The questionnaires contained 20, respectively 24 questions about workload with possible answers on a six-point symmetric Likert scale [12]. An additional questionnaire was handed out asking for subjective evaluation of the display device used, mostly through answers on a seven-point Likert scale. The questionnaire proposed by Bangor [13] was used for assessing aspects of visual fatigue on a continuous scale, while technical affinity was assessed using a questionnaire proposed by Karrer et al. [14] Tables 2, 3, 4, 5 and 6 show relevant excerpts from all questionnaires.

Table 2. Technical affinity questionnaire with scale and item information (Karrer et al.)

Technical affinity questionnaire

Questions	Rating
• I love owning new electronic devices	+
• Electronic devices cause illness	−
• I like to go into the specialist stores for electronic devices	+
• I have or would have comprehension problems when reading electronic and computer magazines	−
• Electronic devices enable a high standard of living	+
• Electronic devices lead to mental impoverishment	−
• Electronic devices make much more cumbersome	−
• I inform myself about electronic devices, even if I have no intention to buy them	+
• Electronic devices make me independent	+
• I enjoy trying out an electronic device	+
• Electronic devices make my everyday life easier	+
• Electronic devices increase safety	+
• Electronic devices reduce the personal contact between people	−
• I know most of the functions of the electronic devices I own	+
• I am excited when a new electronic device is released	+
• Electronic devices cause stress	−
• I know my way around electronic devices	+
• It's easy for me to learn how to operate an electronic device	+
• Electronic devices help to get information	+

Scale type	Values		Meaning	
	Min	Max	Min	Max
5-point-Likert	0	4	Absolutely true	Does not apply at all

Table 3. Prior knowledge and expectancy questionnaire with item information

Prior knowledge and expectancy questionnaire

Questions
• Have you ever heard of the term "industry 4.0"?
• Have you ever heard of the term "digitalization"?
• Have you ever heard of "data glasses"?
• Have you ever heard of any of the above terms in connection with data glasses (e.g. Google Glass)?
• Have you ever heard of areas in which data glasses are used?
• Have you already used the possibility to use data glasses?
• After reading the articles: How do you personally estimate the increase in the application of data glasses in the next 10 years?
• Were you able to understand the content of the articles?
• After working with both setups: How do you personally estimate the increase in the application of data glasses in the next 10 years?

Table 4. Perceived workload questionnaire with scale and item information

Perceived workload questionnaire			
Questions	Likert-scale		
	From	To	# of stages
How physically demanding did you perceive the work?[a]	−3 (very undemanding)	3 (very overstraining)	7
The physical workload was influenced by the ...			
Setup of the work place	−3 (very little)	3 (very much)	6
Type of movement	−3 (very little)	3 (very much)	6
CUELA - measuring suit	−3 (very little)	3 (very much)	6
Data glasses[b]	−3 (very little)	3 (very much)	6
How physically stressful did you perceive the work?	−3 (very low)	3 (very high)	6
How cognitively demanding did you perceive the work?[a]	−3 (very undemanding)	3 (very overstraining)	7
The cognitive workload was influenced by the ...			
Setup of the work place	−3 (very little)	3 (very much)	6
Type of movement	−3 (very little)	3 (very much)	6
CUELA - measuring suit	−3 (very little)	3 (very much)	6
Data glasses[b]	−3 (very little)	3 (very much)	6
How cognitively stressful did you perceive the work?	−3 (very low)	3 (very high)	6
How high did you perceive the workload during work on the following regions?			
Eyes	−3 (very low)	3 (very high)	6
Neck	−3 (very low)	3 (very high)	6
Shoulders	−3 (very low)	3 (very high)	6
Lumbar spine	−3 (very low)	3 (very high)	6
Hands	−3 (very low)	3 (very high)	6
Upper back	−3 (very low)	3 (very high)	6

[a]Note for participants: A demanding job does not necessarily have to be stressful.
[b]Question was asked after use of data glasses

Table 5. Visual fatigue questionnaire with scale and item information

Visual fatigue questionnaire			
Question			
Do you notice that you are currently affected by any of these symptoms?			
Symptoms asked for			
• Dry eyes	• Tearing eyes	• Eyes are irritable or burning	
• Difficulties in following lines	• Mental fatigue	• Blurred letters	
• Double vision	• Headaches	• Pain in the neck	
• Pain in or around the eyes	• Heavy eyes	• Difficulties to see sharply leaping text	
• Blinding effects	• Blurred vision		
Scale type	Values		Meaning	

Scale type	Values		Meaning	
	Min	Max	Min	Max
Continuous	0	10	Not noticeable	Strongly noticeable

Table 6. Hardware and Software Ergonomics Questionnaire with scale and item information

Hardware and software ergonomics questionnaire			
Questions	Likert-scale		
	From	To	# of stages
How physically demanding did you perceive the work?[a]	−3 (very undemanding)	3 (very overstraining)	7
The physical workload was influenced by the ...			
Setup of the work place	−3 (very little)	3 (very much)	6
Type of movement	−3 (very little)	3 (very much)	6
CUELA - measuring suit	−3 (very little)	3 (very much)	6
Data glasses[b]	−3 (very little)	3 (very much)	6
How physically stressful did you perceive the work?	−3 (very low)	3 (very high)	6
How cognitively demanding did you perceive the work?[a]	−3 (very undemanding)	3 (very overstraining)	7
The cognitive workload was influenced by the ...			
Setup of the work place	−3 (very little)	3 (very much)	6
Type of movement	−3 (very little)	3 (very much)	6
CUELA - measuring suit	−3 (very little)	3 (very much)	6
Data glasses[b]	−3 (very little)	3 (very much)	6
How cognitively stressful did you perceive the work?	−3 (very low)	3 (very high)	6
How high did you perceive the workload during work on the following regions?			
Eyes	−3 (very low)	3 (very high)	6
Neck	−3 (very low)	3 (very high)	6
Shoulders	−3 (very low)	3 (very high)	6
Lumbar spine	−3 (very low)	3 (very high)	6
Hands	−3 (very low)	3 (very high)	6
Upper back	−3 (very low)	3 (very high)	6

[a]Note for participants: A demanding job does not necessarily have to be stressful.
[b]Question was asked after use of data glasses

3.6   Procedure

Prior to the study, the participants were asked to wear everyday clothing including pants and a t-shirt for the experiment. Before the experiment the participants were informed about the procedure. After giving informed consent, the participants filled out questionnaires about their prior experience with data glasses as well as some personal data such as age, information about technical affinity, information about work stress and a questionnaire about existing physical strain. If there was any prior knowledge about data glasses the participants answered the question "How do you personally estimate the increase in the use of data glasses over the next 10 years?". Afterwards participants read two newspaper articles reporting the application of data glasses in logistics in a positive way. After reading the articles, the previous question was answered a second time. Weight and height of the subjects were measured using an anthropometer and a personal scale. For measuring the resting heart rate, the participants were equipped with a fitness tracker (Fitbit Surge). Subsequently, they had a 20-min time period to relax on a deck chair in a separated part of the laboratory.

If the participants chose to relax, they were allowed to listen to music. After this procedure the motion-capturing-system (CUELA) was fit to the subject followed by a brief theoretical introduction to the picking task and respectively to working with the data glasses of about five to ten minutes. Prior to starting to work on the workplaces, the participants performed a 15-min practice phase during which they were allowed to ask questions concerning the task and getting used to the working procedure. The subjects had to work on their order picking tasks for 40 min. After this the participants had a break of about 30 min in which questionnaires were answered. Then the participants switched the workplace setup to with or without data glasses dependent on what they had not yet worked on. They were granted an additional 15-min practice phase before starting the second measurement. After the second measurement the same questionnaires were filled out again and the participants were asked about the expected increase of data glass usage in the next 10 years a third time. Afterwards participants where debriefed having the opportunity for comments and criticism about the study. All participants received a 120€ compensation. The complete measuring procedure took about 5 h from introduction to debriefing.

Please Note: Heart rate and motion detection are not evaluated in this article. However, they are mentioned here for reproductive purposes.

3.7   Data Analysis and Statistics

All data was analyzed using IBM SPSS 25. For comparisons between monitor and data glass setup different repeated measures ANOVA-models were calculated. Other between-subject factors (e.g. age-groups, order-of-device-usage) were considered, but have been removed from the models for greater power if no interaction could be shown. Models were also examined to see whether they could be improved by the introduction of covariates where this seemed meaningful. When neither covariates nor between-subject factors had an influence on the model, t-tests where applied alternatively. P-Values where adjusted using a Bonferroni correction. Cohen's d was calculated as the effect size, where significant or near significant results were found.

Homoscedasticity was assessed through visual analysis of the residual plots. Normality was checked through visual analysis of qq-plots. Minor violations of the normality condition were ignored due to the robustness of the ANOVA.

Sphericity was tested with the means of a Levene-test and the Greenhouse-Geisser correction was used where sphericity was violated. Significance level was set to $\alpha = .05$ for all tests.

Boxplots where used to analyze the data for outlier and if no more than two outliers were found, they were removed using 90%-winsorizing. Spearman correlations were applied where a relationship between variables was investigated.

The questionnaire on technical affinity was summarized and standardized to a value of 0–100. For this the individual questions were evaluated as negative or positive impact towards technical affinity, then added or subtracted and rescaled to the new scale.

4 Results

Professional workers evaluated the laboratory setup very comparable to their real workplace (M = 2.00, SD = .93) and thought that the task was almost realistically represented (M = 2.38, SD = .92). Overall work environment (e.g. noise and light conditions) was rated less comparable but still similar although participants had strongly varying opinions on this concern (M = .88, SD = 2.2).

All subjects had heard of the term "digitalization of the industry" and 17 participants (15 np, 2 p) had heard of "industry 4.0". 25 participants (19 np, 6 p) had heard of data glasses prior to the study and 21 (15 np, 6 p) could associate these terms with each other. 11 participants (10 np, 1 p) had used data glasses before but all except for one had a one-time-only use.

Of the 25 participants who knew data glasses only 8 (4 np, 4 p) heard of their usage in logistics whilst the others knew about their usage for leisure activities, other research projects, military usage, customer service or for educational purposes.

These participants thought that the use of data glasses will increase moderately over the next 10 years (M = 2.56, SD = 0.76) prior. There was no significant difference between professional and non-professional participants, $U(n_1 = 19, n_2 = 6) = 44.5$, p = .437. These values increased after reading the articles about data glasses in logistics and pick-by-vision (M = 2.84, SD = .69) and again after using data glasses (M = 3.04, SD = .74). The increase between before and after reading the articles was significant as an within subject factor, $F(1,24) = 5,204$, p = .032, $\eta_p^2 = .178$, while the increase after working with data glasses only showed a slight trend, $F(1,24) = 5,204$, p = .067, $\eta_p^2 = .133$.

The difference in technical affinity of professional (M = 66.29, SD = 18.54) was not significantly different from non-professionals (M = 55.42, SD = 11.00), $t(28) = 1.937$, p = .066. There was a significant negative correlation between technical affinity and age ($r_s = -0.436$, p = .018, n = 29).

Neither the fact that the participants were professional order pickers, Workload * Professional, $F(1,27) = .006$, p = .259, nor the order of device-usage, Workload * Order, $F(1,27) = .458$, p = .504, showed significant effects on the main questions ("How physically/cognitively demanding/stressful did you perceive the work?") concerning physical and cognitive workload, which also had no significant differences for the use of data glasses and the standard setup. All following questions were therefore analyzed using a paired t-test.

No significant differences (lower M_{M-D} stand for higher workload values of data glasses and represents the mean of differences in the paired t-test) on physical workload could be found when rating the impact of the workplace setup ($M_{M-D} = 0.138$, SD = 1.46), $t(28) = 0.510$, p = .614, the type of movement during work ($M_{M-D} = -0.138$,

SD = 1.46), t(28) = 0.493, p = .626, and the motion capturing system (M_{M-D} = −0.241, SD = 1.704), t(28) = 0.763, p = .452. When participants rated the setup in respect to cognitive workload all of these parameters were significantly higher when working with data glasses, e.g. workplace setup (M_{M-D} = −0.966, SD = 1.957), t(28) = 2.636, p = .014, d = 0.494, the type of movement during work (M_{M-D} = −1.483, SD = 1.957), t(28) = 4.080, p < .001, d = −0.76 and the motion capturing system (M_{M-D} = −0.621, SD = 1.590), t(28) = 2.102, p = .045, d = −0.39. The subjects were asked if there was any strain on certain parts of the body. They reported significant higher strain on the eyes, (M_{M-D} = −1.586, SD = 2.383), t(28) = 3.584, p = .001, d = −0.67, while they also reported significant lower strain on the neck (M_{M-D} = 1.621, SD = 2.470), t(28) = 3.533, p = .001, d = 0.66. Impacts on self-reported shoulder workloads (M_{M-D} = 0.483, SD = 1.353), t(28) = 1.922, p = .065, upper back workloads (M_{M-D} = 0.172, SD = 2.089), t(28) = 0.445, p = .660, lower back workloads (M_{M-D} = −0.069, SD = 1.907), t(28) = 0.195, p = .847, and workload on hands (M_{M-D} = 0.172, SD = 2.237), t(28) = 0.415, p = .681, had no significant differences.

The evaluation of the data glasses and some aspects of software ergonomics was perceived rather positive. Participants reported the display size of the monitor (M = 1.45, SD = 1.55) and of the data glasses (M = 1.41, SD = 1.50) as good. Similar positive results were reported for the brightness of the display, comprehensibility of the information and responsiveness of the application. The information itself was rated adequate for its purpose concerning size of the information, amount of information presented and the clearness in depiction of work instructions.

The participants could imagine themselves working with data glasses on a daily basis for an average of 163.72 min (SD = 105.39) but there were great differences in the indication of this duration between subjects and between non-professional participants and professional order pickers (Fig. 4).

In the visual fatigue questionnaire almost all differences were non-significant except that par-

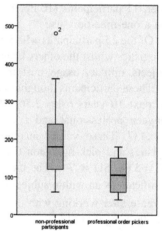

Fig. 4. Distributions of the time professional order pickers and non-professional participants think they can work with data glasses on a daily basis in minutes

ticipants reported significantly less neck pain when using data glasses (M_{M-D} = 2.25, SD = 2.49), t(28) = 4.878, p < .001, d = 0.90. Small tendencies towards differences could be seen when participants were asked about experiencing blinding or blurred vision after using data glasses.

5 Discussion

It can be summarized that the expectations towards using data glasses are quite high and there are indicators that the use of data glasses can convince people that this would be an appropriate tool to enhance workplaces in logistics. Used in a proper way and with the right focus on software ergonomics, data glasses have the potential to even eliminate awkward postures (e.g. looking at a monitor for instructions) as we have seen with a strong effect in this investigation. With this knowledge it becomes obvious that this involves clever design in software engineering. An approach that does not only consider human factors but rather puts them in the center of attention is to be preferred. Age or technical affinity did not show any effect on our findings with respect to the acceptance of data glasses. The protocol indicates that informing the people about the appearance of future workplaces can potentially raise their expectations about the quality of their future workplace as indicated by the results for the question if data glasses will be used more in 10 years. The increase of this expectation after using the data glasses in a simulated workplace environment suggests an overall positive first impression on working with data glasses.

Having this positive motion in mind other factors have to be taken into account as well. We could also see that self-reported cognitive workloads go up when using data glasses. While in this case the participants reported the workload was too low to be satisfying and just right with data glasses, this fact has to be seen as critical as cognitive fatigue could be a result, if the timespans using data glasses get larger. This suggestion has to be looked at thoroughly in further experiments.

The subjective reports of an increase in eye exposure may be an indicator that the use of data glasses could lead to objective problems in this area. This is particularly the case as the analysis of self-reported symptoms related to eye strain shows only small trends of differences. These were negative for the use of data glasses, as some participants felt dazzled and complained about blurred vision. The only significant differences were in the reported neck pain and seem more related to differences in awkward posture as to other factors since the difference was strongly positive for usage of data glasses.

The positive overall picture is also contradicted by the fact that the reported time of how long data glasses can be used is rather short with roughly under 3 h compared to a normal working day. Participants may not have taken into account that companies might want them to use data glasses for an entire working day. The large differences in answers also show that employers have to take a close look at the needs and stress limits of the individual employees.

5.1 Limitations

This study has the following limitations. The fact that using only one certain type of data glasses cannot be ignored especially since these products have product cycles which may address different problems our subjects might have had with the current model. Although monocular data glasses such as the Vuzix M300 are predominantly used in logistics there are also completely different types of data glasses regarding to size, form and weight, which may impact stress levels or even physical workloads.

Although it can be argued that this study is confined to one particular workplace environment several visiting experts from the field stated the work principles of this setup are widely spread throughout companies.

The subjects were not completely randomized to have differing range in age, job qualification and gender on purpose. Inviting more focused groups (e.g. only order pickers) or completely randomizing may yield different results. Randomizing seems a good way to look at all aspects of the study but in reality, some of these job groups will probably not come in contact with data glasses on a regular basis.

Formulating and testing of hypotheses is indispensable especially for the findings about eye strain. Due to the lack of reported effect sizes in the literature this was not possible when the study was launched. In addition, the relevance of the differences in perceived workload have to be investigated and further discussed and criteria have to be formulated what a tolerable limit of strain might be.

6   Conclusion

In this article, we presented the results of a study conducted to examine the first impressions and parameters of acceptance of the use of data glasses in a simulated picking task. Experiences from our protocol purpose that the systematics of introducing data glasses in the workplace with expectable software and hardware ergonomics should be looked at more in detail because it could raise acceptance. Most of our results about impacts on workload seem to have small effects and therefore need further investigation with higher sample sizes if there is any effect to be found. An exception to this is reported eye strain and some parameters related to cognitive load.

When asked for an estimation on how long data glasses could be used on a daily basis, large differences were found between professional and laymen order pickers. This shows that future studies should focus even more on groups of professionals even when conducting laboratory-only studies if feasible.

References

1. Schwerdtfeger, B., Reif, R., Günthner, W., Klinker, G.: Pick-by-vision: there is something to pick at the end of the augmented tunnel. Virtual Real. **15**, 213–223 (2011)
2. Reif, R., Walch, D.: Augmented and virtual reality applications in the field of logistics. Vis. Comput. Int. J. Comput. Graph. **24**, 987–994 (2008)
3. Bretschneider-Hagemes, M., Gross, B.: Smartglasses used by forklift operators: digital accident hazard or efficient work equipment? A pilot study. In: Nah, F.H., Tan, C.H. (eds.) HCIBGO 2017, Part I. LNCS, vol. 10293, pp. 299–307. Springer, Cham (2017). https://doi.org/10.1007/978-3-319-58481-2_23
4. Volkswagen rolls out 3D smart glasses as standard equipment (2015). http://www.ubimax.com/en/references/volkswagen-casestudy.html. Accessed 22 Mar 2018
5. Glockner, H., Jannek, K., Mahn, J., Theis, B.: Augmented reality in logistics, DHL research (2014). http://www.delivering-tomorrow.de/wp-content/uploads/2015/08/dhl-report-augmented-reality-2014.pdf. Accessed 22 Mar 2018

6. Theis, S., Pfendler, C., Alexander, T., Mertens, A., Brandl, C., Schlick, M.: Head-Mounted Displays - Bedingungen des sicheren und beanspruchungsoptimalen Einsatzes. Physische Beanspruchung beim Einsatz von HMDs. Bundesanstalt für Arbeitsschutz und Arbeitsmedizin (2015). ISBN 978-3-88261-162-5

7. Wille, M.: Head-Mounted Displays - Bedingungen des sicheren und beanspruchungsoptimalen Einsatzes: Psychische Beanspruchung beim Einsatz von HMDs. 1. Auflage, p. 136. Bundesanstalt für Arbeitsschutz und Arbeitsmedizin, Dortmund (2015). ISBN 978-3-88261-163-2

8. Sunwook, K., Nussbaum, M.A., Gabbard, J.L.: Augmented reality "Smart Glasses" in the workplace: industry perspectives and challenges for worker safety and health. IIE Trans. Occup. Ergon. Human Factors 4(4), 253–258 (2016). https://doi.org/10.1080/21577323.2016.1214635

9. Terhoeven, J., Wischniewski, S.: Cognitive load by context-sensitive information provision using binocular smart glasses in an industrial setting. In: Nah, F.H., Tan, C.H. (eds.) HCIBGO 2017, Part I. LNCS, vol. 10293, pp. 387–399. Springer, Cham (2017). https://doi.org/10.1007/978-3-319-58481-2_30

10. Friemert, D., Ellegast, R., Hartmann, U.: Data glasses for picking workplaces: impact on physical workloads. In: Nah, F.H., Tan, C.H. (eds.) HCIBGO 2016, Part II. LNCS, vol. 9752, pp. 281–289. Springer, Cham (2016). https://doi.org/10.1007/978-3-319-39399-5_27

11. Dalkey, N., Helmer, O.: An experimental application of the Delphi method to the use of experts. Manag. Sci. 9(3), 458–467 (1963). https://doi.org/10.1287/mnsc.9.3.458

12. Likert, R.A.: Technique for the measurements of attitudes. Arch. Psychol. 140(22), 5–55 (1932)

13. Bangor, A.W.: Display technology and ambient illumination influences on visual fatigue at VDT workstations. Virginia Polytechnic Institute and State University, Virginia (2000)

14. Karrer, K., Glaser, C., Clemens, C., Bruder, C.: Technikaffinität erfassen – der Fragebogen TA-EG. Beiträge 8. Berliner Werkstatt Mensch-Maschine-Systeme, pp. 194–199 (2009)

Continuous Measurement of Muscle Fatigue Using Wearable Sensors During Light Manual Operations

Jiawei Fu[1], Liang Ma[1($\boxtimes$)], Liuxing Tsao[1], and Zhanwu Zhang[2]

[1] Department of Industrial Engineering, Tsinghua University,
Beijing 100084, People's Republic of China
liangma@tsinghua.edu.cn
[2] Hon Hai Precision Industry (Zhengzhou) Co., Ltd.,
Zhengzhou 451100, China

Abstract. Optimization of the temporal aspects of task design requires a better understanding of the development of muscle fatigue over time. The study was aimed to use wearable devices to continuously investigate muscle fatigue in the right forearm of 12 assembly workers. Indicators of fatigue were obtained through surface electromyography (sEMG) and ratings of perceived discomfort during daylong assembly tasks. Average EMG amplitude increased over the work day while median frequency decreased. Local perceived fatigue in the shoulder, upper arm, forearm and wrist increased over the course of the day. However, no clear relationship between perceived fatigue and objective indicators of fatigue was found. Using the wearable monitoring sensors, it is promising to improve worker-supervisor fatigue management in real time. This study might further help in the definition and justification of temporal interventions such as changing the length of the working day, adding extra pauses or task variation across time.

Keywords: Muscle fatigue · Light manual work · Electromyography · Wearable device

1 Introduction

Although technological advancements have reduced the number of heavy manual operations for workers, work-related musculoskeletal disorders (WMSDs) remain a widespread issue leading to increased financial and societal costs [1, 2]. Several risk factors are known to be associated with WMSDs. Among the most commonly accepted physical risk factors are exposure to tasks involving high force demands, tasks involving high rates of repetition, tasks involving awkward postures, and tasks of long duration [3–5]. Light-assembly work is a clear example of work with low force demand, high rates of repetition and long duration. Therefore, assembly workers are exposed to elevated risks of WMSDs [6–8].

To reduce WMSDs risk and to improve health and performance at the workplace, the work intensity of musculoskeletal loads should be ensured within safety limits. When work intensity is too high for workers, industrial manager should affect the

© Springer Nature Switzerland AG 2019
V. G. Duffy (Ed.): HCII 2019, LNCS 11581, pp. 266–277, 2019.
https://doi.org/10.1007/978-3-030-22216-1_20

temporal pattern of the load using effective strategies, which may concern the length of the working day, the work pace, the work-rest scheme or variations in tasks [9].

Work intensity could be estimated by preventive measurements concerning physical fatigue. Muscle fatigue is an important initiating factor in the development of WMSDs. Muscle fatigue, when measured during work, may provide a relevant biomarker for cumulative exposure to repetitive work [10]. A good understanding of the development of muscle fatigue over the course of a working day might be helpful to define the optimal time pattern of the work.

The development of muscle fatigue at repetitive and low-intensity tasks in real or simulated work conditions has been studied on the basis of objective measurements (mainly electromyography (EMG)) and subjective rating scales. Suurküla and Hägg [11] investigated the development of muscle fatigue in the trapezius and infraspinatus muscles after 2 h working at the workplace. EMG variables measured in a test contraction showed a trend towards fatigue, but this was not statistically tested. Mathiassen and Winkel [9] studied the assembly of starters of power saws. In a laboratory setting, they also found a trend towards increased muscle fatigue in the trapezius muscle over the course of a simulated 6-h working day (with a 10% increase of amplitude and a 2.5% decrease in frequency content) but these changes were only partially significant. Perceived fatigue increased significantly during the working day. Bennie et al. [12] and Dennerlein et al. [10] investigated an isolated repetitive ulnar deviation task at a low intensity level during a simulated 8-h working day. Electrostimulation and EMG measurements of the extensor carpi ulnaris were used to detect muscle fatigue. A subjective rating scale was used to investigate the development of local perceived fatigue. Both objective measurements showed an increase in muscle fatigue over the course of an 8-h working day in the absence of perceived fatigue.

The EMG signals in previous studies were obtained in test contractions during breaks at work, not in the real dynamic assembly tasks [10, 11]. These test contractions cannot represent the workload and thus of the muscle behavior during the real tasks [13, 14]. In addition, the EMG measurement in previous studies just took place at several moments during the working day. The discrete measurements of EMG cannot provide the continuous real-time information for muscle fatigue management.

The difficulty of measuring EMG continuously in the real assembly tasks may be due to the disadvantage of the traditional EMG equipment. Traditional EMG devices are expensive and delicate and have many wires connected with electrodes which would disturb normal action of workers. Therefore, it is unrealistic for assembly workers to operate, move or take a coffee as normal when they are equipped with electrodes and wires.

The wearable sensors could be a solution for EMG measurement in industrial settings [15, 16], since it is cheap and easy to use, equipped with wireless transmission capabilities, which minimizes the disturbance caused by instrumentation to the users. Wearable sensors are becoming stretchable and easy to attach to the human body [17]. Montoya et al. [18] showed the feasibility of using one kind of new wearable physiological computing systems, the Myo Armband to measure EMG where high accuracy levels of EMG signal were not required.

Wearables device is an emerging approach and suitable to be applied in natural manufacturing settings, but few pieces of research have been conducted till this day on using wearable devices for detecting/predicting muscle fatigue. Therefore, this paper aimed to use wearable armbands with built-in EMG electrodes to measure muscle fatigue of assembly workers in a mobile phone manufacturing company during a 10-h working day. The general questions that this study tried to answer were:

- how do objective estimates of muscle fatigue in the forearm develop over a 10-h low-intensity assembly work?
- how do subjective feelings of local fatigue develop during a 10-h low-intensity assembly work?

2 Methods

This study was carried out in a production line of a Chinese manufacturer of electrical products. Twelve subjects (four males and eight females) participated in the study. Table 1 shows the demographics of the sample. None of the subjects reported any musculoskeletal disorders. All subjects were experienced assemblers (with 1.61 ± 1.11 years of experience). The subjects gave their written informed consent prior to the start of the study.

Table 1. Demographics of the samples in the case studies.

	Range	Mean	SD
Age (years)	19–46	33.2	8.1
Stature (cm)	152–172	162.9	5.8
Weight (kg)	50–94	65.8	13.0
BMI (kg/m^2)	19.53–39.13	24.8	5.3

These subjects assembled electrical products by picking and placing small parts (Fig. 1). They also performed the quality control for their own work by visual inspection. The work was monotonous, low-intensity with static neck posture and repetitive arm lifting. There was no regular task rotation. Workers were paced by a driven production line. The work pace was indirectly defined by a target (products per hour), but employees could take micro-breaks during the day. The intensity of the trapezius muscle load was estimated at 5% MVC. The subjects worked 10 h per working day which started at 07:30 and ended at 17:30. Two rest breaks of 15 min were taken in the morning and the afternoon. There was a standard 60 min lunch break. Each subject's measurements (described in Fig. 2) took the whole working day.

Fig. 1. A production line for the assembly of electrical products.

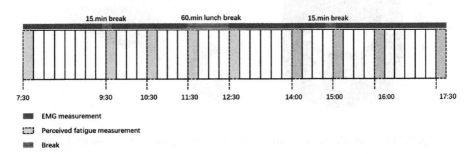

Fig. 2. The working days for the assembly workers. EMG = electromyography.

2.1   Measurements

Electromyography. Surface EMG was measured by wearable EMG devices for nearly 9 h (Myo Armband; Thalmic Labs, Waterloo, Ont). The Myo Armband was placed at the end of the right forearm near the elbow (see Fig. 3(a, b)). The EMG signals were collected by eight electrodes embedded in the Myo armband. These electrodes collected mixed signals from all muscle groups in the forearm (the extensor carpi radialis longus, flexor carpi radialis longus, extensor carpi redialis brevis, flexor carpi redialis brevis, extensor digitorum communis, flexor digitorum communis, extensor digiti minimi, flexor digiti minimi, extensor carpi ulnaris and flexor carpi ulnaris). The electrodes embedded in the armband were cleaned with alcohol each working day. Before the electrodes were applied, the skin was shaved, scrubbed and cleaned with alcohol. Skin resistance was not measured. Raw EMG signals were sampled with a frequency of 200 Hz. The EMG data were recorded as a unitless integer for each sensor representing "activation" and did not translate to volts (V) or millivolts (mV). The EMG signals obtained by eight electrodes were highly correlative, then we used the average EMG signal to describe the fatigue of forearm muscles.

The processing of the EMG signals was performed using the Matlab (R2014, MathWorks, Natick, MA). For the signal filtering, a fourth order Butterworth filters were used with cutoff frequencies from 20 Hz to 100 Hz. A fourth-order rejection Butterworth was applied to signals from 58 Hz to 72 Hz, which filters the noise of the cardiac signal and the signal from the power line [19]. The amplitude values were normalized to the maximum EMG value obtained from the same muscle. To find the muscle fatigue markers (average EMG amplitude (AEMG) and the median frequency (MF)), a moving average window of 200 samples and an overlap of 50 samples was applied to the filtered EMG signals. The median frequency (MF) was analyzed using a fast Fourier transformation in each sliding window.

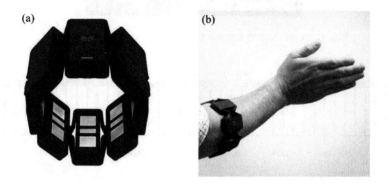

(a)   (b)

Fig. 3. The electrodes of the Myo Armband and its wearing position on the forearm.

Perceived Exertion. Fatigue was also measured using the Borg Rating of Perceived Exertion [20]. A body map consisting of four regions was presented to the subjects, including the shoulder, right upper arm, right forearm and right wrist. Subjects were asked to rate perceived exertion in the regions identified on a 6–20 point-scale (ranging from 6 = no exertion at all to 20 = maximal exertion). In this study, perceived exertion measurements were performed every one or two hours (before starting, 09:30, 10:30, before and after the lunch break, 14:00, 15:00, 16:00 and at the end of the day). The highest perceived exertion score in the four regions was defined as the fatigue score.

2.2   Statistical Analysis

Data were analyzed with a repeated measures ANOVA to compare the independent variables (time moments) for all dependent variables (EMG median frequency (MF), mean amplitude (AEMG) and local perceived fatigue). p-Values were based on degrees of freedom corrected with Greenhouse-Geisser's epsilon to compensate for the effects of violations of the sphericity assumption. A Student t-test was used as the follow-up test for comparisons of means. Pearson's product moment correlation was calculated to determine the relation-ships between objective EMG variables and discomfort. Significance was accepted at $p < 0.05$.

3   Results

3.1   Mean Power Frequency and Amplitude of the Electromyography

As shown in Fig. 4(a) and (b), for the mean amplitude (AEMG) of the EMG signal, a main effect of time was found ($F(9.25, 101.77) = 14.23$, $p < 0.001$, $\eta^2 = .56$). A post-hoc test revealed a significant increase in three periods: from 08:30 to 09:00 ($p < 0.05$), from 10:30 to 11:00 ($p < 0.05$), from 14:30 to 14:50 ($p < 0.001$), and a significant decrease in the period from 14:50 to 15:05 ($p < 0.01$).

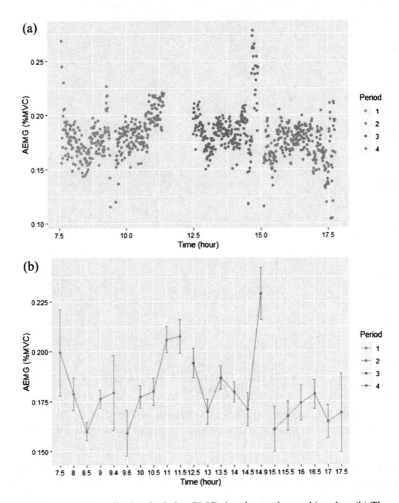

Fig. 4.   (a) The average amplitude of relative EMG signal over the working day; (b) The average amplitude of relative EMG signal at several moments during the working day. Bars represent SD.

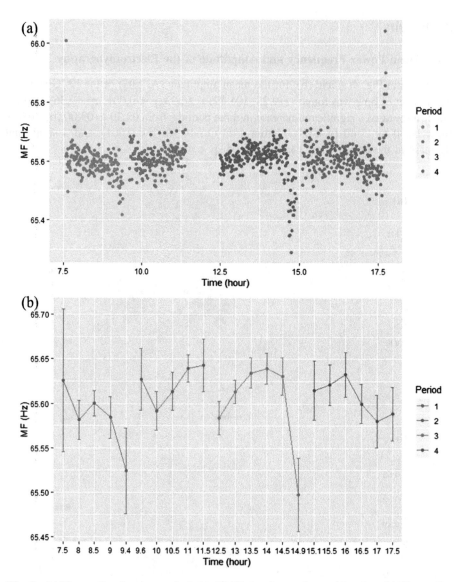

Fig. 5. (a) The median frequency of relative EMG signal over the working day; (b) The median frequency of relative EMG signal at several moments during the working day. Bars represent SD.

As shown in Fig. 5(a) and (b), a significant main effect of time in the MPF were found (F(8.65, 95.15) = 3.3, p < 0.001, η^2 = 0.23). A post-hoc test revealed a significant decrease in the period from 14:30 to 14:50 (p < 0.001), and a significant increase in the period from 14:50 to 15:05 (p < 0.01).

3.2 Perceived Fatigue

Figure 6 shows the development of fatigue in the shoulder, right upper arm, right forearm and the right wrist. A main effect of time on fatigue in the four regions was found ($F(3.6, 39.5) = 21.3$, $p < 0.001$). Post-hoc tests with the Bonferroni adjustment revealed significant increases after the 10:30 ($p < 0.05$), before the lunch ($p < 0.01$), 14:00 ($p < 0.001$), 15:00 ($p < 0.001$), 16:00 ($p < 0.001$) and at the end of the day ($p < 0.001$), compared with scores before starting. The decrease in discomfort during the lunch period, which may have indicated recovery, was not significant ($p = 1.0$).

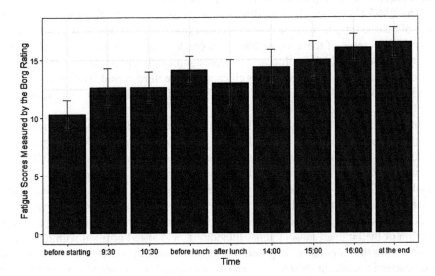

Fig. 6. Perceived fatigue in the four regions (shoulder, right upper arm, right forearm and right wrist) during the working day.

3.3 Correlations Between Variables

Pearson's correlation coefficients were determined for the difference between the start and the end of the day for average EMG amplitude, MPF and perceived fatigue rating (Table 2). No relationship was found between subjective and objective estimates of muscle fatigue. Correlation coefficients were low and not significant.

Table 2. Correlation coefficients between objective estimates and subjective ratings of fatigue.

	r	p
AEMG – Fatigue rating	−0.14728	0.1282
MF – Fatigue rating	−0.03401	0.7268

4 Discussion

In the current study, the development of muscle fatigue in realistic assembly work was continuously investigated using a wearable device. This type of field research has some limitations in comparison with controlled laboratory experiments. The time period as well as the number of subjects is often restricted. In addition, there are many confounding factors related to production planning, capacity utilization, variation in products, (technical) disturbances and absence of subjects. These confounders are hard to control and have large effects. Conversely, field research has the obvious advantage that it requires no extrapolation of results to practice.

The EMG signals obtained in this field study showed indications of the development of muscle fatigue over the course of a working day. Indications of muscle fatigue include an increase of the average EMG amplitude and a decrease of the MF [21]. In this study, average EMG amplitude increased significantly during the first three periods of the day while MF only changed significantly in the third period. The production line slowed down after 16:30, and thus the AEMG and MF had a recovery trend at the fourth period of the day.

Incidences of muscle fatigue (RMS, MF and perceived fatigue) were found different between subjects. The interindividual differences are consistent with the results of other studies in which much interindividual variability in muscle activities was found in a standardized machine-paced work at a packing machine [6, 22, 23]. The variability of fatigue incidences between subjects could be due to individual fatigue patterns, which means muscle motor units recover from fatigue at different speeds for participants, or each participant would use different muscle motor units to take over the function of the fatigued muscle units. In addition, a changed position within the range of motion for the subjects could possibly explain the variable pattern of muscle fatigue. Differences in working postures, working speed and work outputs were observed during the experiment. The variability of fatigue incidences between subjects could also be due to electrodes positions. For each participant, electrode locations were visually controlled carefully, but small changes in electrode positions may have occurred and skin resistance was not controlled.

In addition to the indications of the development of objective muscle fatigue, local perceived fatigue in the shoulder, upper arm, forearm and wrist was also found to increase. Remarkably, there was no clear relationship between subjective indicators (perceived fatigue in the four regions) and the objective indicators (MF and amplitude of the EMG signal) of muscle fatigue. Sundelin and Hagberg [24] were able to find a significant relationship between subjective and objective indicators. However, that study used a 1-h strictly controlled laboratory task with a relative high intensity. No such relationship has been established so far, to the present authors' knowledge, in field research over the course of a working day.

The absence of a relationship might be explained by several factors. First, the ratings of local perceived fatigue obtained in occupational settings might be the result of other issues rather than fatigue. For instance, the subjective interpretation of an intervention (e.g. longer working hours) might influence the subjects' feelings of fatigue. Moreover, fatigue also encompasses sensations of other sensory experiences such as pain and pressure as well as discomfort in tissues other than the muscles. Conversely, EMG measurements reflect only a small part of the physiological state of the muscle. Changes in the MF and AEMG of the EMG signal are less consistent during pro-longed low-level dynamic contractions than during high-force contractions [13, 25]. Physiological processes not reflected in the EMG signal (e.g. local blood flow, local metabolic changes, changes in the mechanical properties of the excitation contraction coupling) may play an important role in the development of fatigue during low-intensity work.

EMG is only one objective method to estimate muscle fatigue. To get comprehensive estimate of muscle fatigue, complementary objective methods may be needed in the future research. Blangsted et al. [14] used mechanomyography (MMG) to detect fatigue during short, low-intensity static contractions. Physiological features such as motor unit recruitment and synchronization of motor units are thought to be reflected by MMG measurements [26] and could provide additional information on fatigue processes. Rosendal et al. [27] used micro dialysis to investigate intramuscular metabolism of the trapezius muscle during a 20 min repetitive low-force contraction exercise. An increase in pain was accompanied by a rise in local anaerobic metabolism. However, the use of micro dialysis in field studies is likely to be limited. An increase in discriminatory power may be required here and these methods (micro dialysis and MMG) could help to achieve field applications.

In conclusion, this study measured signs of fatigue over the whole working day using the wearable devices. Using these wearable monitoring sensors, it is promising to improve worker-supervisor fatigue management in real time. This study might further help in the definition and justification of temporal interventions such as changing the length of the working day, introducing extra pauses or task variation across time.

Acknowledgements. This work was supported by the National Natural Science Foundation of China [grant number 71471095] and Ministry of Science and Technology of China [grant number 2017YFC0820200 and 2016IM010200].

References

1. Andersson, G.: The Burden of Musculoskeletal Diseases in the United States: Prevalence, Societal and Economic Cost. American Academy of Orthopaedic Surgeons, Rosemont (2008)
2. Horton, R.: GBD 2010: understanding disease, injury, and risk. Lancet **380**(9859), 2053–2054 (2012)
3. Putz-Anderson, V., Bernard, B.P., Burt, S.E., et al.: Musculoskeletal disorders and workplace factors. National Institute for Occupational Safety and Health (NIOSH), p. 104 (1997)
4. Hoogendoorn, W.E., van Poppel, M.N., Bongers, P.M., Koes, B.W., Bouter, L.M.: Physical load during work and leisure time as risk factors for back pain. Scand. J. Work Environ. Health **25**, 387–403 (1999)
5. Punnett, L., et al.: Estimating the global burden of low back pain attributable to combined occupational exposures. Am. J. Ind. Med. **48**(6), 459–469 (2005)

6. Aarås, A., Westgaard, R.H.: Further studies of postural load and musculoskeletal injuries of workers at an electro-mechanical assembly plant. Appl. Ergon. **18**(3), 211–219 (1987)
7. Hagberg, M., Wegman, D.H.: Prevalence rates and odds ratios of shoulder-neck diseases in different occupational groups. Occup. Environ. Med. **44**(9), 602–610 (1987)
8. Mathiassen, S.E., Winkel, J., Sahlin, K., Melin, E.: Biochemical indicators of hazardous shoulder-neck loads in light industry. J. Occup. Med. Off. Publ. Ind. Med. Assoc. **35**(4), 404–407 (1993)
9. Mathiassen, S.E., Winkel, J.: Physiological comparison of three interventions in light assembly work: reduced work pace, increased break allowance and shortened working days. Int. Arch. Occup. Environ. Health **68**(2), 94–108 (1996)
10. Dennerlein, J.T., Ciriello, V.M., Kerin, K.J., Johnson, P.W.: Fatigue in the forearm resulting from low-level repetitive ulnar deviation. AIHA J. **64**(6), 799–805 (2003)
11. Suurküla, J., Hägg, G.M.: Relations between shoulder/neck disorders and EMG zero crossing shifts in female assembly workers using the test contraction method. Ergonomics **30**(11), 1553–1564 (1987)
12. Bennie, K.J., Ciriello, V.M., Johnson, P.W., Dennerlein, J.: Electromyographic activity of the human extensor carpi ulnaris muscle changes with exposure to repetitive ulnar deviation. Eur. J. Appl. Physiol. **88**(1–2), 5–12 (2002)
13. Søgaard, K., Blangsted, A.K., Jørgensen, L.V., Madeleine, P., Sjøgaard, G.: Evidence of long term muscle fatigue following prolonged intermittent contractions based on mechano- and electromyograms. J. Electromyogr. Kinesiol. **13**(5), 441–450 (2003)
14. Blangsted, A.K., Sjøgaard, G., Madeleine, P., Olsen, H.B., Søgaard, K.: Voluntary low-force contraction elicits prolonged low-frequency fatigue and changes in surface electromyography and mechanomyography. J. Electromyogr. Kinesiol. **15**(2), 138–148 (2005)
15. Tsao, L., Ma, L., Papp, C.T.: Using non-invasive wearable sensors to estimate perceived fatigue level in manual material handling tasks. In: Ahram, T. (ed.) AHFE 2018. AISC, vol. 795, pp. 65–74. Springer, Cham (2019). https://doi.org/10.1007/978-3-319-94619-1_7
16. Tsao, L., Li, L., Ma, L.: Human work and status evaluation based on wearable sensors in human factors and ergonomics: a review. IEEE Trans. Hum. Mach. Syst. **49**(1), 72–84 (2018)
17. Amjadi, M., Kyung, K.U., Park, I., Sitti, M.: Stretchable, skin-mountable, and wearable strain sensors and their potential applications: a review. Adv. Func. Mater. **26**(11), 1678–1698 (2016)
18. Montoya, M., Henao, O., Muñoz, J.: Muscle fatigue detection through wearable sensors: a comparative study using the myo armband. In: Proceedings of the XVIII International Conference on Human Computer Interaction, p. 30. ACM, September 2017
19. Merletti, R., Farina, D.: Surface Electromyography: Physiology, Engineering, and Applications. Wiley, New York (2016)
20. Borg, G.: Borg's Perceived Exertion and Pain Scales. Human Kinetics, Champaign (1998)
21. Basmajian, J.V., De Luca, C.J.: Muscles Alive: Their Functions Revealed by Electromyography, 5th edn. Lippincott Williams and Wilkins, Baltimore (1985)
22. Kilbom, Å., Persson, J.: Work technique and its consequences for musculoskeletal disorders. Ergonomics **30**(2), 273–279 (1987)
23. Veiersted, K.B., Westgaard, R.H., Andersen, P.: Pattern of muscle activity during stereotyped work and its relation to muscle pain. Int. Arch. Occup. Environ. Health **62**(1), 31–41 (1990)
24. Sundelin, G., Hagberg, M.: Electromyographic signs of shoulder muscle fatigue in repetitive arm work paced by the methods-time measurement system. Scand. J. Work Environ. Health **18**, 262–268 (1992)

25. Nussbaum, M.A.: Static and dynamic myoelectric measures of shoulder muscle fatigue during intermittent dynamic exertions of low to moderate intensity. Eur. J. Appl. Physiol. **85** (3–4), 299–309 (2001)
26. Orizio, C., Gobbo, M., Diemont, B., Esposito, F., Veicsteinas, A.: The surface mechanomyogram as a tool to describe the influence of fatigue on biceps brachii motor unit activation strategy. Historical basis and novel evidence. Eur. J. Appl. Physiol. **90**(3–4), 326–336 (2003)
27. Rosendal, L., et al.: Increase in muscle nociceptive substances and anaerobic metabolism in patients with trapezius myalgia: microdialysis in rest and during exercise. Pain **112**(3), 324–334 (2004)

Level of Robot Autonomy and Information Aids in Human-Robot Interaction Affect Human Mental Workload – An Investigation in Virtual Reality

Mara Kaufeld[1(✉)] and Peter Nickel[2]

[1] Human Factors, Fraunhofer Institute for Communication,
Information Processing and Ergonomics FKIE, Bonn, Germany
mara.kaufeld@fkie.fraunhofer.de
[2] Accident Prevention - Product Safety, Institute for Occupational
Safety and Health of the German Social Accident Insurance (IFA),
Sankt Augustin, Germany
peter.nickel@dguv.de

Abstract. In future work systems, humans may interact with scalable industrial robots. In a virtual reality simulation study, human mental workload effects were analyzed in human-robot interactions (HRI) with variations in design requirements regarding human factors and ergonomics (HFE) as well as occupational safety and health (OSH). Each of 20 participants performed his/her own task while interacting with two virtual robots in a manufacturing environment. Results on task performance indicated relative lower human mental workload when robots acted on lower level of robot autonomy (lower LORA) and the human operator was informed about upcoming HRI by multi-modal signaling (Information Aid 'on'). However, this pattern of workload reflected in performance measures, was not reflected in mental workload ratings. Hence, compensational adjustments in operator performance were assumed. It was concluded, that a combination of less autonomous robots and multi-modal feedback result in relatively less operator distraction from task performance and, thus, less impairment in operator workload. HFE and OSH may improve when HRI is audio-visually indicated and robot activities are adapted to human operator task requirements (low LORA). Therefore, results have the potential to inform future design of HRI regarding HFE and OSH at different workplaces in industry and services.

Keywords: Human-robot interaction · Work systems design ·
Occupational safety and health · Virtual reality · Mental workload ·
Human-automation interaction · Human-system interaction

1 Introduction

1.1 Human-Robot Interaction

Human-robot interaction (HRI) concerns interdisciplinary investigations with the aim to understand, design, and evaluate robotic systems for use by or with humans [1].

© Springer Nature Switzerland AG 2019
V. G. Duffy (Ed.): HCII 2019, LNCS 11581, pp. 278–291, 2019.
https://doi.org/10.1007/978-3-030-22216-1_21

Over the last decades, it has been an active topic in an expanding field with a great need for human factors and ergonomics (HFE) involvement. HRI encloses a range of new developments in supporting, assisting, supplementing, representing and scaling human behavioral competencies in interaction processes in industry, services and leisure time [2]. The design of interactions as mutual exchange of information should be guided along an iterative design process for human-centered solutions in practice, referring to HFE design criteria (e.g. freedom from impairment [3, 4]), strategies (e.g. task orientation [5, 6]) and principles (e.g. compatibility [6, 7]).

Traditionally, individual operators interact tightly coupled with individual technical systems with regard to both, access to, and control of system resources [8]. Future work systems, such as smart and mobile manufacturing and interlinked installations in an industry 4.0 context, however, will include scalable multi-user, multi-technical system architectures with HFE design requirements still in its infancy. HRI becomes even more complex as robot types increase and classifications become broader.

With regard to technical developments, robots may be categorized as industrial robots, professional and personal service robots, and collaborative including managerial robots [9]. Industrial robots are automatically controlled, reprogrammable, multipurpose manipulators, programmable in three or more axes, which can be fixed in place or mobile for use in industrial automation applications [10]. Key hazards are mechanical hazards due to movement and force of the robot as well as hazards referring to poor consideration of HFE design strategies and principles due to engineering errors, poor work place design, and interaction errors [9, 11]. A broad range of safety measures for industrial robots is included in international standards and guidelines [10].

Unlike industrial robots, professional and personal service robots often operate outside industrial settings in unstructured and unpredictable environments [9]. Applications for professional service robotics are, among others, in military, agriculture, healthcare, and logistics and those in personal service refer to settings with robotic toys, vacuum and floor cleaners, camera drones or lawn movers etc. Although user task requirements differ across applications and HRI includes mobility of both, humans and robots, key hazards remain similar. Substantial standardization and guidance on safety requirements is still work in progress, especially for personal or private applications. In some cases, safety measures are different due to smaller robots with lower level of forces and due to different legislation for the context of use.

Collaborative workspaces are part of a safeguarded space where robots and human workers can perform simultaneously during production operations [12]. Benefit for industrial human-robot collaboration is seen in time and space savings due to closer and joint movement areas without fences, in motivation for development of innovative robotic systems, in a lower potential for defeating safeguards, and in potential physical ergonomics improvements such as assistance in flexible, repetitive, or heavy materials handling and positioning [13]. While human-robot collaboration is dominant in industrial settings, the number of personal care robots (e.g. mobile servant robots, person carrier robots, exoskeleton or other assistants) increases, but there is still dispute about managerial robotics as a related approach in administrative or business settings [9]. Safety requirements for the prevention of mechanical hazards have already been agreed upon [12], however, the specification does not yet allow guidance along HFE design strategies and principles [7, 14].

Design of HRI in work systems refers to three different but interrelated interfaces; i.e. the task, the interaction, and the information interface [4, 15]. HFE and occupational safety and health (OSH) in work systems design set the operator task in the center of the design strategy (primacy of task design [16]) that should be supported by technical and organizational components of the system to serve task completion, optimize physical and mental workload, and improve overall system performance. Even though solutions are available for human-automation interaction [7], different arrangements for function allocation in HRI are not yet widely used. It may not be too early for OSH professionals to be involved in HFE and OSH in HRI [9].

1.2   Level of Robot Autonomy and Information Aids

Primacy of Task Design. Designing the task interface means analyses of system goals, functions as well as activities and information required before allocating functions to the operator and/or to technical components of a work system such as machinery [5]. Taking into account task design requirements in ergonomics [5, 17] promotes feasible tasks with low physical and mental impairment for the operator [6, 14, 15]. Among others, 'provide autonomy' is one of the relevant task design requirements in human-automation interaction in the given context [5, 17]. It calls for tasks that can be performed autonomously if they allow the human operator a certain amount of freedom and independence. Decisions about processing part-tasks or the way in which tasks are executed should be left to the human operator's discretion. Provision of autonomy on the interaction interface level is closely linked to the design requirement 'controllability' [17]. 'Controllability' refers to a human operator being able to start a dialogue procedure and to influence its direction and speed until the goal has been achieved. The design of the information interface supports upper level task and interaction interfaces with the requirement to present information that is reliably detected by the human operator [6, 17]. Combinations of modalities potentially improve coding and encoding in feedback information [7, 18], however, arrangements require adaptations to the context of use.

Level of Robot Autonomy. Among task design requirements in HFE [4, 5], autonomy is a critical construct related to HRI with wide variations across robot platforms. The concept of autonomy, however, already differs across disciplines. The understanding used in engineering is that of being independent of the environment. In contrast, the understanding in psychology goes beyond and refers to self-control, self-governance, free will and a person's ability to attribute mental states to self and others [19]. A definition of autonomy in HRI both disciplines may agree upon is proposed as: "The extent to which a robot can sense its environment, plan based on that environment, and act upon that environment with the intent of reaching some task-specific goal (either given to or created by the robot) without external control." [19, p. 77] Levels of robot autonomy (LORA), ranging from teleoperation to fully autonomous systems [19], influence the way in which humans and robots interact with one another. LORA taxonomies seem to be more suitable in HRI than level of automation taxonomies [7, 19], because capabilities such as mobility, environmental manipulation, and social interaction separate robots from other automated systems in both function and physical form.

Information Aids. Feedback in HRI is required to inform both, the human operator and the robot, about events in the work environment, interaction activities and consequences for the work process. Robots act relatively silent and provide relatively poor cues that enable humans to infer detailed information about robot's state, location and intention with regard to work place and process of performance [20]. Therefore, information presentation or signaling about robot activities is key not only to mutual interactions, but also to human safety referring to HFE design requirements [6].

When humans work alongside robots, however, some safety measures (e.g. auditory warning, separating protective devices) will not be suitable or even insufficient [12]. Several modes of information presentation (e.g. visual, auditory, haptics) could be appropriate for feedback with regard to HFE; however, advantages and disadvantages vary across applications. Multi-modal information presentation aids may alert humans in HRI to important information that is either necessary for task completion or helpful in interacting more effectively [21]. Some information aids simply present the user visual and auditory warnings more salient. Consequently, appropriate information or feedback provided to the user potentially serves to optimize mental workload in HRI [7].

1.3 Investigations of HRI in Virtual Environments (for OSH)

Virtual reality (VR) has matured into a simulation tool for humans to interact with dynamic, three-dimensional virtual environments. In industry and services, VR supports applied research in work systems analysis, design, and evaluation for training, for demonstration, for visualization and design purposes [22–24]. Since workplaces with humans interacting or even collaborating with robots in time or space on common tasks are still rare, VR simulation studies have been conducted to investigate HFE issues with regard to OSH in future work environments [1, 25, 26].

With future work systems including scalable multi-user, multi-technical system architectures HFE design requirements and recommendations for HRI becomes a challenging endeavor. In order to contribute to HFE design in the context of HRI, the interaction of two industrial robots with a single operator working on his/her own task is investigated in a mixed reality manufacturing environment [27]. The impact of two LORA combined with Information Aids (multi-modal feedback) on human mental workload is addressed in the present study. It is assumed that human mental workload is relatively reduced when robots interact less autonomous, thus, adapt their request to human tasks. As compared to more robot autonomy when robot's requests are random which is forcing the human operator to perform tasks in parallel. Information aids such as audio-visual signaling about the robot's state may also relatively reduce human mental workload. Hence, when robots intend to interact, this is indicated to the human operator. A combination of lower LORA that adapt their request to human tasks and signaling of tasks (Information Aid) in HRI is also expected to relatively reduce human mental workload.

2   Methods

2.1   Participants

A virtual simulation study was conducted, with 20 participants (age: $M = 30.9$ years, $SD = 10.3$; balanced gender ratio) working together with two robots in a manufacturing environment [27]. All participants provided informed consent to take part in the study, reported adequate or corrected visual acuity, and passed vision tests.

2.2   Task Environment

The Mixed Reality Task Environment. The study was scheduled in the VR laboratory of the Institute for Occupational Safety and Health of the German Social Accident Insurance (IFA; www.dguv.de/ifa/sutave) equipped with a 7 m² operating space in front of a curved presentation wall of 24 m² (3 m × 8 m) (see Fig. 1). The design of the lab supported operator experience of presence and immersion in the mixed virtual environment [28].

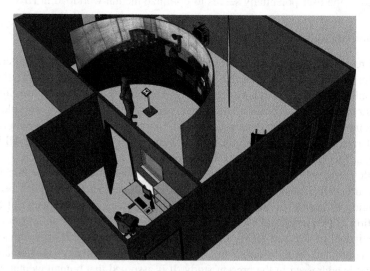

Fig. 1. Bird view perspective of the VR laboratory in the IFA.

The task environment was composed in mixed reality with two industrial robots (R 30-16, Reis Robotics, Kuka AG, Germany) in 1:1 scale in the central part of the manufacturing scenario. A control desk with controls for the human operator enabled haptic feedback during task performance. Vizard Virtual Reality Toolkit (WorldViz LLC, USA) and Python (Python Software Foundation, USA) composed components necessary for contexts of use in the environment (e.g. boxes, storage areas), kinetical and environmental models (e.g. collision, gravity, illumination) and the animation of moving parts of machinery (e.g. two industrial robots). Real and virtual objects cooperated in real-time, i.e. movements of the virtual robots within the virtual work scenario was directly controlled by the operator through real control actuators.

Tasks by the Human Operator and by HRI. During the experiment, the participants performed two tasks. The first was a grammatical reasoning task [29, 30], presented on a virtual display unit in front of the participant (see Fig. 2). The task of the human operator (HT) ran on a notebook using a commercially available software-based generating system (ERTS, [31]). Each trial presented two line statements (e.g. "# BEFORE &" and "# AFTER *") describing the arrangement of characters (e.g. "& # *").

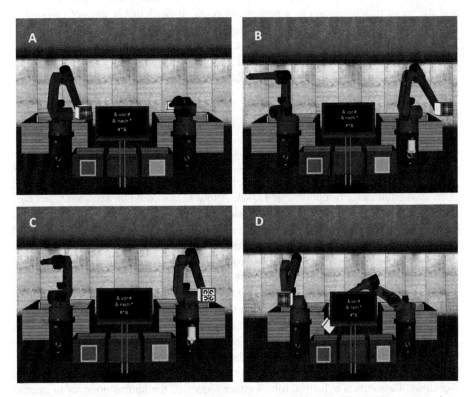

Fig. 2. Virtual environment for the combined HT and HRT tasks. The HRT sequence is as follows: A: robot takes cube from box; B: robot is moving cube in rotational movement; audio-visual cue by warning light and short sound; C: bottom side of the cube is aligned to the participant; Landolt rings are discernible; D: end of the task; robot sorts cube in the designated box. (Color figure online)

Participants were instructed to compare the statements with the third line and press the key "same" if both statements were true, or if both are false. If one of the sentences was true but the other was false, participants were requested to press the key "different". Participants were encouraged to respond to each trial within 10 s. If a trial was answered earlier, the next task followed immediately. The inter-trial interval was 3 s. Functional components of grammatical or logical reasoning are relevant in complex assembly tasks including planning, selecting and implementing various sequences.

For the secondary task, an interaction between the participant and the virtual robots was created. In the human-robot task (HRT), the robot took a cube from a box and guided it in a rotational movement in front of the participant (see Fig. 2). The procedure represents choice reactions and resembles quality control tasks in manufacturing settings. For three seconds, the bottom side of the cube was aligned in the direction of the participant and thus discernible. On the bottom side, a matrix with four rings (Landolt shape; standard vision signs for vision tests was displayed. Participants were instructed to identify whether one of the four rings had an opening to the top (green key) or not (red key) and to press the corresponding key placed on the control desk. Following this, the robot sorted the cube into the corresponding colored box (see Fig. 2). The task ended when the participant had either pressed one of the keys or not and the robot finally moved to a predefined point. If participants did not respond in time, the cube was transported into the grey box (see Fig. 2).

The experimental scenario represents a manufacturing environment with a human operator interacting with two robots (HRT) while performing his/her own task (HT). Since HRT is carried out on a random basis, the operator only shifts his attention to the robots when necessary and possible.

2.3   Variables

Independent Variables. Interaction task settings at the shop floor level with the human operator performing his/her task while performing other tasks in parallel in HRI open up the full range of options for *LORA*. A low *LORA* could be assumed when e.g., robots in HRI present quality control tasks and the human operator can choose to decide during idle time, decides, and initiates action implementation. In terms of *LORA* taxonomy, this describes the range of 'teleoperation' [19]. The *LORA* is higher when the robot presents the control task, the robot chooses when to decide, decides and initiates action implementation (in case the human does not act in time). In the lower *LORA*, at task design level, the human operator retains a certain amount of freedom and independence and some decisions are remaining. At interface design level, the human operator retains controllability in so far as to start a dialogue procedure and to influence its direction and speed until the goal has been achieved [17].

The aim of the study was to investigate the effect of *LORA* (low versus high), *Information Aid* (on versus off) and the interaction of these two factors on human mental workload. Two virtual industrial robots either requested the human operator to interact whenever required (high *LORA*), or adapted the request for interaction to idle times between individual operator tasks (low *LORA*). At low *LORA*, the HRT started during the inter-trial interval of the HT. At high *LORA*, the HRT began randomly.

Requirements for interaction were indicated either audio-visually or not (*Information Aid*). The audio-visual cue included a sound and a yellow warning light attached to the bottom of the virtual robots (see Fig. 2). To avoid order effects the sequence was counterbalanced. Different *LORA* combined with different *Information Aids* were investigated regarding their impact on human mental workload.

Dependent Variables. Human mental workload in terms of work stress is the total of all assessable influences impacting human beings from external sources and affecting that person mentally [3, 32]. Mental strain is the immediate effect of mental stress within the individual and is usually measured by ratings of perceived mental workload, task performance and psychophysiological parameters [3, 30]. Compensatory control models (e.g. [33]) point out that in the process of mental workload and under specific circumstances of high work stress are associated with performance protection. This may cause variations in measurements of psychophysiology and perceived workload not being reflected in task performance and vice versa. In the present study, perceived mental workload was assessed using the multidimensional rating NASA-TLX [34]. LimeSurvey™ (LimeSurvey GmbH, Hamburg) in an off-line version was used to present the ratings and acquire data. Performance data such as response times, error rates and the number of missed trial for HT and HRT were analyzed using ERTS [31] and spreadsheet analysis.

2.4 Procedure and Data Analysis

In the beginning, participants were asked to fill in information forms and questionnaires (e.g. vision, SSQ [35], ITQ [36], PSAM [37], NASA-TLX [34]). Participants got training on separate and combined HRT and HT. Next, participants completed two experimental runs of 20 min each and concluded always with NASA-TLX, SSQ and

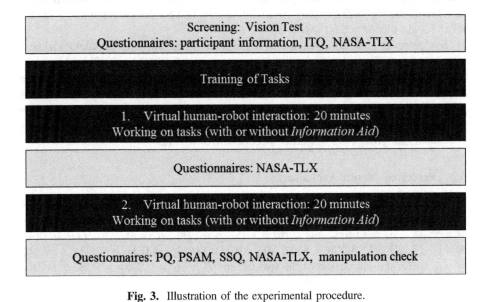

Fig. 3. Illustration of the experimental procedure.

PSAM. Finally, participants filled in other forms and questionnaires including a manipulation check and finished with debriefing (see Fig. 3).

For the measures of human mental workload the effects of a mixed 2 (*LORA*) × 2 (*Information Aid*) analysis of variance (ANOVA; IBM® SPSS® Statistics 23, USA) were evaluated. *LORA* was set as a between-subject factor. *Information Aid* was set as a within factor with the sequence counterbalanced to avoid order effects with the sequence counterbalanced to avoid order effects. The groups high *LORA* and low *LORA* revealed to be similar in terms of age ($M = 30.1, SD = 8.9; M = 31.7, SD = 11.9$) and profession distribution. Hence, groups are comparable and possible differences are unlikely due to differences in age or profession. In ANOVA calculations Bonferroni correction was applied to adjust p-values and avoid issues of multiple testing.

3 Results

3.1 Manipulation Check and VR Assessments

Questionnaires referring to a successful manipulation showed that every participant realized the audio cue, which was combined with the visual cue. Most participants (85%) realized the visual cue through the yellow shining warning light. None of the participants described the signal as disturbing and most of the participants (85%) stated that the signal was helpful.

The immersive tendencies taken from the 7-point Likert scales of the ITQ (immersive tendencies questionnaire, [36]) ratings showed a total score of $M = 4.39$ ($SD = 1.03$). The PQ (presence questionnaire, [36]) asked for the experienced presence in the end of the experiment. The averaged total score was $M = 3.87$ ($SD = 1.29$) on a 7-point Likert scale. The PSAM Scale (presence self-assessment manikin, [37]) is a non-verbal tool to measure the participant's sense of presence. On a 9-point scale, pictograms display different degrees of immersion in VR. The average score for the PSAM scale was $M = 6.68$ ($SD = 1.94$).

Symptoms of simulator sickness were measured using the SSQ (simulator sickness questionnaire, [35]) and revealed a total score of $M = 5.62$ ($SD = 9.48$) which is relatively low compared to other simulators [38]. For the immersive tendencies, the sense of presence, and the simulator sickness score t-tests were calculated for the two *LORA* groups (low and high) to ensure that differences between the groups are not due to different experiences in VR. With no significant differences between the groups, it was concluded that groups did not differ in experiences in VR.

3.2 Perceived Mental Workload

No significant effects were found for perceived mental workload measured by the NASA-TLX. This applies to *Information Aid* (off: $M = 57.45$, $SD = 10.39$; on: $M = 55.48$, $SD = 11.01$), $F(1, 16) = 1.15$, $p = .300$, $\eta^2 = .07$, to *LORA* (low: $M = 57.27$, $SD = 11.84$; $M = 54.88$, $SD = 9.71$), $F(1, 16) = 0.33$, $p = .573$, $\eta^2 = .02$, as well as for the interaction of the two factors: $F(1, 16) = 0.09$, $p = .758$, $\eta^2 = .01$.

3.3 Performance Measures

Results for the HT and the HRT are summarized in Table 1. For main effects of LORA, evidence was found in errors as well as combined errors and missed trials in the HRT. A main effect of *Information Aid* was found for errors and response times of the HT and combined errors and missed trials and response times for HRT. An interaction effect of LORA and *Information Aid* revealed to be significant for missed trials and response times of the HT.

Table 1. Significant (bold) and marginal significant main and interaction effects with p-values and effect sizes presented (Degrees of freedom (Dof) = 16; Dof for error variance = 1).

Performance measures	Main effect *LORA*	Main effect *Information Aid*	Interaction effect *LORA* × *IA*
HT			
Errors and missed	–	–	–
Missed	–	–	$p = .044$, $\eta^2 = .23$
Errors	–	$p = .014$, $\eta^2 = .32$	–
Response time	–	$p = .004$, $\eta^2 = .42$	$p = .002$, $\eta^2 = .47$
HRT			
Errors and missed	$p = .005$, $\eta^2 = .39$	$p = .003$, $\eta^2 = .43$	$p = .064$, $\eta^2 = .20$
Missed	$p = .059$, $\eta^2 = .33$	–	$p = .098$, $\eta^2 = .16$
Errors	$p = .025$, $\eta^2 = .28$	–	–
Response time	–	$p = .027$, $\eta^2 = .27$	$p = .060$, $\eta^2 = .20$

Main effects for *LORA* show that task performance is higher when *LORA* is low, i.e. robot behavior is at lower autonomy. Figure 4 (left) depicts exemplary that errors in the HRT were fewer for the low *LORA* condition. The same pattern is found for *Information Aid* and resulting in higher performance. Figure 4 (right) shows that errors in the HT were fewer for *Information Aid* 'on' condition.

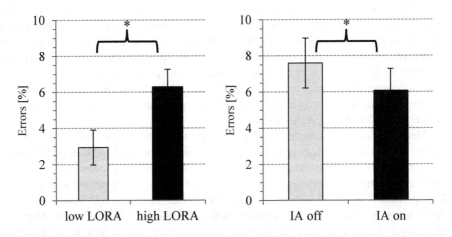

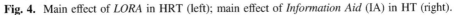

Fig. 4. Main effect of *LORA* in HRT (left); main effect of *Information Aid* (IA) in HT (right).

Interaction effects for the different performance measures revealed best performance for a combination of relatively lower *LORA* with *Information Aid* 'on'. In Fig. 5 the response times of HT are depicted to show the pattern of the interaction effect.

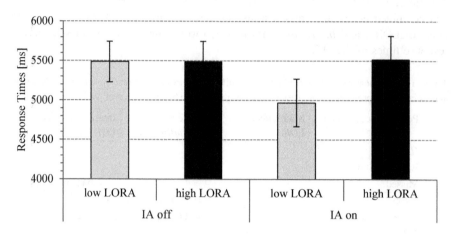

Fig. 5. Interaction effect of *LORA* and *Information Aid* (IA) for the response times of the HT.

4   Discussion and Conclusions

The aim of the present study was to evaluate human mental workload effects for two levels of robot autonomy (LORA) either supported by informational aids (IA) or not. In a virtual manufacturing scenario, two robots interacted with one human operator who is performing his/her own task in parallel. The results provided initial empirical evidence for relative lower mental workload when robots acted on lower LORA while the human operator was informed about upcoming HRI by audio-visual signals (Information Aid 'on').

In this low LORA scenario, robots were limited in their autonomy and required to adapt to the human task demands. This avoided the human operator being required to take on both HT and HRT in parallel and allowed to actively plan, choose and implement sequential task performance [3, 7, 14]. In addition, upcoming HRI was informed by an audio-visual signal, aiding the human operator to recognize the request and to organize HRI in ongoing activities. LORAs adapted to human task requirements and feedback design supported the human operators, improved HFE in work systems design and OSH in the given context.

Mental workload measures available to investigate effects of LORA and Information Aid in the present study were perceived mental workload and task performance. Systematic experimental variation was recognized according to questionnaires about experimental manipulations. However, it was not reflected in mental workload ratings. Task performance for HT and HRT showed variations in LORA and Information Aid. A combination of less autonomous robots and multi-modal feedback may have resulted in relatively less operator distraction from task performance and, thus, less impairment in mental workload. With regard to the compensatory control model, it could be assumed that human operators adjusted their task performance strategy and shifted to simpler or more imprecise procedures requiring lower level working memory [33]. This may have led to performance decrements while perceived mental workload was maintained at above average level.

The present study indicates that simulation environments such as VR are suitable to investigate future HRI for different purposes. Basic HFE and OSH requirements for the design of VR simulation environments refer to simulation sickness and the sense of presence [22]. Simulator sickness revealed a total score, which categorized the virtual environment as causing negligible to minor symptoms [38]. The level of perceived presence has a strong impact on human experience and performance in virtual environments as well as a high relevance for effects in real world environments [36, 37]. Measures resulted in well above average ratings, indicating that participants immersed in the virtual world and were present in the manufacturing environment. Therefore, in general, VR enables creating scenarios not desirable or too dangerous to face in reality, or providing past, present and future systems in the context of use [7, 24].

In the present context of HRI, simulation studies are also suitable because workplaces with humans interacting with scalable robots in time or space on common tasks are still rare. There are, however, methodological issues why care must be taken, when results related to simulations should be applied in practice. One issue refers to scenario selection, which cannot be a full representation of future work scenarios. The other refers to VR as simulation techniques, which will always be simplifications and reductions due to complexity of reality [22, 23]. Nevertheless, both issues provide advantages such as that even those work environments can be investigated that do not yet exist and that simulation environments may to a certain extent represent and augment HRI concept design according to HFE and to OSH.

Acknowledgements. It is a pleasant duty to acknowledge all participants for taking part in the study and for immersing in the virtual work environment. The authors are grateful to the efforts of Mr Andy Lungfiel for technical development of VR scenarios.

References

1. Goodrich, M.A., Schulz, A.C.: Human-robot interaction: a survey. Found. Trends Hum.-Comput. Interact. **1**(3), 203–275 (2007)
2. Lee, J.D., Seppelt, B.D.: Human factors and ergonomics in automation design. In: Salvendy, G. (ed.) Handbook of Human Factors and Ergonomics, pp. 1615–1642. Wiley, Hoboken (2012)
3. Hacker, W.: Mental workload. In: Stellmann, J.M. (ed.) ILO Encyclopaedia of Occupational Health and Safety, vol. 1, pp. 29, 41–43. International Labour Office, Geneva (2011)
4. Nickel, P., et al.: Human-system interaction design requirements to improve machinery and systems safety. In: Arezes, P.M. (ed.) Advances in Safety Management and Human Factors. Advances in Intelligent Systems and Computing (AISC), vol. 969, pp. 3–13. Springer, Cham (2020). https://doi.org/10.1007/978-3-030-20497-6_1
5. EN 614-2: Safety of machinery – Ergonomic design principles – Part 2: Interactions between the design of machinery and work tasks. CEN, Brussels (2008)

6. Sanders, M.S., McCormick, E.J.: Human Factors in Engineering and Design. McGraw Hill, New York (1993)
7. Wickens, C.D., Hollands, J.G., Banbury, S., Parasuraman, R.: Engineering Psychology and Human Performance. Pearson, Upper Saddle River (2013)
8. Tews, A.D., Matarić, M.J., Sukhatme, G.S.: A scalable approach to human-robot interaction. In: Proceedings of the IEEE International Conference on Robotics & Automation, 14–19 September 2003, Taipei, pp. 1665–1670 (2003)
9. Murashov, V., Hearl, F., Howard, J.: Working safely with robot workers: recommendations for the new workplace. J. Occup. Environ. Hyg. **13**(3), D61–D71 (2016)
10. EN ISO 10218: Robots and robotic devices - Safety requirements for industrial robots - Part 1: Robots. Part 2: Robot systems and integration. CEN, Brussels (2012)
11. Vasic, M., Billard, A.: Safety issues in human-robot interactions. In: IEEE International Conference of Robotics Automation (ICRA), 6–10 May 2013, Karlsruhe, Germany, New York, pp. 197–204 (2013)
12. ISO/TS 15066: Robots and robotic devices - collaborative robots. ISO, Geneva (2016)
13. Fryman, J., Matthias, B.: Safety of industrial robots: from conventional to collaborative applications. In: Proceedings of the 7th International Conference on Safety of Industrial Automated Systems (SIAS 2012), 11–12 October 2012, Canada, pp. 198–203. Institut de recherche Robert-Sauvé en santé et en sécurité du travail (IRSST), Montréal (2012)
14. EN ISO 10075-2: Ergonomic principles related to mental workload – Part 2: Design Principles. CEN, Brussels (2000)
15. Nachreiner, F., Nickel, P., Meyer, I.: Human factors in process control systems: the design of human–machine interfaces. Saf. Sci. **44**, 5–26 (2006)
16. Ulich, E., Schüpbach, H., Schilling, A., Kuark, J.: Concepts and procedures of work psychology for the analysis, evaluation and design of advanced manufacturing systems: a case study. Int. J. Ind. Ergon. **5**(1), 47–57 (1990)
17. Wichtl, M., et al.: Improvements of machinery and systems safety by human factors, ergonomics and safety in human system interaction. Adv. Intell. Syst. Comput. (AISC) **819**, 257–267 (2019)
18. EN 894 Series (ISO 9355 Series): Safety of machinery – Ergonomics requirements for the design of displays and control actuators – Part 1: General principles for human interactions with displays and control actuators, Part 2: Displays, Part 3: Control actuators, Part 4: Location and arrangement of displays and control actuators. CEN, Brussels (2010)
19. Beer, J.M., Fisk, A.D., Rogers, W.A.: Toward a framework for levels of robot autonomy in human-robot interaction. J. Hum.-Robot. Interact. **3**(2), 74–99 (2014)
20. Cha, E., Fitter, N.T., Kim, Y., Fong, T., Mataric, M.J.: Effects of robot sound on auditory localization in human-robot collaboration. In: 2018 Proceedings of ACM/IEEE International Conference on Human-Robot Interaction, 5–8 March 2018, Chicago, USA, pp. 434–442. ACM, New York (2018)
21. Johnson, R.C., Saboe, K.N., Prewett, M.S., Coovert, M.D., Elliott, L.R.: Autonomy and automation reliability in human-robot interaction: a qualitative review. In: Proceedings of the 53rd Annual Meeting of the Human Factors and Ergonomics Society, 19–23 October 2009, San Antonio, USA, pp. 1398–1402. HFES, San Diego (2009)
22. Hale, K.S., Stanney, K.M. (eds.): Handbook of Virtual Environments: Design, Implementation, and Applications. CRC Press, Boca Raton (2015)
23. Miller, C., et al.: Human-machine interface. In: Hockey, G.R.J. (ed.) THESEUS Cluster 2: Psychology and Human-Machine Systems – Report, pp. 22–38, Indigo, Strasbourg (2012)

24. Nickel, P., Lungfiel, A.: Improving occupational safety and health (OSH) in human-system interaction (HSI) through applications in virtual environments. In: Duffy, Vincent G. (ed.) DHM 2018. LNCS, vol. 10917, pp. 85–96. Springer, Cham (2018). https://doi.org/10.1007/978-3-319-91397-1_8

25. Naber, B., Lungfiel, A., Nickel, P., Huelke, M.: Human Factors zu Robotergeschwindigkeit und -distanz in der virtuellen Mensch-Roboter-Kollaboration. In: GfA (ed.) Chancen durch Arbeits-, Produkt- und Systemgestaltung – Zukunftsfähigkeit für Produktions- und Dienstleistungsunternehmen, pp. 421–424. GfA-Press, Dortmund (2013)

26. Koppenborg, M., Nickel, P., Naber, B., Lungfiel, A., Huelke, M.: Effects of movement speed and predictability in human-robot-collaboration. Hum. Factors Ergon. Manuf. Serv. Ind. **27**(4), 197–209 (2017)

27. Kaufeld, M.: Auswirkungen von Aufgabenpassung und Informationssignalisierung in der Mensch-Roboter-Interaktion auf die psychische Beanspruchung. Eine empirische Studie in virtueller Realität (Master thesis). Rheinische Friedrich-Wilhelms-Universität, Bonn (2016)

28. Nickel, P., Lungfiel, A., Trabold, R.-J.: Reconstruction of near misses and accidents for analyses from virtual reality usability study. In: Barbic, J., D'Cruz, M., Latoschik, M.E., Slater, M., Bourdot, P. (eds.) EuroVR 2017. LNCS, vol. 10700, pp. 182–191. Springer, Cham (2017). https://doi.org/10.1007/978-3-319-72323-5_12

29. AGARD: Human performance assessment methods (AGARDograph-308, and addendum of 1991). NATO-AGARD, Neuilly sur Seine (1989)

30. Nickel, P., Nachreiner, F.: Sensitivity and diagnosticity of the 0.1-Hz component of heart rate variability as an indicator of mental workload. Hum. Factors **45**(4), 575–590 (2003)

31. Beringer, J.: Experimental runtime system, ERTS: a flexible software tool for developing and running psychological reaction time experiments on IBM PCs. Behav. Res. Methods Instrum. Comput. **26**(3), 368–369 (1994)

32. EN ISO 10075-1: Ergonomic principles related to mental workload – Part 1: General issues and concepts, terms and definitions. CEN, Brussels (2017)

33. Hockey, G.R.J.: Compensatory control in the regulation of human performance under stress and high workload: a cognitive-energetical framework. Biol. Psychol. **45**(1–3), 73–93 (1997)

34. Hart, S.G., Staveland, L.E.: Development of the NASA task load index (TLX): results of empirical and theoretical research. In: Hancock, P.A., Meshkati, N. (eds.) Human mental workload, pp. 139–183. North-Holland, Amsterdam (1988)

35. Kennedy, R.S., Berbaum, K.S., Lilienthal, M.G.: Simulator sickness questionnaire: an enhanced method for quantifying simulator sickness. Int. J. Aviat. Psychol. **3**(3), 203–220 (1993)

36. Witmer, B.G., Singer, M.J.: Measuring presence in virtual environments: a presence questionnaire. Presence **7**(3), 225–240 (1998)

37. Wissmath, B., Weibel, D., Mast, F.W.: Measuring presence with verbal vs. pictorial scales: a comparison between online and ex post ratings. Virtual Reality **14**, 43–53 (2010)

38. Stanney, K.M., Kennedy, R.S., Drexler, J.M.: Cybersickness is not simulator sickness. In: Proceedings of the 41st Annual Meeting of the Human Factors and Ergonomics Society (HFES 1997), 22–26 September 1997, Albuquerque, USA, pp. 1138–1142. HFES, San Diego (1997)

OSH and the Future of Work: Benefits and Risks of Artificial Intelligence Tools in Workplaces

Phoebe V. Moore[(✉)]

School of Business, University of Leicester, Leicester, UK
Pm358@leicester.ac.uk

Abstract. There are significant possibilities for workplace progress and growth in productivity with the integration of artificial intelligence (AI) applications and tools in workplaces. However, there are also important occupational safety and health (OSH)-related questions arising as AI is integrated into workplaces. Stress, discrimination, heightened precariousness, musculoskeletal disorders, and the possibilities of work intensification and job losses have already been shown to pose psychosocial risks, including physical violence in digitalised workplaces. These risks are exacerbated when AI augments already existing technological tools or are newly introduced for workplace management and design. Indeed, AI exaggerates OSH risks in digitalised workplaces, because it can allow increased monitoring and tracking and thus may lead to micro-management, which a prime cause of stress and anxiety. AI stresses the imperative of giving more credibility and potentially authority to prediction machines, robotics and algorithmic processes at work. But it is worth stressing that it is not technology in isolation that creates OSH benefits or risks. It is instead the *implementation* of technologies that creates negative or positive conditions.

Keywords: Artificial intelligence · Health and safety · Human resources · Robotics · Work design · Stress · Workplace tracking

1 Introduction

Artificial intelligence (AI) was born, or at least its name was, in 1956, at a series of academic workshops organised at Dartmouth College in New Hampshire, United States. At that conference a group of scientists set out to teach machines to use language, form concepts, improve themselves (as machines) and solve problems originally 'reserved for humans' (McCarthy et al. 1955). John McCarthy and his colleagues had high hopes that they could achieve this within a few weeks. The conference was not successful on its own terms, but, nevertheless, a significant field of research and development in AI was launched.

We might now laugh at this optimism, but interest in AI did not disappear. Indeed, AI debates and experimentation have gone through a series of phases, from the peak of hope that machines could be trained to behave exactly like people and achieve an equivalent level of intelligence to humans, as seen at the Dartmouth workshops, to the troughs of disillusionment. The first experimental robots, such as 'WOBOT' and

© Springer Nature Switzerland AG 2019
V. G. Duffy (Ed.): HCII 2019, LNCS 11581, pp. 292–315, 2019.
https://doi.org/10.1007/978-3-030-22216-1_22

'Shakey', did not achieve the universal AI they were aiming for. Two so-called AI winters lasted from 1974 to 1980 and from 1987 to 1993 as various experiments failed and funding waned. But now, in 2019, a revived interest is bubbling.

Nowadays, advanced countries are allocating significant pots of funding, in the order of billions, to research and development in AI, with the United States in the lead, closely followed by China and Israel (Delponte 2018). AI is predicted to provide a 26% boost to gross domestic product (GDP) by 2030 in China. North America is predicted to see a 14.5% boost (PwC 2018a), and some predictions indicate that AI will create as many jobs as it eliminates (PwC 2018b). Consultancies' and thinktanks' forecasts run alongside a series of governmental, regional and international organisations' high-level reports that predict the significant impact of AI on economies and societies, including the United States (White House Office of Science and Technology Policy 2018); (the United Kingdom's Department for Business, Energy and Industrial Strategy and Department for Digital, Culture, Media and Sport 2018); the International Labour Organization (ILO) (Ernst et al. 2018); and the European Union (European Commission 2018).

In most cases, high-level governmental and organisational reports are predicting that AI will improve productivity. Discussions of productivity involve direct implications for workers and working conditions, of course, but there is little discussion yet for how the introduction of AI into workplaces will benefit or create risks for occupational safety and health (OSH) for workers themselves. To lay the foundations for this expert report, which addresses this gap in research, the paper starts by discussing the meaning of AI to provide a clear steer for discussions of its impact on workers. Then we outline where AI is being used in a series of applications and tools used for assisted work, as well as workplace decision-making and the OSH risks and benefits arising. We start with human resources (HR) via people analytics and interview filming, then look at the integration of AI-augmented robotics, including collaborative robots (cobots) and chatbots in factories, warehouses and call centres. Next, we identify uses of wearable technologies and assistive tablets on the production assembly line and then outline algorithmic processes in work in the gig economy. Then, we outline international stakeholder responses to the rising risks and benefits of AI at work. In conclusion the report provides some recommendations for how to best manage and mitigate the worst risks that could arise from using AI in workplaces.

2   What Is AI?

There is debate today about 'what is AI' and 'what is not AI'. It may even appear that there is more hype around AI than reality. Nonetheless, as governments are pouring huge amounts of capital into research and development and publishing high-level reports making notable predictions about the contributions that AI will make to GDP and productivity, it is worth taking AI seriously. The dispute around the authenticity of AI is relevant, however. So, rather than waver on the definition throughout this report, the original discussion about what AI 'could be', is recalled. McCarthy and his colleagues, mentioned in the introduction, defined the 'artificial intelligence problem' as one that 'is taken to be that of making a machine behave in ways that would be called intelligent if a human were so behaving' (McCarthy et al. 1955). Since the authors of the Dartmouth document invented the concept of AI, recalling their definition lends much to the discussion. Can machines behave like humans? This philosophical question is not extensively dealt with in this article, but it is worth noting that wider questions about humans and our relationship with machines were central to this research area's early incarnations (see, for example, Simon 1969; Dreyfus 1972 and Weizenbaum 1976), and they still operate in the background of AI experimentation and application today. Central to these questions is the fairly obvious, but rarely vocalised, question: why do we want machines to behave like us and even better than us? Socially, what is missing that we need such improvements? In any case, while there are a number of definitions of AI, for the purposes of this report, McCarthy's definition will be used as a general insight to locate the emerging issues epistemologically.

The European Commission's definition, as provided in its 2018 Communication, is adopted for this report, whereby AI 'refers to systems that display intelligent behaviour by analysing their environment and taking actions—with some degree of autonomy—to achieve specific goals' (European Commission 2018). Another 2018 report entitled European artificial intelligence leadership, the path for an integrated vision further defines AI as a 'cover term for techniques associated with data analysis and pattern recognition' (Delponte 2018, p. 11). That report, which was requested by the European Parliament's Committee on Industry, Research and Energy, differentiates AI from other digital technologies in that 'AI are set to learn from their environments in order to take autonomous decisions' (Delponte 2018, p. 11). These definitions facilitate a clear discussion about what is at stake as AI systems and machines are integrated into workplaces, where systems demonstrate competences that allow decision-making and prediction much faster and more accurately than humans and provide human-like behaviour and assistance for workers.

There are various levels of AI now discussed by experts: weak and strong. 'Weak AI' is where a machine relies on software to guide its investigation and responses. This type of AI does not reach a level of consciousness or full sentience as such, but it acts as a problem-solver within a specific field of application. 'Weak AI' thus applies to expert systems and text and image recognition. 'Strong AI', also called 'universal AI' (Hutter 2012), on the other hand, refers to when a machine can demonstrate behaviour that equals or exceeds the competence and skill of humans, and this is the type of AI that most intrigued researchers such as Alan Turing. Even before McCarthy and his colleagues' conference in 1956, in 1950, Alan Turing had asked himself, 'Can machines think?' (Turing 1950). The stage of universal AI is reached when a single universal agent can learn to behave optimally in any environment, where universal competences are demonstrated by a robot, such as walking, seeing and talking. Today, as computer memory capacity increases and programmes become more sophisticated, universal AI is becoming increasingly likely. This is an advance that could complete the automation process, whereby robots become as good at working as people and do not exemplify human characteristics such as tiredness or sickness, and so on. People appear to feel more comfortable with weak AI, which enhances machines and means that they behave like assistants to humans, rather than replacing us as workers or replacing human management.

We now outline the uses of AI at work and the potential and evidence for risks and benefits for OSH, based on desk-based research and a series of expert interviews carried out by the author.

3   AI in the Workplace

Although there are significant possibilities for workplace progress and growth in productivity, there are also important OSH safety and health-related questions arising as AI is integrated into workplaces. Stress, discrimination, heightened precariousness, musculoskeletal disorders, and the possibilities of work intensification and job losses have already been shown to pose psychosocial risks, including physical violence in digitalised workplaces (Moore 2018a). These risks are exacerbated when AI augments already existing technological tools or are newly introduced for workplace management and design. Indeed, AI exaggerates OSH risks in digitalised workplaces, because it can allow increased monitoring and tracking and thus may lead to micro-management, which a prime cause of stress and anxiety (Moore 2018a). AI stresses the imperative of giving more credibility and potentially authority to what Agarwal and colleagues (2018) call 'prediction machines', robotics and algorithmic processes at work. But it is worth stressing that it is not technology in isolation that creates OSH benefits or risks. It is instead the implementation of technologies that creates negative or positive conditions.

3.1   AI in Human Resources

In the area of HR business execution, one increasingly popular area of AI integration is called 'people analytics', defined broadly as the use of big data and digital tools to 'measure, report and understand employee performance, aspects of workforce planning, talent management and operational management' (Collins et al. 2017). Computerisation, data gathering and monitoring tools allow organisations to conduct 'real-time analytics at the point of need in the business process … [and allow] for a deeper understanding of issues and actionable insights for the business' (ibid.). The prediction machine algorithms applied for these processes often reside in a 'black box' (Pasquale 2015), and people do not fully understand how they work, but, even so, computer programs are given the authority to make 'prediction[s] by exception'[1] (Agarwal et al. 2018).

Not all people analytics have to be, strictly speaking, AI. However, programmes' intelligent responses to algorithmic equations allow machine learning, which generates predictions and asks associated questions that emerge without human intervention except at the data input phase, and are AI in the sense of the EU's definition above. Big data has been seen as a lucrative growth area for some years, whereby the collection of information about everything, all the time, has been an attractive investment. Now, the

---

[1] 'Prediction by exception' refers to processes whereby computers deal with large data sets and are able to make reliable predictions based on routine and regular data and also to spot outliers and even send notifications 'telling' the user that checks should be made or that human assistance or intervention should be provided.

big data era is paying off in HR circles, because the extensive pools of data now available can be used to train algorithms to form analyses and make predictions about workers' behaviour via machine learning and thereby assist management decision-making. On the basis of the patterns identified, AI enables an algorithm to produce solutions and responses to enquiries about patterns across data much more quickly than people could. Machine learning responses are often unlike those that a human alone would, or perhaps even could, generate. Data about workers can be gathered from various sources both in and outside the workplace, such as number of keyboard clicks, information from social media, number of and content of telephone calls, websites visited, physical presence, locations visited outside the workplace through GPS (global positioning system) tracking, movements around the office, content of emails and even tone of voice and bodily movements in sociometrics (Moore 2018a, 2018b).

Also called 'human analytics', 'talent analytics' and 'human resource analytics', in an era of 'strategic HR', this application of AI-enabled tools is defined broadly as the use of individualised data about people to help management and HR professionals make decisions about recruitment, i.e. who to hire, for performance appraisals and promotion considerations, to identify when people are likely to leave their jobs and to select future leaders. People analytics are also used to look for patterns *across* workers' data, which can help to spot trends in attendance, staff morale and health issues at the organisational level.

About 40% of HR functions in international companies are now using AI applications. These companies are mostly based in the United States, but some European and Asian organisations are also coming on board. A PwC survey shows that more and more global businesses are beginning to see the value of AI in supporting workforce management (PwC 2018a). One report shows that 32% of personnel departments in tech companies and others are redesigning organisations with the help of AI to optimise 'for adaptability and learning to best integrate the insights garnered from employee feedback and technology' (Kar 2018) Recent IBM research indicates that in the world's 10 largest economics, even as many as 120 million workers may need to be retrained and reskilled to deal with AI and intelligent automation. This report indicates that two thirds of CEOs believe AI will drive value in HR (IBM 2018). A Deloitte report shows that 71% of international companies consider people analytics a high priority for their organisations (Collins et al. 2017), because it should allow organisations to not only provide good business insights but also deal with what has been called the 'people problem' (ibid.).

'People problems' are also called 'people risks' (Houghton and Green 2018), which are divided into seven dimensions in a Chartered Institute for Personnel Development (CIPD) report (Houghton and Green 2018) as:

1. talent management,
2. health and safety,
3. employee ethics,
4. diversity and equality,
5. employee relations,
6. business continuity, and
7. reputational risk.

But perhaps people are not the only 'problem'. Based on the original definition of AI, in which machines are predicted to eventually have the capability of behaving as a human would, if humans are discriminating and biased, then we should not be surprised when AI provides biased answers. In other words, machine learning operates only on the data that it is fed, and if those data reveal past discriminatory hiring and firing practices, then the results of the algorithmic process are likely to also be discriminatory. If the information gathered about workers is not buffered with qualitative information about individuals' life experiences and consultation with workers, unfair judgements could be made (see below for more on this).

AI-enhanced HR practices can help managers obtain seemingly objective wisdom about people even before they hire them, as long as management has access to data about prospective workers, which has significant implications for tailoring worker protection and preventing OSH risks at the individual level. Ideally, people analytics tools can aid employers to 'measure, report and understand employee performance, aspects of workforce planning, talent management and operational management' (Collins et al. 2017). Indeed, algorithmic decision-making in people analytics could be used to support workforces by aligning employee performance feedback and performance pay—and workforce costs—with business strategy and support for specific workers (Aral et al. 2012, cited in Houghton and Green 2018, p. 5). Workers should be personally empowered by having access to new forms of data that help them to identify areas for improvement, that stimulate personal development and that achieve higher engagement.

However, if processes of algorithmic decision-making in people analytics do not involve human intervention and ethical consideration, this human resource tool could expose workers to heightened structural, physical and psychosocial risks and stress. How can workers be sure that decisions are being made fairly, accurately and honestly, if they do not have access to the data that their employer holds and uses? OSH risks of stress and anxiety arise if workers feel that decisions are being made based on numbers and data that they have neither access to nor power over. This is particularly worrying if people analytics data leads to workplace restructuring, job replacement, job description changes and the like. People analytics are likely to increase workers' stress if data are used in appraisals and performance management without due diligence in process and implementation, leading to questions about micro-management and workers feeling 'spied on'. If workers know that their data are being read for talent spotting or for deciding possible layoffs, they may feel pressurised into improving their performance and begin to overwork, posing OSH risks. Another risk arises with liability, in which companies' claims about predictive capacities may later be queried for accuracy or personnel departments held accountable for discrimination. One worker liaison expert[2] indicated that worker data collection for decision-making such as that seen in people analytics has created the most urgent issues arising with AI in workplaces. Often, works councils are not aware of the possible uses of such management

---

[2] Dr Michael Bretschneider-Hagemes, Head of the Employees Liaison Office of the German Commission KAN spoke to the author of this report in an interview on 18 September 2018.

P. V. Moore

tools. Or, systems are being put into place without consulting with works councils and workers. Even more OSH risks arise, such as worker stress and job losses, when technologies are implemented in haste and without appropriate consultation and training or communication. In this context, it is interesting to consider a project run at the headquarters of IG Metall, in which workplace training curricula are being reviewed in 2019 in the context of Industrie 4.0. (see also Sect. 3.4)[3]. the Findings Demonstrate that Training Needs Updating not Only to Prepare Workers for Physical Risks, as Has Been Standard in Heavy Industry OSH Training, but also for the Mental and Psychosocial Risks Introduced by Digitalisation at Work, Which Includes People Analytics Applications[4].

Another form of people analytics involves filming job interviews. This practice is carried out by organisations such as Nike, Unilever and Atlantic Public Schools. These companies are using products that allow employers to interview candidates on camera, in which AI is used to judge both verbal and non-verbal cues. One such product is made by a group called HireVue and is used by over 600 companies. The aim is to reduce bias that can arise if, for example, an interviewee's energy levels are low or if the hiring manager has more affinity for an interviewee based on similar, for example, age, race and related demographics. However, there is evidence that preferences from previous hiring managers are reflected in hiring, and heterosexual white men are, a report by Business Insider reveals, the hiring preference, other things being equal (Feloni 2017). If the data provided to an algorithm reflect the dominant bias over time, then it may score someone with 'in group' facial expressions higher and give a lower rating to other cues tied to sexual orientation, age and gender that do not resemble a white male.

Overall, people analytics poses both benefits and risks for OSH. As this tool uses algorithms, machines should be subject to extensive testing before they are used for any of the HR applications outlined. Another possibility is for a people analytics algorithm to be designed specifically to eliminate biases, which is not an easy task. Risk assessments are already being experimented with in criminal systems in which AI informs sentencing and parole boards to attempt to eliminate bias. IBM has recently publicised a tool that likewise intends to reduce risks of discrimination. It is hoped that these types of initiatives will deal with rising risks for OSH in AI-assisted HR decision-making. Nonetheless, AI's strength is also its weakness.

---

[3] *Industrie 4.0* is a much-debated term that originated in German manufacturing circles, designed to advance manufacturing in marketing terms. Some critics argue that it is a narrative rather than a reality today. Nonetheless, it is commonly accepted that, if there is to be a trajectory of industrial revolutions, *Industrie 1* is the term for the first industrial revolution and thus the invention of the steam engine. The second is linked to advancements in science and the third to digitalised inventions incorporated into production. Today, the 'Internet of Things', whereby machines technically communicate with another, advanced robotics and increased capacity for memory and processing power are seen as the driving force for the concept of *Industrie 4.0*.

[4] Antje Utecht, who works in the training and policy department at the headquarters of IG Metall in Frankfurt, Germany, shared these insights with the author of this report during an interview on 16 October 2018.

3.2   Cobots in Factories and Warehouses

We can picture the scene: huge orange robot arms in factories whirring away in expansive warehouses in industrial landscapes, building car parts and assembling cars where conveyor belts lined with humans once stood. Robots have directly replaced workers on the assembly line in factories in many cases, and sometimes AI is confused with automation. Automation in its pure sense involves, for example, the explicit replacement of a human's arm with a robot arm. EU-OSHA's report *Foresight on new and emerging occupational safety and health risks associated with digitalisation by 2025* (EU-OSHA 2018, p. 89) indicates that robots allow people to be removed from dangerous physical work and environments with chemical and ergonomic hazards, thus reducing OSH risks for workers. Lower skilled, manual work has historically been most at risk and is still at a high risk of automation. Now, automation can be augmented with autonomous machine behaviour or 'thinking'. So, the AI dimension of automation reflects where workers' brains, as well as their limbs, may no longer needed. Now, as one EU-OSHA discussion paper on the future of work regarding robots and work indicates that, while robots were at first built to carry out simple tasks, they are increasingly enhanced with AI capabilities and are being 'built to think, using AI' (Kaivo-oja 2015).

Cobots are now being integrated into factories and warehouses where they work alongside people in a collaborative way. They assist with an increasing range of tasks, rather than necessarily automating entire jobs. Amazon has 100,000 AI-augmented cobots, which has shortened the time taken to train workers to less than 2 days. Airbus and Nissan are using cobots to speed up production and increase efficiency.

As a recent Netherlands Organisation for Applied Scientific Research (TNO) report states, there are three types of OSH risks in human-cobot-environment interactions (TNO 2018, pp. 18–19):

(a) robot-human collision risks, in which machine learning can lead to unpredictable robot behaviour;
(b) security risks, in which robots' internet links can affect the integrity of software programming, leading to vulnerabilities in security; and
(c) environmental risks, in which sensor degradation and unexpected human action in unstructured environments can lead to risks to the environment.

AI-permitted pattern and voice recognition and machine vision mean that not only are unskilled jobs at risk of replacement but now a range of non-routine and non-repetitive jobs can be carried out by cobots and other applications and tools. In that light, AI-enhanced automation enables many more aspects of work to be done by computers and other machines (Frey and Osborne 2013). One example of the protection of workplace OSH through AI-augmented tools is found in a chemicals company that makes optical parts for machines. The miniscule chips that are produced need to be scanned for mistakes. Previously, one person's job was to detect mistakes with their own eyes, sitting, immobile, in front of repeated images of chips for several hours at a time. Now, AI has fully replaced this task. The OSH risks, which have now been of course, eliminated, include musculoskeletal disorders and eye strain and damage[5].

Cobots can reduce OSH risks, as they allow AI systems to carry out other types of mundane and routine service tasks in factories, which historically create stress, over-work, musculoskeletal disorders and even boredom as a result of repetitive work. However, AI-augmented robots in factories and warehouses can create stress and a range of serious problems if they are not implemented appropriately. Indeed, one UK-based trade unionist indicated that digitalisation, automation and algorithmic management when 'used in combination ... are toxic and are designed to strip millions of folks of basic rights'[6]. Potential OSH issues may also include psychosocial risk factors if people are driven to work at a cobot's pace (rather than the cobot working at a person's pace) and collisions between cobots and people[7]. Another cobot-related case of machine-human interaction creating new working conditions and OSH risks is when one person is assigned to 'look after' one machine and is sent notifications and status updates about machines on a personal device such as a smartphone or a personal laptop. This can lead to risks of overwork, whereby workers feel compelled to take note of notifications in out-of-work hours and their work-life balance is disrupted[8].

One expert[9] in AI and work discussed developments around the Internet of Things in workplaces, in which machine-to-machine connected systems work alongside human labour in factories and warehouses. Data input problems, inaccuracies and faults with machine-to-machine systems create significant OSH risks as well as questions of liability. Indeed, sensors, software and connectivity can be faulty and unstable, and all vulnerabilities raise questions about who is legally responsible for any damage that emerges. Is it a cobot's fault if it runs into a worker, the worker's fault, the company who manufactured the cobot originally or the company that employs the worker and integrates the cobot? The complexities abound. Human-robot interaction creates both OSH risks and benefits in the physical, cognitive and social realms, but cobots may someday have the competences to reason and therefore must make humans feel safe. To achieve this, cobots must demonstrate perception of objects versus humans and the ability to predict collisions, adapt behaviour appropriately and demonstrate sufficient memory to facilitate machine learning and decision-making autonomy (TNO 2018, p. 16) along the lines of the previously explained definitions of AI.

3.3   Chatbots in Call Centres

Chatbots are another AI-enhanced tool that can deal with a high percentage of basic customer service queries, freeing up humans working in call centres to deal with more complex questions. Chatbots work alongside people, although not only in the physical

---

[5] Information obtained from interview with Antje Utecht (fn 4).

[6] Interview with Maggie Dewhurst of the Independent Workers Union of Great Britain (IWGB) in 2017.

[7] Based on an interview with Dr Sam Bradbrook, specialist at the United Kingdom's Health and Safety Executive's Foresight Centre, in September 2018.

[8] Interview with Antje Utecht (fn 4).

[9] Interview with Dr Sam Bradbrook (fn 7).

sense;. Tithin the back end of systems, they are used to deal with customer queries over the phone using natural language processing. Dixons Carphone uses a conversational chatbot now named Cami that can respond to first-level consumer questions on the Currys website and through Facebook Messenger. Insurance company Nuance launched a chatbot named Nina to respond to questions and access documentation in 2017. Morgan Stanley has provided 16,000 financial advisers with machine learning algorithms to automate routine tasks.

Call centre workers already face extensive OSH risks because of the nature of the work, which is repetitive and demanding and subject to high rates of micro-surveillance and extreme forms of measurement (Woodcock 2016). An increasing number of activities are already recorded and measured in call centres. Words used in emails or stated vocally can be data-mined to determine workers' moods, a process called 'sentiment analysis'. Facial expressions likewise can be analysed to spot signs of fatigue and moods that could be used to make judgements and thus lower OSH risks emerging with overwork. But chatbots, while designed to be assistive machines, still pose psychosocial risks around fears of job loss and replacement. Workers should be trained to understand the role and function of workplace bots and to know what their collaborative and assistive contributions are.

3.4   Wearables and AI in (Lot Size) Manufacturing

Wearable self-tracking devices are increasingly seen in workplaces. The market for wearable devices in industrial and healthcare wearables has been predicted to grow from USD 21 million in 2013 to USD 9.2 billion by 2020 (Nield 2014). Between 2014 and 2019, 13 million fitness devices are predicted to be incorporated into workplaces. This is already happening in warehouses and factories where GPS, radio-frequency identification and now haptic sensing armbands, such as that patented by Amazon in 2018, have replaced the use of clipboards and pencils.

One new feature of automation and *Industrie 4.0* processes in which AI-enhanced automation is under way is in the area of lot size manufacturing[10]. This process involves workers being provided with glasses with screens and virtual reality functionality, such as HoloLenses and Google Glasses, or computer tablets on stands within the production line, which are used to carry out on-the-spot tasks on production lines. The assembly line model, in which a worker carries out one repeated, specific task for several hours at a time, has not disappeared completely, but the lot size method is different. Used in agile manufacturing strategies, this method involves smaller orders made within specific time parameters, rather than constant bulk production that does not involve guaranteed customers.

In lot size manufacturing, workers are experiencing the introduction of visual on-the-spot training enabled by a HoloLens screen or tablet, where they are invited to carry out new tasks that is learned instantly and carried out only for the time required to manufacture the specific order a factory receives. While at first glance these assistance

---

[10] Interview with Dr Michael Bretschneider-Hagemes, cited above (fn 2).

systems may *appear* to provide increased autonomy, personal responsibility and self-development, this is not necessarily the case (Butollo et al. 2018). The use of on-the-spot training devices, worn or otherwise, means that workers need less pre-existing knowledge or training, because they carry out the work case by case. The risk of work intensification thus arises, as head-mounted displays or tablet computers become akin to live instructors for unskilled workers. Furthermore, workers do not learn long-term skills, because they are required to perform on-the-spot, modular activities in custom assembly processes, needed to build tailor-made items at various scales. While this is good for the company's efficiency in production, lot size methods have led to significant OSH risks in that that they deskill workers, because skilled labour is needed only to design the on-the-spot training programmes used by those workers who no longer need to specialise themselves.

OSH risks can further emerge because of a lack of communication, meaning that workers are not able to comprehend the complexity of the new technology quickly enough, particularly if they are also not trained to prepare for any hazards arising. One real issue is in the area of small businesses and start-ups, which are quite experimental in the use of new technologies but often overlook ensuring that safety standards are adhered to before accidents occur, when it is, of course, too late[11]. An interview with those involved in the IG Metall Better Work 2020 project (Bezirksleitung Nordrhein-Westfalen/NRW Projekt Arbeit 2020) revealed that trade unionists are actively speaking to companies about the ways they are introducing *Industrie 4.0* technologies into workplaces (Moore 2018a). The introduction of robots and worker monitoring, cloud computing, machine-to-machine communications and other systems have all prompted those running the IG Metall project to ask companies:

- What impact will technological changes have on people's workloads?
- Is work going to be easier or harder?
- Will work become more or less stressful? Will there be more or less work?

These IG Metall trade unionists indicated that workers' stress levels tended to rise when technologies are implemented without enough training or dialogue with workers. Expertise is often needed to mitigate the risks that new technologies in workplaces introduce.

Next, we turn to another arena in which AI is making an impact, namely in 'gig work' environments.

3.5 Platform Applications Enabling Gig Work

'Gig work' is obtained by using online applications (apps), also called platforms, made available by companies such as Uber, Upwork or Amazon Mechanical Turk (AMT). The work can be performed *online*—obtained and carried out on computers in homes, libraries and cafes, for example, and includes translation and design work—or *offline*—

---

[11] Prof. Dr Dietmar Reinert, PEROSH Chairman, Institute for Occupational Safety and Health of the German Social Accident Insurance, indicated this in an interview with the author on 13 September, 2018.

obtained online but carried out offline, such as taxi driving or cleaning work. Not all algorithms utilise AI, but the data produced by client-worker matching services and customer assessment of platform workers provide data that train profiles that then result in overall higher or lower scores that then lead, for example, clients to select specific people for work over others.

Monitoring and tracking have been daily experiences for couriers and taxi drivers for many years, but the rise in offline gig workers carrying out platform-directed food delivery by bicycle, delivering orders and taxi services is relatively new. Uber and Deliveroo require workers to install a specific application onto their phones, which perch on vehicle dashboards or handlebars, and they gain clients through the use of mapping satellite technologies and by matching algorithmically operated software. The benefits of using AI in gig work could be driver and passenger protection. DiDi, a Chinese ride hailing service, uses AI facial recognition software to identify workers as they log on to the application. DiDi uses this information to ensure the identities of drivers, which is seen as a method of crime prevention. However, there was a very serious recent failure in the use of the technology in which a driver logged in as his father one evening. Under the false identity, later in his shift, the driver killed a passenger. Delivery gig workers are held accountable for their speed, number of deliveries per hour and customer rankings, in an intensified environment that has been proven to create OSH risks. In *Harper's* magazine a driver explains how new digitalised tools work as a 'mental whip', noting that 'people get intimidated and work faster' (The Week 2015). Drivers and riders are at risk of deactivation from the app if their customer rankings are not high enough or they do not meet other requirements. This results in OSH risks including blatant unfair treatment, stress and even fear.

Algorithms are used to match clients with workers in online gig work (also called microwork). One platform called BoonTech uses IBM Watson AI Personality Insights to match clients and online gig workers such as those gaining contracts using AMT and Upwork. Issues of discrimination have emerged that are related to women's domestic responsibilities, when carrying out online gig work at home, such as reproductive and caring activities in a traditional context. A recent survey of online gig workers in the developing world conducted by ILO researchers shows that a higher percentage of women than men tend to 'prefer to work at home' (Rani and Furrer 2017, p. 14). Rani and Furrer's research shows that 32% of female workers in African countries have small children and 42% in Latin America. This results in a double burden for women, who 'spend about 25.8 h working on platforms in a week, 20 h of which is paid work and 5.8 h considered unpaid work' (ibid., p. 13). The survey shows that 51% of women gig workers work during the night (22.00 to 05.00) and the evening (76% work from 18.00 to 22.00), which are 'unsocial working hours' according to the ILO's risk categories for potential work-related violence and harassment (ILO 2016, p. 40). Rani and Furrer further state that the global outsourcing of work through platforms has effectively led to the development of a 'twenty-four hour economy … eroding the fixed boundaries between home and work … [which further] puts a double burden on women, since responsibilities at home are unevenly distributed between sexes' (2017, p. 13). Working from home could already be a risky environment for women who may be subject to domestic violence alongside the lack of legal protection provided in office-based work.

Indeed, 'violence and harassment can occur ... via technology that blurs the lines between workplaces, "domestic" places and public spaces' (ILO 2017, p. 97).

Digitalising non-standard work, such as home-based online gig work, and taxi and delivery services in offline gig work, is a method of governance that is based on quantification of tasks at a minutely granular level, where only explicit contact time is paid. Digitalisation may appear to formalise a labour market in the ILO sense, but the risk of underemployment and underpay is very real. In terms of working time, preparatory work for reputation improvement and necessary skills development in online gig work, is unpaid. Surveillance is normalised but stress still results. and Noronha (2016) present a case study of online gig workers in India, in which 'humans-as-a-service' (as articulated by Jeff Bezos, see Prassl 2018) is critiqued for being the kind of work that dehumanises and devalues work, facilitates casualisation of workers and even informalises the economy. Online gig work such as work obtained and delivered using the AMT, relies on non-standard forms of employment (ibid., p. 46) which increases the possibilities for child labour, forced labour and discrimination. There is evidence of racism, whereby clients are reported to direct abusive and offensive comments on the platforms. Inter-worker racist behaviour is also evident: gig workers working in more advanced economies blame Indian counterparts for under-cutting prices (ibid.). Further, some of the work obtained on online platforms is highly unpleasant such as the work carried out by content moderators who sift through large sets of images and are required to eliminate offensive or distributing images, with very little relief or protections around this. There are clear risks of OSH violations in the areas of heightened psychosocial violence and stress, discrimination, racism, bullying, unfree and underage labour, because of the lack of basic protection in these working environments.

In gig work, workers have been forced to register as self-employed workers, losing out on the basic rights that formal workers enjoy such as guaranteed hours, sick and holiday pay and the right to join a union. Gig workers' online reputations are very important because a good reputation is the way to gain more work. As mentioned above, digitalised customer and client ratings and reviews are key to developing a good reputation and these ratings determine how much work gig workers obtain. Algorithms learn from customer rankings and quantity of tasks accepted, which produces specific types of profiles for workers that are usually publicly available. Customer rankings are deaf and blind to the consideration of workers' physical health, care and domestic work responsibilities, and circumstances outside workers' control that might affect their performance, leading to further OSH risks where people feel forced to accept more work than is healthy, or are risk of work exclusion. Customer satisfaction rankings, and number of jobs accepted, can be used to 'deactivate' taxi drivers' use of the platform, as is done by Uber, despite the paradox and fiction that algorithms are absent of 'human bias' (Frey and Osborne 2013, p. 18). Overall, while there are benefits for integrating AI into gig work including driver identity protection and allowing flexible hours of work, good for people's life and work choices. However these same benefits can result in rising risks, such as the case of the DiDi driver and the case of a double burden of work for women online workers. OSH protections are generally scarce in these working environments and the risks are many (Huws 2015 and Degryse 2016) and involve low pay and long hours (Berg 2016), endemic lack of training (CIPD 2017) and a high level of insecurity (Taylor 2017). Williams-Jimenez (2016) warns that labour and OSH laws have not adapted to the emergence of digitalised work, and other studies are beginning to make similar claims (Degryse 2016). The successes of AI are also its failures.

Having outlined where AI is entering the workplace and the benefits and risks for OSH, the report now turns to look at responses from the wider OSH community, identifying the policy developments, debates and discussions underway on these topics.

4 Policy Developments, Regulation and Training

The emergence of AI and in particular the ecosystem and features of autonomous decision-making require a 'reflection about the suitability of some established rules on safety and civil law questions on liability' (European Commission 2018). So, horizontal and sectoral rules need to be reviewed to identify any risks arising as well as to protect and ensure benefits from the integration of AI-enhanced technology at work. The Machinery Directive (2006/42/EC), the Radio Equipment Directive (2014/53/EU), the General Product Safety Directive (2001/95/EC) and other specific safety rules provide some guidance, but more will be needed to ensure workplace safety and health. Indeed, a report in *IOSH Magazine* emphasises that AI risks are 'outpacing our safeguards' (Wustemann 2017) for workplace safety. In that light, this chapter looks at the perspectives of policy-makers and experts from the wider community and emerging recommendations for regulating AI to reduce OSH risks, and then it outlines some suggestions for training linked to AI and OSH at IG Metall.

4.1 European Commission

The digital single market is an important vehicle for the expansion of AI, and the mid-term Commission review of the implementation of the digital single market (European Commission 2017a) indicated that AI will provide substantive technological solutions to risky situations such as fewer fatalities on the roads, smarter uses of resources, less use of pesticides, a more competitive manufacturing sector, better precision in surgery and assistance in dangerous situations such as earthquake and nuclear disaster rescue. Surrounding debates across Europe involve questions about the legal and liability issues, data sharing and storage, the risks of bias in machine learning's competences and the difficulty of allowing for the right to an explanation, including how data about workers are used, firmed up by the General Data Protection Regulation (GDPR).

So, the arena that is covered by the mid-term review of the digital single market, which has implications for AI, OSH and work, is the discussion of the risks of bias and the right to an explanation of how data are used, in which informed consent for the use of data and the right to access data held about the person is paramount. The socio-economic and ethical issues of AI have been further highlighted in more recent European Commission Communications, particularly since the April 2018 Communication on artificial intelligence for Europe and conclusions on the coordinated plan for the development and use of artificial intelligence made in Europe, which emphasise ethics for competitive advantage.

4.2   International Standards

A committee within the International Organization for Standardization (ISO) in 2018 and 2019 has been working on designing a standard that will apply to uses of dashboards and metrics in workplaces. The standard will include regulations on how dashboards can be set up and on gathering and using data from workers. Quantification tools are becoming increasingly of interest to employers, but the data are of no use if they are not standardisable. Representatives from the manufacturers of the software used to standardise data, SAP, are active in the ISO discussions, but it will be important for further actors to participate in order to ensure co-determination in Germany, for example, and to ensure workers' representation more broadly across the international landscape. One expert in this area indicated that international standards can be an effective way to ensure that the benefits of these tools are achieved, and an important step is to ensure that international corporate practices are equivalent at some level, that data is standardisable and that workers are involved in the discussions and implementation processes[12]. Furthermore, risks assessments should be carried out on the basis of the extensive data gathered by these dashboards, which are a clear benefit for OSH protection.

4.3   International Labour Organization

The ILO has produced a number of reports suggesting best practice in integrating AI into workplaces, for member states. In the report named Digital Labour Platforms and the Future of Work (Berg et al. 2018), the human side of AI is revealed, where many of the jobs or microtasks obtained with online platform work (outlined above), is similar to unskilled work that can also be, in many cases, automated. The report indicates that microtask platforms were in fact invented in part to deal with the failures of algorithms of Web 2.0 to 'classify the nuances of the images, sounds and texts' which companies wanted to store and classify (Irani 2015, p. 225, cited in Berg et al. 2018, p. 7). Work can range from bulk tasks like a survey requiring thousand of replies, or image recognition. Amazon actually calls the kind of work performed by people using its AMT platform as 'artificial artificial intelligence', or 'an on-demand, scalable, human workforce to complete jobs that humans can do better than computers, for example, recognising objects in photos' (Berg et al. 2018, p. 7). The report recommends regulation of crowdwork platforms (which are argued to, as indicated above, substitute AI and automated work), listing 18 criteria for 'fairer microwork' which includes such recommendations as eliminating misclassification as 'self-employed' when workers are employees in practice; rights to union membership and collective bargaining; minimum wage; fee transparency (wage theft is a common problem in gig work); workers should be allowed to accept some tasks and decline others and not be penalised for it; protections for computer failure; platform terms should be readable and concise; protections from misuse of worker evaluations and ratings; codes of conduct should be made available; workers should be permitted to contest non-payment and other issues;

---

[12] Interview with Rolf Jaeger, European Industrial Relations Intercultural Communication and Negotiation 18 September 2018.

workers should have access to information about clients; platforms should review task instructions before posting; workers should be able to export reputation histories; workers should have the right to work with a client after working via the platform; customers and operators should respond to worker requests promptly and politely; workers should know the purpose of their work; and any tasks involving psychologically stressful work should be labelled clearly (Berg et al. 2018, pp. 105–109).

The Global Commission on the Future of Work 'Work for a brighter future' report indicates that any actions involving technology and work must take a human-centred agenda. Cobots, the report notes, can actually reduce worker stress and risks of injury. However, technology can also reduce the availability of work for humans, which ultimately will alienate workers and stunt workers' development. Workplace decisions should never rely on data produced by algorithms and any AI at work should be integrated with a 'human-in-command' approach, where any 'algorithmic management, surveillance and control, through sensors, wearables and other forms of monitoring, needs to be regulated to protect the dignity of workers' (ILO 2019, p. 43). The report goes on to state, building on the ILO Declaration of Philadelphia statement that labour is not a commodity: 'Labour is not a commodity; nor is it a robot' (ibid.).

4.4 World Economic Forum and GDPR

The World Economic Forum (WEF) Global Future Council on Human Rights and Technology reported in 2018 that, even when good data sets are used to set up algorithms for machine learning, there are considerable risks of discrimination if the following occur (WEF 2018):

1. choosing the wrong model;
2. building a model with inadvertently discriminatory features;
3. absence of human oversight and involvement;
4. unpredictable and inscrutable systems;
5. unchecked and unintentional discrimination.

The WEF emphasises that there is a distinct need for 'more active self-governance by private companies', which is in line with the ILO's Tripartite Declaration of Principles concerning Multinational Enterprises and Social Policy—5th Edition (Rev. 2017), which provides direct guidance for enterprises in the areas of sustainable, responsible and inclusive working practices and social policy surrounding these, whereby the Sustainable Development Goal (SDG) target 8.8 aims to achieve safe and secure working environments for all workers by 2030. The prevention of unfair and illegal discrimination clearly must be ensured as AI is increasingly introduced and the WEF (2018) and ILO reports mentioned above are vital for steering the course. The first error a company can make when using AI, which could lead to discrimination as listed by the WEF, is in a situation in which a user applies the same algorithm to two problems that may themselves not have identical contexts or data points. A possible workplace example of this could be where potential hires are considered using an algorithm that looks for clues about personality types via searches through social media, videos that detect facial movements and data that are collated across data sets of curriculum vitae, perhaps extending back a few years of hiring. As Dr Cathy O'Neil pointed out in an interview with the author[13], the algorithm then has to be designed to be discriminatory or at least selective, because hiring practices require that at a basic level. However, if, for example, the algorithm is looking for extroverted people for a call centre job, the same algorithm would not be appropriate to find the right lab assistant, where talkativeness is not inherent to the job description. While applying the algorithm would not necessarily lead to illegal discrimination as such, it is not difficult to extrapolate the possibilities for misallocation.

The second error, 'building a model with inadvertently discriminatory features', can refer to, for example, using a databank that already exemplifies discrimination. For example, in the United Kingdom, the gender pay gap has been exposed recently, revealing that for years women have been working for lower salaries and in some cases doing the same work as men for less pay. If the data that demonstrates this trend were used to create an algorithm to make decisions about hiring, the machine would 'learn' that women should be paid less. This demonstrates the point that machines cannot make ethical judgements independently of human intervention. Indeed, there is a growing arena of research that demonstrates that discrimination is not eliminated by AI in decision-making and prediction but instead that codification of data perpetuates the problem (Noble 2018). The third error emphasises human intervention, which is now required across Europe. In May 2018, the GDPR became a requirement, whereby workers' consent for data collection and use applies. While the GDPR looks primarily at consumer data rights, there are significant applications for the workplace, because workplace decisions cannot be made using automated processes alone.

Section 4 of the GDPR outlines the 'Right to object and automated individual decision-making'. Article 22, 'Automated individual decision-making, including profiling', indicates that:

22(1): The data subject shall have the **right not to be subject to a decision based solely on automated processing**, including profiling, which produces legal effects concerning him or her or similarly significantly affects him or her.

The foundations for the Regulation, listed in the first sections of the document, make it clear that:

(71): The data subject has the **right not to be subject to a decision**, which may include a measure, evaluating personal aspects relating to him or her which is based solely on automated processing and which produces legal effects concerning him or her or similarly significant affects him or her, such as... **e-recruiting practices without any human intervention**. Such processing includes profiling that consists of any form of automated processing of personal data evaluating the personal aspects of a natural person, in particular to analyse or predict aspects concerning the data subject's performance at work... reliability or behaviour, location or movements, where it produces legal effects concerning him or her or similarly significantly affects him or her.

---

[13] Dr Cathy O'Neil, author of *Weapons of maths destruction* and CEO of ORCAA (O'Neil Risk Consulting and Algorithmic Auditing), interviewed by the author on 14 October 2018.

Failure to apply these criteria could lead to unfair or illegal discriminatory decisions.

With regard to the fourth error, 'unpredictable and inscrutable systems', the description in the WEF (2018) report indicates that 'when a human makes a decision, such as whether or not to hire someone, we can *inquire* as to why he or she decided one way or the other' (italics added). Obviously, a machine cannot discuss its 'rationale' for decisions it reaches based on data mining. The elimination of qualified judgements and lack of human intervention therefore creates a clear route to discrimination.

The final error in the implementation of AI can be when 'unchecked and intentional discrimination' occurs. This could happen, for example, when a company in fact does not want to hire women who are *likely* to become pregnant. While this explicit position would not hold up in court, a machine learning system could provide covert tactics to make it happen through an algorithm designed to out to filter out a subset of women candidates where that might be the case, based on age and relationship data. It is not difficult to see how this opens the door to not only the risks, but in fact the likelihood, of technically illegal discrimination.

4.5   Training for AI and OSH

IG Metall is working with companies on its OSH training programmes to accommodate the latest technological changes in workplaces in 2019. Discussions with the expert leading this initiative indicated that training for OSH has typically been seen as an arena solely populated by the one or two safety and health officers in workplaces and has not been fully integrated into all systems. Findings now demonstrate that people need to be trained to acquire fast learning capabilities, because technology changes quickly and skills thus must adapt[14]. This expert indicated that training must be adjusted for relevance in the era of *Industrie 4.0* and digitalisation, so that workers are prepared to deal with emerging risks. However, this is not a panacea and must be part of a larger implementation plan. If there is no plan to actually implement and use any new knowledge and skills delivered by training, new skills will be lost. In that light, better alignment between OSH training and integrated technologies is necessary. That being said, training pedagogy should also be adjusted, as learning is a process that will need to continue throughout workers' lifetimes, particularly in the current climate of job uncertainty. It will also be important for workers to acquire problem-solving skills and principles as well as traditionally understood 'skills'. These days, workers should understand and choose their own learning pathways and styles[15]. Only time will tell just how ubiquitous AI in workplaces becomes, but it is worth remaining alert to OSH risks and benefits and involving workers in these processes by providing training at every juncture.

---

[14] Interview with Dr Maike Pricelius, Project Secretary, Better Work 2020, IG Metall, 12 October 2018.

[15] Duncan Spencer, Head of Advice and Practice, Institution of Occupational Safety and Health, based in Leicester, United Kingdom, talked about this with the author in an interview on 15 October 2018.

5 In Conclusion

Even as far back such as the 1920s, the writer Forster, painted a dystopian picture of technology and humanity. Forster's classic story *The machine stops* talks about a world where humans must live underneath the Earth's surface, within a machinic apparatus that the protagonist of this novel celebrates, because the machine (Forster 1928):

> ... feeds us and clothes us and houses us; through it we speak to one another, through it we see one another, in it we have our being. The Machine is the friend of ideas and the enemy of superstition: the Machine is omnipotent, eternal; blessed is the Machine!

But the omnipotent, all-housing contraption soon begins to decay in this classic literary masterpiece, and human expertise is not sufficient for its maintenance, leading to a grim ending for all of humanity.

While this is a classic piece of science fiction, today, technology's seeming invisibility and potential power are seemingly endlessly perpetuated, because its operations are often hidden within a black box, where its workings are often considered beyond comprehension but seem, still, to be accepted by the majority of people. Most people are not engineers, so they do not understand how computers and AI systems work. Nonetheless, human experts are surprised by AI actions, such as the chess Go player who was beaten by a computer programme.

In China, the government will soon give each person a citizen score, or an economic and personal reputation scoring, which will look at people's rent payments, credit rankings, phone use, and so on. It will be used to determine conditions for obtaining loans, jobs and travel visas. Perhaps people analytics could be used to give people 'worker scores' to be used for decision-making in appraisals, which would introduce all sorts of questions about privacy and surveillance. The 'algorithmic condition' is a term also coined in a recent EU report (Colman et al. 2018) that refers to the increasingly normalised logic of algorithms, in which symbols are transformed into reality. Today, this condition is beginning to impact many workplaces, in which online reputations are subject to algorithmic matching and people's profiles subject to data-mining bots. The problem is that algorithms do not see the qualitative aspects of life nor the surrounding contexts. Dr O'Neil (cited in fn 13) made an insightful observation in a recent interview with the author. While watching Deliveroo riders hurtle past her in the rain, Dr O'Neil considered the platforms directing the riders' work, which operate on the basis of efficiency and speed and thus instigate riders to cycle in unsafe weather conditions. This clearly puts riders' very lives at risk. Dr O'Neil calls algorithms 'toy models of the universe', because these seemingly all-knowing entities actually only know what we tell them, and thus they have major blind spots.

Google co-founder Brin (Vincent 2018) addressed investors in his annual founder's letter earlier in 2018 stating that:

> ...the new spring in AI is the most significant development in computing in my lifetime ... however, such powerful tools also bring with them new questions and responsibilities. How will they affect employment across different sectors? How can we understand what they are doing under the hood? What about measures of fairness? How might we manipulate them? Are they safe?

Ethical questions in AI must be discussed beyond the corporate sphere, however, and this report has covered these questions surrounding OSH and the risks as well as benefits that are introduced. The mythical invention of E. M. Forster's all-encompassing machine in his classical science fiction story was not, of course, subject to a range of ethical and moral review panels before all of humanity began to live within it under the Earth's crust. This dystopia is not exactly what we face now, of course, but current discussions—from those held to inform the European Commission Communications and European Coordinated Plan on Artificial Intelligence to trade union curriculum review groups such as those at IG Metall—show significant interest in preventing the worst risks and facilitating the benefits of OSH, as AI is increasingly implemented for workplace decision-making and assisted work.

In conclusion, as the implementation of AI at work is relatively new, there is only nascent evidence of OSH risks and benefits. Nonetheless, this report has covered some of the arenas where benefits are being noted and supported and risks are highlighted, as well as caution and regulation being applied. In HR decision-making with the use of AI-augmented people analytics, the risk of unfair treatment and discrimination is flagged up. In automation and *Industrie 4.0*, risks involve unsuitable or unavailable training leading to overwork and stress (Downey 2018), unpredicted accidents such as collisions between humans and robots. Deskilling of work is at stake in manufacturing and other industries, with the integration of lot size processes and the use of wearable technologies for machinised training practices. Risks of privacy relating to intensified surveillance and feelings of micro-management have been reported, as management is able to access more intimate data about workers because of wearable technologies in factories and offices alike. In gig work, algorithms cannot be posed as sole decision-makers. The benefits should be emphasised in all cases.

Indeed, it will be important for all stakeholders to maintain focus on the assistive possibilities of business application and ensure government and other regulatory oversight of AI tools and applications in the workplace. The positive effects of AI, when it is implemented with appropriate processes, are that it can help management reduce human bias in interviewing processes, if algorithms are designed to identify evidence of past discrimination in decision-making and decisions are made with full human intervention and even affirmative action. AI can help to improve relationships with, and between, employees when data collected demonstrates potential for collaboration. AI-enhanced HR tools can improve decision-making using prediction by exception and can allow people more time for personal and career development, if AI can start to take over repetitive and unfulfilling work. To avoid risks for OSH, the author recommends focusing on implementing assistive and collaborative AI rather than heading for the general and widespread competences of universal AI. Appropriate training must be provided at all points, and checks must also be made consistently, including by OSH departments and authorities. Workers must be consulted at all points whenever new technologies are integrated into workplaces, sustaining a worker-centred approach and prioritising a 'human in command' approach (De Stefano 2018). Business owners and governments should keep an eye on international standardisation, government regulation and trade union activities, in which significant progress is already being made to mitigate against the worst risks of AI and to develop positive and beneficial gains. In conclusion, it is not AI technology itself that creates risks for the safety and health of workers, it is the *way* that it is implemented, and it is up to all of us to ensure a smooth transition to increased integration of AI in workplaces.

References

Agarwal, A., Gans, J., Goldfarb, A.: Prediction Machines: The Simple Economics of Artificial Intelligence. Harvard Business Review Press, Boston (2018)

Berg, J.: Income security in the on-demand economy: findings and policy lessons from a survey of crowdworkers. Conditions of Work and Employment Series No 74. International Labour Organization, Geneva (2016)

Berg, J., Furrer, M., Harmon, E., Rani, U., Silberman, M.S.: Digital labour platforms and the future of work: towards decent work in the online world. ILO, Geneva (2018)

Butollo, F., Jürgens, U., Krzywdzinski, M.: From lean production to Industrie 4.0: More autonomy for employees? Wissenshanftszentrum Berlin für Socialforschung (WZB) Discussion Paper SP 111–303 (2018)

CIPD (Chartered Institute for Personnel Development): To gig or not to gig? Stories from the modern economy (2017). www.cipd.co.uk/knowledge/work/trends/gig-economy-report

Collins, L., Fineman, D.R., Tshuchica, A.: People analytics: recalculating the route. Deloitte Insights (2017). https://www2.deloitte.com/insights/us/en/focus/human-capital-trends/2017/people-analytics-in-hr.html

Colman, F., Bülmann, V., O'Donnell, A., van der Tuin, I.: Ethics of coding: a report on the algorithmic condition. European Commission, Brussels (2018)

D'Cruz, P., Noronha, E.: Positives outweighing negatives: the experiences of Indian crowdsourced workers. Work. Organ. Labour Glob. **10**(1), 44–63 (2016)

De Stefano, V.: Negotiating the algorithm: automation, artificial intelligence and labour protection. ILO working Paper No 246/2018. International Labour Organization, Geneva (2018)

Degryse, C.: Digitalisation of the economy and its impact on labour markets. European Trade Union Institute (ETUI), Brussels (2016)

Delponte, L.: European artificial intelligence leadership the path for an integrated vision. Policy Department for Economic, Scientific and Quality of Life Policies, European Parliament, Brussels (2018)

Downey, K.: Automation could increase workplace stress, unions warn. IOSH Magazine (2018). https://www.ioshmagazine.com/article/automation-could-increase-workplace-stress-unions-warn. Accessed 23 Apr 2018

Dreyfus, H.L.: What Computers Can't Do. Harper and Row, New York (1972). (Reprinted by MIT Press (1979/1992))

Ernst, E., Merola, R., Samaan, D.: The economics of artificial intelligence: implications for the future of work. ILO Future of Work Research Paper Series. International Labour Organization, Geneva (2018). https://www.ilo.org/global/topics/future-of-work/publications/research-papers/WCMS_647306/lang–en/index.htm

EU-OSHA (European Agency for Safety and Health at Work): Foresight on new and emerging occupational safety and health risks associated with digitalisation by 2025. Publications Office of the European Union Luxembourg (2018). https://osha.europa.eu/en/tools-and-publications/publications/foresight-new-and-emerging-occupational-safety-and-health-risks/view

European Commission: Communication on artificial intelligence for Europe. European Commission, Brussels (2018)

European Commission: Communication on the mid-term review on the implementation of the digital single market strategy: a connected digital single market for all (2017a). https://eur-lex.europa.eu/legal-content/EN/TXT/?qid=1496330315823&uri=CELEX:52017DC0228

European Commission: Attitudes towards the impact of digitisation and automation on daily life (2017b). https://ec.europa.eu/digital-single-market/en/news/attitudes-towards-impact-digitisation-and-automation-daily-life

Feloni, R.: I tried the software that uses AI to scan job applicants for companies like Goldman Sachs and Unilever before meeting them, and it's not as creepy as it sounds. Business Insider UK (2017). https://www.uk.businessinsider.com/hirevue-ai-powered-job-interview-platform-2017-8?r=US&IR=T/#in-recorded-videos-hirevue-employees-asked-questions-like-how-would-you-describe-your-role-in-the-last-team-you-worked-in-4. Accessed 23 Aug 2017

Forster, E.M.: The Machine Stops. Penguin Books, London (1928/2011)

Frey, C., Osborne, M.A.: The future of employment: how susceptible are jobs to computerisation? University of Oxford, Oxford Martin School, Oxford (2013). https://www.oxfordmartin.ox.ac.uk/downloads/academic/The_Future_of_Employment.pdf

Houghton, E., Green, M.: People analytics: driving business performance with people data. Chartered Institute for Personnel Development (CIPD) (2018). https://www.cipd.co.uk/knowledge/strategy/analytics/people-data-driving-performance

Hutter, M.: One decade of universal artificial intelligence. Theor. Found. Artif. Gen. Intell. **4**, 67–88 (2012)

Huws, U.: A review on the future of work: online labour exchanges, or "Crowdsourcing"—Implications for occupational safety and healths. Discussion paper. European Agency for Safety and Health at Work, Bilbao (2015). https://osha.europa.eu/en/tools-and-publications/publications/future-work-crowdsourcing/view

IBM: IBM Talent Business Uses AI To Rethink The Modern Workforce. IBM Newsroom (2018). https://newsroom.ibm.com/2018-11-28-IBM-Talent-Business-Uses-AI-To-Rethink-The-Modern-Workforce

ILO (International Labour Organization): Work for a brighter future – Global Commission on the Future of Work. ILO, Geneva (2019)

ILO (International Labour Organization): Ending violence and harassment against women and men in the world of work, Report V. In: 2018 International Labour Conference 107th Session, Geneva (2017). http://www.ilo.org/ilc/ILCSessions/107/reports/reports-to-the-conference/WCMS_553577/lang–en/index.htm

ILO (International Labour Organization): Final Report: Meeting of Experts on violence against women and men in the world of work. MEVWM/2016/7. ILO, Geneva (2016). http://www.ilo.org/gender/Informationresources/Publications/WCMS_546303/lang–en/index.htm

Kaivo-oja, J.: A review on the future of work: Robotics. Discussion paper. European Agency for Safety and Health at Work, Bilbao (2015). https://osha.europa.eu/en/tools-and-publications/seminars/focal-points-seminar-review-articles-future-work

Kar, S.: How AI is transforming HR: the future of people analytics. Hyphen (2018). https://blog.gethyphen.com/blog/how-ai-is-transforming-hr-the-future-of-people-analytics. Accessed 4 Jan 2018

McCarthy, J., Minsky, M.L., Rochester, N., Shannon, C.E.: A proposal for the Dartmouth Summer Research Project on Artificial Intelligence (1955). http://www-formal.stanford.edu/jmc/history/dartmouth/dartmouth.html

Moore, P.V.: The threat of physical and psychosocial violence and harassment in digitalized work. International Labour Organization, Geneva (2018a)

Moore, P.V.: The Quantified Self in Precarity: Work, Technology and What Counts. Routledge, Abingdon (2018b)

Nield, D.: In corporate wellness programs, wearables take a step forward. Fortune (2014). http://fortune.com/2014/04/15/in-corporate-wellness-programs-wearables-take-a-step-forward/. Accessed 15 Apr 2014

Noble, S.A.: Algorithms of Oppression: How Search Engines Reinforce Racism. New York University Press, New York (2018)

Pasquale, F.: The Black Box Society: The Secret Algorithms that Control Money and Information. Harvard University Press, Boston (2015)

Prassl, J.: Humans as a Service: The Promise and Perils of Work in the Gig Economy. Oxford University Press, Oxford (2018)

PwC: Artificial intelligence in HR: a no-brainer (2018a). https://www.pwc.com/gx/en/issues/data-and-analytics/publications/artificial-intelligence-study.html

PwC: AI will create as many jobs as it displaces by boosting economic growth (2018b). https://www.pwc.co.uk/press-room/press-releases/AI-will-create-as-many-jobs-as-it-displaces-by-boosting-economic-growth.html

Rani, U., Furrer, M.: Work and income security among workers in on-demand digital economy: issues and challenges in developing economies. Paper presented at the Lausanne University Workshop 'Digitalization and the Reconfiguration of Labour Governance in the Global Economy', 24–25 November 2017 (2017, unpublished)

Simon, H.: The Sciences of the Artificial. MIT Press, Cambridge (1969)

Taylor, M.: Good work: the Taylor review of modern working practices. Department for Business, Energy and Industrial Strategy, London (2017). https://www.gov.uk/government/publications/good-work-the-taylor-review-of-modernworking-practices

The Week: The rise of workplace spying (2015). http://theweek.com/articles/564263/rise-workplace-spying

TNO (Netherlands Organisation for Applied Scientific Research): Emergent risks to workplace safety; Working in the same space as a cobot, Report for the Ministry of Social Affairs and Employment, The Hague (2018)

Turing, A.M.: Computing machinery and intelligence. Mind **49**, 433–460 (1950)

United Kingdom (UK) Department for Business, Energy and Industrial Strategy and Department for Digital, Culture, Media and Sport, AI sector deal policy paper (2018). https://www.gov.uk/government/publications/artificial-intelligence-sector-deal/ai-sector-deal

Vincent, J.: Google's Sergey Brin warns of the threat from AI in today's 'technology renaissance' (2018). https://www.theverge.com/2018/4/28/17295064/google-ai-threat-sergey-brin-founders-letter-technology-renaissance

WEF (World Economic Forum): How to prevent discriminatory outcomes in machine learning. World Economic Forum Global Future Council on Human Rights 2016–2018. WEF, Cologny, Switzerland (2018)

Weizenbaum, J.: Computer Power and Human Reason: From Judgment to Calculation. W. H. Freeman, San Francisco (1976)

White House Office of Science and Technology Policy. Summit on artificial intelligence for American industry (2018). https://www.whitehouse.gov/articles/white-house-hosts-summit-artificial-intelligence-american-industry/ Summary of report. https://www.whitehouse.gov/wp.../Summary-Report-of-White-House-AI-Summit.pdf

Williams-Jimenez, I.: Digitalisation and its impact on psychosocial risks regulation. Paper presented at the Fifth International Conference on Precarious Work and Vulnerable Workers. Middlesex University, London (2016)

Woodcock, J.: Working the Phones: Control and Resistance in Call Centers. Pluto Press, London (2016)

Wustemann, L.: AI and nanotech risk outpacing our safeguards. IOSH Magazine (2017). https://www.ioshmagazine.com/article/ai-and-nanotech-risk-outpacing-our-safeguards. Accessed 25 Aug 2017

Cooperation Between Design and Neuroscience: Contributions to Current Project Methodologies Applied to Automotive Design

Carolina Vieira Liberatti Rosa[1]([⊠])[iD] and Rachel Zuanon[2][iD]

[1] Graduate Program in Design, Anhembi Morumbi University, Sao Paulo, Brazil
ca_liberatti@yahoo.com.br
[2] Art Institute, State University of Campinas (UNICAMP), Campinas, Brazil
rachel.zuanon@gmail.com

Abstract. Currently, the project methodologies applied to Automotive Design indicate measurement limitations of car users' emotional responses, specifically in terms of correlating such responses to product project parameters. The purpose of this article lies in the mapping and elucidation of the neurophysiological data measurement techniques adopted by Automotive Design research, developed between the years 2000 and 2017, in order to identify relevancies to project development in this field. The main outcomes achieved in each investigation are discussed, as well as the main obstacles to the advancement of studies of this nature. Moreover, it reflects on the importance of Automotive Design and Neuroscience cooperation in the analysis and evaluation of products, mostly in regards to understanding the perceptive, cognitive and behavioral processes of human beings in this context; the obtention of relevant subsidies for the project parameter definition aligned to requirements of the human organism, addressing his well-being and quality of life.

Keywords: Automotive design · Neuroscience · Project methodologies · Neurophysiological data measurement

1 Introduction

In the automotive design field, as well as in the creation and development of any other product, there are limitations to the user's perception in regards to new proposals and design concepts. Specifically referring to their emotional response measurement, which aims to correlate between such responses to project parameters in relation to the product in question.

Such evidence is gathered through literature review [32], during the period between 1995 and 2017. It indicates the following project methodology applications in the automotive design field, hereby organized by decreasing order of recurrence: Kansei Engineering [1, 3, 5, 15, 22, 24, 29, 30, 34, 35, 41–45, 47, 48, 54], Semantic Differential Technique [23, 26, 49, 50], Environment Semantic Description [2, 25], Citarasa [16, 17, 28], Quality Function Deployment integrated to Fuzzy Kano Model

© Springer Nature Switzerland AG 2019
V. G. Duffy (Ed.): HCII 2019, LNCS 11581, pp. 316–334, 2019.
https://doi.org/10.1007/978-3-030-22216-1_23

[33, 53], Robust Design Methodology [31], MCDAC [10], Zaltman Elicitation Metaphor [13], Product Emotion Measure [8, 9], Fuzzy Set Theory [18, 19], and Quantification Analysis Type I [55]. In the methodological context, which employs questionnaires and interviews to gather data related to user perception, participants are asked to evaluate their emotions in a pre-defined numerical and semantical scale.

However, emotions consist of a complex set of chemical and neural reactions, primarily expressed through automatic reactions of physical and behavioral patterns, and after expressed in verbal responses [7, 38]. In addition, emotions are a complex feedback, generated by different brain systems, with variable timing, specific to each individual, culturally motivated, experience driven, and therefore, cannot be measured by just one technique [27].

From this perspective, this article aims to discuss the context of researches that employ neurophysiological data measurement, as a step in the process of automotive design development. This reinforces that the comprehension of the complex mechanism involved in the emotional process of individuals is able to bring significant contributions to project methodologies, specifically relevant information to designers' teams – responsible for the concept and development of a range of automobiles from a specific brand. The relevancy of this information lies in the analysis and interpretation of neurophysiological data delivered by the users' biological signals, through their experiences with product prototypes. Such responses may provide: (a) preview of emotional and behavioral reactions, by pattern mapping; (b) identification of wishes and/or corresponded or not expectations; (c) project guidelines in regards to consistent and affective interactions with the product; (d) extension of well-being and the identification to the product, as a result of the reduction in discrepancy between user emotional response and intentional project concept; among others, also capable of positively impacting individual habits and life quality in this context.

To broaden the knowledge of neurophysiological measurement techniques able to be applied to the automotive design field, consider the following table (Table 1).

2 Automotive Design and Neurophysiological Assessment Techniques: Scope Investigated [2000–2017]

The research is dedicated to identifying neurophysiological data assessment techniques applied in the automotive design field, between the years 2000–2017. Twelve researches express the totality of the available scope in international literature, in the referred period. It should be emphasized that, in this context, there were no studies dedicated to data measurement through: Heart Rate (HR); Magnetoencephalography (MEG) and Positron Emission Tomography (PET). From those, seven researches apply eye tracking (ET) technique [6, 11, 20, 21, 36, 39, 52]; one of them employs, simultaneously, the eye tracking technique, galvanic skin response (GSR) and facial electromyography (fEMG) [40]; three investigate the application of Functional Magnetic Resonance Imaging (fMRI) [12, 14, 46]; and one employs the Electroencefalography (EEG) [4].

Furthermore, only Normark et al. [36] study focuses on the collaboration of neurophysiological assessment technique and project methodology, specifically in the

Table 1. Neurophysiological measurement techniques.

Technology	Activity measured	Mapped state (in real time)
Eye Tracking (ET)	Time and trajectory of gaze, pupil diameter Alteration and blinking frequency	Attention, interest, complexity and visual memory
Galvanic Skin Response (GSR)	Electric skin conductivity	Arousal state and emotion intensity
Facial Electromyography (fEMG)	Facial muscle movements	Positive and negative emotions
Electroencephalography (EEG)	Brain wave frequency	Attention level, alert and relaxing states
Heart Rate (HR)	Cardiac frequency	Attention, positive and negative emotions
Magnetoencephalography (MEG)	Electromagnetic brain activity	Relates area and brain function
Positron Emission Tomography (PET)	Brain activity by radioactivity	Relates area and brain function

application of Eye Tracking associated to Environment Semantic Description methodology. It is also important to emphasize that, from the totality of researches mentioned, only 3 investigations involve authors from the automotive sector. This fact also indicates the interaction between the automotive industry and academic areas: Fiat Brazil and Colleges and Foundation of Minas Gerais, in Brazil [11]; Daimler-Chrysler Research Center and Ulm University, in Germany [12]; and Hyundai-Kia Motors and National Institute of Science and Technology ULSAN, in South Korea [4]. The table below summarizes the scope that will be discussed in sequence. It is organized by technology recurrence and presents each research in regards of neurophysiological data assessment applied in the automotive design sector (Table 2).

2.1   Eye Tracking and Semantic Environment Description

Normark et al. [36] employed the eye-tracking equipment Tobii x50, associated with two semantic evaluation methods, SMB – Semantic Environment Description and PSA – Product Semantic Analysis, in addition to interviews oriented by heat-maps reached through ocular assessment, to evaluate the visual appearance of eight instrumentation clusters, attached to the automotive panel. The categories "pleasantness", "complexity", "unit", "social status", "affection" and "originality" were classified in a 7-point Likert scale by 23 young participants, divided in four groups. Group 1 and 3 had access to left instrument panels, while groups 2 and 4 analyzed panels on the right. Two of the instrument panels, B and F are used as references in both scenarios.

We can infer that the participants follow a western reading trajectory, as they focus their attention from left to right, and from top to bottom, as showed in the following picture. However, it is not possible to correlate the gaze time and the attractiveness of the clusters, once the screen projection is downscaled and the visual perception of

Table 2. Researches in automotive design, which apply neurophysiological assessment techniques [2000–2017]

Technology	Researcher/Affiliation	Context of evaluation	Results
Eye Tracking (ET) and Semantic Environment Description (SMB)	Normark et al. [36] Lulea University, SWE	8 instrumentation clusters	ET as an interview support
Eye Tracking	Windhager et al. [52] EFS Company; Vienna University; Salzburg University, AT Bamberg University, DE	38 digital models, front view	Anthropomorphic perception; headlamp receives more attention
Eye Tracking	E Sousa et al. [11] Fiat Automobile, FAPEMIG University, USP University, BR	3 hatchback, front view	Preference order: Hyundai i30, Ford Focus and Fiat Bravo
Eye Tracking	Purucker et al. [39] Würzburg University, DE Washington University, USA St. Gallen University, SWZ	8 images, front view	Anthropomorphic perception
Eye Tracking	Chassy et al. [6] Liverpool Hope University, UK	50 mid-size cars, front view	visual complexity and gaze trajectory; aesthetic pleasure and dwelling time
Eye Tracking	Hyun et al. [20, 21] KAIST Advanced Institute of Science and Technology, KOR	119 cars from 23 brands, front, side and rear view	Front bumper and fender, side silhouette
Eye Tracking, Galvanic Skin Response, Facial Electromyography	Schmitt et al. [40] RWTH Aachen University; WZL Laboratory, DE Universitat Politècnica de València, ES	Production line SUV image and modified, ¾ view	Bumper and 'power'
Functional Magnetic Resonance Imaging	Gauthier et al. [14] Vanderbilt University; Yale University, USA	Cars, birds, familiar objects and human faces	Fusiform gyrus and facial recognition
Functional Magnetic Resonance Imaging	Erk et al. [12] Daimler-Chrysler Research Center; Ulm University, DE	Limousine, sporty and compact car images	Sporty cars activate reward brain area

(*continued*)

Table 2. (*continued*)

Technology	Researcher/Affiliation	Context of evaluation	Results
Functional Magnetic Resonance Imaging	Sylcott et al. [46] Carnegie Mellon University, USA	Car silhouette, side view	Anterior cingulate gyrus activated for form and function; insula activated for form
Electroencephalography	Chae et al. [4] Hyundai-Kia Motors; Ulsan National Institute of Science and Technology, KOR	HUD display	Information quantity activates central lobe; temporal lobe associated to concentration level

details may be affected, such as font variations in the text. The reduced number of subjects could compromise the studies validation. On the other hand, this investigation identifies eye tracking as a tool to guide interview discussions, by contrasting it with the user heat-map and its evaluation in regards to areas of interest and each element rating (Fig. 1).

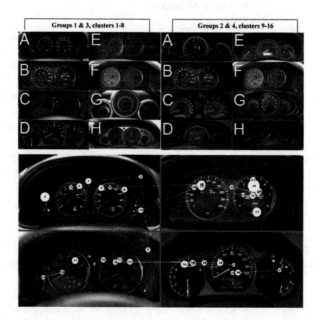

Fig. 1. Above: Cluster panels used in the study; bottom: visualization order of a participant. Font: adapted from Normark et al. [36]

2.2 Eye Tracking

The studies conducted by Windhager et al. [51, 52] aim to evaluate the human tendency of anthropomorphic perception. In other words, the investigation relies on identifying human face characteristics in front car view, through the following associations: 'headlamp and eyes', 'front grille and nose', 'air intake and mouth', and 'side view mirror and ears'.

In the study the IView X Hi-Speed tracking column camera is used to assess and analyze the eye-tracking data of 49 participants, while they evaluate 38 three-dimension digital car models from 26 different brands, related to existing cars on the market between the years 2004 and 2006. As a result, the tendency for anthropomorphic perception in visual interpretation is confirmed, through analogy identification between human faces and inanimate objects, such as the 'headlamp-eye'. Moreover, in human face perception, the eyes get more attention from the individuals (Fig. 2).

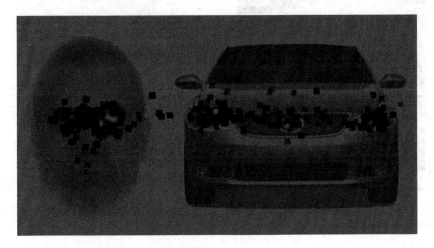

Fig. 2. Anthropomorphic perception: participants answer to the following question "Do the face and the car have the same eyes?" Font: Windhager et al. [52]

E Sousa et al. [11] investigates pupil diameter and heat-map from 30 participants, when in contact with three front view images from hatchback cars sold in Brazil: Fiat Bravo, Ford Focus and Hyundai i30.

The data gathering employs the Viewpoint of Arrington Tracker Research equipment, constituted by a pair of glasses with three cameras. Two of them are orientated to the participants' eyes, through two infrared Leds (invisible to the human eye) that read the pupil diameter, without distracting or disturbing the viewer. The third camera captures scenes analyzed by the individual in real time. The main goal is to examine the attention and interest area of each observer in relation to headlamps, brand logo, front bumper, front grill, hood and outside mirrors. And when measuring the pupil diameter, direction and gaze time of each individual, it is intended to identify elements of preference, with a view to future design solutions.

In the figure below, the red dots represent the left eye data assessment, and the yellow ones, the right eye. Next to it, there is data exported from the software. The results obtained from eye tracking equipment, associated to questionnaire answers with scale variation between 'like' and 'do not like', indicate the following participants preference order: (1) Hyundai i30; (2) Ford Focus; and (3) Fiat Bravo.

Only when each car was assessed individually, not side by side, it became possible to identify the relationship between the interest and preference points from viewers. According to the findings, the most preferred item in the Fiat Bravo was the headlamps, while the least one was the outside mirror. Such preference is measured from the correlation between the visualization of these items and the alterations caused in the pupil diameter (Fig. 3).

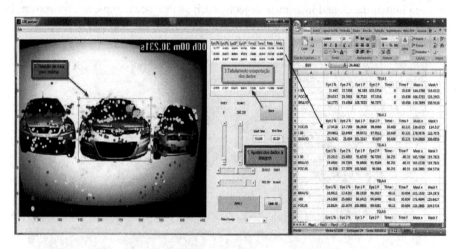

Fig. 3. Visual stimulus analysis by eye tracking (left): red – left eye; yellow – right eye. Data output (right). Font: adapted from E Sousa et al. [11] (Color figure online)

Purucker et al. [39] study investigated automatic responses in the observer evoked by car frontal views. Specifically, responses similar to those evoked by the human face and identified by anatomic structures of fusiform gyrus, according to the evolutionary mechanism of facial perception. The study seeks to comprehend if initial exposure to design characteristics qualified as 'threatening' attract observer attention, and if pro-longed exposure to the same stimuli result in avoidance of those areas.

Modified frontal view images are used as stimuli for the participant to analyze. Eight combinations set the visual scope to be evaluated, in which there are variations in elements such as flipped headlamp, air intake and side air intake.

Tobii X120 eye tracking equipment is employed in the 8 images analyzed by 39 individuals. Primarily, it can be confirmed that subjects focus their attention on the 'threatening' elements. Besides that, participants prefer 'threatening' headlamps and 'non-threatening' air intake. In a second phase, it was found that 32 subjects avoided long periods of observation to design elements deemed as 'threatening'.

According to evolutionary biological preparedness perspectives researchers [39] suggest that threatening facial expressions are processed faster and more accurately, if compared to friendly faces.

In conclusion, anthropomorphic car frontal design may attract attention and manifest specific behavior in the subject. In other words, the visual patterns associated to gaze activate the affective dimension and, thereby, are relevant in capturing the attention and reaching satisfactory evaluation from the user (Fig. 4).

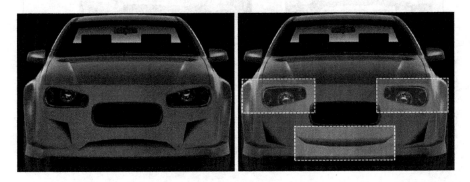

Fig. 4. 'Threatening' design (left); and 'non-threatening' (right), with headlamp, lower and side air vent variation. Font: Purucker et al. [39]

Chassy et al. [6] investigate the relationship between visual complexity and aesthetic pleasure, associated to two eye-tracking parameters: trajectory and gaze permanence. The device 'EyeLink1000' is attached to a head mounted feature to monitor and analyze left eye behavior, when visualizing 50 images of different mid-size car frontal views. Twenty-six students, 13 men and 13 women without art background or professional experience in automotive sector, evaluated the attraction degree of each image. A 9-point Likert scale was used with the following parameters: aesthetic appraisal – evaluated between −4 (ugly) and +4 (beautiful); and visual complexity – between 1 (simple) and 9 (complex). As a result: (a) the relationship between visual complexity and aesthetic pleasure are characterized by a U inverted curve calculated by a quadratic equation; (b) gaze is an objective behavior measure related to visual complexity; (c) dwelling time is correlated to aesthetic pleasure. Meaning, the observer spends more time exploring the image elements when the object is considered attractive (Fig. 5).

Hyun et al. [20, 21], via eye-tracking, identify the relationship between the visual observation patterns of 10 participants, familiar with automotive design, and the exterior design elements in 119 medium-sized sedans (on the market between 1999 and 2013) from 23 different brands.

Each car selected for the study is represented by 3 drawings: frontal, lateral and rear view. These drawings are used as a visual stimulus to the participants during the experiment with the Tobii X120. Nineteen design elements are analyzed, from the parameters: (a) duration of gaze on the area of interest; and (b) mapping of gaze

Fig. 5. Left – eye trajectories (visual complexity); right – eye tracking heat-map reflecting dwelling time (aesthetic pleasure). Font: Chassy et al. [6]

permanence. As a result, the most relevant exterior elements are the side silhouette, front fender and front bumper. Specifically, for luxury brands, participants focus attention on the silhouette, window and side taillamp (Fig. 6).

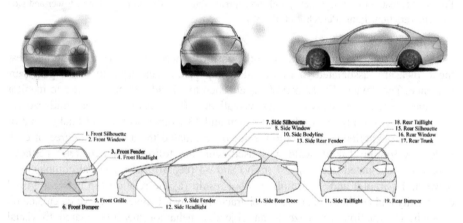

Fig. 6. At the top: red - long gaze time and green – short gaze time; at the bottom: most relevant elements in bold (3, 6, 7). Font: Hyun et al. [20, 21] (Color figure online)

2.3   Eye Tracking, Galvanic Skin Response, Facial Electromyography

The research of Schmitt et al. [40] seeks to identify the relevance of the external components of the sports utility vehicle (SUV), when assessing the emotions elicited by its elements. In addition, the study investigates the applicability of the screen-based eye-tracking system in the measurement of the degree of attention. Furthermore, they check the influence of the semantic concepts in the evaluation of the product mediated by the measurement of biological signals, in this case, through the association between facial electromyography (EMG) and galvanic skin response (GSR) techniques.

In the first phase, 25 participants holistically analyze the exterior image of two sports utility vehicles, one of which is the production model and the other a modified model. In this context, they evaluate their impression with the semantic concepts: "dynamic", "powerful", "sporty" and "modern", in a 5-point scale. The explicit results were combined with the eye-tracking technique (ET), and it was concluded that the modified car is considered significantly more "potent" in terms of power when compared to the production model.

The second stage of the study focuses on the identification of quality attributes associated with certain concepts by users, either voluntarily or involuntary. To this end, areas of interest of the participants are mapped, via ET, during free visualization of the product image, and after presentation of the "dynamic" semantic concept. The figure below indicates relevant information regarding the attention, order and frequency of fixation of each individual's gaze (Fig. 7).

Fig. 7. Individual gaze track for one user (free interaction vs. 'dynamic' concept). Font: Schmitt et al. [40]

Subsequently, the emotions are investigated via galvanic skin response (GSR) and facial electromyography (EMG), with the objective of verifying the quality of the users' evaluation (positive or negative), in relation to specific design alternatives. In addition, they seek to identify the influence of the semantic concept on the behavior of neurophysiological signals. Fourteen students participate in this measurement (Fig. 8).

Fig. 8. Placement of sensors for detecting bio-signals. Left: Skin Galvanic Response (GSR); Center and right: Facial Electromyography (fEMG). Font: Schmitt et al. [40]

The results of the study suggest that semantic concepts affect eye-tracking and attention span over the relevant attributes of the product, as well as the signs of galvanic skin response and facial electromyography. The diagram below confirms the possibility of obtaining, for each attribute of the product in question, design recommendations regarding the attention evoked by the semantic concepts. In this case, the front bumper is mentioned as an example. The evaluation indicates it as a relevant attribute to the perception of the modified car as more "powerful" when compared to that of the production model (Fig. 9).

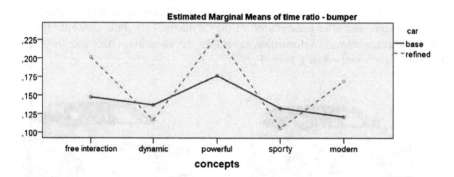

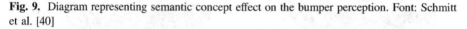

Fig. 9. Diagram representing semantic concept effect on the bumper perception. Font: Schmitt et al. [40]

2.4   Functional Magnetic Resonance Imaging

Gauthier et al. [14] confirm that the tasks of identifying and categorizing animals and cars, by specialists in these domains, activate the brain areas involved in facial recognition. With the use of the fMRI technique, they observe the brain activity of eight specialists in the identification of bird species and eleven professionals in the automotive sector, who are skilled at recognizing car models, when both groups are exposed to 4 categories of visual stimuli: human faces (Caucasian and without hair); familiar objects; cars (in models from years 1995 to 1998); and birds (from New England). All images are displayed in the chromatic scale of gray.

In conclusion, both categorization and identification, aside from experience, determine the specialization of fusiform gyrus, located in parts of the temporal and occipital lobes in area 37 of Broadmann, which is responsible for facial recognition (Fig. 10).

While the studies by Erk et al. [12] investigate the connection between the brain mechanism associated with reward and ownership of cars and the image of wealth and social dominance.

The fMRI technique is used through the 1.5 T Siemens Magnetom Symphony device to observe the brain activity of twelve male drivers, during the observation of 66 gray scale car images. The images are equally distributed in the following categories: sport; limousine; and compact. Associated with the fMRI technique, a 5-point scale

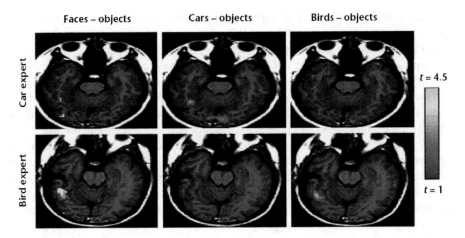

Fig. 10. Brain activation for cars and birds identification specialists, accessed by fMRI. Font: Gauthier et al. [14]

aims to assess the attractiveness of these models, based on the responses attributed by the drivers.

The rating obtained from the attractiveness scale indicates a better evaluation of sports cars, when compared to the other categories. In parallel, the results obtained through the fMRI technique express that cultural objects, associated with wealth and social dominance, modulate the reward dopaminergic circuit by stimulating brain-related areas: ventral striatum; orbitofrontal cortex; anterior cingulate gyrus; and occipital region. It is known that the reward mechanism induces subjective feelings of pleasure and contributes to trigger positive emotions (Fig. 11).

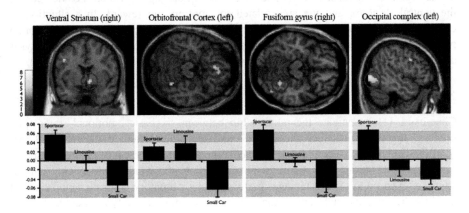

Fig. 11. Image of brain regions mapped for contrasting sports cars > small cars, accessed by fMRI. Font: Erk et al. [12]

The research of Sylcott et al. [46] investigates the preference and judgment processes, as well as consumer decision-making in regards to stimuli related to aesthetic (form) and automotive performance (function). The first phase employs the statistical technique of joint analysis and self-report, and the second adopts the fMRI technique.

The primary phase identifies the aesthetic preference of 14 participants considering 36 options of automobile silhouettes, with the following variations: shoulder, ramp angle, distance from the ground, body height, ceiling height, hood length, and trunk length. Of the total number of options, the distance between wheels and the wheel size remain constant. In this context, the functional preference is also identified, in which the performance specifications are observed, such as: acceleration, fuel consumption, power and braking. Subsequently, 25 combinations of preferences are observed, both aesthetic and functional, in order to evaluate the balance between decision-making and the above-mentioned attributes. The result of the first phase indicates the preference for the function, coming from the majority of participants.

In the second phase, validation of the first experiment occurs, through self-report, reading and interpretation of the brain activity of 7 individuals by fMRI. The collection of data is performed during the visualization of 24 stimuli, which focus on conflicts between form and function. Using the Siemens 3T Verio Scanner, the fMRI technique aims at highlighting the brain areas involved in the mechanisms associated with logic and emotion, and at the same time, relating the decision-making between form and function.

When analized individually, form and function activate the dorsal region of the anterior cingulate gyrus (involved in conflict monitoring, error detection in both domains, cognitive and emotional, and decision making) and the dorsolateral prefrontal cortex (cognitive reasoning). However, the insula (area of the limbic system associated with emotion derived from visceral experience) is exclusively activated during the analysis of the form. When evaluated simultaneously, form and function activate the dorsal region of the anterior cingulate gyrus; the limbic region, which includes part of the ventral striatum; and the area related to emotion and reward. In a situation of conflict between form and function in the process of decision making, the midbrain regions were activated, as well as the orbitofrontal cortex, the parahippocampal gyrus and the amygdala, which are associated with emotion and its regulation (Fig. 12).

2.5   Electroencephalography

Chae et al. [1] investigate the relationship between six basic emotional states (joy, sadness, anger, disgust, fear and neutral) and the brain signals evoked by different head-up display (HUD) configurations - technology that projects information on speed, fuel level, navigation, gear position, and others onto the windshield. Twenty participants are exposed to 18 HUD images performed in a laboratory-controlled environment and in a driving simulator. These images differ according to the type of content, color and source, according to (Fig. 13).

Sixteen localized channels in the participants' scalps are monitored through electroencephalography (EEG) technique. Three of them, associated with the indexes of mental activity, level of concentration and relaxation, are analyzed more in-depth from the PolyG-A equipment. In addition, participants report their emotions on a 7-point

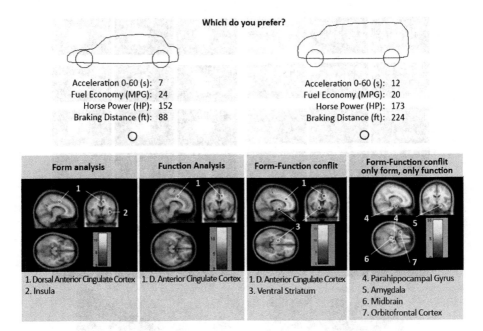

Fig. 12. Form vs. function: brain activity assessed by fMRI technique. Font: adapted from Sylcott et al. [46]

scale using the semantic differential technique, utilizing dichotomous adjectives such as "modern-old fashioned", "masculine-feminine", "comfortable-uncomfortable", "smooth-rough", "clear- ambiguous". The study shows that HUD images evoke different brain signals, concentration levels, and emotions. Moreover, color proves to be the main factor in determining the type of emotion evoked, while the amount of information determines the level of activation in the brain's central lobe. The brain activities in the temporal lobe are positively associated with the level of concentration. In this sense, it is possible to affirm that discoveries in the association between emotions and EEG signals can be used in the design of new driver-vehicle interfaces.

In order to clarify the understanding of the investigations that analyze human neural activity, through fMRI and EEG techniques, consider the following illustration of the brain areas and their correlation to perceptive, cognitive and behavioral processes (Fig. 14).

3   Conclusion

The mapping carried out by this research facilitates the formulation of inferences about the role and use of neurophysiological data verification techniques in the scope of Automotive Design and its association with design methodologies currently applied, specifically in the period between the years of 2000 to 2017.

Fig. 13. Top: 18 HUD images and brain activity induced by each image. Bottom: Electroencephalography experiment in laboratory and in simulator. Font: Chae et al. [1]

Although the twelve investigations covered here demonstrate the cooperation between the fields of Automotive Design and Neuroscience, and how promising and rich this research pathway proves to be, only two of them have professionals working in the automotive sector on their research team. This indicates an existing gap between the productive (automobile industry) and research (laboratories/universities) sectors, which endorses the reduced number of studies available in international literature.

Another factor that also corroborates this limitation lies in the main obstacles to the advancement found by research of this nature: (a) expressive sampling of participants to validate data collection; (b) limitations to the sampling of participants due to the use of technologies that require high investment of time and financial resources, and invasive radioactive material employment, such as PET; (c) limitations to the comparison of research results obtained through the same technology, caused by the adoption of different methods of induction, measurement and data processing, as cited by Phan et al. [37].

Despite the above mentioned adversities, the contributions of neurophysiological data assessment techniques are notorious when associated with design methodologies and, consequently, incorporated into product design and development stages. Such contributions emphasize, but are not limited to: (a) enable 'access' to brain areas related

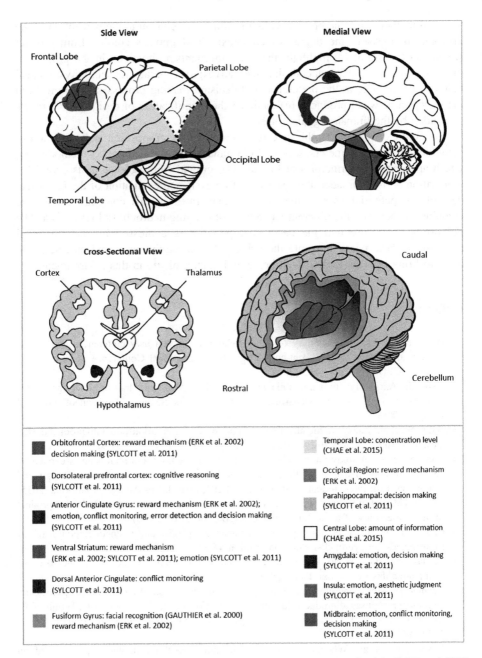

Fig. 14. Anatomy of brain areas and their respective functions, described in fMRI and EEG investigations. Font: the author (2018)

to visual memory and, thereby, providing information relevant to the perception of the product; (b) measure the degree of complexity and impacts coming from product stimuli on the brain; (c) highlight the brain mechanisms involved in the process of distinguishing between product design alternatives; (d) evaluate the neurophysiological behavior of the user in the preference and decision making processes, resulting from the selection between products; (e) facilitate the identification of design requirements demanded by the human organism itself.

For future development, this research focuses on the proposition and validation of automotive design parameters, seeking to formulate an integrated project methodology, which articulates the principles of Product Design and Neuroscience at its core. This articulation aims to broaden the spectrum of analysis and evaluation of the biological data of the potential user to the products elaborated in this context, through the combination between the different techniques of gauging neurophysiological data. The purpose is to ensure that the needs and preferences expressed by the emotional response of these users, integrate the vehicle design requirements and parameters in order to bring benefits to their well-being and quality of life in this environment.

References

1. Antoine, D., Petiot, J.F.: Study of the correlations between user preferences and design factors: application to cars front-end design. In: International Conference of Engineering Design, ICED 2007, pp. 1–12 (2007)
2. Asfallah, A.: Design of automobile instrumentation. Master in Industrial Design, Luleå University of Technology, Department of Human Work Sciences, Division of Industrial Design (2008)
3. Bahn, S., et al.: Incorporating affective customer needs for luxuriousness into product design attributes. Hum. Factors Ergon. Manuf. Serv. Ind. 19(2), 105–127 (2009)
4. Chae, S., et al.: A study on the relationship between emotions and brain signals evoked by head-up display images.. In: Proceedings of Human-Computer Interaction, Design end evaluation, 17th International Conference, HCI 2015, Part I, Los Angeles, California (2015)
5. Chang, H.C., et al.: Expression modes used by consumers in conveying desire for product form: a case study of a car. Int. J. of Ind. Ergon. 36, 3–10 (2006)
6. Chassy, P., et al.: A relationship between visual complexity and aesthetic appraisal of car front images: an eye-tracker study. Perception 44(8–9), 1085–1097 (2015)
7. Damásio, A.: O mistério da consciência: do corpo e das emoções ao conhecimento de si. Companhia das Letras, São Paulo (2000)
8. Desmet, P.: Measuring emotion: development and application of an instrument to measure emotional responses to products. In: Blythe, M.A., Overbeeke, K., Monk, A.F., Wright, P.C. (eds.) Funology, vol. 3, pp. 111–123. Springer, Dordrecht (2005). https://doi.org/10.1007/1-4020-2967-5_12
9. Desmet, P., et al.: When a car makes you smile: development and application of an instrument to measure product emotions. In: Hoch, S.J., Meyer, R.J. (eds.) Advances in Consumer Research, 27, pp. 111–117. Association for Consumer Research, Provo (2000)
10. Ensslin, L., et al.: Identificação das necessidades do consumidor no processo de desenvolvimento de produtos: uma proposta de inovação ilustrada para o segmento automotivo. Produção (São Paulo, Impresso), 21(4), 555–569 (2011)

11. E Sousa, C.V., et al.: Using the eye tracking for analysis of preference for vehicles. In: International Conference on Marketing and Consumer Behaviour ICMC (2013)

12. Erk, S., et al.: Cultural objects modulate reward circuitry. NeuroReport **13**(8), 2499–2503 (2002)

13. Furlaneto, F., et al.: Análise de Consumidores Por Meio do ZMET Confirmam Conforto e Segurança como Itens de Preferência na Escolha de Automóveis. PMKT – Revista Brasileira de Pesquisas de Marketing, Opinião e Mídia (ISSN 1983–9456 Impressa e ISSN 2317-0123 On-line), São Paulo, Brasil, vol. 14, pp. 57–72 (2014)

14. Gauthier, I., et al.: Expertise for cars and birds recruits brain areas involved in face recognition. Nat. Neurosci. **3**(2), 191 (2000)

15. Gentner, A., et al.: Mapping a multi-sensory identity territory at the early design stage. Int. J. Affect. Eng. **12**(2), 191–200 (2013)

16. Helander, M.G., et al.: Emotional needs of car buyers and emotional intent of car designers. Theor. Issues in Ergon. Sci. **14**(5), 455–474 (2012)

17. Helander, M.G., et al.: Citarasa engineering model for affective design of vehicles. In: IEEE International Conference on Industrial Engineering and Engineering Management, pp. 1282–1286 (2007)

18. Hsiao, S.-W.: Fuzzy set theory on car-color design. Color Res. Appl. **19**(3), 202–213 (1994)

19. Hsiao, S.-W., Wang, H.-P.: Applying the semantic transformation method to product form design. Des. Stud. **19**(3), 309–330 (1998)

20. Hyun, K., et al.: The gap between design intent and user response: identifying typical and novel car design elements among car brands for evaluating visual significance. J. Intell. Manuf. **28**(7), 1729–1741 (2017)

21. Hyun, K., et al.: Style synthesis and analysis of car designs for style quantification based on product appearance similarities. Adv. Eng. Inform. **29**(3), 483–494 (2015)

22. Jindo, T., Hirasago, K.: Application studies to car interior of Kansei engineering. Int. J. Ind. Ergon. **19**, 105–114 (1997)

23. Jindo, T., Nagamachi, M.: Analyses of automobile interiors using a semantic differential method. In: Human Factors and Ergonomics Society Annual Meeting Proceedings, October 1989

24. Jung, G., et al.: Effects of design factors of the instrument cluster panel on consumers' affection. In: Proceedings of the International MultiConference of Engineers and Computer Scientists IMECS 2010, vol. 3 Hong Kong (2010)

25. Karlsson, B., et al.: Using semantic environment description as a tool to evaluate car interiors. Ergon. **46**(13–14), 1408–1422 (2003)

26. Khalid, H.M., Helander, M.G.: A framework for affective customer needs in product design. Theor. Issues Ergon. Sci. **5**(1), 27–42 (2004)

27. Khalid, H.M., Helander, M.G.: Customer emotional needs in product design. Concurrent Eng. **14**(3), 197–206 (2006)

28. Khalid, H.M., et al.: Elicitation and analysis of affective needs in vehicle design. Theor. Issues Ergon. Sci. **13**(3), 318–334 (2012)

29. Kim, C., et al.: Affective evaluation of user impressions using virtual product prototyping. Hum. Factors Ergon. Manuf. Serv. Ind. **21**(1), 1–13 (2011)

30. Kim, S., et al.: The relationship between preference and Kansei values. Kansei Eng. Int. J. **11**(4), 259–266 (2012)

31. Lai, H.-H., et al.: A robust design approach for enhancing the feeling quality of a product: a car profile case study. Int. J. Ind. Ergon. Taiwan **35**(5), 445–460 (2005)

32. Liberatti, C., Zuanon, R.: Engenharia Kansei no design automotivo de exterior. In: 13° Congresso Pesquisa e Desenvolvimento em Design, Joinville (2018)

33. Liu, S.F., Lee, M.H.: User-oriented prospective smart electric vehicles innovating design development. J. Balk. Tribol. Assoc. **22**(1), 111–121 (2016)
34. Mohamed, M.S.S., Mustafa, S.: Kansei engineering implementation on car center stack designs. Int. J. Educ. Res. **2**(4), 355–366 (2014)
35. Nagamachi, M.: Kansei engineering: a new ergonomic consumer-oriented technology for product development. Int. J. Ind. Ergon. **15**, 3–11 (1995)
36. Normark, C., et al.: Evaluation of car instrumentation clusters by using eye-tracking. In: European Automotive Congress, EAEC (2007)
37. Phan, K.L., et al.: Functional neuroanatomy of emotion: a meta-analysis of emotion activation studies in PET and fMRI. Neuroimage **16**(2), 331–348 (2002)
38. Pérez, P.M., et al.: Álvarez González, Miguel Ángel. In: ¿ Cómo el diseño puede utilizar las neurociencias? Arquitectura y Urbanismo **37**(2), 83–87 (2016)
39. Purucker, C., et al.: Consumer response to car fronts: eliciting biological preparedness with product design. RMS **8**(4), 523–540 (2014)
40. Schmitt, R., et al.: Objectifying user attention and emotion evoked by relevant perceived product components. J. Sens. Sens. Syst. **3**(2), 315–324 (2014)
41. Schütte, S.T.W., Eklund, J.: Design of rocker switches for work-vehicles—an application of Kansei engineering. Appl. Ergon. **36**(5), 557–567 (2005)
42. Shen, K.S., et al. In: Measuring the functional and usable appeal of crossover B-Car interiors. Hum. Factors Ergon. Manuf. Serv. Ind. 1–17 (2012)
43. Shen, W., et al.: A cross-cultural study of vehicle front mask design using Kansei engineering approach. In: Proceedings of the Human Factors and Ergonomics Society Annual Meeting, vol. 44, no. 33, pp. 6-372–6-375 (2000)
44. Sihombing, H., et al.: The product design preferences based on KE: car products in Malasiya. In: Proceedings of Mechanical Engineering Research Day, pp. 200–201 (2017)
45. Smith, S., Fu, S.-H.: The relationships between automobile head-up display presentation images and drivers' Kansei. Displays **32**(2), 58–68 (2011)
46. Sylcott, B., et al.: Understanding of emotions and reasoning during consumer tradeoff between function and aesthetics in product design. In: ASME 2011 International Design Engineering Technical Conferences and Computers and Information in Engineering Conference. American Society of Mechanical Engineers, pp. 165–176 (2011)
47. Tanoue, C., Ishizaka, K., Nagamachi, M.: Kansei engineering: a study on perception of vehicle interior image. Int. J. Ind. Ergon. **19**, 115–128 (1997)
48. Vieira, J., et al.: Kansei engineering as a tool for the design of in-vehicle rubber keypads. Appl. Ergon. **61**, 1–11 (2017)
49. Wellings, T., et al.: Customer perception of switch-feel in luxury sports utility vehicles. Food Qual. Prefer. **19**, 737–746 (2008)
50. Wellings, T., et al.: Understanding customers' holistic perception of switches in automotive human-machine interfaces. Appl. Ergon. **41**, 8–17 (2010)
51. Windhager, S., et al.: Face to face: the perception of automotive designs. Hum. Nat. **19**(4), 331–346 (2008)
52. Windhager, S., et al.: Laying eyes on headlights: eye movements suggest facial features in cars. Collegium Antropol. **34**(3), 1075–1080 (2010)
53. Yadav, H.C., et al.: Prioritization of aesthetic attributes of car profile. Int. J. Ind. Ergon. **43**, 296–303 (2013)
54. Yogasara, T., Valentino, J.: Realizing the Indonesian national car: the design of the 4×2 wheel drive passenger car exterior using Kansei engineering type 1. Int. J. Technol. **2**, 338–351 (2017)
55. You, H., et al.: Development of customer satisfaction models for automotive interior materials. Int. J. Ind. Ergon. **36**(4), 323–330 (2006)

An Integrated Ergonomics Evaluation Method of HWDs

Hongjun Xue[1(✉)], Hua Zhao[1(✉)], and Xiaoyan Zhang[1,2,3(✉)]

[1] School of Aeronautics, Northwestern Polytechnical University,
Xi'an, China
xuehj@nwpu.edu.cn, 1046445923@qq.com,
zxyliuyan@163.com
[2] Institute of Human Factors and Ergonomics, Shenzhen University,
Shenzhen, China
[3] Key Laboratory of Optoelectronic Devices and Systems of Ministry
of Education and Guangdong Province, Shenzhen University, Shenzhen, China

Abstract. As one of the new human-computer interaction devices in advanced cockpit, the design and application of HWDs (Head-Worn Display System) must ensure that pilots can complete flight tasks comfortably, efficiently and safely with acceptable workload. However, to our knowledge, the thorough evaluation methods of HWDs have not been found. Therefore, an integrated ergonomics evaluation method of HWDs was established in this paper. Firstly, the main factors affecting ergonomics in HWDs had been analyzed to establish a preliminary index system by combining the working principle of the system with the related criterions in GJB. And then a final integrated ergonomics evaluation index system of HWDs was established based on modified Delphi method. Gl method was used to determine the weight vector of each index, which provides a good foundation for further evaluation of the HWDs' design.

Keywords: Head-Worn Display System ·
Integrated ergonomics evaluation index system · Modified Delphi

1 Introduction

Head-Worn Display System (HWDs) is an important device to realize virtual-real fusion display. According to the working principle, it can be divided into two types: optical transmission and video transmission [1, 2]. A HWD system typically is mainly composed of the source of image display system, positioning sensor system, optical imaging system, computing system and shell components. With the help of glasses or helmet, the display system is fixed on the user's head, and presenting a complete dynamic image in front of the user's eyes to create a feel of immersion and interaction [3, 4]. For a long time, in order to enhance the ability of interaction between pilots and cockpits, and improve the performances for flight, scholars in the aviation field are keen to apply the HWD of optical transmission to the new concept design of cockpit, so that the primary flight information and the real view of pilot can be combined into one and moving along with the movement of pilot' head, which can realize all-round observation and improve situation awareness for pilots [5–7].

© Springer Nature Switzerland AG 2019
V. G. Duffy (Ed.): HCII 2019, LNCS 11581, pp. 335–344, 2019.
https://doi.org/10.1007/978-3-030-22216-1_24

With the help of combined glasses, the HWD system applied in the cockpit collects the information of the real situation and measures the movement of the pilot's head by sensing system, and, stores and processes the data through the computing system to make tracking and registering combined with the data of head posture. Then, the optical lens and the image source are used to fuse the information of characters, icons, images, alarms and other information of flight into the external view, which present in front of the pilot's eyes to realize the interaction between the pilot and the situation around. Researches [7, 8] show that pilots using HWD often suffer from eye swelling, dizziness, nausea and difficulty in distinguishing and reading displayed information, which makes an influence on pilots' performance in the status of comfort, efficiency and safety. Therefore, it is an indispensable thing to evaluate the ergonomics of HWD before putting it into use. At present, there is no a thorough integrated evaluation index system for the ergonomics of HWDs. This paper puts up an integrated ergonomics evaluation index system of HWDs from the way of meeting the three requirements of comfort, efficiency and safety, which provides an important reference for further evaluating whether the design and application of HWDs can meet the ergonomics requirements.

2   Method

2.1   Preliminary Index System

Through literature research and analysis of the structure and working principle [4, 8, 9], it is found that the HWD worn on the pilot' head makes a combination of reality and virtuality and the transmission of information into the pilot' eyes by spectacle display. In this way, the comfort of man-machine interaction, the efficiency of display and control, as well as the safety of design all make an influence on the ergonomic of HWD system, which decides whether the pilots can complete the flight task comfortably, efficiently and safely. According to relevant reference with GJB 4052, GJB 1062A, GJB 301 and so on [10–14], it is found that the main factors including operation of wearing, weight and center of gravity, degree of tightness, mode of transmission, components of structure and visual representation will have impact on whether pilots can complete task in a comfortable state. The main factors including quality of brightness, angle of observation, distance of exit pupil, field of view, coding of icon, coding of character, coding of color, coding of distribution, mode of interaction and time of delay will affect the speed of obtaining information for pilots, which determines the efficiency of completing missions. And the main factors including protection of head, protection of eyes and design of quick detachment will have impact on whether pilots can work in a safe condition. Therefore, a preliminary evaluation index system for ergonomics of HWDs can be established on purpose by taking the comfort, efficiency and safety as the first-level indexes, and taking its main influencing factors and detailed factors as the second-level and third-level indexes respectively, which contains 3 first-level indexes, 19 second-level indexes and 49 third-level indexes actually.

2.2   Integrated Ergonomics Evaluation Index Method

Delphi [15] is the most representative and authoritative method in the construction of index system because of its goodness of making full use of the wisdom and experience of experts in the field. In order to ensure the scientificity and rationality of the index system established, this paper implements the analysis and selection of all the indexes based on the modified Delphi method, as described next.

(1) Organize a coordinating group

The coordinating group is composed of three members including one professor and two postgraduates to mainly complete the work of explaining the terms of indexes, determining the group of the experts, making questionnaires, organizing consultation and collecting data.

(2) Identify consulting experts

Experts who have certain professional knowledge and rich practical experience, and are willing to participate in the implementation of Delphi method are the key to success. Members of experts in this paper are all researchers with rich experience in ergonomics, including 2 doctoral students and 10 master students.

(3) Contents of consultation

Consultation questionnaires and questionnaires are made by the coordinating group according to each round of consultation, and the importance and operability of the all levels indicators are scored with the 5-point Likert scale by experts. The influence levels indicated by 1 to 5 were "not", "general", "average", "very" and "great". At the same time, the level of judgment Ca (theoretical analysis 0.9, practical experience 0.7, peer understanding 0.3, intuition 0.1) and familiarity Cs (0.9/0.7/0.5/0.3/0.1) of experts should be evaluated by their own to determine the authority Cr of experts.

(4) Screening criteria

On the basis of above, we collect the data and result of consultation each round, and evaluate the degree of authority for experts, and the degree of coordination and concentration for experts' opinions respectively by statistical analysis.

① Degree of authority for experts

The authority of experts is expressed by the coefficient Cr, which is generally determined by two factors: Ca, the basis on which experts make their judgment on the problem, and Cs, the familiarity of experts with the index. There are:

$$C_r = \frac{(C_a + C_s)}{2} \tag{1}$$

Where, $C_r \geq 0.7$ is an acceptable value. The degree of authority for experts has a certain functional relationship with the prediction accuracy, and the prediction accuracy increases with the improvement of the degree of authority of experts generally.

② Degree of coordination for experts' opinions

The degree of coordination of experts' opinions indicates whether there are big differences in the evaluation of each index among the experts in the study, which is reflected by the coefficient of variation V_j and the coefficient of coordination W.

$$V_j = \frac{\delta_j}{M_j} \tag{2}$$

Where, M_j denotes the arithmetic average value of index j, δ_j denotes the standard value of index j. The smaller the V_j, the higher the degree of coordination of experts, if $V_j > 0.25$, it is recognized that the degree of coordination of experts is not enough.

$$W = \frac{12}{m^2(n^3 - n) - m \sum_{i=1}^{m} T_i} \sum_{j=1}^{n} d_j^2 \tag{3}$$

Where, n denotes the number of indexes, m denotes the total number of experts, T_i is the correction coefficient, d_j is the difference of the arithmetic average value between index j and the sum of all index. Whether the evaluation opinions of experts have great differences is reflected by W, which can be tested by Kendall W test with SPSS. Taking the significance level ($p < 0.01$) as the test standard, it is believed that the test value >0.01, the coordination degree of experts' opinions on the indexes meets the requirements.

③ Degree of concentration for experts' opinions

The degree of concentration of experts' opinions on the relative importance of each index is generally expressed by the arithmetic mean M_j, median and full mark frequency K_j.

$$M_j = \frac{1}{m_j} \sum_{i=1}^{m} C_{ij} \tag{4}$$

Where, m_j denotes the number of experts, C_{ij} denotes the evaluation value of expert i for indexes j. $M_j > 3$ means that experts' recognition of the importance of the index meets the requirements.

$$K_j = \frac{m_{j'}}{m_j} \tag{5}$$

Where, $m_{j'}$ donates the number of experts given full marks. The higher the K_j, the higher the experts' recognition of the index generally.

2.3   Calculation of the evaluation index weight

The weight of index is an accurate description of the impact degree between the indicators and the target, which determines the effectiveness of the results for evaluation. G1 method is an improvement of AHP to get the weight quickly and accurately. In this paper, the weight of each index is determined based on G1, as described next.

(1) Determine the set of evaluation index

Note that U is the set of index which is composed of the first-level evaluation index u_i. U_i is the set of index which is composed of the second-level evaluation index u_{ij}. U_{ij} is the set of index which is composed of the third-level evaluation index u_{ijz}. There are:

$$U = \{u_1, u_2, \ldots u_i\} \tag{6}$$

$$U_i = \{u_{i1}, u_{i2}, \ldots u_{ij}\} \tag{7}$$

$$U_{ij} = \{u_{ij1}, u_{ij2}, \ldots u_{ijz}\} \tag{8}$$

Where, i donates the number of first-level indexes, j donates the number of second-level indexes, z donates the number of third-level indexes.

(2) Organize experts and determine its credibility

In order to determine the credibility of experts, the background of education (a_t), the basis of evaluation (b_t), the understanding degree of the problem (c_t), and the confidence of the evaluation (d_t) for each experts is comprehensively evaluated by the Expert Comprehensive Assessment Form. Assuming that the number of experts is m, and the self-evaluation value of the t-th expert is G_t ($G_t = a_t \cdot b_t \cdot c_t \cdot d_t$), and the credibility of the t-th expert is:

$$R_t = \frac{G_t}{\sum_{t=1}^{m} G_t}, \quad t = 1, 2, 3, \ldots, m \tag{9}$$

Then, the experts' confidence vector is determined as $\boldsymbol{R} = (R_1, R_2, R_3, \cdots R_m)$.

(3) Calculate the single weight of index

The weight questionnaires are full in by each experts to complete the importance ranking of sub-indexes under each set of indexes and the comparison and assignment of importance (defined r_i) between indexes u_i and u_{i-1}

$$w_n^* = \left(1 + \sum_{k=2}^{n} \prod_{i=k}^{n} r_i\right)^{-1} \tag{10}$$

$$w_{i-1}^* = r_i w_i^*, \quad i = n, n-1, \ldots, 2 \tag{11}$$

Through Eqs. (10–11), the relative weight coefficient of each index under its set can be determined and the vector W^* can be obtained.

$$W^* = \{w_1^*, w_2^*, \ldots, w_n^*\} \tag{12}$$

(4) Calculate the integrated weight of index

The integrated weight of each index can be obtained by combining the single weight of index from every expert and its credibility. Taking the single weight of the index i evaluated by the t-th expert is w_i^{t*}, then the integrated weight of index i is determined as w_i, there is:

$$w_i = \sum_{t=1}^{m} w_i^{t*} R_t \tag{13}$$

2.4   Implementation of method

12 experts including 2 doctoral students and 10 master students major in ergonomics participated in this research. They were informed of the purpose and main contents of the modified Delphi method and G1 method so that all works could be performed better.

Firstly, based on the modified Delphi method, each expert was required to analyze the importance and operability of each indexes in preliminary system to the ergonomic of HWDs. According to the Consultation Questionnaires, experts evaluated the influence of the indexes with a score of 1–5, and the level of judgment and familiarity with a score of 0.1–0.9. The indexes with high scores by screening criteria were retained and the indexes with low scores were deleted, then the final integrated ergonomics evaluation index system was established by several round of consultation until experts are unanimous.

After that, based on the G1 method, each expert was required to compare and sort the sub-indexes under each index set by its importance to HWDs and evaluated the assignment between index u_i and u_{i-1} with a score of r_i (in Table 1) according to the Weight Questionnaires, one the other hand, the credibility of each expert was also evaluated with a score of 8–10 by the Expert Comprehensive Assessment Form. Then, the integrated weight of each index were calculated by formula 13.

Table 1. The reference for the value of r_i

r_i	Importance of w_{i-1}/w_i
1.0	Equally
1.2	Slightly
1.4	More
1.6	Very
1.8	Extremely

3 Result and Discussion

3.1 Results of Consultation for Delphi

The first round of consultation evaluated the importance and operability of 3 first-level indexes, 19 second-level indexes and 49 third-level indexes under the preliminary index system to the ergonomics of HWDs. The evaluation data were tested by Kendall W from SPSS (importance: P = 0.384, operability: P = 0.301), which indicated that experts had a high degree of coordination and authority on the proposed indexes, so the evaluation results of this round were in high credibility.

Taking the M_j of importance ≥ 3, the M_j of operability ≥ 3, and the $V_j \leq 0.3$ were used as screening criteria. The results showed that 3 first-level indexes and 19 second-level indexes were all in conditions. In the third-level indexes of comfort, the importance and operability of "ease of wearing" (M_j = 2.750, 2.583) and "normalization of parts" (M_j = 1.750, 2.667) did not meet the screening requirements because of its weaker impact on comfort, the importance of "transmission wired/wireless" (M_j = 2.250) as well as the operability of "coordination of component" (M_j = 1.583) also did not meet the requirements, which were decided to be deleted in the next round of consultation therefore. The evaluation results of the three-level indexes of efficiency showed that "types and quantities of interaction" did not meet the importance requirements (M_j = 2.750), so it was decided to delete. The three-level indexes of safety all met the screening requirements of importance and operability and were retained.

Combining with the expert' opinions of the first round, the importance and operability of the remaining 3 first-level indexes, 19 second-level indexes and 44 third-level indexes to the ergonomic of HWDs were re-evaluated in the second round of consultation. Test of Kendall W (importance P = 0.314, operability P = 0.260) showed that experts' opinions on the indexes were consistent and had high credibility. The results showed that all indexes retained were all in conditions of importance and operability. Moreover, in the three-level indexes, "compression on head and ear" (M_j = 4.583), "compression uniformity on head and ear" (M_j = 4.417) and "fit of display size and head size" (M_j = 4.167) all had a larger influence on comfort. "Coordination between brightness and illuminance" (M_j = 4.083), "contrast between image and background" (M_j = 4.333), "angle of view" (M_j = 4.250), "readability of height of character" (M_j = 4.133) and "size of total delay time" (M_j = 4.417) all had great influence on efficiency. And, "shock resistance of shell" (M_j = 3.583) and "preventive measures of eye" (M_j = 3.750) also affected the safety of the HWD to varying degrees.

No new index added in this round, so there was no need for the next round of consultation, then an integrated evaluation index system of evaluation for Head-Worn Display system was established successfully.

3.2 Results of weight for G1

Based on the index system, the results of index weight at all levels determined by formula (9–13) were shown in Table 2.

Table 2. The results of index weight at all levels

First-level indexes		Second-level indexes		Third-level indexes	
Name	Weight	Name	Weight	Name	Weight
Comfort	0.315	Operation of wearing	0.144	Flexibility of wearing	0.474
				Time-saving and labor-saving of wearing	0.527
		Weight and center of gravity	0.227	Compression on head and ear	0.495
				Compression uniformity on head and ear	0.506
		Degree of tightness	0.189	Fit of display size and head size	0.394
				Stability during turning	0.351
				Breathability of display	0.256
		Mode of transmission	0.150	Speed of transmission	0.478
				Stability of transmission	0.523
		Component of structure	0.138	Roughness/smoothness of parts	0.241
				Firmness and reliability of connections	0.414
				Flexibility of adjusting knob	0.345
		Visual representation	0.152	Load of visual information	0.496
				Fatigability of vision	0.505
Efficiency	0.380	Quality of brightness	0.121	Coordination between brightness and illuminance	0.360
				Self-regulation of brightness	0.305
				Contrast between image and background	0.336
Efficiency	0.380	Angle of observation	0.079	Angles of observation in up and down direction	0.316
				Angles of observation in left and right direction	0.344
				Self-regulation of angles	0.341
		Distance of exit pupil	0.095	Distance of eye-to-screen	0.433
				Accurate alignment of virtual and real images	0.568
		Field of view	0.120	Size of angle of field	0.395
				View of activities	0.330
				Coordination with resolution	0.276
		Coding of icon	0.074	Figurativeness of icon	0.420
				Understandability of icon	0.581
		Coding of character	0.116	Readability of height	0.305
				Readability of stroke width	0.249
				Readability of character spacing	0.248
				Standardization of fonts	0.200
		Coding of color	0.104	Psychological feeling of color	0.337
				Rationality of collocation	0.364
				Salience of color	0.300
		Coding of distribution	0.073	Centrality/dispersion of contexts	0.503
				Spacing of contents	0.498
		Mode of interaction	0.068	Maneuverability of interactivity	0.486
				Coordination of interoperability	0.515
		Time of delay	0.152	Size of total delay time	1.000

(*continued*)

Table 2. (*continued*)

First-level indexes		Second-level indexes		Third-level indexes	
Name	Weight	Name	Weight	Name	Weight
Safety	0.305	Protection of head	0.326	Preventive measure of head	0.319
				Shock resistance of shell	0.366
				Buffer capacity of liner	0.316
		Protection of eyes	0.404	Preventive measures of eye	1.000
		Detachment	0.271	Quick detachment	1.000

Comparing the weights of the above indexes, it was obvious that "weight and center of gravity" and "degree of tightness" had a greater impact on comfort, "time of delay", "quality of brightness" and "coding of character" had great influence on efficiency, and the impact of "protection of eyes" on safety was also clear, which was basically consistent with the above results of importance by modified Delphi method. Therefore, more attention should be paid to the impact of the above important indexes in actual design and application.

4   Conclusion

In order to establish an excellent integrated ergonomics evaluation index system of Head-Worn Display system, this paper used improved Delphi method and finally established an integrated evaluation index system with 3 first-level indexes, 19 second-level indexes and 44 third-level indexes starting from the way of meeting the requirements of comfort, efficiency and safety. On this basis, the weights of indexes at all levels were determined by the G1 method, and the influence degree was clear and definite, which provids a certain reference for the design and evaluation as well as the subsequent in-depth researches of HWDs, therefore.

References

1. Ronald, A., Yohan, B., Reinhold, B., et al.: Recent advances in augmented reality. IEEE Comput. Graph. Appl. **11**, 34–47 (2001)
2. Julier, S., Baillot, Y., Lanzagorta, M., et al.: BARS: battlefield augmented reality system. In: NATO Symposium on Information Processing Techniques for Military Systems (2000)
3. Kalich, M.E., Rash, C.E.: A limited flight study for investigating hyperstereo vision. Head Helmet Mounted Displays VII **6557**, 1–14 (2007)
4. Huxford, R.B.: Wide FOV head-mounted display using hybrid optics. Opt. Des. Eng. **5249**, 230–237 (2004)
5. Jarvis, J.A., Lawrence, J.P., Randall, E.B., et al.: Head-Worn display concepts for surface operations for commercial aircraft. National Aeronautics and Space Administration (2008)
6. Jarvis, J.A., Lawrence, J.P., Williams, S.P., et al.: Enhanced/synthetic vision and head-worn display technologies for terminal maneuvering area NextGen operations. In: Display Technologies and Applications for Defense, Security, and Avionics V; and Enhanced and Synthetic Vision (2011)

7. Sarma, K.R., Grothe, S., Gannon, A.: Avionics displays. In: Chen, J., Cranton, W., Fihn, M. (eds.) Handbook of Visual Display Technology, pp. 253–274. Springer, Cham (2016). https://doi.org/10.1007/978-3-319-14346-0_168

8. Geiselman, E.E., Haig, P.R.: Rise of the HMD: the need to review our human factors guidelines In: Proceeding of SPIE, vol. 804, pp. 102–111 (2011)

9. Wang, Y.S.: On dynamic, performance of airborne helmet-mounted display and sight system. Electron. Opt. Control **20**, 1–4 (2013)

10. GJB 1062A-2008, General Requirements for Ergonomic Design of Military Visual Display

11. GJB 4052-2000, General Specification for Airborne Helmet/Aiming Display System

12. GJB 300-1987, Head-up Display Characters for Aircraft

13. GJB 2020A-2012, General Specification for Aircraft Internal and External Lighting Equipment

14. Nanyan, L.: Summary of key technologies and related design problems of HMD. Infrared Laser Eng. **31**, 237–243 (2002)

15. Yajun, G.: Theory and Method of Comprehensive Evaluation. Science Press, Beijing (2002)

Evaluation of the Advising Doctor for Operating of Medical Student by Laparoscopic Surgery Simulator

Kazuaki Yamashiro[1]([✉]), Koichiro Murakami[2], Hisanori Shiomi[3], and Akihiko Goto[4]

[1] Kyoto Institute of Technology,
Goshokaido-cho, Matsugasaki, Sakyo-ku, Kyoto, Japan
k.yamashiro546@gmail.com
[2] Tesseikai Neurosurgical Hospital,
28-1 Nakanohomma-chi, Shijonawate, Osaka, Japan
[3] Nagahama Red Cross Hospital,
14-7 Miyamae-cho, Nagahama-shi, Shiga, Japan
[4] Osaka Sangyo University, Daito-shi, Osaka, Japan

Abstract. Laparoscopic surgery is less intraoperative hemorrhaging and pain than open surgery, reducing the patient's burden. However, laparoscopic surgery requires time for practicing to acquire the procedure due to restrictions such as work through instruments or limited viewing. In this study, we elucidate the relationship of evaluation of simulator and evaluation of advising doctor, and verified the possibility of constructing educational system including education as guidance. In this experiment, the subjects were surgeons with 18 years of experience of laparoscopic surgery to qualify as an instructor. The content of the experiment was the 5-grade evaluation for the work by viewing the candidate movie. The 5-grade evaluation is "A", "B", "C", "D", "E", and it is an evaluation that it is bad from "A" to "E". We compared them with the evaluation items of the simulator and focused on the items of moving distance of forceps considered to be related to the medical student's skill. It was found that the shorter the moving distance, the better the evaluation by the advising doctor depending on the moving distance of the forceps. However, in "D" as well, it was a value approximate to "B". From this, it is considered that the reason why the forceps movement distance was short in the medical students of "D" evaluation is because they forceps are not operated (not moving). Therefore, it is thought that more accurate evaluation can be made by evaluating no only the evaluation of the simulator but also the evaluation judgment of the advising doctor, that is, the operation of the forceps.

Keywords: Evaluation · Advising doctor · Laparoscopic surgery simulator

© Springer Nature Switzerland AG 2019
V. G. Duffy (Ed.): HCII 2019, LNCS 11581, pp. 345–354, 2019.
https://doi.org/10.1007/978-3-030-22216-1_25

1   Introduction

Japanese doctors counted statistics on the number of doctors by the Ministry of Health, Labor and Welfare [1]. According to it, the number of surgeons, especially those under 29 years old decreased from 3,383 in 1998 to 1,422 in 2016. That means that medical students and residency who wish for surgeons are getting less. As one of these causes, it will take time to acquire skills. One of the factors that raises the difficulty of acquiring skills will be surgical techniques. In addition, in recent years, surgery of another method such as laparoscopic surgery as well as open surgery will be performed, and surgical techniques for it must be acquired. Laparoscopic surgery differs from open surgery in the following points.

- Work with forceps.
- Obtain surgical field with video of endoscope camera.

For the above reasons, the field of vision is restricted and you have to get used to operating forceps. The eye-hand coordination is regarded as important, and there is a problem that it takes time to familiarize.

The aim of the research was to construct a self-learning educational support system that feedbacks the evaluation results to the learner for laparoscopic surgery. We measured the medical student's eye movement in practice and reported the results of gaze point and gaze time in last year's HCII [2]. Thereby, we clarified the medical student's eye movement and the guidance content of the advising doctors and suggested that we can see the proficiency level by gaze time and evaluation of simulation. And we compared the moving distance of forceps obtained by the simulator and the evaluation by the surgeon in the japan ergonomics society kansai branch [3]. The moving distance of forceps was shorter as a surgeon evaluated good medical student. However, medical students with low evaluations also had short the moving distance. Besides whether the medical student is good or bad, there is a possibility that the work may be complicated, and as a result, the moving distance may be shortened. We reported that we need to evaluate them differently and clarify the difference.

In this research, we clarified the relationship between the evaluation items of the simulator obtained by the previous research and the evaluation of the advising doctors and searched for a new evaluation axis.

2   Experimental Method

In this content of implementation, participants watched target videos and evaluated it. Participants were a surgeon of 18 years' experience with qualification of advising doctors. Figure 1 shows the videos watched by participants. The target videos was 37 medical students targeted in previous research. The content of the videos was a practice of laparoscopic cholecystectomy using a surgical simulator. Evaluation method was set to 5 grades of "A", "B", "C", "D" and "E". It is an evaluation that "A" is the best and it is bad with E.

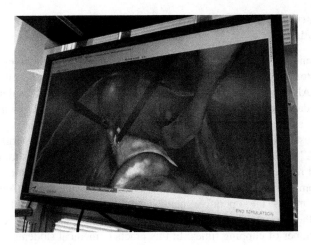

Fig. 1. Target video watched by participants

3 Result

3.1 Comparison of Evaluation of Simulator and Evaluation by Surgeon

Among the evaluation items of the simulator, comparisons were made on 9 items considered to be related to skills. Table 1 shows item names and their contents. The value of the evaluation item is evaluated by a numerical value or "01". For example, "Actual Result for time.complete.task" is expressed by working time. "Actual result for Duct.First" is expressed by "0" or "1", indicating whether or not it is done. "0" indicates that it is not for the item, and "1" indicates what it was done for the item.

Table 1. Focused evaluation item of the simulator

Evaluation item	Evaluation method
Actual result for Time.Complete.Task	Numerical value
Actual result for Time.Cautery.Used	Numerical value
Actual result for Duct.Proximal.Clipped	01 notation
Actual result for Duct.Distal.Clipped	01 notation
Actual result for Artery.Proximal.Clipped	01 notation
Actual result for Artery.Distal.Clipped	01 notation
Actual result for Duct.First	01 notation
Actual result for Blood.Loss	Numerical value
Actual result for Clips.Placed	Numerical value
Actual result for Clips.Dropped	Numerical value

3.2   Comparison Between Numeric Data and Advising Doctor's Evaluation

The average and the standard deviation (SD) were calculated with the evaluation value of the simulator of each evaluation divided by the advising doctors in order to make a comparison. Also, since there is only one medical student of "E" evaluation, average and standard deviation are not calculated. Figures 2, 3, 4, 5 and 6 show the comparison between each evaluation item and the advising doctor's evaluation.

"Actual result for Time.Complete.Task" means working time, working time was long from "A" evaluation to "C" evaluation. And "D" evaluation shortened working time. "Actual result for Time.Cautery.Used" means the operating time of acusector.

No predominant difference was seen between the evaluations. "Actual result for Blood.Loss" means the operative hemorrhage. The worse bleeding amount was increased as the advising doctor's evaluation was bad. "Actual result for Clips.Placed" means the number of clipping times. In this practice, medical students were instructed to do 6 times in total, 3 times to the cystic duct and 3 times to the cystic artery. The worse the advising doctor's evaluation, the less the number of clipping was filled. "Actual result for Clips.Dropped" means the number of clipping dropout intraoperatively. The worse the advising doctor's evaluation, the more dropped out.

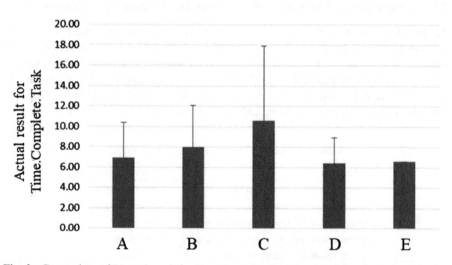

Fig. 2. Comparison of "Actual result for Time.Complete.Task" and advising doctor's evaluation

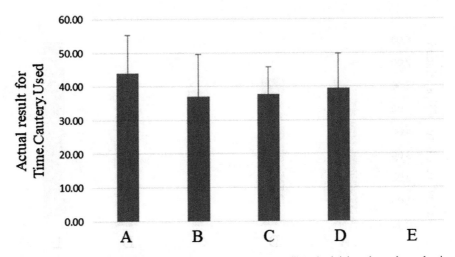

Fig. 3. Comparison of "Actual result for Time.Cautery.Used" and advising doctor's evaluation

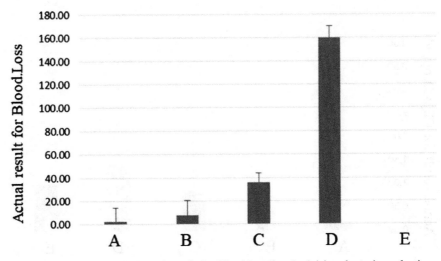

Fig. 4. Comparison of "Actual result for Blood.Loss" and advising doctor's evaluation

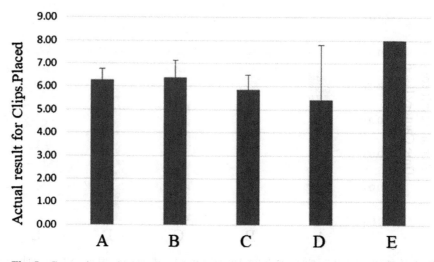

Fig. 5. Comparison of "Actual result for Clips.Placed" and advising doctor's evaluation

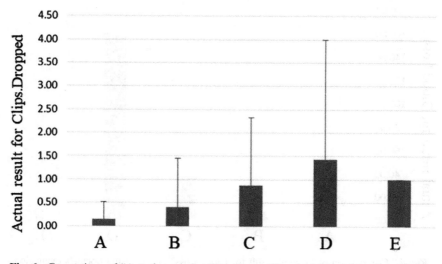

Fig. 6. Comparison of "Actual result for Clips.Dropped" and advising doctor's evaluation

3.3 Comparison with "01" Data and Advising Doctor's Evaluation

Next, we calculated the rate of the medical student who was "1" in each evaluation and the medical student who was "0". Figures 7, 8, 9, 10 and 11 show to compare the rate of the evaluation item of the simulation and the advising doctor's evaluation. "Actual result for Duct. Proximal. Clipped" and "Actual result for Duct. Distal. Clipped" means clipping at a position close to the cystic duct or clipping to a distant position. "Actual result for Artery.Proximal.Clipped" and "Actual result for Artery.Distal.Clipped" have the same meaning and do for the cystic artery. Doing these tasks makes easier to cut the cystic duct and the cystic artery. The results show that the worse the advising doctor's evaluation, the more medical students are not doing it. Finally, "Actual result for Duct. First" means that the cystic duct was worked before the cystic artery. It is said that the cystic duct is located on the near side of the gallbladder artery and working with the gallbladder earlier is easier to work. There was a medical student who could not work the cystic duct earlier in every evaluation. Also, the worse the advising doctor's evaluation, the higher the proportion of "0" was.

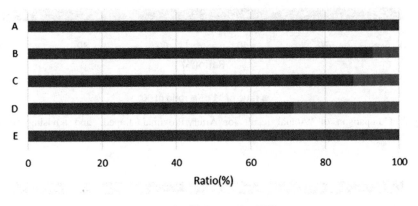

Fig. 7. Comparison of "Actual result for Duct.Proximal.Clipped" and advising doctor's evaluation

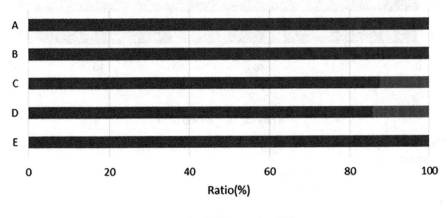

Fig. 8. Comparison of "Actual result for Duct.Distal.Clipped" and advising doctor's evaluation

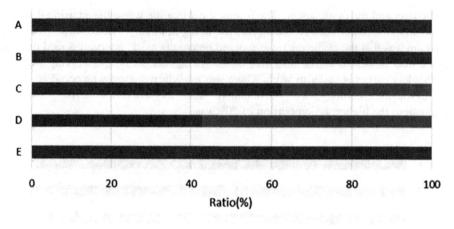

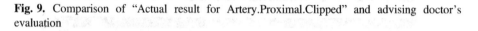

Fig. 9. Comparison of "Actual result for Artery.Proximal.Clipped" and advising doctor's evaluation

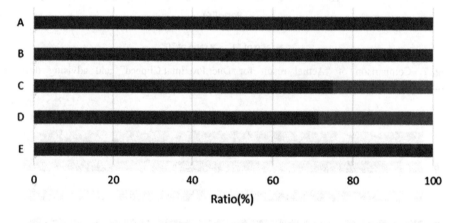

Fig. 10. Comparison of "Actual result for Artery.Distal.Clipped" and advising doctor's evaluation

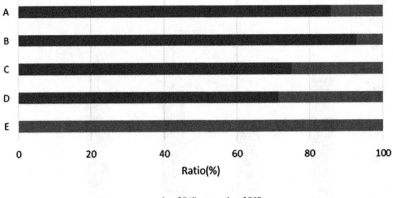

Fig. 11. Comparison of "Actual result for Duct.First" and advising doctor's evaluation

4   Discussion

There was a tendency similar to each item compared. Table 2 summarizes the evaluation for each trend. First, "1" filled the criteria. Also, they are items that the advising doctor's evaluation was bad with the increase and decrease of the numerical value. We think that it is possible to see the evaluation of the simulator and the advising doctor's evaluation as the same evaluation. "2" was that the advising doctor's evaluation grow worse according to the increase and decrease of the numerical values. However, it was an approximate value for D evaluation and B evaluation. Almost, there were no predominant differences. We think quantitative evaluation is difficult in these items. As mentioned in the previous study, medical students did complicated working, so good evaluation and bad evaluation will be approximate values, or it may be difficult to evaluate without difference. It is considered that it is also necessary to evaluate these items according to the manipulation method of the forceps (the holding time of organs, etc.).

Table 2. Evaluation items for each trend

No.	Evaluation item
1	Actual result for Duct.Proximal.Clipped
	Actual result for Duct.Distal.Clipped
	Actual result for Artery.Proximal.Clipped
	Actual result for Artery.Distal.Clipped
	Actual result for Duct.First
	Actual result for Blood.Loss
	Actual result for Clips.Placed
	Actual result for Clips.Dropped
2	Actual result for Time.Complete.Task
	Actual result for Time.Cautery.Used

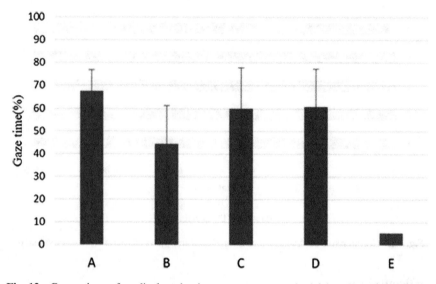

Fig. 12. Comparison of medical student's eye movement and advising doctor's evaluation

5 Conclusion

This study revealed that items evaluated by advising doctor coincide with those of simulators. On the other hand, there were items that did not fit with the evaluations of the simulator and the advising doctor. The item of operation of the forceps is easy to evaluate the skill of medical students. However, an advising doctor's evaluation is necessary to judge whether the work is good or bad. It is important to evaluate these quantitatively.

In addition, Fig. 12 shows a graph that divides the results of the eye movement of medical students obtained by previous studies for each the advising doctor's evaluation. This shows that medical students with the highest evaluation are more frequent in medical students who are closely watching organs. In the future, we will consider whether the result of eye movements can be used for evaluation.

References

1. Ministry of Health, Labour and Welfare. https://www.mhlw.go.jp/toukei/list/33–20c.html. Accessed 22 Jan 2019
2. Yamashiro, K., Goto, A., Shiomi, H., Murakami, K.: Construct of learning model for laparoscopic surgery. In: Duffy, Vincent G. (ed.) DHM 2018. LNCS, vol. 10917, pp. 558–566. Springer, Cham (2018). https://doi.org/10.1007/978-3-319-91397-1_45
3. Yamashiro, K., Murakami, K., Shiomi, H., Goto, A.: Japan Ergonomics Society Kansai Branch, pp. 106–107 (2018). ISSN 1344-4565

Research on Path Planning Algorithm for Two-Dimensional Code Guidance Model of Automated Guided Vehicle

Wei-Dong Zheng[1], Ben Yan[1(✉)], Zhi-Xian Li[1], Hua-Ping Yao[1],
Li-Li Wei[1], and Masahide Nakamura[2]

[1] LuoYang Institute of Science and Technology, No. 90 Wangcheng Road,
Luolong District, Luoyang 471023, Henan, China
yanbenjp@gmail.com
[2] Kobe University, 1-1 Rokkodai, Nada, Kobe, Hyogo 657-8501, Japan
masa-n@cs.kobe-u.ac.jp

Abstract. With the development of industrial automation technology, the automated guided vehicle (AGV) has been widely used in industrial transport, warehouse logistics and other fields. As a new guidance model for AGV, the two-dimensional code guidance model has been discussed in many fields. Two-dimensional code guidance model is a type of free path guidance technology. Under this guidance model, the work area of AGV can be divided into multiple rectangle regions, a two-dimensional code is deployed at each intersection of these regions, which carries the guidance information for its neighborhood regions. The AGV walks along a path which is obtained from the central server, and by scanning the two-dimensional code it encountered, it acquires the way to the next node in the path, until it reaches the endpoint. This guidance model has many advantages, such as low-cost, high re-usage, high flexibility etc., it is a competitive technology to replace the traditional track bedding and laser guidance technology.

Although the use of the two-dimensional code technology avoids or solves a lot of problems compared to the traditional guidance technologies, there are still many potential problems to be tackled, such as matching the actual environment, arranging AGV in place etc. Especially, because there is no track for the AGV to follow, a new path planning algorithm should be designed to solve the above problems.

In this paper, we propose a path planning algorithm under the two-dimensional code guidance model. It allows us to find an optimal path for the AGV to follow from the start point to the end point. To demonstrate the feasibility and advantages of this solution, a simple simulation platform is built and the algorithm is tested and verified by experiments.

Keywords: AGV · Path planning · Dijkstra's algorithm · Shortest path ·
Two-dimensional code guidance technology

V. G. Duffy (Ed.): HCII 2019, LNCS 11581, pp. 355–365, 2019.
https://doi.org/10.1007/978-3-030-22216-1_26

1 Introduction

Automated guided vehicle (AGV) is a kind of wheeled autonomous mobile robot, which is widely used in automation production line, warehousing logistics etc. It is an important unit of flexible manufacturing system, automated storage and retrieval system of logistics transport. At present, there're several mature guidance technologies, such as are electromagnetic guidance, magnetic guidance, optical guidance, laser guidance, inertial guidance and vision guidance, but each of the above guidance technologies has its drawbacks (shown in Table 1).

Table 1. The type and weakness of guidance technologies

Type	Guidance model	Technology	Weakness
Electromagnetic guidance	Fixed path guidance	Electromagnetic	Difficult to change guiding, easy to wear, susceptible to interference
Guidance magnetic	Fixed path guidance	Magnetic Rubber strip belt	
Optical guidance	Free path guidance	Image recognition	High cost, Strict external requirements
Laser guidance	Free path guidance	Laser	
Inertial guidance	Free path guidance	Ground assisted location facility	Accuracy instability
Vision guidance	Free path guidance	Image recognition	Technical bottleneck

As the table above, since the limitations of traditional AGV guidance model, such as difficult to change guiding path, easy wearing, susceptible to interference, high cost, strict external requirements and accuracy instability etc., it can not meet the needs of modern electricity suppliers to discrete heterogeneous picking, then a new guidance model, which employs the two-dimensional code technology is proposed recently.

Two-dimensional code guidance model is a type of free path guidance technology. It does not have strict external environment requirement, and have the advantages of low cost, flexibility, and high efficiency. What it requires is just the network access of AVG cars and the two-dimensional code for each small region, which carries the guidance information for its neighborhood regions [23].

Our research aims to present a complete technical solution of "the path planning and guidance of AGV cars based on two-dimensional code dispersion visual identity model", which can be effectively applied to the logistics robots of the modern storage centers, and enhance logistics efficiency and productivity.

In order to achieve the above research objectives, first of all, we need to solve the optimal path selection problem for AGV, then the two-dimensional guidance system should be designed and implemented.

For this purpose, we propose a path planning algorithm under the two-dimensional code guidance model. It allows us to find an optimal path for the AGV to follow from the start point to the end point. And to demonstrate the feasibility and advantages of this solution, a simple simulation platform is built and the algorithm is tested and verified by experiments.

2 Preliminaries

2.1 Dijkstra's Algorithm

The Dijkstra's algorithm is a classic single-source shortest path algorithm proposed by Dutch computer scientist Edsger W. Dijkstra, which is mainly used to calculate the shortest path form one node in a connected graph to all other nodes. It is used in the breadth of the first search ideas from the inside to the outside of the traversal search, until traversing to the end [1].

The core idea of this algorithm is to record the distance from the source point to any point in real time by means of the edge expansion method. The working process of Dijkstra's Algorithm are described as following steps:

Let the node at which we are starting be called the initial node. Let **the distance of node Y** be the distance from the initial node to Y. Dijkstra's algorithm will assign some initial distance values and will try to improve them step by step.

Step 1. Mark all nodes unvisited. Create a set of all the unvisited nodes called the unvisited set.

Step 2. Assign to every node a tentative distance value: set it to zero for our initial node and to infinity for all other nodes. Set the initial node as current.

Step 3. For the current node, consider all of its unvisited neighbors and calculate their tentative distances through the current node. Compare the newly calculated tentative distance to the current assigned value and assign the smaller one. For example, if the current node A is marked with a distance of 6, and the edge connecting it with a neighbor B has length 2, then the distance to B through A will be 6 + 2 = 8. If B was previously marked with a distance greater than 8 then change it to 8. Otherwise, keep the current value.

Step 4. When we are done considering all of the unvisited neighbors of the current node, mark the current node as visited and remove it from the unvisited set. A visited node will never be checked again.

Step 5. If the destination node has been marked visited (when planning a route between two specific nodes) or if the smallest tentative distance among the nodes in the unvisited set is infinity (when planning a complete traversal; occurs when there is no connection between the initial node and remaining unvisited nodes), then stop. The algorithm has finished.

Step 6. Otherwise, select the unvisited node that is marked with the smallest tentative distance, set it as the new "current node", and go back to step 3 [2].

Figure 1 is an example of Dijkstra's algorithm.

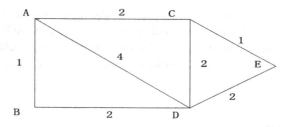

Fig. 1. Dijkstra's algorithm example

The above figure (Fig. 1) requires us to use the Dijkstra algorithm to find the shortest distance from point A to any other point (Where S = {A(source)}, U = {points other than A}). Proceed as follows (number in parenthesis denotes the distance from point A to other points):

STEP 1. Initialize the set S: S = {A (0)}

Set U: U = {B (1), C (2), D (4), E (∞)}

STEP 2. Since there's a direct path from A to B, and the distance is the shortest, move B to the set S,

Set S: S = {A (0), B (1)}

Set U: U = {C (2), D (4), E (∞)}

STEP 3. Update the distance values for each point in the U collection with B as the middle point,

Set S: S = {A (0), B (1)}

Set U: U = {C (2), D (3), E (∞)}

STEP 4. Since there's a direct path from A to C, and the distance is the shortest, movie C to the set S,

Set S: S = {A (0), B (1), C (2)}

Set U: U = {D (3), E (∞)}

STEP 5. Update the distance values for each point in the U set with C as the middle point,

Set S: S = {A (0), B (1), C (2)}

Set U: U = {D (3), E (3)}

STEP 6. There're three paths from A to D, and the path with B as middle point is the shortest, then move C to the set S,

Set S: S = {A (0), B (1), C (2), D (3)}

Set U: U = {E (3)}

STEP 7. Update the distance value for each point in the U collection with D as the middle point,

S set: S = {A (0), B (1), C (2), D (3)}

U set: U = {E (3)}

STEP 8. Move the updated E to S

S set: S = {A (0), B (1), C (2), D (3), E (3)}

U set: U = {}

Finally, we get the shortest distance form source A to other points through the set S.

2.2   Two-Dimensional Code Guidance Model for AGV

Two-dimensional code guidance technology is a free guidance technology which is proposed recently. There're two important parts in the two-dimensional code guidance model, one is a central server, which is a computer which computes and send the path information to each AGV car whenever it requires; another are the AGV cars, which have wireless network access, could communicate with the central server, and walk along given path to perform actual actions.

In the Two-dimensional Code Guidance Model, the work area of AGV is usually divided into many rectangle regions, and a two-dimensional code, which contains the location information and path information to the adjacent regions, is deployed at the intersection of each region. When the AGV walks along a certain path (code sequence) given by the central server, it just need to reach the next point in the path, recognize the two-dimensional code it encountered, acquires the working information (corner degree, speed etc.), obtain the path to the next node, and repeat the same action of the last step, until it reaches the end point.

Compare with traditional guidance model, two-dimensional code guidance model has a lot of advantages, such as low cost, flexible layout, easy controlling of density, easy to modify, having a wider range of application prospects etc.

In view of these advantages, assuming that there is an irregular warehouse, in the cargo-intensive place, the code can be placed more closely, and in the place where the goods cannot put the two-dimensional code, they can be arranged more relaxed, so that the cost of laying down can be controlled, and the working efficiency can be higher.

3   Research Goal and Approach

3.1   Research Goal

As mentioned above, the traditional guidance models for AVG cars have many disadvantages. So our research goal is to design a novel guidance model based on two dimensional code technology which has the following features: low cost, dynamic path planning, low requirement for external environment.

The core points for the above idea are:

Design of the dynamic path planning algorithm;
Combined with above algorithm and network technology, design the guidance model based on two-dimensional code technology.

3.2   Key Idea

Based on Dijkstra's Algorithm, a new path planning algorithm is proposed to better meet the needs of AGV cars, to better match the actual working environment, and to improve work efficiency.

According to the path determined by the above algorithm, the two-dimensional guidance model is designed so that the AGV cars could walking along the given path with low cost, high flexibility and high efficiency.

3.3   The Path Planning Algorithm

The two-dimensional code guidance technology is a free guidance technology, the travel route can be very flexible, which is different from the traditional guidance technology. Therefore, the path planning algorithm of AVG cars plays a vital role as it should choose a suitable path from the initial point to the target point so that both the total cost and the efficiency can be optimized.

The so-called suitable path selection, not only refers to the length of the path, but also means that the time spent should be as short as possible. Usually the walking path of AGV cannot be a straight line, there may be many factors which influence the final result, such as the speed of AGV, the time to slow down and speed up, the rotation speed and times, all the above factors should be taken into account during the design of the path planning algorithm.

The proposed algorithm is based on the Dijkstra's algorithm, which is a classic single-source shortest path algorithm proposed by Edsger W. Dijkstra. The core idea of Dijkstra's algorithm is to record the distance from the source point to any point in real time by means of the edge expansion method, and it is mainly used to calculate the shortest path from one node in a connected graph to all other nodes. The Dijkstra's algorithm only focused on the sum of the edge weight or the length of the path between the start point and end point, so it is not suitable for AGV application.

In our proposal, we not only consider the length of the path, but also consider the whole time spent which is influenced by the cruising speed of AGV, the turn angle and frequency of AGV, the time of speedup and slowdown of the AGV etc.

The key idea of our proposal algorithm is defined as follow:

For a start point SP(X,Y) and a goal point GP(X,Y), the path between SP and GP can be defined as a set of coordinate PATH = $\{sp(x_1,y_1), pp(x_2,y_2)...pp(x_n,y_n), gp(x_m, y_m)\}$.

STEP 1. In the initial state, the AGV is at SP(X,Y), and PATH = $\{sp(x_1,y_1)\}$.

STEP 2. Set current start point as $sp(x_1,y_1)$, find appropriate points from its adjacent points, which can make the AGV walk close to GP(X,Y), either from the X-axis, or from the Y-axis, or both. If only one point is found, add it to the PATH as pp (x_2,y_2), then PATH = $\{sp(x_1,y_1), pp(x_2,y_2)\}$; If multiple suitable points are found, name the paths as $PATH_1$, $PATH_2$,......, $PATH_n$ respectively, and add the corresponding point to the corresponding path set.

STEP 3. Set the current start point as the last point for each path set, repeat the same behavior as STEP 2, until GP(X,Y) is reached, add it to the path set, and the path can be denotes as $PATH_i = \{sp(x_1,y_1), pp(x_2,y_2)...pp(x_n,y_n), gp(x_m,y_m)\}$.

STEP 4. Repeat the behavior of STEP 3, until all the path reaches GP(X,Y).

STEP 5. For each path found in above steps, compute the time spent for the AGV to run from SP(X,Y) to GP(X,Y) along each found path, then select the path with the shortest time as the final result. In this step, the whole time not only consider the time spent walking along the given path, but also consider the cruising speed of AGV, the turn angle and frequency of AGV, the time of speed up and slowdown of the AGV etc.

STEP 6. The AGV walk along the selected path PATH f = $\{sp(x_1,y_1), pp(x_2,y_2)...pp(x_n,y_n), gp(x_m,y_m)\}$. If the AGV is at $pp(x_i,y_i)$, and encounters an obstacle, then set $pp(x_i,y_i)$ as the new start point, obtain a new path to GP(X,Y), then continue to walk along the new path until GP(X,Y) is reached; if no path can be found, set pp(x_{i-1}, y_{i-1}) as new start point and repeat the same action, until a path is found, and then continue to walk along the new path.

In a warehouse deployed with a two-dimensional code, the shortest path from the initial point to the target point can be derived from the Dijkstra algorithm without considering other factors except for the distance problem. However, taking into account the characteristics of two-dimensional code guidance technology, this study will be based on our proposed algorithm as the main algorithm for path planning. First of all, the core of Dijkstra algorithm is the comparison of weights. The weight of our proposed algorithm is no longer a simple distance problem. Instead, it joins the parameters such as vehicle speed and corner time, that is T[S] = T[run timing] + T[rotate]. These parameters together determine the weight problem between two points. And the choice of the optimal path is determined by comparing the weights.

Our Path planning algorithm differs from the Dijkstra algorithm for the following reasons:

The Goal is Different. Our algorithm only needs to find the optimal path from the start point to the end point, but the Dijkstra algorithm aims to find the shortest path from one start point to all other points in a connected graph.

The requirement is Different. In our algorithm, there's a rule, that is, for every step forward, the AGV should be closer to the endpoint either from the x-axis, or the y-axis, or both. But the Dijkstra algorithm doesn't have this requirement.

The Measurement of Cost is Different. In Dijkstra algorithm the total length of edges in the path is its cost. But in our algorithm, the speed of AGV, the time of speed up and slow down, the rotating angle, rotating speed, time of rotation, all the above factors should be taken in account, and is a part of the total cost.

4   Case Study

In practical applications, there may exist two conditions for the AGV in two-dimensional guidance model, one is the AGV get a path without any obstacle, another is that there is one or more obstacles in the path.

For the first condition, once the AGV gets its path from the central server, it just needs to walk along the given path until it reaches the end point.

For the second condition, each time the AGV encounter an obstacle along the given path, it returns to the last point in the path, and asks the central server for a new path, which set the current position of AGV as the start point, and the end point as the initial end point, and walks along the new path, until it reaches the end point.

4.1   Case 1: Path with no Obstacle

In the absence of obstacles, we set the trolley's initial point (3,1) and the target point coordinates (26,14), according to the optimized Dijkstra's Algorithm. The AGV car is simulated with three successive points, the red one denotes the front, blue for the rear, and black for the body. This can reflect the characteristics of the car in the steering. The working process of the algorithm is simulated by setting the running parameters in Table 2. The horizontal point time in the Table 2 means the time needed for the car between adjacent point in horizontal direction.

Table 2. Setting of AVG parameters

Endpoint coordinate	Horizontal point time	45°	90°	135°	180°	225°	270°	315°	360°
(26,14)	1	1	2	3	4	5	6	7	8

As can be seen from Fig. 2:

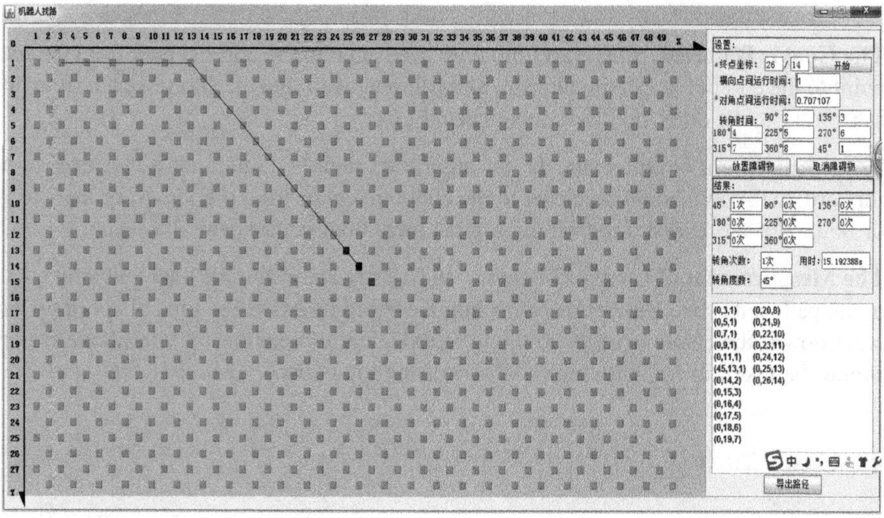

Fig. 2. Simulation of path without obstacle

Starting point: (3,1)

Target: (26,14)

Optimal path: (3,1), (5,1), (7,1), (9,1), (11,1), (13,1), (14,2), (15,3), (16,4), (17,5), (18,6), (19,7), (20,8), (21,9), (22,10), (23,11), (24,12), (25,13), (26,14)

There is one corner in the path, and the turning angle is 45°. If for any reason there exists another corner in the path, the total time spent must be greater than the previous path. Therefore, the path shown in the figure is the optimal path for the car.

4.2 Case 2: Path with Obstacles

The path planning algorithm has the obstacle avoidance function, which could simulate the more actual case. Because in practical case, there may be many goods or shelves placed here and there in the warehouse, and there may be many obstacles for a given path.

In the case of obstacles, we set the initial point (3,1) and the target point coordinates (23,15), and simulate the real environment by setting different obstacles on the simulation platform. The optimal path of the car is simulated by setting the run parameter the same as in Table 2. The blue line represents the optimal path without obstacle, and the red line denotes the optimal path with one obstacle.

It can be seen from the above Fig. 3 that when there is an obstacle, the car:

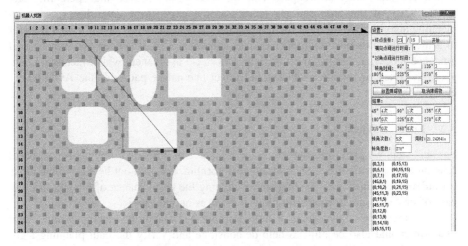

Fig. 3. Simulation of path with obstacles

Starting point: (3,1)

Target: (23,15)

Optimal path: (3,1), (5,1), (7,1), (9,1), (10,2) (11,3), (11,7), (12,8), (13,9), (14,10), (15,11), (15,13), (15,15), (17,15), (19,15), (21,15), (25,13), (23,15).

There're five corners in the path, of which four corner is 45°, and one is 90°. Therefore, it can be seen from the figure that the car has successfully avoided the obstacle and has chosen the shortest path between the running time and the turning time.

4.3 Case Analysis

As show in the figure, case 1 and case 2, we set the distance between the coordinate points in the matrix, including the horizontal distance and the diagonal distance, as well as the setting of the corner time. The purpose of above settings is trying to simulate the actual behavior of the real AGV.

According to the case study, we can obviously find that in the case of with or without obstacles, the proposed algorithm makes the correct judgments, and find the suitable path in both conditions.

Therefore, in practical application, the proposed algorithm can be tested in certain cases, for the logistics industry or large warehouse, to provide more efficient transport tools, improve work efficiency, and acquire more data to further improve the algorithm.

5   Discussion

5.1   Summary

In our previous study and experiment, we successfully proved the operability and practicability of the proposed algorithm. As the experiment data shows, the path planning algorithm could meet the requirement of path planning, and it makes it easier to achieve the previously complicated path planning of AGV under two-dimensional guidance model, and it has the function of obstacle avoidance, which means it could avoid the fixed or mobile obstacles and select alternative paths for the AGV to run along with.

5.2   Further Work

For next step, we plan to further study the influence of different combination of speed, rotation times, laying down method on the algorithm, and find out better combinations for different circumstance. Testing and evaluating the performance of the algorithm in case of obstacles under more complex situation is another topic.

To achieve the above goals, a more complicated and fully functional simulation platform should also be built to help demonstrate and verify the path planning algorithm for AGV, and to deal with more complicated conditions.

Acknowledgements. This work was supported by the National Natural Science Foundation of China under Grant U1604149; and the International Science and Technology Cooperation Project (2015) (152102410053) supported by Science and Technology Department of Henan Province, China.

References

1. Dijkstra, E.W.: A note on two problems in connexion with graphs. Numer. Math. **1**(1), 269–271 (1959)
2. Description of Dijkstra's Algorithm on Wikipedia.org. https://en.wikipedia.org/wiki/Dijkstra%27s_algorithm. Accessed 20 Jan 2019
3. Yan, W.: Data Structure (C Language Edition), 1st edn. Tsinghua University Press, Beijing (1997)
4. Wang, H., Huang, Q., Li, C.: Graph Theory and Its MATLAB Implementation, 1st edn. Beijing University of Aeronautics and Astronautics Press, Beijing (2010)
5. Zhou, X.: The shortest path problem and its solution. Comput. Knowl. Technol. **06**, 1403–1405 (2010)
6. Chaorui, W.: Graph Theory, 2nd edn. Beijing Institute of Technology Press, Beijing (1997)
7. Feng, L.: Shortest path algorithm classification system and research progress. J. Surv. Mapp. **3**, 269–275 (2001)

8. Chen, X., Cai, X., Tang, D.: Shortest path algorithm analysis and its application to bus route query. J. Eng. Graph. **3**, 20–24 (2001)
9. Song, X., Yu, L., Sun, H., Li, J.: Advanced path search algorithm in the case of congestion path in traffic network. J. Shenyang Jianzhu Univ. (Nat. Sci. Edn.) **25**(4), 776–780 (2009)
10. Zhang, C., Yang, Y., Zhao, H.: Improvement and implementation of shortest path algorithm based on path dependence. Comput. Eng. Appl. **25**, 56–58 (2006)
11. Li, Q.: An adaptive genetic algorithm. J. Univ. Sci. Technol. Beijing **11**, 1082–1086 (2006)
12. Xie, B., She, X.: Algorithm and Data Structure, 1st edn. Higher Education Press, Beijing (2001)
13. Chen, Y., Lu, X., Ding, H.: Study on optimization strategy of Dijkstra algorithm. Comput. Technol. Dev. **16**(9), 73–75, 78 (2006)
14. Zhang, Y.: Dijkstra shortest path algorithm optimization. J. Nanchang Inst. Technol. **25**(3), 30–33 (2006)
15. Hu, S., Zhang, X., Zhao, Y.: Sector optimization Dijkstra algorithm. Comput. Technol. Dev. **16**(12), 49–51 (2006)
16. Wang, P., Sun, L., Huang, B.: Ground mobile robot system research status and key technology. J. Mech. Des. **23**(7), 1–4 (2006)
17. Wang, S.: Graph Theory, 2nd edn. Science Press, Beijing (2009)
18. Yin, J., Wu, K.: Graph Theory and its Algorithm, 1st edn. Press of University of Science and Technology of China
19. Yao, E., He, Y., Chen, S.: Mathematical Planning and Combinatorial Optimization, 1st edn. Zhejiang University Press, Hangzhou (2001)
20. Zhu, J., Zhang, G.: Mathematical Modeling Method, 1st edn. Zhengzhou University Press, Zhengzhou (2003)
21. Yang, Yu.: Bar code and automatic identification technology. Enterp. Stand. **6**, 35–36 (2002)
22. Jiao, Y., Zhang, C.: Two-dimensional Bar Code Technology, 1st edn. China Price Press, Beijing (1996)

Risk Assessment and Safety

A Framework to Quantitatively Assess Safety Performance for Civil Aviation Organization

Mingliang Chen[1,2(✉)], Min Luo[1,2], Yuan Zhang[1,2], and Yanqiu Chen[1,2]

[1] China Academy of Civil Aviation Science and Technology,
Beijing 100028, China
{chenml,luomin,zhangyuan,chenyq}@mail.castc.org.cn
[2] Engineering and Technical Research Center of Civil Aviation Safety Analysis
and Prevention of Beijing, Beijing 100028, China

Abstract. As many other high-risk industries, safety is the most important prerequisite and foundation for the development of civil aviation. A systematic framework is presented to quantitatively assess the safety performance and operation risk for civil aviation organizations. The safety performance indicator program life cycle is introduced. A comprehensive safety performance assessment model is proposed to evaluate a civil aviation organization's safety status and operation risk based on safety performance indicator system. A safety performance assessment tool is developed to realize the function of safety performance indicator definition, data filling of safety performance indicators, and data statistics and presentation. A case of a civil airport in Central and Southern Regional of China is studied to illustrate the efficiency and flexibility of the proposed model. The assessment results are consistent with the actual operation state of the airport.

Keywords: Civil aviation · Airport · Safety performance ·
Safety performance indicator

1 Introduction

The civil aviation industry plays a major role in global economic activity and development. As many other high-risk industries, safety is the most important prerequisite and foundation for the development of civil aviation. Despite several high-profile accidents, the year 2018 is one of the safest years according to the Aviation Safety Network data. There is a total of 18 fatal airliner (14+ passengers) hull-loss accidents excluding corporate jet and military transport accidents/hijackings, resulting in 561 fatalities in 2018. The statistics of number of fatal accidents and fatalities from 1990 −2018 is showed in Fig. 1 below [1]. Though there is a decrease trend in the overall number of fatal accidents as well as fatalities, dealing with safety in civil aviation is a continuous and never-ending challenge because civil aviation industry is open, complex, and evolving.

Safety is typically managed through continuous risk management, including hazard identification, risk evaluation, risk mitigation and risk monitoring [2]. Control measures

© Springer Nature Switzerland AG 2019
V. G. Duffy (Ed.): HCII 2019, LNCS 11581, pp. 369–381, 2019.
https://doi.org/10.1007/978-3-030-22216-1_27

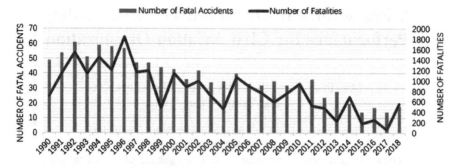

Fig. 1. Number of fatal accidents and fatalities from 1990–2018 (Data from the Aviation Safety Network)

in different dimensions have been used to control technical risk, personnel risk, organizational risk, and so on. Industry has found that the traditional emphasis on personnel safety will not prevent the low probability and high consequence accidents [3].

The International Civil Aviation Organization (ICAO) revised Annexes 1, 6, 8, 11, 13, and 14 to refine the framework requirements for implementing Safety Management System (SMS) in 2008. With the wide promotion of safety management system (SMS) in civil aviation, more and more attention has been paid to safety performance management. Safety performance management has been recognized as playing a key role in achieving an acceptable level of safety in civil aviation organizations.

According to the ICAO Doc 9859 Safety Management Manual [4], safety performance is 'A State or a service provider's safety achievement as defined by its safety performance targets and safety performance indicators'. Safety performance indicator is 'A data-based parameter used for monitoring and assessing safety performance'. ICAO describes indicators as two levels, the State level, which monitor its safety indicators, and the individual service provider that monitors safety performance indicators as part of its SMS.

Safety performance indicators play an important role in providing information on a civil aviation organization's current safety status, motivating people to work on safety and increasing the efficacy of an organization's safety improvement efforts. The establishment of a safety performance indicator system allows a civil aviation organization to assess whether it is implementing appropriate safety programs and policies, whether these programs and policies are achieving their desired objectives, and to assess the effectiveness of its SMS. On the other hand, the development of a safety performance indicator system is an important management responsibility that will prevent civil aviation accidents by identifying, measuring, analyzing, and adjusting key activities or indicators [5].

In recent years, there is increasing interest for researchers and industries to paid more and more attention to safety performance management in different domains. Enoma et al. [6] collected data from a series of interviews, workshops, the internet and other media to develop and test a set of key safety and security performance indicators for airport facility management. Lu et al. [7] evaluated airport safety risk based on modification of quantitative safety management model. In the proposed model, airport safety risk evaluation indicator system was established. Reiman et al. [8] presented a theoretical framework for utilizing safety performance indicators in safety-critical organizations. Kim et al. [9] built a structure of safety performance indicators to measure the safety performances of airline. In the safety performance assessment proposed by the Safety Management International Collaboration Group (SMICG) [10], safety performance indicators are divided into three tiers, where tier 1 measure the outcomes of the whole civil aviation system, tier 2 indicators depict safety management performance of operators and tier 3 address the activities of the regulator. McDonald et al. [11] introduced the overall Proactive Safety Performance for Operations project concept and high level system requirements as they emerged from industry needs. Gander et al. [12] provided the first comprehensive description of how sleep/wake history and circadian phase influence measures of pilot fatigue pre-flight and at the TOD on long trans-meridian flights by combining data sets from four airline studies using the same measures. Chang et al. [13] used a two-stage process to evaluate the performance of the SMS operations at Taiwan's three international airports by using the Analytic Network Process and the fuzzy Technique of Ordering Preference by Similarity to Ideal Solution. Chen et al. [14] proposed a specific method based on the analytic hierarchy process and Delphi method to measure the safety management of civil aviation unit with a series of safety performance indicators. Panagopoulos et al. [15] introduced an integrated, conceptual framework for measuring and improving aviation system's safety performance by adapting and combing classical Quality Management tools, a leading indicators program and Lean-six Sigma methodology. Thekdi et al. [16] presented and discussed an enhanced framework for unification of performance management and risk management principles based on analysis of combinations of different risk management and performance management practices/polices. Rong et al. [17] established an airport operational risk warning model based on determining ten key modules affecting the airport operational safety and designing 165 airport operational risk monitoring indicators. MacLean et al. [18] developed a benchmark from the aggregation of failure data on a set of comparable airports to compare airports' performance with the benchmark using the defined safety measures. Sun et al. [19] established a safety performance index system based on Reason's model and a safety performance evaluation model to compare fleet safety performance from five dimensions quantitatively. Gerede et al. [20] adopted the Delphi Method to produce a list of safety performance indicators used to measure safety in flight training organizations in Turkey. Sun et al. [21] established a comprehensive evaluation model based on the subjective and objective combination weight method for quantitatively assess the safety state of the maintenance department. Chen et al. [22, 23] proposed comprehensive risk evaluation models to evaluate civil airport's operation risk.

The remaining of this paper is organized as follows. The framework to assess safety performance, safety performance indicator life cycle, weight assignment for different types of safety performance indicators, and the comprehensive risk evaluation model are presented in Sect. 2. Then, Sect. 3 introduces the safety performance assessment tool. In Sect. 4, a case study is given to verify the proposed model. Finally, conclusions are provided in Sect. 5.

2   A Framework for Assessing Safety Performance

A systematic framework is presented to quantitatively assess the safety performance and operation risk for civil aviation organization as shown in Fig. 2. In this framework, four main assessment steps are given. In the first step, safety performance indicators and corresponding metrics of different departments/posts of a civil aviation organization are defined. Second, the severity of the event, deviation, management represented by each safety performance indicator is different. In this step, weights for different types of safety performance indicator will be assigned. Third, a comprehensive assessment model will be established based on safety performance indicators and corresponding weights. The last step is verifying the proposed model by case study. Safety performance indicators, metrics, weights, and the assessment model would be adjusted if the verification results are inconsistent with the actual operation of civil aviation organization.

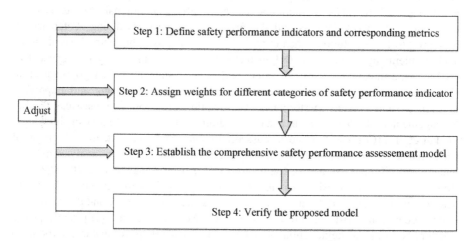

Fig. 2. Steps for the safety performance assessment framework

2.1   Safety Performance Indicator System

The Organization for Economic Cooperation and Development (OECD) proposed a step-by-step approach to create and implement the safety performance indicators programs [24, 25]. There are seven steps in the proposed approach from establishing a safety performance indicator team to evaluating and refining safety performance indicators. In this paper, the safety performance indicator system will be established according to a six steps process illustrated in Fig. 3.

The first step is to establish a safety performance management team. In the establishment process of safety performance indicator system, the involvement of management is critical to ensure resources are committed to the program. Appropriate team members should be involved in the safety performance management team, including an individual leader or leader group, technical experts and front-line

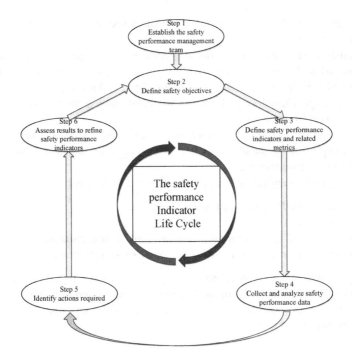

Fig. 3. Six steps to define safety performance indicators

employees. Additionally, employee participation is an excellent learning and motivating experience.

Once the safety performance management team are in place, the next step is to
define safety objectives. Safety objectives are brief, high-level statements of safety
achievements or desired outcomes to be accomplished. The safety performance management team should focus on what to monitor rather than how to monitor and avoid
the pitfall of measuring what they can measure instead of what they should measure.

In the next step, the safety performance management team should define safety
performance indicators and related metrics. Safety performance indicators should be
related to the safety objective based on available data and reliable measurement.
A metric, which defines the unit of measurement, should be assigned to each safety
performance indicator. When establishing safety performance indicators, the safety
performance management team should consider the following factors: measuring the
right thing, availability of data, reliability of the data, and common industry safety
performance indicators.

Once the safety performance indicators and corresponding metrics have been
defined, the next step is to collect and analyze safety performance-related data. The
data should be collected frequently enough to identify critical changes in a timely
manner so actions can be taken to ensure safety.

Results from collection and analyzation safety performance data must be monitored
to identify actions required. This information is important to ensuring quick follow-up

action on adverse findings to fix problems in the associated policies, procedures, and operation processes.

The safety performance indicators and corresponding metrics should be periodically reviewed and assessed. These reviews help to ensure the safety performance indicators and corresponding metrics are well-defined and respond to safety objectives. It will identify specific safety performance indicators which are no longer needed and adjust safety performance indicators.

For key safety performance indicators, more does not mean better. The right number for organizations should depend on how many is manageable by organizations' safety performance management team.

Signs of good safety performance indicators are as follows:

- It is aligned directly with safety objectives;
- It is quantifiable;
- Data sources used to monitor and track are reliable and measurable; and
- Few or no other organizations will have this exact same statistic.

Safety performance indicators can be categorized into four types: unsafe event type, foundation type, management type, and operation type. Different methods can be used to define these four types of safety performance indicators mentioned above. The methods are list in Table 1.

Table 1. Different methods for defining safety performance indicators

Safety performance indicator type	Method
Unsafe event type	Decomposition of safety objectives
	Analyzation of historical operation data
Operation type	Forward analysis
	Backward analysis
	Bow-tie
	Statistical method
Management type	Brainstorming
	System elements
	SMS elements
Foundation type	Brainstorming
	System elements
	SMS elements

It can be found that safety performance indicators can be defined through forward analysis process and backward analysis process from Table 1. The forward analysis process is a logical technique that starts from hazard identification and lays a path to unsafe activities or status, then lead to unsafe events. Safety performance indicators and corresponding metrics are defined based on the event chain. Many methods can be used in the forward analysis process, includes: system and job analysis, What-if analysis, event tree analysis (ETA), hazard and operability analysis (HAZOP), etc. The backward analysis process starts from unsafe events and lays a path to direct or indirect causes. Then, safety performance indicators and corresponding metrics are defined. Methods used in the backward analysis process include: Reason model, SHELL model, fault tree analysis (FTA), etc.

2.2 Weights for Different Types of Safety Performance Indicators

In order to assign weights for different types of safety performance indicators, Heinrich's Law is used as baseline while taking into account 'Civil aircraft incident standard' and 'Event sample' published by Civil Aviation Administration of China (CAAC). According to Heinrich's Law, there are about 29 minor injuries and 300 near misses and 1000 potential hazards behind every serious accident. As mentioned above, safety performance indicators can be categorized as four types. For the unsafe event type, it can be classified as accident, serious incident, general incident, and serious error. Based on Heinrich's Law and in conjunction with experts' evaluation, different weights for different types of safety performance indicators are listed in Table 2.

Table 2. Weights for different types of safety performance indicators

Safety performance indicator type		Severity
Unsafe event type	Accident	1000
	Serious incident	300
	General incident	100
	Serious error	25
Operation type		[0.5,1]
Management type		5
Foundation type		30

2.3 Comprehensive Safety Performance Assessment Model

For a typical civil aviation organization, there are a number of departments with several posts. According to the hierarchy of a civil aviation organization, a multi-level safety performance assessment model is proposed. At the post level, safety performance of different posts can be calculated based on safety performance indicator system. At the department level, safety performance of different departments can be calculated based on posts' safety performance. And for the organization level, safety performance can be assessed based on departments' safety performance.

At the post level, safety performance indicators mainly include unsafe event type and operation type. For each safety performance indicator related to a certain post, its statistical value can be obtained every month. According to the evaluation standard of safety performance indicator, every safety performance indicator of a post will be evaluated as one of these five grades, namely 'very poor', 'poor', 'average', 'good' and 'very good'. Correspondingly, values for these five grades can be assigned as 100,80,60,40, and 0 in the hundred-mark system.

Then, the safety performance of a certain post can be calculated as follow.

$$R_p = R_{pc} + R_{pp} = \sum_{i=1}^{l} w_{pci} \times S_{pci} + \sum_{i=1}^{r} w_{pnci} \times S_{ppi} \qquad (1)$$

In Eq. (1), R_{pc} is the assessment value of unsafe event type of safety performance indicators, R_{pp} is the assessment value of non-unsafe event types, w_{pci} is the weight of unsafe event type, w_{ppi} is the weight of non-unsafe event types, l and r are the number of unsafe event type and operation type of safety performance indicators, respectively.

At the department level, safety performance indicators mainly include unsafe event type, operation type, management type, and foundation type. Then, the safety performance of a certain department can be calculated as follow.

$$R_d = R_{dc} + R_{dnc} = R_{dc} + R_{db} + R_{dm} + R_{dp}$$

$$= \frac{1}{m} \sum_{j=1}^{m} R_{pcj} + \sum_{i=1}^{s} w_{dbi} \times S_{dbi} + \sum_{i=1}^{t} w_{dmi} \times S_{dmi} + \sum_{j=1}^{m} w_{dj} \times R_{ppj} \qquad (2)$$

R_{dc} is the assessment value of unsafe event type of safety performance indicators, R_{dnc} is the assessment value of non-unsafe event types, R_{db} is the assessment value of foundation type, R_{dm} is the assessment value of management type, R_{dp} is the assessment value of operation type, w_{dj} is the weight of different post, R_{pcj} is the assessment value of unsafe event type for post j, w_{dbi} is the weight of foundation type, w_{dmi} is the weight of management type, and R_{ppj} is the assessment value of operation type for post j.

At the civil aviation organization level, safety performance indicators mainly include unsafe event type, operation type, management type, and foundation type. Then, the safety performance of the civil aviation organization can be calculated as Eq. (3).

$$R_o = R_{oc} + R_{onc} = \frac{1}{k} \sum_{i=1}^{k} R_{dci} + \sum_{i=1}^{k} w_{oi} \times R_{dnci} \qquad (3)$$

R_{oc} is the assessment value of unsafe event type of safety performance indicators, R_{onc} is the assessment value of non-unsafe event types, w_{oi} is the weight of different department, R_{dci} is the assessment value of unsafe event type for department i, and R_{dnci} is the assessment value of non-unsafe event type for post i.

3   Safety Performance Assessment Tool

A safety performance assessment tool is developed to realize the function of safety performance indicator definition, data filling of safety performance indicators, and data statistics and presentation. The structure of this safety performance tool is illustrated as Fig. 4.

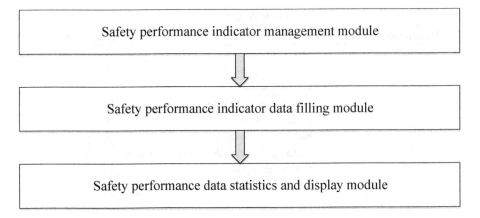

Fig. 4. Structure of the safety performance assessment tool

4   Case Study

Civil airports are important infrastructures in the civil aviation industry. In order to verify the proposed comprehensive safety performance assessment model, a case of a civil airport in Central and Southern Regional of China is studied. There are six departments and twenty key posts involving in the safety performance assessment. For each key post, there are several unsafe event type and operation type of safety performance indicators. The numbers of safety performance indicators for these twenty key posts of different departments are listed in Table 3 below.

Table 3. Numbers of safety performance indicators for different departments and posts

Department	Post	Number of SPIs
Operation Control Center	Command and coordinate post	9
	Supervisory post	8
Airfield management	Inspection and release post	10
	Runway pavement post	10
Security guard	Jet bridge guard post	10
Cargo	Loading and uploading post	10
	Loading and uploading supervisory post	10
	Baggage towing tractor post	10
	Belt loader post	9
	Cargo loader post	8
Airport food service	Catering truck post	9

(continued)

Table 3. (*continued*)

Department	Post	Number of SPIs
Aircraft Maintenance	Shuttle driver post	10
	Passengers steps post	9
	Tow tractor post	9
	Tow bar operation post	10
	Ramp agent post	10
	Water truck driver post	10
	Watering and blowdown operation post	8
	Maintenance post	10
	Follow me car post	10

The total number of safety performance indicators for different posts is 189. The numbers of management type and foundation type of safety performance indicators for each department are 8 and 4, respectively.

According to the safety performance assessment model described above, the airport's operation data is used to assess safety performance of the airport, six departments, and 20 key posts. The assessment results are presented in Figs. 5, 6 and 7.

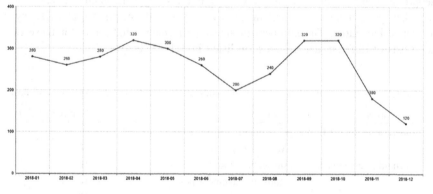

Fig. 5. Safety performance assessment result of follow me car post

Figure 5 presents the safety performance assessment result of follow me car post, other 19 posts' assessment results can be shown as Fig. 5. Figure 6 presents the safety performance assessment result of aircraft maintenance department; other 5 departments' assessment results can also be shown as Fig. 6.

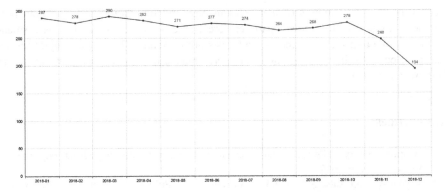

Fig. 6. Safety performance assessment result of aircraft maintenance department

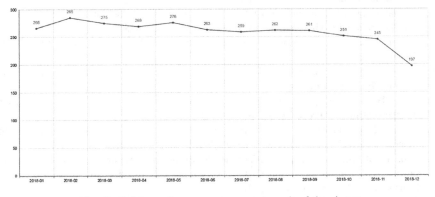

Fig. 7. Safety performance assessment result of the airport

5   Conclusion

Safety performance management plays an important role in revealing a civil aviation organization's current safety status and safety level. In order to assess safety performance of civil aviation organizations, the research progress of safety performance management is summarized. A framework used to assess safety performance is proposed. The life cycle of safety performance indicator is presented to defining/refining safety performance indicators for civil aviation organizations. Safety performance indicators have been classified into four types: unsafe event type, operation type, management type, and foundation type. Weights for different types of safety performance indicators have been assigned based on Heinrich's Law and in conjunction with experts' evaluation. A novel safety performance assessment model is proposed to assess the safety performance of a civil aviation organization, departments and key posts. The developed safety performance assessment tool can improve efficiency of safety performance assessment process and realize data visualization. A civil airport in Central and Southern Regional of China is used to illustrate the efficiency and flexibility of the proposed model. 189 safety performance indicators have been defined for

20 key posts. The numbers of management type and foundation type of safety performance indicators for each department are 8 and 4, respectively. The assessment results for the airport, departments, and posts are presented. These assessment results can be used to further analyze the safety performance level and causes, and make the improvement plan.

References

1. Aviation Safety Network. https://aviation-safety.net/statistics/period/stats.php?cat=A1. Accessed 27 Jan 2019
2. Boelen, A., Van Aalst, R., Karanikas, N., Kaspers, S., Piric, S., De Boer, R.J.: Effectiveness of risk controls as indicators of safety performance. AUP Adv. 1(1), 175–189 (2018)
3. Kubias, F.O., Louvar, J.F.: Upgrading education and safety performance: SACHE at 17. Process Saf. Prog. 21(4), D2–D4 (2002)
4. International Civil Aviation Organization: ICAO Doc 9859 Safety Management Manual, 4th edn. International Civil Aviation Organization, Montreal (2018)
5. Louvar, J.: Guidance for safety performance indicators. Process Saf. Prog. 29, 387–388 (2010)
6. Enoma, A., Allen, S.: Developing key performance indicators for airport safety and security. Facilities 25, 296–315 (2007)
7. Lu, X., Huang, S.: Airport safety risk evaluation based on modification of quantitative safety management model. Procedia Eng. 43, 238–244 (2012)
8. Reiman, T., Pietikainen, E.: Leading indicators of system safety-monitoring and driving the organizational safety potential. Saf. Sci. 50(10), 1993–2000 (2012)
9. Kim, S., Oh, S., Suh, J., Yu, K., Yeo, H.: Study on the structure of safety performance indicators for airline companies. In: Proceedings of the Eastern Asia Society for Transportation Studies, pp. 1–17 (2013)
10. Safety Management International Collaboration Group. A system approach to measuring safety performance: The regulator perspective. Technical report, Safety Management International Collaboration Group (2014)
11. McDonald, N., Corrigan, S., Ulfvengren, P., Baranzini, D.: Proactive safety performance for aviation operations. In: Harris, D. (ed.) EPCE 2014. LNCS (LNAI), vol. 8532, pp. 351–362. Springer, Cham (2014). https://doi.org/10.1007/978-3-319-07515-0_36
12. Gander, P., et al.: Effects of sleep/wake history and circadian phase on proposed pilot fatigue safety performance indicators. J. Sleep Res. 24, 110–119 (2015)
13. Chang, Y., Shao, P., Chen, H.: Performance evaluation of airport safety management systems in Taiwan. Saf. Sci. 75, 72–86 (2015)
14. Chen, W., Li, J.: Safety performance monitoring and measurement of civil aviation unit. J. Air Transp. Manag. 57, 228–233 (2016)
15. Thekdi, S., Aven, T.: An enhanced data-analytic framework for integrating risk management and performance management. Reliab. Eng. Syst. Saf. 156, 277–287 (2016)
16. Rong, M., Luo, M., Chen, Y.: The research of airport operational risk alerting model. In: Duffy, Vincent G.G. (ed.) DHM 2016. LNCS, vol. 9745, pp. 586–595. Springer, Cham (2016). https://doi.org/10.1007/978-3-319-40247-5_59
17. MacLean, L., Richman, A., MacLean, S.: Benchmarking airports with specific safety performance measures. Transp. Res. A 92, 349–364 (2016)

18. Panagopoulos, I., Atkin, C., Sikora, I.: Developing a performance indicators lean-sigma framework for measuring aviation system's safety performance. Transp. Res. Procedia **22**, 35–44 (2017)
19. Sun, Y., Luo, M., Chen, Y., Sun, C.: Safety performance evaluation model for airline flying fleets. In: Duffy, Vincent G. (ed.) DHM 2017. LNCS, vol. 10287, pp. 384–396. Springer, Cham (2017). https://doi.org/10.1007/978-3-319-58466-9_34
20. Gerede, E., Yasar, M.: Evaluation of safety performance indicators of flight training organizations in Turkey. Int. J. Eurasia Soc. Sci. **8**(29), 1174–1207 (2017)
21. Sun, Y., Zhang, Y., Zhao, R., Chen, Y.: Safety performance evaluation for civil aviation maintenance department. In: Duffy, Vincent G. (ed.) DHM 2018. LNCS, vol. 10917, pp. 635–646. Springer, Cham (2018). https://doi.org/10.1007/978-3-319-91397-1_52
22. Chen, M., Luo, M., Sun, H., Chen, Y.: A comprehensive risk evaluation model for airport operation safety. In: The proceedings of 12th International Conference on Reliability, Maintainability and Safety (ICRMS). IEEE (2018)
23. Chen, M., Zhang, Y., Chen, Y.: Apron operation risk assessment based on safety performance. J. Civil Aviat. **2**(6), 90–94 (2018)
24. Organization for Cooperation and Development. Guidance on developing safety performance indicators related to chemical accident prevention, preparedness and Response. Technical report, Organization for Cooperation and Development (2008)
25. Jennings, K., Schulberg, F.: Guidance on developing safety performance indicators. Process Saf. Prog. **28**, 362–366 (2009)

Modeling Vehicle-Pedestrian Encountering Risks in the Natural Driving Environment Using Machine Learning Algorithms

Priyanka Gandhi[1], Xiao Luo[2(✉)], and Renran Tian[2]

[1] Department of Computer and Information Science, Indiana University Purdue University Indianapolis, Indianapolis, IN 46077, USA
[2] Department of Computer Information Technology, Indiana University Purdue University Indianapolis, Indianapolis, IN 46077, USA
luo25@iupui.edu

Abstract. For modern automated driving systems, interaction with pedestrians in the mixed traffic conditions is one of the most challenging problems. Potential conflict cases have been widely used to study vehicle-pedestrian encountering scenarios in natural road environment. However, these relatively dangerous cases between human drivers and pedestrians are not necessarily the dangerous cases for automated driving systems, especially when trained artificial intelligence systems can predict the potential risks and prepare in advance. In this study, we investigate the performance of machine learning algorithms in detecting potential conflicts between vehicle and pedestrians, as well as prioritizing passing sequences during the conflicts. A total of five commonly-used machine learning algorithms are tested. The results show that Deep Neural Network can predict the potential risk and passing priority very accurately (93% and 96% respectively) solely based on descriptive scenario variables. A set of wrongly classified cases (False Negative) are also collected for further study which represent unpredictable risks for automated driving systems.

Keywords: Naturalistic driving study ·
Vehicle-pedestrian interaction · Autonomous driving · Machine learning

1 Introduction

As the most commonly-seen vulnerable road users, pedestrian safety is always a big concern in the transportation-related research. Especially with the progress in the development of automated driving systems (ADS), how to fit the autonomous vehicles into mixed traffic conditions with other human-driven cars and pedestrians becomes one of the most critical challenges now [1]. Without exclusive road design for autonomous cars, it is necessary for these ADS to

© Springer Nature Switzerland AG 2019
V. G. Duffy (Ed.): HCII 2019, LNCS 11581, pp. 382–393, 2019.
https://doi.org/10.1007/978-3-030-22216-1_28

behave similarly as human drivers, in terms of understanding the road scenes, estimating encountering risks, communicating with other road users, and providing human-like responses in different situations. Thus, there is imminent research need to model the encountering scenarios between human drivers and pedestrians to direct the design and testing of ADS.

A list of studies has been published focusing on pedestrian-vehicle interaction scenarios and processes [2–4]. Most of the work relies on crash database, videos recorded from fixed cameras, or naturalistic driving study. In these studies, the scenarios are usually modeled either based on actual crashes [3] or unclassified encountering cases [2,4], with some limitations:

- Although crash data can reflect the actual dangerous situations, these data are usually recorded retrospectively after the events which are not only biased but also missing many details, as summarized in [5]. These make construction of comprehensive and complete scenarios difficult.
- In other studies, unclassified encountering cases are randomly selected and analyzed from recorded road videos. Because these data do not represent the encountering risk levels, the modeled encountering scenarios mainly represent safe cases, whereas most crashes will not happen in these circumstances. The results have reduced implications in training AI for emergent situations.

One option is to investigate the vehicle-pedestrian encountering scenarios through the potential conflict cases [5], which can represent the actual crashes to some extent [6] while also provide details recorded from the on-board or roadside cameras and other vehicle sensors. A number of representative pedestrian-vehicle encountering scenarios have been published using these types of data.

Although these potential conflict cases reflect actual dangers between particular driver and pedestrian(s), they are not necessarily the dangerous cases for ADS. Most applied AI system uses machine-learning algorithms to understand and predict the new event based on the experiences (training data). Thus, ADS will have experiences from a lot of drivers in different scenarios. This makes it interesting to investigate that after trained with the potential and actual dangerous scenarios collected from the naturalistic data, how AI algorithms can predict the encountering risks. The idea is that some more dangerous cases may become less risky if the AI algorithms can predict the danger based on the scenario conditions; while on the other hand, some less dangerous cases to the human drivers may be riskier for ADS if the condition is hard to be predicted by the AI algorithms.

To our best knowledge, most naturalistic driving studies investigate pedestrian-vehicle interactions based on all potential conflicts or near-miss events, and do not further classify them to look for more risky cases for ADS system. In this study, we try to open the discussions about the differences in potential conflict cases collected between human drivers and pedestrians in terms of their risk levels for ADS.

2   Research Objectives and Scope

ADS can predict the encountering risks with pedestrians at micro and macro levels. At the micro level, ADS analyses instantaneous sensing results of surrounding road objects with short-range movement prediction to detect and mitigate imminent conflicts. While in this study, we mainly focus on the prediction at macro level, which relies on descriptive scenario variables to classify the encountering cases into different risk levels. The main idea is that without consuming large amount of computational resources, the ADS shall be able to read the encountering cases based on scenario variables that are easier to acquire, and prepare necessary follow-up steps.

Based on a pre-labeled naturalistic driving data set focusing on pedestrian behaviors [5], this study will try to apply different machine-learning algorithms including Naive Bayes, Logistic Regression, Random Forests, Support Vector Machines, and Deep Neural Network to classify vehicle-pedestrian encountering risks in natural road environment. There are two research questions:

- **First research question:** based on a list of descriptive variables without detailed movement and posture data, to what extent can machine learning algorithms classify potential conflict cases from all vehicle-pedestrian encounters?
- **Second research question:** towards the potential vehicle-pedestrian conflicts, to what extent can machine learning algorithms classify passing priorities between the pedestrians and cars?

Towards the proposed research questions, a multi-step process is adopted to carry out the study. The first step is to classify between safe cases and potential conflict cases based on a list of environment, traffic, and behavior variables in the encountering scenario. The potential conflict is defined as "that the contact between the vehicle and pedestrian(s) will occur if neither the driver nor the pedestrian(s) changes the moving speed/moving direction, or the trajectories of the vehicle and the pedestrian are adjacent to each other during the time period which results in the movement responses from the driver and/or the pedestrian(s) to avoid the contact, although the responses may not be necessary" [7]. As illustrated in Fig. 1, vehicle-pedestrian encounters can be classified as three categories, safe cases, cases with predictable risks, and cases with unpredictable risks, which are corresponding to true negative, true positive, and false negative classification results about potential conflict events. Both true negative and false positive classifications will not post additional risks. True positive cases represent the potential conflict dangers that can be predictable by the AI system, which may not cause the same level of risk as for the human drivers. However, false negative cases represent the unpredictable potential dangers for the AI system, and shall be further studied.

The second step is to further classify the potential conflict cases into vehicle-pass-first and pedestrian-pass-first cases. We will follow the same logic of predictable and unpredictable potential conflicts for the analysis. A series of variables describing more encountering details will be used at this step. Again, the

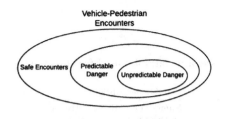

Fig. 1. Vehicle-pedestrian encountering risk model

goal focuses on studying the capability of machine learning algorithms in classifying vehicle-pedestrian encountering risks based on easy-to-acquire descriptive scenario variables to prepare the system with more challenging training data set. At this level of classification, special interests fall on the false negative classification results for pedestrian-pass-first cases, representing the risks that AI algorithms wrongly underestimate pedestrian crossing priority and suggests the vehicle to cross first. This type of wrong decisions may cause increased danger for pedestrians.

3   Methodology

3.1   Data Set Description

Based on the TASI 110-car naturalistic driving study, as described in [5, 7], this work used the full data set of more than 50,000 pedestrian-vehicle encounters, containing both safe cases (N = 49,631) and potential conflict cases (N = 1,472) (following the definition described above). For all of these cases, descriptive scenario variables are manually labeled as shown in Table 1.

In the first step of classification, all of these 18 descriptive scenario variables listed in Table 1 are used to classify safe and potential-conflict encountering cases. In the second step of data analysis, all the potential conflict cases are firstly labeled with ground-truth data about the passing priority between vehicles and pedestrians. Then, another list of variables with more encounter details are used to train the machine learning algorithms to classify the passing priorities, including:

- Time-to-potential-collision: the time duration from pedestrian appearance moment or first potential conflict point to the moment that potential collision will happen if no avoidance behavior is performed.
- Pedestrian and Vehicle Relative Moving Direction
- Vehicle Speed: actual vehicle speed
- Pedestrian Moving Action: walking, running, biking, standing
- Pedestrian Moving Speed Category: fast, slow, normal
- Pedestrian Moving Direction
- Pedestrian Appearance Location
- Driver Avoidance Behavior

Table 1. Descriptive scenario variables used for classifying potential conflict cases

Variable name	Variable description	Values
Number of adult pedestrians	Number of adult pedestrians involved in the encounter	
Number of child pedestrians	Number of child pedestrians involved in the encounter	
Main pedestrian status	The main pedestrian activity	Standing, Running, Walking, etc.
Pedestrian facing direction	Which side of the pedestrian is visible to the vehicle	Face, Back, Side, Others
Walking speed	Pedestrian walking speed	Fast, Slow, Normal, Unknown
Driving environment	The environment that the counter occurs	Rural, Urban, Other
Pedestrian walking direction	Pedestrian moving directions	Against traffic, With traffic, Cross the road, No movement, Combinations of multiple direction
Pedestrian entering the road	If the pedestrian moves into the road during the encountering process	In road (at least partially), Not in road at all
Pedestrian moving location	Where the pedestrian moves during the whole encountering process	Left Side, Middle of the road, Right Side, Combinations of the locations
Pedestrian appearance location	Where the pedestrian(s) was initially seen from the vehicle's point of view	Behind right-hand parked vehicle, Behind opposite moving vehicle, Behind other obstacle, Not obscured
Vehicle moving direction	Driving direction of the vehicle during the encountering process	Straight, Left Turn, Right Turn, etc.
Road alignment	The road alignment that the encounter occurs	Straight, Left curve, Right curve, Others
Road location	The road location that the encounter occurs	Mid-block cross-walk, Intersection, Junction, Mid-block others, etc.
Road infrastructure	Some road features that may affect the encountering risk	Median, Separator, Shoulder, etc.
Weather condition	The weather condition when the encounter occurs	Clear, Cloudy, Fog/Smog, Raining, Snowing, etc.
Light condition	The light condition when the encounter occurs	Daylight, Night-Headlight only, Night-Street light, etc.
Vehicle action	The vehicle acceleration situation during the encountering case	Faster, slower, no change, full stop, etc.
Traffic control condition	The traffic control condition when the encounter occurs	No traffic control, With traffic control

- Pedestrian Avoidance Behavior
- Driving Environment
- Road Type
- Light Condition
- Traffic Control Device
- Weather
- Traffic Density Level
- Road Infrastructure: divided traffic, non-divided traffic, one-way traffic
- Car Direction: straight, turning left, turning right

3.2 Machine-Learning Algorithms Implemented

A total of 5 different machine learning algorithms are applied towards the prior-described data set in the two-step classification process.

Naive Bayes. Naive Bayesian Classifier is a kind of probabilistic classifier [8]. Known for its simplicity, Naive Bayes can often outperform more sophisticated classification methods. It works as computing the probability of a data instance of n features: $d = (f_1, f_2, \ldots, f_n)$ belongs to category C. The probability is computed by applying the Bayes' theorem, given by Eq. 1:

$$P(C|d) = \frac{P(C)P(d|C)}{P(d)} \tag{1}$$

$P(C|d)$ is thus the probability that the data instance d belongs to category C. $P(d)$ is the probability that a randomly picked data instance has vector $d = (f_1, f_2, \ldots f_n)$ as its representation, and $P(C)$ is the probability that a randomly picked document belongs to C. $P(d|C)$ is the probability that a data instance belongs to category C has the representation d. In order to alleviate the problem, it is common to assume that $f_1, f_2, \ldots, f_n$ are conditionally independent given the category C. As a result, the $P(d|C)$ is computed as Eq. 2. $P(f_i|C)$ and $P(C)$ are estimated from the training set.

$$P(d|C) = \sum_{i=1}^{n} P(w_i|C) \tag{2}$$

Logistic Regression. Logistic Regression [9] is an efficient way for binary classification and uses predictive analysis for assigning observations to a discrete set of classes. Unlike linear regression which gives continuous number values, logistic regression transforms its output using the sigmoid function to return a probability value. This probability value can then be mapped to two or more discrete classes. Given a data instance with n features $f_1, f_2, \ldots, f_n$, the probability of it belongs to one category C is calculated as Eq. 3, where $\alpha_0, \ldots, \alpha_n$ are estimated from the training set.

$$\frac{1}{1 + exp(\alpha_0 + \alpha_1 f_1, + \cdots + \alpha_n f_n)} \tag{3}$$

Random Forests. Random forests algorithm is very similar to decision tree algorithms. The one main difference was the amount of trees that were used to determine the error. Research has shown that when decision trees grow very deep to learn irregular patterns, they can over fit to the training sets [10]. Random forests take one third of the data from the sample and uses them to calculate an unbiased estimate of error. Then, it uses this information while creating the next tree to improve accuracy. They provided a way of averaging deep decision trees with the goal of reducing the variance [10]. The combination of the multiple trees created a "forest" which gave a much more accurate approximation of the data. On the other hand, they also showed tree like models for visualizing the results.

Support Vector Machines. Support Vector Machines (SVMs) [11] was one of the classification algorithms evaluated. The SVMs classifier aims to separate the input data using hyperplanes. In order to generate a less complex hyperplane function for classification, the maximum margin between the hyperplane and the support vectors is required. When the samples are not linearly separable, support vector machines was used to non-linearly transform the training features from a low dimensional space 'd' to a higher dimensional feature space '$\phi(d)$' using a factor $\varphi : d \rightarrow \phi(d)$ and a function called 'Kernel', an inner product of two examples in the feature space. The ability to learn from large feature spaces and the dimensional independence make the support vector machines a universal learner for data classification. Another characteristic of SVMs is the use of soft margins to protect from over fitting caused by the misclassification of noisy data in such large feature spaces [12].

Deep Neural Networks. The Deep Neural Network [13] is similar to other machine learning algorithms. During the training phase, the network accepts inputs and feed forward mathematical operations that ultimately set off an activation function on each node of the network. The activation of the node relies on the weights associated with itself. Normally, higher weight results in greater activation. The activation of the final layer is then compared to the inputs, and a cost or a loss is computed. The weights of the final layer and the preceding layers are adjusted based on the cost function in order to minimize the cost of the next prediction. Once the training phase is done, the trained model can be loaded into a system for testing. Each deep neural network extracts useful information from the input data elements automatically. Hence, no other data pre-processing is involved in the process. Figure 2 provides an example of a DNN classier. M components are the number of neurons at the input layer. Normally, they equal to the number of features $f_l, f_2, \ldots, f_n$ in the data set. N components at the output layers correspond to the number of classes to predict. Given an input, there is a associated probability of each class C at the output layer. The probability to a class is between 0 and 1. In this research, we use three hidden layers, and each layer contains 500 neurons.

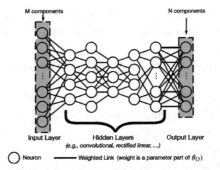

Fig. 2. Deep neural networks

3.3   Classification Process

In this research, we have explored classification of whether there are potential conflicts and whether pedestrian or vehicle passes first when there is potential conflict. The classification process consists of two levels, first level is to classify whether there are potential conflict, whereas the second level is to classify whether pedestrian or vehicle passes first. The classifier that performs the best at the first level is used for the second level. In this research, the deep neural network performs better at the first level. Hence, it is used for the second level classification.

Since there are much more no potential conflict instances, The data set for the first level classification is extremely unbalanced. In order to balance the data set to train the learning models, we duplicate the instances of the potential conflict to balance the data set. Afterwards, the data set is randomly split into training and test data. In this research, 60% of the data is used as training data to train the learning models, 40% of the data is used for testing. Five different learning

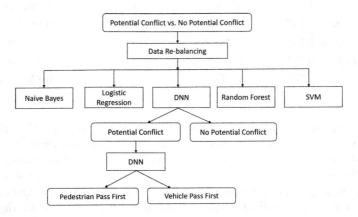

Fig. 3. Classification process

algorithms described in Sect. 3.2 are used for classify the potential conflict versus no potential conflict instances. Figure 3 demonstrates the classification process.

4   Machine-Learning Classification Results

In this research, we use true positive (TP), true negative (TN), false negative (FN), false positive (FP), accuracy ($\frac{(TN+TP)}{(TN+TP+FN+FP)}$), precision ($\frac{TP}{(TP+FP)}$), recall ($\frac{TP}{(TP+FN)}$) and F1 ($\frac{TP}{(TP+FN+FP)}$) to evaluate the performance of all five learning algorithms. Since both levels are binary classification, we calculate the TP, TN, FN and FP according to class potential conflict and pedestrian pass first.

4.1   Classification Results for Potential Conflict Cases

The following Tables 2 and 3 show the results of first-level classification towards potential conflict cases. For four commonly used machine learning algorithms, the classification accuracy is in the range of 0.75 to 0.81; however, deep neural network successfully achieves a accuracy rate of more than 93% for the testing data set. This suggests that only with the descriptive scenario variables listed in Table 1, AI system can recognize potential conflict at a very high accuracy level. Considering that the precision, recall, and F1 rates for DNN are also very high, the high accuracy rate is achieved with low False Positive rate.

Table 2. Classification results of training data

	Naive Bayes	Logistic regression	Random forest	SVM	DNN
TN	15106	14885	14694	15726	20369
FP	6057	6278	6469	5437	876
FN	4671	3824	3909	2419	1099
TP	16655	17502	17417	18907	20146
Accuracy	0.747	0.762	0.756	0.815	0.953
Precision	0.733	0.736	0.729	0.777	0.958
Recall	0.781	0.821	0.817	0.886	0.948
F1	0.756	0.776	0.770	0.828	0.953

Based on the results, we can answer the first research question that both traditional machine learning algorithms and deep neural network can classify potential conflict between vehicles and pedestrians based on easy-to-acquire descriptive scenario variables. Comparing to 4 machine learning algorithms, deep learning algorithm shows better performance. Thus, in one hand, the cases that can be successfully classified by deep neural network will be used for the second-level data analysis. In the other hand, the False Negative cases will be collected for more detailed investigations.

Table 3. Classification results of test data

	Naive Bayes	Logistic regression	Random forest	SVM	DNN
TN	10182	9985	9945	10466	13150
FP	4063	4260	4300	3779	1013
FN	3035	2551	2549	1662	739
TP	11047	11531	11533	12420	13424
Accuracy	0.749	0.760	0.758	0.808	0.938
Precision	0.731	0.730	0.728	0.767	0.930
Recall	0.784	0.819	0.818	0.882	0.948
F1	0.757	0.772	0.771	0.820	0.939

4.2 Classification Results for Passing Priority

The following Table 4 reports the classification results of passing priority between pedestrians and vehicles for potential conflicting cases, using deep neural network. With intensive training, the constructed network is able to achieve an accuracy level of 96% for the testing data set. This suggests that it is possible for AI system to classify passing priority to a very high accuracy level with enough details provided, even when the actual pedestrian moving trajectories and/or body postures are not available. Please note that the precision rate in this case is also very high, suggesting that the high accuracy is not sacrificing a high false positive rate.

Table 4. Classification results of training and test data

	TN	FP	FN	TP	Accuracy	Precision	Recall	F1
Training	337	0	0	157	1	1	1	1
Test	554	10	23	234	0.960	0.959	0.911	0.934

5   Conclusions and Future Work

Based on a large-scale naturalistic driving data set focusing on vehicle-pedestrian encountering cases, this study tries to investigate the possibility to detect potential conflict and prioritize passing sequences using only descriptive scenario variables, without involving quantitative data like pedestrian moving trajectories or body postures which consume large amount of computing resources and are difficult to acquire all the time. The main goal is to investigate if these relatively easy-to-acquire scenario variables can provide enough information to help ADS decide when to prepare for potential conflicts or give away right-of-way. Also, some wrongly classified cases may provide important features representing unpredictable risks.

Five different machine learning algorithms, including Naive Bayes, Logistic Regression, Random Forests, Support Vector Machines, and Deep Neural Networks, are applied towards the pre-labeled data set. The results show that the tested algorithms, especially the constructed deep neural network, can classify the potential conflict cases from safe cases at a very high accuracy level (93%) with low false positive rates (93% precision). Also, deep neural network can prioritize the passing sequences correctly at the accuracy level of 96% (at 96% precision level). The results prove that the descriptive scenario variables can be efficiently used to classify vehicle-pedestrian encountering risks.

As a preliminary study, there are some limitations in the work requiring additional investigations. There are some wrongly classified cases, especially the FN cases, which can represent additional risk for ADS as the corresponding risk is not predicted via the AI algorithms. The features of these cases will be further studied in comparison with other cases. Also, feature reduction process can be applied for all the scenario variables to further improve the performance of the machine learning algorithms.

References

1. Chen, D., Ahn, S., Chitturi, M., Noyce, D.A.: Towards vehicle automation: roadway capacity formulation for traffic mixed with regular and automated vehicles. Transp. Res. Part B Methodol. **100**, 196–221 (2017)
2. Sherony, R., Tian, R., Chien, S., Fu, L., Chen, Y., Takahashi, H.: Pedestrian/bicyclist limb motion analysis from 110-car TASI video data for autonomous emergency braking testing surrogate development. SAE Int. J. Transp. Saf. **4**(1), 113–120 (2016)
3. Schram, R., Williams, A., Van Ratingen, M.: Implementation of autonomous emergency braking (AEB), the next step in Euro NCAP'S safety assessment. In: Proceedings of the 23rd International Technical Conference on the Enhanced Safety of Vehicles (ESV), Seoul, Republic of Korea, 27–30 May 2013 (2013)
4. Rasouli, A., Kotseruba, I., Tsotsos, J.K.: Understanding pedestrian behavior in complex traffic scenes. IEEE Trans. Intell. Veh. **3**(1), 61–70 (2018)
5. Tian, R., Li, L., Yang, K., Jiang, F., Chen, Y., Sherony, R.: Single-variable scenario analysis of vehicle-pedestrian potential crash based on video analysis results of large-scale naturalistic driving data. In: Duffy, V.G. (ed.) DHM 2015. LNCS, vol. 9185, pp. 295–304. Springer, Cham (2015). https://doi.org/10.1007/978-3-319-21070-4_30
6. Feng, G., Sheila, K., Jon, H., Thomas, A.D.: Near crashes as crash surrogate for naturalistic driving studies. Transp. Res. Rec. J. Transp. Res. Board **2147**(1), 66–74 (2010)
7. Tian, R., Li, L., Yang, K., Chien, S., Chen, Y., Sherony, R.: Estimation of the vehicle-pedestrian encounter/conflict risk on the road based on TASI 110-car naturalistic driving data collection. In: IEEE International Conference on Intelligent Vehicles Symposium, Dearborn, pp. 623–629 (2014)
8. Rish, I.: An empirical study of the Naive Bayes classifier. In: IJCAI 2001 Workshop on Empirical Methods in Artificial Intelligence, vol. 3, no. 22, pp. 41–46 (2001)
9. Kleinbaum, D.G., Klein, M.: Logistic Regression. SBH. Springer, New York (2002). https://doi.org/10.1007/b97379

10. Breiman, L.: Random forests. Mach. Learn. **45**(1), 5–32 (2001)
11. Cortes, C., Vapnik, V.: Support-vector networks. Mach. Learn. **20**(3), 273–297 (1995)
12. Joachims, T.: Making large-scale SVM learning practical (No. 1998, 28). Technical report, SFB 475: Komplexitätsreduktion in Multivariaten Datenstrukturen, Universität Dortmund (1998)
13. LeCun, Y., Bengio, Y., Hinton, G.: Deep learning. Nature **521**(7553), 436 (2015)

Innovative and Comprehensive Support System for Training People Working in Dangerous Conditions

Andrzej Grabowski[✉] [ID]

Central Institute for Labour Protection – National Research Institute,
Warsaw, Poland
angra@ciop.pl

Abstract. The visuals used in the virtual environment keep the trainees interested and facilitates the memorization of information as well as consolidates their skills. Wireless HMD (Head Mounted Display) and the motion capture technology are used in order to involve muscle memory and improve the effectiveness of trainings. All training scenarios are fully integrated with ICT training assessment system. The possibility of practical application of the VR-based training into the educational process of workers can have a significant impact on improving collective and individual work safety. VR-based training is a particularly valuable for people working in dangerous conditions, where the accident rate is clearly higher than in other branches of the economy. Moreover VR-based training allows to support the rehabilitation and physiotherapy process in order to accelerate the return to work after injuries.

Keywords: Virtual reality training · Training scenarios · Safety at work

1 Introduction: Virtual Reality as Training Tool

The use of Virtual Reality technology makes it possible to acquire and practice the workers' correct actions even in emergency situations. This is done in a controlled and safe circumstances. The visuals used in the virtual environment keep the trainees interested and facilitates the memorization of information as well as consolidates their skills. The training system will allow to simulate different conditions in hazardous situations. Using the VR (Virtual Reality) technologies will enable observing the trainees' behavior in stressful situations.

Efficacy of new technologies can be further enhanced thanks to the experience in the field of gamification, research processes and training. Gamification – this term refers to the mechanics of computer games which are used to modify people's behavior in tasks which aren't related to entertainment or games. Worldwide research shows that the use of gaming elements in a training environment helps improve the usability experience and participants' commitment. For some time, the gaming technology are used for a much wider range of applications rather than just entertainment. Evidence of such trend shows a growing market for so-called serous games, which are applications-like games, but used for research or training purposes. The newest psychological

© Springer Nature Switzerland AG 2019
V. G. Duffy (Ed.): HCII 2019, LNCS 11581, pp. 394–405, 2019.
https://doi.org/10.1007/978-3-030-22216-1_29

research analysis shows that playing computer games and using game-like training applications improves the cognitive functioning of individuals (e.g. increasing the individuals attention). These results are in agreement with reports on the effect of games on the cognitive functioning (it is related with improvement of visual attention performance, especially for first-person perspective games). It has been proven that the effectiveness of such applications supports gaining knowledge and skills. Gamification became a method for creating more engagement in work environment, whose main feature is natural and facilitated cooperation with other users [1, 2].

One of the most frequent causes of accidents in the industry (e.g. in mining) is the lack of workers' attention. The complexity of the environment in which people (especially miners) work, has an extreme burden on cognitive processes. Limited visibility, high temperature and humidity, the necessity of wearing protective clothing and equipment are conditions in which miners are pushed to the limit. In such a situation, some tasks can be easily overlooked, which may result in an accident. For the past 10 years, many studies show that people with gaming experience are more successful with achieving cognitive tasks [3]. This applies especially to the visual attention and the ability to switch to different tasks. It is particularly interesting what the experimental studies show. Trainees can improve their attention just after relatively short trainings. The improvements last for several weeks or even months after the training [4, 5].

Positive effects of gamification are also visible in the area of improving the ability to perform many tasks simultaneously [6] and cognitive skills, especially in the case of elderly [7]. Therefore, interactive games and virtual environments are increasingly used for cognitive rehabilitation in order to improve cognitive abilities and resources of various groups of people, including children [8] or people after stroke and other brain injuries [9, 10]. Rehabilitation activities based on computer simulations have the potential to provide patients with enriched training environments that motivate to a longer, heavier and regular activity aimed at overcoming subsequent challenges in the field of motor control. Particularly good adaptation to the defined requirements of effective rehabilitation are achieved by systems using virtual reality technologies. The reason for this is the possibility of stimulating many senses of the patient within the simulation: sight, sound, sensory experience. Rehabilitation with the use of immersive virtual environments, based on the experience of conventional rehabilitation techniques, provides tools that intensively stimulate patients and more effectively maintain motivation for exercise. An important aspect of the assessment of the impact of physical training in virtual environments, on changes in behaviors observed in the natural environment, is the determination of the correctness of kinematics of movements performed in the context of 2D interfaces and more immersive 3D solutions. The improvement of the motor performance of the upper limbs is most often measured by the parameters of speed, precision, smoothness of movements and the degree of coordination between changes in the position of individual components of the musculoskeletal system [25]. Movements of upper limbs performed in the context of three-dimensional interfaces are more similar to natural ones than the same movements realized using two-dimensional interfaces (in our work we are using VR-equipment to track upper limb movement in three dimensional space, but the image of the virtual environment can be presented in HMD, as a stereoscopic image, or on the two dimensional screen – see Fig. 1). This is evidenced by the studies in which the kinematics of the movements of indicating various points in the field of the arm's work in the natural environment were compared to movements performed in the immersive virtual environment presented in the HMD [26, 27]. Virtual environments allow for precise measurement of behavior parameters while performing complex but safe tasks in simulations, the realism of which is similar to real situations [28, 29]. In many solutions based on virtual reality technologies and computer games, feedback is provided by both visual and auditory stimuli. In the case of upper limb rehabilitation, users can interact with virtual objects directly through the hand and body movement, through interfaces that enable sensory feedback, performing activities that give the impression of immersion in simulation, which increases the probability of transfer of learning outcomes to natural situations [30].

Fig. 1. An image of a virtual environment can be presented in many ways, e.g. on the screen or in the HMD. The choice of the display method and image depends on the type of training scenario, e.g. it is not possible to force all trajectories of the upper limb movement by presenting only a two-dimensional image.

Virtual reality is often used as a training tool, and also in this study we are using virtual reality-based training methods. It is assumed that immersive simulations in virtual environment enhance trainee ability to modify inefficient and false working procedures [11], mainly because the support acquisition and transfer of tacit knowledge and enhance human abilities and motivation to absorb new knowledge [11]. Results of many studies show that training is effective in reducing accidents at work and this effect is increased by the level of engagement of the training methods [12] and the virtual reality is one of the most engaging and immersive training method. A review of 95 quasi-experimental studies was performed to determine the relative effectiveness of different methods of worker safety and health training aimed at improving safety knowledge and performance and reducing negative outcomes (accidents, illnesses, and injuries) [13]. The main outcome of this study is following: as training methods became more engaging (i.e., requiring trainees' active participation), workers demonstrated greater knowledge acquisition, and reductions were seen in accidents, illnesses, and injuries [13]. Results of virtual reality-based pilot training of underground coal miners [14] show that in almost all cases high immersive VR, especially combined with wide FoV, is assessed as better solution for training, than less immersive training methods. Moreover, trainees consider used system useful and feel the positive effects of training even after three months [14].

It should be noted that virtual reality is only a tool and in some cases it is not working as it is supposed to be. At the current stage of technology it is impossible to use virtual reality to all possible training scenarios and always achieve expected results. It was even more complicated in the past with big, heavy equipment, especially head mounted displays and motion tracking systems. Some studies show lack of transfer of positive effects of virtual reality training. For instance in [15] real-world training, virtual reality training, and no training in the transfer of learning to the same task performed in real-world conditions were compared. The results show that there was no significant difference between the virtual reality training group and the group that received no training on the task, indicating that improvements to virtual reality for the purpose of enabling the transfer of training are needed. Moreover it is still difficult to train manual tasks due to poor mechanical performance of the simulated haptic feedback [16]. In some cases problems with quality of simulation may lead to learn improper practices and as a result control group achieve better rating scores than group trained with the simulator [16]. However in most cases positive effects of virtual reality training is clearly visible, e.g. the use of virtual reality surgical simulation significantly improved the operating room performance of residents during laparoscopic cholecystectomy [17]. Outcomes of 10 laparoscopic cholecystectomies performed by novices shows that The VR-trained group consistently made significantly fewer errors. Moreover, residents in the control group made, on average, 3 times as many errors and used 58% longer surgical time [18]. It indicates that virtual reality based simulation significantly improves performance and error rate. Results of systematic review of 91 articles, which all reported on training in arthroscopic surgery, shows that VR training leads to an improvement of technical skills in orthopaedic surgery [19]. Interactive virtual reality training was found to be a relatively inexpensive and effective mode for teaching operating room fire prevention and management scenarios [20]. Even if both groups have reached the same level of cognitive knowledge, when tested in the mock operating room fire scenario, 70% of the simulation group subjects were able to perform the correct sequence of steps in extinguishing the simulated fire whereas only 20% subjects in the control group were able to do so. The simulation group was better than control group in correctly identifying the oxidizer and ignition source [20]. Virtual reality is also used in many safety training applications [21, 22] and military applications [23]. In the case of soldiers training the stress during training is an important factor [23] and it is possible to lower the stress level by proper (even virtual) training. It should be noted that virtual reality has potential not only in the case of workers training to increase safety and work efficiency. It is also useful to simulate of different potentially dangerous events. Virtual reality seems to be advantageous for observations of near misses and accidents at work. Use of VR for accident investigations facilitate new insights into cause of events and thereby provide new perspectives for the development of measures of hazard and risk reduction [24].

2   Methods and Results

The implementation of an effective training system requires precise preparation of assumptions regarding the scope of functionality of the products planned to be implemented. In the case of people working in dangerous conditions, the key task is also to describe the specificity of the work environment to be transferred to virtual reality. For this reason, the assumptions for the training scenarios were first developed. In this way, the process of training simulators was defined. The source data necessary for the simulation of the work process of self-propelled mining machinery operators was collected and analyzed. These data included technical, photographic, film documentation and 3D scans.

Fig. 2. For the training a wireless HMD and gloves are used. Since the heavy machinery chamber has a very large surface, and mining machines such as a loader have a length of about 10 m, it is advisable to use sufficiently large training rooms. Equipped with a vision based motion capture system, the room shown in the picture is 16 × 11 m.

The principle of operation of the training and examination system is be based on the use of a hybrid motion tracking system allowing to determine the movement of the entire figure of people participating in the simulation, as well as the location and orientation of any items in space (e.g. physical surrogates of virtual object can be used). HMDs (Head Mounted Display) are used to observe the virtual environment, wireless gloves allow full interaction with the virtual environment (e.g. moving virtual objects). The belt with battery for wireless data transmission system is also used. The analysis of data from the motion tracking system (which is based on passive markers) allows to determine the position of the entire body, i.e. the position and orientation of all limbs, torso and head, with particular attention to the head and hands. Special gloves monitoring the degree of flexion of the fingers allow for advanced interaction with the environment, e.g. turning machines on or off, gripping, moving and throwing virtual objects. The use of commanding gestures is also possible. Immersive interaction with virtual environment is possible because the collected data is transferred to a specially adapted physics engine operating in real time.

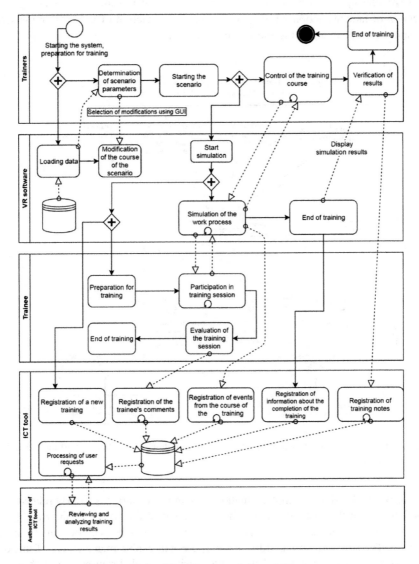

Fig. 3. A simplified diagram of the training course.

The use of the wireless system (Fig. 2) allows the trainee to freely explore the virtual environment, the size of which does not have to be limited to the size of the room in which the training or examination takes place. The trainee can go, and even run, in any direction. This approach gives a unique opportunity to build scenarios such as exploring a large area. A redirected walking algorithm will allow free movement even in very large virtual environments. This is possible due to the domination of the sense of sight over the sense of proprioception associated with the sense of touch and the vestibular system, which allows a certain degree of invisible manipulation of the direction of human motion while maintaining the conviction of a person immersed in the simulation of maintaining the chosen direction.

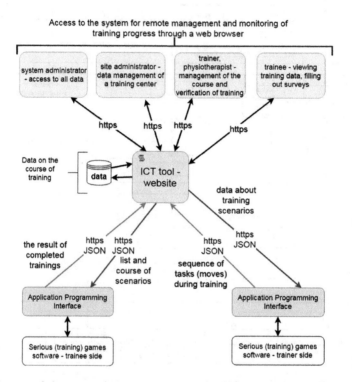

Fig. 4. Diagram of data transmission between different users of the supporting the training process system.

Software related to the implementation of training scenarios is closely related to the functioning of a ICT tool to support the assessment of the course of the training. All important events and decisions made by the trainee will be recorded in the central database. The software prepared for this purpose will enable management of this data, and above all their display and description using a web browser (i.e. a thin-client application paradigm will be used). Authorized persons will have access to the collected data, which can be used, among others to assess changes in the knowledge and skills of trained people. A simplified diagram of the training course is presented in Fig. 3. Using such ICT it is possible to easily change training scenarios and adapt them to the needs and capabilities of the trainees (this is especially important in the case of training games supporting rehabilitation process). Users of the system have easy access to almost all that through a web browser (diagram of data transmission is shown in Fig. 4). The accessible functionalities depend on user role, e.g. the training scenario can be changed only by a trainer.

The described above methods are used to support the rehabilitation and physiotherapy process in order to accelerate the return to work after injuries. Such training is a particularly necessary for people working in dangerous conditions (e.g. in underground mines), where the accident rate is clearly higher than in other branches of the economy. It should be noted that the same VR-technology combined with ICT tools supporting training process is used to teach employees how to do their job safely, and this is also particularly necessary for people working in dangerous conditions. We are preparing training applications for miners working in different types of underground mines (e.g. coal mines and copper mines – see Fig. 5) as well as firefighter (Fig. 6) were training of cooperation in a team is very important.

Fig. 5. Training application for miners working in underground coal mine (left) and a 3D model of one of the mining machine in underground copper mine. A control panel is visible through the glass (right).

Fig. 6. Virtual reality with motion capture technology allow to train group of people. Such cooperation training is very important in the case of people working in dangerous conditions, like firefighters. On the right side the use of physical surrogates of virtual objects is visible. Trainee can use real nozzle to change properties of the water stream.

3 Summary

Evaluation of the effectiveness of solutions based on virtual reality technologies as an effective tool for acquiring mobility skills requires evidence of effective transfer of acquired skills to behavior in the natural environment. Nowadays, only a few studies control important indicators of learning effectiveness, such as long-term maintenance of increased mobility, transfer of training effects and their generalization to untrained tasks [31]. In one of the studies of this type, the relationship between exercises performed using the interface in the form of a specialist glove has been proven and overall improvement in the efficiency of functioning outside the virtual environment, but undoubtedly more research is needed on the issue of the generalization of training effects. Another example of the transfer is a study [32], in which after training in a virtual environment, patients with side-shedding syndrome coped better with the task of crossing the street in real situations, despite the lack of significant differences in other range tests and the degree of deficit.

Despite the considerable diversity of individual studies in the field of correctness of movements performed in virtual environments (2D vs. 3D interfaces), a suggestion emerges that the movements performed in the simulation may translate into significant changes in everyday functioning [33]. Therefore, it can be assumed that it is not essential that the movement in the simulation reflects the kinematics of movement in the natural environment, nor is the role of the natural rotational behavior of individual joints necessary for the movement. The potential for transfer of skills learned in virtual environments may be related to other advantages possible thanks to virtual reality technologies.

The described challenges and the lack of unambiguous evidence on the effectiveness of the transfer of training effects remain an important area of research on the possibility of using virtual environments in training and rehabilitation. A separate problem is the further integration of these solutions in clinical practice, because rehabilitation tools in the first place must serve the effectiveness of the activities of professionals choosing the training variants of each patient.

In summary, there is a lot of evidence that it is possible to effectively use virtual reality technologies to create enriched training environments in accordance with established principles of physical control and movement learning, to support upper limb rehabilitation processes. The flexibility of computerized solutions gives therapists the opportunity to precisely determine the goals and scope of the exercise, while providing feedback that effectively induces neuroplasticity and motivates patients.

The possibility of real and practical application of the project into the educational process of people working in dangerous conditions will have a significant impact on improving collective and individual work safety among people identified as target groups. It should be emphasized that this does not apply only to people subjected for training. The long-term effect of it would be to increase the safety of all employees. The results of global research on the effectiveness of training show that trained staff have a positive impact on the people in their environment who did not participate in the training. In this way the knowledge is transferred naturally among people who work together. It will also affect the level of their own potential to improve knowledge of the diversity of threats and the ability to react to a specific threat through acquired skills and competences. In real work environment it is not possible to carry out a number of simulation events. It results from the organization and labor productivity, the cost-efficiency requirements for employees, as well as the production cycle that takes into account the natural movement of the rock mass. These restrictions do not apply to VR technology.

It should be noted that all training scenarios are fully integrated with ICT training assessment system. This is a clear step ahead to a fully comprehensive approach to a complex training which is based on knowledge and skills which come directly from experience and not from a theoretical course.

Acknowledgement. Publication based on the results of the fourth stage of the multi-annual program "Improving safety and working conditions", financed in the years 2017–2019 in the field of state services by the Ministry of Family, Labor and Social Policy.

Program coordinator: Central Institute for Labor Protection - National Research Institute.

References

1. McGonigal, J.: Reality is Broken: Why Games Make us Better and how they can Change the World. Penguin, London (2011)
2. Reeves, B., Read, J.L.: Total Engagement: Using Games and Virtual Worlds to Change the way People Work and Businesses Compete. Harvard Business School Press, Boston (2009)
3. Green, C.S., Bevalier, D.: Action video game modifies visual selective attention. Nature **423** (6939), 534–538 (2003)
4. Feng, J., Spence, I., Pratt, J.: Playing an action video game reduces gender differences in spatial cognition. Psychol. Sci. **18**(10), 850–855 (2007)
5. Li, R., Polat, U., Makous, W., Bavelier, D.: Enhancing the contrast sensitivity function through action video game training. Nat. Neurosci. **12**(5), 549–551 (2009). https://doi.org/10.1038/nn.2296
6. Abbott, A.: Gaming improves multitasking skills. Nature (2013). https://www.nature.com/news/gaming-improves-multitasking-skills-1.13674
7. Anguera, J.: Video game training enhances cognitive control in older adults. Nature **501**, 97 (2013)
8. Boivin, M.J., et al.: Neuropsychological benefits of computerized cognitive rehabilitation training in Ugandan children surviving severe malaria: a randomized controlled trial. Brain Res. Bull. **145**, 117–128 (2018). https://doi.org/10.1016/j.brainresbull.2018.03.002
9. Bonnechère, B.: Serious Games in Physical Rehabilitation: From Theory to Practice. Springer, Cham (2018). https://doi.org/10.1007/978-3-319-66122-3
10. De Luca, R., et al.: Cognitive rehabilitation after severe acquired brain injury: current evidence and future directions. Neuropsychol. Rehabil. Int. J. **28**(6) (2018). https://doi.org/10.1080/09602011.2016.1211937
11. Podgórski, D.: The use of tacit knowledge in occupational safety and health management systems. Int. J. Occup. Safety Ergonom. **16**, 527–543 (2010)
12. Brahm, F., Singer, M.: Is more engaging safety training always better in reducing accidents? Evidence of self-selection from chilean panel data. J. Saf. Res. **47**(0), 85–92 (2013). https://www.sciencedirect.com/science/article/pii/S0022437513001515

13. Burke, M., et al.: Relative effectiveness of worker safety and health training methods. Am. J. Public Health **96**(2), 315–324 (2006). https://doi.org/10.2105/ajph.2004.059840

14. Grabowski, A., Jankowski, J.: Virtual reality-based pilot training for underground coal miners. Saf. Sci. **72**, 310–314 (2015)

15. Kozak, J., et al.: Transfer of training from virtual reality. Ergonomics **36**(7), 777–784 (1993). https://doi.org/10.1080/00140139308967941

16. Våpenstad, C., et al.: Lack of transfer of skills after virtual reality simulator training with haptic feedback. Minim. Invasive Ther. Allied Technol. **26**(6), 346–354 (2017). https://doi.org/10.1080/13645706.2017.1319866

17. Seymour, N., et al.: Virtual reality training improves operating room performance. Ann. Surg. **236**(4), 458–464 (2002)

18. Ahlberg, G.: Proficiency-based virtual reality training significantly reduces the error rate for residents during their first 10 laparoscopic cholecystectomies. Am. J. Surg. **193**(6), 797–804 (2007). https://doi.org/10.1016/j.amjsurg.2006.06.050

19. Aim, F., et al.: Effectiveness of virtual reality training in orthopaedic surgery. Arthroscopy J. Arthroscopic Relat. Surg. **32**(1), 224–232 (2016). https://doi.org/10.1016/j.arthro.2015.07.023

20. Sankaranarayana, G., et al.: Immersive virtual reality-based training improves response in a simulated operating room fire scenario. Surg. Endosc. **32**(8), 3439–3449 (2018). https://doi.org/10.1007/s00464-018-6063-x

21. Leder, J., et al.: Comparing immersive virtual reality and powerpoint as methods for delivering safety training: Impacts on risk perception, learning, and decision making. Saf. Sci. **111**, 271–286 (2019). https://doi.org/10.1016/j.ssci.2018.07.021

22. Silliker, A.: Virtual reality shakes up safety training. Canadian Occupational Safety. https://www.cos-mag.com/personal-process-safety/36967-virtual-reality-shakes-up-safety-training/. Accessed 06 Apr 2018

23. Lackey, S., et al.: The stress and workload of virtual reality training: the effects of presence, immersion and flow. Ergonomics **59**(8), 1060–1072 (2016). https://doi.org/10.1080/00140139.2015.1122234

24. Nickel, P., Lungfiel, A., Trabold, R.: Reconstruction of near misses and accidents for analyses from virtual reality usability study. In: Barbic, J., D'Cruz, M., Latoschik, M., Slater, M., Bourdot, P. (eds.) EuroVR 2017. LNCS, vol. 10700, pp. 182–191. Springer, Cham (2017). https://doi.org/10.1007/978-3-319-72323-5_12

25. Levin, M.F., Kleim, J.A., Wolf, S.L.: What do motor "recovery" and "compensation" mean in patients following stroke? Neurorehabilitation Neural Repair **23**(4), 313–319 (2009)

26. Knaut, L.A., Subramanian, S.K., McFadyen, B.J., Bourbonnais, D., Levin, M.F.: Kinematics of pointing movements made in a virtual versus a physical 3-dimensional environment in healthy and stroke subjects. Arch. Phys. Med. Rehabil. **90**(5), 793–802 (2009)

27. Subramanian, S.K., Levin, M.F.: Viewing medium affects arm motor performance in 3D virtual environments. J. Neuroeng. Rehabil. **8**(1), 36 (2011)

28. Weiss, P.L., Sveistrup, H., Rand, D., Kizony, R.: Video capture virtual reality: A decade of rehabilitation assessment and intervention. Phys. Ther. Rev. **14**(5), 307–321 (2009)

29. Weiss, P.L., Keshner, E.A., Levin, M.F.: Applying virtual reality technologies to motor rehabilitation. In: Sharkey, P., (ed.) Virtual Reality Technologies for Health and Clinical Applications, vol. 1, Springer, New York (2014)

30. Slater, M.: Place illusion and plausibility can lead to realistic behaviour in immersive virtual environments. Philos. Trans. R. Soc. Lond. B Biol. Sci. **364**(1535), 3549–3557 (2009)

31. Abdollahi, F., et al.: Error augmentation enhancing arm recovery in individuals with chronic stroke: a randomized crossover design. Neurorehabilitation Neural Repair **28**(2), 120–128 (2014)
32. Katz, N., et al.: Interactive virtual environment training for safe street crossing of right hemisphere stroke patients with unilateral spatial neglect. Disabil. Rehabil. **27**(20), 1235–1244 (2005)
33. Henderson, A., Korner-Bitensky, N., Levin, M.: Virtual reality in stroke rehabilitation: a systematic review of its effectiveness for upper limb motor recovery. Top. Stroke Rehabil. **14**(2), 52–61 (2007)

Development and Evaluation of a Tablet-Control for a Surgical Workstation in the Open Integrated Operating Room

Johanna Hemmeke$^{(\boxtimes)}$, Philipp Krumholz, Armin Janß,
and Klaus Radermacher

Chair of Medical Engineering, RWTH University Aachen, Aachen, Germany
janss@hia.rwth-aachen.de

Abstract. In the complex and safety-critical environment of the operating room the increasing use of technology and the interactions are significant causes for critical incidents and adverse events. Thus, the usability needs to be optimized, e.g. by enhancing the Human-Machine-Interaction, the workflow and therefore the safety for users and patients. Hence, big companies offer integrated operation room systems, with harmonized safety- and HMI-concepts. Unfortunately, these systems come along with closed proprietary communication solutions. This prevents flexible design for the hospital operator and easy integration of medical equipment from small and medium-sized enterprises. To open this market, a safe and dynamic networking approach of medical devices has been established on the basis of an open communication standard (IEEE 11073-SDC). Within the OR.NET follow-up project ZiMT (Certifiable integrated Medical Technology), a mobile control in addition to the central surgical workstation use concept has been developed. The requirement analysis for the tablet concept considers existing integrated OR systems and the development and evaluation of human-machine interfaces, regarding the usability engineering process as well as related standards (e.g. Machinery Directive 2006/42/EC, DIN EN ISO 9241-110, IEC 62366). The graphical user interface provides inter alia a flexible und workflow-oriented assembly of a function group view. To evaluate the developed concept in comparison to the user interface of the workstation, an interaction-centered usability test with nine participants (surgeons and OR nurses) has been conducted. The results show a comparable effectiveness and efficiency. Moreover, the intuitiveness of the tablet control is estimated to be higher and most test subjects prefer to work with the tablet control.

Keywords: Human-Machine-Interaction · Human factors ·
Usability evaluation · Risk analysis · Integrated operating room ·
Dynamic and open surgical network · Tablet control · IEEE 11073-SDC

1 Introduction

The technical progress within the last 25 years has fundamentally changed the way medicine and surgery are practiced nowadays. Results of this development are e.g. a better understanding of diseases, higher efficiency, therapeutic results, lower mortality rates and less invasiveness of interventions and treatments [1].

© Springer Nature Switzerland AG 2019
V. G. Duffy (Ed.): HCII 2019, LNCS 11581, pp. 406–419, 2019.
https://doi.org/10.1007/978-3-030-22216-1_30

The increasing use of technology in medicine results in even higher demands regarding the usability and safety of medical devices. This development is also reflected in regulatory and normative standards regarding safety, risk analysis and usability engineering in the field of medical technology [2].

One of the consequences for doctors and nursing staff is the increasing Human-Machine-Interaction in their everyday work [2]. Especially in the OR, the complexity of technical equipment is constantly increasing. Surgical procedures are performed by interdisciplinary teams, based on documents from various sources and highly specialized medical equipment from various manufacturers. The technical equipment and deficient usability within of the OR is in these days is a significant cause of incidents and malfunctions [2–4].

In order to avoid additional stress on medical personnel and nursing staff through the use of an increasing number of new medical devices, the user interface must be designed to support the work process through system integration and consistent user interfaces [5].

An integrated workstation with a central control unit can help to facilitate the control of a large number of devices. Currently there are only closed, proprietary systems of big manufacturers on the market, which prevent a flexible and open exchange of different medical devices [6].

Within the framework of the OR.NET follow-up project ZiMT (Certifiable integrated medical technology and IT systems based on open standards in OR and clinics) the research and development regarding a safe and open networking of medical devices is continued. The interaction of the devices with medically approved software is an important part of the project. In cooperation with companies from NRW (North Rhine Westphalia), a surgical cockpit is developed in order to centrally control medical devices. As a part of the Workstation a tablet control is being developed, which can be used as a mobile and flexible addition to the central cockpit, shown in Fig. 1 [7, 8].

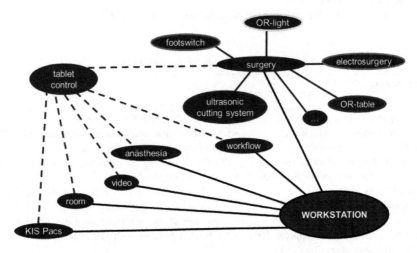

Fig. 1. Overview tablet control and surgical workstation

2   Materials and Methods

2.1   Requirements

The requirement analysis consisting of literature analysis and use process analysis includes additionally considering the principles of dialogue design according to DIN EN ISO 9241-110, a detailed examination of existing user interfaces and systems on the market and an evaluation of tablets, which are used in the medical context. Furthermore, the analysis of the structure and usage process of the existing surgical workstation demonstrator at the Chair of Medical Engineering, trials on existing surgical workstations exhibited at the MEDICA and the results of an online survey (conducted by the Chair of Medical Engineering at the Helmholtz Institute for Biomedical Engineering, RWTH Aachen) influenced the requirements for the tablet control.

On the tablet GUI all functions of the Workstation need to be shown, but on a considerably smaller screen of 10" simultaneously the virtual buttons therefore need to be of appropriate size (min 13 × 13 mm).

In order to avoid random interaction with the medical devices, e.g. by blood droplets on the screen, a safety concept has to be considered. For some functions, especially when energy is introduced into the body or when the position of devices and components is changed in the OR (e.g. OR table and C-arm), at least one separate confirmation switch must be provided complementary to the touch control. This kind of trigger is necessary in order to avoid endangering the patient, user and third parties. This way, the control complies with the following requirement of the Machinery Directive: "Particular attention must be given to the following points: - the machinery must not start unexpectedly" [9].

Another important aspect is the fast access to various functions. Especially in an emergency it is important to be able to control the corresponding device as quickly as possible, in other words to get to the right screen to operate the required device with as few interactions as possible.

In summary, the following requirements result (see Table 1).

Table 1. Requirements for the tablet concept

Requirements	
GUI of the tablet	Tablet in the OR
• All Operating functions of the existing surgical workstation	• Shockproof, sterilizable sleeve
• Safe and usable control	• Lightest possible weight at a size of approx. 10"
• Control elements of sufficient size	• Possibility of setting a key lock
• Easy and fast navigation between the different pages	• Existing hard keys for triggering certain functions
• If possible use of pictograms, arrows and labels	• Additional sterilizable holder
• Intended screen size of approx. 10" with high resolution	• Long battery life and easy replacement of the battery or existing redundant control unit
	• If possible charge without a plug e.g. via induction
	• Multitouch gestures with gloves and cover possible

2.2   Tablet Design Concept

The design concept has been developed in several iteration loops. It started out as a structured overview where the properties of different functions and their interactions are displayed and their arrangement on the screen.

Based on that structure and also on the design for the existing workstation a first concept has been developed. That concept has been reviewed and evaluated in accordance with heuristics and criteria-based usability assessment (DIN EN ISO 9241-110). Based on that review the next step of the concept has been developed and after another iteration loop regarding AAMI-HE75 the following concept has been elaborated [10].

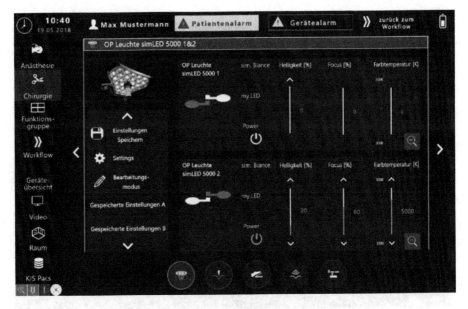

Fig. 2. GUI concept for the tablet control

Basic Elements. Figure 2 shows the panel of the OR-lamp. At the top of the screen the status bar is located. In addition to time and date, the patient name, examples for the display of a patient alarm and a device alarm, a navigation field, in which a quick navigation back to a selected workflow is possible, and a status display with battery indicator, WLAN, Bluetooth and more are provided.

The menu bar is located on the left side, where the corresponding buttons can be used to quickly access the control panels of the corresponding category (e.g. the menu item "Surgery" guides the user to the surgical equipment).

The miniature view of the universal footswitch is positioned at the lower left end of the screen below the menu bar. Since the foot switch, developed within the ZiMT project, can be configured to operate different devices and functions, it is important to see the status of the function and pedal mapping. At the same time, the control panel of the universal footswitch can be called up directly by clicking on the miniature view.

In the lower edge of the control panel (shown in Fig. 2) the page-navigation is shown. If a menu item (on the left) is selected, circle areas appear for navigation between the different pages of the menu item. The number of circles is equivalents to the number of pages that can be found. The page navigation is therefore comparable to a submenu. The momentarily selected page is highlighted in a light color. It is possible to navigate between the different pages either by swiping to the next or previous page or by selecting the circle symbolizing the corresponding page. To facilitate navigation, labels, images or icons can be added to the respective circle area. For example, a small icon of the operating table can be found in the circle that allows navigation to the operating table.

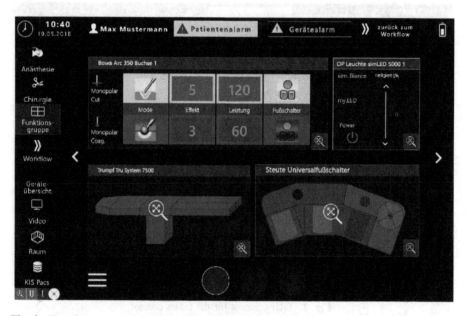

Fig. 3. Function group view (the selected function group at the left bar is illustrated at the centered main layout frame) (Color figure online)

Function Group View. In the function group view (see Fig. 3), smaller views of the devices can be aligned next to each other on a grid by using drag and drop. There is always a predefined minimum and maximum size of the respective device view that can be aligned to the grid in the group view according to the user's needs. If the space that is left becomes too small, the device that is added must be placed on the next page. Depending on the device, controlling it is possible directly at the function group view or the window, shown in the overview, is only used to display a current status and allows the access to the device's control panel more quickly (e.g. the operating table). To guarantee an optimal GUI setup for the surgeons and the anesthetic personnel, information from anesthesia and surgery can be provided in each workstation. In general, the function group overview allows a better overview and faster navigation between the different devices. A navigational shortcut to the different control panels is achieved via zoom-in two-finger gesture, and back to the function group overview via zoom-out two-finger gesture. However, these gestures could not be realized in the prototype yet, therefore the magnifying glass buttons for zooming in and out symbolize them.

Workflow. Regarding the aim of a safe and intuitive GUI, the workflow of the pre-, intra- and postoperative phases in the OR and clinic has to be considered. In addition to a defined workflow by the networked system, a workflow can be individually generated, adapted or saved during and after completing the planning process for the surgery. This simplifies the work process during surgery – especially for routine operations. Beside of the particular data of the workflow, e.g. name of procedure or preselected device configurations, a short description can also be added to the overview, for example to highlight and explain the special features of the saved workflow more detailed.

If one of the predetermined workflows is selected, the corresponding workflow overview appears (see Fig. 4). There is a start and an end box, between which the individual steps of the operation are provided. Furthermore, milestones for the three parts of the Surgical Safety Checklist are provided during the planning process at the between the various steps.

During the composition of workflows, only devices that were already connected to the surgical workstation can be used. If a device contained in the workflow is not connected when the workflow is activated, an error message is issued and the device concerned is "greyed out" in the corresponding workflow steps, i.e. displayed in significantly lower color intensity and cannot be selected.

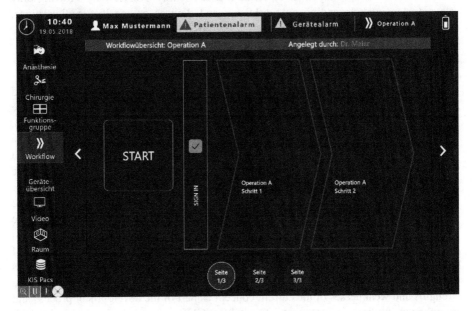

Fig. 4. Workflow overview

If the intended part of the Surgical Safety List has been completed (see Fig. 3), the color of the checkbox icon changes from red to green and the entire box of the finished workflow-step is outlined in green and therefore marked as completed. In addition, the name of the currently shown workflow overview is displayed in the header as well as the user who generated this workflow. As a result the status indicates the current workflow procedure by listing the title, instead of the "back to the current workflow"-button.

The steps of the surgery can be combined individually. For each of them, the relevant devices can be selected and additionally be combined to a function group for that workflow, so that the device selection is reduced to sow only the devices currently necessary for surgery. If required, any devices that may be needed can still be easily accessed in the section for surgical device via menu item "surgery". The user can then return to the workflow with just one click via the "back to the current workflow"-button in the status bar. In addition to the reduced device selection, presets can be saved for each step for a simultaneous change of several settings. If the user switches from one step to the next or select a new step in the workflow overview, the changing settings need to be actively confirmed. For example, if an operating table preset is stored, the hard button must be held until the preset position is reached and the change thus is confirmed.

Auxiliary it is possible to provide emergency settings parallel to critical steps of a surgery. In this way, a parallel workflow step can be created that is never used in the ideal case, but which triggers a reaction within seconds in an emergency, thus precious time can be saved and action can be taken as quickly as possible.

By providing a workflow, the individual planning of an operation is supported and it is possible to switch easily and quickly between different stages during a surgery. The aim of the shown GUI layout is to create a user-friendly overview by showing only relevant elements, depending on workflows and devices or specific configurations, instead of an overloaded 10″ display with any possible information.

2.3   Usability Evaluation

The developed tablet control concept for the integrated surgical workstation is tested regarding effectiveness, efficiency and learnability using the created mock up. The methods to determine these usability criteria regarding various norms (60601-1-6, 62366, 9241-11, 25062) are described in detail in the results section. Aside from the tablet concept, the existing surgical workstation is used as a comparative GUI to perform defined tasks. The user-centered formative usability tests are carried out in the laboratory of the Chair of Medical Engineering at the Helmholtz Institute for Biomedical Engineering at RWTH Aachen University. The test group consists of nine participants (surgeons and nursing staff) from the Uniklinik RWTH Aachen, who are familiar with the working environment of the OR as well as with GUI such as from smartphones. As a first step, the aim is to generate an understanding and orientation of the navigation between the different dialogues, functionalities, pages and control panels of the GUI. The formative tests are conducted with the intention to identify the strengths and weaknesses of the current concept as part of the development process and to enhance further development. The tablet GUI concept is implemented with

Adobe XD [11]. Therefore, the tablet mock up runs on a 5th-generation iPad with 10.1″ display, while the workstation is typically equipped with 22″ touchscreens.

The test framework is divided into four parts, where the subjects must perform three tasks on the GUI and afterwards fill out questionnaires (see Table 2). The walkthroughs are guided and observed by two investigators, who also apply the different evaluation methods.

Table 2. Framework of the usability test

Task number	Subtask	Performance		Topic	Evaluation method
		Tablet	Workstation		
1 /2 (task 1 and 2 are identical)	1 2 3 4	x x x x	x x	OR-light OR-table Patient data Workflow	• Operating steps (both) • Number of errors (both) • Thinking aloud (task 1) • Time (task 2)
3	n = 8	x		Configuration and navigation through GUI	• Thinking aloud • Tracking of Eye/input/process-steps
4	/	x	x	• General question through tasks and GUI • Direct comparison (multiple-choice) • Free text options	Questionnaire (Likert-Scale)

The four subtasks of the first and second task are identical, only differing by the methods. Furthermore, the learnability can be detected rudimentarily by repeating the four subtasks within the second task. In total five subtasks (1.1, 1.2, 2.1, 2.2 and second paragraph of the questionnaire) are intended to enable a direct comparison of the tablet and the workstation.

The third task includes eight subtasks and is only performed on the tablet. Therein the test subjects have to navigate through the GUI, select different functions and also configurate different parameters, e.g. workflow settings or checkmarks of the Surgical Safety Checklist. To track the eye-movement and every input of the user, the tablet concept is performed on a notebook. Thereby, the test subjects' focus and reorganization of alerts and changes, e.g. colors or status, as well as their logic of navigation and search for items can be detected [12, 13].

Subsequent to that, questionnaires are employed. Regarding the main objective (design characteristics, structure, color settings and different features of the GUI), customized questionnaires instead of standardized are developed. However, standardized questionnaires as like SUS or NASA TLX served as blueprints [14, 15].

3 Results

3.1 Effectiveness

To identify the effectiveness of both systems, the amount of errors made during the tasks has been counted [16, 17]. An error was assessed when a task was performed in such a way that it could potentially have led to a hazard. While performing on the tablet, a total of three test subjects made an error at task 1.2. Another participant aborted this subtask, due to fear of releasing a dangerous function. In comparison to that, two errors were made on the workstation (1.1). Furthermore, half of the test subjects were not able to fulfill the task 1.2 completely. The thinking aloud method, where test subjects are instructed to think aloud while performing a given task, confirmed the measured data. Most of the participants hardly found specific features on the tablet, e.g. the Mayfield lock for the OR table (1.2). Likewise, they faced difficulties identifying the correct status of this feature on the workstation. Furthermore, they did not find the required settings for the OR lights (1.1), which led half of them to abort the subtask. In conclusion the effectiveness of both systems is comparable.

Regarding the third task, as all subtasks has been passed, a complete effectiveness was determined. By evaluating the eye- and input-tracking, the user's understanding of the GUI structure and logic was analyzed. The successful identification by the test group of different items at the toolbar and navigation path was investigated.

3.2 Efficiency

The efficiency of both systems has been identified by measuring the time during the test procedure. With the time for completing the second task, a time-based efficiency index can be calculated (see Eq. 1) [2, 17].

$$time - based\ efficiency = \frac{\sum_{j=1}^{R} \sum_{i=1}^{N} \frac{n_{ij}}{t_{ij}}}{NR} \tag{1}$$

$$N = Number\ of\ tasks$$

$$R = number\ of\ test\ subjects$$

$$n_{ij} = results\ of\ task\ and\ user,\ if\ the\ task\ was\ sucsessfully\ completed\ n_{ij}$$
$$= 1,\ if\ not\ n_{ij} = 0$$

t_{ij} = time the test subject j needed to complete task i. If the test subject was,
   not able to complete the task the time is used at which the test subject aborted the task

Comparing the overall average of all test subjects at the second task, both systems showed similar results (see Fig. 5).

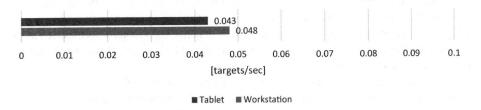

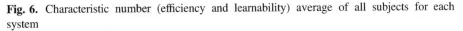

Fig. 5. Time-based efficiency average of all subjects for each system

Another method to evaluate the efficiency is to generate a characteristic number [17]. Therefore, the workarounds of the subjects are compared to the minimum required steps to pass the task. This keyfigure gives an idea if the test subjects could avoid unnecessary steps, where a score of zero presents perfect efficiency, independent from the overall required steps of both systems. The results of the calculation (see Eq. 2) are shown in the next paragraph.

$$characteristic\ number = \frac{number\ of\ steps\ used\ -\ minimal\ number\ of\ steps\ needed\ for\ completion}{minimal\ number\ of\ steps\ needed\ for\ completion} \quad (2)$$

3.3   Learnability

Within the subsequent second task, which is similar to the first, potential learning effects can be identified. Therefore, the characteristic numbers of both tasks for each system has been compared (see Fig. 6). As a conclusion, the average numbers indicate a given learnability of both systems. However, the high tendency to avoid any workaround, especially by operating the workstation, presents a high efficiency of both GUI.

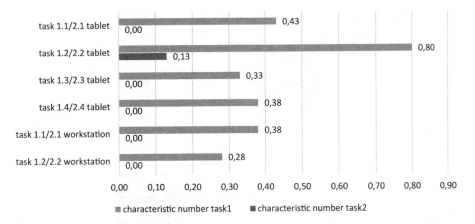

Fig. 6. Characteristic number (efficiency and learnability) average of all subjects for each system

3.4 User Satisfaction

In the questionnaire different panels, control elements, their navigation and their usage are assessed by the test subjects. As a conclusion, the majority of the test subjects valued those items at a neutral to good range, but for some questions the variance was high. Concerning the direct comparison of both systems, the test subjects experienced a more intuitive and easy to use GUI by operating the tablet concept. However, the safety of both was rated similar.

Furthermore, specific design proposals are rated. For example several colors were used in the prototype each for a different device, so the participants should evaluate the assignment of these (see Fig. 7). As a result, none of the subjects was bothered by the color selection and more important, almost half of them found it useful.

■ "i did not notice" [55%]   ▪ "was useful" [45%]   ▪ "was bothersome" [0%]

Fig. 7. Rating of the assignment of colors for different devices (Color figure online)

When asking for the chosen tablet size, most of the test group found 10,1" reasonable (Fig. 8). This could also be confirmed by the thinking aloud method at the previous tasks, as everyone were satisfied with the tablet size. The surgeons of the test group appreciated the possibility, to operate different devices or retrieve information on the tablet by themselves. Therefore, they favored a mobile and configurable device as the tablet over the workstation for their daily usage.

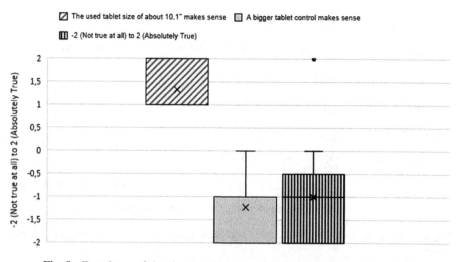

Fig. 8. Experience of the chosen tablet size of 10,1″ on a 5-point Likert Scale

During the test and subsequent discussion, some of the participants mentioned satisfying but also critical thoughts:

- A tablet can be an additional equipment to the workstation, with the advantage to be used by the surgeons, especially when unsterile OR staff (e.g. operation department assistants) are missing and a function needs to adjust immediately.
- Tablet does not require much space, but needs an option to be mounted (e.g. for the nurse table).
- Concerned about a solid sterile solution (must be maintained during the entire operation).
- Tablet should provide more functions for the OR-room and connection to the clinical data system.

4 Discussion

Two different GUI concepts to operate an integrated OR system have been compared, the developed tablet concept against the regular touchscreen control of the surgical workstation. The results show overall t comparable effectiveness and efficiency. Although the majority of the test subjects fulfilled the given tasks, usability gaps are revealed, e.g. locating and selecting the correct functions at times. The user satisfaction (while operating the tablet GUI) is rated partially higher, which is mainly substantiated by the provided configurable function group view. As the subjects were able to handle the repeated tasks more efficient, a possible learnability of both systems is indicated. It should be mentioned, that the whole test procedure took approximately 45 min per test subject. Thus, the learning effects may be caused by short-term memories. Some of the participants state, that the use of GUI in medical context, e.g. the OR, requires an acclimatization period. Beside of the test group size (n = 9), further limitations have to be taken into account. All test subjects work at the same clinic and the demo OR test environment at the laboratory does not represent real clinical OR conditions. Furthermore, the eye- and input-tracking method did not provide a complete dataset of any procedure made by the subjects. Nevertheless, an insight how the participants used the tablet concept has been given.

Regarding common integrated OR solutions, there are only a few concepts of integrated mobile touch-devices. Thus, manufacture-independent approaches should be the future aim. As a conclusion of the evaluation, a further development of the tablet concept as an additional operating device within the central workstation approach should considered.

5 Conclusion

In this paper, the development of a concept for a safe and usable GUI for an OR tablet device is illustrated. The evaluation showed similar effectiveness and efficiency compared to the touch display of the surgical workstation. Hence, the possibility of scaling down the 22″ GUI to a 10″ display has been approved, involving modifications regarding the interface design. A high degree of acceptance towards the tablet concept has been observed, which indicates an advantage of multiple controls for the workstation (central touch unit and mobile devices). In addition, weaknesses of the current concept have been identified as well. Further investigations concerning the understanding and acceptance of the clinical usage of graphical user interfaces by surgeons, anesthetics and other OR personnel are mandatory. Furthermore, evaluations regarding learnability have to be considered.

Another important issue is to provide an optimal procedure to configure the interface and the workflow. The evaluation suggests a systematic processing of the workflow data as well as a requirement analysis on how to implement and visualize the data on the GUI. Furthermore, the subjects favor to configure or adjust special checkmarks of the workflow by themselves.

Acknowledgments. This research work has been funded within the project "ZiMT - Certifiable Integrated Medical Technology and IT Systems based on Open Standards in the Operating Room and Hospital" (State of North-Rhine Westphalia and the European Commission - European Regional Development Fund (EFRE); grant no.: EFRE-0800454).

References

1. Lemke, H.U., Berliner, L.: Systems design and management of the digital operating room (No. S1) (2011). https://link.springer.com/content/pdf/10.1007%2Fs11548-011-0608-y.pdf. Accessed 09 Jan 2019
2. Backhaus, C.: Usability Engineering in der Medizintechnik-Grundlagen Methoden Beispiele. Springer, Heidelberg (2010). https://doi.org/10.1007/978-3-642-00511-4
3. Rockstroh, M., et al.: From SOMDA to application - integration strategies in the OR.NET demonstration sites. Biomed. Eng. Biomed. Tech. (Berl) **63**(1), 69–80 (2018)
4. Blaar, M., et al.: Bottlenecks and needs in human-human and human-machine interaction - a view from and into the neurosurgical OR. J. Biomed. Eng. Biomed. Tech. **61**(2), 135–146 (2015)
5. Janß, A., Benzko, J., Merz, P., Dell'Anna, J., Strake, M., Radermacher, K.: Development of medical device UI-profiles for reliable and safe human-machine-interaction in the integrated operating room of the future. In: Proceedings of the 5th International Conference on Applied Human Factors and Ergonomics, pp. 1855–1860 (2014)
6. Mildner, A., Janß, A., Dell'Anna-Pudlik, J., Merz, P., Leucker, M., Radermacher, K.: Device- and service profiles for integrated or systems based on open standards (Current directions in biomedical engineering No. 1) (2015). https://www.degruyter.com/downloadpdf/j/cdbme.2015.1.issue-1/cdbme-2015-0128/cdbme-2015-0128.pdf. Accessed 10 Jan 2019
7. Rockstroh, M., et al.: OR.NET: Multi-perspective qualitative evaluation of an integrated operating room based on IEEE 11073 SDC (No. 8) (2017). https://link.springer.com/content/pdf/10.1007%2Fs11548-017-1589-2.pdf. Accessed 11 Jan 2019
8. Janß, A., et al.: Extended device profiles and testing procedures for the approval process of integrated medical devices using the IEEE 11073 communication standard. J. Biomed. Eng. Biomed. Tech. **63**(1), 95–103 (2018)

9. Directive 2006/42/EC of the European Parliament and of the Council of 17 May 2006 on machinery, and amending Directive 95/16/EC (recast), The European Parliament and the Council of the Euro- Pean Union (2006)

10. ANSI/AAMI HE75:2009/(R), Human factors engineering – Design of Medical Devices (2013). my.aami.org/aamiresources/previewfiles/he75_1311_preview.pdf. Accessed 10 Jan 2019

11. Adobe XD. https://www.adobe.com/de/products/xd.html. Accessed 12 Jan 2019

12. Majaranta, P., Bulling, A.: Eye tracking and eye-based human–computer interaction. In: Fairclough, S., Gilleade, K. (eds.) Advances in Physiological Computing. HIS, pp. 39–65. Springer, London (2014). https://doi.org/10.1007/978-1-4471-6392-3_3

13. Eyetracking Software. https://www.eyesdecide.com/. Accessed 12 Jan 2019

14. Sarodnick, F.; Brau, H.: Methoden der Usability Evaluation: Wissenschaftliche Grundlagen und praktische Anwendung (2016)

15. Brooke, J.: SUS: ar retrospective. J. Usability Stud. olumen **8**(2), 29–40 (2013)

16. Wiklund, M., Kendler, J., Strochlic, A.: Usability Testing of Medical Devices. CRC Press, Boca Raton (2016)

17. Tullis, T., Albert, B.: Measuring the User Experience: Collecting, Analyzing, and Presenting Usability Metrics. Elsevier (2013)

Developing Real-Time Face Identification Device Composable with Distributed Applications

Kosuke Hirayama[1]([envelope]), Sachio Saiki[1], and Masahide Nakamura[1,2]

[1] Graduate School of System Informatics, Kobe University,
1-1 Rokkodai, Nada, Kobe, Japan
hirayama@ws.cs.kobe-u.ac.jp, sachio@carp.kobe-u.ac.jp,
masa-n@cs.kobe-u.ac.jp
[2] Riken AIP, 1-4-1 Nihon-bashi, Chuo-ku, Tokyo 103-0027, Japan

Abstract. In recent years, many applications which using face identification are developed. However, development load in creation of an
application program using the face identification is high because of the
tight coupling of each functions and lack of sharability of imaging device.
To address this problem, in this research, we propose a new device
named "face identification sensor box" which can realize loose coupling
of function and high sharability. The proposed device uses cognitive API
for face identification and notifies the result to application with Pub-
lish/Subscribe messaging model. Using this architecture, face identification results can be shared among with applications and design of application becomes easier.

Keywords: Face identification · Cognitive API · Pub/Sub · IoT ·
Edge computing

1 Introduction

For the rapid improvement of image processing and AI technology, many applications start to incorporate face identify function, which identifies a person from
images obtained from image sensors, by using computer vision. Face identification
is a method of finding and extracting a face and calculating positions of face parts,
which can be a characteristic part when identifying a person, like eyes or a nose
from extracted faces as feature points, and identifying persons by comparing feature points with that of other people registered in advance. In our life, face identification is often used for user authentication, for example, iPhone X, a smartphone
released by Apple Inc., has Face ID function which uses face identification to unlock
their lock and complete online payment [4]. Furthermore, Universal Studio Japan,
a theme park in Japan, have incorporated face identification in the identity confirmation process which is needed when annual pass holders enter the park to improve
work efficiency related to identity confirmations and prevent abuses [7]. In addition to user authentication, various usages are emerging. For example, developing a

© Springer Nature Switzerland AG 2019
V. G. Duffy (Ed.): HCII 2019, LNCS 11581, pp. 420–432, 2019.
https://doi.org/10.1007/978-3-030-22216-1_31

personal talking robot which is capable of comprehending the target user and generate proper subjects for them by providing face identification on the robot [3], and making a system which can prevent dementia patients' going out and wandering without permission [5], and so on.

Face identify function offers novel added values to applications, but on the other hand, when implementing these function to applications, some problems such as high development load due to low reusability of the function, and lack of sharability of resources such as cameras and devices, often occur. To address these problems, in this research, we propose a new device named *Face identification sensor box* which can offer a face identification service which various applications can use. The sensor boxes keep taking photos by a connected camera and trying to detect faces. Then, when a face is detected, the sensor box does face identification and identifies whose face is this. The face identification process is executed by using external cognitive service. After the face identification completed, the sensor boxes notify the result of the identification to subscribed external applications with Pub/Sub messaging model. By using the Face identification sensor box, multiple applications that need face identification in the same space can use the results at their desired timings by using a single sensor box. Also, since we can delegate face identification process to the sensor box, developers can reduce the working load in designing applications, and they may be able to focus on the essence of the services they want to offer. Moreover, we can reduce dependency within the application and expect improvement of scalability. As an example of a set of service which can be realized by using the Face identification sensor box, for instance, in an office, put the device on an entrance, and identify faces when someone pass there, then create attendance management and entering or leaving room record, after that, unlock the computer of the corresponding user's and give information about their schedule and reminder. In this paper, to realize the Face identification sensor box, we design a functional requirement and confirm the effectiveness of the proposed method by a prototype implementation. We have checked that we can offer face identification service to external applications which require these service by using the prototype.

2 Preliminaries

2.1 Pub/Sub Type Messaging

Pub/Sub (Publish/Subscribe) [9] is one of the messaging models used for asynchronous exchanging messages between multiple devices and services. We show a conceptual diagram of Pub/Sub in Fig. 1. In Pub/Sub messaging model, sender clients creating messages and sending them are called *Publisher*, and recipient clients receiving messages are called *Subscriber*. Messages sent by Publishers are stored in the destinations called Topic. On the other hand, Subscribers register (subscribes) to topics in which necessary messages are sent. When a message stored in a topic, this message is sent (delivered) to Subscribers of this topic. By using this messaging model, both Publishers and Subscribers can send and receive messages with no dependency on each other's state. Basically, Publishers

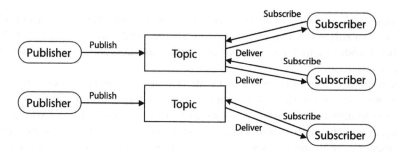

Fig. 1. A conceptual diagram of Pub/Sub

can send messages sequentially regardless of Subscribers' status, and Subscriber can receive only necessary messages. As a result, the performance and scalability of applications can be improved.

2.2 MQTT

MQTT (Message Queue Telemetry Transport) [6] is a protocol to realize asynchronous communication between two endpoints with Pub/Sub messaging model. Since MQTT is an asynchronous communication protocol, MQTT communication can be stable regardless of network reliability, and since MQTT is a lightweight protocol, many IoT (Internet of Things) devices with not high-performance use MQTT.

MQTT defines two entities in the network: Broker and Client. Client corresponds to Publishers and Subscribers in Pub/Sub. Broker works as a Client's mediator and manages the destinations of messages for each of topics. In actual connection, Publishers send messages to Subscribers through Broker. When sending messages, Publishers set a topic of each message. Broker sends the message to Subscribers only which subscribe to the message's topic. In this way, MQTT makes able to Pub/Sub type messaging.

2.3 Cognitive API

With the rapid technological growth of cloud computing, now we can use cloud services to process various tasks which are previously executed on edge sides. Under such a kind of background, various services utilizing artificial intelligence, which becomes explosively popular in recent years, are now getting available as a cloud service. One of the actual cases of cloud service using artificial intelligence is cognitive services. Cognitive services extract useful information from visual/sound/linguistic/knowledge data by analyzing them and enable computers to recognize these types of information. Using cognitive services can realize functions about cognition which are previously difficult for computers. The cognitive service based on images can extract various information from images, and a lot of public clouds provide this kind of services. In general, cloud services are available from outside as APIs. Likewise, users of cognitive services can get various information by sending images to the API. With cognitive services, for example, it is able to analyze human face images and estimate the age, gender, and emotional value of the face. It is also possible to recognize various items such as appliances, furniture, foods, and colors from images. Furthermore, It is able to output tags about the place and weather from the background of an image.

3 Proposed Method

In this chapter, we provide a detailed explanation for the face identification device mentioned in Sect. 1, which various applications can use.

3.1 Problems with Existing Face Identification Application

Face identification function offers novel added values to applications. Currently, many companies such as NEC [8] and Panasonic [2] are offering face identification solutions. However, when implementing these function to applications, developers have to implement services, photo taking and face identification functions for each application. Therefore, each function has tight coupling with applications, and as a result, the reusability of these function may deteriorate. For example, we cannot reuse photo taking and face identification functions although these are a general function. In addition, Occupying one camera by one application makes another problem. In the case where multiple face identification functions required within the same space, although the object person is in the same place, many cameras will be required.

3.2 Face Identification Sensor Box

Based on the problems of existing applications, in this research, we propose Face identification sensor box. The Face identification sensor box is a device to provide some functions to share cameras and face identification services. The sensor box has to be able to provide the same face identification function to multiple applications. In addition, considering when there are multiple sensor boxes, it is required that we can configure the face identification and add or delete users for each device all at once. Then, we make the sensor boxes delegate face identification processes to an outside service, and execute and manage the face identification function in there, to reduce the load of managing sensor boxes. The sensor box also has to be able to deal with many pollings at the same timing, assuming the sensor box is called by multiple applications. And in order to improve the scalability, the sensor box should be able to continue to notify the results of identification. Then, we adopt a connection framework which realizes asynchronous communication.

  We show a conceptual diagram of the whole architecture of the sensor box in Fig. 2. "Face identification process" is the component which represents APIs for face identification process with the sensor box, such as Pub/Sub connection

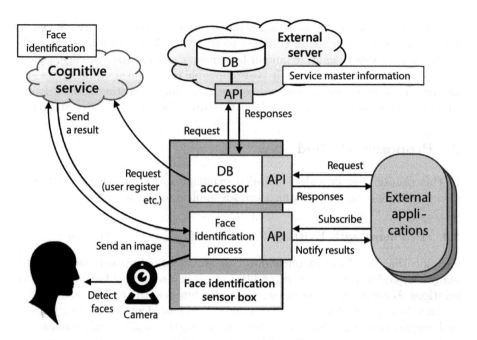

Fig. 2. A conceptual diagram of the whole architecture

(described later) or using a cognitive service. "External server" shown on the sensor box is for building the database which uniquely stores user information and so on separately from the cognitive service. "DB accessor" is used for exchanging data between the database on the external server and external applications.

3.3 Functional Requirement

The face identification with the sensor box has these function:

Service Exposure with Pub/Sub. When applications need face identification function, applications have to register itself to the sensor box. The sensor box stores subscribed applications. After the face identification process, when the sensor box obtains the result, the sensor box notifies the result to all subscribed applications. After that, applications can process their tasks with received result. We adopt Pub/Sub in the connection between the sensor box and applications and make it asynchronous.

In addition to the function to subscribe, we equip the sensor box with a function to unsubscribe for when applications no longer need the results.

Photo Taking and Face Detection at Fixed Intervals. The sensor box keeps getting images from the connected camera. Before the face identification, as a preparation, the sensor box executes face detection locally because it is inefficient to execute face identification for all obtained images. In the face detection process, *whether an image contains a face is only judged.* Thereby, the sensor box can execute face identification only for images containing a face.

Face Identification with Cognitive API. The sensor box executes face identification with face images obtained on the previous section. We use a cognitive API for the face identification to delegate face identification processes to the outside. When the face identification process finished, the sensor box receives the result.

By the way, to execute face identification with cognitive API, we have to register the name and face images of object people and train the machine learning model used for identification beforehand. We can do these operations by accessing endpoints of cognitive API, but, to make applications can do it easily, we have to create wrapper APIs on the sensor box. Also, when we add a new user on cognitive API, some problem may occur on the API side, for example, the API does not accept non-latin characters for user's name, or the API cannot register a detailed profile of users such as a birthday. Therefore, we build a database with a unique data format on an external server. When we add a new user of identification, the sensor box sends only the necessary information to the cognitive API and registers to the API, and, at the same time, sends full information to the external server's database and make it stored also in there. Furthermore, in order to enable applications to use the information stored in the database, we have to prepare ways to refer the database via the sensor box as APIs. To prepare such necessities, we make DB accessor which is a group of APIs to use the database. In addition to user information, we put various setting information such as API key and endpoint to use a cognitive API in the external server and make the external server provide this information as a service master, to enhance the convenience when accessing from each sensor box. All user information is stored in Face API and the external server. As a result, the sensor box itself does not store any user information.

The above is the functions necessary for the Face identification sensor box.

4   Implementing the Prototype

4.1   Implementation

Based on the proposed method, we implement a prototype of the Face identification sensor box.

We use the following technologies.

- Development languages: Python 3.5, HTML5, JavaScript, PHP 5.3
- Database: MySQL 5.7

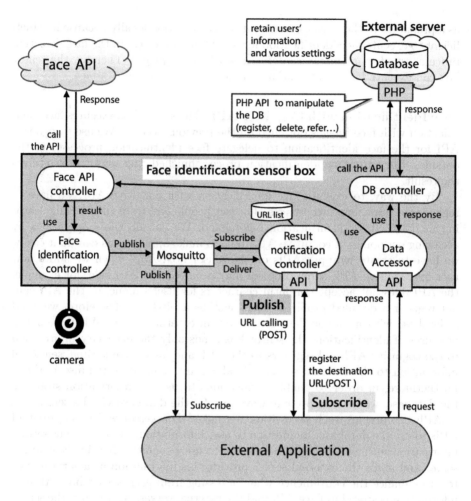

Fig. 3. The overall implementation

- Libraries: Paho MQTT[1], Flask[2], Flask-SocketIO[3], OpenCV[4]
- MQTT broker: Mosquitto[5]
- Cognitive API: Microsoft Face API [1]

Paho MQTT, Mosquitto is an open source implementation of MQTT protocol. Paho MQTT serves as Publisher and Subscriber, and Mosquitto serves as Broker. Flask is one of the web application frameworks. We use Flask to make each

[1] https://www.eclipse.org/paho/.

[2] http://flask.pocoo.org/.

[3] https://flask-socketio.readthedocs.io/en/latest/.

[4] https://opencv.org/.

[5] https://mosquitto.org/.

function WebAPIs. Flask-SocketIO is a library which enables WebSocket connection with Socket.IO on Flask applications. We use Flask-SocketIO to connect with a browser. We use Raspberry Pi 3[6] (OS : Raspbian 9.4), which is a small single board computer, as the prototype edge device.

4.2 Notification Flow of Identification Results

For the prototype, we make the part which notifies results of face identification Pub side, and we make external applications Sub side, then Pub/Sub communication is performed between both side. Inside of the sensor box, the Face identification controller notifies the results to Mosquitto, and Mosquitto assigns them to the specific topic, and the Result notification controller which subscribes this topic receives the results of face identification asynchronously. The Result notification controller works as Publisher to external applications and notifies the identification results to URLs of subscribed external applications. By these process, the Result notification controller works as Broker simulatively.

Actually, the Face identification sensor box also supports Pub/Sub by using MQTT. Mosquitto can be Publisher and send the identification results to external applications. However, we do not assume that MQTT used from applications directly for this time, and we do not use this function.

4.3 Preparation

For the implementation of the prototype, as cognitive API, we use Microsoft Face API (hereinafter called "Face API") which is one of the services of Microsoft Azure. Face API can detect faces, identify faces, analyze emotions, and so on. We can use these functions easily via the cloud. To use face identification function of Face API, firstly we have to make a group (=PersonGroup) and add users (=Person) who are object people of identification. On the registration, an ID (=personId) used by Face API is assigned to each user. By selecting the Person registered, uploading one's face images, training of the learning model of the PersonGroup enables face identification.

We can complete these operations by sending requests including various parameters to the correspondent Face API endpoints. However, to simplify this, we make the Face API controller which is a set of utilities including various operations to Face API.

And we build a database to store users' information and various setting values on an external MySQL server, and we make PHP APIs on the server so that the sensor box can access the database. The database keeps information of users who use face identification in the form [uId, personId, name, reading, birthday, gender, nickname, description]. uId is the unique Id used in the Face identification sensor box, and personId is the Id used in Face API. We make applications which subscribe to the sensor box to use uId mainly. Regarding the

---

use of the database, to simplify it, we make the DB controller which is a set of utilities to get, write, modify, delete, search data and convert id mutually.

Furthermore, with the Face API controller and the DB controller, we implement the Data accessor as a WebAPI to use these controllers and use functions to register and delete users and so on from external applications. In addition to user registration and deletion, the Data accessor has some functions such as to convert between uId and personId, and to confirm and acquire the existence of user information corresponding to each Id, and applications can get information from the database as needed. The reason why we avoid making each controller API directly is that, when registering new entries, after registering to Face API, we have to store it also in the database, but by gathering these operations together with the controllers, we can register necessary information collectively by POST. As a result, we can simplify the implementation of applications. Also, we can prevent inconsistency between registered information of Face API and of the database.

We show the overall implementation of face identification sensor box described above in Fig. 3.

4.4   Details About the Operation

In this section, we explain the functions of the prototype while associating functional requirements mentioned in Sect. 3. Note that we use URL call for Pub/Sub connection of the prototype.

Service Exposure with Pub/Sub. Applications which need to use the Face identification sensor box have to register their destination URL to the endpoint of the Result notification controller. To complete this operation, applications have to connect to the endpoint such as (DeviceURL):(PORT):/reg_app_url with POST request. After the registration, when face identification is executed, the sensor box notifies the result to all registered URLs. Applications can cancel their registration in the same way at any time.

Photo Taking at Fixed Intervals and Face Detection. The sensor boxes keep getting images by a connected camera and detecting a face. For face detection, we use OpenCV which is an image processing library and use Haar Cascade [10] classifier with preliminarily prepared classifier file. When a face is detected in the image, the face identification process starts.

In the face detection, the sensor box does not execute face identification immediately when a face is detected. Instead, we introduce Face counter to stable face identification. We show the role and behavior of Face counter in Fig. 4. The Face counter increases when a face is detected in the image, and the sensor box considers the face detection completed only after Face counter exceeds a certain threshold. Once the face is detected, the Face counter decreases while the face detection does not succeed, and until the value of Face counter becomes 0, the sensor box does not detect the next face. With the Face counter,

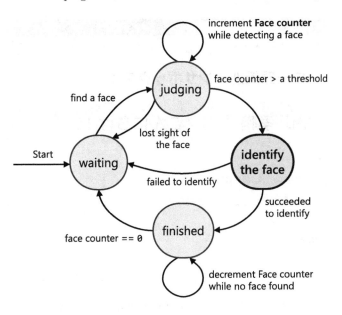

Fig. 4. The role and behavior of Face counter

the sensor box can get face images when users keep still in front of the camera, and the face identification becomes stable. Besides, since Face API (described later) has restrictions on the number and interval of calls, it is impossible to execute massive face identification in a short time, but by using the Face counter, we can reduce the number of face identifications and therefore we can deal with this problem.

Face Identification with Cognitive API. The Face identification controller sends images which are obtained by the face detection to the Face API controller. The Face API controller executes some processes to use Face API, and receive the personId of the person with the highest confidence.

Before identify faces using Face API, we have to register users. We register users through the Data accessor. The Data accessor has an endpoint for user registration in form like (DeviceURL):(PORT):/register and by sending necessary information there, we can register new users. The Data accessor also has endpoints to add and delete face images, and these functions are callable by external accesses. The sensor box only notifies uId to applications as a result of the face identification, and does not notify detailed information such as name. Therefore, when applications need detailed information about users, applications have to use the Data accessor to obtain these information using uId as the key. If Face API received a face image of a not registered person and failed to identify, the sensor box notifies "unknown" as a result.

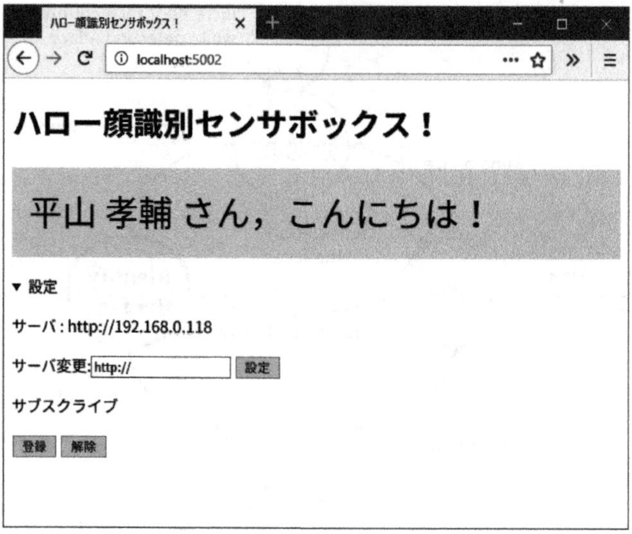

Fig. 5. A screenshot of the sample program

4.5   A Sample Application and Testing

For samples using functions of the prototype of the Face identification sensor box, we made two sample web applications for clients, one is for user registration, and the other is to receive the result of face identification and display the name of the user. These applications access to functions of the sensor box from the outside. We tested whether the sensor box works properly by using these applications.

Firstly, we use the user registration application and register some users on a browser. This application sends information which filled in a certain form to the Data accessor. The Data accessor stores the information to the database, and registers it to Face API. Then, Face API issues personId. personId is represented in hexadecimal form like

```
c0a094ab-e8b0-4368-...
```

After that, a user takes some face photos on the browser, then, this application sends the photos to Face API through the Data accessor.

Next, we start the results receiver application and send its URL to the Result notification controller to subscribe the sensor box. If the subscribe process succeeds, the sensor box returns 200 HTTP status code.

After the above preparations are completed, the user turns one's face to the camera connected to the sensor box, then the sensor box executes face identification. When the face identification completed, Face API returns personId as result. The sensor box converts the personId to uId and sends it to subscribed URLs. The result receiver application receives the result and sends it to the Data accessor to get various information from uId. The Data accessor has an

API which returns various information of a user registered in JSON format by using uId as a key. By sending a uId to URL /get_data_by_uid by POST, the Data accessor returns the JSON including information of the user registered in advance. The JSON is like

```
{'description':None, 'personId':'c0a094ab-e8b0-...',
'gender':'m', 'uId':'hirako', 'birthday':'1996-01-24',
'nickname':None, 'name':'平山 孝輔',
'reading':'ヒラヤマ コウスケ'}
```

Finally, this application extracts the 'name' attribute from the JSON and displays (It means "Hello, Kosuke Hirayama !" in Japanese.)

```
平山 孝輔 さん, こんにちは！
```

We show the screenshot of this application in Fig. 5.

5   Conclusion

In this paper, we proposed the Face identification sensor box which can realize development efficiency, effective use of resources and so on in developing applications which has face identification function. In the proposed method, by using the cognitive API of cloud service for face identification, we can easily realize high-quality face identification function and manage it. Also, by incorporating Pub/Sub for communication with applications, the sensor box can asynchronously send the identification results and secure scalability capable of bearing uses from many applications. The future tasks are not only to incorporate this system we implemented into a large scale external application and evaluate its performance, but also to expand the sensor box to cognitive sensor box which can realize various cognitive service other than face identification. In addition, considering the security risk, we will have to put an authentication process before accessing functions of the sensor box from outside, and, to prevent abuses in face identification, we will also have to make the method by which the sensor box can combine authentication methods other than face identification, such as password, with user authentication process.

Acknowledgments. This research was partially supported by the Japan Ministry of Education, Science, Sports, and Culture [Grant-in-Aid for Scientific Research (B) (16H02908, 18H03242, 18H03342), Grant-in-Aid for Scientific Research (A) (17H00731)], and Tateishi Science and Technology Foundation (C) (No.2177004).

References

1. Face API - Facial recognition software – Microsoft Azure. https://azure.microsoft.com/en-us/services/cognitive-services/face/
2. Faceproface recognitionpanasonic security system. https://security.panasonic.com/Face_Recognition/
3. Facial recognition: coming to a gadget near you. https://techxplore.com/news/2019-01-facial-recognition-gadget.html
4. iphone xr - face id - apple. https://www.apple.com/iphone-xr/face-id/
5. A measure to use face identification system to prevent going out from medical/care facilities without permission – face identification based wandering prevention system for dementia patients [lykaon]. https://www.facial-lykaon.com/topics/wandering_prevention.php (in Japanese)
6. MQTT. http://mqtt.org/
7. New biometric identification tools used in theme parks — NEC. https://www.nec.com/en/global/about/mitatv/03/2.html
8. Public safety: Products & solutions — NEC. https://www.nec.com/en/global/solutions/safety/Technology/FaceRecognition/index.html
9. Birman, K., Joseph, T.: Exploiting virtual synchrony in distributed systems. SIGOPS Oper. Syst. Rev. **21**(5), 123–138 (1987)
10. Viola, P., Jones, M.: Rapid object detection using a boosted cascade of simple features. In: Proceedings of the 2001 IEEE Computer Society Conference on Computer Vision and Pattern Recognition, CVPR 2001, vol. 1, p. I, December 2001

An Integrated Approach of Multiple Correspondences Analysis (MCA) and Fuzzy AHP Method for Occupational Health and Safety Performance Evaluation in the Land Cargo Transportation

Genett Jimenez-Delgado[1(✉)], Nidia Balmaceda-Castro[2],
Hugo Hernández-Palma[3], Emiro de la Hoz-Franco[4],
Jesus García-Guiliany[5], and Jairo Martinez-Ventura[6]

[1] Department of Engineering in Industrial Processes, Engineering Faculty,
Institución Universitaria ITSA, Soledad, Atlántico, Colombia
gjimenez@itsa.edu.co
[2] Department of Basic Sciences,
Institución Universitaria ITSA, Soledad, Colombia
nebalmaceda@itsa.edu.co
[3] Faculty of Economic Sciences,
Corporación Universitaria Reformada CUR, Barranquilla, Colombia
hugo.hp83@yahoo.com
[4] Department of Electronic and Computer Science,
Universidad de la Costa CUC, Barranquilla, Atlántico, Colombia
edelahoz@cuc.edu.co
[5] Faculty of Administration and Business,
Universidad Simón Bolívar, Barranquilla, Colombia
jesus.garcia@unisimonbolivar.edu.co
[6] Faculty of Engineering, Corporación Universitaria Latinoamericana CUL,
Barranquilla, Colombia
jairoluis2007@gmail.com

Abstract. Land cargo transportation is one of the components of the logistics chain with high impact on economic and social development worldwide. However, problems such as top logistics costs, deficiencies in transportation infrastructure and the failure to adopt good operating practices in aspects such as quality, environment, and occupational safety and health affect the ability of companies to comply with the agreements, requirements, and regulations of the clients and other interested parties. One of the most relevant problems for the sector is associated with the high accident rates that make this medium less advantageous compared to other means of transport with impact on operational costs, on logistics indicators, on compliance with legal regulations and customer satisfaction. However, although there are legal standards and management standards in occupational safety and health, evaluating performance can become a difficult and subjective process, due to the complexity of the land cargo transportation and the different interest groups involved. Besides, there is little information in the literature that provides solutions for the industry. Therefore,

V. G. Duffy (Ed.): HCII 2019, LNCS 11581, pp. 433–457, 2019.
https://doi.org/10.1007/978-3-030-22216-1_32

this document presents an integrated approach between multi-criterion decision making models (MCDM) and the Multiple Correspondences Analysis (MCA) to facilitate the evaluation and improvement of occupational health and safety performance, with a logical process, objective, robust and using both qualitative and quantitative techniques, with real application in the land cargo transportation sector. First, the multivariate method of Multiple Correspondences Analysis (MCA) was used for the evaluation of a sample of companies in the industry, considering the factors and sub-factors identified in the first stage and performing correlational analyzes among the variables. Subsequently, a multicriteria decision-making model was designed to determine the factors and sub-factors that affect occupational health and safety performance through the technique of the Fuzzy Analytic Hierarchy Process (FAHP). Finally, improvement strategies are proposed based on the approaches suggested in this document.

Keywords: Fuzzy Analytical Hierarchy Process · Fuzzy AHP ·
Multicriteria decision making · MCMD · Factorial analysis ·
Multiple Correspondence Analysis (MCA) · Occupational health and safety ·
ISO 45001 · Land cargo transportation · Cargo logistics ·
Performance evaluation

1   Introduction

Land cargo transportation represents one of the links in the logistics chain of great importance at the regional, national and global levels, due to its impact not only at an economic level but a social level [1]. In this sense, statistics show that the road freight transport sector represents 90% of the movements of goods in countries such as Argentina, Spain, Greece, South Korea, Bulgaria, Canada, China, Colombia, Denmark, Finland, France, Italy. In other countries such as the United Kingdom, the Czech Republic, and South Africa, land transport concentrates between 75% and 80% of traffic. Besides, in Germany, Austria, Belgium, Brazil, Croatia, the United States, India, Japan, the Netherlands, it is estimated that more than 50% of the modal distribution is by land [2].

However, this sector shows operational deficiencies that affect aspects such as productivity, competitiveness, and safety compared to other transport services. In this regard, Dinero Magazine [3], highlights the problems of the land transport sector, which affect its capacity to adapt to new challenges such as globalization, customer demands, legal regulations, and society. Among the problems identified is the deficiency in the implementation of management standards to continuously improve their performance and comply with current regulations in areas such as quality, safe trade, environment, safety, and occupational health. In this sense, this last aspect of safety and health at work is of great importance due to the complexity of the land cargo transportation and the surveillance and control by official bodies, customers and others involved in the logistics chain.

According to the research of International Labor Organization [2], the land transport sector presents different safety and occupational health problems, such as a high risk of traffic accidents, psychosocial factors associated with long working hours, stress, drugs, and alcohol. Concerning the conditions of the vehicle conditions, external factors that include the state of the roads, physical hazards, violence, dangerous work situations and internal factors related to the methods of enlistment and location of cargo, traffic infractions, among others, are problems that should be considered. These health and safety risks at work can directly affect other users of roads, traffic and public safety in general, as well as operating costs for companies derived from accidents at work and occupational diseases. Also, an increase in the lead time and inventory volume, which generate delays, operational inefficiencies, economic losses, loss of reputation and decrease in competitiveness, leading to a negative impact on the economic and social development of a country [4].

These aspects justify the carrying out of research that contributes to the development and implementation of management methodologies, focused on the prevention of accidents and occupational diseases in the land cargo transportation. In this regard, we found different investigations carried out for the transport sector in general, oriented towards the analysis of root causes for accidents and risk management. Besides, in the literature review, we found several studies with the application of the Multicriteria Decision Methods (MCDM) and Multiple Correspondence Analysis (MCA). However, the development of studies in the use of hybrid methodologies based on MCDM and MCA for Occupational Health and Safety Performance Evaluation in Land Cargo Transportation sector is still minimal and with scarce information.

In this work, we propose an integrated methodology based on the application of the Multicriteria Decision Methods based on Multiple Correspondences Analysis (MCA) approach and Fuzzy Analytic Hierarchy Process (FAHP) to evaluate the Occupational Health and Safety performance in the land cargo transportation sector, analyzing the case study of Colombia, under a quantitative methodological, of descriptive and correlational scope.

The design of the methodology is based on the approach of the ISO 45001 standard and the PDCA (Plan-Do-Check-Act) methodology, through the design of a performance evaluation model and its application in 25 companies in the sector.

First, the Multiple Correspondence Analysis (MCA) was used, after validation of the reliability and significance of the evaluation instrument, to classify the companies in differentiated groups considering their performance in occupational health and safety. Likewise, to correlate the influence of critical variables such as seniority, size, number of employees with the level of performance, with which improvement strategies are defined by companies in the sector analyzed. Then, the Fuzzy Analytic Hierarchy Process (FAHP) was applied to reconcile human subjectivity and the multiple criteria in the evaluation process. In this regard, FAHP is used to estimate the global and local weights of criteria and sub-criteria under uncertainty in the ponderation.

The results show that the methodology allows not only to evaluate the performance of companies through significant key variables, but also critical variables can be identified that affect the management, in this case, the implementation and improvement for occupational safety and health security, which is reflected quantitatively and through 4 groups of companies according to their performance. Likewise, the findings show that aspects such as size, seniority, and the national or international scope of the companies, affect the level of performance in Occupational safety and health. Considering the previous point, this integrated methodology facilitates the decision-making process Managers for the improvement in the management of health and safety at work, through the use and interaction of computational tools and statistics.

2 Approaches of MCDM and Multivariate Methods for Occupational Health and Safety Performance Evaluation: A Brief Literature Review

In spite of the advances of the last years, the land cargo transportation, presents high accident rates, in comparison with other modalities of transport like the rail transport, maritime transport, and air transport at world-wide level. In Colombia, accident statistics exceed both the number of accidents and the number of deaths recorded in other transport systems [5]. The leading causes of accidents and occupational diseases are related to insecure acts by drivers, faults in vehicles and transportation systems, poor road conditions, high workloads and stress [2], affecting significantly, the quality-life of workers, the competitiveness of transportation sector and, consequently, the value chain of production and services of many organizations.

In this regard, the identification of risks and dangers, the control measures at the source, the environment, and the worker, procedures and protocols, education and awareness, among other aspects, are vital to generate a culture of prevention of accidents and occupational diseases. In this sense, the management of occupational safety and health, allows an employer or independent undertakings create an optimal relationship between the economy and security while respecting the employer's responsibility for protection [6].

In recent years, the use of different regulations and standards to support the implementation of occupational health and safety management has become increasingly common due to the demands of the government, customers and other stakeholders in the chain of logistics value. At an international level, standards such as the OHSAS 18001, and more recently, the ISO 45001 standard, help organizations improve their safety and health performance at work to prevent injuries and deterioration of workers' health and to provide places of safe and healthy work [7].

In Colombia, these standards have facilitated the creation of legal regulations applicable to the cargo transport sector such as the Decree No 1072 of 2015. This normativity establishes and regulates the Occupational Health and Safety Management for companies. In the same way, the Resolution 1565 of 2014 (it contains the guidelines for the implementation of the Strategic Plan of Road Safety to reduce the accident rate), and Resolution No 0302 of 2019 (this legislation lays down the rules for the compliance of minimum standards in Occupational Health and Safety in organizations).

All such considerations have led to the development of different studies that contribute to the development and implementation of management methodologies, focused on the prevention of accidents and occupational diseases in the transport sector. In this regard, we found different research oriented towards the analysis of risk management in maritime ports using Fuzzy techniques [8], analysis of transport risk by checking probabilistic models [9], develop approach of root causes for accidents in the maritime industry [10], and use of techniques to increased safety and operability of inland terminals for containers with dangerous goods [11].

In the land cargo transportation, the focus of the identified studies is aimed determining the safety risks management in the road transport [6, 12–14], to analyze the elements that affect the successful implementation of occupational health and safety management. Likewise, there are other objectives such as identifying the literature review that support the safety management for heavy vehicle transport [15], recognizing the safety and health perceptions in work-related transport activities in industries [16], and evaluate the initial conditions for implementation of the Integrated Management System based on quality, health and safety [1]. All these studies highlight the need to continually identify and evaluate performance and propose improvement strategies to reduce accidents and work-related illnesses in the land transport sector, so the evaluation of overall performance is shown as an alternative to investigate with greater depth.

Regarding the object of this research, we found in the literature review evidence of studies oriented to apply the Multicriteria Decision Methods (MCDM) in occupational health and safety management (OHS). In this regard, one of the most recent studies conducts a critical state-of-the-art review of OHS risk assessment studies using MCDM-based approaches, includes fuzzy versions of MCDM approaches applied to OHS risk assessment [17]. The results of this study, which analyzed a total of 80 papers cited in high-impact journals, demonstrated the growing trend in the use of MCDM in the evaluation of risks, especially in the use of FAHP-based approaches, with application mainly in the manufacturing sector. On the other hand, the potential to continue developing methods of evaluation in occupational health and safety based on MCDM in an integrated way with different approaches was also identified.

On the other hand, we review the literature in the use of Multivariate Correspondence Analysis in Occupational Health and Safety. In this sense, we found several works with the application of the MCA method in the identification of areas of intervention for public safety policies using multiple correspondence analysis [18], use of multiple correspondence analysis and hierarchical clustering to identify incident typologies about the biofuel industry [19]. We also found other studies about pattern extraction for high-risk accidents in the construction industry: a data-mining approach [20], and decision support system for safety improvement using multiple correspondence analysis, t-SNE algorithm and K-means clustering [21].

However, the use of the integrated approaches of Multiple Correspondences Analysis (MCA) and MCDM such as Fuzzy AHP does not have an extended application, especially in the occupational health and safety performance evaluation in the land cargo transportation. Therefore, this research contributes to the scientific literature and provides a hybrid methodology for overall performance evaluation in occupational health and safety management and provides to managers procedures and techniques to generate a culture of prevention and healthy environments, through strategic alignment, driving the behavior and performance of people towards the achievement of the strategic objectives of land cargo transportation [22].

3 Proposed Methodology

The proposed approach aims to evaluate the overall performance in occupational health and safety management in the land cargo transportation sector by the integration of the Multiple Correspondence Analysis (MCA) and the Fuzzy Analytic Hierarchy Process (FAHP). In this regard, the methodology is comprised of four phases (refer to Fig. 1):

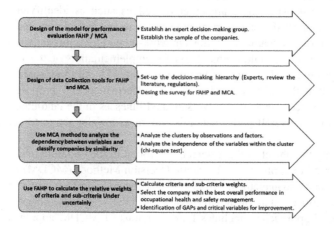

Fig. 1. Methodological approach for evaluating the overall performance in occupational health and safety management in the land cargo transportation

- **Phase 1 (Design of the model for performance evaluation FAHP/MCA):** A decision-making group is chosen based on their experience in occupational health and safety. The experts will be invited to be part of the decision-making process through Fuzzy Analytical Hierarchy Process (FAHP) technique. Subsequently, a sample of companies of the land cargo transportation was selected for the application of the MCA method.
- **Phase 2 (Design of data collection tools for FAHP and MCA):** In this step, the criteria and sub-criteria are established to set up a decision hierarchy considering the personal opinion of the expert decision-makers, the literature review and regulations in occupational health and safety management [23]. Then, the surveys for the application of the FAHP and MCA methods were designed.
- **Phase 3 (MCA application):** In this step, the Multivariate Correspondence Analysis (MCA) method was implemented to analyze from a graphical point of view the dependency and independence relationships of a set of categorical variables and the classification of observations or individuals in clusters considering the similarity in their responses for each variable (described in Sect. 3.2). For this purpose, we designed a survey considering the personal opinion of the expert decision-makers, literature review and regulations. Then, collecting of data set of 25 companies and finally, applied the MCA method using R 3.5.0 software.
- **Phase 4 (FAHP application):** FAHP is used to estimate the global and local weights of criteria and sub-criteria under uncertainty in the ponderation. In this

phase, the experts were invited to perform pairwise comparisons, which are subsequently processed following the FAHP method, as detailed in Sect. 3.1. Also, in this phase, GAPs and critical variables were identified with the goal of improving the overall performance in the evaluation of occupational health and safety management [1, 24, 25].

3.1 Fuzzy Analytic Hierarchy Process (FAHP)

Fuzzy AHP is an extension of Analytic Hierarchy Process (AHP) proposed by Thomas L. Saaty as an integrated methodology between the AHP and Fuzzy Logic with the aim of improving decision-making process since inability of AHP to deal with the imprecision and uncertainty of human judgments and with multiple criteria in the pair-wise comparison process [26, 27]. In this regard, according to Ortiz-Barrios et al. [28], the fuzzy logic theory was introduced due to its capability of representing imprecise data. Fuzzy AHP uses a range of value to incorporate the decision maker's uncertainty [29, 30].

In FAHP, the paired comparisons are represented in a matrix using fuzzy triangular numbers [31–33] as described below (Refer to Table 1). Considering the findings from the literature review, a reduced AHP scale has been adopted by the decision makers when making comparisons [28].

Table 1. Linguistic terms and their fuzzy triangular numbers

Reduced AHP scale	Definition	Fuzzy triangular number
1	Equally important	[1, 1, 1]
3	More important	[2, 3, 4]
5	Much more important	[4, 5, 6]
1/3	Less important	[1/4, 1/3, 1/2]
1/5	Much less important	[1/6, 1/5, 1/4]

The steps of the FAHP algorithm as follows:

- Step 1: Perform pairwise comparisons between criteria/sub-criteria by using the linguistic terms and the corresponding fuzzy triangular numbers established in Table 1. With this data, a fuzzy judgment matrix $\tilde{A}^k (a_{ij})$ is obtained as described below in Eq. 1:

$$\tilde{A}^k = \begin{bmatrix} \tilde{d}_{11}^k & \tilde{d}_{12}^k & \cdots & \tilde{d}_{1n}^k \\ \tilde{d}_{21}^k & \tilde{d}_{22}^k & \cdots & \tilde{d}_{2n}^k \\ \cdots & \cdots & \cdots & \cdots \\ \tilde{d}_{n1}^k & \tilde{d}_{n2}^k & \cdots & \tilde{d}_{nn}^k \end{bmatrix} \tag{1}$$

$\tilde{d}_{ij}^k$ indicates the *kth* expert's preference of *ith* criterion over *jth* criterion via fuzzy triangular numbers.

- Step 2: In this phase, GAPs and critical variables were identified, and improvement strategies were defined with the goal of improving the overall performance in the evaluation of occupational health and safety management.
- Step 3: In the case of a focus group, the judgments are averaged according to Eq. 2, where K represents the number of experts involved in the decision-making process. Then, the fuzzy judgment matrix is updated as shown in Eq. 3.

$$\tilde{d}_{ij} = \frac{\sum_{k=1}^{K} \tilde{d}_{ij}^{k}}{K} \tag{2}$$

$$\tilde{A} = \begin{bmatrix} \widetilde{d_{11}} & \cdots & \widetilde{d_{1n}} \\ \vdots & \ddots & \vdots \\ \widetilde{d_{n1}} & \cdots & \widetilde{d_{nn}} \end{bmatrix} \tag{3}$$

- Step 4: Calculate the geometric mean of fuzzy judgment values of each factor by using Eq. 4. Here, $\tilde{r}_i$ denotes triangular numbers.

$$\tilde{r}_i = \left(\prod_{j=1}^{n} \tilde{d}_{ij} \right)^{1/n}, \ i = 1, 2, \ldots, n \tag{4}$$

- Step 5: Determine the fuzzy weights of each factor $(\tilde{w}_i)$ by applying Eq. 5.

$$\tilde{w}_i = \tilde{r}_i \otimes (\tilde{r}_1 \oplus \tilde{r}_2 \oplus \ldots \oplus \tilde{r}_n)^{-1} = (lw_i, mw_i, uw_i) \tag{5}$$

- Step 6: Defuzzify $(\tilde{w}_i)$ by performing the Centre of Area method [34] via using Eq. 6. M_i is a non-fuzzy number. Then, normalize M_i via applying Eq. 7.

$$M_i = \frac{lw_i + mw_i + uw_i}{3} \tag{6}$$

$$N_i = \frac{M_i}{\sum_{i=1}^{n} M_i} \tag{7}$$

3.2   Multivariate Correspondence Analysis (MCA)

The Multiple Correspondence Analysis (MCA) is a statistical technique used in the analysis of multivariate exploratory data. According to Rueda and Balmaceda [35], its objective is to reduce the dimension of the space of the observed characteristics in a small number of variables related to the set of variables and to represent in a factorial plane the maximum information contained in a Table of Burt (TB). This process is done to obtain typologies of the rows or typologies of the columns that are related to each other [35], facilitating the identification of groups of observations or groupings considering the correspondence in their responses and the variables that affect their classification. From there the correspondence term is justified, that is, the technique that seeks that the rows or columns correspond in information. The MCA is based on the direct results of matrix theory. It mainly uses the decomposition of a matrix in singular values.

In this regard, according to [21], "Multiple Correspondence Analysis. MCA uses a data matrix as its input to develop point clouds where data are clustered by similarity. Let N be the number of individual records (i.e. row) and Q be the number of categorical variables (i.e. column) and J_q be the number of categories for q^{th} categorical variable, then the total categories for all variables are, $J = \sum_{q=1}^{Q} J_q$ 'N multiplied by J' forms the indicator matrix (A) with elements aij such that aij $= 1$ if $= i^{th}$ observation contains the category, otherwise aij $= 0$". The mathematical procedure of MCA is given as follows [21].

- Step 1: The indicator matrix is transformed to matrix Z such that each element z_{ij} of Z is derived as $z_{ij} = \frac{a_{ij}}{W}$ where W is the total count $W = \sum_{i=1}^{N} \sum_{j=1}^{J} a_{ij}$. Z is also known as the correspondence matrix.
- Step 2: Row and column masses of Z, denoted by r_i and c_j respectively, are obtained by summing up the row and column point profiles as described below in Eqs. 8 and 9:

$$r_i = \sum_{j=1}^{J} z_{ij} \tag{8}$$

$$c_j = \sum_{i=1}^{N} z_{ij} \tag{9}$$

Where i = 1, 2, ..., N and j = 1, 2, ... J.
- Step 3: Row and column profiles, denoted as r and c are the vectors containing the row and column masses as an individual element, respectively.
- Step 4: Using singular value decomposition (SVD) principles, U, Dα, and VT can be calculated from the matrix D where (refer to Eq. 10)

$$D = D_r^{-1/2}(Z - rc^T)D_c^{-1/2} \tag{10}$$

D_r and D_c are diagonal matrices having r_i and c_j as diagonal elements. U, V are the orthogonal matrices of N × N and J × J dimensions respectively, and D_α is diagonal matrix of N × J dimension.
- Step 5: Principal inertia of the retained components K = (J − Q) are in the diagonal of $D_\lambda = D_\alpha^2$. Total inertia is the total sum of squares of the diagonal elements of D_λ.
- Step 6: For obtaining correspondence plot of row and column categories in low dimensional space, SVD will give us first coordinates as given below in Eq. 11:

$$W = D_r^{-\frac{1}{2}}UD_\lambda^{\frac{1}{2}}, \quad X = D_c^{-\frac{1}{2}}VD_\lambda^{\frac{1}{2}} \tag{11}$$

Where W and X are the coordinate matrices of individual observations and variables with dimension K, respectively.

The maximum possible number of MCA dimensions are calculated by the difference between the sum of variable categories and the number of variables. The number of dimensions to retain can be determined by calculating inertia, which is a measure of variance explained and choosing from the cumulative percentage of variance explained. Further, to aid the visualization, the first two dimensions are usually considered for interpretation. The coordinates of each category on selected dimensions are displayed to determine similarity amongst categories.

4   Application of the Integrating Proposed Approach

4.1   Design of the Model for Performance Evaluation FAHP/MCA

In this stage, it began with the selection of companies belonging to the land cargo transportation sector. This allowed, in the first place, the choice of some representatives of these companies as experts for the validation process of the criteria and sub-criteria through the FAHP technique and then, for the application of the MCA method through a survey.

In this regard, the survey was applied to a sample of 25 companies of the land cargo transportation sector in Colombia using Eq. 12 for the calculation of the sample size (p = 0,5; q = 0,5; e = 0,05; k = 1.96; N = 27).

$$n = \frac{k^2 * p * q * N}{(e^2 * (N - 1)) + k^2 * p * q} \tag{12}$$

Subsequently, a decision-making group was selected with the aim of validating the criteria and sub-criteria through the application of FAHP technique, for the overall performance evaluation in occupational health and safety management given they expertise in these topics.

This project was presented to the selected companies. The chief executive of each organization gave informed consent for participation. Then, the expert team was selected. The selection process of these participants began with the identification of decision-maker profiles. In this regard, four types of experts were found to be meaningful for the decision-making process: leaders of occupational health and safety departments of the selected companies (three experts were selected, one expert representing small companies, and one expert from medium-sized companies and one representative from large companies), two experts consultors in health and safety management, and two representatives of academic sector linked to the occupational health and safety in companies. The team of experts was comprised of:

- Participants 1, 2 and 3 are industrial engineers with specialization in occupational health and safety and minimum 5 years of experience as a leader in occupational health and safety departments. Participant 1 in representation of small companies, Participant 2 as part of medium-sized companies and Participant 3 in representation from large companies.

- Participants 4 is an industrial engineering with specialization in Occupational Health and more than seven years of experience in the management of health and safety programs in companies as a leader of department and as a consultant.
- Participant 5 is a professional in occupational health and safety with a master's degree in Management Systems and 10 years of experience as a consultant in both private and public organizations in the diagnostic, design implementation and improve health and safety programs in companies.
- Participants 6 is industrial engineering, specialist in occupational health and Auxiliary Professor with knowledge and 10 years of experience in health and safety in work, regulations and standards in occupational health and safety management (OHS), risk assessment, and industrial hygiene.
- Participant 7 industrial engineering, specialist in quality and engineering management, master's degree in industrial engineering, Auxiliary Professor, and Associated Research with experience and knowledge in occupational health and safety management, multivariate methods and multi-criteria models for performance evaluation. The industrial engineer acted as a facilitator to take over the judgment process.

Specifically, the facilitators established a decision-making hierarchy that would assist the researchers and practitioners in identifying and predicting the criteria and subcriteria in the occupational health and safety management evaluation. In addition, they trained the team members to undertake paired comparisons employing the FAHP. Complementary to these activities, the participants were also invited to enroll in the decision-making team based upon their expertise to provide precise information about the evaluation criteria, which should be included in the decision process to assess the performance in occupational health and safety in companies.

The decision-making group identified four criteria (C1, C2, C3, and C4) and 23 sub-criteria (S1, S2... S23) to evaluate the performance in occupational health and safety management in companies of land cargo transportation. The criteria and subcriteria were established based on the personal experience of experts, the regulations applicable to the cargo transport sector such as the Decree No 1072 of 2015 (this normativity establish the and regulates the occupational health and safety management for companies), Resolution 1565 of 2014 (it contains the guide-lines for the implementation of Strategic Plan of Road Safety to reduce the accident rate), Resolution No 0302 of 2019 (this legislation lays down the rules for the compliance of minimum standards in Occupational Health and Safety in organizations), requirements of the international standard ISO 45001 [7] and the pertinent scientific literature. The experts took into account all the aforementioned health and safety regulations, and the literature review presented by the experts of the academic sector in order to provide an MCDM model responding to the current needs of land cargo transportation.

The multi-criteria hierarchy was then verified and discussed during multiple sessions with the expert decision-making team to establish if it was accurate and comprehensible. The final decision model is presented in Fig. 2.

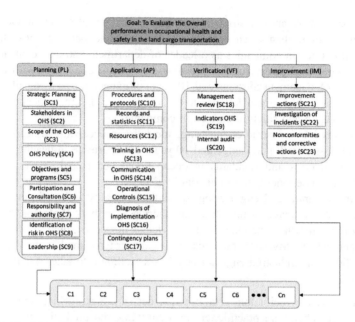

Fig. 2. Multi-criteria decision-making model to evaluate the overall performance in occupational health and safety management in the land cargo transportation

Particularly, the aforementioned criteria and sub-criteria were labeled and described as stated in Table 2.

Table 2. Description of criteria

Criterion (C)	Subcriteria (SC)	Criterion description
Planning (C1)	Strategic planning (SC1) Stakeholders in OHS (SC2) Scope of the OHS system (SC3) OHS Policy (SC4) Objectives and OHS programs (SC5) Participation and consultation (SC6) Responsibility and authority in OHS (SC7) Identification of risks in OHS (SC8) Leadership (SC9)	Is defined as the capacity of the company to establish the strategic elements that allow proactive and prospective planning of the company in occupational health and safety management and the degree to which the OHS system meets the government regulations and stakeholder's requirements
Application (C2)	Procedures and protocols (SC10) Records and statistics (SC11) Resources (SC12) Training in OHS (SC13) Communication in OHS (SC14) Operational Controls (SC15) Diagnosis of implementation OHS (SC16) Contingency plans (SC17)	Considers the implementation of procedures, protocols, registers, and statistics, for operational control of processes in occupational health and safety. This criterion also taking into account the resources (infrastructure, technology, financial, human), training and communication activities necessary to the operation of the management system in health and safety

(continued)

Table 2. (*continued*)

Criterion (C)	Subcriteria (SC)	Criterion description
Verification (C3)	Management review (SC18) Indicators OHS (SC19) Internal audits (SC20)	This criterion measures the company capability to evaluate its performance in order to achieve the expected results of the system, through mechanisms such as review by management, indicators, and audits in occupational health and safety
Improvement (C4)	Improvement actions (SC21) Investigation of incidents (SC22) Nonconformities and corrective actions (SC23)	Criterion considers the company's ability in the implementation of recurrent activities to improve performance in occupational health and safety management in coherence with the OHS policy and the objectives in OHS

4.2   Design of Data Collection Tools for FAHP and MCA

For the data collection, a survey for evaluation of conditions in occupational health and safety management was designed based on the personal experience of the selected experts, the occupational health and safety regulations, and the literature review. This instrument consists of two components, as shown in Fig. 3. In the first item, general aspects or profile of the companies were analyzed, such as antiquity, size, type of company, and export orientation. In the second item, the objective is to diagnose the companies of the land cargo transportation based on the criteria and sub-criteria validated with the experts concerning the application of occupational health and safety management, to identify the critical variables in the evaluation of the companies and recognize the clusters of companies taking into account the similarities in their answers with the use of MCA methodology (refer to Fig. 3). This item consists of four components, each with questions associated with the sub-criteria within each criterion as shown in Fig. 2. Each question is rated by the companies taking into account the following evaluation scale adapted from [36] (refer to Table 3).

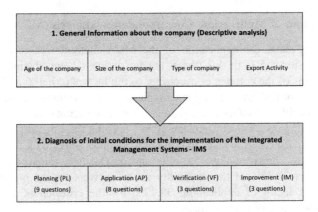

Fig. 3. Structure of the survey for diagnosis of the occupational health and safety management (MCA methodology)

Table 3. Rating scales

Rating scale	Level	Description
1	Without application	Not implemented
2	Basic	There are plans to implement it at the related levels
3	Advanced	It is beginning to be implemented at related levels
4	Expert	It is applied in most of the related levels of the company
5	Mature	It is applied at all levels of the company

Likewise, a data-collection instrument (refer to Fig. 4) was created to gather the paired comparisons performed by the expert team. Then, by using Eqs. 1–7, criteria and sub-criteria weights were determined. For each pairwise judgment it was asked: Concerning goal/factor, how important is each element on the left over the item on the right? The participants answered by using the scale described in Table 1. This process was then repeated until completing all the judgments. Mainly, the design of this instrument contributed to minimizing discrepancies and lack of comprehension. Additionally, it excluded intransitive comparisons during the decision-making process.

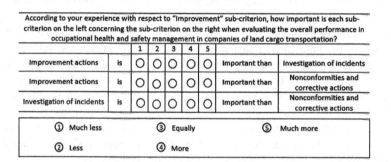

Fig. 4. Data-collection instrument implemented for FAHP judgments

4.3 Application of Multivariate Correspondence Analysis (MCA)

After collecting data, the application of the MCA method was carried out, using software R version 3.5.1. In this phase, the factor maps were obtained to show the relative positions of the companies according to the factors (criteria) and the variables (sub-criteria) identified by the experts in phase 1, to evaluate the performance in Occupational health and safety in the land cargo transportation sector. The factor maps classified the companies into clusters, taking into account the similarity in the responses associated with each criterion and sub-criteria in the questionnaire for the application of MCA method, as shown in Figs. 5a, b, c, and d. The two dimensions of the questionnaire, collect 27.33% of the variability in the answers for the planning criterion, 40.18% for the factor of application, 38.42% for the criterion of verification and 44.11% for the factor of improvement.

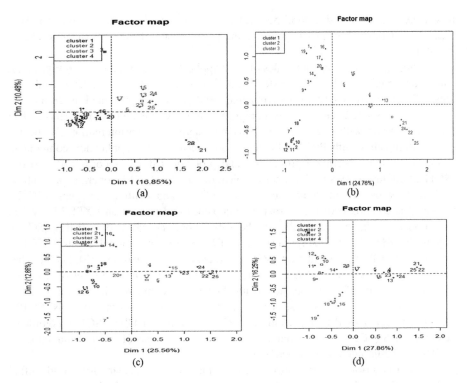

Fig. 5. Factor map for criterions (a) Planning; (b) Application; (c) Verification; (d) Improvement

Considering the results from "Planning" criteria (refer to Fig. 5a), we identified 4 clusters: Cluster 1, comprised of 56% of the companies analyzed, group 2 composed of 4% of the companies, cluster 3 represented by the 32% of the companies and cluster 4 made up of 8% of the companies analyzed. In this regard, cluster 1 is characterized by the presence of large companies, with more than 20 years old and constituted as companies by shares. In this cluster, companies with PREMIUM levels are located in the planning component, especially in the sub-criteria of strategic planning (SC1), the scope of the OHS system (SC3), OHS policy (SC4), objectives and OHS programs (SC5), participation and consultation (SC6), responsibility and authority in OHS (SC7), identification of risks in OHS (SC8), and leadership (SC9). Cluster 2 is comprised of a large company, between 11–20 years old, that presents an EXPERT level in the planning factor, in the OHS policy sub-factors (SC4), objectives and OHS programs (SC5), and participation and consultation (SC6). Cluster 3 is made up of companies of a limited nature, with a national scope in their operations. This group is at the EXPERT level in the subcriteria of leadership, strategic planning, and responsibility and authority in OHS and INITIAL level in the sub-factors objectives and OHS programs, OHS policy, and participation and consultation. Finally, cluster 4 is formed by small companies, with antiquity between 6 and 10 years and a BASIC level in the planning component, particularly in the sub-criteria related to the scope of the OHS system, stakeholders in OHS, strategic planning and responsibility and authority in OHS. In this sense, it is observed a good performance in the planning criterion, but it is necessary to establish strategies to improve the performance of the companies in cluster 3 and 4.

Taking into account the outcomes of the "Application" criterion (refer to Fig. 5b), it can be observed in 3 clusters. Cluster 1, made up of 32% of the companies analyzed, cluster 2 composed of 40% of the companies, and cluster 3 represented by 28% of the companies evaluated. Group 1 is comprised of large companies, with more than 20 years old and with operations not only nationally but also internationally. In this cluster, companies with PREMIUM levels are located in the application component, especially in the sub-criteria procedures and protocols (SC10), records and statistics (SC11), training in OHS (SC13), communication in OHS (SC14), operational controls (SC15), diagnosis of implementation OHS (SC16), and contingency plans (SC17). Cluster 2 is composed of medium-sized companies that present an EXPERT level in the application factor, especially in the sub-factors records and statistics (SC11), training in OHS (SC13), communication in OHS (SC14), operational Controls (SC15), diagnosis of OHS implementation (SC16), and contingency plans (SC17). On the other hand, cluster 3 is represented by small companies, with antiquity between 6 and 10 years and scope of operations at a national level. The companies in this cluster are at the INITIAL and BASIC levels, in the sub-criteria procedures and protocols (SC10), records and statistics (SC11), resources (SC12), training in OHS (SC13), communication in OHS (SC14), operational controls (SC15), diagnosis of implementation OHS (SC16), and contingency plans (SC17).

Another criterion is "verification" (refer to Fig. 5c). In this category, we identified 4 clusters: Cluster 1, made up of 32% of the companies analyzed, cluster 2 integrated by 20% of the companies, cluster 3 represented by 28% of the companies evaluated and the cluster 4 with 20% of the observations. Cluster 1 is integrated by large companies, which obtained a PREMIUM performance in the sub-criteria of management review (SC18), OHS indicators (SC19) and internal audits (SC20). In the cluster 2, companies with an EXPERT level were located in the sub-factors of management review (SC18), OHS indicators (SC19) and at the initial level in the sub-criterion of internal audits (SC20). For cluster 3, the companies obtained the INITIAL level in the sub-factor of internal audits (SC20) and the ADVANCED level in the OHS indicators sub-criterion (SC19). In cluster 4, most of the small companies, with antiquity between 6 and 10 years old, obtained BASIC and INITIAL levels in the subcriteria associated with the "verification" factor.

Based on the results of the "Improvement" category (refer to Fig. 5d), we observed 4 clusters: Cluster 1, made up of 4% of the companies analyzed, cluster 2 composed of 40% of the companies, cluster 3 represented by 20% of the companies evaluated and cluster 4 with 36% of the observations. Cluster 1 is made up of a large company, with more than 20 years old and with an international scope in its operations. However, in the "improvement" factor, it obtained BASIC level results in the subcriteria associated with the investigation of incidents (SC22), and nonconformities and corrective actions (SC23). Cluster 2 is represented by companies with more than 20 years of seniority and international presence. These companies obtained award levels in the subcriteria investigation of incidents (SC22), nonconformities and corrective actions (SC23) and to a lesser extent, in improvement actions (SC21). In cluster 3, companies with

EXPERT levels were located in the sub-factors investigation of incidents (SC22), nonconformities, and corrective actions (SC23). Group 4 is made up mostly of small companies, with antiquity between 6 and 10 years and national operations. These companies obtained ADVANCED performance levels in the sub-factor improvement actions (SC21) and an INITIAL level in the investigation of incidents (SC22), and nonconformities and corrective actions (SC23).

Finally, the chi-squared test was performed to analyze the independence of the variables or sub-criteria for each criterion or factor. The dependent or significant variables were those that obtained a p-value lower than the level of significance (p-value < 0.05). Table 4 shows the significative subcriteria in the evaluation of occupational health and safety performance. In this sense, the results obtained show that all the criteria and sub-criteria validated by the experts, taking into account the legal regulations, the ISO 45001 Standard and the pertinent literature, are significant in the evaluation of Occupational Health and Safety performance and the formation of business clusters. On the other hand, we identified other significative variables were also found in the survey for the MCA method, such as the age of the company, the legal nature of the company, the size of the company and the export orientation, which affect the level of Overall performance in OHS. These results allow us to conclude that the factors and sub-factors identified are relevant in the evaluation of occupational health and safety performance and that, through these criteria and sub-criteria, groups of companies can be identified and characterized to design multivariate strategies for the improvement in the management of health and safety in the land cargo transport sector.

Table 4. Rating scales Chi-squared test for independent analysis in software R 3.5.1.

Criterion (C)	Subcriteria (SC)	p-value
Planning (C1)	Strategic planning (SC1)	0.00000218
	Stakeholders in OHS (SC2)	0.00131
	Scope of the OHS system (SC3)	0.0000102
	OHS Policy (SC4)	0.0000000282
	Objectives and OHS programs (SC5)	0.0000000282
	Participation and consultation (SC6)	0.000000124
	Responsibility and authority in OHS (SC7)	0.0000214
	Identification of risks in OHS (SC8)	0.00831
	Leadership (SC9)	0.00139
Application (C2)	Procedures and protocols (SC10)	0.00109
	Records and statistics (SC11)	0.0000461
	Resources (SC12)	0.00203
	Training in OHS (SC13)	0.000000452
	Communication in OHS (SC14)	0.00000694
	Operational Controls (SC15)	0.00000000470
	Diagnosis of implementation OHS (SC16)	0.000935
	Contingency plans (SC17)	0.00000328

(continued)

Table 4. (*continued*)

Criterion (C)	Subcriteria (SC)	p-value
Verification (C3)	Management review (SC18)	0.00000513
	Indicators OHS (SC19)	0.0000000153
	Internal audits (SC20)	0.000446
Improvement (C4)	Improvement actions (SC21)	0.00219
	Investigation of incidents (SC22)	0.00000000127
	Nonconformities and corrective actions (SC23)	0.000000110

4.4   Calculating the Relative Weights of Criteria and Sub-criteria Using FAHP

Via the FAHP method, the local and global contributions of sub-criteria were determined to take into account importance, and uncertainty environments. To do this, the fuzzy judgment matrixes were initially calculated based on the pairwise comparisons performed by the selected experts. An example of this matrix is shown in Table 5. An illustration of a fuzzy reciprocal comparison matrix is presented in Table 6 where the judgments derived from the questionnaire were aggregated by applying Eqs. 1–3. The geometric means of fuzzy comparisons were then computed for each criterion/sub-criterion (refer to Table 6). The normalized priorities of criteria and sub-criteria were estimated after defuzzification by use of Eq. 4 and Eqs. 5–7 (refer to Table 7). Table 8 depicts the local (LW) priorities of sub-criteria as well as the global weights (GW) of all the decision elements of the model; a result of multiplying their local priority by the GW of its respective parent criterion.

Table 5. Fuzzy reciprocal comparison matrix for criteria

	C1	C2	C3	C4
C1	[1, 1, 1]	[1.64, 2.19, 2.69]	[1.64, 2.19, 2.69]	[1.64, 2.19, 2.69]
C2	[0.30, 0.39, 0.55]	[1, 1, 1]	[1.35, 1.60, 1.81]	[0.47, 0.58, 0.74]
C3	[0.45, 0.53, 0.67]	[0.55, 0.62, 0.74]	[1, 1, 1]	[0.41, 0.53, 0.74]
C4	[0.37, 0.46, 0.61]	[1.64, 2.02, 2.34]	[1.81, 2.56, 3.28]	[1, 1, 1]

Table 6. Geometric means of fuzzy comparisons for criteria

Criterion	C1	C2	C3	C4
Geometric mean of fuzzy comparisons	[1.64, 2.19, 2.69]	[0.54, 0.68, 0.88]	[0.66, 0.82, 1.05]	[0.78, 0.96, 1.19]

Table 7. Normalized fuzzy priorities for criteria

Fuzzy weight				Non-fuzzy weight	Normalized weight
C1	9.54	10.19	9.74	9.82	0,463
C2	3.15	3.15	3.17	3.16	0,149
C3	3.82	3.82	3.80	3.81	0,180
C4	4.54	4.46	4.32	4.44	0,209
Total				21.23	

Table 8. LW and GW of criteria and sub-criteria

Cluster	GW	LW
Planning (C1)	**0.463**	
Strategic management (SC1)	0,068	0,148
Stakeholders (SC2)	0,021	0,046
Scope of OHS (SC3)	0,018	0,040
Policy of OHS (SC4)	0,068	0,148
Objective of OHS (SC5)	0,064	0,138
Participation of workers (SC6)	0,029	0,064
Responsibilities and authority (SC7)	0,032	0,070
Risk management (SC8)	0,040	0,087
Leadership (SC9)	0,121	0,261
Application (C2)	**0.149**	
Procedures and protocols (SC10)	0,014	0,097
Records and statistics in OHS (SC11)	0,013	0,088
Resources for OHS (SC12)	0,024	0,164
Education and Training (SC13)	0,014	0,096
Communication in OHS (SC14)	0,009	0,061
Operational Controls (SC15)	0,028	0,189
Diagnosis in OHS (SC16)	0,029	0,197
Contingency plans (SC17)	0,016	0,109
Verification (C3)	**0.180**	
Management review (SC18)	0,040	0,221
Evaluation of OHS (SC19)	0,067	0,375
Audit od OHS (SC20)	0,073	0,404
Improvement (C4)	**0.209**	
Improvement plans (SC21)	0,128	0,613
Incident investigation (SC22)	0,052	0,247
Nonconformities and corrective plans (SC23)	0,029	0,140

Considering the FAHP results, first, the global weights of criteria were graphed in Fig. 6. By analyzing this bar diagram, it can be said that "Planning" is the most relevant criterion (NF = 46.3%) when assessing the overall performance in occupational health and safety. This criterion presents a difference of more than 20% compared to the other factors of the model. These results indicate that planning is an essential aspect for the success in the implementation of Occupational health and safety management systems so that companies in the sector must generate strategies and actions aimed at realizing effective planning processes in OHS. "Improvement" was also identified as an important factor in the evaluation (NF = 20.9%). However, there is a big difference (6%) between this factor and the last one in the "Implementation" ranking. These results demonstrate that the overall performance in occupational health and safety is the result of different strengths that underpin the companies in the prevention of accidents and occupational diseases, taking into account the regulations and standards in OHS, contributing in the corporate competitive plans and the decision making process in the land cargo transportation sector. Therefore, it is essential to design multi-criteria strategies aimed at continuous improvement in occupational health and safety taking into account different aspects of the P-D-C-A (Plan-Do-Check-Act) cycle (planning, application, verification, improvement)

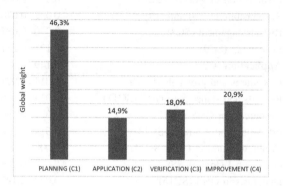

Fig. 6. Global weights of criteria when assessing the overall performance in occupational health and safety in companies of land cargo transportation

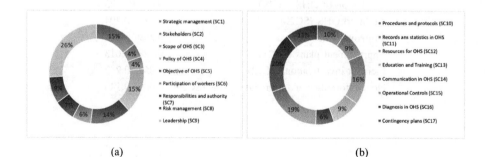

(a)   (b)

Fig. 7. Local contributions for factors (a) Planning (b) Application

Considering the results from "Planning" cluster (refer to Fig. 7a), "Leadership" was selected as the most important sub-criterion (26%). Other subfactors such as "Strategic management" (15%), Policy of OHS (15%) and "Objective of OHS" (14%) were identified as important sub-criteria in the planning cluster. This result means that the aforementioned sub-criteria are equally relevant in the overall performance evaluation in the planning cluster because these elements are conditions of compliance in mandatory national regulations and international standards in occupational health and safety that must be fulfilled by the companies in the land cargo transportation sector. In the "Application" category (refer to Fig. 7b), "Diagnosis in OHS" was chosen as the most relevant sub-factor (20%). Although there is a slight difference between this sub-category and other sub-factors as "Operational controls" (19%) and "Re-sources for OHS." These factors being relevant when evaluating the performance in terms of application, since these sub-criteria are requirements of national regulations in OHS and the standard ISO 45001, with the objective of identifying the initial conditions to implement the standard, establish the work plans, and ensuring physical, technological and infrastructure resources for occupational health and safety. Therefore, these variables must be controlled and monitored to generate a culture of prevention in companies and obtain good outcomes in performance evaluation.

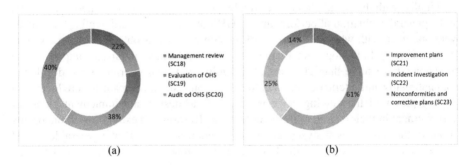

(a)   (b)

Fig. 8. Local contributions for factors (a) Verification (b) Improvement

Taking into account the results of the "Verification" criterion (refer to Fig. 8a), it can be observed that "Audit of OHS" (40%) represents the highest preference even though there are no significant differences between the decision elements of this cluster for example with the sub-factor "Evaluation" (38%). In this regard, both the legal regulation and the standard ISO 45001 define the audit as a systematic process of evaluation of evidence to compare against the criteria and objectives of the system, in order to establish the actions for continuous improvement. This means that the audit involves in itself an evaluation process and serves as a basis for management review, which is why it is a relevant sub-criterion in the evaluation. Finally, in the "Improvement" cluster, (refer to Fig. 8b), "Improvement plans" contribute with 61% of the total criterion weight. In this sense, this sub-criteria allows the development of strategies to promote the continuous improvement in occupational health and safety, which also involves the analysis of accidents and the identification of nonconformities, but with a focus on prevention and development.

On the other hand, consistency values were estimated (refer to Table 9) to verify the reliability of the judgments provided by the participants. The results revealed that all matrices yielded good consistency values (CR ≤ 0.1). Consequently, considering the above-mentioned findings, the data-collection procedure can be regarded as robust and the outputs derived from the decision-making process can be hence concluded as highly reliable regarding the calculated priorities of criteria and sub-criteria. Therefore, the data-gathering process can be considered satisfactory and subsequently, the decision-making process with highly reliable results.

Table 9. Consistency values for FAHP matrices

Cluster	Consistency ratio (CR)
Criteria	0.015
Planning	0.092
Application	0.088
Verification	0.086
Improvement	0.031

Finally, with the calculation of the weights of the criteria and sub-criteria, the scores of the general evaluation of performance in OHS of each of the participating companies were obtained, with which the ranking of the companies was obtained. of these results (refer to Fig. 9). In the top 5 are 4 large companies and a medium-sized company, these companies have more than 20 years of antiquity, and their operations are developed both nationally and internationally. On the other hand, small companies were located in the last places of the ranking, so it is necessary to design and implement plans for improvement in their overall performance. Table 10 shows an example with the results of one of the companies analyzed and the calculation of the GAP, at a general level and by the factor, which serves as the basis for the approach to improvement strategies.

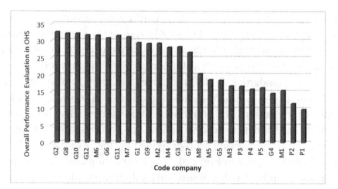

Fig. 9. Ranking of classification companies when assessing the overall performance in occupational health and safety of land cargo transportation sector

Table 10. Example of results overall performance evaluation in OHS

Code company	C1	C2	C3	C4	Total score
G1	20	5	2	3	29
Score max	21	25	13	8	67
% of compliance	95,2%	20.0%	15.3%	37.5%	43,8%
GAP	4,8%	80.0%	84.7%	62.5%	56,2%

5 Conclusions and Future Work

The land cargo transportation presents a high rate of accidents due to the risks inherent to the sector (psychosocial factors, mechanical and physical hazards, risks of security, among others) which hurt the welfare of workers, on operational costs, on logistics indicators, on the compliance with legal regulations and customer satisfaction. In this sense, it is necessary to develop integrated models cuali-cuantitative that provide information on occupational health and safety performance in the land cargo transportation to detect critical points, classify companies considering their levels of management and, subsequently, design strategies of improvement.

This research enriches the scientific literature and contributes to the evidence base related to the use of integrated approaches based on Multivariate Correspondence Analysis (MCA) and Fuzzy AHP for evaluation of performance in occupational health and safety in the companies of land cargo transportation sector with the aim of reduce the rates of accidents and incidents, losses for companies, increasing the competitiveness of the industry. In this regard, as future work, the integrated methodology will be extended in other economic sectors. In addition, we propose a comparison of the approach proposed in this project with different hybrid methods as DEMATEL, TOPSIS, and VIKOR to validate and improve the performance of the method.

The results showed that the factors associated to planning, application, verification, and improvement are dependent factors in the overall evaluation in occupational health and safety, and different clusters were identified considering the factors of evaluation. In addition, it was evidenced that the size, seniority and international scope of the companies are related to the level of performance in occupational health and safety. The outcomes of the FAHP showed that the factors with the most significant weight in the evaluation of occupational health and safety performance are Planning (46.3%) and Improvement (20.9%). The criterions associated to Verification (10.8%) and Application (14.9%) present few differences regarding the weights in the evaluation, which evidences the preventive nature of this proposed integrated model for the assessment of the performance in occupational health and safety in the companies of land cargo transportation.

References

1. Jimenez, G., Novoa, L., Ramos, L., Martinez, J., Alvarino, C.: Diagnosis of initial conditions for the implementation of the integrated management system in the companies of the land cargo transportation in the City of Barranquilla (Colombia). In: Stephanidis, C. (ed.) HCI 2018. CCIS, vol. 852, pp. 282–289. Springer, Cham (2018). https://doi.org/10.1007/978-3-319-92285-0_39
2. International Labour Office ILO: Priority safety and health issues in the road transport sector. 1a Ed. Geneva (2015)
3. Los altos costos del comercio interno. https://www.dinero.com/pais/articulo/los-costos-transportar-mercancia-colombia/208736. Accessed 21 Ene 2019
4. Perez, G.: Seguridad de la cadena logística terrestre en América Latina, Comision Económica para América Latina y el Caribe (CEPAL), Santiago de Chile (2013)
5. Ministerio de Transporte: Transporte en cifras: Estadísticas (2017)
6. Šukalova, V.: Safety risks management in the road transport. Logistyka **3**, 2131–2135 (2012)
7. International Standardization Organization ISO. Standard ISO 45001. Occupational Health and Safety Management Systems (2018)
8. Mokhtari, K., Ren, J., Roberts, C., Wang, J.: Decision support framework for risk management on sea ports and terminals using fuzzy set theory and evidential reasoning approach. Expert Syst. Appl. **39**(5), 5087–5103 (2012)
9. Soeanu, A., et al.: Transportation risk analysis using probabilistic model checking. Expert Syst. Appl. **42**(9), 4410–4421 (2015)
10. Kececi, T., Arslan, O.: SHARE TECHNIQUE: a novel approach to root cause analysis of ship accidents. Saf. Sci. **96**, 1–21 (2017)
11. Molero, G., Santarremigia, F., Aragonés, P., Pastor, J.: Total safety by design: increased safety and operability of supply chain of inland terminals for containers with dangerous goods. Saf. Sci. **100**(B), 168–182 (2017)
12. Van Schagen, I., Janssen, T.: Managing road transport risks: sustainable safety in The Netherlands. IATSS Res. **24**(2), 18–27 (2000)
13. Vaiana, R., et al.: Road safety performance assessment: a new road network risk index for info mobility. Procedia – Soc. Behav. Sci. **111**(5), 624–633 (2014)
14. Conca, A., Ridella, C., Sapori, E.: A risk assessment for road transportation of dangerous goods: a routing solution. Transp. Res. Procedia **14**, 2890–2899 (2016)
15. Mooren, L., Grzebieta, R., Williamson, A., Olivier, J., Friswell, R.: Safety management for heavy vehicle transport: a review of the literature. Saf. Sci. **62**, 79–89 (2014)
16. Atombo, C., Wu, C., Tettehfio, E., Nyamuame, G., Agbo, A.: Safety and health perceptions in work-related transport activities in Ghanaian industries. Saf. Health Work. **8**(2), 175–182 (2017)
17. Gul, M.: A review of occupational health and safety risk assessment approaches based on multi-criteria decision-making methods and their fuzzy versions. Hum. Ecol. Risk Assess. Int. J. **24**(7), 1723–1760 (2018). https://doi.org/10.1080/10807039.2018.1424531
18. Carrillo, J., Rubio, J., Guadix, J., Onieva, L.: Identification of areas of intervention for public safety policies using multiple correspondence analysis. DYNA **83**(196), 31–38 (2015)
19. Riviére, C., Marlair, G.: The use of multiple correspondence analysis and hierarchical clustering to identify incident typologies pertaining to the biofuel industry. Biofuels Bioprod. Biorefin. **4**(1), 53–65 (2010)
20. Amiri, M., Ardeshir, A., Hossein, M., Zarandi, F., Soltanaghaei, E.: Pattern extraction for high-risk accidents in the construction industry: a data-mining approach. Int. J. Inj. Control Saf. Promot. **23**(3), 264–276 (2015). https://doi.org/10.1080/17457300.2015.1032979

21. Dhalmahapatra, K., Shingade, R., Mahajan, H., Verma, A., Maiti, J.: Decision support system for safety improvement: an approach using multiple correspondence analysis, t-SNE algorithm and K-means clustering. Comput. Ind. Eng. **128**, 277–289 (2019)
22. Jimenez, G., Zapata, E.: Metodologia integrada para el control estratégico y la mejora continua, basada en el Balanced Scorecard y el Sistema de Gestión de Calidad: aplicacion en una organizacion de servicios en Colombia. In: 51a Asamblea Anual del Consejo Latinoamericano de Escuelas de Administracion CLADEA 2016, Medellin, Colombia, pp. 1–20 (2016)
23. Ortiz-Barrios, M.A., Herrera-Fontalvo, Z., Rúa-Muñoz, J., Ojeda-Gutiérrez, S., De Felice, F., Petrillo, A.: An integrated approach to evaluate the risk of adverse events in hospital sector: from theory to practice. Manag. Decis. **56**(10), 2187–2224 (2018)
24. Jimenez, G., Hernandez, L., Hernandez, H., Cabas, L., Ferreira, J.: Evaluation of quality management for strategic decision making in companies in the plastic sector of the Colombian Caribbean Region using the TQM diagnostic report and data analysis. In: Stephanidis, C. (ed.) HCI 2018. CCIS, vol. 852, pp. 273–281. Springer, Cham (2018). https://doi.org/10.1007/978-3-319-92285-0_38
25. Jimenez, G.: Procedimientos para el mejoramiento de la calidad y la implantación de la Norma ISO 9001 aplicado al proceso de asesoramiento del Centro de Investigaciones y Desarrollo Empresarial y Regional en una Institucion de Educacion Superior basados en la gestión por procesos. In: Congreso de Gestion de la Calidad y Proteccion Ambiental GECPA 2014, Habana, Cuba, pp. 1–22 (2014)
26. Demirel, T., Demirel, N., Kahraman, C.: Fuzzy analytic hierarchy process and its application. In: Kahraman, C. (ed.) Fuzzy Multi-Criteria Decision Making: Theory and Applications with Recent Developments. Springer Optimization and its Applications, vol. 16, pp. 53–83. Springer, Boston (2008). https://doi.org/10.1007/978-0-387-76813-7_3
27. Ertuğrul, İ., Karakaşoğlu, N.: Performance evaluation of Turkish cement firms with fuzzy analytic hierarchy process and TOPSIS methods. Expert Syst. Appl. **36**(1), 702–715 (2009)
28. Ortiz-Barrios, M.A., Kucukaltan, B., Carvajal-Tinoco, D., Neira-Rodado, D., Jiménez, G.: Strategic hybrid approach for selecting suppliers of high-density polyethylene. J. Multi-Crit. Decis. Anal. **24**, 1–21 (2017). https://doi.org/10.1002/mcda.1617
29. Kuswandari, R.: Assesment of different methods for measuring the sustainability of forest management. International Institute for Geo-Information Science and Earth Observation Enschede, Netherlands (2004)
30. Izquierdo, N.V., et al.: Methodology of application of diffuse mathematics to performance evaluation. Int. J. Control Theory Appl. (2016). ISSN 0974-5572
31. Kusumawardani, R., Agintiara, M.: Application of fuzzy AHP-TOPSIS method for decision making in human resource manager selection process. Procedia Comput. Sci. **72**, 638–646 (2015)
32. Ayhan, M.B.: A fuzzy AHP approach for supplier selection problem: a case study in a gear motor company. arXiv preprint arXiv:1311.2886 (2013)
33. Kilincci, O., Onal, S.A.: Fuzzy AHP approach for supplier selection in a washing machine company. Expert Syst. Appl. **38**(8), 9656–9664 (2011)
34. Vahidnia, M.H., Alesheikh, A.A., Alimohammadi, A.: Hospital site selection using fuzzy AHP and its derivatives. J. Environ. Manage. **90**(10), 3048–3056 (2009)
35. Rueda, D., Balmaceda, N.: Analisis de Correspondencias Multiples aplicado a la prueba Saber Pro 2017 en el programa de matematicas de las universidades del Departamento del Atlantico. Universidad del Atlantico (2019)
36. AENOR Norma No. 66177. Guía para la integración de sistemas de gestión (2005)

The Relevance of Cybersecurity for Functional Safety and HCI

Sebastian Korfmacher[✉]

Commission for Occupational Health and Safety and Standardization (KAN),
St. Augustin, Germany
Korfmacher@KAN.de

Abstract. Our world is being accelerated and changed massively by digitalization. We must therefore consider possible changes in the world of work and the impact on OSH. A changing world of work will also lead to changes in the work equipment. Digitalization will cause an increase in networked work equipment. If products are networked to the world wide web, possible threats originating from the web must be considered.

Cybersecurity is not only realized by technical solutions and requirements. Humans are also a key element for cybersecurity. The design of the HCI interface is therefore essential for minimizing the impact on cybersecurity and OSH.

The conference contribution gives a fundamental explanation of why functional safety & cybersecurity is important for OSH and HCI, especially in the context of digitalization and scenarios such as Smart Manufacturing or Industry 4.0.

The contribution of standardization and the current discussion concerning functional safety & cybersecurity will also be illustrated.

Keywords: Digitalization · Safety · Functional safety · Security · IT security · Cybersecurity · Standardization · Smart Manufacturing · Industry 4.0 · Work equipment · World of work

1 The Impact of Digitalization to the World of Work

Many developments are currently taking place in the context of digitalization: Homes are becoming smart, cars will be connected to one another and autonomous driving is being developed. In the healthcare sector, digitalization will make diagnostics more reliable and efficient. In the future robots will not only assist humans in their own home, but will also taking care of them.

Digitalization also has a strong impact on the world of work. There is an increase in "mobile work" and "crowd working", and their consequences are being discussed. We also see a massive change in work equipment due to digitalization. These changes must be considered adequately. This also leads to the question of whether digitalization affects safety (see Sect. 1.1).

© Springer Nature Switzerland AG 2019
V. G. Duffy (Ed.): HCII 2019, LNCS 11581, pp. 458–466, 2019.
https://doi.org/10.1007/978-3-030-22216-1_33

1.1   Possible Changes in Work Equipment

To answer the question regarding the effect of digitalization on safety, possible changes in work equipment must first be determined. The following example will illustrate this:

In the past, machines were controlled by the machine operator. Machine control systems did not exist. Today, processes are often automated and computers are essential for this.

Robots for example are often used within factories for process automation. The safety of the humans also working in this factory is ensured by a safety fence. When the door of the safety fence is opened the robot stops immediately. This safety function must function correctly at all times. This is guaranteed by the so called "functional safety", which refers to the safety of the control system.

Functional safety is a subsystem of safety and contributes to preventing hazards.

In view of the current progress in digitalization, we cannot however focus on machines or robots that are fenced in anymore. Robots are being developed which collaborate with humans to assist and support them. Robots will therefore no longer be fenced in at every workplace. Use of collaborating robots is not only conceivable in the industrial sector. They are also developed for the healthcare sector to assist humans in hospitals and in their homes.

In general, work equipment is changing and will increasingly be networked. Examples are drones used for transportation or smart personal protective equipment for firefighters intended to increase safety. Tablets are being used in various scenarios to provide additional information and can be used for setting up machine parameters.

As work equipment will be connected to the world wide web, possible threats originating from the world wide web must be considered. Possible consequences for functional safety must also be considered, because

- what happens if a collaborating robot makes unexpected moves due to a hacker attack?
- what happens if the speed of travel of a machine/robot is manipulated?
- what happens if functional safety is impaired by malware or a hacker attack?
- what happens if a machine or system can no longer be controlled because of malware or a hacker attack?

These questions lead to a new field which must be considered adequately if work equipped is being networked via the world wide web: cybersecurity.

A detailed description of why cybersecurity is relevant for functional safety is presented in the following chapter.

1.2   Why Cybersecurity Is Relevant for Functional Safety

To understand the relevance of cybersecurity for functional safety, a closer look should be taken at the history of electronics:

In the beginning, electronics (such as control systems) consisted purely of hardware components. Changes could only be made by changing the hardware. Then technology changed and electronic components became programmable. Today electronic

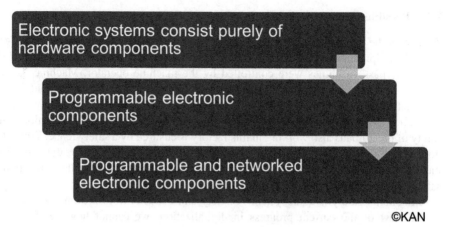

©KAN

Fig. 1. Changes in electronic components

components are not only programmable, they are also connected to the world wide web (see Fig. 1).

This is the real problem, because cyberattacks or malware may have a negative impact on control systems – including those for safety. Safety functions may not perform correctly as result and humans could be at risk.

The types of attack can be differentiated and will be described in the following paragraph.

Types of Attack
Cybersecurity attacks can be differentiated into two groups: selective attacks and random attacks.

Selective attacks focus on one specific target. They are performed by a hacker who knows how to paralyse or manipulate machines or systems. However, they do not necessarily have an overview of possible negative effects on safety.

Random attacks do not focus on one specific target. They are intended to affect as many systems as possible and are called malware. Malware can lead to an unfavourable situation if machines or systems are paralysed.

Both types of attack can represent a possible hazard for humans. However, random attacks constitute a greater problem because in contrast to hacker attacks, targets are not selected based on attractiveness. Even small companies can be a target of random attacks. They should not suppose that they will never be affected by this kind of attack. Random attacks try to have a negative effect on the availability of systems of as many targets as possible. However, apart from the availability of the system, safety functions may also be affected negatively in case of an unfortunate combination of circumstances.

The different types of attack lead to the question of how significant cybersecurity is. The answer is given in the following paragraph.

Significance of Cybersecurity and the Relevance for HCI

Within the scenario of attacks coming from the world wide web, the question of the relevance and frequency of these attacks arises.

The German Federal Office for Information Security (BSI) communicates that 70% of companies and organisations in Germany were a target of cyber attacks in 2016 and 2017. Attackers did not only gain access to the IT system to influence them. Every second successful attack also led to a loss of production or a system breakdown [1].

There are also attacks which may not have been detected until now. Many companies will probably not admit a successful attack because this would have a negative impact on their image.

Cybersecurity is therefore very significant and must be considered adequately. Examples of possible gateways for hackers and malware are:

- insufficient security standards for hardware components
- remote maintenance
- unchanged standard passwords
- missing software updates
- obsolete operating systems
- vulnerable operating systems

This list of possible gateways for hackers and malware is by no means exhaustive. It can never be complete because threats for cybersecurity can change from one minute to the next. As possible ways of attacks are constantly changing, the cybersecurity will never cease to be relevant.

The aspects mentioned above focus on technical solutions and requirements to ensure cybersecurity. Humans and their behaviour and knowledge about the mechanisms employed by hackers and malware must not be ignored, however [2].

Humans are often a key element for the success of malware or hackers. Clicking on a faked link that was sent by e-mail, for example, can open doors to hackers. Likewise, the execution of malware can be started and the computer be encrypted until a ransom is paid. The design of the HCI interface is therefore essential not only for office computers, but for any kind of machine and system. Furthermore, HCI has the opportunity to take account of cybersecurity and to facilitate the prevention of wrong decisions made by humans which would open the door to potential threats (e.g. malware, hacker attacks).

Standardization contributes to cybersecurity and functional safety. Section 2 will illustrate important documents and the current progress of standardization activities concerning cybersecurity of industrial automation and control systems and functional safety.

2 Contribution of Standardization to Functional Safety and Cybersecurity

Standardization documents provide a contribution to functional safety and cybersecurity. Functional safety and cybersecurity are two independent spheres that are being brought together through the increasing development of systems that are connected to the world wide web. Functional safety and cybersecurity use different mechanism however to achieve their particular aims.

The following chapters will illustrate the different mindsets and methodologies.

2.1 Standardization of Functional Safety

The safety of a system as a whole is achieved by different individual systems. These systems can consist of different technologies such as hydraulic, mechanical, electrical, electronic or programmable electronic components.

ISO/IEC Guide 51 defines safety as the freedom from unacceptable risk. Functional safety applies to all kinds of control systems and is aimed at the reduction of unacceptable risk. Functional safety guarantees that safety functions (see example of Sect. 1.1) are functioning at all times. Only then is functional safety able to contribute to safety and to ensure human health.

The key element of safety is the risk assessment, during which the necessary input of every safety function in the control system is defined.

In the event of a fault, the safety function must perform correctly. Necessary methods are described in full detail by standardization documents:

- IEC 61508 series: Functional safety of electrical/electronic/programmable electronic safety-related systems (generic standard) [3]

- IEC 61508-1:2010: Functional safety of electrical/electronic/programmable electronic safety-related systems - Part 1: General requirements
- IEC 61508-2:2010: Functional safety of electrical/electronic/programmable electronic safety-related systems - Part 2: Requirements for electrical/ electronic/programmable electronic safety-related systems
- IEC 61508-3:2010: Functional safety of electrical/electronic/programmable electronic safety-related systems - Part 3: Software requirements
- IEC 61508-4:2010: Functional safety of electrical/electronic/programmable electronic safety-related systems - Part 4: Definitions and abbreviations
- IEC 61508-5:2010: Functional safety of electrical/electronic/programmable electronic safety related systems - Part 5: Examples of methods for the determination of safety integrity levels
- IEC 61508-6:2010: Functional safety of electrical/electronic/programmable electronic safety-related systems - Part 6: Guidelines on the application of IEC 61508-2 and IEC 61508-3
- IEC 61508-7:2010: Functional safety of electrical/electronic/programmable electronic safety-related systems - Part 7: Overview of techniques and measures [4]

- IEC 61511 series: Functional safety - Safety instrumented systems for the process industry sector (process industry)

- IEC 61511-1:2016 + AMD1:2017 CSV Consolidated Version: Functional safety - Safety instrumented systems for the process industry sector - Part 1: Framework, definitions, system, hardware and application programming requirements [5]
- IEC 61511-2:2016: Functional safety - Safety instrumented systems for the process industry sector - Part 2: Guidelines for the application of IEC 61511-1:2016 [6]

- IEC 61511-3:2016: Functional safety - Safety instrumented systems for the process industry sector - Part 3: Guidance for the determination of the required safety integrity levels [7]
- ISO 13849 series: Safety of machinery – Safety-related parts of control systems (machinery)
- ISO 13849-1:2015: Safety of machinery – Safety-related parts of control systems – Part 1: General principles for design [8]
- ISO 13849-2:2012: Safety of machinery – Safety-related parts of control systems – Part 2: Validation [9]

and

IEC 62061: Safety of machinery - Functional safety of safety-related electrical, electronic and programmable electronic control systems [10]
  (machinery)

2.2   Standardization of Cybersecurity

Cybersecurity describes the resistance of an IT system to attacks and the disruptions and malfunctions caused by them. To reach cybersecurity different strategies can be applied, e.g. security by design or defense in depth. All strategies and measures which can be applied depend on the motivation of the attacker, however. A distinction between coincidental maloperation and intentional attacks is therefore drawn and expressed by different security levels (SLs) specified in the international (draft) standard IEC 62443-3-3: Industrial communication networks - Network and system security - Part 3-3: System security requirements and security levels.

The IEC 62443 series constitutes very important standardization documents for IT security for industrial automation and control systems. The series is currently under development and not all parts have been published yet.

Comparison of the strategies of functional safety (Sect. 2.1) and cybersecurity (Sect. 2.2) illustrates the different mindsets: Security is faced with continually changing attack scenarios. By contrast threats addressed by functional safety will not change unless the state of the art changes. Owing to the described change of digitalization (see Sect. 1), functional safety and cybersecurity must be applied at the same time to guarantee safe products.

Owing to the different histories and strategies of functional safety and cybersecurity, further standardization documents exists that are very important in this context and will be described in the next chapter.

2.3   Developments Within Standardization of Functional Safety and Cybersecurity

Standardization documents for functional safety have existed for a very long time, but they do not consider possible threats arising due to the fact that machines are connected directly or indirectly to the world wide web. Dedicated standards for cybersecurity are therefore being developed.

Many standardization activities are currently taking place regarding functional safety and cybersecurity. Some of them will be presented in this chapter and can be categorized as follows:

The documents are categorized into "Guides" and "Technical Reports" (TR). Guides represent an internal rulebook of the particular standardization organization and assist standards writers during the developing process [11, 12].

Technical reports contain collected data, e.g. regarding the "state of the art", and are entirely informative and not normative [13, 14]. They can also serve as an aid for people applying standards.

Some key facts on some of the documents in Fig. 2 are given below to demonstrate the wide range of topics covered by these documents:

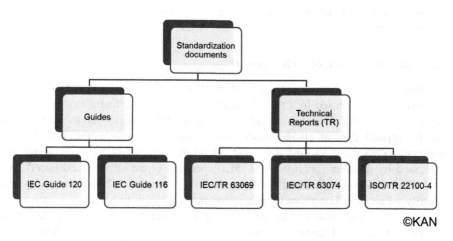

©KAN

Fig. 2. Documents for functional safety and cybersecurity

- **IEC/TR 63069: Industrial-process measurement, control and automation – Framework for functional safety and security**

As mentioned in (Sect. 2.1) the standard IEC 61508 describes generically the safety of a whole system. In contrast, IEC 62443 describes security for industrial automation and control systems (Sect. 2.2).

Today's challenge is to apply both standards at the same time to guarantee functional safety & security.

"This Technical Report (TR) explains and provides guidance on the common application of IEC 61508 and IEC 62443 in the area of industrial-process measurement, control and automation. This document may apply to other industrial sectors where IEC 61508 and IEC 62443 are applied." [15].

- **IEC/TR 63074:2017-12 Draft (44/793/CD:2017): Safety of machinery - Security aspects related to functional safety of safety-related control systems**

This draft TR contains general requirements regarding such aspects of security threats and vulnerabilities that could affect functional safety (realized by the safety-related control system (SCS)) and lead to a loss of the ability to maintain the safe operation of a machine [16].

- **ISO/TR 22100-4:2018: Safety of machinery – Relationship with ISO 12100 – Part 4: Guidance to machinery manufacturers for consideration of related IT-security (cyber security) aspects**

"This document gives machine manufacturers guidance on potential security aspects in relation to safety of machinery when putting a machine into service or placing on the market for the first time. It provides essential information to identify and address IT-security threats which can influence safety of machinery.

This document gives guidance but does not provide detailed specifications on how to address IT-security aspects which can influence safety of machinery.

This document does not address the bypass or defeat of risk reduction measures through physical manipulation." [17].

Due to the diversity of different standardization activities, a coordinated procedure must be followed to avoid duplication or overlap in the development of standards. Close cooperation between experts and standardization organizations must continue for this purpose [18].

3   Conclusions

In conclusion, the proportion of networked machines and systems is going to increase. As a result, the probability of successful attacks will also increase – especially in scenarios of Industry 4.0 or Smart Manufacturing. Cybersecurity can no longer be ignored because a cybersecurity problem can lead to a potential risk for humans if functional safety is affected.

Standards are an appropriate resource for the consideration of functional safety and cybersecurity. During the current development of functional safety and cybersecurity standards, documents overlapping and duplication of work must be avoided.

As cybersecurity is relevant for a broad range of products, some organisations propose a horizontal implementation of a cybersecurity directive. The German Electrical and Electronic Manufacturers Association (ZVEI) has recently published a whitepaper regarding this proposal [19]. The idea behind this proposal is that cybersecurity problems would affect not only one component or product. The problem can have a negative impact on a whole system. ZVEI therefore considers it necessary to have a common horizontal solution which is valid across the European Union.

Independent of the solution for cybersecurity it is necessary that manufacturer, user, integrator and operator are adequately involved to prevent that only one of them bears responsibility. Only then can cybersecurity be applied holistically.

In addition, questions of liability and guarantee must be resolved. This lies outside the scope of standardization, however.

Technical measures and concepts are essential for cybersecurity. Humans are equally important, however. In consequence, the design of HCI interfaces is not negligible. The opportunity to design HCI interfaces such that they consider cybersecurity and the possible consequences for the safety of humans should therefore be taken.

References

1. BSI. https://www.bsi.bund.de/DE/Presse/Pressemitteilungen/Presse2018/Cyber-Angriffe_haben_erhebliche_Konsequenzen_fuer_die_Wirtschaft_31012018.html. Accessed 26 Nov 2018
2. Moallem, A.: Human-Computer Interaction and Cybersecurity Handbook, pp. 18–19. CRC Press, Boca Raton (2019)
3. IEC. https://www.iec.ch/functionalsafety/explained/page1.htm. Accessed 23 Jan 2019
4. IEC. https://www.iec.ch/functionalsafety/standards/page2.htm. Accessed 23 Jan 2019
5. IEC. https://webstore.iec.ch/publication/61289. Accessed 23 Jan 2019
6. IEC. https://webstore.iec.ch/publication/25521. Accessed 23 Jan 2019
7. IEC. https://webstore.iec.ch/publication/25479. Accessed 23 Jan 2019
8. ISO. https://www.iso.org/standard/69883.html. Accessed 23 Jan 2019
9. ISO. https://www.iso.org/standard/53640.html. Accessed 23 Jan 2019
10. IEC. https://webstore.iec.ch/publication/22797. Accessed 23 Jan 2019
11. IEC. https://www.iec.ch/standardsdev/publications/guide.htm. Accessed 12 Dec 2018
12. ISO. https://www.iso.org/iso-guides.html. Accessed 12 Dec 2018
13. IEC. https://www.iec.ch/standardsdev/publications/tr.htm. Accessed 12 Dec 2018
14. ISO. https://www.iso.org/deliverables-all.html#TR. Accessed 12 Dec 2018
15. Danish Standards Foundation. https://standards.globalspec.com/std/10392180/dsf-iec-tr-63069. Accessed 16 Jan 2019
16. Beuth. https://www.beuth.de/de/norm-entwurf/din-en-63074/280563956. Accessed 16 Jan 2019
17. ISO. https://www.iso.org/standard/73335.html. Accessed 16 Jan 2019
18. KAN. https://www.kan.de/en/publications/kanbrief/digitalization-and-industry-40/aspects-of-safety-and-security-in-the-emergence-of-industrie-40/. Accessed 16 Jan 2019
19. ZVEI. https://www.zvei.org/presse-medien/publikationen/horizontale-produktregulierung-fuer-cybersicherheit-whitepaper/. Accessed 26 Nov 2018

Highway End-of-Queue Alerting System Based on Probe Vehicle Data

Keyu Ruan[1,3], Zahra Yarmand[2,3], Renran Tian[2,3], Lingxi Li[1,3(✉)],
Yaobin Chen[1,3], Feng Li[2,3], and Jim Sturdevant[4]

[1] Department of Electrical and Computer Engineering, Indiana University Purdue
University Indianapolis, Indianapolis, IN 46202, USA
ll7@iu.edu
[2] Department of Computer Information and Graphics Technology, Indiana
University Purdue University Indianapolis, Indianapolis, IN 46202, USA
[3] Transportation Active Safety Institute (TASI), Purdue School of Engineering
and Technology, IUPUI, Indianapolis, IN 46202, USA
[4] Indiana Department of Transportation Traffic Management Center, Indianapolis,
IN 46219, USA

Abstract. Back-of-queue crashes are one of the main reasons for fatal
accidents on US highways, which are commonly caused by driver inattention or distraction. It is important to improve driver's situation awareness when approaching slow traffic or traffic queues when cruising on
highways. In this paper, we propose a novel approach for developing a
prototype end-of-queue alerting system that is based on the probe vehicle
data. Speed changes among different road segments are used to identify
slow traffic queues, which are compared with vehicle locations and moving directions to detect potential back-of-queue crashes. This system is
designed to issue alerting messages to drivers approaching the queues via
an Android-based smartphone App and an Android Auto device. Preliminary road test has proved the effectiveness of the prototype system.
For the future work, the system functionality and reliability will be further improved, and multi-modal alerting parameters will be optimized
via human subject tests.

Keywords: End-of-queue crashes · Real-time detection · Alerts

1 Introduction

1.1 Background of End-of-Queue Crashes

Recent studies [1] concluded that highway congestion is causing a much higher
crash rate compared to un-congested driving conditions. For the highway congestion, back-of-queue crashes are the main sources for fatal accidents, which stand
for about 13% of all highway fatal accidents [1]. A variety of factors including
low visibility, slippery road surface, and driver distraction/drowsiness during
highway cruising, all contribute to this type of fatal crashes.

© Springer Nature Switzerland AG 2019
V. G. Duffy (Ed.): HCII 2019, LNCS 11581, pp. 467–478, 2019.
https://doi.org/10.1007/978-3-030-22216-1_34

The role of common ADAS (advanced driver assistance systems) features such as adaptive cruise control (ACC) and lane keeping assist (LKA) have two-sided effects in these back-of-queue crash scenarios. On one hand, some onboard sensors may help issue imminent crash warnings or braking assist to mitigate the crash consequences. On the other hand, these features may also cause increased driver distraction and inattention that potentially delay appropriate driver responses.

1.2 Feasible End-of-Queue Alerting Solutions

Investigation of feasible end-of-queue alert solutions has been completed. Typical highway traffic-queue scenarios, road characteristics, and environmental factors are considered. Three main approaches have been investigated:

1. Broadcast through the 4G network. In this approach, alerting messages on the current traffic-queue information will be broadcasted using 4G network through base stations. A 4G base station can be identified close to the detected highway traffic queue. The smartphones of drivers approaching the queue can receive alerts with the upcoming traffic information;
2. Adopting onboard alerting devices. In this approach, an onboard device (e.g., dedicated-short-range-communication (DSRC)-based device) can be installed in the vehicle and uses velocity information (combined with real-time highway data) to produce a warning threshold.
3. Portable and changeable off-road message signs. When the traffic-queue is identified and located, a portable off-road sign can be placed a few miles upstream of the end-of-queue location. For instance, the messages on these signs can read as "Slow Traffic – 3 miles," or "Stopped Traffic Ahead." Approaching highway drivers can be warned in advance of the end-of-queue.

Researchers have developed and evaluated end-of-queue alerting systems [2,3] showing good potentials in smoothing the transition from free flow to congestion as well as improving drivers' situational awareness. Authors of [4] implemented a queue warning system that is used to give alert to motorists with variable message signs. A high bandwidth, a long-haul communication system is designed to transmit data over 100 km. The system was proved to be successful and the number of rear-end collision has been notably reduced. Khan in [5] has proposed a queue-end warning system that is based on a combination of sensors and an artificial neural network model-based algorithm. The warning messages are issued on portable variable message sign boards. Simulation has been done and the approaches are suitable for traffic operations in a work zone. Liu et al. [6] have proposed an EOQ warning system with dedicated short-range communications. The system is established using velocity-related information combined with real highway data. The authors have also proposed an evaluation model to consider the influence of factors like traffic parameters, communication range, and penetration rate. There are also other researches that have a contribution to improving the performance of the end-of-queue detection algorithms. Researchers in [7] developed an algorithm that can estimate the queue lengths for a given time period, the time needed to clear individual vehicles from a vehicle queue and the total and average traffic delays of a queue. The output of this algorithm could be very useful as the method as the input of the end of queue alerting systems. Amini et al. from the University of California Berkeley [8] has also proposed an algorithm that could be used to estimate the queue length at an intersection. The algorithm is based on stochastic gradient descent. Their theoretical contribution is supported by simulations. Another research has been done in [9] to investigate the effects of using officer and vehicle at upstream of work zones. Traffic speed, deceleration, and erratic maneuvers of traffic approaching the queue were investigated. The conclusion was that the enforcement vehicle is a reasonable alternative but a different analytic approach is needed.

However, the published studies lack a systematic investigation on alarm timing/modality/frequency, driver status, as well as the corresponding driver responses, which significantly affect the effectiveness of the crash warnings [10].

1.3 Development Based on Probe Vehicle Data

In this paper, we want to introduce an end-of-queue alert system using probe vehicle data, which are acquired through freight, smartphones, and in-vehicle GPS units, when the movement information is sampled from in-road vehicles, as shown in Fig. 1:

Fig. 1. Probe vehicle data points on the highway

These data are collected and integrated, which can then be used to monitor average vehicle driving speeds at all separated road segments that cover the whole highway network and detect highway congestion, queue starting locations, and queue lengths [11] based on speed changes [12]. Although this information is available now, there are no currently available methods to effectively distribute these potential hazards to on-road drivers.

In order to achieve the objective, the first step is to implement hardware and software for pilot alerting systems. The potential prototype system will consist of the following functionalities that (1) has an Android/iOS-based application which can be installed on smart-phones of highway drivers, (2) can obtain vehicle locations and directions, (3) can access and integrate with real-time highway traffic-queue data, (4) can issue on-board multimodal alerts.

The next step focuses on highway traffic-queue scenario modeling and testing. With the help of real-time historical highway traffic data collected from probe vehicles, typical highway traffic-queue scenarios will be modeled with support from other GIS/Map databases. The scenario development will focus on road levels, road conditions, lane availability, roadside conditions, weather conditions, lighting conditions, and other infrastructure/environment variables. This information is crucial for evaluating the appropriate approach for delivering alerting messages to highway drivers.

2   Research Objectives

The objective of our research focuses on developing an end-of-queue alerting system towards drivers approaching congestion queues on highways based on probe data. The research aims to

- Investigate feasible solutions to apply end-of-queue alarms considering both in-car and road-side options;
- Determine the best practice for end-of-queue alarms by examining technical requirements and limitations for different feasible solutions, focusing on the aspects of queue data acquisition, vehicle localization, communications, and adaptive alarms;
- Develop a prototype end-of-queue alerting system based on probe vehicle data.

2.1   Research Plan

Based on the objectives, the overall plan for this project has been settled as shown in Fig. 2:

Following this plan, our research has been divided into several different tasks:

1. Probe vehicle queue data acquisition. In this task, first, we need to fetch vehicle probe data from the server. Indiana Department of Transportation (INDoT) has provided the real-time queue data on all Indiana highways, including highway names, highway directions and the coordinates of congestion starting points. After we obtain the geo-locations of the end of queues, we need to develop a data visualization software to show the end of queues on a map.

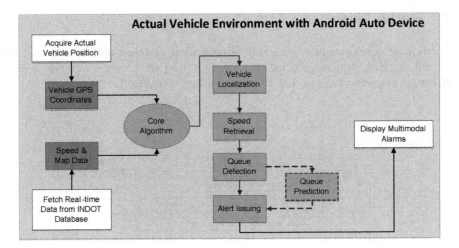

Fig. 2. Overall project plan

2. Investigation of feasible End-of-Queue alerting solutions. After many possible solutions have been investigated, we have at last chosen the method with the 4G network and onboard alerting device. A smartphone will be used as the platform to receive real-time data through the 4G signal and give out pilot alerting.

3. Hardware/Software implementation for pilot alerting. As we have mentioned above, a smartphone will be used as the platform of data receiving and alerting generating. To achieve it, a smartphone app is needed. Currently, only Android OS has been considered. To make the alerting system multimodal and more compatible for driving, an Android Auto device will be deployed as an extension of the smartphone.

4. Evaluation of pilot alerting systems in a driving simulator. We would like to test the system in a driving simulator with a controlled in-lab environment as the first stage of testing. The advantages of driving simulator are as follows:
   - It is much easier to have customized road networks following our requirements.
   - It is more convenient to generate traffic congestion on demanded locations.
   - Subjects can have more concentration on the tests because of zero driving risk.

   The subjects will be with different demographical information to make the testing data more comprehensive and convincing.

5. Evaluation of refined pilot alerting system with limited road testing. To obtain an optimized system, road testing will be necessary. Our plan is to do eight weeks daily driving tests on different Indiana highways, with a small sample of subjects with alerts off for four weeks and alerts on for 4 weeks.

3   Methodology

The flow of development of the end-of-queue alert system could be divided into several sections: data acquisition, car location, and alert triggering. The overall flowchart of method design has been shown below in Fig. 3:

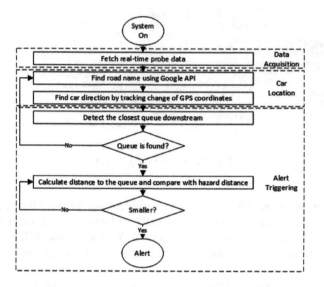

Fig. 3. Flowchart of methodology design

3.1   Probe Vehicle Queue Data Acquisition

INDoT has provided us the real-time probe vehicle queue data that is open to the public [13]. The data, which will be updated every minute, could be accessed on a server with the *.json* format. Programs have been developed to fetch the data automatically. One segment of the data is as shown in Fig. 4:

In Fig. 4, we can see that each segment that starts with *"geometry"* represents a traffic queue on the highway, which includes the geo-location of the queue starting point, the road name, road direction, mileage of the probe site and the previous and current traffic speed.

3.2   Car Location

In order to generate correct pilot alerts, we need to acquire the location of ego car. The on-board smart-phone has the GPS module to obtain real-time geolocation. Then a method is needed to do reverse-geocoding from geolocation to road name and direction.

```
{ ⊟
    "tstamp":"2019-02-19T17:54:18.470Z",
    "type":"PointFeatureCollection",
    "version":"1.0.0",
    "features":[ ⊟
        { ⊟
            "geometry":{ ⊟
                "coordinates":[ ⊟
                    -86.5169800067561,
                    39.3040097858985
                ],
                "type":"point"
            },
            "properties":{ ⊟
                "assettype":"delta",
                "description":"I-69 SB @ MM 128.54",
                "directions":"south",
                "from":72,
                "icon":"delta-icon",
                "message":"from:72 to:53",
                "mile":128.54,
                "road":"I-69",
                "to":53
            }
        },
```

Fig. 4. Real-time queue data from server

There are many feasible solutions to solve the reverse-geocoding problem. Our current solution is to use Google API. Google has provided the API and has integrated it into their Android SDK. We can use it by simply call the function in our code and obtain its output as a road name in a certain format. We have also implemented the visualization of ego car location on the map, which can visualize the real-time location of ego car and display the current road, as shown in Fig. 5.

In Fig. 5(b), we can see that the current driving direction is also accessible. Although a highway will not be constantly in one direction, with a reference segment that is long enough, the changing of latitude and longitude values could be used to estimate the overall driving direction. For example, when a highway has northbound and southbound, although the car could be toward east or west sometimes, driving direction will also be mostly north or south.

3.3 Alert Triggering Algorithm

After we have obtained the real-time queue data and ego car location, it is possible to determine whether the ego car has the risk of rear-end collision. First of all, target queue selection. All the queues from current fetched data will be scanned to find the ones on the same highway as the ego car. Among these queues, only the ones downstream will be considered, which could be determined

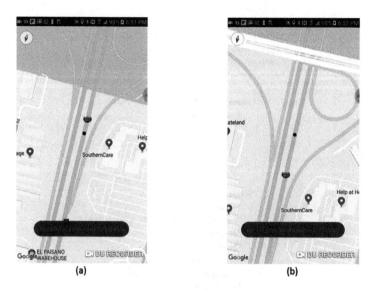

(a)   (b)

Fig. 5. Visualization of ego car with Google API: (a) Current road is I-465; (b) Current driving direction is South

by whether the distance between ego car and the queue is getting smaller. Based on the distance, the closest queue will be selected.

Second, the determination of hazard distance. The hazard distance represents the distance reserved for the driver to reduce the speed with relatively low acceleration. Depending on the reaction time of different drivers and the deceleration design of different vehicle manufacturers, the minimum distance for deceleration could be quite different. Hence the hazard distance should not be to close to the queue. Based on the distance for portable message board placement provided by INDoT [14], for queues on freeways, the distance should be at least one mile before the queue end. In our case, we also take the distance of one mile as the hazard distance for alert triggering.

At last, the third step is to iteratively compare the distance to the closest queue with the hazard distance. When the closest queue distance is no larger than the hazard distance, the alert will be triggered.

4   Pilot Alerting System

The pilot alerting system consists of messaging and tone on both cellphone and Android Auto display. When ego car approaching an end-of-queue, a message box will be shown on the middle of the phone screen, with content "Attention! Traffic ahead! Please reduce your speed!", as shown in Fig. 6.

On the other hand, the Android Auto display can also generate pop-up message banner on top of the display, with similar warning content on the phone, as shown in Fig. 7.

Fig. 6. Alerting on an Android phone

Fig. 7. Alerting on an Android Auto display

Through the function of message voice interaction that Google provided, this alerting message could be read by tapping the banner, or dismissed by saying "I'm done", which could give the driver more freedom while driving and reduce the risk of distraction.

4.1   Unit Testing

Several groups of unit testing have been done in order to debug the program and evaluate the performance of the system. The tests were mostly done in rush hours from 4 pm to 7 pm EST in highways I-65, I-70, and I-465 around Indianapolis downtown area. The app on the smartphone could show all queues based on the data on INDoT database as shown in Fig. 8. By tapping on the red icon, the detailed information about the queue, including its road name, road direction and delta speed, could also be shown (Fig. 8(c)).

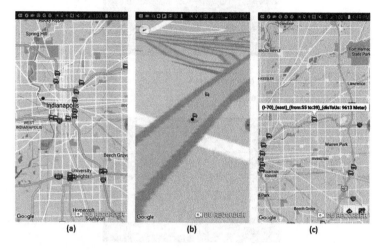

(a)   (b)   (c)

Fig. 8. Queue visualization on Android phone: (a) All queues nearby; (b) One queue ahead; (c) Detailed information of one queue (Color figure online)

4.2 Pilot Road Testing Results

The images in Fig. 9 shows that the system works as expected. The pilot alert was given (in Fig. 9(b)) before the end-of-queue could be observed. By changes the threshold, we can set the *Time to Queue* (TTQ), which represents the time of driving before the end-of-queue is actually reached. Therefore, with the proper value of TTQ, the objective of reducing the rate of an accident caused by highway congestion could be achieved.

5   Discussions and Future Work

In this paper, we implemented a system to detect End-of-Queue on the highway. This system could give pilot alert with message and tone with multiple platforms before the queue could be observed by eyes. Visualization of all queuing sites can also be shown on the map with detailed location information. On-road unit tests have been done in order to evaluate the system. From the current results, it has been proved that this system works as expected and could provide accurate alerts in time.

For future work, there are still many aspects that could be improved. First, the stability and reliability of the Android app need to be improved. Second, we

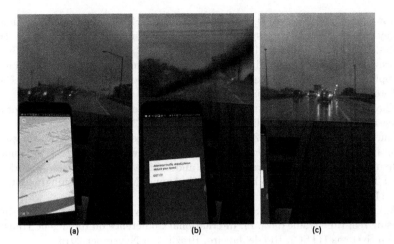

Fig. 9. Highway testing results: (a) Normal driving; (b) Pilot alert; (c) Traffic queue

would like to use our custom algorithm to determine ego car location instead of using Google API since although it is simple to use, it requires Internet access all the time, which could be slow and cause more data cost of the user's cellphone. At the same time, Google API is provided by a third party, which could cause confidential problems. Third, the Android Auto device needs to be integrated with the cellphone. After we have finalized the system setting, the evaluation will be needed on both driving simulator and on road.

Evaluation in a driving simulator will involve controlled in-lab tests. Road scenarios and queue locations could be designed following our demands. Real human subjects with different demographic information will be hired. After the evaluation in the driving simulator, the refined alerting system will be deployed to several testing vehicles which will be used in limited road testing. The road testing will last for eight weeks with the system on for four weeks and off for four weeks, in order to evaluate the effects that the system has on the drivers.

Acknowledgments. The authors would like to thank the Indiana Department of Transportation (INDoT) for the support of this research.

References

1. Mekker, M.M., Remias, S.M., McNamara, M.L., Bullock, D.M.: Characterizing interstate crash rates based on traffic congestion using probe vehicle data. In: Transportation Research Board 95th Annual Meeting, Washington DC, USA, January 2016
2. Tampere, C.M.J., Hoogendoorn, S.P., van Arem, B.: Continuous traffic flow modeling of driver support systems in multiclass traffic with intervehicle communication and drivers in the loops. IEEE Trans. Intell. Transp. Syst. **10**(4), 649–657 (2009)

3. Nowakowski, C., Vizzini, D., Gupta, S., Sengupta, R.: Evaluation of real-time freeway end-of-queue alerting system to promote driver situational awareness. Transp. Res. Rec. **2324**, 37–43 (2012)
4. Browne, R., Byrne, A.: Highway 402 queue warning system (wireless long haul application). In: Annual Conference of the Transportation Association of Canada, Toronto, ON, Canada (2008)
5. Khan, A.M.: Intelligent infrastructure-based queue-end warning system for avoiding rear impacts. IET Intell. Transp. Syst. **1**(2), 138–143 (2007)
6. Liu, Y., Zhang, W., Wang, Z., Chan, C.: DSRC-based end of queue warning system. In: IEEE Intelligent Vehicles Symposium, Los Angeles, CA, USA, 11–14 June 2017
7. Jiang, Y.: Estimation of traffic delays and vehicle queues at freeway work zones. In: Transportation Research Board 80-th Annual Meeting, Washington DC, USA, 7–11 January 2001
8. Amini, Z., Pedarsani, R., Skabardonis, A., Varaiya, P.: Queue-length estimation using real-time traffic data. In: International Conference on Intelligent Transportation Systems (ITSC), Rio de Janeiro, Brazil, 1–4 November 2016
9. Ullman, G.L., et al.: Enforcement effectiveness for queue-end protection. In: Traffic Law Enforcement in Work Zones: Phase II Research, vol. 3, pp. 35–57 (2013)
10. Lee, J.D., McGehee, D.V., Brown, T.L., Reyes, M.L.: Collision warning timing, driver distraction, and driver response to imminent rear-end collisions in a high-fidelity driving simulator. Hum. Factors **44**(2), 314–334 (2002)
11. Mekker, M., Li, H., McGregor, J., Kachler, M., Bullock, D.: Implementation of a real-time data driven system to provide queue alerts to stakeholders. In: IEEE 20th International Conference on Intelligent Transportation Systems (ITSC), Yokohama, Japan, October 2017
12. Li, H., Remias, S., Day, C., Mekker, M., Sturdevant, J., Bullock, D.: Shock wave boundary identification using cloud-based probe data. Transp. Res. Rec. J. Transp. Res. Board **2526**, 51–60 (2015)
13. Traffic Slowdown Database from Indiana Department of Transportation (INDoT). http://content.trafficwise.org/json/deltas.json
14. Indiana Department of Transportation (INDoT): INDoT Guidelines for Portable Changeable Message Signs, Section III: Placement (2012)

Creating and Testing Objective Performance Metrics for the Manual Teleoperation of Robotic Arms

Shuqi Xue[1](✉), Guohua Jiang[1], Ting Jiang[1], Chunhui Wang[1], and Zhiqiang Tian[2]

[1] Astronauts Research and Training Center of China,
Key Laboratory of Human Factors, Beijing 100094, China
xavierxuper@163.com
[2] China Institute of Marine Technology and Economy,
Laboratory of Marine Human Factors Engineering, Beijing 100089, China

Abstract. Facing with the background of robotic arms teleoperation task, 11 items of performance metrics in operation were put forward, and an experiment of operating the simulated robotic arm to dock a target was carried out to testify the usability of these metrics. The experimental results show that: providing numerical information promotes several metrics, and the layout plan with 4 cameras is superior to 2 cameras on the metric of the times of reaching joint limitation; whether the mission could be successfully completed can be predicted by the times of reaching joint limitation, the times of incorrect operation and the efficiency of operating the hand controllers; the efficiency of operating the hand controller, which are put forward in this study, is able to predict the completion time and the risk of reaching joint limitation, hence it can be used in the evaluation of an operator's ability in this robotic arm operation.

Keywords: Teleoperation · Robotic arm · Performance metrics · Ergonomics

1 Introduction

For delicate operations of robotic arms under unstructured working environment, such as the Space Station Remote Manipulation System (SSRMS) [1], teleoperation surgeries, computer automation system itself is not able to fully meet the task demand. In these cases, manual teleoperation mode in which human operators obtain information through Human Computer Interface (HCI) still plays an indispensable role [4]. In order to evaluate operators' performance effectively, objective metrics of robotic arm teleoperation are essential. Valid objective metrics help not only improve operator's ability, but improve the system design accordingly as well, in this way, the success probability, the operation efficiency, and the safety risk, will achieve better states.

When teleoperating a robotic arm, operators mainly depend the visual information which is captured by the cameras to obtain the perception of the working environment [6]. There are 2 basic kinds of cameras: the cameras which provide local views, and the fixed cameras which provide overall views. An operator should do the cognitive

© Springer Nature Switzerland AG 2019
V. G. Duffy (Ed.): HCII 2019, LNCS 11581, pp. 479–490, 2019.
https://doi.org/10.1007/978-3-030-22216-1_35

processing and spatial imagination based on these visual information [7]. In addition to that, an operator must pay attention to the running state information, the value information, warning information of the robotic arm. Hence, teleoperation of a robotic arm, is a complicated task requires highly developed operation skills of human. And the evaluation of operators' operation becomes an important issue of system design and training [8].

In the past 20 years, the training of SSRMS mainly depended on the subjective evaluation of NASA trainers who observed operator's operation and gave their scores [5]. And a Genetic Robotic Training (GRT) handbook was created by NASA, Table 1 showed partial content of it. There were a few objective metrics in GRT such as whether a collision occurred, the times of reaching joint limitation, but still GRT was mostly consist of subjective metrics, which was not suitable for standardized assessment as well as self-study.

Table 1. NASA GRT standards (excerpts).

Skill	Standard
According to the input of hand-controllers (HC), predict the moving trends of end-effector (EE)	According to the cameras' image, predict the moving trends of EE correctly
Select and control cameras for ideal observation	Use the perspective in accordance with the control frame
	Select and control the camera which is able to cover 6 DOFs
Situation Awareness Watch available HCI displays (especially cameras' view)	Be able to scan all the displays and warning information in 10 s
	Be able to pause immediately in response of warning
	Shall not hit the space station
	Be able to find and correct a potential joint limitation risk before warning

Besides NASA, several researches explored the utility of objective metrics of robotic arm teleoperation were carried out. Fry et al. [10] picked and verified smooth operation input and multi-axes input as metrics in their study. Lamb and Owen [11] picked completion time, operation error times, and deviation as objective metrics in their study using SSRMS simulation environment. Akagi et al. [12] picked completion time, correct control times, moving distance and other 3 metric in a 3 Dimension of Freedom (DOF) robotic arm experiment. Yet these studies didn't treat the metrics themselves as primary research goal, and their experiment tasks were mainly focused on fly-to mission, which didn't consider the delicate moving operation of robotic arm's end-effector.

In faced with teleoperation task of robotic arms, this paper summarized and created several objective operational performance metrics. And on a simulated robotic arm operation environment an experiment which asked operators to control the end-effector dock a target was carried out, the metrics were collected accordingly; by analyzing the differences of these metrics under different experimental conditions, this paper on one hand seek key display factors influencing this task, and on the other hand testified the validity of the objective metrics.

2   The Objective Metrics of a Robotic Arm Teleoperation Task

Based on the above-mentioned studies and the ISO standard: Ergonomics of human-system interaction – Usability methods supporting human-centered design [16], considering the feathers of robotic arm teleoperation task with hand-controllers, this paper raises 11 items of objective performance metrics, among which four items (8–11) are originally proposed, see Table 2.

Table 2. Objective performance metrics of robotic arm operation with hand controllers.

The metric of whether succeed	Whether succeed (No. 1)	Whether complete the task in time
The metrics of safety	Collision times (No. 2)	The total times of colliding the environment or target objects
	Reaching joint limitation times (No. 3)	The total times of reaching joint limitation
The metrics of accuracy	Position accuracy (No. 4)	The final position deviation between the end-effector and the target
	Angle accuracy (No. 5)	The final angle deviation between the end-effector and the target
The metrics of efficiency	Completion time (No. 6)	Completion time of docking task
	Multi-axes operation ratio (No. 7)	The ratio of multi-axes operation time and completion time
	Incorrect operation times (No. 8)	**Moving HC towards one direction but realizing it is a wrong move then change to the opposite direction**
	Translation efficiency of EE (No. 9)	**The ratio of the whole travel distance of end-effector and completion time**
	Efficiency of translation HC (No. 10)	**The ratio of the total operation output of translation HC and the origin position deviation**
	Efficiency of orientation HC (No. 11)	**The ratio of the total operation output of orientation HC and the origin angle deviation**

Metric 8 (incorrect operation times) reflects operators' cognitive ability of mental rotation when watching the video information provided by virtual cameras; less incorrect operation times means better awareness of the location and orientation relationship between the target and the robot arm. Metric 9 (translation efficiency of end-effector) reflects the operating efficiency on the three translation DOF, higher value of Metric 9 means longer moving distances in certain time which suggests a smoother operating of translation hand-controller. Lower values of Metric 10 and Metric 11 (operating efficiency of translation hand-controller and orientation hand-controller) mean less operating of the hand-controllers of certain deviation which means the efficiency is higher. These metrics will be tested and analyzed in the experiment.

3   Method

3.1   Experimental Environment

The experimental scene was simulated on V-Rep software platform. The robotic arm was built based on the Xinsong SR6C industrial robot which had 6 joints so as to ensure the end-effector was able to move inside the workspace with 6 DOF (3 translation DOF and 3 orientation DOF). In the experiment, subjects must observe the visual information provided by virtual cameras on HCI and operated two hand-controllers (Laishida PNX-2103) with both hands to control the movement of the robotic arm. The terminate frame was set as the control frame.

3.2   Subject

16 subjects were selected to do this experiment. They were all male, right-handed, and their average age was 24.4 (s = ±1.5). The subjects had no experience of teleoperating a robotic arm and thus need a standard process of operation training.

3.3   Task

The operation task was designed as followed: in the simulated scene, a cross-shaped facility for docking was connected to the end-effector, and its direction was marked by a colored block, see Fig. 1. There were 2 docking target cubes whose surfaces were set with cross-shaped grooves, each cube had 3 grooves therefore a total number of 6 target grooves were in the working space. In each simulation trail, one groove would be selected randomly to be the docking target, and a colored block would be marked on it. An operator needed to control the end-effector till the cross-shaped facility moved into the groove with the 2 colored marks in the same direction. The success criteria were: the relative translation deviation was less than 0.004 m and the relative orientation deviation was less than 4° in each DOF. If the task could not be done in 240 s, it was considered a failure. During the operation, if any joint of the robotic arm reached the limitation position, or the robotic arm had a collision with other objects (especially the target cubes), a warning window would appear to remind the subject to move away the robotic arm to a suitable state.

Fig. 1. The simulated experimental scene.

The manual operation of the task could be vaguely divided into 2 phases: firstly the subject watched the video image (mostly the overall cameras), controlled the robotic arm till the target surface appeared in the local camera's view; secondly the subject mainly depended the local camera's view, as well as the value information (when provided), adjusted the position and orientation of the end-effector, and completed the task.

The speed of end-effector was constant, and the difficulty of each trail was in the same level.

3.4   Design

The experiment was interclassed with 2 factors and 2 levels. The 2 factors were whether the value information was provided, and different number of virtual cameras (2 or 4), the layout plans were shown in Fig. 2.

The value information included: relative deviation value of 6 DOF, joint angle value of 6 joints (and their limitation range), running time of task and others. In the 2 cameras condition, one was the local view cameras which moved with the end-effector, and the other was the overall view camera which was fixed and able to see all 6 target surfaces. In the 4 cameras condition, besides the mentioned 2 cameras, 2 fixed cameras which respectively observed the 2 cubes from another position were added, since in one trial there was only one target cube, in this condition, only 3 cameras were valid.

Based on the attention allocation theory of Xu et al. [13], an operator should not pay attention to more than 4 items of information in the same time. On the condition of numerical value and 4 cameras, since only 3 cameras functioning, it reached this limit.

16 subjects operated 2 trails on each of the 4 conditions. In order to balance the study effect, the sequence of experiment was in Latin square design. The original performance data was recorded by the software system, and the data was calculated into the metrics in Table 2.

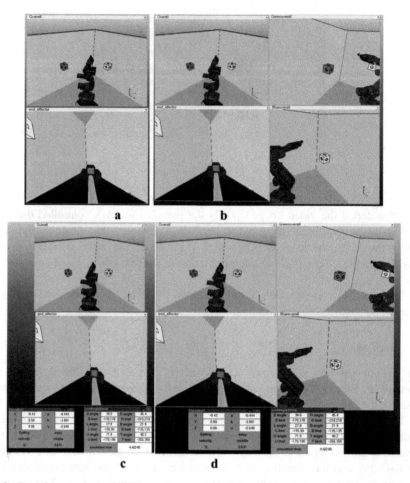

Fig. 2. Four layout plans of HCI. a: no numerical information + 2 cameras (staring interests areas: end-effector camera + big global camera); b: no numerical information + 4 cameras (staring interests areas: end-effector camera + big global camera + far global camera); c: numerical information + 2 cameras (staring interests areas: end-effector camera + numerical information); d: numerical information + 4 cameras (staring interests areas: end-effector camera + big global camera + numerical information)

4   Results

The analysis of variance (ANOVA) towards 11 performance metrics showed that with value information all metrics except translation efficiency of end-effector were better than without value information, and 5 metrics (whether succeed, collision times, operation time, efficiency of translation hand-controller and efficiency of orientation hand-controller) were significantly better ($p < 0.050$). A larger number of metrics on 4 cameras condition were better than those on 2 cameras condition, yet only the metric of reaching limitation times was statistically significant better ($F = 4.299$, $p = 0.040$). The interaction analysis of the 2 factors showed that interaction effect significantly influenced the metric of translation efficiency of end-effector ($F = 4.690$, $p = 0.032$). The 7 metrics that showed significant differences were shown in Table 3.

Table 3. Comparison of performance metrics (who have significant difference) under 4 different experimental conditions.

	a. No numerical information + 2 cameras	b. No numerical information + 4 camera	c. Numerical information + 2 cameras	d. Numerical information + 4 cameras
Success rate	0.66 ($s = \pm0.48$)	0.63($s = \pm0.49$)	0.77 ($s = \pm0.43$)	0.87 ($s = \pm0.35$)
Collision times	0.90 ($s = \pm1.40$)	0.50($s = \pm1.36$)	0.23 ($s = \pm0.43$)	0.30 ($s = \pm1.12$)
Completion time/s	197.18 ($s = \pm46.23$)	187.66 ($s = \pm52.64$)	173.91 ($s = \pm56.02$)	165.44 ($s = \pm43.53$)
Efficiency of translation HC	1980.81 ($s = \pm446.85$)	2104.23 ($s = \pm850.00$)	1876.98 ($s = \pm570.73$)	1767.13 ($s = \pm410.50$)
Efficiency of orientation HC	1039.92 ($s = \pm297.36$)	1028.01 ($s = \pm304.39$)	953.49 ($s = \pm351.33$)	854.64 ($s = \pm143.78$)
Reaching joint limitation times	1.56 ($s = \pm3.32$)	1.20 ($s = \pm2.75$)	1.26 ($s = \pm3.79$)	0.30 ($s = \pm1.47$)
Translation efficiency of EE/(mm/s)	4.33 ($s = \pm1.41$)	5.22 ($s = \pm2.35$)	5.12 ($s = \pm1.76$)	4.97 ($s = \pm1.48$)

The success rate of all trails was 73.17%. Comparing the other 10 metrics between the success trails and fail trails, the significance analysis showed that all the metrics in success trails except collision times, multi-axe operation ratio, and translation efficiency of end-effector were significantly better than those in fail trails ($p < 0.003$). ANOVA within the success trails showed that whether to provide value information had significant influences ($p < 0.026$) on the metrics of collision times, angle accuracy and efficiency of orientation hand-controller, seen Fig. 3; while different camera layout plans merely significantly influenced ($F = 5.417$, $p = 0.022$) the metric of collision times. In the fail trails, the 2 factors had significant influence on none of the metrics.

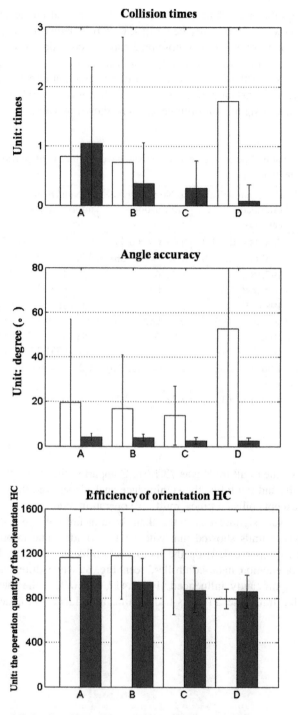

failed trails, white, n=33; succeeded trails, grey, n=90

Fig. 3. The metrics (times of collision, angle accuracy, efficiency of orientation HC) comparison under different experimental conditions.

Whether succeed, collision times, reaching limitation times and operation time were 4 basic and important metrics, and using the efficiency metrics to do the correlation analysis with the 4 basic metrics would help to find which efficiency metrics benefited the basic metrics, and the most 3 related metrics to the 4 basic metrics are listed in Table 4. The results showed whether succeed and operation time were significantly correlated to all the other metrics. However, for the 2 safety metrics (collision times and reaching limitation times), the majority of efficiency metrics were not able to predict them, only 2 metrics (translation efficiency of end-effector and efficiency of orientation hand-controller) were significantly correlated to reaching limitation times.

Table 4. The 3 most correlated metrics to vital performance metrics.

Vital performance metric	The 3 most correlated metrics		
Whether succeed	Reaching joint limitation times ($r = -0.474**$)	Incorrect operation times ($r = -0.352**$)	Efficiency of translation HC ($r = -0.34**$)
Collision times	translation efficiency of EE ($r = -0.175*$)	multi-axes operation ratio ($r = -0.111$, $p = 0.116$)	reaching joint limitation times ($r = -0.092$, $p = 0.163$)
Reaching joint limitation times	translation efficiency of EE ($r = -0.269**$)	efficiency of orientation HC ($r = 0.256**$)	incorrect operation times ($r = 0.167*$)
Completion time	incorrect operation times ($r = 0.513**$)	translation efficiency of EE ($r = -0.493**$)	efficiency of translation HC ($r = 0.450**$)

r: correlation coefficient, $*p < .05$, $**p < .01$

5 Discussion

5.1 The Influence of Experimental Factors

For the trails providing value information, subjects usually began to focus on the value information (mostly relative deviation value) and operated the robotic arm as to make the relative deviation value decline till meet the success criteria, hence the trails with value information had a significant higher success rate ($F = 4.545$, $p = 0.035$). In the task, collision only occurred when the end-effector was close enough to the target, and value information helped subjects to judge if there existed the risk of collision, hence the collision times were significantly decreased ($F = 5.214$, $p = 0.024$). Value information also helped subjects decide whether they were operating the hand-controllers correctly, if the relative deviation values were decreasing, it generally (not always) means the current moving direction of the hand-controllers were correct, hence the trails with value information had significant better metrics of efficiency of hand-controllers ($F = 4.043$, $p = 0.047$; $F = 7.015$, $p = 0.009$).

As introduced in Sect. 3.3, different camera layout plans mainly affected the task in the first phase. In the 4 cameras (3 valid cameras) layout trails, subjects could observe whether a joint was likely to reach the limitation more directly (than observe value information), so the metric of reaching limitation times was significantly lower ($F = 4.299$, $p = 0.040$). Besides this, despite that 4 cameras plan showed superiority than 2 cameras plan in most metrics, no statistically significant difference appeared. Additional cameras didn't help the subjects to do the task much, the reason might be that the local camera which moved with the end-effector played a most important role in this operation, operators almost need to rely on it all the time, whereas the importance of overall cameras was weakened respectively, hence the overall cameras' influence on performance declined accordingly.

On the interaction of the 2 experimental factors, there was a significant change ($F = 4.690$, $p = 0.032$) in the metric of translation efficiency of end-effector. It indicated that in the first phase of the operation, subjects' comprehension of value information interacted with their observation of camera views, and it might cause the overload of information which made it difficult for the subjects to allocate their attention [13], hence the performance suffered a significant decline.

5.2 Analysis of the Performance Metrics

According to the task analysis, the experimental factors analysis, and the results of the metrics, the performance metrics will be discussed in the following:

(1) Whether succeed and completion time. Whether an operation is successful or not is a core metric in this experiment as well as in any other robotic arm teleoperation task. In our task, completion time and docking accuracy (distance and angle) make no sense unless the operation succeeds, therefore correlations between these 3 metrics and whether succeed are not taken into consideration. Reaching limitation times has a significant influence on whether succeed (seen Table 3), it is because when a joint reaches its limitation, a subject need to do complicated decisions and operations to get rid of the unsafe state, which will usually cost much time and make the task failed. The operation efficiency metrics put forward in this article, especially incorrect operation times and efficiency of hand-controllers, can straightly reflect the effectiveness of a subject's operation, hence they are able to predict the metric of whether succeed and completion time well.

(2) Safety metrics. Collisions are unacceptable accidents in most actual robotic arm teleoperation tasks, in this experiment, the efficiency metrics don't have strong correlations with the metric of collision times, which means collision times should be an independent metric to investigate. Another important safety metric is reaching limitation times [9], more times a joint reaches its limitation position means more easily the joint will be damaged. To avoid that, it demands subjects keep their situation awareness (SA) [15] of the gesture of the robotic arm, which reflects onto the efficiency metrics, especially translation efficiency of end-effector and efficiency of hand-controllers (seen Table 3).

(3) Incorrect operation times and multi-axe operation ratio. Similar metrics have been used in GRT and other researches [9, 11, 12], [15], yet in different tasks their

detailed definitions differ. In our experiment, incorrect operation times is able to predict whether succeed, completion time and reaching limitation times, this metric reflects the subjects' proficiency of operating the hand-controllers and comprehension of situational information. The metric of multi-axe operation ratio doesn't show significant predictability in this task.

(4) Translation efficiency of end-effector. This metric primarily functions in the first phase of the operation, and it is affected under the interaction of the 2 factors. This metric indicates the fluency of an operator's control, so that reflects the consistency of his decision-making, hence this metric is a significant prediction of the 2 safety metrics and the metric of completion time.

(5) Efficiency of hand-controllers. These 2 metrics (which were defined in this article) indicate operators' ability of situation perceiving, and hand-controllers operation during the whole task. Less operation of hand-controllers (under the same task difficulty) indicates a more effective and adequate operation. These 2 metrics are significantly correlated with the metric of whether success, completion time and reaching joint limitation times (see Table 4), which means trainings towards the improvement of the metrics of efficiency of hand-controllers would benefit the performance in the robotic arm teleoperation task displayed equations are centered and set on a separate line.

6   Conclusion and Future Work

Facing with the background of robotic arms teleoperation task (especially the space station robotic arm), this article abstracted and analyzed 11 items of objective performance metrics for evaluating an operation. These metrics were collected in a simulated experiment whose factors were whether providing numerical information and different camera layout plans (2 or 4). Under this experimental task and condition, primary conclusions are as follows:

(1) With numerical information, operators perform better on the metrics of whether succeed, collision times, as well as many operation efficiency metrics. Under 4 camera layout plans, reaching joint limitation times decrease. Hence in this task 4 camera layout with numerical information is the better HCI design plan.

(2) The metrics of reaching joint limitation times, incorrect operation times, and efficiency of hand-controllers are able to predict the metric of whether succeed. The metric of collision times is relatively independent with the other metrics; therefore, it should be examined individually.

(3) The metrics of translation efficiency of end-effector and efficiency of hand-controllers which are put forward in this article, are able to predict the crucial metrics including whether succeed, reaching joint limitation times and completion time. So, they can be used to evaluate operation efficiency in this task and give instructions in operation training.

In future studies, the objective metrics in this article can be used to build a quantitative model for comprehensively evaluate the space station robotic arm tele-operation. Furthermore, operators' situation awareness and the relationship between SA and performance metrics should be analyzed.

References

1. Shuqi, X., Guohua, J., Zhiqiang, T., et al.: Progress of the key technologies in human-computer interface in space teleoperation. Manned Spaceflight **20**(5), 497–502 (2014)
2. Sheridan, T.B.: Telerobotics, Automation, and Human Supervisory Control, pp. 145–212. MIT Press, Cambridge (1992)
3. Sheridan, T.B.: Telerobotics. Automatica **25**(4), 487–507 (1989)
4. Menchaca-Brandan, M.A.: Influence of spatial orientation and spatial visualization on space teleoperation performance. Thesis, Massachusetts Institute of Technology (2007)
5. Van Woerkom, P.T.L.M., Misra, A.K.: Robotic manipulator in space: a dynamics and control perspective. Actaastronautica **38**(4), 411–421 (1996)
6. Zak, H., Das, H.: Towards a training methodology for skilled teleoperation. IEEE Trans. Syst. Man Cybern. **25**(2), 313–327 (1995)
7. Fry, T.L., Schlegel, R.E., Shehab, R.L., et al.: Developing metrics to evaluate NASA RMS training performance. In: IIE Annual Conference, Proceedings, p. 1. Institute of Industrial Engineers-Publisher (2003)
8. Lamb, P., Owen, D.: Human performance in space telerobotic manipulation. In: Proceedings of the ACM Symposium on Virtual Reality Software and Technology, pp. 31–37. ACM (2005)
9. Akagi, T.M., Schlegel R.E., Shehab, R.L., et al.: Toward the construction of an efficient set of robot arm operator performance metrics. In: Proceedings of the Human Factors and Ergonomics Society Annual Meeting, vol. 48, no. 10, pp. 1194–1198. SAGE Publications (2004)
10. ISO/TR 16982:2002 standard: Ergonomics of human-system interaction – Usability methods supporting human-centred design
11. Wu, X., Xiaoru, W., Damin, Z.: Attention allocation modeling under multi-factor condition. J. Beijing Univ. Aeronaut. Astronaut. **39**(8), 1086–1090 (2013)
12. National Aeronautics and Space Administration, Generic Robotics Training Evaluation. NASA (2010)
13. Endsley, M.R.: Toward a theory of situation awareness in dynamic systems. Hum. Factors J. Hum. Factors Ergon. Soc. **37**(1), 32–64 (1995)

A Method of Designing Outdoor Safety Way Guidance Sign Layout Information Based on Human Factors Engineering

Jiliang Zhang[1], Yongquan Chen[2(✉)], and Jingquan Liu[1(✉)]

[1] Department of Engineering Physics, Tsinghua University, Beijing, China
zhangjiliang0727@126.com, jingquan@tsinghua.edu.cn
[2] China National Institute of Standardization, Beijing, China
chenyongquan@cnis.gov.cn

Abstract. Outdoor safety way guidance sign's guidance function benefits from its reasonable layout information design. In order to get an effective design method, a series of analyses were done as follows. Based on the theory of human factors engineering, an interactive mode between individual and sign was proposed, dividing the interaction process into four stages: Capturing Sign, Reading Information, Making Decision, and Taking Action. Based on Shannon information theory, a method on how to measure a sign's information and its loss caused by obstacles was put forward, and 305.2 bit was pointed out to be the allowed information maximum value when designing a sign under the consideration of human's ability to deal with information. Signs were classified to be 11 kinds according to corresponding evacuation environment and psychological needs, and what information should each kind show on layout was analyzed with several typical design examples following. A simulation model was created by 3dsmax to verify obstacle's influence on information transferring from signs to individuals, and to analyze improved design methods. The research results were expected to be useful to instruct designers in designing outdoor safety way guidance signs and to improve evacuation efficiency.

Keywords: Human factors engineering · Layout information · Outdoor safety way guidance sign · Information amount · Emergency evacuation

1 Introduction

In recent years, various disasters occurred more and more frequently, leading to huge losses in people's lives and property. It appears to be particularly important to carry out effective evacuation in sudden disasters. Safety way guidance signs are designed for emergency evacuation, aiming to guide the public to safe areas in a safe and quick way.

Currently, a series of relevant standards have been promulgated internationally. ISO 16069 [1], newly issued in 2017, is mainly for the setting standards of indoor environmental safety way guidance signs. ISO 7010 [2], a standard dedicated to graphical symbols, gives a large number of safety symbols that can be used in safety signs. ISO 20712-1 [3], a standard dedicated to water safety signs and beach safety flags, gives design methods for water-related signs. However, existing standards are

© Springer Nature Switzerland AG 2019
V. G. Duffy (Ed.): HCII 2019, LNCS 11581, pp. 491–508, 2019.
https://doi.org/10.1007/978-3-030-22216-1_36

mainly for indoor or some other specific environmental evacuation, and none is for general outdoor environmental evacuation. In the other words, based on existing standards, the public can be guided just from a building's inside to its exit, but how to get to emergency shelters then, is still a problem.

Layout information of a safety way guidance sign plays a great role in achieving the sign's guidance function. Reasonable layout information design contributes to the interactive effect between individuals and signs. Therefore the evacuation efficiency can be greatly improved.

In order to improve the standardization construction of safety way guidance system, a design method for layout information of outdoor safety way guidance sign (OSWGS) was analyzed, aiming to be helpful in establishing OSWGS design standards.

2 Design Principles

To ensure the design effect, design principles for OSWGS layout information were analyzed first of all as follows.

Information Correctness. Wrong information causes erroneous decisions and wrong actions. Information correctness is the basic requirement of OSWGS design.

Information Clarity. Clearly defined layout information helps the public speed up their understanding, and reduce the probability of misunderstanding.

Information Amount. Too little information leads to the public not fully understanding, while too much information leads to the public a slower understanding. In order to get a balance, the minimum and maximum values of information should be determined by some methods.

3 Interactive Mode

3.1 Interaction Model

Base on Jun Liang's research [4] on evacuation behavior of people in building fires, and according to the interaction mode between driver and traffic sign, an interaction model between public and OSWGS has been proposed, dividing the interaction process into four stages: Capturing Sign, Reading Information, Making Decision, and Taking Action. The interaction model is shown in Fig. 1.

Capturing Sign. Capturing sign stage refers to the process that evacuators evacuate from the capturing point A to the reading point B. The capturing point is the position where the evacuators notice the sign for the first time and complete the first interaction with the sign. The reading point is the position where the evacuators start reading the information on the sign and complete the first interaction with the guidance information. The meaning of this stage for evacuators is finding and noticing the sign, and achieving their psychological verification that the direction they have selected is right,

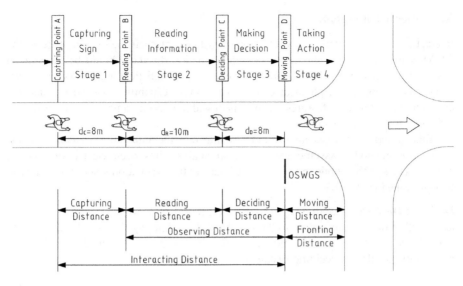

Fig. 1. OSWGS interaction model

so that they should make some physiological and psychological preparation for the stage of reading information.

Reading Information. Reading information stage refers to the process that the evacuators evacuate from the reading point B to the deciding point C. The deciding point is the position where the evacuators finish their reading information and start thinking about the meaning of the guidance information and considering how to make decisions next for themselves. The meaning of this stage for evacuators is getting the guidance information from OSWGS. As a much important stage of the interaction process, this stage can be regarded as the information input stage of evacuators' cognitive process.

Making Decision. Making decision stage refers to the process that the evacuators evacuate from the deciding point C to the moving point D. The moving point is the position where the evacuators finish their making evacuation decisions and start taking action as the instruction of the guidance information. Different from driving behavior, emergency evacuation doesn't have to consider the distance between moving point and sign position point for walking's low speed, so the two positions overlap in the interaction model. The meaning of this stage for evacuators is understanding infor-mation and making decisions, and it can be regarded as the information processing stage of evacuators' cognitive process.

Taking Action. Taking action stage refers to the process after the moving point D. Based on the information comprehension and evacuation decision, the evacuators take specific action in this stage, and it can be regarded as the information output stage of evacuators' cognitive process.

3.2 Interaction Distance

Interaction distance refers to the evacuation distance of each interaction stage in the OSWGS interaction model. The values of interaction distance should be determined based on the actual statistics, including the evacuators' statistical features (such as age, gender, education level, physical condition, response capability, and so on) and the environment's statistical features (such as path width, crossing amount, road condition, lighting situation, and so on).

Take a certain case as an example to illustrate the interaction distance values' calculation methods. Assume that statistical analysis has been carried out on the characteristics of the public in the area of China and the evacuation velocity v value can be determined as 3.5 m/s.

Deciding Distance. Deciding time t_D can be divided into two parts: thinking time t_t and reaction time t_r. According to the measured data, thinking time can be determined from 1.0 s to 1.5 s, while reaction time may be roughly determined as 1.0 s. The method of calculating deciding distance d_D is as follow.

$$d_D = v \times (t_t + t_r) \tag{1}$$

Approximate the result of the calculation as an integer: $d_D = 8$ m.

Reading Distance. According to Posner [5], the average reading speed of regular English article is 330 words/min. According to Liao and Zhang [6], the average reading speed of regular Chinese article is 309 words/min. Having considered an OSWGS's information amount and the corresponding relationship between other information elements (such as Arabic numeral, graphic, symbol, and so on) and words, the reading time t_R may be roughly determined as 3.0 s. The method of calculating reading distance d_R is as follow.

$$d_R = v \times t_R \tag{2}$$

Approximate the result of the calculation as an integer: $d_R = 10$ m.

Capturing Distance. Capturing time is similar to deciding time, so t_C may be roughly determined as 2.25 s. The method of calculating deciding distance d_C is as follow.

$$d_C = v \times t_C \tag{3}$$

Approximate the result of the calculation as an integer: $d_C = 8$ m.

4 Information Amount

4.1 Shannon Information Theory

Shannon [7], the founder of information theory, gave a method for information measurement from the perspective of probability.

Consider that there's a discrete random variable X, whose possible output is x_i, $i = 1, 2, \ldots, n$. The information amount of $X = x_i$ is as follow.

$$I(x_i) = -logP(x_i) \tag{4}$$

When the base is 2, the unit is bit.

4.2 Information Amount Calculation

OSWGS mainly includes 7 types of information: English, Local Language, Arabic numeral, Color, Shape, Direction Arrow, and Graphic Symbol. Particularly, Local Language varies from country to country, aiming to be better understood by the locals. In this paper, Local Language takes Chinese as an example.

Calculate each type of information separately. Take the calculation of English as an example. There are a total of 26 English letters, and in order to simplify the calculation, assume that each letter appears to be independent of each other. In the other words, the probability of each letter appearing is 1/26 when there's some English Language on an OSWGS. The information amount of a single English letter is calculated as follow.

$$\begin{aligned} I(x_1) &= -log_2^{P(x_1)} \\ &= -log_2^{\frac{1}{26}} \\ &= 4.7\,bit \end{aligned} \tag{5}$$

Similarly, the calculation results of all unit information amounts are shown in Table 1.

Table 1. OSWGS unit information amount summary table

x_i	x_1	x_2	x_3	x_4	x_5	x_6	x_7
Information type	English	Chinese	Arabic numeral	Color	Shape	Direction arrow	Graphic symbol
Amount/bit	4.7	11.3	3.3	3.0	3.3	4.6	5.9

In order to calculate an OSWGS's information amount, count its unit number of each information type separately, and record it as n_i. Take Color as an example. Assume that an OSWGS contains several types of information. Having observed it carefully, we find that it contains three kinds of colors altogether: blue, green, and white, and we can point out that n_4 equals 3. The method of calculating the amount of an OSWGS's layout information is as follow.

$$I_{OSWGS} = \sum_{i=1}^{7} n_i \cdot I(x_i) \tag{6}$$

4.3 Allowed Maximum Information Amount

Too much information extends evacuators' reading and understanding time. Due to human's limited ability to process information and the importance of evacuation time in emergency escape, it is necessary to get a reasonable value of an OSWGS's allowed maximum information amount.

Considering that an OSWGS may contain uncertain types and quantities information units, in order to simplify the calculation, we may unify all types of information into one type, such as language information. Due to the familiarity with English differing from country to country, local language may be the best choice. In this paper, assume that an OSWGS includes only Chinese character information.

According to the reading speed of Chinese (309 words/min) and the OSWGS's interaction model, the allowed information process time during evacuation is the sum of reading time and decision time (3.0 s + 2.25 s = 5.25 s). The allowed maximum number of Chinese character may be determined as 27 (309 $\div$ 60 $\times$ 5.25 $\approx$ 27). The allowed maximum information amount I_{max} is as follow.

$$
\begin{aligned}
I_{max} &= \sum_{i=1}^{7} n_{imax} \cdot I(x_i) \\
&= n_2 \times I(x_2) \\
&= 305.2 \, bit
\end{aligned} \tag{7}
$$

It is recommended to control the amount of information within 305.2 bit when designing an OSWGS.

4.4 Occlusion Information Loss Amount

Considering the impact of occlusion on the information transfer effect during the information input stage, it is necessary to analyze the information loss amount caused by occlusion. The method of calculating occlusion information loss amount I_{loss} is as follow.

$$
I_{loss} = \sum_{k}^{n} \frac{I_k \cdot d_k}{d_R} \tag{8}
$$

In the equation above, k refers to the kth occluded information unit, and I_k refers to the kth unit's information amount, and d_k refers to the kth unit's obscured distance, and n refers to the number of obscured units in the reading information stage, and d_R refers to the reading distance.

Occlusion information loss amount can be used to measure the information transmission loss caused by occlusion and evaluate the occlusion disposal methods.

5   Information Design

5.1   OSWGS Classification

OSWGSs in different positions provide different guidance functions and meet evacuators' different psychological needs. As shown in Table 2, OSWGSs are classified into 11 kinds based on different evacuation environments.

Table 2. OSWGS classification

Main procedure	Evacuation environment	OSWGS
Starting point	Disaster area	Disaster Type Sign
	Risk area	Evacuation Plan Sign
		Description Sign
En route	Straight road	Midway Indication Sign
	Curved road	
	Vertical multilayer	Vertical Indication Sign
	General intersection	Intersection Indication Sign
	Optional intersection	Optional Route Sign
	No entry	No Entry Sign
	Dangerous section	Danger Warning Sign
	Safe area	Temporary Area Sign
Terminal point	Refuge place	Emergency Shelter Sign

5.2   Necessary Information Element

Disaster Type Sign. Compared with other areas, disaster areas are much more dangerous, so it is necessary to set Disaster Type Signs at these locations to alert the public to caution. The disasters mainly include fires, floods, landslides, typhoons and mudslides.

The main function of Disaster Type Sign is to quickly attract the public's attention. Their layout information should be as simple as possible and their features should be much prominent. Therefore, besides color and shape, only the Disaster Type Symbol element should be selected when designing its layout information.

To be more acceptable, the symbols prefer the corresponding symbols in the current standards. Fires Symbol selects W021 in ISO7010, and Floods Symbol selects WSW014 in ISO20712-1. Symbols not found in current standards need to be designed based on the principle of simple and vivid.

Disaster Type Symbols are shown in Fig. 2. From left to right, there are Fires, Floods, Landslides, Typhoons, and Mudslides.

Color and shape play an important role in attracting public's attention. As shown in Yuchang Han's eye movement experiments [8], yellow and triangle are easier to be found first. Disaster Type Signs corresponding to the Disaster Type Symbols are designed as shown in Fig. 3.

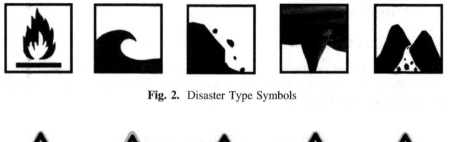

Fig. 2. Disaster Type Symbols

Fig. 3. Disaster Type Signs (Color figure online)

Evacuation Plan Sign. Sudden disasters cause public bad mood such as panic and anxiety, leading to a decline in cognitive ability. Evacuation Plan Sign can increase the public's awareness of the surroundings and help them adjust their mood. Evacuation Plan Sign should provide real and streamlined information within the evacuation scope and highlight the information that is important for evacuation.

Road Network Information. According to this information, evacuators can familiarize themselves with the surrounding road network in advance, and reduce their strangeness during the evacuation.

Current Location Information and Emergency Shelter Location Information. According to this information, evacuators can specify the relative location of the emergency shelter and quickly determine the best evacuation route.

Best Evacuation Route Information. Generally speaking, a short and good road conditions path can contribute to evacuation. Marking the best evacuation route on the evacuation plan can help evacuators make their best choices in complex road networks.

Distance Information. Distance information shows the distance from the current location to the emergency shelter. It can help evacuators get certain expectations for evacuation intensity in advance.

Relative Safe Areas Information. According to this information, evacuators can know the location of temporary rest areas on the way to the emergency shelter, and they can decide whether to have a short rest at the right point during their evacuation.

Other Potential Disaster Information, Dangerous Areas Information, and No Entry Information Within the Evacuation Scope. They can remind evacuators to be vigilant about unsafe environments and bypass them in advance.

Other Information. Other information such as scale information and compass information should also be contained. Since the Evacuation Plan Sign is mainly used before the disaster, its information should be as detailed as possible and not subject to the allowed maximum information amount.

Evacuation Plan Sign is designed as shown in Fig. 4.

Fig. 4. Evacuation Plan Sign

Description Sign. In general, the Description Sign is designed to match the Evacuation Plan Sign. It can deepen the public's understanding of the evacuation environment.

The Description Sign should contain the following information: Emergency Shelter Symbol, Disaster Type Symbols, and other precautions. Emergency Shelter Symbol and Disaster Type Symbols indicate that the Description Sign is applicable to emergency evacuation situations in the event of such types of disaster.

Description Sign is designed as shown in Fig. 5.

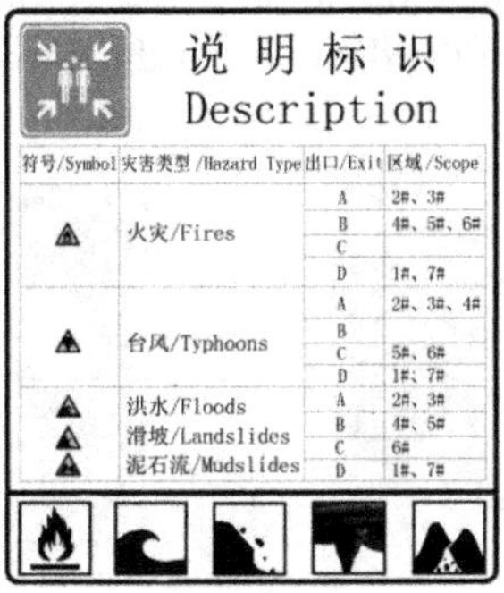

Fig. 5. Description Sign

The setting effect of Evacuation Plan Sign and Description Sign in a scene is shown in Fig. 6.

Midway Indication Sign and Vertical Indication Sign. Setting Midway Indication Signs and Vertical Indication Signs at appropriate locations helps evacuators

Fig. 6. The setting effect of Evacuation Plan Sign and Description Sign

continuously obtain guidance information during their evacuation process and achieve the psychological verification of their evacuation direction's correctness.

According to their functions, the Midway Indication Sign and the Vertical Indication Sign should be designed as simple as possible. They should contain only Emergency Shelter Symbol information and Direction Arrow information. The Emergency Shelter Symbol indicates that the sign is suitable for emergency evacuation and the Direction Arrow indicates that the direction indicated by the arrow is the correct evacuation direction.

They are designed as shown in Fig. 7. Midway Indication Sign is the left one, and it means going straight in the direction of the arrow. Vertical Indication Sign is the right one, and it means going up in the direction of the arrow.

Fig. 7. Midway Indication Sign and Vertical Indication Sign

The setting effect of Midway Indication Sign and Vertical Indication Sign in a scene is shown in Fig. 8.

Intersection Indication Sign. The intersection is one of the most confusing locations for evacuators due to its multiple selectivity. Intersection Indication Sign's function is to guide the evacuators to correctly select their evacuation route. It should contain the

Fig. 8. The setting effect of Midway Indication Sign and Vertical Indication Sign

following information: Direction Arrow, Distance, Text, Emergency Shelter Symbol, and Disaster Type Symbols.

Direction Arrow Information. According to this information, evacuators can select a right evacuation route at the intersection. It improves the accuracy of the public's evacuation direction selection.

Distance Information. In order to avoid the homing behaviors of the evacuators, it is necessary to provide distance information on the sign. Distance information also contributes to adjusting evacuators' anxiety during their evacuation.

Text Information. As an auxiliary function, text information can further clarify the meaning of the sign.

Symbol Information. Symbol information of the Intersection Indication Sign includes Emergency Shelter Symbol and Disaster Type Symbols, indicating that the sign is suitable for emergency evacuation of such disasters.

Intersection Indication Sign is designed as shown in Fig. 9.

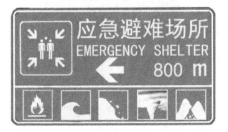

Fig. 9. Intersection Indication Sign

The setting effect of Intersection Indication Sign in a scene is shown in Fig. 10.

Fig. 10. The setting effect of Intersection Indication Sign

Optional Route Sign. The density of personnel during evacuation has a certain impact on evacuation efficiency. Diverted evacuation helps relieve congestion. When there are routes similar to the best evacuation route's length, they can also be used for evacuation. To illustrate this situation, it is necessary to set an Optional Route Sign at the selection point.

Optional Route Sign should include the information of Emergency Shelter Symbol, Disaster Type Symbols, Text, and Optional Route Sketch. Optional Route Sketch should fully reflect the start point and the terminal point, and clearly mark the optional routes.

Optional Route Sign is designed as shown in Fig. 11.

Fig. 11. Optional Route Sign

The setting effect of Optional Route Sign in a scene is shown in Fig. 12.

Fig. 12. The setting effect of Optional Route Sign

No Entry Sign and Danger Warning Sign. In order to indicate the no entry road sections and the dangerous locations caused by the disaster around the evacuation route, it is necessary to set No Entry signs and Danger Warning Signs at the corresponding locations.

No Entry Sign/Danger Warning Sign should include the information of Emergency Shelter Symbol, Disaster Type Symbols, No Entry Symbol/Danger Warning Symbol. No Entry Symbol and Danger Warning Symbol are each selected from P004 and W001 in ISO 7010.

They are designed as shown in Fig. 13. No Entry Sign is the left one, and Danger Warning Sign is the right one.

Fig. 13. No Entry Sign and Danger Warning Sign

Temporary Area Sign. When the evacuation distance is a little far, it is necessary to set Temporary Area Signs in relatively safe positions to prompt the needy evacuators to take a short break there.

Temporary Area Sign should include the information of Text, Temporary Area Symbol, and Disaster Type Symbols. Temporary Area Symbol is selected from 1–1 in DB12/330 [9].

Temporary Area Sign is designed as shown in Fig. 14.

Fig. 14. Temporary Area Sign

Emergency Shelter Sign. Emergency Shelter is the evacuation terminal point. In order to clarify to the evacuators that they can gather here, it is necessary to set up an Emergency Shelter Sign in the corresponding position.

Emergency Shelter Sign should include the information of Text, Emergency Shelter Symbol, and Disaster Type Symbols. It states that the emergency shelter is suitable for such disasters.

Emergency Shelter Sign is designed as shown in Fig. 15.

Fig. 15. Emergency Shelter Sign

5.3   Information Amount Verification

In order to verify whether the designed information meets the requirement of allowed maximum information amount, the information amount of each sign is calculated and compared with 305.2 bit. Particularly, considering the function and application conditions of Evacuation Plan Sign and Description Sign, their information amount does not participate in this verification.

Take Fires Sign as an example. It includes only 2 kinds of colors (yellow and black), and a symbol (Fires Symbol), and a shape (triangle). According to Table 1, the information amount of Fires Sign is calculated as follow.

$$
\begin{aligned}
I_{FiresSign} &= \sum_{i=1}^{7} n_i \cdot I(x_i) \\
&= 2 \times 3.0 + 1 \times 3.3 + 1 \times 5.9 \\
&= 15.2 \, bit
\end{aligned}
\tag{9}
$$

Compared with 305.2 bit, the information of designed Fires Sign meets the requirement of allowed maximum information amount. The information of other designed signs can be calculated in the same way, and the results are shown in Table 3.

Table 3. Designed OSWGSs' information amount verification

Sign name	Information amount/bit	Meet(Y) or Not(N)
Disaster Type Sign	15.2	Y
Midway Indication Sign	23.1	Y
Vertical Indication Sign	23.1	Y
Intersection Indication Sign	230.0	Y
Optional Route Sign	305.2	Y
No Entry Sign	83.0	Y
Danger Warning Sign	83.0	Y
Temporary Area Sign	196.7	Y
Emergency Shelter Sign	210.8	Y

5.4   Information Occlusion Disposal

Effective transmission of information should also be considered in information design. Occlusion is one of the most important reasons that affect OSWGS's information transmission.

Simulation Model. A simulation model was created by 3dsmax software to simulate the effect of occlusion on information. The model is shown in Fig. 16.

In the simulation model, an OSWGS and two obstacles were created, and a camera 1.6 m above the ground was used to simulate the human eyes. Observe the occlusion of the OSWGS information by the obstacles when the camera is gradually moved from the distance to the OSWGS.

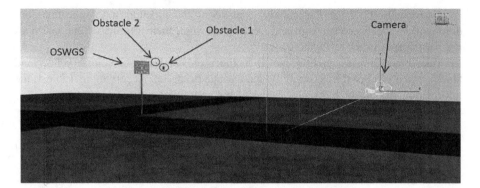

Fig. 16. The simulation model of information occlusion

Table 4. The information occlusion by obstacle 1

Occlusion element	Occlusion start position (m)	Occlusion end position (m)	Occlusion distance (m)
m	18.00	10.09	7.91
T	18.00	11.42	6.58
E	18.00	8.85	9.15
R	18.00	8.00	10.00
所	15.17	8.00	7.17

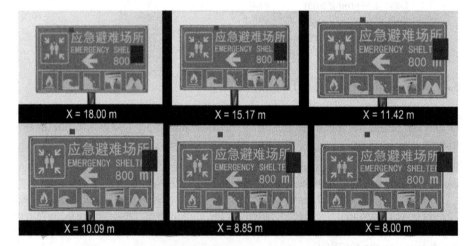

Fig. 17. Vision screenshots of key positions

While the camera moving in the entire stage of Reading Information, the obstacle 2 obscures the sign for a period of time, but it has no effect on the information at all, because there is no information in the area it blocks.

The occlusion of the information by obstacle 1 is shown in Table 4.

Several vision screenshots of key positions during the camera's movement are shown in Fig. 17.

The OSWGS's occlusion information loss can be calculated based on the Eq. (8) in this paper as follow.

$$
\begin{aligned}
I_{loss} &= \sum_{k}^{n} \frac{I_k \cdot d_k}{d_R} \\
&= \frac{4.7 \times (7.91 + 6.58 + 9.15 + 10.00) + 11.3 \times 7.17}{10.00} \\
&= 23.91 \text{ bit}
\end{aligned}
$$

Obstacles Disposal. Since the obstacle 2 has no effect on the information transmission, it is judged that no treatment is required. In order to reduce occlusion information loss caused by obstacle 1, several solutions are as follows.

Remove Obstacle 1. If obstacle 1 is easy to remove, direct removal can reduce the occlusion loss to zero.

Move OSWGS. If obstacle 1 is not easy to remove, moving the OSWGS's design position to the left a little bit can also reduce the occlusion loss to zero, but be careful not to create new occlusions due to this operation.

Adjust Layout. If obstacle 1 and OSWGS's position are not easy to change, moving the Text information and the Distance information on the layout to the left a little bit can perfectly reduce the occlusion loss to zero.

6 Conclusion

In this paper, we have analyzed the design principles and a design method of OSWGS's layout information based on human factors engineering and psychology.

Through the analysis of the interaction mode between evacuator and OSWGS, the interaction process is divided into four stages, and we have gotten the conclusion that the main research stage of information transmission should be the stage of Reading Information, and the range is about $8 \sim 18$ m away from the front of OSWGS.

Based on Shannon information theory, a method of calculating an OSWGS's information amount and its loss caused by occlusion has been proposed, and 305.2 bit has been pointed out to be the recommendation value of the allowed maximum information amount, which can be used to evaluate an OSWGS's design rationality.

OSWGSs have been divided into 11 categories. What necessary information elements should each kind of OSWGS provide has been analyzed, and typical design examples and setting effects in some scenes have been given in this paper to explain the application of the analysis results.

Particularly, focusing on the influence of occlusion on information transmission, the application of occlusion information loss calculation method in occlusion effect evaluation and occlusion disposal has been given by simulation. It shows that the occlusion information loss calculation method helps to guide the OSWGS's information design to the occlusion problem.

The method of designing an OSWGS's layout information proposed from the perspective of Interactive mode and information quantification can be used to guide OSWGS's design and it is of great significance to improve evacuation efficiency. Further statistical analysis of the basic characteristics of personnel in different countries and regions will help to improve the accuracy of the method and expand its application scope.

Acknowledgement. This research is supported by National Key R&D Program of China (2016YFF0201700) and Presidential Foundation Program of China National Institute of Standardization "Research on Standardization and Application of Safety signs Based on the Needs of Winter Olympic Games".

References

1. Graphical symbols-Safety signs-Safety Way Guidance Systems (SWGS). ISO 16069 (2017)
2. Graphical symbols-Safety colors and safety signs-Registered safety signs. ISO 7010 (2011)
3. Water safety signs and beach safety flags-part 1: Specifications for water safety signs used in workplaces and public areas. ISO 20712-1 (2008)
4. Liang, J.: Analysis on people's evacuating behavior during the building fire. Fire Sci. Technol. **28**(11), 866–869 (2009)
5. Posner, M.I.: Foundations of Cognitive Science, 3rd edn. MIT Press, Cambridge (1991)
6. Liao, J., Zhang, W.: On the reading speed of Chinese. Chin. J. Ergon. **2**(1), 38–41 (1996)
7. Bose, R.: Information Theory, Coding and Cryptography, 1st edn. China Machine Press, Beijing (2005)
8. Zhu, Y.: Experimental Psychology, 2nd edn. Peking University Press, Beijing (2001)
9. Design standard for emergency shelter. DG/TJ 08-2188 (2015)

Memories and Brain Maps

Representations of Fear, Risk and Insecurity in Downtown Areas

Rachel Zuanon[1] , Melissa Ramos da Silva Oliveira[2(✉)] ,
Cláudio Lima Ferreira[1] , Evandro Ziggiatti Monteiro[1] ,
and Haroldo Gallo[1]

[1] Universidade Estadual de Campinas, Campinas, São Paulo, Brazil
{rzuanon,limacf,evanzigg}@unicamp.br,
haroldogallo@uol.com.br
[2] Universidade Vila Velha, Vila Velha, Espírito Santo, Brazil
melissa.oliveira@uvv.br

Abstract. Departing from an approach focused on the cooperation between Architecture, Urbanism and Neuroscience, we investigate the impacts of the urban environment of the city of Campinas (São Paulo, Brazil) downtown area on the declarative semantic memories consolidated in the brain maps of the city's inhabitants/users. Through field research with two hundred and sixty-six participants, the memories about this space/place are evoked and recorded in the testimonies made by these individuals, as well as represented in drawings made by themselves. We focused on the modulation of these memories through the emotions and feelings, respectively related to fear, risk and insecurity in this urban space. The main results are: the absence of identification with and the repulsion of the inhabitants/users of the public space; the restricted use of the urban space and the remote possibility of citizens "experiencing" the city; and the threat to the homeostatic balance of these individuals. Such discussions evince the responsibility of public policies, as well as of architects, designers and urban planners in the ways human beings feel, perceive, and appropriate the urban space.

Keywords: Architecture, Urbanism and Neuroscience cooperation ·
Memories · Brain maps · Emotions, feelings and affections ·
Space/Place appropriation

1 Introduction

Walking around the different downtown areas that make up the Brazilian urban realm is entering a world in which shapes, colors, textures, odors and sounds blend together. They arouse emotions, feelings and affections from multiple sensations and perceptions. It means dealing with the confrontation of contradictory and antagonistic worlds embedded into a single reality. The new lives alongside the old, not always harmoniously. Those who have presence and visibility try to impose themselves on the world of destitute and outcast people. The speed and ephemerality of capitalist production,

V. G. Duffy (Ed.): HCII 2019, LNCS 11581, pp. 509–523, 2019.
https://doi.org/10.1007/978-3-030-22216-1_37

which shape the urban spaces, clash in the coexistence with the slow men[1]. The formal city coexists with the informal one. Public spaces that are not legitimized, and therefore underutilized, become territorialities of crime and prostitution.

As in other Brazilian cities, walking around the downtown area of the city of Campinas[2], located in the state of São Paulo, means strolling through congested and paralyzed roads; through narrow pavements and streets, which crush the heavy flow of vehicles and people; through antagonistic worlds and times: hurried executives; worried housewives; untroubled consumers gaze at storefronts, while others rush to hunt for sales; autonomous salespeople dispute spaces among cars and pedestrians; car watchers perform their duty while waiting for the drivers to return; preachers blare in the middle of the squares, alongside the street performers and their artistic works, while beggars earn some change for their livelihood.

The intense noise comes from the entangled sound of voices and screams; the horns; the roaring of the engines; the megaphones of politicians and the loudspeakers of the stores. Graffiti and advertisements are juxtaposed in the visual pollution, which hides the facades of buildings and impacts the referentials and the sense of location in the urban space. The fast pace doesn't coexist with the time to observe the surrounding landscape. Public spaces cease to be social areas to become places of transit. Sociability vanishes with the ephemerality of the public life. Dirtiness, pollution and noise. Excess of information. Haste and confusion. Alternating movements of use and emptying. Diversities built in the attraction and repulsion of differing emotions and feelings.

Similar to other Brazilian cities, the downtown area of Campinas corresponds to a physical space organized and reorganized by urban interventions carried out by political and economic forces. In the past, it housed both instances of government, commerce and leisure, and the dwellings of wealthier families. With the expansion, the city is now characterized by a residential model of suburbanization and the more eminent activities move to different regions. Whereas the downtown area popularizes and becomes the go-to place for discount stores, public services and informal workers, especially during business hours. The scant night activity goes hand in hand with the expansion of violence and prostitution, helping to define a scenario of degradation. "It's a bitter irony that often the city may look like a scary place. Built to remedy the apparent confusion and chaos of nature, the city itself becomes a disorienting physical environment (...)" [3].

All these characteristics expose the lived space, defined by the daily space practices. Such practices simultaneously establish places; the relationship between local and global; the representation of common everyday spaces and privileged spaces, affected by their existence as a favorable or unfavorable symbol. By taking this scenario as our

---

[1] "Slow men" is a category defined by geographer Milton Santos [1] to refer to subjects who are outside the speed of hegemonic processes, that is, they are part of the spatial dynamics that "come from below"—it personifies the ordinary, poor man.

[2] Campinas is a municipality in the countryside of the state of São Paulo, located roughly 100 km off the capital city, São Paulo. According to the website of the City Hall of Campinas (http://www.campinas.sp.gov.br) [2] the municipality has 1,091,946 inhabitants, and the Metropolitan Region of Campinas, comprising 20 municipalities, has 3,094,181 inhabitants. Campinas has a high level of industrialization and approximately 70% of its economy comes from the service sector.

object, we can advance to the concept of space/place appropriation, which corresponds to the way in which it is occupied by objects, activities (uses), individuals, classes or other social groups [4].

This way of appropriating space/place is intimately related to the emotions and feelings this space/place arouses, and how these emotions and feelings modulate the brain maps and the memories of its inhabitants/users. In the case of the present article, it focuses on the sentiment of fear and the feelings of risk and insecurity that modulate the declarative semantic memories present in the brain maps of inhabitants/users of the downtown area of the city of Campinas. These memories, which contain information about the surrounding environment, are evoked in the participants of this research, and gain materiality in the content reported by them in interviews, as well as in the graphic representations made by them, and which comprise the drawings of this space/place. In this context, urban problems such as social and political oversight, violence, infrastructure and environment deterioration erupt like involuntary tattoos, which embed the mental images that inhabit the brain maps of these residents and users, injure the city's 'skin' and distort the affections related to it.

Departing from this perspective and from an approach focused on the cooperation between Architecture, Urbanism and Neuroscience, this article discusses the impacts of these urban problems on the organism of the inhabitants/users of the downtown area of Campinas, especially regarding: the absence of identification with and the repulsion of public space; the restricted use of the urban space and remote possibility of citizens "experiencing" the city; and the threat to the homeostatic balance. It is understood that investigations of this nature aid the urban socioeconomic development by evincing the responsibility of public policies, as well as of architects, designers and urban planners in the ways human beings feel, perceive, and appropriate such space.

2 Memories Modulated by Emotions and Feelings

The word memory expresses a process that involves information acquisition, formation, conservation and evocation. Memories are the only collection of data coming from personal experience. Associated with genetic characteristics, memories define the individual, influence his personality. The identity of peoples comes from the memories which are common to all of its members. Memories encompass the story of every city, country, people, civilization, as well as the individual memories of animals and people. Memories are encoded by neurons, stored in neural networks and evoked by the same networks in which they were stored or by others [5].

Emotions, moods, alertness, anxiety, and stress strongly modulate human being's memories. An individual who is not alert or is stressed will not form memories correctly. Another, subject to a high level of anxiety, may forget everything he has learned. Yet another, stressed at the time of evocation of his memories, will have difficulty recalling them. On the other hand, an alert individual will remember them promptly. That is, several modulator systems act, satisfactorily or not, on the mechanisms that control human memories. The modulation of the acquisition and of the early stages of memory consolidation occurs at almost the same time and involves two aspects: (1) the distinction between the memories with greater emotional load from the others, in order to guarantee that the first ones are better recorded than the others; (2) the addition of neurohumoral or hormonal information to the contents of memory in situations of anxiety or stress [6].

The role of emotions, positive or negative, as well as the feelings that follow, as modulators of human memories and also as requisite components of our social experiences is thus emphasized [7].

Emotions conform subjective experiences in the short term. Humors, in turn, define a persistent, subjective, and sustained emotional experience. Whereas memory functions are widely distributed through the limbic and non-limbic areas of the brain, emotions are mediated within the limbic system by the amygdala, areas of the hypothalamus, the septal area, anterior nuclei of thalamus, anterior portion of the cingulate cortex and the limbic association cortex [8]. The amygdala plays a crucial role in the social body, interpreting facial expressions and social cues [9].

Emotions are triggered by images of people, animals, objects, environments or phenomena, present or past, when recalled. They shape our perceptions about the beings and things of the world, and influence our actions. The mental images of a particular situation and/or environment in which the individual finds himself affect his emotional machinery. Whether these images are formulated at the present moment, evoked from memory, or created by imagination, all carry the potential to trigger emotional chain reactions in the human body [10]. Each life experience, especially those linked to social problems, is accompanied by some degree of emotion, however small [7].

In this context, it is important to emphasize the impacts on the functions of all human organs resulting from the thoughts and emotions experienced by the individual. This is due to two-way communication between the nervous system and the immune system. For example, the immediate body responses to feelings of threat, risk, and insecurity involve somatic, autonomic, and hormonal changes, which include increased muscle and heart rate, pupil dilation, and disruption of digestion. Such responses can disrupt homeostasis, that is, disrupt the processes of life regulation, as well as the conditions that arise from a well-regulated life.

This disruption can also be considered a response to stress. When an individual feels threatened, for any reason present or past, this response to stress ensures an increase in strength and energy of this individual in order to provide him with organic conditions favorable to coping with the threatening situation. Such response triggers the return of the organism to homeostasis. However, the stress response often remains active, either as a result of the individual's thinking patterns or due to the circumstances surrounding him [8]. In other words, however much the individual's body employs strength and energy to handle adversity, it will only be fully overcome when the external and internal environments, which keep the threat alive, are fully and positively transformed. At this point, it is relevant to emphasize the strong connection between emotional states and decision-making. Emotional signals do not decide, but do affect our decision-making process [8]. That is, even the decision to transform oneself and its surroundings is modulated by the emotional states. This leads us to the thorough reflection on the crucial role of Architecture, Design, and Urban Planning and Management, associated with the municipal and state policies, regarding the definition of the quality of emotions that will modulate our brain maps and our memories, as well as our decision-making in the urban space, and how to appropriate it or not.

3 Methodology

This research aims to examine the impacts of the urban environment of the downtown area of the city of Campinas (São Paulo, Brazil) on the consolidated memories in the brain maps of its inhabitants/users, especially regarding the modulation of these maps and memories by the emotions and feelings, respectively related to fear, risk and insecurity in such urban space. In order to accomplish that, the semantic declarative memories of the participants of this research about this space/place are evoked and recorded in the statements made by these individuals, as well as represented in drawings made by themselves.

In this sense, the methodology comprises three distinct phases: (a) preparation of the material for field research; (b) collecting information from 266 individuals, among city inhabitants and users; (c) compilation, analysis and systematization of the data collected.

In the **(a) preparation phase**, the spatial focus of the research is delimited[3]: beginning at Aquidaban Avenue; then through Antônio Cesarino Street, Itu Street, Júlio de Mesquita Avenue; moving around Centro de Convivência (Community Center); continuing through José Évilagelin Junior Street; down Guilherme da Silva Street up to Anchieta Avenue; continuing along Orosimbo Maia Avenue, Culto à Ciência Street, Hércules C. Florence Street, Saldanha Marinho Street, Marquês de Três Rios Street, Barão de Parnaíba Street, Dr. Mascarenhas Street; finally, following the Fepasa Railway until returning to Aquidaban Avenue. In this phase, the strategy for data collection is also defined: semi-structured interviews with the research participants and free-hand drawings.

In the **(b) information collection phase**, 266 questionnaires were distributed, during three months of work conducted in the field, within the spatial focus delimited by the research, as detailed above. The selection of the target audience considers the diversity of people, social classes, races and genres, who experience the city's downtown area. The interviewees' age bracket encompasses the minimum age of 16 and the maximum of 80 years of age. The researchers, through a direct approach to the inhabitants/users in this public space, started the interviews by collecting of their demographic information. Afterwards, the interviewees receive the questionnaire printed on paper, to be filled in by themselves, and to include the freehand drawings. In this process, there is no demand or limitation regarding the drawing technique, or in relation to the time reserved to complete the questionnaire. This procedure intends to avoid any interference in the emotional reaction or in the memory evocation process of the interviewees.

---

[3] Throughout the research we identified that the Secretariats of Campinas City Hall adopt different perimeters to define the downtown area. These perimeters were superimposed and we opted for an extended spatial focus that encompassed all of them.

The (c) **data compilation, analysis and systematization phase** initially consists in compiling the information recorded in the interviews and questionnaires. After that, the analysis of this set of compiled data is aimed at identifying: (1) spaces/places evoked from the participants' memories; (2) associations between the evoked spaces/places and the sentiment of fear and the feelings of risk and insecurity expressed by the participants; (3) possible correlations between all the testimonies and the drawings made. Finally, the quantitative and qualitative results are systematized. The quantitative results, systematized in a table, show the thematic predominance of the evoked memories in the brain maps of the inhabitants/users. The qualitative results, on the other hand reveal the main problems identified in this urban space and its impacts on the well-being, quality of life and health of the inhabitants/users of the city of Campinas, as detailed in the next section.

4   Results/Discussions

Populations of large cities such as Campinas (São Paulo, Brazil) face many difficulties resulting from accelerated urbanization without a proper urban planning and management. The problems are diverse, among which the following stand out: negative impacts on the environment; social inequality; unemployment; lack of investment in such areas as health, education, law enforcement and infrastructure, among many others. This wide gamut of urban problems is articulated in a system that triggers negative chain reactions. Such reactions can only be contained and reversed with the extensive enforcement of public policies aimed at providing the resources and conditions necessary for the preservation and maintenance of the quality of life of the city's inhabitants/users.

In the opinion of the interviewees of this research, problems such as these are observed on a daily basis in the downtown area of Campinas. It was the group of younger people (up to 40 years of age), regardless of social class and gender, who expressed the strongest sentiment of fear and declared feelings of risk and insecurity. The predominant income bracket of this group is 3 to 5 minimum wages[4].

A more detailed examination allows us to point out some relevant elements (triggers) that conform the environment of fear, risk and insecurity described by the inhabitants/users of the downtown area of Campinas. Violence is a source of great concern on the part of frequenters of the downtown area. To Vinícius (18 years old, student), "the beggars and thieves" are the worst problems about the downtown area. To him, it is necessary to "take the beggars out of the streets and put more police to avoid having too much robberies." According to Ruan (19 years old, student), the problems with the downtown area are "thieves and people that ask for money on the streets." To Aline (16 years old, student), the problems are "the lack of security, the beggars, the robberies, visual and noise pollution, and dirty streets and pavements." According to Carlos (16 years old, student), the problems are "too many beggars, street

---

[4] The minimum wage in Brazil corresponds to R$998.00, which is equivalent to approximately US $257.00.

children and pollution." When asked about what they enjoyed about the downtown area, which is no longer present, Rafael (37 years old, 5–10 wages, office assistant) claims that he misses the "tranquility of walking around downtown Campinas without fear;" Cassiana (26 years old, 1–3 wages, receptionist) wishes "to be able to walk around downtown without having to worry about robberies" and João (68 years old, 10 + wages, retired) "the easiness of strolling safely".

The table below shows, in the first column, the question asked to the interviewees; in the second, the problems classified into categories; and, in the third, the general tabulation of the answers obtained (Table 1).

Although it is a frequent aspect of this central region as a whole, violence is more pronounced in certain territories, such as around Silvia Simões Square and in the area known as Boca do Lixo (Skid Row). The downtown area of the city of Campinas is still marked by several prostitution spots, a fact that also adds to its physical deterioration.

Regarding the main problems related to the infrastructure of the downtown area, the following testimonies stand out: Ingrid (19 years old, student), who claims that "(there is) lack of organization, too much graffiti and dirt", João Carolino (58 years old, 1–3 wages, doorman), who points out the inefficacy of the existing structure for rainwater drainage, "when it rains the streets flood easily".

Now we will further discuss the main urban problems raised by the research participants and their impact on the consolidated memories and, consequently, on the balance and quality of life of the inhabitants/users of the city's downtown.

4.1   Vandalism and Graffiti: Inducers to the Absence of Identification and Repulsion to the Public Space

The feeling of identification, affection and belonging to the space/place reserved in the individual and/or collective memory is consolidated in the brain maps of the inhabitants/users of a city, from constructions and reconstructions of meanings, senses and values that are attributed to this space/place throughout their lives. This process traces back its origin to the appropriation of the space/place by these inhabitants. Such appropriation drives individuals to experience this space/place in its totality and to establish with it a concrete and/or subjective identity relationship. For instance, this occurs when the inhabitants/users are able to develop, in this space/place, values close to their feelings and their cultural and symbolic identity.

In our social experiences, emotions, whether positive or negative, as well as feelings that arise afterwards, become mandatory and fundamental components for the feeling of affection and of belonging or not belonging to a given space/place.

Currently, several urban problems identified in Downtown Campinas accompany social experiences that trigger negative emotions in their inhabitants/users and arouse the feeling of not belonging to the space/place, as in the cases related to the presence of graffiti on properties. The Palácio dos Azulejos (Tile Palace), less than a year after the end of its renovation, had its facade tiles graffitied. The headquarters of the Carlos Gomes Band had its facade graffitied, just the week following its reinauguration. The same happened with the neoclassical facade of the Roque de Marco Building, in front of Estação Cultura (Culture Station) (Fig. 1).

Table 1. Problems identified by the interviewees from the questions in the questionnaire. Source: the authors

Question	Problems	Identified aspects
When hearing about downtown, what is the first thing that comes to your mind?	*Insecurity (11)*	Fear, violence (11)
	Pollution (12)	Atmospheric, visual and noise pollution (12)
	Infrastructure deterioration (14)	Dirtiness (6); narrow streets/pavements (3); lack of urban improvements (3); poor state of conservation (2)
	Social and political neglect (17)	Beggars/street children (9); disorganization (5); public neglect (3)
What did you like about downtown that has disappeared?	*Security (98)*	Absence of violence (69); tranquility (29)
	Planning and infrastructure (62)	Cleanness (38); more pleasant (11); more beautiful (4); lighting (3); better conserved pavements (2); with public toilets (2); less rough roads (2)
	Social equality (56)	Organized (29); no beggars (16); no street vendors (8); no prostitution (3)
	Salubrity/cleanness (19)	No vandalism/graffiti (7); no visual pollution (5); no noise pollution (5); no atmospheric pollution (2)
What does the downtown area you want feel like?	*Security (6)*	Safer/no fear (3)
	Social equality (6)	No beggars (3); no prostitution (3)
	Planning (5)	Clean (2); better state of conservation (2); more trees (1)
In your opinion, what are the main problems in the downtown area?	*Violence (122)*	Fear/insecurity
	Infrastructure deterioration (106)	Dirtiness (42); rough pavements/streets (19); narrow pavements/streets (9); floods (7); lack of space (5); lack of public toilets/smell of urine (5); lack of trees (4); lack of infrastructure (4); lack of signaling (3); unsightliness (3); lack of conservation (3); lack of lighting (2)
	Social and political neglect (71)	Beggars (33); street vendors (14); lack of organization (11); people lacking civility (9); prostitution (4)
	Infrastructure deterioration/pollution (59)	Vandalism/graffiti (22); atmospheric pollution (15); visual pollution (10); noise pollution (6); damage to public property (6).

Fig. 1. Graffiti on the facades of properties recognized as Cultural Heritage of Campinas. 1. Facade of the Carlos Gomes Band. 2. Facade of the Roque de Marco Building [11].

Even with the Anti-Graffiti Plan, implemented by the City Hall, the buildings remain damaged and the city's downtown has an unsightly aspect. Both facts strongly add to the image of total disregard for the public property, which back-feeds the loss of identification and affection, as well as the feeling of not belonging to this space/place on the part of the inhabitants/users.

In the drawings made by the participants, graffiti is a significant element in regard to urban problems. In Fig. 2, Lucas and Gabriel show graffitied buildings, with reference to visual pollution. Lucas also adds his critical opinion to this practice, with the phrase: "to me, downtown Campinas has too much graffiti." In Fig. 3, in turn, posters and signs of commercial buildings blend together and the graffiti is again portrayed, in an evident demonstration of visual pollution as a deprecating element to the city. Gabriella, in her drawing, also expresses her criticism of urban vandalism through the phrase "we is vandal (sic)".

If on the one hand, these drawings denounce the lack of identity and affection of the inhabitants/users toward Downtown Campinas, on the other they function as externalization of the interviewees' concerns with the negative effects to the city resulting from the feeling of 'not belonging' to it. As one interviewee points out: (downtown Campinas) "is ugly and that's why it's lost its appeal. Why can't we have a pretty and appealing downtown as there exist or as we see in other cities?" (Ana, 41–50, 3–5 wages, maid). Regarding this point, we must return to the concepts of appropriation and backfeeding in order to understand that the feeling of identification and belonging to a space/place is also something to be constructed. That is, something that demands that we abandon our passive condition, in the public and private spheres, to reach perspectives directed at reformulating the space/place in which we live, as an act of legitimizing and appropriating it.

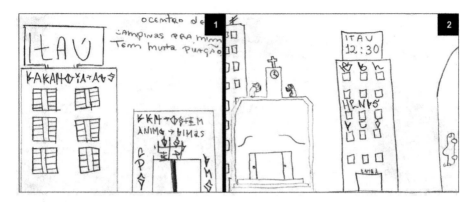

Fig. 2. Images criticizing graffiti: 1. Lucas, 20 years old, 1–3 wages, bricklayer; 2. Gabriel, 29 years old, 1–3 wages, security guard. Source: the authors.

Fig. 3. Visual pollution and vandalism: 1. Gabriella, 28 years old, up to 5 wages, stylist; 2. Gabriella, 20 years old, up to 1 wage, store supervisor. Source: the authors.

4.2   The Perception and Feeling of Violence as Restricting Factors for the Use of Urban Space and the Possibility of Citizens to "Live" the City

Most of the objects around us are capable of triggering emotions: good or bad, strong or weak, conscious or unconscious. While some "objects are emotionally competent" for evolutionary reasons, that is, they carry within themselves the potential to evoke emotions and play a relevant role in the history of human development, others act as competent emotional stimuli throughout our individual experiences. For example, an intense sentiment of fear experienced in a childhood space/place can be evoked in the future, when the individual returns to the same space/place, and trigger a feeling of malaise in him without any immediate and apparent reason for that. Or yet, be evoked in another space/place similar to that of childhood. That is, even without an immediate and apparent cause existing in this space/place in the present justifying the fear felt by the individual at that moment, his brain maps record the emotional memory of his childhood in that environment, and the slightest stimulus may be enough to evoke it [7].

From this context the graphic representations present in the figure below (Fig. 4) emerge, which portray scenes of robbery and violence in the downtown area of the city of Campinas. In his drawing, Richard depicts a pavement, bounded by a graffitied wall. Behind the wall we can see a series of tall buildings with no lateral setback. In the foreground, a street with several cars circulating, two of them taxi cabs. On the pavement, a violent scene is depicted when a burglar, shouting the word "die," shoots a person with his arms raised. Rafael's image portrays, in the central part, the intersection of three streets. In one of them, a car lets smoke out its tailpipe, an allusion to air pollution. At the top we see two billboards, highlighting the names of the stores Hot Point and C&A. At the bottom of the image we see the scene of a robbery, in front of the C&A store, where one person shoots another, in a typical demonstration of violence.

These scenes portray violent situations that emerge from the emotional memories of these inhabitants/users, here evoked and related to the fear triggered by urban violence in the downtown area of Campinas. Implicit mental images that form the brain maps of these two participants, from the experiences lived in that space at different moments of their lives. Such mental images are now made explicit in the memories evoked and recorded in their respective drawings.

Melgaço [12] defines violence as "all acts that are detrimental to individual and social interests, whether recognized by law or not". Yázigi [13], in turn, argues that violence is organized in multiple interrelations: "with established and informal trade; with the drug network; with the male and female prostitution scheme". The fact is that these harmful practices, articulated in these multiple interrelations, alter the routine of several inhabitants/users of the city's downtown area. Merchants are forced to close their doors earlier, and students to return from school in groups, both intending to minimize the chances of being robbed. According to an article in Correio Popular (Campinas, May 23, 2010), violence imposes "curfew in the downtown area." Antônio Cardoso Júnior, a merchant in this region of the city, reports:

> One begins to close up shop and the others follow. It's a kind of curfew indeed (...) we used to close later. But we started closing (our businesses) at 6 p.m. for fear of violence. I'm closing at a time when I could still make many sales, when people leave work and walk through here to go back home [14].

As Jacobs points out [15], bakery owners, cafés, shops, grocery stores and other small establishments are the ones who keep "attentive eyes" and assume the position of "natural owners of the street," who use and monitor the urban space the whole time.

In the words of Melgaço [12], "it is the culture of fear, a result of the violence of information promoted by the media the main incentive for the emergence of segregating and violent urban forms". Such as this 'implicit curfew,' recorded as a conditioned stimulus in the emotional memories of the merchants in downtown, especially in the perimeter between Francisco Glicério Avenue and the former Fepasa Station (east–west), and between the Central Terminal to the immediate vicinity of the old bus station (north–south). It is important to emphasize that, within this perimeter, in the surroundings of the Railway Complex (when traversing Saldanha Marinho, Visconde do Rio Branco, Ferreira Penteado and Costa Aguiar Streets, and the Marechal Floriano Peixoto Square region) "Boca do Lixo" is located, a region that concentrates activities

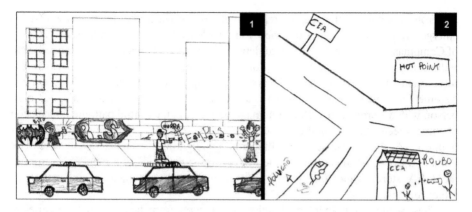

Fig. 4. Emphasis on violence: robbery in the midst of the traffic and scenes of armed robbery, in a polluted urban setting. 1. Richard, 18 years old, 3–5 wages, student; 2. Rafael, 18 years old, up to 1 wage, student. Source: the authors.

such as smuggling, counterfeiting and prostitution, which corroborate the consolidation of these memories in the brain maps of the city's inhabitants/users.

As a result, this region remains an obstacle to the revitalization of the downtown area. In an interview to the Campinas newspaper, Correio Popular, on May 2, 2010, architect Débora Frazatto points out:

> People don't want to live in an unappealing region. Banks and shops close by late afternoon. And deserted streets have become fertile ground for marginal activities. The community needs cultural attractions, commercial establishments open at any time. The downtown area must have life [16].

In other words, this 'implicit curfew' not only restricts the use of urban space, but also prevents inhabitants/users from 'living the city' and, consequently, 'giving life' to its equipment.

4.3   Desire for Health and Well-Being as a Strategy to Achieve Homeostatic Balance

Homeostasis consists of a set of regulation processes and, at the same time, in the resulting state of well-regulated life. Homeostatic reactions detect difficulties or opportunities and, through actions performed in and/or by the body, solve the problem of eliminating difficulties or seizing opportunities. At its inception, human life is regulated by natural and automatic homeostasis devices, such as metabolism, appetites and emotions. In adulthood, on the other hand, this regulation becomes more complex, given our need to deal with and seek solutions, both physically and socially, for a significant number of conflicts.

The mechanisms of social homeostasis emerge in this context, extending the drastic limits of automatic life regulation, when the physical and social environments become complex. That is to say, the basic mechanisms of life regulation articulate with the mechanisms of social homeostasis imbued with the responsibility of ensuring balance to human survival. By contrast, this regulation not only occurs in the individual, but in the collective. That is, beyond their own desires and feelings, as well as in the concern for the desires and feelings of others. Such concern is organized in the form of social conventions and ethical rules, and in turn, these conventions and rules are managed by institutions, whether a social, political, legal or religious organization. It is these conventions, rules and institutions that act in the social group as homeostatic instruments [7].

In Image 1, Fig. 5, when drawing three garbage cans, Patrícia symbolizes the importance of homeostatic instruments, represented here by the urban furniture in the city's public spaces. In this case, the goal is to organize and facilitate garbage collection. Behind the cans, a paradoxical moment is depicted, common to the urban scene: the presence of a tree, which refers to the idea fresh air and greenery, is opposed to the mall's chimney, which releases polluting smoke to the environment and denotes an evident threat to the health of the city's inhabitants/users. In the same direction, the three garbage cans, present in drawing 2, made by Camila, allude to dirtiness; while at the top there is an emphasis to air pollution, represented by continuous lines and the phrase "polluted air." Both drawings denounce, in their representations, the absence, fully or partially, of homeostasis mechanisms dedicated to the regulation of social life in downtown Campinas. Whereas the scene portrayed by Patricia synthesizes the clear desire of the city's inhabitants/users for homeostatic instruments capable of guaranteeing the well-being and health of the population.

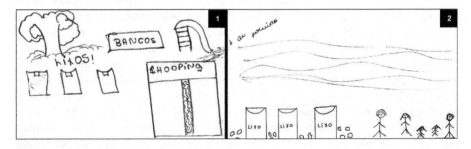

Fig. 5. Urban paradox: presence and absence of homeostatic instruments: 1. Patricia, 14 years old, up to 1 wage, student; 2. Camila, 21 years old, 1–3 wages, accounting assistant. Source: the authors.

5 Conclusion

This paper intends to show the influence of urban problems as actual triggers, that is, as stimuli that spark negative emotions and feelings in the inhabitants/users of a city, specifically represented here by the downtown area of the Brazilian city of Campinas.

Such triggers set off a slow, silent but intense chain reaction. Gradually, the experiences lived in the downtown area of Campinas, reconfigured by numerous problems, accumulate as the successive mental images that the brains of its inhabitants/users are capable of storing. Images that trigger sentiments of fear. Sentiments of fear that are felt as life threatening and dangerous. These are the predominating mental images in the brain maps of the participants of this research, and here they emerge as memories externalized in the testimonies and/or drawings made by the interviewees. Downtown Campinas, popularly recognized as the space/place in the city that concentrates the consumption of goods, as well as leisure activities, is evoked from the memories of its inhabitants/users as the space/place of fear, risk and danger. These memories, clearly modulated by this set of emotions and sentiments, evoke violence, pollution, traffic jams, unemployment, social inequality, precarious infrastructure, lack of urban beautification, among many other problems, which lie in the physical spaces of the city and within the minds of its residents.

The slow, silent, but intense chain reaction erupts in the involuntary hostility towards the central region. A hostility based on the set of emotions, feelings and memories mentioned earlier and slowly built up in the popular imagery. This hostility, even if involuntary, compromises the desire for the space/place that would guide the inhabitant/user to the decision of appropriating this urban environment. On the contrary, repulsion prevails and sustains the obstacles to the downtown area's refunctionalization. In other words, the feeling of insecurity arising from the fear of violence and the risk to life itself leads individuals to avoid residing in, as well as frequenting the bars, restaurants and cultural activities available in downtown. Consequently, properties deteriorate for lack of use; historical and social values are forgotten, or kept in the background; the image of the downtown area as the most important and safe place in the city—as it actually was in the past—deteriorates; and the chain reaction is back-fed.

But how can we cut short and reverse this cyclical process of degradation and abandonment? We must insist in the importance of understanding that the feeling of identifying with and belonging to the space/place is something to be revived and rebuilt progressively. That the dynamic brain maps of the inhabitants/users be reconfigured. And that the old mental images, fueled by fear, be replaced by new ones. That is, by mental images formed from positive emotions and feelings, arising from the pleasurable experience in the space/place. Something that asks us to abandon our passive condition, in the public and private spheres, to break the barriers erected by the urban problems and to build a different landscape, this time matching the voluntary desires of the city's inhabitants/users. Here lies the significant contribution that the cooperation between the fields of Architecture, Design, Urban Planning and Management, and Neuroscience can bring to the fore, by making available to these spheres instruments capable of ensuring the well-being and quality of life in the everyday relations between people and spaces/places, as well as the general health of the population.

In this path, as a future development, the research will add other possible layers of interpretation to the results discussed here, derived from the neurophysiological information obtained through eye tracking devices and through the monitoring of the emotional variability of the city's inhabitants/users.

References

1. Santos, M.: Técnica, espaço e tempo: globalização e meio técnico-científico informacional [Technique, space and time: globalization and technical-scientific informational medium]. Hucitec, São Paulo (1994)
2. Prefeitura Municipal de Campinas. http://www.campinas.sp.gov.br. Accessed 21 Dec 2018
3. Tuan, Y.-F.: Paisagens do medo [Landscapes of Fear]. Unesp, São Paulo (1995)
4. Lefebvre, H.: La production de l'espace [The Production of Space], 15th edn. Anthropos, Paris (1974)
5. Cammarota, M., Bevilaqua, L.R.M., Izquierdo, I.: Memória [Memory]. In: Lent, R. (Coord.) Neurociência da mente e do comportamento [Neuroscience of Mind and Behavior]. Guanabara Koogan, Porto Alegre (2008)
6. Izquierdo, I.: Memória [Memory]. Artmed, Porto Alegre (2011)
7. Damásio, A.: Em busca de Espinosa: prazer e dor na ciência dos sentimentos [In Search of Espinosa: Pleasure and Pain in the Science of the Feelings]. Companhia das Letras, São Paulo (2004)
8. Lundy-Ekman, L.: Neurociência: fundamentos para reabilitação [Neuroscience: Fundamentals for Rehabilitation]. Elsevier, Rio de Janeiro (2004)
9. Young, A.W., Aggleton, J.P., Hellawell, D.J., Johnson, M., Broks, P., Hanley, J.R.: Face processing impairments after amygdalotomy. Brain J. Neurol. 118(1), 15–24 (1995). https://doi.org/10.1093/brain/118.1.15
10. Damásio, A.: E o cérebro criou o homem [And the Brain Created Man]. Companhia das Letras, São Paulo (2011)
11. Costa, M.T.: Prefeitura vai bancar nova pintura: lei que limita venda de spray e pune quem for flagrado pichando fica no papel [City Hall to pay for new painting: a law that limits the sale of spray paint and punishes whoever is caught graffitiing remains on the drawing board]. Correio Popular, Campinas, Cidades section, 4 October 2006
12. Melgaço, L.M.: Território em atrito: a violência sob o olhar da complexidade dialética [Territory in conflict: violence under the perspective of dialectical complexity]. In: Souza, M.A.A. (ed.) A Metrópole e o futuro: refletindo sobre Campinas [The Metropolis and the Future: Reflecting on Campinas]. Territorial, Campinas (2008)
13. Yázigi, E.: O mundo das calçadas. Por uma política democrática de espaços públicos [The world of sidewalks. Toward a democratic politics of public spaces]. Humanitas/FFLCH/Imprensa Oficial do Estado, São Paulo (2000)
14. Gallacci, F.: Violência impõe toque de recolher no Centro [Violence imposes curfew in the downtown area]. Correio Popular, Campinas, Cidades, 23 May 2010
15. Jacobs, J.: Morte e vida de grandes cidades [The Death and Life of Great American Cities]. Martins Fontes, São Paulo (2001)
16. Félix, L., Verzignasse, R.: Boca do lixo expõe a decadência do centro [Skidrow exposes the deterioration of the downtown area]. Correio Popular, Campinas, Cidades, 2 May 2010

Author Index